SPECIAL EDITION
USING®

Macromedia®
Director® MX

Gary Rosenzweig

800 East 96th Street
Indianapolis, Indiana 46240

SPECIAL EDITION USING MACROMEDIA DIRECTOR MX

International Standard Book Number: 0-7897-2903-2

Library of Congress Catalog Card Number: 2002117820

Printed in the United States of America

First Printing: June 2003

06   05   04   03   4   3   2

Bulk Sales

Que Publishing offers excellent discounts on this book when ordered in quantity for bulk purchases or special sales. For more information, please contact

> U.S. Corporate and Government Sales
> 1-800-382-3419
> corpsales@pearsontechgroup.com

For sales outside of the U.S., please contact

> International Sales
> 1-317-428-3341
> international@pearsontechgroup.com

Trademarks

Warning and Disclaimer

Acquisitions Editor
Betsy Brown
Candace Hall

Development Editor
Laura Norman

Managing Editor
Charlotte Clapp

Project Editor
George E. Nedeff

Copy Editor
Geneil Breeze

Indexer
Erika Millen

Proofreader
Benjamin Berg

Technical Editor
Allison Kelsey

Team Coordinator
Vanessa Evans

Multimedia Developer
Dan Scherf

Designer
Anne Jones

Page Layout
Kelly Maish
Michelle Mitchell

Illustrator
William Follett

Contents at a Glance

Chapters on Bonus CD

TABLE OF CONTENTS

VI Production Process

ABOUT THE AUTHOR

Gary Rosenzweig is the chief engineer, founder, and owner of CleverMedia, a game and multimedia development company in Denver, Colorado. This is his 10th book on Macromedia Director and Flash.

Gary has degrees from both Drexel University in Philadelphia and the University of North Carolina in Chapel Hill. He has been building multimedia projects since 1989. CleverMedia was founded in 1995 and has produced more than 250 Shockwave and Flash games for CleverMedia's sites and other companies.

Gary lives in Denver, Colorado, with wife Debby, daughter Luna, cat Lucy, and dog Natasha. Debby owns The Attic Bookstore (`http://atticbookstore.com/`), a used bookstore in Denver. Other than computers and the Internet, Gary also enjoys film, camping, classic science fiction books, writing, and video games.

Some of Gary's other books are

- *Advanced Lingo for Games* (Que Publishing)

- *Flash MX ActionScript for Fun and Games* (Que Publishing)

- *Sams Teach Yourself Flash MX ActionScript in 24 Hours* (Sams Publishing)

Personal Home Page: `http://www.garyrosenzweig.com/`

Email: `http://www.garyrosenzweig.com/email.html`

DEDICATION

Dedicated to my newest inspiration: my daughter Luna.

ACKNOWLEDGMENTS

Very special thanks go to William Follett and Jay Shaffer, my co-workers at CleverMedia and to all the people I have had the pleasure of working with in the past. They make developing games even more fun than playing them.

Thanks to my family for their continuing lifetime of support: Jacqueline, Jerry, and Larry Rosenzweig; Rebecca Jacob; Barbara and Richard Shifrin.

The most thanks go to my wife, Debby, for her never-ending love and support.

WE WANT TO HEAR FROM YOU!

As the reader of this book, *you* are our most important critic and commentator. We value your opinion and want to know what we're doing right, what we could do better, what areas you'd like to see us publish in, and any other words of wisdom you're willing to pass our way.

You can email or write me directly to let me know what you did or didn't like about this book—as well as what we can do to make our books stronger.

Please note that I cannot help you with technical problems related to the topic of this book, and that due to the high volume of mail I receive, I might not be able to reply to every message.

When you write, please be sure to include this book's title and author as well as your name and phone or email address. I will carefully review your comments and share them with the author and editors who worked on the book.

Email: feedback@quepublishing.com

Mail: Mark Taber
          Associate Publisher
          Que Publishing
          800 East 96th Street
          Indianapolis, IN 46240 USA

READER SERVICES

For more information about this book or others from Que Publishing, visit our Web site at www.quepublishing.com. Type the ISBN (excluding hyphens) or the title of the book in the Search box to find the book you're looking for.

INTRODUCTION

ABOUT DIRECTOR MX

I love working with Macromedia Director. By education, I am a computer scientist and a journalist. By nature, I am a problem solver. I love using both logic and imagination. Director requires me to use all these things.

If you have a job in which you work all day with Director, consider yourself lucky. You probably already do. In fact, you have probably said to yourself before: "I can't believe I get paid for this!"

Director is a great tool for creating software. On one hand, you can quickly bring to life your ideas. On the other hand, Director is an environment that inspires new ideas as you explore it.

The possibilities for animators are incredible, even if they never choose to do any programming. Director also has built-in programs called *behaviors* that expand the possibilities a thousand times for those looking to make interactive presentations.

If you are willing to go on to learn Lingo, the programming language of Director, the possibilities for your creations become virtually limitless. There are more than 800 keywords in Lingo including all standard programming language structures. This makes Lingo every bit as powerful as languages such as C++, Pascal, and Java. In some cases, it's even more powerful.

The results of your work can be easily distributed to the world. You can create standalone applications to send over the Internet or burn into CD-ROMs. You can embed your creations into HTML pages for the Web. You can even create a Java applet.

Many people in the computer industry still think of Director as it was in version 3: an animation tool with a simple scripting language. However, each version since then has added a huge array of powerful features. Director is now the most advanced animation tool ever, with one of the most advanced programming languages.

Anyone who says, "You can't do that in Director," doesn't really understand the power or depth of Director MX.

WHO IS THIS BOOK FOR?

This book is for people who use Macromedia Director. It is a comprehensive reference guide to using Director.

This book is not a beginner's tutorial nor is it a series of hands-on examples. It is a reference. That means you can find out about almost every aspect of Director.

But this book is not meant to *teach* you how to use Director. It can certainly do that, especially if you combine it with the tutorials that come with Director and a self-motivated desire to learn.

For advanced subjects, this book can act as a guide for developers who are already using Director or those who feel that beginner's books are too simple.

Inside, you will find detailed sections of various aspects of Director, such as communicating with Flash movies, using imaging Lingo, altering the appearance of text members, reading and writing files, creating and controlling 3D worlds, communicating with servers, and incorporating Xtras into your projects.

My goal with this book is to make it the ultimate reference for Director developers. Every serious Director developer will want to have this book on her desk. It will save her time, effort, and many headaches.

HOW HAS THIS BOOK CHANGED FROM THE PREVIOUS EDITION?

This book is the fourth edition of this series, which started with *Special Edition Using Director 7* several years ago. The second and third revisions added new material. This fourth edition, however, is a complete overhaul of the book.

I've combined much of the beginner's materials into a few chapters, condensing sections on using the Paint panel and using the Score and Cast.

I've added large new sections on advanced topics such as imaging Lingo and 3D topics. I've also added many more tables that quickly summarize the Lingo used in various aspects of Director Lingo programming.

I've completely reorganized sections on Xtras, FileIO, Lingo data structures, and MIAWs. My goal was to make these sections more useful to people using this book as a reference.

I've also added new sections on accessibility and the Flash Communication Server, which are new features of Director MX.

No part of this book was untouched. Every word and paragraph was examined, updated or, in some cases eliminated. Some material, such as the applied examples of the previous editions, was moved to the CD-ROM as bonus chapters. The Lingo Reference section was moved there as well. So if you think this book is pretty thick, keep in mind that there is a lot more on the CD-ROM as well.

WHAT IS NEW IN DIRECTOR MX?

Director MX is major advancement over Director 8.0. However, the most impressive feature is 3D, which was added in version 8.5. The MX version, also known as Director 9, adds a whole new user interface and a few new powerful features.

- New interface—The MX interface brings Director in line with other Macromedia products. Instead of tons of small windows and dialog boxes, things are arranged in panel sets. It takes some getting used to, and requires more screen space, but the new interface grows on you.

- Flash ActionScript access—Director can now use Flash MX (Flash 6) movies, and Lingo has access to many ActionScript objects. You can communicate with the Flash Communication Server and other Flash-related features.

- Flash linked editing—You can automatically launch Flash MX to edit Flash members.

- Text-to-speech—As part of the new accessibility features, you can easily access text-to-speech functionality on both Mac and Windows.

- Object Inspector—The Object Inspector allows you to watch variables and properties as the movie plays. You can drill down to see properties of properties.

- Debugger integration—The debugger is now part of the Script panel. In addition, the Script panel now has numbered lines and improved syntax-finding menus.

- OS X authoring and playback—For Mac developers, Director MX is now an OS X program. In addition, both OS 9 and OS X are supported for playback.

CONVENTIONS USED IN THIS BOOK

I've tried to make it clear in the text which words are actual Lingo keywords. Any time I mention a Lingo command, function, property or other syntax, it will appear `monospaced`. When I mention variable or handler names that can be user-defined, they are also monospaced but in *`italics`*.

At the end of most chapters you will find two sections: "Troubleshooting" and "Did You Know?" The first presents some common problems that developers face and how to avoid them. This is in addition to troubleshooting advice found throughout many chapters.

The "Did You Know?" section is something a little different. It contains extra information about the topic. Sometimes the information is a little more advanced than the level of the chapter. Other times it highlights little-known facts or undocumented Lingo. On occasion it simply contains an idea for an interesting application of the information taught in the chapter. In addition, Tips and Notes placed throughout the chapters provide interesting ideas and methods you might not have considered. Caution notes are also found in places to help you avoid common pitfalls.

When keyboard shortcuts are mentioned, the shortcut in curved parenthesis are for Mac users, while the shortcut in the square brackets are for Windows users.

BEFORE YOU BEGIN

The first thing you will want to do is to copy the book source files from the CD-ROM to your hard drive. This way you have them readily available as you refer to different chapters.

You'll probably want to copy the bonus chapters as well. The Lingo Reference PDF file should open easily with Adobe Acrobat. Try to get the version of the free reader that includes the text search function. This way you can quickly search the document for what you need to know.

UPDATES AND SUPPORT

There are a lot of pages in this book and it was produced in a very short amount of time. Several editors and the author have worked very hard to make sure that all of the information is correct and complete.

But it is likely that issues will arise as readers use the book. I've created a Web page that will contain any updates and corrections. You can find it at this address:

`http://garyrosenzweig.com/books/`

You can also check my site at `http://director-online.com/` for up-to-date information about Director, lists of Xtras, and support forums.

DIRECTOR ESSENTIALS

IN THIS PART

1

USING THE DIRECTOR INTERFACE

IN THIS CHAPTER

THE MACROMEDIA DIRECTOR METAPHOR

Macromedia Director MX is a complete environment for the creation of multimedia. Think of it as an artist's canvas. Or, to use the metaphor that Director follows, a stage.

You can fill this stage with your own production. Any element in the production is called a *cast member* or simply a *member*. The computer screen where the action takes place is a window called the *Stage*.

The rest of the elements in Director also follow a theater/film metaphor, although some element names follow it better than others.

Assume that you have an image drawn in another program that you want to place in Director. Let's look at how this is done, leaving the details for later.

When you import this image into Director, it becomes a *cast member*. A cast member, usually referred to as just a *member*, is an individual media element such as a bitmap, sound, Flash movie, or video clip.

The Cast panel displays a list of all the cast members. This list is called the *cast library* or sometimes simply the *Cast*.

Now that the bitmap is a member stored in the Cast, it will be included in the Director file, which is also called a *movie*. You can use the terms Director *file* and Director *movie* interchangeably.

To use this bitmap in the movie, you'll need to place it on the *Stage*. The Stage is the main Director window. It represents what the end-user will see when they view the movie.

You can place this bitmap onto the Stage by simply dragging and dropping it there. Once it is one the Stage, you can drag it to any position on the stage.

> Every element in a Director movie is stored in a cast library. This is unlike other programs such as Flash that can have shapes and scripts that only appear on the Stage and not in the library.

Members that are placed on the stage are also placed in the *Score*. The Score is a chart that shows which members appear on the Stage at certain times.

Figure 1.1 shows the Stage, with the Cast and Score in separate windows on top of the Stage. You can see three members in the Cast, each member placed both on the Stage and in the Score as sprites.

The Score has rows and columns, as you can see in Figure 1.1. The columns represent frames. If you are using Director for animation, a frame represents a moment in time. If you are using Director to build presentations, applications, or games, then a frame represents one screen.

The rows represent *sprite channels*. A member that is in the Score is called a *sprite*. This term does not describe the member, but rather the combination of the member and its placement in the Score and on the Stage. A member is simply a bitmap or other media element, whereas a sprite is the description of which member is being used, which frame of the Score it is in, and where it is located on the stage, as well as many other properties. For instance, a member might be a picture, and a sprite is that picture placed on the Stage.

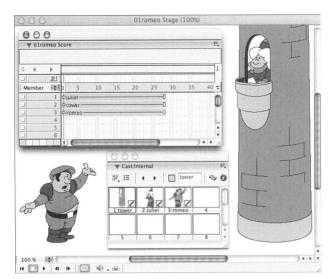

Figure 1.1
The Stage, Cast, and Score work together to make your Director movie.

A Director production is called a *movie*. This term is more accurately used to describe the file that contains all your work. A Director project can actually contain many movies, or just one. A movie can have many cast members, but only one Score.

Understanding Director's terminology is the first step toward learning to use the program:

- **Movie**—The primary Director file. It contains one or more Casts and a Score. It's the only Director file you need for most productions. Also called the *movie file*.

- **Cast**—The list of cast members used in a movie. Also called the cast library.

- **Member**—A single element, such as a bitmap, some text, a sound, a shape, a vector drawing, a Flash movie, or a piece of digital video. Also called a *cast member*.

- **Score**—A chart showing which members appear on the Stage at certain times.

- **Frame**—An instant of time in Director. While you are working on a movie, the stage shows a single frame. While the movie is animating, the stage moves through frames to create the visual effect of animation.

- **Channel**—A numbered position in the Score. Every sprite occupies a channel over a series of frames. The score can have as many as 1,000 channels, as well as a few special channels at the top. The specific channel a sprite is in determines whether it gets drawn on top of or underneath another sprite. Also called a *sprite channel*.

A bitmap would typically appear once in the Cast. But that cast member can be used in many sprites in the Score. Many sprites with the same member can appear on the same frame or different frames. For instance, a snowflake bitmap would be in the Cast once, but 100 sprites using it might appear in the Score.

An author can make changes to a sprite without affecting the cast member that is the source of the sprite. Conversely, changes to a cast member are immediately reflected among all the sprites created from it.

- **Sprite**—The description of which member is shown, where it is in the Score, where it appears on the Stage, and many other properties.

Using only the preceding elements, you can create animations with Director. They are the primary parts of the program and are used in the simplest of movies as well as in the most complex.

However, several other important elements are required to create more complex projects in Director. The most critical element is the *script*.

> **Caution**
>
> It can be easy to get your "movies" confused. A Director file is a movie. A Flash file or cast member is also called a movie. A digital video file is also called a movie.

Sticking with the theater/film metaphor, a script is like stage direction. Using a programming language in Director called *Lingo*, you can tell sprites what to do. Although it is possible to animate a sprite using only the Stage and Score, more complex movements and user interaction require you to learn and use Lingo.

A Lingo script that is attached to a sprite in the Score is called a *behavior*. This type of script tells a sprite how to behave under different circumstances. A script attached to a whole frame is called a *frame script*, and a script that controls the entire movie is called a *movie script*. You'll find more information about scripts and scripting later in the book.

These terms will become important to you after you have mastered the basic skills of Director and begin to make professional projects. Here is a review of some more advanced Director terms:

- **Script**—A set of Lingo commands that controls sprites and other elements of the movie.

- **Lingo**—The programming language of Director.

- **Behavior**—A script that controls a sprite.

- **Frame Script**—A script that controls a frame.

- **Movie Script**—A script that controls the entire movie.

- **Projector**—A standalone application program created from a Director movie.

- **Shockwave**—Technology that enables users to play Director movies in Web browsers.

The Director user interface is essentially several groups of windows and panels. Let's take a look at how windows and panels work. Using them efficiently is the key to working in Director.

EXPLORING WINDOWS AND PANELS

One of the major changes from Director 8.5 to Director MX is the user interface. In the past, working in the Director environment meant using windows and palettes, which were small windows.

Director MX features a whole new user interface to bring it in line with Macromedia's other MX products such as Flash and Fireworks. There are now three types of windows: A normal window, of which the Stage is the only example; document window panel groups; and tool window panel groups.

The document window panels are typically large windows that have large title bars, although no title appears in this bar. Examples are the Cast and the Score, shown back in Figure 1.1.

Tool window panels are smaller windows with small title bars. Examples are the Property Inspector and the Text Inspector.

If panels seem familiar, it is because they have been adopted across almost all Macromedia products. Flash MX and Fireworks MX use them.

Document and Tool window *panel groups* can have one or more items, or panels, inside them. For instance, one window can contain both the Property Inspector and the Message panel. They are stacked vertically and each has its own header bar, a gray area with a title such as "Property Inspector" or "Message." Figure 1.2 shows a panel window with several panels, some open and some closed.

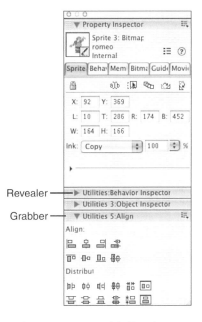

Revealer

Grabber

Figure 1.2
This panel window contains several tools.

You can group together panels any way you wish. But document window panels can only be grouped with other document window panels, and tool window panels can only be docked with other tool window panels.

To open a panel, choose it in the Window menu. If it is already on the screen as part of a panel group, this will either expand or collapse the panel. You can also click on the *revealer*, a small triangle on the left side of every panel's header bar, to expand or collapse the panel. If the panel is not on the screen anywhere, a new panel window will open containing only that panel.

You can combine or detach a panel from a panel window by clicking and dragging on its *grabber* area. This is a rough-looking spot at the very left of the header bar of each panel, just to the left of the revealer. Click it and drag it away from any other window to place the panel in its own new window. Or, you can drag it to an existing panel window of the same type.

Each panel also includes a small context menu on the right side of the header bar. Click there to bring up this options menu, which contains varying commands about hiding, collapsing, and regrouping the panel window.

Some panels have tabs in them. These are a series of buttons at the top of the panel that allow you to view different parts of the panel's functionality. For instance, the Property Inspector panel has tabs for the selected object's various types of properties. Figure 1.2 shows several tabs for the Property Inspector panel.

Tabs also appear at various times when a panel window contains related panels. For instance, if you try to open several cast library panels, you might get a single panel with multiple tabs, one for each cast library.

One panel that is different from all the rest is the Tool panel. It appears in its own narrow and title-less window, usually at the upper left corner of the screen.

Spend some time getting used to these panels, panel groups, and their various functionality. Being able to open, group, and regroup these panels is one of the keys to using Director MX efficiently.

> You can save and recall the positions of panel sets by choosing Window, Panel Sets.

The three main parts of Director are the Cast, Stage, and Score. Lets take a closer look at each, and then look at the various supporting panels.

UNDERSTANDING THE CAST AND CAST MEMBERS

The most basic elements of any Director movie are the cast members. You can't do any work in the Score or on the Stage without first having some members to work with.

Almost any form of media can be represented in Director as a cast member. Each type of cast member can be viewed or edited in the Media Editors panel. For instance, a bitmap member can be edited, pixel for pixel, using tools on the Paint tab of the Media Editors panel. This tab resembles a standalone image-editing application, but with an emphasis on editing the bitmap for use in Director. In some cases, you can assign external editors to cast member types.

⇨ *For more information on the Media Editor, see "Using Bitmaps," p. 34.*

The Cast Panel

The Cast panel has two modes. The default mode shows all members in a list. This list view allows you to sort the members in the Cast by any attribute, such as name, modification date, or type. Figure 1.3 shows the Cast in list mode, while Figure 1.1 showed it in thumbnail mode. To switch to thumbnail mode, use the Cast View Style button at the upper left corner of the Cast panel. In thumbnail mode, each square in the grid shows a simple preview of the member, plus the name and/or number of the cast member.

Cast view style   Cast member properties

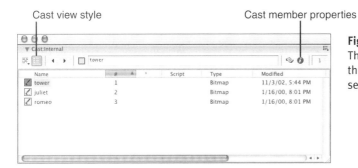

Figure 1.3
The Cast can be shown in thumbnail or list mode, as it is seen here.

You can add a member to the Score or Stage by dragging it from the Cast panel to the Score or Stage. Double-click a member's thumbnail or icon to edit it. A single click on a member selects it, and then you can click the information button in the Cast panel to view the member's properties.

The information button—a blue box with a lowercase *"i"*—appears in the upper-right corner of many windows in Director. Clicking it shows you the properties of the selected cast member in the Property Inspector. This is how you edit important properties of the member.

> You should always assign every cast member a unique name. Named cast members will come in handy when you begin scripting with Lingo.

The appearance of the Cast panel can be changed by choosing Director, Preferences, Cast. The dialog that comes up allows you to change the size of the thumbnails and the columns of the list view.

▭⟩ *If it seems that the Cast preferences keep switching on you each time you open another movie, see "Cast Preferences Won' t Stick" in the "Troubleshooting" section at the end of this chapter.*

Cast Member Types

How you work with cast member types vary greatly. Some can be created and edited in Director. Others need to be created in programs such as video or sound-editing tools and then imported. The following table summarizes most of the possible member types.

Table 1.1 Types of Cast Members

Member Type	Editable in Director?	Description	Similar To
Bitmap	Yes, using the Paint tab of the Media Editors panel	A drawing, photograph, or even an image generated by an advanced graphics program	Photoshop or Fireworks documents
Text	Yes, using the Text tab of the Media Editors panel	Rich text or HTML. Text members can have smooth edges and use a variety of formatting styles	Word processor documents

Table 1.1   Continued

Member Type	Editable in Director?	Description	Similar To
Fields	Yes, using the Field tab of the Media Editors panel	Basic text data with limited formatting options	Notepad, Text Editor, or BBEdit documents
Sounds	No, but simple recording and playback of new sounds are supported	Director supports a variety of different sound formats, such as WAV, AIFF, and MP3	
Shockwave Audio	No	A link to an external file of of streaming, compressed audio	
Shapes	Only type of shape and fill	Lines, ovals, rectangles, and rounded rectangles	Simple shapes created in old drawing programs
Vector Graphics	Yes, with the Vector Shape tab of the Media Editors panel	A collection of lines and curves	Adobe Illustrator or Macromedia Freehand documents
Flash	No, must be edited in Flash	Complete Flash .swf files, created with Flash MX or earlier	Compressed Flash MX files
Shockwave 3D	No, but can be viewed in the Media Editors panel, and cameras and lights can be modified there	Complete 3D worlds, featuring multiple models, cameras, lights, bone structures, and animation	3D Studio Max, Maya, Lightwave, Alias Wavefront
Buttons	Only size, color, and text	Simple buttons that show a highlight when clicked	
Video	No, but can be viewed with the Media Editors panel	QuickTime or Windows AVI video	Video created with Final Cut Pro or Adobe Premiere
Fonts	No, but can be created by choosing Insert, Media Element, Font	A complete font outline that will ensure that text members look the same on any machine	Macromedia Fontographer
Scripts	Yes, with the Script panel	Lingo instructions that control the elements of the movie	
Xtra Members	Sometimes, depending on the Xtra	Director extensions that allow you to use other types of media as members	

As you explore Director's different cast members, you will find that they relate to one another in many ways. For instance, most cast members can have a script attached to them. The script is not a separate cast member, but a property of that single cast member. You can, therefore, create a bitmap image that has a script in it. That script enables it to react to the user's mouse click. But you can

1

also use that bitmap without any script attached to it. Instead, you attach a separate script member, known as a behavior, to the same sprite in the Score.

Another example of cast members relating to each other would be a bitmap image and a 3D world. The bitmap might be used as a texture to paint the surface of a 3D object in the 3D world.

Multiple and External Casts

Director MX allows you to break your members up into multiple cast libraries. You start with a default Cast named "Internal." To create a new Cast, open the Cast panel and use the Choose Cast button menu at the upper left to choose the New Cast option. You can also choose File, New, Cast from the main menu bar.

Once you have more than one Cast, tabs will appear at the top of the Cast panel to allow you quickly select the Cast being shown in the panel.

When you create a new cast, you have the choice of whether this new cast should be internal or external. An *internal cast* is stored in the same Director file as your default cast and the rest of the movie's information. An *external cast* is stored in its own file. These files typically have a .cst extension and reside in the same directory as the movie file.

You can use external casts to organize your media, allow others to work on a cast while you work on the rest of the movie, or easily swap out media in a movie. For instance, you could have a cast with all English text and graphics, and then swap it out for a cast with all Russian text and graphics.

You can also create an external cast and choose not to use it in the current movie. You will have the option to do so when creating the cast. This means that you have temporary access to the cast library, but it will not reappear the next time you open the movie. You will not be able to access all of its functionality either. This is a good way to quickly remove members from your cast while still saving them in a file for later reference.

USING THE STAGE

The Stage is the only window that the end users will actually see. It is where all the visual action of a movie takes place, at least until you start using some advanced techniques.

During authoring, the Stage has two main purposes. The first is to show you a preview of what the users will see. While the movie is stopped, you see a frozen moment in time: one single frame of the movie. The second main use for the Stage is to allow you to position sprites on the screen.

The Stage also acts as your primary placement tool. You can drag cast members to either the Stage or the Score to use them on the Stage. However, you can only use the Stage to position sprites with the mouse. With the Score and other tools, you are limited to positioning the sprites by tweaking numbers. On the Stage, you can position sprites by dragging them with the mouse.

It is important to differentiate the Stage window in Director from the actual Stage. The Stage is the area where your

The Stage in Director MX is the only normal window. Everything else is a panel. You can make the window temporarily disappear by pressing (Command-1) [Ctrl+1]. You can make it reappear the same way.

Director movie is seen. The end user will see only this area. However, the Stage window in Director MX can show this area, plus the area that surrounds it.

Figure 1.4 shows the Stage window. In this case, the Stage window is slightly larger than the Stage area. The white area represents the Stage, which is the area the user will see in the final product. The gray area around it is an off-Stage area that you can still use during authoring. Sprites can be positioned anywhere in the Stage window or beyond it, even if that position is outside of the white area.

Figure 1.4
The Stage is shown inside the Stage window at 100% zoom, along with some extra gray area around the Stage itself.

Zoom amount

You can stretch the Stage window just like most other windows on the Mac or Windows operating systems. You can use the scrollbars of the window to see different areas of the Stage or the off-Stage area.

Stage Properties

While zooming in and out changes the scale of the Stage for editing purposes, changing the actual Stage size is done by choosing Modify, Movie, Properties and looking at the Movie tab of the Property Inspector. A common Stage size is 640 pixels wide and 480 pixels high, because that screen size was the standard for personal computers for a long time. Today, 800×600 seems to be a more common size for presentations, or even 1024×768.

The Stage window can also be shrunk or magnified in a number of ways. One way is to use the pop-up menu shown previously at the bottom left of Figure 1.4. You can also use the keyboard shortcuts (Command-=) [Ctrl+=] and (Command--)

You don't have to decide on a Stage size at the beginning of a project. Just keep in mind that the top-left corner of the Stage stays still if you readjust the Stage size. Only the width and height from this top-left corner can change.

[Ctrl+-]. This zooming feature helps you arrange objects on the Stage, but does not affect playback for the end user.

Another property of the Stage is its background color. You can set the background color of the Stage in the same place where you set the Stage size. The default is white and the second most common setting is black, but you can use any color.

Grids and Guides

Using grids and guides is a way to quickly position sprites. Find the menu items that pertain to grids and guides by choosing View, Guides and Grids. This will open the Property Inspector to the Guides panel, which you can see in Figure 1.5.

Figure 1.5
The Guides tab of the Property Inspector allows you to add guides and a grid to the Stage window.

The *grid* is a set of evenly spaced lines on the Stage that serves as a visual guide, or as something that your sprites lock to as you rearrange them on the Stage. You can set horizontal and vertical amounts for the grid, and then specify whether you want to have sprites snap to the grid. This is useful when you want to quickly lay out items in precise positions relative to each other.

Guides are like the grid, but each guide line can be individually placed. You can place horizontal and vertical guides, and you have the option to display them visibly, or not, and have sprites snap to them, or not.

Turn grids and guides on and off and set their preferences by selecting View, Guides and Grid, Settings. This brings up the Property Inspector with the Guides and Grid settings properties. Change the color of the grid and guides here. You can also click the horizontal and vertical guide buttons, next to the New label and beside the Remove All button, to add guides.

To align the sprites in a movie, you can simply turn on grids or guides. You can set the vertical grid to 60 pixels and space each sprite by just dragging it until it locks onto a grid line. You can position

1

the sprites to a vertical grid line as well, which accomplishes the left-side alignment. Or, use guides and create a custom guide line that you want the sprites to snap to.

Stage Tools

The bottom of the Stage includes a set of interface elements that control movie playback. In Director 8.5 and earlier, these items were in a separate control palette.

From left to right, the controls are explained in Table 1.2. Not all of the controls are visible in the Stage window. The frame and tempo displays will only be seen if you detach the controls from the Stage by (Control-clicking) [right-clicking] on the controls and selecting Detach Control Panel.

Table 1.2   Stage Window Controls

Control	Description	Keyboard Shortcut
Rewind	Rewinds the movie to frame 1.	(Command-Option-R) [Ctrl+Alt+R]
Stop	Stops the movie on the current frame.	(Command-.) [Ctrl+.]
Play	Plays the movie from the current frame.	(Command-Option-P) [Ctrl+Alt+P]
Step Backward	Moves the playback head backward one frame. Holding down either button scans the movie quickly.	(Command-Option-Left Arrow) [Ctrl+Alt+Left Arrow]
Step Forward	Moves the playback head forward one frame. Holding down either button scans the movie quickly.	(Command-Option-Right Arrow) [Ctrl+Alt+Right Arrow]
Frame	Displays the current position of the playback head. Entering a number in the frame counter and pressing Return/Enter advances you to that frame.	When dragging the mouse in the frame counter, (Option-dragging) [Alt+dragging] moves the playback head quickly forward or backward.
Tempo Mode	This pop-up menu determines how the tempo is displayed. The choices are frames per second (fps) or seconds per frame (spf).	
Tempo	This is the assigned speed of the selected frame in either fps or spf. Entering a new tempo into the field and pressing Return or clicking the arrow buttons changes the tempo.	
Actual Tempo Mode	This pop-up list sets the display mode of the actual tempo to the right of this setting. The choices are frames per second (fps), seconds per frame (spf), Running Total, and Estimated Total. Running Total is the elapsed time since the start of the movie. Estimated Total is a more accurate, although slower, calculation of elapsed time.	

Table 1.2 Continued

Control	Description	Keyboard Shortcut
Actual Tempo	This number shows the actual tempo that Director is achieving in the current frame. Depending on how much activity is taking place on the Stage, the actual tempo could be less than the assigned tempo on slower machines. It never exceeds the assigned tempo.	
Loop	Sets whether the movie should play again after the last frame, or play only once.	(Command-Option-L) [Ctrl+Alt+L]
Volume	This pop-up menu sets the volume for the entire movie. It can be overridden by Lingo commands.	(Command-Option-M) [Ctrl+Alt+M] will toggle the sound on and off.
Play Selected Frames Only	Toggle this button on or off to set the movie to play only the selected frames in the Score panel. A green line at the top of the sprite channels indicates the selected frames. If the movie is looped, only the selected frames play over and over.	

⇨ *If you have noticed that some of the features mentioned in this chapter aren't showing up in your version of Director, see "Missing Interface Elements" in the "Troubleshooting" section at the end of this chapter.*

USING THE SCORE

The real heart and soul of a movie is the Score. As you can see in Figure 1.6, it really is just a chart of the contents of the movie. Time, represented by frames, goes across the Score, whereas sprite channels and other elements are listed as rows in the chart.

Score Panel Basics

The Score panel shown in Figure 1.6 contains more information than the default Score panel. To reveal all of this extra information, choose View, Sprite Toolbar and also click the Hide/Show Effects Channels button at the right edge of the Score (it looks like two small arrows pointed at each other). We'll review the effects channels as we use the functions that each channel represents. Right now, the part to focus on is the main area with sprite channels and frames.

The left side of the Score shows channel numbers. By default, the score has 150 sprite channels. You can change the number of channels in a movie by choosing Modify, Movie, Properties and changing the Channels property.

Hide/show effects channels

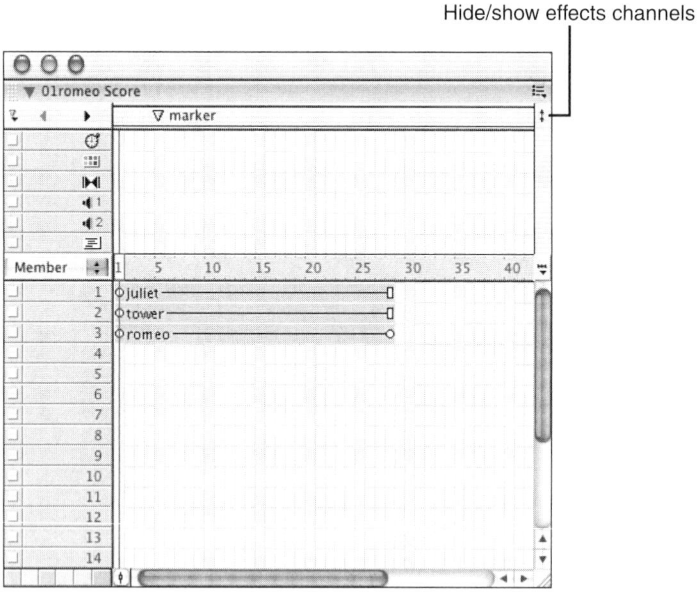

Figure 1.6
The Score panel shows frames horizontally and channels vertically. Other elements appear near the top.

When a sprite is added to the Score, it appears as a horizontal series of cells in the grid. You can see an example in Figure 1.6.

A sprite often spans more than one frame. For instance, a sprite may start on frame 1 and stop on frame 5. You can adjust a sprite's span by clicking and dragging each end of the sprite span. Click in the middle of the span and drag it up or down to move the sprite in a channel. In Figure 1.6, the sprite span is 28 frames long.

Near the top of the Score panel is the marker area. You can mark special frames in your movie with text called *labels*. A typical marker label might be "introduction" or "main animated loop." You add a marker by simply clicking in the marker area. The small down-arrow button on the left enables you to see a list of markers. The two other arrows enable you to jump between frames that have markers.

Effects Channels

Under the marker area are some rows that contain special channels. Table 1.3 details what each of these channels does.

The default sprite span for new sprites is 28 frames. But you can change that in the Preferences panel for the Score.

To get rid of a marker label, just click it and drag it away from the marker area.

Markers can be used to organize your project. When you begin programming with Lingo, markers are even more important because you can refer to them in your code.

Table 1.3   Effects Channels

Channel	Description
Tempo	Use this channel to specify the speed at which the movie moves through this frame. Double-clicking this row brings up a dialog box. Specify the rate at which this movie should be progressing in frames per second (fps). This setting persists until another frame contains a new setting to override it. You can also set the Tempo channel to pause for a certain number of seconds. This is useful for slow animations, such as automatic slideshows. Other settings include having the movie stop altogether until the mouse is clicked, and having the movie wait for a sound or video cue point.
Palette	This channel controls the palettes. Color palettes, rarely needed with today's computers, are used if a computer is capable of displaying only 256 colors. You can use the Palette channel of the Score to set which palette is used in which frame. There are also a few palette special effects that can be performed.
Transition	Director has a number of predefined visual transitions that can be applied to a frame. The transition defines how that frame appears as the movie goes from the preceding frame to the current one. For instance, you can have the screen wipe from left to right, or have one frame dissolve into the next.
Sound	The two Sound channels enable you to define sounds that automatically play when a frame is shown. For example, you can have background music playing in Sound channel 1, and voice narration in Sound channel 2. With Lingo, you can use even more Sound channels.
Frame Script	In the Frame Script channel, you can place Lingo script members that are meant to control that specific frame, the sprites on it, and the entire Director environment, as long as the movie is passing through that frame.

Modifying the Score Panel

The Score panel is by far the most customizable panel in Director. There are a number of ways to add or remove controls and fields.

Table 1.4   Score Customization

Score Element	How to Customize	Use
Effects Channels	Button to the right of markers	If you do not need to use the effects channels, you can hide them to make more room for sprite channels. Animators will typically use the effects channels while Lingo programmers typically do not.
Zoom Menu	Pop-up menu to the right of the frame numbers	This allows you to expand the width of the frames in the score. This is useful if you need room to display the names of members in the Score.
Sprite Toolbar	Choose View, Sprite Toolbar	The Sprite toolbar is an alternative view of the Sprite tab of the Property Inspector.
Sprite Labels	Choose View, Sprite Labels	You can specify when information is shown in sprite spans. For instance, you can show the member name at only the start of the sprite, or at every keyframe.

1

Table 1.4 Continued

Score Element	How to Customize	Use
Sprite Information Display	Pop-up menu to the left of frame numbers	Allows you to select how much information to display in each sprite span. You can show the member, the ink, the blend, the location, or the behavior.

The Sprite Information Display pop-up's last choice is "Extended." This means that each sprite span can display a whole set of information. To determine which information is displayed, choose Director, Preferences, Score.

An alternative way to hide or show many of the modifications in the preceding table is to (Control-click) [right-click] on an inactive part of the Score panel to bring up a context menu. It can be hard to find an inactive part of the Score to click on, but the frame number area will work.

Other Score Functionality

Next to each channel in the score is a small square. Click on it to make the channel invisible. This will remove the sprite from the movie, just as if it wasn't there. Scripts will not be executed on these sprites.

You can also use this square to deactivate any effects channel, such as scripts or sounds. The channel itself will remain unaltered, so you can turn off a channel temporarily without actually changing the Score.

At the bottom left corner of the Score are six color chips. When you select one or more sprites in the Score, you can change their color by clicking on one of these color chips. This is strictly an organizational tool, and doesn't affect movie playback. Only the color of the sprite in the Score changes, not the color of the sprite on the Stage.

Another Score function that doesn't affect playback is the ability to lock sprites. Lock a sprite by selecting it, then clicking the lock button in the Sprite toolbar or Property Inspector. You can also (Control-click) [right-click] on the sprite and choose Lock.

The reasons you would want to lock a sprite include preventing yourself or a co-worker from accidentally changing the sprite, and allowing yourself to easily select other sprites near or behind that sprite.

WORKING WITH TOOL PANELS

To complement the major parts of Director—the Stage, Score, and Cast—the tool window panels are small controls that allow you to edit sprites and other objects.

Property Inspector

The most versatile and most useful tool panel in Director is the Property Inspector. This panel contains information about the current sprite selected. So its appearance and function change constantly.

For instance, if you have a bitmap sprite selected, the Property Inspector will have Sprite, Behavior, Member, Bitmap, Guides, and Movie tabs.

Figure 1.7 shows a typical view of the Property Inspector. A bitmap sprite has been selected in the Score, so the panel reflects that by displaying the proper tabs that have to do with that sort of sprite.

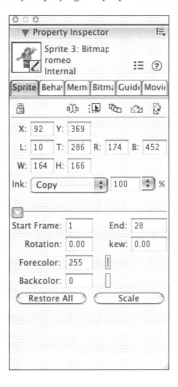

Figure 1.7
The Property Inspector shows all of the tabs associated with the selected bitmap sprite.

If you think your movie is running too slowly, it may be because you have too many tool panels open, see "Movies Run Too Slow" in the "Troubleshooting" section at the end of this chapter.

Tool Palette

The Tool Palette, shown in Figure 1.9, contains a variety of buttons. Most of them enable you to quickly create both a cast member and a sprite at the same time by placing a new element on the Stage. To open or close the Tool Palette, press (Commmand-7) [Ctrl+7].

Table 1.5 explains each tool, from top to bottom and left to right.

If you are ever unsure which icon matches which tool in any of the toolbars in the Director interface, all you need to do is simply move the cursor over that tool and wait for the tool tip label to appear next to your cursor.

1

Figure 1.8
The Tool Palette allows you to quickly create new members on the Stage.

Table 1.5   The Tool Palette

Tool	Use
Arrow	Enables you to select sprites on the Stage with the arrow cursor.
Rotate and Skew	Enables you to grab certain types of sprites and rotate them at any angle. You can also grab the corners of sprites and pull them to distort the image.
Hand	Allows you to drag the actual Stage around inside the Stage window.
Magnifying Glass	Allows you to zoom in on a spot of the Stage. Hold the (Option) [Alt] key to zoom back out.
Text	Allows you to click and drag in the Stage window to create a new text member. Text members can use embedded fonts, advanced styles, and anti-aliasing.
Line	Allows you to click and drag in the Stage window to create a new line member.
Shape Tools	These six tools allow you to create ovals, rounded rectangles, and rectangles, both filled and unfilled.
Check Box	Allows you to create Director-style check boxes. You can use Lingo to determine the state of a check box.
Radio Button	Allows you to create Director-style radio buttons. You can use Lingo to link radio buttons and read their states.
Field	Enables you to create field members. Field members are more basic than text members, but have a few special features of their own.
Push Button	Lets you create simple buttons with text labels inside them.
Color Chips	Allows you to change the foreground and background color of the selected sprite. Different types of sprites react differently to color changes.
Pattern	Enables you to select a pattern for the sprite. Patterns are tiled bitmap images that repeat over the duration of the sprite area. You can use them only on filled shape sprites.
Line Width	You can set the line width of any line or outlined shape. The options here are limited, but Lingo enables you to use other sizes as well.

Other Panels

Director includes many other small panels that can be used to modify sprites and members. Table 1.6 presents a summary of all of these panels and their keyboard shortcut for easy access.

Table 1.6   Tool Panels

Panel	Keyboard Shortcut	Description
Behavior	(Command-Option-;) [Ctrl+Alt+;]	View, add, or edit behaviors applied to a frame or a sprite.
Text	(Command-T) [Ctrl+T]	Edit the font, size, and style of selected text in text members, fields, and some panels.
Object	(Shift-Command-`) [Shift+Ctrl+`]	View the properties of a sprite or Lingo object.
Align	(Command-K) [Ctrl+K]	Aligns, centers, or spaces sprites on the Stage.
Color Palettes	(Shift-Command-7) [Shift+Ctrl+7]	View color values and edit palette members.
Library	None	Lists premade behaviors that can be applied to frames and sprites.
Markers	(Shift-Command-M) [Shift+Ctrl+M]	Lists the labeled markers in the Score.

SETTING DIRECTOR PREFERENCES

Director has several preferences dialog boxes that you can use to change the Director environment. There are no correct or incorrect ways to set these preferences; it's all a matter of personal taste. The best approach is experimentation to find what suits you best.

You can bring up most of the preferences dialog boxes by choosing Director, Preferences on the Mac, and File, Preferences in Windows, and then choosing the appropriate category.

General Preferences

The General Preferences dialog box is shown in Figure 1.9. It contains some settings similar to those seen when creating a projector.

The Stage Size set of options has to do with the Stage size and position. You can set the Stage to either use the settings of each movie that is opened (Use Movie Settings option), or match only the current movie (Match Current Movie option).

You can use the Center option to set the Stage to automatically center when a new movie is opened and force the monitor to change color depths for each movie with the Reset Monitor to Movie's Color Depth option. The Animate in Background option tells Director to keep playing the movie even when Director is not the front-most application.

Figure 1.9
The General Preferences dialog box enables you to specify a few general options.

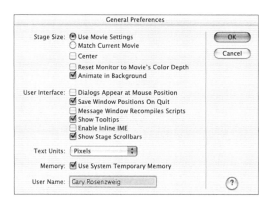

The next set of options in the dialog box is the User Interface options:

- **Dialogs Appear at Mouse Position**—Determines whether dialog boxes appear at the mouse position or centered on the monitor.

- **Save Window Positions On Quit**—Tells Director to remember the window positions when you quit, so when you return to Director the next time, they are in the same places.

- **Message Window Recompiles Scripts**—Automatically recompiles all scripts when you enter something in the Message panel. Although it makes sense to always do this, if you are working on a movie that is filled with errors, you cannot use the message window for much until you fix the errors.

- **Show Tooltips**—Turns Tooltips on or off. Tooltips are the little yellow boxes that appear as you hover the mouse over buttons in the interface. They can be useful, but you might find them annoying.

- **Enable Inline IME**—An IME is an Input Method Editor. Turning this option on allows you to use special hardware or software to enter characters in some languages that use other alphabets, such as Japanese.

- **Show Stage Scrollbars**—You can turn this option off to make the Stage look more like it did in Director 7. You can still zoom in and out with the Magnifying Glass tool and move the Stage inside the Stage window with the Hand tool.

The Text Units list in the General Preferences dialog box also enables you to set the ruler measurement for panels that use a ruler. You can select inches, centimeters, or pixels.

The Use System Temporary Memory check box enables Mac users to tell Director to use memory outside its normal memory block. This doesn't work with virtual memory turned on, however, and it is unclear whether it works in OS X at all.

At the bottom of the dialog box is a space to change the username. It starts off with the username that was entered when Director was installed. However, you can change this here.

I set the text units to pixels. Using inches just doesn't make sense. If you want to create a small margin in your text boxes, you can easily specify 2 pixels, but it is hard to figure out the equivalent in inches (.03 is close).

When you modify a cast member, the name of the user is recorded in the Modified By property of that member. This name is also permanently attached to a movie as the "Created By" information when it is created.

Network Preferences

The Network Preferences dialog box enables you to set the network preferences for Director. Figure 1.10 shows this dialog box. It has settings similar to those found in a Web browser.

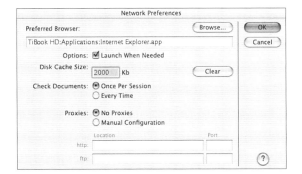

Figure 1.10
The Network Preferences dialog box enables you to set the default browser and cache options.

The Preferred Browser option sets the default browser used by Director. Primarily, this comes into play only when you use a `gotoNetPage` Lingo command. It is also used when you choose File, Preview in Browser to check how your movie works in Shockwave.

The Launch When Needed option specifies whether Director should automatically launch the browser when it is required by the movie, such as a `gotoNetPage` command. If you turn it off, the browser will not launch.

The Disk Cache Size text box enables you to define the size of the disk cache. Like browsers, Director movies can access files from the Internet and store them in a cache for later retrieval. You can set Director to check the file on the Internet for new versions Every Time or only Once per Session. Choosing Once per Session means that if a document on the Internet is updated after you access it once, you might get the older copy of it when accessing it the second time during the same session.

For those who have to work behind a firewall of some sort, the Proxies set of options enables you to set proxies to get files through the firewall. Consult your network administrator about these settings if you need them.

Editors Preferences

If you double-click a bitmap member, it brings up the Paint Editor to enable you to edit the bitmap. However, you can have it launch Photoshop instead by associating bitmaps with Photoshop. You can edit that member in Photoshop and then save the changes back into the cast member.

The Editors Preferences dialog box, shown in Figure 1.11, enables you to select different editors for different cast types. You can access this dialog box by choosing File, Preferences, Editors. This dialog also features some options for some Director-only member data.

Figure 1.11
The Editors Preferences dialog box enables you to choose external editors for some cast member types.

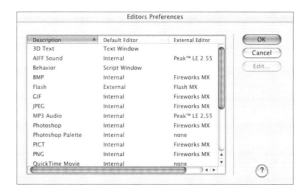

For example, a common setting is to use Peak LE to handle sound members. You can point Director to your copy of that application using this window. Then, when you double-click a sound member, you will launch Peak LE.

Certain member types have special settings. Behaviors, for instance, enable you to pick between opening the Behavior Inspector or the Script window.

You can even tell Director to scan your computer for applications that can be used to edit a type of file. You will be presented with a list and asked to choose your preferred editor.

I always change the Behavior editor to Script Window. If you leave it at its default of Behavior Inspector, it takes an extra step to get to the Script editor every time you select a behavior. As a Lingo programmer, this gets very annoying.

Script Window Preferences

The last preference dialog box listed in the File menu enables you to set a few options for the Script panel. Figure 1.12 shows the Script Window Preferences dialog box.

Figure 1.12
The primary use of the Script Window Preferences dialog box is to control coloring.

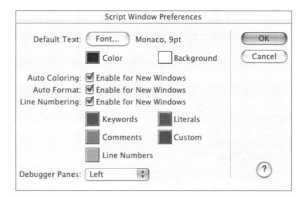

With the Default Text option, you pick a default font for the Script panel. You are still able to change the font of any script; this option just establishes the font to be used when a new script is created.

The bulk of the settings are for script colorization. Director MX automatically colors your scripts to make them easier to read. These settings determine what colors you want Director to use. You can also turn this option off and color the scripts on your own.

The default settings are blue for keywords, red for comments, light blue for line number, dark gray for literals, and green for custom variable and function names.

The last setting determines where the debugger will appear when the Script panel becomes a combined Script panel/Debugger panel. This will happen if you get a Lingo error during playback, or you force the debugger to be used by setting a breakpoint. You can place the debugging panes above, below or to either side of the script pane.

There are many other preference windows, specific to a part of Director such as the Paint Editor. Details of those preference windows will be discussed in other areas of the book where they apply.

Movie Properties

Each movie has some global properties that can be altered. To access these, choose Modify, Movie, Properties. The Property Inspector appears, showing the movie's properties. The settings here affect only the current movie. Figure 1.13 shows the Property Inspector.

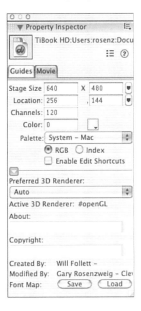

Figure 1.13
In the Property Inspector panel, you can change the size, location, and color of the Stage.

The first group of settings lets you change the palette, size, and location of the Stage. You can also set the background color of the Stage.

The palette is simply the default palette that the movie will use to display itself on an 8-bit monitor. The palette setting is not very important anymore because most computers have monitors set to a higher bit depth.

The last item in the top portion of the Property Inspector enables you to change the number of sprite channels in the movie. The default is 150, but you can set it as high as 1,000.

The color selection option is very important. If you select RGB, the movie does not use a specific color palette, but instead displays with thousands or millions of colors. If you

The only reason to set the number of sprite channels to less than 1,000 is because movies will play slightly faster with fewer channels to examine.

select Palette Index, however, you can specify a default movie palette. These settings affect mostly Lingo commands that need to specify color numbers.

The Remap Palettes If Needed setting enables Director to display a bitmap image on the Stage with the best possible colors even when the bitmap's palette and the Stage's palette are different. This would only be needed if the user's monitor is set to 256 colors for some reason.

The Enable Edit Shortcuts option allows the user to use standard cut, copy, and paste functions in editable text members on the Stage.

You can use the About and Copyright options to set an information message and a copyright line in the Director movie. This will be embedded in the file and seen by people looking for more information about the movie within some playback methods. The Created By and Modified By information is set by Director according to the registration of the Director application.

The buttons at the bottom of the dialog box enable you to define a font map for the movie. A *font map* is a small text file that you can save out from this dialog box and edit. After it is edited, it can be loaded into the movie with this same dialog box.

The font map was once very important. It tells Director, Shockwave, or a projector exactly how to deal with fonts when the movie is played back on a different platform: Mac or Windows. The file is well commented and easy to edit. The font map is no longer very important because text members can use fonts that are embedded into the movie as cast members.

Movie Playback Properties

The Movie Playback Properties dialog box, shown in Figure 1.14, offers even more movie settings. You can get to it by choosing Modify, Movie, Playback.

Figure 1.14
The Movie Playback Properties dialog box gives you control over streaming and Shockwave menu settings of a movie.

The first setting, Lock Frame Durations, enables the movie to remember the speed at which it played back on your machine. Every frame that is played remembers how long it was on the screen. When the movie is on another computer, it plays back at the same speed, no matter how much the speed might differ from frame to frame. This setting enables you to prevent faster computers from playing your movie back too fast, but it does not enable your movie to gain any extra speed on slower machines.

The next setting, Pause When Window Inactive, determines whether the movie keeps playing when it is a movie in a window (MIAW) and it is not the frontmost MIAW. A *MIAW* is a Director movie that is run in a separate window rather than on the Stage. You can read more about them in Chapter 10.

The next set of options has to do with streaming movies over the Internet. Play While Downloading Movie enables streaming. Download X Frames Before Playing enables the machine to download a specified number of frames before the movie begins playing. Show Placeholders enables you to show placeholders, usually boxes, in place of media that has not yet been loaded. When the graphics arrive, the boxes are replaced with the graphics.

GETTING HELP

Director comes with full-featured online help in the form of a Mac OS X Help Center volume and a Windows Help volume. Although the manuals and this book contain just about everything you need to know, sometimes the online help is the quickest way to find the details of a feature. The Director help files are informative and comprehensive.

To access help, use the Help menu. Or, on most computers, you can press Alt+H or the Help key.

In addition, a lot of information is available in the support section of Macromedia's Web site (http://www.macromedia.com). The Web site has a Tech Notes section that includes a variety of helpful tips and tricks. When you are having a problem and you think, "I bet I'm not the first one to run into this!" check the Tech Notes. They are compiled by Macromedia tech support from common and interesting support calls.

> Caution
>
> Using Play While Downloading Movie is really meant for movies that are simple animations. If you use this option with a Lingo-driven movie, you may get errors when users on modems play the movie back since some of the cast members your Lingo code needs may have yet to be downloaded.

> The online help for Director is really just a digital copy of the printed manuals. But, unlike the manuals, it is searchable and has cross-referenced links you can click on.

Also, many other Web sites offer information, tips, and developer forums. See the Appendix "Online Resources," for more information and a list of places to start.

TROUBLESHOOTING

Missing Interface Elements

For some reason I don't seem to have the same panels and tools available as what this chapter covers. Why aren't they there?

If you cannot find some feature mentioned in this chapter, it might be because your copy of Director has its preference settings set in a different way. Many preferences show or hide different features of the authoring environment.

Cast Preferences Won't Stick

I'm certain that I set my Cast panel preferences to show thumbnail rather than list view, but when I open a movie I did a while back, it reverts back to list view again. Why?

Some preferences, such as Cast panel thumbnail sizes, do not persist across movies. If you change this preference, and then open an old movie, the Cast panel reflects the preferences set for that movie.

Movies Run Too Slow

I thought I had a system that was sufficient to run Director, but my movies are running so slowly, I'm concerned that I don't have enough memory.

You can cause your movie run very slowly by having too many windows and panels open. For instance, if your movie changes a text member as it animates, the thumbnail in the Cast panel will update and the frame indicator in the Score will update. The view of the member in the Property Inspector may also be updating. So instead of Director just updating the Stage like it would for the end-user, it may have to update several windows. By using (Command-Shift-Option-P) [Ctrl+Shift+Alt+P] to run your movie, you can isolate the Stage for better test conditions.

DID YOU KNOW?

- Most preference windows can be reached by (Ctrl-clicking) [right-clicking] on the element, window, or panel that you want to affect. Many times the contextual menu brought up by this click will have some commonly used options available in the menu, in addition to a menu item that will bring up the complete preferences window.

- Grids always start in the upper-left corner. If you want to have a grid that starts a little farther in, such as a 20×20 grid that starts at 10×10, you can just use the 20×20 grid as is, and then move all the sprites over and down by 10 pixels when you are done. This way, your grid starts at 10 horizontally and vertically, and it continues to 30, 50, 70, and so on.

- If you ever want to reset your preferences to the default settings, and you are using a Mac, just throw away the `User/Library/Preferences/com.macromedia.DirectorMX.plist` file. In the past, this has been the only way to retrieve a window or panel that is lost from sight.

- You can also set the font type, size, and style of text in the Message panel. This is not a preference, but you can select the text in the Message panel and change it. New text placed in the Message panel picks up the font used where the cursor in the Message panel is located.

- You can also find files in a folder called Props that describe the way the Property Inspector creates its property options. They are interesting to look at, but fool around with these at your own risk.

2

WORKING WITH DIRECTOR
MEMBER TYPES

IN THIS CHAPTER

USING BITMAPS

Bitmaps are usually photographs, renderings, scanned images, or non-vector illustrations. You can create bitmaps in a variety of programs, and then bring these images into Director by importing from a variety of standard formats. You can also create and edit bitmaps by using Director's Paint Editor.

Types of Bitmaps

The biggest difference between types of bitmaps is that they can be of different bit depths. There are five different bit depth settings: 1, 4, 8, 16, and 32. *Bits* refer to the amount of information stored for each pixel of a graphic. A 1-bit image has only one piece of information: on or off. An 8-bit image has eight pieces of information, which corresponds to 256 possible combinations.

With today's computers, there is little need to use anything less than 32-bit graphics. These are the best quality, allowing millions of color variations. Plus, with Director's ability to compress 32-bit images in JPG format, the 32-bit images can take up very little space.

8-bit bitmaps use a 256-color palette. This palette usually contains black, white, a small range of grays, and a general selection of basic colors. You can customize an 8-bit palette both on the Macintosh and in Windows. Director ships with a number of built-in 8-bit palettes. You also can import custom 8-bit palettes into your Director movie either with images that use them, or on their own in the standard palette format (PAL). They are then stored as cast members.

A 1-bit bitmap contains only black-and-white pixels. 1-bit bitmaps can be useful because you can define the colors of the two types of pixels to different colors depending on the sprite. So, a single 1-bit member can be used multiple times to display graphics with different colors.

Importing Bitmaps

Even though there is only one bitmap member type, a variety of formats can be imported into this bitmap member type. You can import any one of these types of formatted files:

- **BMP**—A common Windows graphic format.
- **GIF**—A format originally used by CompuServe known as the Graphic Interchange Format. It's now one of the two standard image formats of the Internet.
- **JPEG**—Defined by the Joint Photographic Experts Group as a high-quality compressed image format. It is also a standard image format of the Internet.
- **LRG**—The native format of Macromedia's xRes image editor.
- **Photoshop (PSD)**—The native format of Adobe Photoshop.
- **MacPaint**—An older Macintosh image format.
- **PNG**—Portable Network Graphics format. There is some momentum behind this format to be the new standard for the Internet. It is also the native format for Macromedia Fireworks.
- **PICT**—Originally defined for the Apple Lisa computer, now a standard Macintosh image format.

- **Targa**—Also known as the .tga format. Targa was the name of the Truevision graphics card that first used the .tga format.

- **TIFF**—Tag Image File Format.

After you import any of these file formats into Director as a bitmap, it no longer matters what the original format of the document was; it is now a bitmap cast member.

By default, however, JPEG, GIF, and PNG files retain their original file data inside Director until you edit them. These originals are then used as the compressed image data when a Shockwave movie is made. The result is that the Shockwave movie is far smaller than the original Director movie, which contained both the original file data and the Director-formatted bitmap.

⇨ *For more information about Shockwave movies, see "Publishing Shockwave Movies," p. 687.*

To import a bitmap image, choose File, Import. This brings up Director's Import dialog box. Figure 2.1 shows this complex window. You can import most media from here, including sound and video.

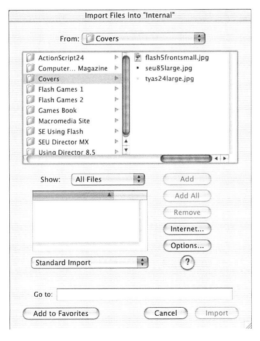

Figure 2.1
The Import dialog box enables you to select the files you want to import into the Cast.

If the graphics are set to the same bit depth as the monitor, and use the same palette as the movie does, they are immediately brought in. Otherwise, you are prompted with the Image Options dialog box where you are given the choice of bringing in the bitmap using its bit depth or palette, or converting it to the bit depth of the movie. The Trim White Space option allows you to remove any excess white pixels from around the image. Selecting the Dither option smoothes over any color changes that need to be made. The final option, Same Settings for Remaining Images, enables you to bypass this dialog box for the rest of the images that you have selected in that single import.

After you have imported a bitmap, you can still change its bit depth or palette. Just select a bitmap or bitmaps in the Cast and choose Modify, Transform Bitmap. This command also enables you to resize the image.

Editing Bitmaps with the Paint Editor

The Paint Editor panel allows you to edit bitmap images right in Director. You can open the Paint panel by double-clicking a bitmap cast member or using (Command-5) [Ctrl+5].

Figure 2.2 shows an empty Paint Editor panel. Note that it has toolbars both on the top and on the left side of the panel. It also has a typical set of buttons and the name field at the top of the panel.

The Trim White Space feature of the Image Options dialog box defaults to on. You might want to turn it off when you are importing graphics that use whitespace around them to cause each graphic to line up on the screen with the others. This often happens when importing a group of related images, such as images exported from PowerPoint, or a set of images exported from a 3D graphics tool.

Figure 2.2
The Paint panel has more than 50 buttons and other items that enable you to alter bitmap images.

The tools on the left side of the panel are used to edit or add to the bitmap. Notice that some of them have a small arrow at the right-bottom corner of the button. This means that you can click and hold over that button to see a small pop-up list of tool options. Table 2.1 shows all of these tools and what they are used for.

Caution

If you edit a bitmap that was originally imported from an external file, you will permanently convert that cast member to a plain internal bitmap, removing its compressed original format. Also, you cannot edit 32-bit images that have alpha channels, as there is no way to edit the alpha channel component.

Table 2.1   Paint Editor Tools

Tool	Use
Marquee, Shrink	On selection of an element, the selection marquee shrinks to the outside edges of the artwork to create a rectangular selection. All white pixels contained within this selection are seen as opaque white.
Marquee, No Shrink	On selection of an element, the selection marquee remains in the dragged position as a rectangular selection. All white pixels contained within this selection are seen as opaque white.
Marquee, Lasso	On selection of an element, the color of the pixel where the drag was started and all same-colored touching pixels are ignored. All other colors within the selection are selected within a flat-sided selection. All white pixels contained within this selection are seen as opaque white.
Marquee, See Thru Lasso	This option behaves the same as Marquee, Lasso except all white pixels contained within this selection are seen as transparent (no value).
Lasso, No Shrink	The area drawn with the Lasso tool retains its shape and selects all its content. All white pixels contained within this selection are seen as opaque white.
Lasso, Lasso	On selection of an element, the color of the pixel where the drag was started and all same-colored touching pixels are ignored. All other colors within the selection are selected within the drawn area. All white pixels contained within this selection are seen as opaque white.
Lasso, See Thru Lasso	This option behaves the same as Lasso, Lasso, except that all white pixels contained within this selected area are seen as transparent (no value).
Registration Point Tool	Used to view or reset the registration point of a member. A registration point is a location in the bitmap that the Stage uses to decide the placement of the sprite.
Eraser Tool	Paints white pixels on the bitmap. Double-clicking this button erases the entire image in the panel.
Hand Tool	The hand tool does the same job as the panel's scrollbars by moving around the visible area of the paint panel. You can quickly access the Hand tool by pressing the spacebar.
Zoom Tool	The Paint Editor changes somewhat when you zoom in. The upper-right corner of the panel contains an actual-size version of what you see in the main, zoomed area of the panel. You can also use (Command-=) [Ctrl+=] or (Command—) [Ctrl+-] to zoom.
Eyedropper Tool	Enables you to select a color in the Paint Editor to use as the foreground color. If you hold down the Shift key, that color becomes the background color. If you hold down (Option) [Alt], that color becomes the gradient destnation color. Even when not using this tool, you can hold down the (Option) [Alt] keys to temporarily change to the eyedropper tool.
Paint Bucket	Enables you to fill an area with the foreground color. The fill begins at the hot spot of the fill cursor, which is the tip of the pouring paint. The fill changes the color of the selected pixel and all pixels of that color that surround it. Double-clicking the Paint Bucket button brings up the Gradient Settings dialog box.

Table 2.1   Continued

Tool	Use
Text Tool	Selecting this tool changes the cursor to a text insert cursor. You can then click in the Paint editor to set the start position of the text. You can double-click the Text tool button to bring up the Font dialog box, with which you can change the font, size, and style of the text you are inserting.
Pencil Tool	The simplest, and yet the most useful, tool in the Paint Editor. You can draw one pixel at a time with this tool, something that is not easy to do in Photoshop or other image-editing programs. You can also draw straight lines by holding down the Shift key.
Air Brush Tool	The effect the Air Brush tool creates, at first, might not look like paint being sprayed out of an air brush. To get a very smooth spray, the pixels must be smoothed out or anti-aliased, something you generally don't want to do in a Director animation. The Air Brush tool can create some fun patterns despite its limitations. This tool has five fixed settings, ranging from small to large, and a custom setting dialog box to set up your own air brush pattern. Click the Air Brush tool to activate the pop-up menu. Choose Settings or double-click the Air Brush tool to open the Air Brush Settings dialog box.
Brush Tool	Used for freehand drawing. It uses one of five brush settings. Click and hold the button to choose which setting you want to use, or open the Brush Settings dialog box.
Arc Tool	Draws an arched line on the canvas the thickness of the line set in the line weight selection area of the Tool palette. Pressing the Shift key when an arc is created causes the arc to constrain to a circular radius.
Line Tool	The Line tool creates straight lines. The width of a line in the Paint editor can be between 1 and 64 pixels. Click the default one-, two-, and three-pixel line width settings, or double-click the Other Line Width setting to select a larger width. Pressing the Shift key before starting to draw a line causes the line to constrain to a 45° angle.
Rectangle and Ellipse Tools	The Rectangle and Ellipse tools create basic shapes on the canvas. These bitmapped shapes can be filled or unfilled, depending on which tool you select. The line weight of the shape is set with the Line Weight selectors. Pressing the Shift key as the bitmapped rectangle or ellipse is being created constrains the shape to square or circular, respectively.
Polygon Tool	The Polygon tools create both filled and outlined polygons. Each click you make on the Paint panel with the Polygon tool becomes a corner of the desired shape. The shape can be finished by either double-clicking to close the shape or by clicking the last position over the top of the first position.
Color Chips	Four color chips are in the left-side tool area of the Paint panel. They correspond to the foreground color, the gradient destination color, the foreground color, and the background color. You will notice that two color chips represent the foreground color. They behave as you might expect, with a change made to one of these two affecting both. So, despite the four color chips, there are really only three color settings.
Gradients	Between the first foreground color chip and the gradient destination color chip is a small area in which you can specify a gradient for use with the Paint Bucket tool and some other tools. You can select options such as Top to Bottom, Bottom to Top, Left to Right, Right to Left, Directional, Shape Burst, and Sun Burst. You can also choose to bring up the Gradient Settings dialog box for more control.

Table 2.1   Continued

Tool	Use
Patterns	Director includes a set of patterns that you can use for fills instead of a solid color. Clicking the area directly below the background color chip brings up the palette of patterns.
Line Weight Settings	Five choices for line weights are given at the bottom-left corner of the Paint panel. The first is to have no line. The others are widths 1 through 3. The last line width choice is a custom setting. Double-clicking the last line width choice brings up the Paint Window Preferences dialog box, where you can set it.

> *If you are having trouble with the pencil tool while editing 1-bit images, see "Problems Editing 1-bit Cast Members" in the "Troubleshooting" section at the end of this chapter.*

In addition to these drawing tools, the Paint Editor panel has an ink mode setting. This is a small pop-up menu at the bottom of the Paint Editor that usually reads "Normal." This pop-up enables you to set the ink of a drawing tool, such as the Paintbrush tool or the Rectangle tool. These are different from sprite inks in that they apply only to the result of editing in the Paint Editor. Not all inks are available to all painting tools. The ink options are as follows:

- **Normal**—The default ink draws with the foreground color or selected pattern.

- **Transparent**—When used with a pattern, this ink draws only the foreground color and leaves the background areas (white pixels) of the pattern with their existing colors.

- **Reverse**—This ink reverses the color of anything drawn over. If used with a pattern, only the black pixels of the pattern reverse the pixels under them.

- **Ghost**—This ink draws with the current background color. If you are using black and white, white pixels are drawn in such a way that they show up over a black background.

- **Gradient**—This ink uses the gradient settings and draws appropriately. Use with the Paint Bucket tool or a shape drawing tool.

- **Reveal**—This unusual ink uses the image of the previous bitmap member in the Cast. As you paint, you are actually painting with colors from that member, mapped onto the current bitmap.

- **Cycle**—This ink causes the Paintbrush tool to cycle through colors in the palette as you draw. It starts with the foreground color and cycles through all the colors until it reaches the background color. It can then repeat the sequence or move through the sequence in reverse, depending on your setting in the Paint Window Preferences dialog box.

- **Switch**—This ink causes any pixels that use the foreground color to switch to the destination color. You should have your monitor set to 8 bits for this to work properly.

- **Blend**—This ink enables you to blend the foreground color with the color of the pixels underneath it. It works best with 16- or 32-bit bitmaps.

- **Darkest**—This ink draws the foreground color only when it is darker than the pixels you are drawing over.

- **Lightest**—This ink draws the foreground color only when it is lighter than the pixels you are drawing over.

- **Darken**—This ink darkens the pixels as you paint over them.

- **Lighten**—This ink lightens the pixels as you paint over them.

- **Smooth**—This ink smoothes differences between adjoining pixels. The current color settings have no effect on the operation of this ink.

- **Smear**—This ink creates an effect similar to smearing paint across the image. The current color settings have no effect on the operation of this ink.

- **Smudge**—This ink is similar to smear, but the colors do not carry as far.

- **Spread**—This ink is similar to using the Eyedropper tool and then painting. Each time you click in the Paint editor, the spread ink picks up the color under the brush and uses it to paint that stroke. It even works when several different colors are under the paintbrush. It just repeats that pattern as you draw.

> Not all Paint Editor panel drawing inks can be used at all times. It depends on which tool you are using. The inks that you cannot use will be inactive in the menu.

- **Clipboard**—This ink draws with the clipboard image as the paintbrush shape and color pattern.

Paint Window Preferences

The Paint Window Preferences dialog box, shown in Figure 2.3, enables you to set a variety of options. In the middle, you can see the custom line width setting ("Other" Line Width) mentioned previously. Most of the rest of the options deal with the different inks.

Figure 2.3
Open the Paint Window Preferences dialog box by choosing File, Preferences, Paint or by double-clicking the custom line width tool.

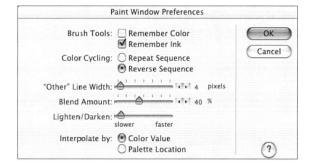

The Remember Color and Remember Ink options enable you to specify whether you want Director to remember the last color set and ink used with each brush. The Interpolate By option determines whether the Cycle ink is to cycle between colors in the palette or real colors.

The Paint Editor also has a ruler that you can turn on or off. You can do this by choosing View, Rulers. After rulers are turned on, you can click a small area in the upper-left corner of the Paint editor to change the type of units that the ruler displays.

You can also hide or show the Paint editor tools in the View menu. The tools still work, but you won't be able to change them unless you use keyboard shortcuts.

The Effects Toolbar

Abovethe paint area is another toolbar space with a few buttons that represent certain tools. To use these tools, first select an area in the bitmap. These tools are defined in Table 2.2.

Table 2.2 Effects Toolbar Buttons

Tool	Use
Flip	The Flip Horizontal and Flip Vertical tools flip a selected element across a horizontal or vertical axis.
Rotate	Selected elements can be rotated 90° clockwise or counterclockwise. The Free Rotate tool enables the selected element to rotate freely around its center. The selection places handles on each of the element's corners. Drag these handles to a new position to produce the rotation.
Distort	The next three buttons can create interesting effects. The Skew tool skews selected elements by slanting the sides of an element equally, leaving the top and bottom of the element perpendicular to one another. The Warp tool enables handles of the selected element to be pulled around to create a smashed or twisted effect. The Perspective tool shrinks or expands the edges of the selected element to give the illusion of depth.
Smooth	This tool enables smoothing of pixels within a selected area of artwork. The smoothing effect functions only when the bit depth of the cast member is set to 8 bits.
Trace Edges	This tool creates a new 1-pixel-thick line around the edges of the original pixels of the artwork, leaving the original pixels white.
Invert	When clicked, Invert causes the selection to change its black pixels to white, and white pixels to black. Colors in the active 8-bit palette flip to the opposite side of the palette. To see the exact place a color occupies in a palette, open the Color Palettes panel from the Window menu. If an image has a color depth higher than 8-bit, the Invert button replaces the colors with their RGB complement colors.
Lighten and Darken	Selected elements grow lighter or darker in their palette of colors. This command is unavailable in a 16-bit color space.
Fill	This tool fills any selected area with the current foreground color or pattern.
Switch Colors	This tool changes the color of identically colored pixels in a selected area. Pixels that match the foreground color are changed to the destination color. Switch Colors works only when the cast member is set to a palette of 256 or fewer colors.

Registration Points

A *registration point* is a location in the bitmap that the Stage uses to decide the placement of the sprite. Figure 2.4 shows a bitmap with the Registration Point tool activated so you can see exactly where the registration point is located.

Figure 2.4
The horizontal and vertical lines
indicate the precise location of
the registration point in the
bitmap.

By default, the registration point is at the center of the image.
A bitmap displayed at location 50, 120 on the Stage, would
then be centered at 50, 120. However, you can use the
Registration Point tool to shift that point from the center of
the image, and thus have it displayed according to the new
registration point.

Why would you want to do this? If you are animating something that requires a series of members—a man jumping, for
example—you would expect the center of the graphic to
change as the animation progresses. In the middle of the
jump, for instance, the center of the man would be higher
than at the start. You can move that portion of the sprite
higher on the Stage when creating the animation.

However, by using different registration points, you can have
each bitmap in the animation stay at the same Stage location,
and let the offset of registration points do the movement for
you. You can then easily reuse this set of cast members as an
animation without having to reposition every sprite.

> Bitmap members use the center
> of the bitmap as the default regis-
> tration point. However, text and
> field members use the upper-left
> corner of the sprite as their regis-
> tration points. You can't change
> the registration points of text or
> field members.

> If you open a bitmap member
> where the registration point is not
> in the center, you can double-click
> the Registration Point tool button
> to re-center it.

Bitmap Member Properties

Bitmaps have a few options that can be set in the Property Inspector, as shown in Figure 2.5. You
bring up the Property Inspector with the bitmap settings showing by clicking the *i* button at the top
of the bitmap Paint Editor.

Figure 2.5
The Property Inspector enables you to set a bitmap's options when a bitmap is selected in the Cast, or the Paint editor is open.

At the top of the Property Inspector bitmap member settings area is a pop-up menu with a list of palettes. This will have an effect on the image only when the bitmap is set to 8-bit. It enables you to change the palette for the member without actually transforming the actual pixels in the member. The new palette is applied, and the pixels in the image will now display on the screen with those palette colors.

The available options for working with bitmaps include

- **Highlight**—enables you to have the bitmap automatically invert itself when users click it. This can be used to make quick-and-dirty buttons that react to mouse clicks.

- **Dither**—This option comes into play if you scale or rotate the image. The image might display better with a dither, but dithering might hurt your animation speed.

- **Trim**—Enables you to retain white pixels around the bitmap, even if it is edited in the Paint Editor.

- **Use Alpha**—Determines whether the Alpha channel of the bitmap is used when it is displayed on the Stage.

Alpha channels are a fourth channel of image data. The others are the Red, Green, and Blue channels. The Alpha channel defines how transparent each pixel is. If you create a 32-bit image with an Alpha channel, you can anti-alias the edges of the image, or make some of it transparent. You can use the Use Alpha option to make graphics that are semitransparent or have edges that blend nicely with any background.

The Compression setting enables you to decide how the image is compressed when the movie is saved as a Shockwave movie. You can use the normal bitmap compression, which is similar to how Director 5 and 6 saved all bitmaps, or you can opt to use JPEG compression for the image. You can also choose the Movie Setting option from the Compression list, which means that the cast member will follow the preferences set by the Publish Settings dialog box.

JPEG compression is best used for photographic images and other things that do not require precision. Depending on the Quality setting, JPEG compression will blur your image more and more to squeeze it into a smaller file space.

In addition to being able to use JPEG compression, you can choose the Optimize button if you have the Macromedia Fireworks program installed. This option allows you to use the excellent compression techniques that Fireworks has available.

> Using JPEG compression with 32-bit images that use an alpha channel could cause the alpha channel to degrade beyond being useful. I've had cases where the alpha channel develops spots of opaqueness after bringing the JPEG compression down too low.

The Alpha Threshold defines how much of a role the Alpha channel plays in defining where the users can click the image. If the image is set to transparent, the Alpha channel is used to define the clickable area.

Photoshop Filters

Although not all the features of programs such as Photoshop are available in the Paint Editor, one powerful feature, *filters*, can be borrowed. If you are a Photoshop user, you probably already know about filters and what they can do. From a simple blur to a complex rendering, filters can alter an entire graphic or part of one. They are really just special effects for still images.

In Photoshop, you place filters in a `Plug-ins` folder and access them through the Filter menu. You can apply the transformation, such as a blur effect, to the entire image, or to just a selected area.

⇨ *If Director keeps crashing when you are trying to use a filter, see "Photoshop Filter Crashes Director" in the "Troubleshooting" section at the end of this chapter.*

Director can borrow these Photoshop filters and use them on cast members or in the Paint Editor. First, you need to tell Director where the filters are. This can be as easy as making an alias or shortcut to your Photoshop filters folder and placing it in the Director Xtras folder. You can also copy filters, or folders of filters, into the Xtras folder.

> **Caution**
>
> Photoshop filters seem to be supported in Director MX, as they are mentioned in the documentation. However, I was unable to get them to work in the final version of Director MX in OS X. Check the Macromedia support area to see if they have recognized the problem and posted a fix.

The simplest way to use filters is to apply them to an entire single cast member. Select that cast member in the Cast and choose Xtras, Filter Bitmap. This brings up the Filter Bitmap dialog box, which organizes the filters into categories.

> In addition to the filters that come with Photoshop, several third-party companies make filters that work with both Photoshop and Director.

If no filters show up in your dialog box, it means that you have no filters in your Xtras folder, or the filters that you have are not compatible with Director. You also might be missing the Photoshop Filters Xtra, which should have been installed when you initially installed Director.

To use a filter, select it and click the Filter button. If the filter has its own dialog box, as most do, you see that dialog box first and can then choose your options. The filter is then applied to the cast member.

A powerful feature of using filters with Director is that you can apply a filter to more than one cast member at a time. Simply select multiple cast members in the Cast panel and apply a filter. Each of the members gets the same filter, with the same settings, applied to it.

You can also apply a filter to a selected area of an image using the Paint Editor. In that case, the filter is applied to only that area in that one bitmap image.

Director also has an auto filter function. Choose Xtras, Auto Filter to use it. Its purpose is to create a series of bitmaps based on a filter that changes slightly over time. However, very few filters are built to have a filter-over-time function. The dialog box that appears lists only the filters that do. Do not be disappointed if no filters are shown. Hopefully, more filters will be written in the future to take advantage of this feature.

If you don't get as nice an effect as you expected, check the bit-depth settings of the bitmap. Most filters only work well with 32-bit images. If you have an 8-bit image that you want to filter, convert it first to 32-bit in the Paint editor panel, filter it, and then convert it back to 8-bit.

When working with filters, use a lot of caution. Filters are written by third-party companies that rarely test their filters on Director. Some filters do not work, others work in strange ways, and some will crash Director. Save your movie and Casts just before trying to apply a filter. If a filter does not work at first, add more memory to the Director application and try again.

USING TEXT MEMBERS

Text members are complex, involving many options and features. However, you can create a simple text member without much trouble. Just select the Text tool in the Tools panel and click the Stage. This creates a text cast member and at the same time places that member on the Stage and in the Score. You are then in edit mode, and can type text into this member directly on the Stage.

After you finish typing your text, click elsewhere on the Stage to deselect the text member. There are two different ways to select a text member. The first, achieved by simply clicking it, enables you to drag the sprite around the Stage. You can also stretch and shrink the sprite's Stage area. If you double-click the sprite, you can once again edit the text inside it. In this mode, you cannot move or resize the sprite.

Text Editing

Although editing on the Stage is quick and easy, it doesn't give you as much control over the text as editing the member in a Text Editor panel. Open the member in a Text Editor panel by double-clicking it in the Cast. You can also (Command-click) [Ctrl+click] the sprite to bring up a context menu. From here, you can select Edit Cast Member.

Figure 2.6 shows the Text Editor panel with the typical options. A simple toolbar at the top of the panel gives you tools to change the font, size, style, alignment, line spacing, and kerning of any selection. A standard text ruler also enables you to add and adjust tabs.

Figure 2.6
The Text Editor has functions similar to that of a simple word processor.

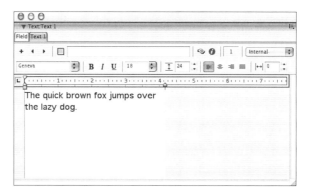

The tools in this toolbar are self-explanatory. Line spacing enables you to set how many pixels apart each line begins. *Kerning* is an adjustment that you can make to the spacing of each character. Although in most fonts each character has a different width—an *m* being wider than a *l* for instance—you can add or subtract from the width of each character space. This does not change the actual shape of the character, only the amount of space between that character and the next.

Using the tabs in the ruler is fairly simple, as well. Click the Tab button, which appears to the left of the ruler, to change the type of tab you want. There are tabs that left-justify, right-justify, and center text. There are also decimal tabs that line up columns of numbers on their decimal points. To add a tab, click in the ruler. To remove a tab, click and drag that tab away from the ruler.

You can specify left, right, and first-line indents for paragraphs in the ruler as well. The thick markers along the top and bottom of the ruler can be dragged left and right. Drag the black bar to the right of the text area to stretch or shrink the page width. This bar brings the right margin along with it.

Justified text, the last option of the four justification buttons, aligns both the left and right sides of lines of text. This is commonly used in newspapers. Although this technique looks nice at first, it can be distracting to the reader if the text columns are too narrow. Make sure you use it only for wide columns of text where many words appear on each line.

When setting any text property, whether it's font, size, tabs, or indents, remember that the property affects only the selected text, or the text in the paragraph in which the cursor is located. To have the change affect the whole member, select all the text first.

Text Importing

Although the Text Editor is great for editing text, larger pieces of text are likely to come from an outside source, such as a word processor. You can easily import text of various formats into Director. Director will even remember most of the various styles and settings of that text.

The three primary file formats can be read by Director are text, rich text (RTF), and hypertext markup language (HTML). The first type of file does not have any formatting; it's just a simple stream of characters. You can still style these characters after they are in a text member, but they have no styling when they first arrive.

➡️ *If you are getting odd results when importing RTF or HTML files, see "Problems Importing Text Files" in the "Troubleshooting" section at the end of this chapter.*

The other two formats can contain a variety of styles and formats. Rich text contains a similar set of styles and formatting options to the Text Editor. There are more advanced forms of RTF files, but the basic idea behind rich text is to accommodate different fonts, sizes, styles, and paragraph formatting. As long as your RTF files stick to these basics, you should be able to import them completely.

Some RTF files, such as those created from complex Microsoft Word documents, can include tables, images, and drawings. Director skips these elements when it imports the RTF file because the text member type does not support these options. All in all, rich text is your best bet for importing general text that uses only some basic formatting.

Since version 7, Director allows you to import HTML files, as well. You can create these files with some modern word processors, but they are commonly created with HTML editing programs.

Director cannot import all the elements and formats used in modern HTML, but it does a fairly good job with those it can. Standard styles, font size changes, paragraphs, line breaks, and the most basic tags are all supported. Director even goes as far as importing tables. This is probably the most powerful aspect of the HTML import.

After the HTML text has been imported, you can edit it in the Text Editor. However, because HTML is more complex than the features of the panel, you might be better off editing the original HTML document in an HTML editor. Of course, if your text is only a few lines or plain paragraphs, it should work just fine.

Text Member Options

You can set a variety of options to change the appearance of your text member. To change text member properties, use the Property Inspector. One way to get to these settings is to click the Information button in the Text Editor, or use the context menu on the Stage. The Property Inspector appears, as shown in Figure 2.7.

Figure 2.7
You can use the Property Inspector to make decisions about how the member will look on the Stage.

Table 2.3   Text Member Properties

Option	Choices	Function
Display	Normal	Displays as a normal text member
Display	3D Mode	Allows you to display the text as a 3D member using the character outlines to make quick 3D models.
Framing	Adjust to Fit	The sprite's height adjusts to automatically fit the amount of text in it.
Framing	Fixed	Allows you to manually stretch or shrink the sprite, and the text in it is cropped if it can't fit.
Framing	Scrolling	Use a scrolling frame, which enables you to set the exact size of the text sprite. If the text doesn't fit, the scrolling bar on the sprite becomes active and the users can scroll through the text.
Editable	On/Off	Making the member editable means that every time the member appears on the Stage, it is editable. However you can also make a sprite editable, which means it is editable only for that single sprite instance.
Tab	On/Off	This property enables the users to use the Tab key to move from editable text member to editable text member on the Stage.
Wrap	On/Off	The Word Wrap option is useful when you have long lines of text that you want to keep to a single line, rather than wrapping them to a second or more. If a line of text is longer than the width of the text member, the rest of the line is simply not seen.
DTS	On/Off	The Direct to Stage option speeds up the presentation of the text by ignoring other sprites drawn under it.
Use Hypertext Styles	On/Off	Any links in the hypertext will appear as blue and underlined, just as they typically do in a Web browser.
Anti-Alias	All Text	Anti-Aliasing means that the text will display with smooth edges when possible.
Anti-Alias	Larger Than	This uses the field next to it to determine at what size to start anti-aliasing text.
Anti-Alias	None	All text in this member appears without smooth edges.
Kerning	All Text	This uses font information to control spacing between characters.
Kerning	None, Larger Than	Uses the field next to the menu to determine at what size to start using font kerning.
Pre-Render	Copy Ink	Enables you to have Director create the image for the text member before it is displayed on the screen, thus speeding up the display. This setting will only work for text members shown with copy ink.
Pre-Render	Other Ink	Creates a static text image that can be used with non-copy inks.
Pre-Render	None	The text member is created on the fly as the movie is played.

Table 2.3　Continued

Option	Choices	Function
Save Bitmap		If you are using pre-rendering, you can choose to have the image created when the movie is saved, rather than when it is loaded. This means that Shockwave playback can be done without the fonts used in the text member.

Working with the Text Inspector Panel

Although the Text Editor's toolbar contains just about everything you need to style and format text, it's not always convenient to have this panel open. Instead, you can edit text directly on the Stage, as shown previously, and use the Text Inspector panel to make some style and format changes. Figure 2.8 shows the Text Inspector. Access it by choosing Windows, Inspectors, Text.

Using the pre-render options means that the text won't be editable or changeable by Lingo during playback.

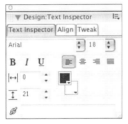

Figure 2.8
The Text Inspector panel can be used to style and format text in text members, fields, scripts, and even in the Paint Editor.

In addition to the style and format tools, the Text Inspector has two color chips. You can use the foreground color chip to change the color of any selected text. The background color chip works on the entire text member that is being edited. A text member can have only one background color. This color is ignored if you are displaying the sprite in a background transparent ink.

You can also use the Text Inspector to add hyperlinks. For now, this just colors and underlines the text for you. When you read about the Lingo involved in hyperlinks, you will see how this can be used for navigation and control.

⇨ *For more information about adding hyperlinks to text members, see "Using HTML and Hypertext," p. 374 (Chapter 13).*

Using the Font Dialog Box

Although you can change fonts with either the toolbar in the Text Editor or the Text Inspector, you can also bring up a Font dialog box that contains detailed information about your selected text. Figure 2.9 shows this dialog box.

You have three more style choices in the Font dialog box: Superscript, Subscript, and Strikeout. Superscript and Subscript adjust the vertical position of the selected text. Strikeout places a line through the center of the text.

Figure 2.9
Choose Modify, Font to access the Font dialog box. You can also use (Command-Shift-T) [Ctrl+Shift+T].

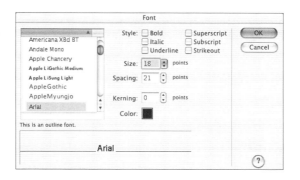

You also have a much nicer font selection method in the Font dialog box. The scrolling list is easier to look through than the pop-up menu. In addition, the Font dialog box will tell you which fonts are capable of displaying as anti-aliased text. Bitmapped fonts cannot be anti-aliased, whereas TrueType fonts can.

Only fonts that can be anti-aliased appear in the list when you choose Insert, Font. If you select some text in a text member and choose Modify, Font, you get the font dialog box seen in Figure 2.9. As you select fonts, you see either "This is an outline font" or "This font cannot be anti-aliased" under the font list.

The Paragraph Dialog Box

The Paragraph dialog box, shown in Figure 2.10, enables you to set the left, right, and first-line indents. Unlike the actual Text Editor, the Paragraph dialog box enables you to set these indents to precise numbers. You will find that this comes in handy when you are trying to match settings between two or more text members. Clicking and dragging the indent tabs does not give you precise enough control.

Figure 2.10
Choose Modify, Paragraph to access the Paragraph dialog box when you have text selected. You can also use (Command-Shift-Option-T) [Ctrl+Shift+Alt+T].

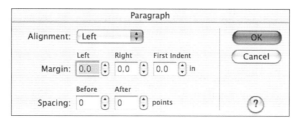

Use the Paragraph dialog box to set extra space between paragraphs. Specified in points, you can set the spacing before and spacing after so that paragraphs are spaced farther apart than normal lines of text. This is a technique sometimes used to increase the readability of large text blocks.

Inches? Yep, the margin settings in the Paragraph dialog box are in inches. If you would rather use pixels, you can change this preference in general preferences dialog using the Text Units setting.

Using 3D Text

Thanks to the 3D engine inside Director and Shockwave, simple text members can now pop out of the 2D world and use a variety of 3D special effects. Making your text members 3D is easy—almost too easy. This is a lavish special effect that should be used rarely.

Figure 2.11 compares two text members that are exactly the same, except that the second member has been set to 3D Mode using the text member's display property seen back in Figure 2.7.

Hello World!

Hello World!

Figure 2.11
The first text member is normal, but the second is the same member with its display type set to 3D Mode.

As you can see, this is an effect that is really meant for screen titles or special highlighting. If you made entire sentences or paragraphs of text that used the 3D mode, it would be very hard for users to read.

Displaying 3D text relies on Director's 3D engine. This engine, in turn, relies of the user's computer's abilities to display 3D. If the user has a 3D video card, for instance, then the 3D text will appear faster and nicer than if the user's computer has to render the text in software mode.

There are a variety of options that you can set for 3D text. They can all be found with the Property Inspector. Select the text member in the score to bring up the Property Inspector, and search the tabs at the top for the 3D Extruder tab. When you select it, you will see a Property Inspector that looks like the one in Figure 2.12.

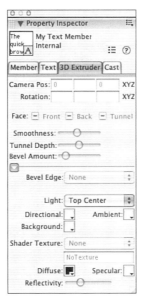

Figure 2.12
The 3D Extruder panel of the Property Inspector displays a variety of options that determine how your 3D text will look.

The first set of options defines the camera position and angle. When talking about any 3D object, such as text in this case, the camera defines the point in space that the user is looking through to see the 3D object. In the case of 3D text, the camera is in front of the text looking straight at the text. This gives you the view seen in Figure 2.12.

There are six parameters that define the camera. The first three are the x, y, and z positions of the camera. The x and y positions are simply the horizontal and vertical location. The z position is the third dimension, so to speak. It is the *depth*. So the position shown in Figure 2.13 is 90 units to the right of center, 55.5 units down from the center, and 177.04 units back from the center. This can also be represented as (90,55.5,177.04).

Why these numbers? Director created them when you decided to set the text to 3D mode. The text itself is placed in the 3D world at such a location so that the bottom left corner of the text is at the world center, (0,0,0). Moving the camera to the position (90,55.5,177.04) places the camera where it appears to be looking directly into the center of the text and the camera is far enough away so that the text appears to be the proper size on the screen.

The six parameters at the top of Figure 2.12 give you complete control over the position of the camera. The most immediately useful are the two z values. The z position will allow you to easily move the camera toward or away from the text. The z rotation value will allow you to spin the text around the visual center of the text.

Shockwave 3D

A much easier way to control the appearance of the 3D text is to use the Shockwave 3D Editor. First select the text member so that it is shown in the Text Editor tab of the panel, and then switch to the Shockwave 3D tab. You can now move and rotate the text. A button called Set Camera Transform at the top of this panel will make any changes to the camera permanent; otherwise, they will not affect the real cast member.

The next set of options are three check boxes called Front Face, Tunnel, and Back Face. These are the three portions of the extruded text. You probably never want to turn off Front Face and leave the other two on, but combinations like Front Face and Back Face or just Front Face could create useful effects.

The Smoothness setting allows you to modify the 3D detail in the model. Larger numbers will mean that the text is constructed with more polygon faces. The downside is that the model is more complex and may be harder for slow, non-3D machines to render.

The Tunnel Depth setting is simply the length of the distance between the front and back face of the text. A smaller amount would mean that the letters simply appear as solid shapes, while a larger amount would suggest flying, zooming text like you sometimes see in movie titles.

The second half of the 3D Extruder properties as seen in Figure 2.12 contains some more advanced options. A Bevel Edge will make the edges of the letters, at the point where the front face and the tunnel meet, look rounded. The effect is very slight, so a figure here would do very little to demonstrate it. Play with the bevel settings, both Round and Miter (angled) and the amounts to see what sort of effect it has on text of your choice.

The Director Light, on the other hand, has a very pronounced effect. You can change the main light that shines on the text to be in a variety of positions. You can also change the color of this light by selecting a color for the Directional light. Unless you want to tint the text a different color, you will want to stick with varieties of white, black, and grays.

The Ambient light is a glow that comes from all directions and hits the text evenly throughout. You can easily set either the Directional or the Ambient light to black (turned off) and just use one of the two lights. Experimentation with these settings will usually pay off by giving you the perfect lighting effect.

The Background color doesn't affect the text at all, but simply changes the color of the pixels behind it. If you set the sprite to use Background Transparent ink, then this setting doesn't matter.

The last set of controls allows you to determine what texture is applied to the text. The default is to use None, which produces an even, solid color. The Diffuse setting controls the overall reaction of the model to light, while the Specular color is used for highlights where the light is hitting the model almost directly. With Shader Texture set to None, these two colors control the color of the model completely.

You can also set the Shader Texture to Default, which will use a red and white checkerboard pattern, or the far more useful Member setting, which allows you to select a bitmap member as the texture.

The last setting, Reflectivity, determines how much light is reflected from the texture. The lower the number, the more washed-out the texture will appear as more of the directional light is reflected from the surface. It will look very shiny, to put it simply.

USING FIELD MEMBERS

Once the only text option in Director, field members are still useful for a variety of tasks. For one, they take up much less file space than text members. A text member with the phrase "This is a test" placed in it is about 1,600 bytes, whereas a field containing the same text is only about 700 bytes. The difference is even more dramatic when you use anti-aliased text in the text member.

Using the Field Editor

The Field Editor, shown in Figure 2.13, looks different from the Text Editor. For one thing, the ruler is gone. Field members do not have the capability to recognize indents or tabs. However, you can still adjust the width of the field.

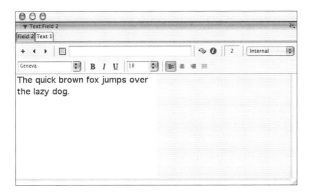

Figure 2.13
The Field Editor is similar to the Text Member tab, except fewer options are available.

You also cannot fully justify text; only left, center, and right justification is possible. The Justify button is inactive.

Fields cannot be imported. Instead you have to copy and paste text into the Field Editor if you want to use text generated by an outside program. You can't anti-alias text within fields either.

⇨ *Developers can use fontmap.txt to have more control over how fonts are mapped on other machines, across platforms. See "Mac and Windows Cross-Platform Issues," p. 718 for more information.*

Figure 2.14 shows the Property Inspector with the field member properties. You do not have as many options available as you do with text members.

Fields are ideal for emulating the small input fields seen in HTML pages. Just set the border to 1 and the margin to 2. With the member or sprite Editable property set to TRUE, this makes a nice standalone input field.

Figure 2.14
The Property Inspector offers different options for field members than text members.

You can take advantage of four settings to add border-like elements to fields. These settings are found in the lower portion of the Property Inspector, shown previously in Figure 2.14. The available border settings are

- **Box Shadow**—Places a black shadow to the bottom and right of the field. This classic computer display effect can help make fields stand out, but can also be easily overused.

- **Border**—Enables you to add a plain black border around the field. You can add a border that is any size from 1 to 5 pixels wide.

If you are using a border, you should always use a margin. One of the most common mistakes that Director developers make is to not include a margin on their fields. This makes the text bump right up against the border, which makes it look unprofessional. A two- or three-point margin should be used.

- **Text Shadow**—Comes in handy when you are trying to display text over a background that makes the text hard to read.

- **Margin**—Adds a margin inside the field. This places extra pixels between the border and the area that contains the text.

Each setting offers six options: None, and 1 through 5 pixels.

Knowing When to Use Text and When to Use Fields

When deciding whether to use text or field members, you must take a variety of factors into account. Table 2.4 can help you decide. In most cases, you will find reasons to use both types. To choose which to use, you must decide which factor is a priority.

Table 2.4 Factors in Deciding Between Text and Field Members

Factor	Which to Use
Must look smooth	Text
Must display quickly	Field
Must not add too much to the file size	Field
Must be capable of displaying indents	Text
Consistent line spacing	Text
Must be capable of displaying tables	Text
Must be capable of receiving imported RTF and HTML files	Text
Must be able to add borders and margins easily	Field
Must be able to add a text shadow easily	Field
Must be able to add hypertext links easily	Text
Must never change appearance from platform to platform	Text

A good rule of thumb is to use text members unless you need to use one of the features of a field. You will find that text members are more versatile and easier to use.

IMPORTING FONT MEMBERS

A powerful feature of Director is the capability to import fonts as cast members. This feature enables you to use fonts in your movies that the users do not have on their machines. Otherwise, you have to use non-editable text members to display special fonts, or stick to fonts that you know the users have on their machines.

To import a font, choose Insert, Media Element, Font. This creates a new font cast member. The Font Cast Member Properties dialog box, shown in Figure 2.15, is immediately displayed. In this dialog box, choose the font that this cast member will display. The only fonts listed are those compatible with your machine.

Figure 2.15
The Font Cast Member Properties dialog box enables you to set the options for a font member.

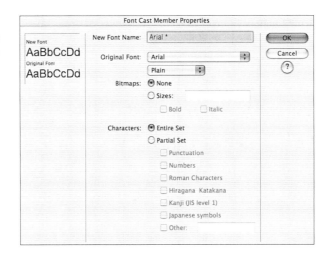

You can choose any font to be represented by that cast member. After import, the font appears in font pop-up menus as a font with the same name, but followed by an asterisk. The asterisk signifies that this is a font internal to this movie. However, Director does not convert existing field and text members to now use the new internal font. You have to change them yourself. When you create new field and text members, you can select the new internal font.

Director also enables you to decide how much of that font to import. If you want only the basic font, leave the Bold and Italic check boxes off. However, if you do want these versions of the font, check them. This increases the size of the font cast member. These members are compressed in Shockwave movies and compressed projectors, but it's a good idea to leave out whatever you don't intend to use.

> According to Macromedia, no legal issues are involved in distributing fonts inside a Director movie. There is no way for users to export and then redistribute them as fonts again. So, as long as you have the right to display the fonts on your authoring machine, you should be allowed to use them in your movies.

🖎 *If you are using embedded font members but the characters look odd when you play the movie in Shockwave, see "Styled Text Looks Wrong" in the "Troubleshooting" section at the end of this chapter.*

You can also specify the exact characters you want to import. This can further shrink the size of the font member. Another option enables you to include bitmap versions of fonts. Many fonts include bitmap versions to display perfect text at certain sizes. Include these by typing in font sizes separated by commas.

A good way to use imported fonts is to decide which fonts you want to use before authoring the movie. Import all your fonts first. You can also create external cast libraries that hold a variety of font members. You can then copy and paste these members into your current movie. This saves you from having to have these fonts on your system.

> **Caution**
> After you have a font member and are using it in text members and fields, do not try to delete or replace the font member. This will confuse your text and field members.

Another useful side-effect of using font members is that you can have custom-built fonts that display a variety of simple images. Using a program such as Macromedia Fontographer, you can create a vector graphic disguised as a font and import it into Director. You can then have text members that use these images. It's like having dozens of vector graphics embedded in a single member.

IMPORTING AND USING SOUNDS

There are many reasons to include sounds in your movies. Sounds can be used in a variety of ways, such as small button feedback noises, background music, audio narration, animation soundtracks, and special effects.

Using Sounds

Like images, sound files come in a variety of formats. Director can import a large number of these formats.

You can access sounds three different ways in Director. The first is to import them as cast members by choosing File, Import. You can place the members in the Score's Sound channels by dragging them to the Score, or you can use Lingo. Although sound members can be large, when you save the movie as a compressed Shockwave file or projector, Director can compress them for you.

Another way to use sound files in Director is as external files. Import sound files using the Link to External File option, which is a check box in the Import dialog box. This action creates a cast member that contains no data, but represents the external file. You can place this member in the Score as well. Director accesses the external file as needed. You can also play external sound files with a Lingo command, even if the sound is not represented by a member.

➪ *For more information about using Lingo to play external sounds, see "Playing External Sounds,"* *p. 217.*

You can also create Shockwave audio files. You create these files by exporting a file from your sound-editing program in Shockwave audio format. The resulting files are pre-compressed external files that can be called with Lingo. These files can also be *streamed*, meaning Director can play them over the Internet as the files are downloaded. Shockwave audio files can be created on the Mac using Peak LE. In Windows, you can use SoundForge.

Importing Sounds

You can import sounds into Director with the same import function used for bitmaps and text. Choose File, Import, and select the sound file or files you want to import. After the sound is in the Cast, you can use the Property Inspector, shown in Figure 2.16, to view information about the sounds.

As you can see in Figure 2.16, sounds have only one available option. The Loop option enables you to tell Director whether the sound is a looping one.

If looping is turned on, Director plays this sound over and over as long as the sound is in one of the Sound channels in the Score. As soon as you jump to a frame that does not have this sound, it stops.

Figure 2.16
Sound Cast Member Properties
can be seen with the Property
Inspector.

You can record sounds in Director only on the Mac. If you choose Insert, Sound, a Mac system sound recording dialog box appears that enables you to record a sound from the current sound source, usually the microphone. No editing options are available, so this technique can be used only to create temporary placeholder sounds.

Using External Sounds

Sounds tend to be large and add significantly to the file size of a Director movie. For this reason, you might want to consider keeping sounds as external files and creating a linked cast member that uses this external sound. Create a linked sound member by choosing File, Import to get the Import dialog box, and then selecting Link to External File instead of Standard Import.

Another method for using an external sound involves no cast member at all, but simply playing a file directly with a Lingo command. You will learn about sound-related Lingo commands in Chapter 7, "Controlling Sound."

An even more compelling reason to use external sounds is that internal sounds need to be completely loaded into memory before being played. If a sound is 1MB, and the user's machine does not have the extra memory to store it, the sound simply does not play. However, an external sound does not have to be completely loaded to start playing. This might be your only option for playing larger sounds.

Starting speed is another issue. A large sound inside the Director movie can take noticeable time to load and begin playing. However, an external file can also take some time to start because hard drives and CD-ROM drives have to search for the beginning of the sound file. It is best to plan for such delays when designing your movie.

Streaming Shockwave Audio

For audio to stream over a network, the data rate has to be small and regular. This means that the size of the file devoted to one second of sound and the next second of sound has to be exactly the same. This is known as the *bit rate* of the sound.

A typical streaming sound may be 16 kilobits per second (Kbps), or 16 times 1,024 bytes of information. A file with this bit rate can be streamed over a 28.8 modem that gets data at 28.8Kbps. However, a 32Kbps sound cannot stream smoothly over a modem.

Even a 24Kbps sound will probably not stream smoothly over a 28.8 modem because a 28.8 modem rarely gets a continuous stream of data at 28.8Kbps. The measurement is really telling you the maximum that the modem can receive.

Shockwave audio is typically produced by SoundEdit 16 or Bias Peak on the Mac and the Shockwave converter Xtra in Director on Windows. You can choose from a range of bit rates between 8Kbps and 128Kbps. The following list will help you decide which to use:

- **8Kbps**—Limited use for voice-only sounds when you need maximum compression.

- **16Kbps**—The only real choice for any type of audio that needs to stream over 28.8 modems. Sound quality supports voice, music, and sound effects.

- **32Kbps**—Should be used only when users are using 56Kbps modems or better. Good quality, although still mono.

- **48Kbps**—Enables you to use stereo sounds, but at a relative 24Kbps per channel rate. Users must have fast connections. This rate and higher can also be used for streaming sounds from the hard drive or CD-ROM.

- **64Kbps**—At this rate, you can do good-quality stereo sound.

- **96 and 128Kbps**—Accommodates excellent-quality audio. 128Kbps is a typical rate used for the popular MP3 format because it sounds pretty close to CD-quality audio.

If you want to get an idea of which bit rate settings match which sample frequency settings, 8Kbps uses 8KHz output sample rate, 14 and 24Kbps use 16KHz output sample rate, and 32Kbps and above try to use the same sample rate as the original sound file. However, if the sound file was at 44.1KHz and the Shockwave audio compression is set to be less than 48Kbps for mono and 96Kbps for stereo, it is forced to use 22.050KHz.

> On the Director MX CD there is a folder named Support in the Macromedia folder that contains sounds and other files that can be used to test such things as bit rate.

You can import a Shockwave audio sound completely into Director as a cast member. You can also import it as a normal linked sound. Shockwave audio files can be streamed, however, only by linking to them as Shockwave audio files.

To link to an external Shockwave audio file, choose Insert, Media Element, Shockwave Audio. This brings up the SWA Cast Member Properties dialog box shown in Figure 2.17.

Figure 2.17
The SWA Cast Member Properties dialog box enables you to link to an external Shockwave audio file.

You can type a full or relative path for the SWA file. The path can be a file on your hard disk or CD-ROM, or a Web address. Use the Browse button to quickly get the path of a local file.

You can also set the volume and Sound channel for the sound. Choosing Any for the Sound channel means the machine will attempt to play the sound in the first unused channel.

You can also set the preload time of the sound. The preload time determines how many seconds of sound have to load before the sound starts. Smaller numbers mean that the sound can begin sooner. However, a larger number reduces the chance that a streaming sound will be interrupted if the user has a bad connection. This occurs because Director buffers that many seconds of sound at the start. If Director buffers 5 seconds of sound, there needs to be only a 5-second interruption in the transmission for the Shockwave audio to need to pause and wait for more data. With a 10-second buffer, Director can take a 10-second interruption, or even two 5-second interruptions before it needs to pause the sound.

If you aren't sure what options to choose, or change your mind during development, you can still change all the Shockwave audio member settings later using the Property Inspector.

CREATING SHAPE MEMBERS

There are eight kinds of shape members: two kinds of lines, and filled and unfilled ovals, rectangles, and rounded rectangles. You can create all these shape members with the Tool palette. If the Tool palette is not already present, choose Window, Tool Panel, and then select a tool and draw on the Stage. This creates a cast member with the shape, as well as a sprite that contains the member. After you have a cast member for a shape, you can drag that member from the Cast panel to the Stage or Score to reuse it in another sprite. You can even stretch or shrink it differently in different sprites.

The ovals, rectangles, and rounded rectangles are fairly straightforward. You can set their colors by selecting the forecolor chip in the Tool palette. This changes the color of the entire shape in the case of filled shapes. However, it changes the color of only the outline in the case of nonfilled shapes. The background color chip has no effect.

Director sometimes refers to round shape members as "ellipses" and sometimes as "ovals." They are, in fact, the same thing.

If you want to create an area that is both filled with a color and uses an outline of a different color, you need to create both shapes, filled and nonfilled, and change their colors separately. The shapes cannot share the same cast member, because one cast member must be filled and the other not.

Most properties of shapes are properties of the shape member, not the sprite. The shape type and filled property, for instance, can be changed in the Property Inspector, but these changes affect all the sprites that use the same shape member. The location, rectangle, and color of the shape are sprite properties and can be set to different values for different sprites that use the same shape member. In addition, normal sprite properties, such as ink and blend, can also be set on a sprite-by-sprite basis.

You can, therefore, have four different sprites—a small blue oval outline, a small black oval outline, a large green oval outline, and a large green oval outline with a thick border—that all use one single cast member. However, if you want an oval outline and a filled oval, you need two separate cast members.

The type of shape and filled property can be changed in the Property Inspector panel. Within this dialog box you can actually change the type of member to another shape type. Although it doesn't make sense to change a line into an oval, having the capability to change a rectangle into a rounded rectangle can be useful at some point.

Line shapes don't have a filled and nonfilled version, of course. The filled property of a line member must always be turned on for the line to be visible. However, there are still two types of line members: lines that draw from the upper-left to the lower-right, and lines that draw from the upper-right to the lower-left.

If you think about it, you can see why these two types are needed. A sprite is placed on the screen at a certain position and with a certain rectangular area. This is all that is needed for a rectangle shape to be drawn, but a line shape does not automatically sense which diagonal direction to use to fill the sprite's shape. When you first draw a line, it uses your drawing motion to determine which type of line to create.

The danger is not immediately apparent. If you draw a line on the Stage from upper-left to bottom-right, and then use that same cast member in another sprite for a second line, you will have one cast member and two sprites. If you then alter one of the sprites to draw from the upper-right to the lower-left, the change is made to the cast member itself. This means that your first sprite will also flip! The solution is to use two different cast members, one for each type of line. Or, you can simply use a new line member each time if you don't mind the extra members.

Most uses for lines are not sensitive to this problem, however. If you draw a straight horizontal or vertical line, as you might use in a presentation screen layout to separate elements, it doesn't matter which line type is used.

Lines can be set to be different widths as well. You won't find this setting in the Property Inspector until you switch it to List view. You can do this by clicking the List icon at the upper-right corner of the Property Inspector.

CREATING VECTOR MEMBERS

Vector members allow you to create complex lines and shapes that can be scaled, anti-aliased, and modified on-the-fly. These shapes also take up a relatively small amount of file space, making them ideal for Internet delivery.

Using the Vector Shape Editor

To create a vector member, choose Insert, Media Element, Vector Shape to bring up the Vector Shape tab of the Editing panel shown in Figure 2.18. You can also choose Window, Vector Shape. Like the Paint Editor, it includes two toolbars. Most of the drawing tools are on the left, and the top toolbar is used to set some special properties of the shape's color fill.

A vector shape is essentially one or more long curves built around two or more points each using a mathematical calculation. Some points also contain curvature information. If the image is set to be closed, and the first and last points of each curve are in the same location, then a fill will be applied to the enclosed area.

Figure 2.18
The Vector Shape editor panel enables you to create and edit vector members.

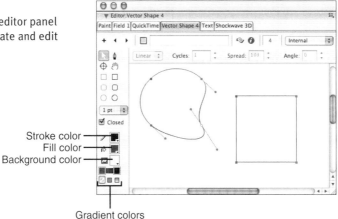

Stroke color
Fill color
Background color

Gradient colors

To create a vector shape, choose the Pen tool. Click in the panel to create the first point of the vector shape. If you click and hold the mouse button down, you can set the curvature amount, or handles, of the point. You can then place other points in different locations. A quick click adds a point with no handles; a prolonged click and hold enable you to set the curve of the line.

After you finish drawing, you can edit any point by selecting it with the Arrow tool. The arrow turns white when it is positioned over an editable point. After you select one point, you can edit its location and the locations of its handles. You can also continue the curve by selecting the Pen tool again and clicking to create another point. To insert a new point between two points that already exist, use the Pen tool with (Option) [Alt].

> Curves defined by points and handles are also known as *Bézier curves*. The first handle of any point determines how the line curves into the point, whereas the second handle determines how the line curves away from a point. So, any section of the curved line will curve depending on the second handle of the preceding point and the first handle of the next point. If neither point has these handles, the line is drawn straight from one to the other.

Six shapes are also shown in the toolbar. You can use them to make some standard shapes. Because these shapes all exist in Director as regular shape members, there is little point to using them here to create plain shapes. Instead, you can use them to create a starting point for a shape that still needs to be edited to get the result you want. For instance, you can use the rectangle shape to create a rectangle that you will edit by adding other points to create a completely new shape.

Another reason to use these standard shapes is that you might want to take advantage of the fill techniques available to vector shapes but not standard shapes. By having a closed shape and turning on the Closed setting, you can apply a fill. Select the type of fill from the toolbar on the left side of the screen. You can have no fill, a solid fill, or a gradient.

If you select a solid fill, you must also select the fill color from the collection of color chips on the left toolbar. The first is the color of the line. The line color does not matter if you set the line to be 0 pixels wide. The second is the color of a solid fill. Having these as two separate colors means that you can have a vector graphic that has one color for the outline and another for the fill. The last color chip enables you to set the color of the background. This color comes into play only if you set the sprite that uses the vector member to Copy Ink.

If you set the fill type to be a gradient, you can also set the destination color with a color chip arrangement that is similar to what is used in the Paint Editor. A host of settings in the top toolbar defines the type of gradients.

You can use a linear or radial gradient and set the number of *cycles*, or the number of times that the gradient is to travel between the initial and destination colors. The Spread setting enables you to restrict the fill to only a small portion of the image, or enlarge it so that only a portion of the gradient fits into the shape. You can also change the angle and offset location of the gradient. This gives you an incredible amount of control over where the gradient is placed and how it looks.

Vector Shape Properties

In addition to the Vector Shape Editor, the Property Inspector, shown in Figure 2.19, has a few other settings you can establish. Access the Property Inspector when you are editing the vector shape by clicking the Info button.

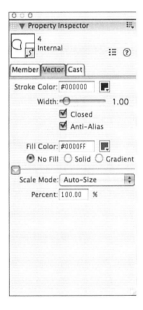

Figure 2.19
The Property Inspector enables you to define what happens when a sprite containing this member is stretched.

One of the settings on the Property Inspector determines whether the shape is drawn using anti-aliasing. Anti-aliasing uses shading to smooth out the line. This type of line is slower to draw, of course, but looks much better than a ragged line of pixels.

The Scale Mode pop-up menu enables you to choose what happens when the member is stretched on the Stage. Here are the options:

- **Show All**—The vector shape keeps the same dimensions, stretching only when it can still fit the entire shape in the sprite.

- **No Border**—The vector shape keeps the same dimensions, but scales to fill the sprite area, even if it means cutting off some of the shape horizontally or vertically.

- **Exact Fit**—The vector scales to the new dimensions of the sprite, stretching horizontally and vertically as needed.

- **Auto Size**—The sprite's rectangle changes its shape to fit the entire member as you rotate, skew, or flip it.

- **No Scale**—The vector does not scale when the sprite is stretched. This keeps the vector looking the same size, even if it means that the shape is cropped if the sprite is shrunk.

The last setting in the Vector Shape Properties dialog box enables you to scale the cast member. This is independent of any scaling on the Stage. Sprite scaling affects each sprite individually, whereas member scaling affects all instances of the member in a sprite.

Unfortunately, you cannot import vectors from other programs, such as Freehand and Illustrator. Vectors created with these programs are usually much more complex than vector cast members.

ADDING FLASH MEMBERS

Another type of vector graphic is the Flash member. Macromedia Flash is a standalone tool for creating vector graphics and animations for Web pages. It uses vectors, rather than bitmaps, to create very small files that are very versatile.

Starting with Director 6.5, developers have had the capability to import Flash members into Director as cast members. A Flash movie can be as simple as a single frame with a vector drawing on it. In this case, you can use Flash members like vector shape members. The advantage is that you can have much more in a Flash member, such as text and bitmap elements.

Flash movies can also be animations, so you can use Flash members as you use digital video. The movie can play once, loop, or even contain interactivity tools, such as simple buttons.

You can also import bitmaps and sounds into Flash movies, but because Director can already use bitmaps and sounds as members, there is little point. However, if you have graphic artists who are accustomed to working in Flash, you can easily import their animations.

After you import a Flash movie, the Property Inspector gives you many options that you can alter for the member, as you can see in Figure 2.20. You can bring up the Property Inspector by selecting the Flash member in the Cast panel and clicking the Info button.

The Rate setting enables you to alter the playback rate for the Flash movie by setting it to either Normal, Lock Step, or Fixed. Normal plays the Flash movie at the speed in which it was created. Lock Step sets its tempo so that it plays one frame of Flash animation for every one frame that the Director movie moves. The Fixed setting enables you to specify a frame rate for the Flash member.

Next, the Scale Mode option enables you to set the scale mode of the member. This determines how the member reacts when a sprite that uses it is stretched. Here are the options available:

- **Show All**—As you stretch, the smaller of the horizontal or vertical scale is used to size the image. The result is that the Flash member will always fit in any rectangle.

- **No Border**—As you stretch, the larger of the horizontal or vertical scale is used to size the image.

Figure 2.20
The Property Inspector offers
many settings for Flash members.

- **Exact Fit**—As you stretch, the image is stretched horizontally and vertically according to the rectangle of the sprite.

- **No Scale**—The image is never stretched, but is instead shown at 100% in the center of the sprite.

- **Auto Size**—Similar to Exact Fit, but if you rotate the sprite, the bounding box of the sprite expands so that the image is not clipped.

Next to the Scale Mode setting is a space for you to type a scale percentage. Unlike sprite stretching, this percentage will affect every sprite that uses the member.

Next, you can turn on or off certain features of the Flash member. You can turn off the sound or the image if your Flash movie needs to have only one or the other. You can have the movie be paused, rather than playing, when it appears on the Stage. This is useful when you want to use Lingo to start the movie. You can also set a Flash animation to loop. Otherwise, it will play through once and then stop.

For the Quality Setting, you can choose High, Low, Auto-High, or Auto-Low. The High setting shows vector lines and text in the Flash member with smooth edges as opposed to jagged edges. If you choose Auto-High, the Flash movie starts by using high quality, but reverts to low quality if it has trouble on a slower computer. Auto-Low does the opposite, starting at low quality, but then switching to high if the computer can handle drawing the graphics quickly.

You might also want to set a Flash member to start paused if the Flash movie is a one-frame static graphic, and not meant to be an animated element. This will speed up performance of the rest of the Director movie's elements.

The Preload option is useful only when the Flash movie is a linked external file rather than an imported member.

The last option is DTS, or Direct to Stage, which will play the Flash movie on top of everything else on the screen. It may give you a performance boost if you need it. You can also use the Static check box to indicate that the Flash movie does not need to animate, so Director does not have to update its image while it sits on the screen. This will definitely speed up playback of your movie.

IMPORTING DIGITAL VIDEO

Like animation, digital video presents successive frames of graphics to create a moving image. Video is typically real-life recordings, but can also be rendered animations. You can use various digital video formats with Director.

Digital Video Formats

Digital video has many aspects to consider, such as file type and compression. Because digital video files tend to be huge, uncompressed video is almost unheard of. Whatever type of file you choose to store and play back the video, you should also choose a video compression algorithm to use with this file type.

Director authors primarily use two digital video formats. The most common is QuickTime: a cross-platform multimedia format created by Apple. The other is the Video for Windows (AVI) format, which is built into Windows 95, 98, 2000, Me, NT and XP.

Both QuickTime and Video for Windows can be imported into Director as cast members. In Windows, you can have either a QuickTime member or a digital video cast member. On Macintosh computers, QuickTime is the only option. In both cases, the cast members are linked to the external video file. Unfortunately, there is no way to import a video file completely in Director; you always have to rely on the external file.

To import a digital video file, just choose File, Import and select a digital video file in the same way you select an image file or a sound. You can import QuickTime files on the Mac, and both QuickTime and AVI files in Windows.

Understanding Digital Video Settings

After a QuickTime or AVI member is in the Cast, you can set a variety of important settings in the Property Inspector. The Property Inspector is shown in Figure 2.21.

An important option to look at is the playback mode of the video. If set to Sync to Sound, the video plays normally. However, setting it to Play Every Frame (No Sound) tells Director to ignore the video timing in the digital video movie, and instead display each frame at a constant frame rate. When you do this, the sound for the video is disabled. This is useful for digital video files that contain simple, silent animation. You can present this video at a speed different than intended in the original file.

Use the Framing options to determine what happens when you stretch the sprite on the Stage. Because the size of the sprite will no longer equal the original size of the digital video, Director needs to know what to do in this case. The first option is to crop the video. Of course, if you are stretching the sprite, a crop will not occur, but neither will the video stretch to fill the space. If you choose Crop, the Center option tells Director whether it should automatically center the video in the sprite rectangle.

Figure 2.21
The Property Inspector dialog box enables you to set a number of QuickTime video options.

If you select the Scale option, Director forces the video to fill the sprite rectangle, even if it's larger or smaller than the original digital video. You can distort the video this way. Note that a digital video member that's playing back in a stretched sprite requires more processor power than one playing back at the original size.

The upper portion of the Property Inspector shows a number of options that you can turn on or off. The first two items enable you to specify whether you want to hide or show the video or sound portions of the video. In case you are using video that does not have one of these two elements, you can turn it off. For instance, if you have a QuickTime movie that contains only a MIDI track, you can turn off the video portion. Or, if you have a video that has both video and sound, you might want to turn off the sound in a situation where it isn't needed.

With the Paused option, you can specify whether you want the movie to begin playing automatically, as soon as it appears on the Stage. If you want it to show up paused on the first frame, be sure to include the controller so that the user can start the video. Alternatively, you can use some Lingo to kick off the video.

With the Loop option, you can tell the movie whether it should automatically loop. If set, this causes the movie to start at the beginning again as soon as it is finished.

The Direct to Stage option, indicated in the panel as "DTS," enables the video to be placed over all other sprites in the frame. This means that Director is telling the QuickTime or Video for Windows portion of the operating system to ignore other sprites. The result is faster, smoother playback. If you are not trying to blend the video in with any other sprites or perform any special effects with the sprites, use this option.

The Controls setting tells Director to place the standard video controller bar under the digital video. This controller is not a part of Director, but a part of QuickTime and Video for Windows.

The Streaming option tells the member to take advantage of the streaming capabilities in QuickTime and stream the movie from the hard drive or the Internet.

Working with Digital Video

To use a digital video member, just drag it to the Score or Stage. A sprite contains the video member and automatically sizes itself to the proportions of the video. If you selected the video controller option, it displays below the sprite.

If you are using the video in a presentation, you are likely to want it to appear on a frame that has a Hold On Current Frame behavior placed on it. This keeps the playback head steady and enables the video to be played back.

You can use the same Wait for Cue Point tempo setting with QuickTime movies that you can with sounds. Many editing tools enable you to place cue points in video and export the video as QuickTime. You can use the {End} setting to have the movie pause on a frame and wait for the video to end. You use this feature, of course, when you are not using the video controller and when you have the movie set so that it is not paused when it appears.

QuickTime videos are cross-platform, so the same files work on both Macintosh computers and Windows, provided that the computer has QuickTime installed. If you create a QuickTime movie on the Mac, be sure to save it following your video software's instructions on how to make a cross-platform video file. Otherwise, your Mac file might not work on Windows machines.

OTHER MEMBER TYPES

Although this chapter has so far covered the most common cast member types, there are actually many more. In fact, with Xtras, you can keep adding cast member types as long as Macromedia and third parties keep developing more Xtras.

Pushbuttons

Director pushbuttons are easy to create and use, but lack a professional appearance, which makes them useless in real-world situations. They are black-bordered, rounded rectangles with text in them. However, they can be useful for quick prototypes or as placeholders until you get around to making the final buttons.

To place a pushbutton on the Stage, use the Tools panel, select the Pushbutton tool, and then draw the pushbutton on the Stage. After you finish, you can adjust the size of the pushbutton by grabbing the corners. You can also double-click and type text into the pushbutton.

You can do a few things to get away from the standardized look of the pushbutton, for example, changing the font and style of the text inside it. As a matter of fact, if you double-click the member, you can edit it directly on the Stage. If you choose to edit it from the Cast, you do so in an editing panel that looks just like the field-editing window. You can select any font and style, and even right-, left-, or center-justify the text.

Pushbuttons are similar to fields with regard to how they handle text. They use the system's installed fonts, so make sure

You can use text members as buttons. In fact, any member can be placed on the Stage and used as a button if the proper behavior is attached. One way to get a text member to actually look more like a button is to set its background color to something other than white and center the text inside it.

that any font you use in pushbuttons is available on all machines that are expected to run the movie. The text is not anti-aliased.

You can customize pushbuttons by setting the foreground and background colors of the text. To do this, you must be editing the text, not just the sprite. Then, use the color chips to set the background color of the button and the foreground color of the text.

Check Boxes

The check box is a small square that users can click to signify a true or false value. You see them all the time in other software programs and even in Director's own dialog boxes.

The check box cast member, however, is like the pushbutton cast member in that it shows a fairly old-fashioned version of a check box that is not used in either Mac or Windows operating systems anymore.

The check box also uses a text editor similar to that of the field member. Adding a background color, however, is fairly useless because the color wraps around the check box area and you are not offered any option for setting a margin or border.

After a check box member is on the Stage as a sprite and the movie is running, you can click it to turn the check on or off. This value is then available for Lingo commands to interpret.

Creating Radio Buttons

Radio buttons are similar to check boxes. They have some text next to an on/off switch. The visible difference is the type of switch. Whereas check boxes have a box with an x in them to signify whether the switch is on or off, radio buttons are circles that have a dot in them to signify whether they are on or off.

In any group of radio buttons, only one should be selected at any time. They are usually used to offer a choice between many options. If you want users to choose one color from three, for instance, clicking the button for one color immediately turns off any other selection.

For this reason, radio buttons are grouped together. In any one group, only one can be selected at any time. Another rule is that one *must* be selected. So, you have to start users with a default setting.

You need Lingo to interpret radio button selections, and to make them work properly. A behavior that enables you to group radio buttons together is included in the Macromedia Director library.

The term radio button comes from the old-style car radios that had a row of pushbuttons on the front. If you pressed down one button, the others would automatically pop up. In fact, you could have only one button down at a time. This made sense, because you could listen to only one radio station at a time.

To make this behavior work, first create two or more radio buttons and place them on the Stage. Then, drag the behavior to the first radio button. You are prompted to assign a group name to the button. The group name should be exactly the same for the other buttons you want to group together. You also need to select the Initially Selected option for one of the radio buttons. Drag the behavior and set the parameters for each of the other buttons.

Now when you run the movie, each of these buttons controls how the others are set. Only one can be selected at a time. You can always add more radio buttons to a group, or start another group on the same frame.

Adding Cursors

Three types of custom cursors are available in Director: built-in cursors, custom bitmap cursors, and animated cursors. Each of these cursor types is discussed in the following sections.

Both radio buttons and check boxes rely on the cast member to determine whether the button is on or off. For this reason, you cannot reuse a cast member, even if it appears exactly the same, in two sprites. Clicking one of the sprites affects any others that use the same member.

Built-In Cursors

Director's built-in cursors include the arrow, the hand, the crosshairs, and the clock. The following is a list of some of the most common built-in cast members and their numbers. Use their numbers to refer to them in behaviors that ask for a cursor type.

Table 2.5   Standard Built-In Cursors

Number	Description
0	Revert to system default.
-1	Arrow cursor.
1	I-beam cursor.
2	Thin crosshair cursor.
3	Thick crossbar cursor.
4	Watch cursor.
200	Blank cursor.
280	Finger cursor.

To use these cursors, you will either need to write some Lingo code or use a prebuilt behavior. One such behavior is the Rollover Cursor Change behavior from Director's built-in library. With this behavior, you don't even have to remember the number of the cursor. Instead, you can choose from a list of names that the Behavior Parameters dialog box provides.

Custom Bitmap Cursors

You can also build your own cursors. The easiest way to do this is to create a single bitmap member that contains a 1-bit image that is no larger than 16 pixels wide and 16 pixels high. Figure 2.22 shows the Paint Editor with a bitmap member that is destined to be used as a cursor. The zoom is turned on to show detail.

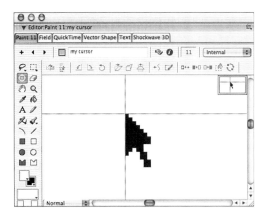

Figure 2.22
The Paint Editor can be used to create 1-bit bitmaps to be used as custom cursors.

Notice the registration point in Figure 2.22. This point is used to determine the control point of the cursor. Even though cursors can be 16×16, only one point (the control point) is the actual clicking area. In an arrow cursor, it is usually the tip of the arrow; in a paint bucket cursor, it is usually the bottom tip of the falling paint.

You can use cursors such as this in the Rollover Cursor Change behavior of the library. Just select the member as the Custom Image for the effect. Note that you can also provide a mask image for the cursor. This is another 1-bit image that shows the cursor where it should be opaque.

Animated Cursors

A third way to create a custom cursor is to use the special cursor Xtra. Choose Insert, Media Element, Cursor to add one of these cast members to your movie. The Cursor Properties Editor, shown in Figure 2.23, appears.

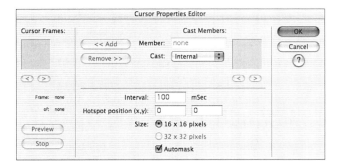

Figure 2.23
The Cursor Properties Editor dialog enables you to create color and animated cursors.

You can add and remove bitmap members from the animated cursor sequence. The members must use 8-bit color. You can add only one bitmap to the cursor if you want it to remain a static cursor. Adding more than one bitmap makes the cursor animate between the two or more members that make it up. You can set the interval time between the frames of the animation.

The Automask option in the Cursor Properties Editor dialog enables you to determine whether the cursor should use a mask that fits around the cursor, just as the matte ink fits around sprites. Turning this off masks the entire cursor rectangle. You cannot make custom masks for animated cursors.

Like the other custom cursor type, you set the control point of the cursor by setting the registration point of the members involved.

Using Animated GIFs

Director comes complete with an Xtra that enables you to add animated GIFs as cast members. When you import a file that is in GIF format, Director prompts you as to whether you want to import it as a bitmap or an animated GIF member.

As you can imagine, animated GIF members have a special tab in the Property Inspector (see Figure 2.24) to handle their properties. You can access it by selecting the member in the Cast panel and clicking the Info button. You then need to click the Options button in the dialog box that appears.

Figure 2.24
The Property Inspector enables you to determine how an animated GIF member is played on the Stage.

You can choose to have the animated GIF file embedded in the Cast, or to have it linked to an external file. You can also choose Direct to Stage for faster playback when you don't need to use special inks.

You have three Rate choices for how you want the animated GIF to keep pace. The first option (Normal) uses the same tempo that it would if it were presented on the Web. The second option (Fixed) throws away its built-in tempo information and makes the GIF move at a consistent rate, which you can define. The third method (Lock-Step) ties the tempo of the GIF to the tempo of the movie.

ADDING NEW CAST MEMBER TYPES WITH XTRAS

Xtras enable third-party companies to develop programs that add to the functionality of Director. Sometimes they add new Lingo commands. Other times they add the possibilities for new types of cast members. Many times they add both.

Xtras that enable you to use new types of cast members are called *asset Xtras*. Some of the cast members that you might think are built in to Director are actually made possible by asset Xtras that come preinstalled with Director. Examples are QuickTime members, Flash members, cursor members, and even vector shape members.

Other Xtras enable you to add even more types of members. You just need to download or purchase them from the companies that make them and then follow their installation instructions. For instance, the AlphaMania Xtra from Media Lab enables you to import anti-aliased images and perform special effects on them. See Chapter 26, "Using Xtras," for a listing of where you can find some asset Xtras.

TROUBLESHOOTING

Photoshop Filter Crashes Director

Everytime I use a certain Photoshop filter on a cast member, Director crashes. I thought I had enough memory allocated to Director—could there be some other problem?

If you are trying to use a Photoshop filter and Director crashes, it's probably because the filter is not compatible with Director. Most filter developers test their products only on Photoshop, and they may not be 100% compatible with Director. Make a note when a filter doesn't work so that you do not crash again.

Problems Editing a 1-bit Cast Members

The Pencil tool does not seem to work correctly when drawing in a 1-bit image. What am I doing wrong?

If you need to edit a 1-bit member in the Paint Editor, note that the Pencil tool does not always switch black to white and white to black as it should. However, converting the image to 8-bit and editing it there works fine; then, you can convert back to 1-bit when you are done.

Problems Importing Text Files

I'm trying to import RTF and HTML files, but they don't look right after importing. What am I doing wrong?

If you are trying to import an RTF file or an HTML file and you aren't getting the results you want, it's probably because the file uses an RTF or HTML feature that Director does not support. Try eliminating that part of the text or converting it to a simpler layout.

Styled Text Looks Wrong

I am using a special font in my text members, and I embedded the font in the Cast. But the text looks odd and characters overlap when I view the movie in Shockwave.

Bolded or italicized text will be displayed completely wrong if you do the following: use an embedded font, set the font member to use the "plain" version of that font, and then go ahead and make the font bold or italic in the displayed text. I've only seen this happen in Windows, so if you are developing on a Mac, make sure you avoid changing the font style if using embedded fonts; otherwise, your text will look very messed up when a Windows user sees it.

DID YOU KNOW?

- Holding down the Shift key before clicking the screen constrains the Pencil tool to drawing a straight line, either horizontally or vertically.

- You can cut, copy, and paste between the Paint Editor and other image programs.

- You can drag and drop a graphics file from the desktop to the Cast panel.

- After you use one of the Distort tools in the Paint editor, you can then choose Xtras, Auto Distort. This creates new cast members that are copies of the original image, but include the distortion you last used. So, if you rotate the image about 10°, and use Auto Distort to create six new members, the new members will be rotated 10, 20, 30, 40, 50, and 60°.

- Convert a color image to black-and-white by using Transform Bitmap and then changing the color depth to 8-bit and the color palette to grayscale. You can then convert it to another palette if you need to.

- You can create a selected area in one bitmap member and then select that same area in another member. First, use the Lasso tool to select the area. Then, copy it. Go to the second bitmap image. Choose Edit, Paste, and then immediately choose Edit, Undo. The pasted image goes away, but the selection lasso remains.

- Some fonts, such as Courier and Courier New, are monospaced, which means that each character is the same width. You can use these fonts to create simple tables in which each column lines up exactly.

- In most fonts, all the number characters are monospaced.

- A common design mistake in Director is to use a field with a border, but not to set a margin. Any field that uses a border should have at least a 2-pixel margin.

- Because you can import fonts and specify which characters you need to keep, you can use the special Dingbats font and keep only one or two members. Then, use these members in text member sprites as graphics. They take up very little space, and are scalable by setting the font size.

- You can create Shockwave audio compressed files and then import them into Director as internal cast members. You can create sounds that are compressed all the way down to 8Kbps in this way. However, be sure you don't lose too much quality.

- You can't export sounds from Director normally, but you can copy a sound cast member and then paste it into another sound program. You can also choose an external editor by choosing File, Preferences, Editors and saving the sound that is referenced when you launch the editor.

■ You can change the fill color of a vector shape member as a sprite on the Stage. Just take a filled vector shape, place it on the Stage, and use the foreground color chip in the Tool palette. You can also tween the fill color over a series of frames. You cannot, however, change the line color.

■ You can apply patterns to standard shape members but not to bitmaps or vector shapes. Just select the shape sprite and use the pattern chip in the Director Tool palette to set a pattern.

■ Using QuickTime movies that contain only a MIDI track is an easy way to use MIDI inside Director. You can convert any standard MIDI file to a QuickTime movie with the QuickTime MoviePlayer application. Simply open a MIDI file with the QuickTime MoviePlayer, and it prompts you to convert the MIDI file to QuickTime format.

■ You can use cue points in QuickTime movies in Director in the same way that you use sound cue points. If a QuickTime movie is present in a frame, double-click the Tempo channel and select Wait for Cue Point. In addition to any Sound channels, you can see any QuickTime sprites listed. You can choose a cue point as well as {Next} or {End}.

■ Remember that there are two types of line shapes: lines that draw from the upper-left to lower-right and lines that draw from the upper-right to lower-left. If you use one line member on the Stage and try to make it go in different directions for different sprites, all the sprites that use that line will turn out to be the same type.

■ Change the background color of a pushbutton by selecting the text in it and then using the background color chip in the Tool palette. This creates more interesting buttons.

2

3

WRITING LINGO SCRIPTS

IN THIS CHAPTER

WHAT IS LINGO?

Lingo is the programming language used in Director movies. Unless you stick to bare bones, PowerPoint-like presentations or linear animations, you need to learn Lingo to use Director to its full capabilities.

Lingo code is stored in cast members called *scripts*. There are three different types of script members: movie scripts, behavior scripts, and parent scripts. In addition, other cast members, such as bitmaps, can have scripts embedded inside them. These are usually referred to as *cast scripts*.

The difference between script types is not in what they look like or how they behave, but in *when* they act. Here is a summary:

- **Movie script**—Contains handlers that can be accessed by any other script. Cannot be assigned to specific sprites or frames.

- **Behavior script**—Assigned to sprites or frames. Controls the sprite or frame that it is assigned to.

- **Parent script**—Can be used only by object-oriented programming techniques.

- **Cast script**—Exists inside a cast member. Only affects that one cast member, but affects every sprite instance of the cast member.

A movie script is a global presence in a movie. If a movie script produces a system beep whenever the mouse is clicked, this script sounds the beep whenever the mouse is clicked anywhere in the movie. Thus the name *movie* script: It acts on the entire movie.

A behavior script does nothing until it is placed on a sprite or in a frame script channel. When a behavior script is placed on a sprite, the Lingo commands inside the script are active only as far as the sprite is concerned. If you have a behavior that plays a beep when the mouse is clicked, for example, and you apply that behavior to a sprite, the beep sounds only when users click that sprite. Behavior scripts are sometimes called sprite or Score scripts for this reason. They act only on a sprite in the Score to which they are assigned.

For more information about behaviors, see "Creating Simple Behaviors," p. 319.

Behavior scripts can also be assigned to the frame script channel of the Score. When they are, they act like movie scripts, but only for the frame or frames to which they are assigned. Behaviors used this way are sometimes called frame scripts.

Parent scripts are a different type of script. They actually don't do anything until you use some object-oriented programming Lingo commands to tell them how and when they are to be used.

You would use parent scripts if you like object-oriented programming. This means that the code and the data exist in special *objects* that can be duplicated and modified.

For more information about parent scripts, see "Using Parent Scripts," p. 345.

Cast scripts, on the other hand, are easy to use. You can create one by selecting a member, such as a bitmap, and clicking the Script button at the top of the Cast panel. This opens the Script panel and enables you to add a script to that particular member.

Cast scripts act only on that one cast member. If you place a script with a cast member that makes the system beep when users click the mouse, that action affects only that one cast member when it is on the Stage. If you use that cast member more than once in the Score, the script that is a part of that cast member is active in all those places.

CREATING SCRIPTS

To create a script, select an empty location in the Cast panel and press (Command-0) [Ctrl+0]. The Script panel appears. The Script panel also appears when you try to edit an exist-

> Cast scripts are not used much with modern Lingo programming. Behaviors can accomplish the same tasks and are much more flexible. However, they do come in useful when you want to create some quick buttons without crowding a Cast with both the button members and the scripts that are assigned to them.

ing cast member, double-click on the frame sprite channel, or use any of the various shortcuts found throughout Director to get access to a frame's, sprite's, or cast member's script.

Using the Script Panel

The Script panel has a few buttons at the top including the typical Director cast member buttons that take you forward and backward in the Cast, enable you to add a new cast member, and enable you to switch cast libraries. Figure 3.1 shows the Script panel.

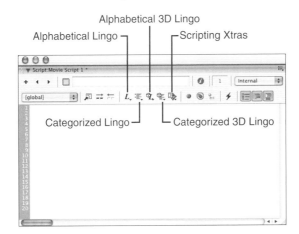

Alphabetical 3D Lingo

Alphabetical Lingo ─┐   ┌─Scripting Xtras

Categorized Lingo ─┘   └─ Categorized 3D Lingo

Figure 3.1
The Script panel enables you to edit movie scripts, behaviors, and parent scripts.

The rest of the buttons deal with more advanced Lingo functions, such as handlers and debugging. You will learn about them as you learn about those functions.

⇨ *For more information about debugging your Lingo code, see "Using Lingo Debugging Tools," p. 671.*

There are five menu buttons that allow you to quickly access various Lingo commands. The first two are for alphabetized and categorized general Lingo, the second two are for 3D-specific Lingo, and the last is for Lingo added to Director via Xtras. These five menus enable you to hunt for and automatically insert any Lingo keywords into your script. They come in handy when you just can't remember the name of a command, but you have a good idea of how it starts or under which category it falls. They are also handy in refreshing your memory as to the proper syntax for using Lingo commands.

Script Cast Member Properties

A script cast member's properties can be changed with the Property Inspector. Script cast members have one script-related property: the type of script. The three options, of course, are Movie, Behavior, and Parent. You can also use the Link Script As button to use an external file, rather than an internal member, as the script text.

Linked scripts can be used to allow several movies to share a single script. The code resides in an external text file that you can edit with any text editor. Linked scripts also permit what is called *source control*—you can check your scripts into a source database, keep track of changes to scripts, perform backups, and so on.

A Typical Frame Script

So what sort of code gets placed in script members? It depends on what the script is used for. For instance, if a behavior script is placed in the Score in the frame's script channel, then it is called a frame script. Here is an example of a very typical frame script:

```
on exitFrame
 go to the frame
end
```

This small piece of code is called a *handler*. A handler starts with on and the name of the handler, in this case exitFrame. A handler ends with the word end.

There are two types of handlers: event handlers and custom handlers. Event handlers use names that match specific events in Director. The exitFrame event occurs when Director is done displaying a frame and is about to move to the next frame.

The other type of handler, a custom handler, is never called by Director, but is instead called by a piece of code that you write. In other programming languages, these are known as procedures or functions.

Everything in between the on and end lines is the code that runs when the handler is called. In this example, go to the frame is the only code. This is a simple command. The go to command tells Director to jump to a new frame in the movie. The the frame portion of the line identifies the current frame by number.

So, go to the frame is basically commanding Director to jump to the frame that it is already on. The exitFrame event is called just before Director is about to leave the current frame and continue on to the next one. Instead, the script tells it to simply repeat the current frame.

The result of this common script is that the movie will repeat the same frame over and over again. This is the preferred technique for getting the movie to pause on a frame. It is

Lingo is very forgiving and will also accept go the frame instead of go to the frame.

used for presentations, applications, games, and just about every other type of Director movie outside of straight animation.

A Typical Button Script

Buttons can be almost anything in Director. For instance, they could be bitmaps, shapes, Flash members, or even Director's own button member. Regardless of the media used, you'll need a script applied to that sprite to make the button work.

A button script can react to a number of events. The most common one would be the mouseUp event. This occurs when the user has completed a mouse click on that sprite. Here's a simple button script:

```
on mouseUp
 go to frame 3
end
```

When the mouseUp event occurs, the on mouseUp handler will be called. The code in it will make the movie jump to frame 3.

You can use a button script like this, along with the previous looping frame code, to build a simple presentation. The movie initially loops on frame 1. When the user clicks on the button, the movie jumps to frame 3. You can see these two scripts in the file called simplescripts.dir on the CD-ROM.

➡️ *For more information about button scripts, see "Creating a Simple Button Behavior," p. 325 (Chapter 12).*

Reusing Scripts

In the simplescripts.dir example, when the user clicks on the button, the movie jumps to frame 3. The movie then loops on frame 3, just as it looped on frame 1. Since the behavior of frame 1 and frame 3 is the same, they can use the exact same script. They don't use a *copy* of the same, script, but instead the exact same script cast member is applied to both frames.

Figure 3.2 shows the score for the simplescripts.dir movie. You can see that the same script has been applied to both frames 1 and 3.

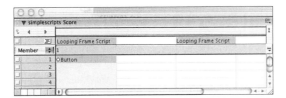

Figure 3.2
The Score shows a simple two-frame presentation that reuses the frame script.

In a simple presentation, the looping frame script may be used on all of your frames. There is never a need to create a new frame script or make a copy of this script.

Testing Lingo with the Message Panel

Although Lingo scripts are usually stored in cast members, you can also run short, one-line programs in something called the Message panel. Open the Message panel by choosing Windows, Message, or by pressing (Command-M) [Ctrl+M].

The Message panel has two modes in Director MX. The split-pane mode divides the panel into two portions: the top typing portion and the bottom output portion. If you have it set to this mode, change it to the single-pane mode by dragging the divider bar down to the bottom of the panel like in Figure 3.3. Or, you can click on the button in the middle of this divider.

Type `put  42` into the Message panel. When you press (Return) [Enter], the Message panel interprets what you just typed and returns `--  42` on the next line. Figure 3.3 shows how the Message panel now looks.

Figure 3.3
The Message panel enables you to type single lines of Lingo code and see the results.

The double dash, --, appears before lines that Director returns to you in the Message panel. Later, you will learn how to use the double dash to comment your code.

▷ *For more information about commenting your code, see "Writing Good Code," p. 662.*

The `put` command is used to place text into the Message panel. It has some other uses that you will learn much later.

▷ *For more information about the put command, see "Using String Variables," p. 295.*

You asked Director to put the number 42 into the Message panel. It did just that. But it did more than just echo a number back at you. It actually understood what you meant by 42. To prove it, try this:

```
put  42+1
--  43
```

Now you see that Director can add. It doesn't merely spit back 42+1, but instead understands that these are numbers and that the plus symbol means that they should be added together.

You can do other things with Lingo besides math. Try this in the Message panel:

```
beep
```

You should hear your computer's default system beep. If you don't, it is probably because your volume is turned down or your system beep is turned off.

Notice that the Message panel does not return anything in the next line, because you didn't ask it to. The command beep simply plays the system beep. It does not place anything in the Message panel as the put command does.

The Message panel is nice for taking your first Lingo steps, and it continues to be useful as you learn new Lingo commands. Even expert Lingo programmers use the Message panel constantly to program in Lingo.

UNDERSTANDING LINGO ELEMENTS

If you have never written a computer program before, there are a few basics you should know about. A computer program is a set of instructions that tells the computer what to do. For Lingo, we can be more specific and say that a Lingo program is a set of instructions that tells the movie what to do.

Commands

Commands are the active part of any program. They are single words or lines that tell the movie to do something.

For instance, the go command will tell the movie to jump to the beginning of a specified frame. Other commands might play a sound or bring up a dialog box.

Handlers

A *handler* is a group of Lingo commands put together and given a name. A handler would be referred to as a procedure, function, method, or subroutine in another programming language.

They are called handlers in Lingo because they handle events. An event can be something like a mouse click or a advancement of the movie from frame to frame. When these events occur, a handler might be called if you as the programmer have created a handler for that event.

When a handler is called, all of the commands inside that handler are run in order. For instance, here is a handler that will issue three system beeps and then show an alert dialog box.

```
on myHandler
 beep(3)
 alert "Testing!"
end
```

Using Variables

Another key element in Lingo and every other programming language is the *variable*. Variables are storage areas for values.

For instance, you can store the number 42 in a variable named *myNumber*. To do this, assign this value with the = symbol. Try it in the Message panel:

```
myNumber = 42
```

The syntax *myNumber* meant absolutely nothing to Director and Lingo before you typed this line. This line, however, told Director to create a variable called *myNumber* and store the numerical value 42 in it. You can now get this value back by using the `put` command to place it in the Message panel.

```
myNumber = 42
put myNumber
-- 42
```

Director remembered that you stored the value 42 in a variable called *myNumber*. When you asked it to place *myNumber* in the Message panel, it looked into its memory, found a variable called *myNumber*, and placed its value in the Message panel. You can do even more complex things with variables. Try this:

```
myNumber = 42+1
put myNumber
-- 43
```

Director performed the arithmetic before placing the value in the variable. You can even do arithmetic with variables that already have a value.

```
myNumber = 5
myOtherNumber = 3
put myNumber+myOtherNumber
-- 8
```

You can also change the value of a variable that already exists.

```
myNumber = 42
put myNumber
-- 42
myNumber = myNumber+1
put myNumber
-- 43
```

Numbers are not the only items that variables can store. They can also store characters. Try this:

```
myName = "Gary"
put myName
-- "Gary"
```

A series of characters is called a *string*. Strings are usually shown with quotation marks around them. Lingo, in fact, insists that these quotation marks be present. So, a number, such as 42, can just be written as 42, but a string, such as my name, must be written with quotes: "Gary".

Variables can be used in handlers as well. For instance:

```
on playWithVariables
  myNumber = 5
  myNumber = myNumber+4
  myNumber = myNumber-2
  put myNumber
end
```

If you have ever used variables in older programming languages, you may think that variables need to hold only one type of data. For instance, once a variable holds a number, it can only hold a number from that point on. This is called *variable typing*. Lingo does not have this restriction. A variable that holds a number can later be assigned a string.

If you place this handler in a movie script, and then type *playWithVariables* in the Message panel, you will see the number 7 placed in the Message panel.

A variable used in this way is called a *local variable*. That means it is used inside only that handler. It exists only when the handler is being used, and is disposed of when the handler ends. If the handler is called again, or the same variable name is used in another handler, the variable is re-created from scratch.

A string can be many characters long, only one character long, or even zero characters long (""). There is no limit to how long a string can be, except your computer's memory.

If you created another handler that also used a variable named *myVariable*, it would in fact be a different variable altogether. Each handler is like a little world all to itself. A local variable inside a handler belongs to it and no other handler.

Type this script in a movie script cast member:

```
on myHandlerOne
 myVariable = 42
 put myVariable
end

on myHandlerTwo
 put myVariable
end
```

Now, try out these handler in the Message panel:

```
myHandlerOne
-- 42
myHanderTwo
```

When you type the last line above, you will get an error message. That is because the variable *myVariable* is not defined in the handler *myHandlerTwo*. This handler knows nothing about the variable because it is local only to the handler *myHandlerOne*.

You can see that *on myHandlerOne* fills the variable with 42 and it knows its contents when you ask it to put the variable to the Message panel. But handler *on myHandlerTwo* doesn't know what the contents of *myVariable* are because that variable was local to *on myHanderOne*. As soon as *on myHander1One* was done, it forgot about the variable and its contents.

You can create another type of variable, called a *global variable*, which is shared by more than one handler. Here are the same two handlers, but the variable being used is a global.

```
on myHandlerOne
 global myVariable
 myVariable = 42
 put myVariable
end

on myHandlerTwo
 global myVariable
```

```
 put myVariable
end
```

Now, try out these handler in the Message panel:

```
myHandlerOne
-- 42
myHandlerTwo
-- 42
```

The variable persisted when *on myHandlerOne* was done and the handler *on myHandlerTwo* was able to read its value.

Rather than declare the global variable with `global` commands in each and every handler, you can place one `global` command outside all the handlers, perhaps in the first line of the script. This declares the global variable for every handler in that script member. Here's how the previous two handlers would look with this technique:

```
global myVariable

on myHandlerOne
 myVariable = 42
 put myVariable
end

on myHandlerTwo
 put myVariable
end
```

> Use the `clearGlobals` command in the Message panel or in a handler to erase all global variables. Use the `showGlobals` command in the Message panel to see a list of all current globals and their values.

⇨ For more information about variables, see *"Using Number Variables,"* p. 288, and *"Using String Variables,"* p. 295.

Custom Handlers

The previous example handlers were not tied to Director events. The handlers in these examples are custom handlers that will only be called when you specifically call them in your code.

When you write your own handler, it can have any name you want, as long as it is not the name of an event.

Creating a Custom Handler

The following example is a movie script. An `on startMovie` handler is called by an event message when the movie starts. It, in turn, calls a custom handler named *on initScore*. The word "score" refers to a game score, in this case, rather than the Director Score. This handler sets a few global variables:

```
on startMovie
 initScore
 go to frame "intro"
end
```

```
on initScore
 global gScore, gLevel
 set gScore = 0
 set gLevel = 0
end
```

You could have all the lines of the `on initScore` handler included in the `on startMovie` handler. However, creating your own custom handler does a couple things. First, it makes the code neater. The `on initScore` handler takes care of one task and one task only. Second, it makes it so that the `on initScore` handler can be called again later in the program. In this case, you might need to reset the score when users start a new game. If you were to place the same lines in `on startMovie`, you would be stuck executing unwanted lines, such as `go to frame "intro"` again, even though that might not be required the next time you want to reset the score.

Using Functions

One type of custom handler is sometimes called a *function*. What makes this type of handler different is that it returns a value. It works in the same way as the math functions shown earlier in this chapter. The difference, of course, is that you can define what the function does.

Two elements of a function are different from a simple handler: input and output. A function handler usually accepts one or more values as input, and sends one value back. The inputs are called *parameters* and the output is simply called the *returned value*.

For a handler to accept parameters, all you need to do is add the variable names to the handler declaration line. This is the line that begins with the word on. Here is an example:

```
on myHandler myNumber
 return myNumber+1
end
```

By placing the variable name *myNumber* in the declaration line of a handler, you are preparing the handler to receive *myNumber*'s value when it is called. If you place this handler in a movie script and then type the following in the Message panel, the handler executes:

```
put myHandler(7)
-- 8
```

You can see that the number 8 was sent to the Message panel. The handler *on myHandler* received the value 7 as the contents of *myNumber*. It then returned that value plus one.

You can also have more than one variable as a parameter. Just use commas to separate them in the declaration line as well as when you are calling the handler. Here is an example:

```
on myHandler myNumber, myOtherNumber
 mySum = myNumber + myOtherNumber
 return mySum
end
```

When you call this handler from the Message panel, place two numbers after the handler name in the parentheses. The handler places both those numbers in the variables specified by the declaration line. In the case of our handler, it then adds them to create a new variable and then outputs that variable to the Message panel.

```
put myHandler(7,4)
-- 11
```

> If a function handler expects a value to be passed into it, and no value is passed, the parameter variables start off with a value of VOID.

`if` **Statements**

Computer programs need to be able to make their own decisions. This is called *conditional branching*. Your code performs a test and executes different instructions depending on the outcome of the test. In Lingo, these tests are done with `if then` statements.

Simple `if then` **Statements**

The `if` and `then` keywords can be used to process comparisons. Here is an example:

```
on testIf num
 if num = 7 then
  put "You entered the number 7"
 end if
end
```

You can probably guess what the result of trying this in the Message panel is:

```
testIf(7)
-- "You entered the number 7"
```

Any commands that you place between the line starting `if` and the line `end if` are executed if the value of the statement between the `if` and the `then` is true.

A natural extension of the `if` statement is the `else` keyword. You can use this keyword to specify commands to be performed when the `if` statement is not true. Here is an example:

> You can also place the entire `if` statement on one line:
>
> `if num = 7 then put "You entered the number 7"`
>
> This works only when you have one line of commands that needs to be inside the `if` statement.

```
on testElse num
 if num = 7 then
  put "You entered the number 7"
 else
  put "You entered a number that is not 7"
 end if
end
```

Here is what happens when you test this function in the Message panel:

```
put testElse(7)
-- "You entered the number 7"
put testElse(9)
-- "You entered a number that is not 7"
```

case **Statements**

if statements can actually get a little more complex. You can use the else keyword to look for other specific situations. For example

```
on testElse2 num
 if num = 7 then
  put "You entered the number 7"
 else if num = 9 then
  put "You entered the number 9"
 else
  put "You entered another number"
 end if
end
```

Now you have a handler that deals with all sorts of different cases. In fact, Director has some special syntax that handles multiple condition statements like those in this handler. Here is a handler that does exactly the same thing:

```
on testCase num
 case num of
  7:
   put "You entered the number 7"
  9:
   put "You entered the number 9"
  otherwise:
   put "You entered another number"
 end case
end
```

The case statement is simply a neater way of writing multiple condition statements. It provides no extra functionality over the if statement.

In the case statement, you enclose the condition between the word case and the word of in the first line. Then, you order your commands under each value, followed by a colon. The otherwise keyword acts like a final else in an if sequence.

Nested if **Statements**

It is important to understand that Lingo commands are very dynamic. An if statement, for instance, can exist inside another if statement. Check out this example:

```
on nestedIf num
 if num < 0 then
  if num = -1 then
   put "You entered a -1"
  else
   put "You entered a negative number other than -1"
  end if
 else
  if num = 7 then
```

```
    put "You entered a 7"
  else
    put "You entered a positive number other than 7"
  end if
 end if
end
```

The preceding example first determines whether the number is less than 0. If it is, it does one of two things depending on whether the number is -1 or another negative number. If the number is not less than 0, it does another one of two things—one if the number is 7, and something else otherwise.

Although this nesting is not really necessary to achieve the desired result, it demonstrates using the if statement in a nested fashion. You could do this to make your code better fit the logic you have in mind, or you could do this because the logic requires nested if statements. You will encounter situations like this as you gain more programming experience.

The nests can even go further. You can go as many levels deep as you want. You can even embed if statements inside case statements and vice versa.

Table 3.1 reviews all of Lingo's syntax dealing with branching.

Table 3.1 Conditional Branching Syntax

Syntax	Description
if x then	Runs the nested code only if the expression x is true.
else if	Performs another test if the previous test(s) in the if statement have failed.
else	Used at the end of an if statement. Runs the nested code only if all other tests have failed.
end if	Ends an if statement
case x of	Begins a case statement. x is the value that will be compared to each section of the case statement.
otherwise	Nested code will run if none of the preceding cases were true.
end case	Ends a case statement.

Loops

Computers are great at doing repetitive tasks. To ask a set of Lingo commands to repeat, you use the repeat command. You can have commands repeat a certain number of times, until a certain condition is met, or forever.

repeat with

If you want to make a Lingo program count to 100, all you need are a few simple lines. Here is an example:

```
on countTo100
 repeat with i = 1 to 100
  put i
 end repeat
end
```

The `repeat with` loop creates a new variable—in this case, *i*—and tells it where to start and where to end. Everything in between the `repeat` line and the end `repeat` is executed that many times. In addition, the variable *i* contains the number of the current loop.

You can also have `repeat` loops count backward from a specific number by using `down` to rather than just to.

The result of this handler is to count from 1 to 100 and place each value in the Message panel.

repeat while

Another type of `repeat` loop is the `repeat while` loop. This operator repeats until a certain statement is true. Here is a handler that does exactly the same thing as the last example:

```
on repeatTo100
 i = 1
 repeat while i <= 100
  put i
  i = i + 1
 end repeat
end
```

This handler starts the variable *i* out as 1, and then repeats over and over, each time outputting the number to the Message panel and increasing it by 1. Each time, before the `repeat` loop begins, the statement *i <= 100* is checked to see whether it is true. When it is, the `repeat` loop ends.

This example is, of course, very simple. If you wanted to do this in real life, you would use the `repeat with` loop in the earlier example. The `repeat with` syntax is good for counting and the `repeat while` syntax is good for a lot of other things, such as in the following simple example. In this case, you are writing a handler that counts until the user presses and holds the Shift key to stop it:

```
on countWhileNoShift
 i = 1
 repeat while not the shiftDown
  put i
  i = i + 1
 end repeat
end
```

This example uses a new property called `the shiftDown`. It returns a TRUE when the Shift key is held down, and a FALSE when it is not. When you run this handler in the Message panel, the *i* variable starts counting. Press and hold the Shift key and it stops. The Message panel contains the history of the count.

Other repeat **Variations**

Suppose you want a handler that counts to 100, but can also be interrupted by the Shift key. The following is one way to do that:

```
on countTo100orShift1
 i = 1
 repeat while (i <= 100) and (not the shiftDown)
  put i
  i = i + 1
 end repeat
end
```

This handler uses a repeat while loop that checks to make sure two conditions are true: *i* is still less than or equal to 100 and the Shift key is not down. Another way to do this is to use the exit repeat command:

```
on countTo100orShift2
 repeat with i = 1 to 100
  put i
  if the shiftDown then exit repeat
 end repeat
end
```

This second handler is much neater. It uses a repeat with loop, which makes more sense for a loop that counts. One line of the loop checks whether the Shift key is down, and then the exit repeat command breaks Director out of that loop.

The exit repeat command works in both repeat with and repeat while loops. It acts essentially as a second way for the loop to end. The loops you are writing now are only a few lines long, but advanced Lingo programmers write loops that are much more involved. Sometimes an exit repeat command is the best way to break out of a loop when needed.

There is also a next repeat command that doesn't go quite as far as the exit repeat. Rather than end the loop, next repeat prevents all the rest of the lines in that loop from executing and goes immediately back to the beginning of the loop. Here is an example:

```
on countTo100WithShift
 repeat with i = 1 to 100
  put "Counting..."
  if the shiftDown then next repeat
  put i
 end repeat
end
```

The preceding handler counts from 1 to 100 like a lot of the previous examples. Each time through the loop it sends a "Counting..." to the Message panel. It then sends the number to the Message panel. However, if you hold the Shift key down while it is running, the next repeat command prevents Director from continuing to the put *i* line. The result is that only "Counting..." goes to the Message panel those times.

Lingo is fast—so fast, in fact, that it might be impossible to interrupt the previous handlers with the Shift key before they get the chance to finish. You might want to try them with 10,000 or an even higher number, instead of 100.

Repeating Forever

Sometimes, it might be necessary to construct a `repeat` loop that keeps going until an `exit repeat` command is executed. In that case, you don't want to use `repeat with`, because that command causes the loop to repeat only a certain number of times. Using `repeat while` demands that you also place a condition on when the `repeat` loop stops.

However, there is a tricky way to use `repeat while` without a condition, but instead basically tell it to repeat forever. Here is an example:

```
on repeatForever
 repeat while TRUE
  put "repeating..."
  if the shiftDown then exit repeat
 end repeat
end
```

This handler doesn't really repeat forever; it just repeats until the Shift key is pressed. However, an `exit repeat` and only an `exit repeat` can terminate the loop, because you have placed TRUE as the condition on the `repeat while` loop. Because TRUE is always true, it repeats forever, or at least until the `exit repeat` command executes.

You need this kind of `repeat` loop when you don't want the conditions that determine when the `repeat` loop ends to be on the same line as the `repeat while` statement. You might want to have a loop like this when the condition is long and involved, or because several conditions exit the `repeat` loop and no one condition is more important than the other.

Table 3.2 reviews all of the different variations of the `repeat` loop and other syntax associated with loops.

If you ever set up a repeat loop to repeat forever and don't give Director a way to get out of it, you can always press (Command-.) [Ctrl+.] to halt Director and Lingo. If you don't, Director might eventually crash.

Table 3.2   Loop Syntax

Syntax	Description
`repeat with a = b to c`	Repeats enough times for the value of a to move from b to c.
`repeat with a = b down to c`	Repeat enough times for the value of a to move from b to c, assuming b is larger than c.
`end repeat`	Ends the nested code inside the loop.
`repeat while x`	Repeats so long as x is true.
`next repeat`	Stops executing the nested code in a loop and starts the next iteration of the loop immediately.
`exit repeat`	Breaks out of the loop.
`repeat with a in alist`	Loops through the items in $alist$ assigning each value to a.

The last item in Table 3.2 will make more sense once you learn about lists in the next section. In this example, the code will loop five times, and i will have the value 7 the first time, then 3, 9, 2 and 12.

```
repeat with i in [7,3,9,2,12]
 put i
end repeat
```

Using List Variables

Every major programming language has the capability to store a series of variables. In some languages, these are called arrays. In Lingo, they are called *lists*. There are two types of lists: linear lists and property lists.

Linear Lists

A linear list is a series of numbers, strings, or data of some other type that is contained in a single variable. Try this in the Message panel:

```
myList = [4,7,8,42,245]
put myList
-- [4, 7, 8, 42, 245]
```

Now that you have created a list, you need a way to access each of the items in it. This is done with some special syntax:

```
put myList[1]
-- 4
put myList[4]
-- 42
```

Lists can also hold strings. In fact, they can hold a combination of numbers and strings. They can even hold structures such as points, rects, and color values. Here are some examples of valid lists:

```
myList = ["apples", "oranges", "peaches"]
myList = [1, 2, 3, "other"]
myList = [point(50,50), point(100,100), point(100,125)]
myList = [[1,2,3,4,5], [1,2,3,5,7,9], [345,725]]
```

The last example shows a list that actually contains other lists. These come in handy in advanced Lingo. Here is an example of a list that holds a small database of names and phone numbers:

```
myList = [["Gary", "555-1234"], ["William", "555-9876"], ["John", "555-1928"]]
```

Here is a handler that shows a somewhat practical use for lists. The list contains a series of member names. When the handler is called, it uses the list to rapidly change sprite 1's member to these members:

```
on animateWithList
 myList = ["arrow1", "arrow2", "arrow3"]
 repeat with i = 1 to 3
  sprite(1).member = member myList[1]
  updateStage
 end repeat
end
```

The handler uses a `repeat` loop to take the variable *i* from 1 to 3. It then sets the member of sprite 1 to the member with the name used in each location of the list. An `updateStage` is used to make the change visible on the Stage.

Another way to create lists is to use commands that add or remove an item from them, rather than create the list all at once. The `add` command places an item in a list that already exists. A `deleteAt` command removes an item from a list. Try this in the Message panel:

```
myList = []
add myList, 5
add myList, 7
add myList, 9
put myList
-- [5, 7, 9]
add myList, 242
put myList
-- [5, 7, 9, 242]
deleteAt myList, 3
put myList
-- [5, 7, 242]
```

The first line in this example creates an empty list. Then, you added three items to it. After taking a look at the contents, you added a fourth item. Finally, you deleted item number 3, which was the number 9, from the list.

Another command you should know about is the `count` property of a list. It tells you how many items are currently in the list. Try this in the Message panel:

```
myList = [5,7,9,12]
put myList.count
-- 4
```

In the preceding handler example, instead of having *i* go from 1 to 3, you could have had *i* go from 1 to *myList*.`count`. This would have made it possible to add or remove items from the list later, without having to worry about changing the hard-coded number 3 in the script as well.

Property Lists

One of the problems with linear lists is that you can refer to the items in the list only by position. A different type of list, called a *property list*, enables you to define a name for each item in the list. Here is a typical property list:

```
myList = [#name: "Gary", #phone: "555-1234", #employedSince: 1996]
```

Each item in a property list contains both a property name and a property value. For instance, the first item in the preceding list is the property *#name*, and its value is "Gary". The property name and the property value are separated by a colon.

To refer to a property in a list such as this, you can use the property name rather than the position. Try this in the Message panel:

```
myList = [#name: "Gary", #phone: "555-1234", #employedSince: 1996]
put myList.name
```

```
-- "Gary"
put myList[#name]
-- "Gary"
```

Add items to a property list with the `addProp` command, and Delete an item in a property list with a `deleteProp` command.

```
myList = [:]
addProp myList, #name, "Gary"
addProp myList, #phone, "555-1234"
put myList
-- [#name: "Gary", #phone: "555-1234"]
deleteProp myList, #phone
put myList
-- [#name: "Gary"]
```

> The properties in this list are called *symbols*. In Lingo, anything prefaced by a # character is a symbol. Anything referred to with a symbol can be accessed by Lingo very quickly. Symbols are ideal for property lists for this reason. However, you can use numbers and strings as property names in property lists as well.

Notice that you use a [:] rather than a [ ] to create an empty property list. You cannot use `addProp` with a linear list and you cannot use `add` with a property list.

To get values from a property list, you can use dot syntax, or the function `getProp`.

```
myList = [#name: "Gary", #phone: "555-1234"]
put myList.name
-- "Gary"
put getProp(myList,#name)
-- "Gary"
```

⇨ *For more information about lists, see "Using List Variables," p. 305.*

NAVIGATION WITH LINGO

One of the simplest tasks you can do with Lingo is to control the flow of your movie. You can tell the movie to jump straight from frame 4 to frame 12, for instance. Or, you could tell it to jump from frame 17 back to frame 9.

Better still, you can tell the movie to wait on a frame, and then let the user control the movie by associating navigation commands with buttons.

Navigation With the go Command

The `go` command is the most basic Lingo navigation command. If you are building a presentation with Director, you will want to use various Lingo navigation commands to allow the user to move through the screens of your presentation.

You can make the movie jump to a frame number by simply telling it to go. Open the Score panel and the Message panel. The playback head should be on frame 1. Now, in the Message panel, type go *5*.

The playback head should proceed to frame 5. A more common form of this command is to use the full statement go to frame 5. This is a little more readable.

You can also tell the movie to go to the next marker. Create a marker label for frame 7 simply called "intro". Do this by clicking on the marker/label bar above the frame numbers in the Score. Then, in the Message panel type go to frame "intro".

You can put this code into a button using the on mouseUp handler. For instance, to create a button that will jump to the "intro" frame, all you need is to attach this script to the button:

```
on mouseUp
 go to frame "intro"
end
```

Use the go command to jump to frames based on the current location of the movie. When you issue a go to the frame command, the frame is actually the frame number of the frame that you are on. You can test this in the Message panel:

```
put the frame
-- 7
```

So in order to go to the next frame, just issue a command like this:

```
go to the frame + 1
```

If you want to jump ahead to the next labeled frame, use the special syntax go next. For instance, if frame 1 is labeled "menu", frame 2 is empty, and frame 3 is labeled "summary", and the movie is on frame 1, then go next will take the movie to frame 3.

Similarly, you can use go previous to jump to the previously labeled frame relative to the current frame. Table 3.3 shows all the variations of the go command.

Table 3.3 The Many Versions of the go Command

Version	Description	Example
go to frame x	The movie goes to frame number X.	go to frame 7
go to frame "x"	The movie goes to the frame labeled X.	go to frame "credits"
go to the frame	The movie begins the current frame over again.	go to the frame
go to the frame + x	The movie jumps ahead X frames.	go to the frame + 1
go to the frame - x	The movie jumps back X frames.	go to the frame - 1
go next	The movie jumps to the next labeled frame.	go next
go previous	The movie jumps to the labeled frame immediately before the current frame	go previous
go loop	The movie jumps back to the currently labeled frame.	go loop
go marker(x)	The movie jumps forward X labeled frames.	go marker(2)
go marker(-x)	The movie jumps back X labeled frames.	go marker(-2)

Table 3.3 Continued

Version	Description	Example
play	Jumps to the frame or movie, and remembers where it came from	play frame 40
play done	Returns to the frame where the last *play* command was issued.	play done

The play and play done commands will be covered in more detail in the next section.

The most confusing concept is the difference between the current label and the previous label. Figure 3.4 shows the Score with some labeled frames. The playback head is between two of them in frame 7. Frame 5 is labeled "that", frame 1 is labeled "this", and frame 10 is labeled "other". If you were to execute a go loop, the movie would jump back to "that", because it is the closest marker just before the playback head. However, a go previous command takes the movie back to "this", which is considered the previous label.

Figure 3.4
The playback head is between two labeled frames. "that" is considered the current label and "this" is the previous one.

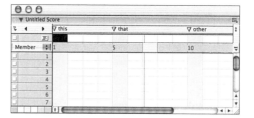

The function marker() is used to get frame label information from the Score. It takes one number as a parameter. If that number is a 0, it returns the name of the current label marker. If it is a -1, it returns the name of the previous marker. A 1 returns the name of the next marker.

play **and** play done

A second way to navigate around a movie is to use the play command. The basic command works just like a go, but there is a major difference. The play command actually remembers which frame the movie was on when the command was issued. That way, the play done command can be used to return the playback head to the original frame.

Suppose you have three labels named "menu", "chapter1", and "chapter2" in the Score. A button on the frame labeled "menu" can issue this command:

```
play frame "chapter1"
```

Then, another button on the frame labeled "chapter1" can issue a play done to have the playback head return to the frame "menu". The same play done button and behavior can be reused in the frame labeled "chapter2".

You could, in fact, issue the initial play command anywhere in the movie and Director will remember that frame and use it with the play done command.

Jumping to Other Movies

Both go and play can be used to jump to another movie as well as a frame in the current movie. The syntax is simply an extension of what you have already read about.

Here is a behavior that opens another movie and starts playing it from frame 1:

```
on mouseUp
 go to movie "nextMovie.dir"
end
```

If you don't want to have the movie start playing on frame 1, you can specify the frame by extending the command a bit:

```
on mouseUp
 go to frame "intro" of movie "nextMovie.dir"
end
```

> Director is actually smart enough to assume the correct extension at the end of a movie name if you leave it off. This way, you don't have to worry about having a .dir extension on a Windows file but not on a Mac file. It also solves the problem of changing the movie's filename to have a .dxr or a .dcr when you protect or compress it later.

You can use the same format with the play command. The power of the play command really shines here. You can have a button that takes users to a completely separate movie and enables them to navigate there. When they are finished, they can press a button that executes a play done command and they will return to the previous movie. The play done command even returns users to the correct frame in that movie.

Example: Creating a Simple Presentation

The set of files presentation1.dir and presentation2.dir contain a simple presentation built in Director. It has been designed to teach basic navigation techniques.

In the first sample movie, you can see the four frames of the presentation. Each contains information about one of four countries. Each frame is labeled in the Score. Figure 3.5 shows what the Score looks like.

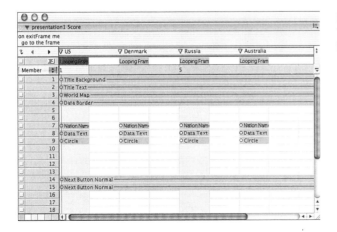

Figure 3.5
The Score shows the four frames in the presentation.

Each frame has a frame script applied to it. This looks like the looping frame script mentioned earlier in this chapter.

```
on exitFrame
  go to the frame
end
```

By using this script, the movie will remain on each frame, without advancing automatically to the next frame in the Score.

Each of the four frames contains several sprites. The first two sprites of the Score are stretched across all four labeled frames. These include the title bar background and the title. You can see the title bar and title at the top of Figure 3.6.

Figure 3.6
This simple presentation shows information about countries.

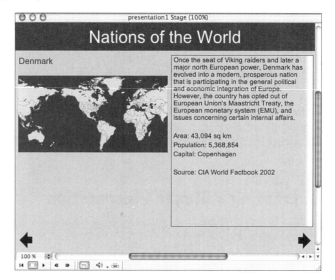

There is also a world map graphic and another border around the text area that are stretched across all frames.

Then each screen contains a separate set of three sprites: the city name, the text information about the city, and a circle to indicate the position of the city on the map.

The city name and text information sprites each use a different cast member on each frame. So there are four city name members and four city information members. The circle for the map is just one member. Each of the four sprites that use this single member have it positioned at the different location on the Stage.

Two other sprites that are stretched across the Score are the two buttons at the bottom of the screen. They look like arrows pointing left and right.

These are actually the same member in the Cast. The right button sprite uses that member as-is. But the left button member uses a sprite ability to flip itself horizontally to create a mirror image. This way we only need one Cast member for both the left and right buttons.

These two buttons are the only other place in the movie where there are scripts. On the left button, we'll use this script:

```
on mouseUp
 go previous
end
```

On the right button, we'll use this script:

```
on mouseUp
 go next
end
```

This will allow the user or presenter to navigate between the four frames. Try the movie out and look at each sprite and script.

Example: A Presentation Menu Screen

This simple presentation movie simulates a basic PowerPoint presentation. However, it would be much more useful if information were available more easily to the user. For instance, the user should be able to jump to any screen in the movie, not just the previous or next screen.

To do this, we'll add a menu frame to the movie. This will be the first frame. The other four frames will be moved down two frames to the right. Do this by selecting the sprites and dragging them to the right. Then drag the markers as well.

Figure 3.7 shows the new Score for movie `presentation2.dir`. The first frame is labeled "menu" and contains the title box and title text sprites just like the four other frames.

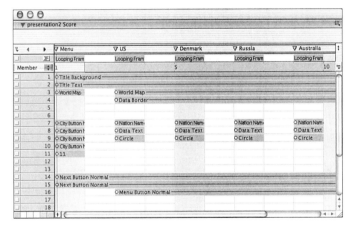

Figure 3.7
This Score includes a menu frame.

The menu frame includes four buttons. These are the same bitmap member, but stacked vertically on the Stage, one under the other. Overlaid on top of that is a text member that gives each button a label. By using the same exact button four times and a text member on top of them, we make it easy to add new buttons or change the text on the existing ones. The end-user doesn't know or care that the text and buttons are really separate elements.

Each button is a rectangular graphic with a triangle on the left and a gray area filling out the rectangle to the right. Figure 3.8 shows the bitmap in the Paint Editor. The reason that the gray area doesn't appear in the previous figure is that the Stage itself is the same shade of gray.

Figure 3.8
The gray part of this bitmap will blend with the gray color of the Stage.

Since the entire area of a button is clickable, making the buttons larger than they appear will give the user a larger space to click on. In this case, the user will be able to click on the area under the text.

The scripts for each button will be very similar. Here is the script for the first one. The rest of the button scripts use different frame names.

```
on mouseUp
  go to frame "US"
end
```

We'll also add another button to the movie to allow the user to get back to the menu frame. This button only needs to be on the content frames, not the menu frame. This menu button will allow the user to jump back to the menu to select another city.

```
on mouseUp
  go to frame "menu"
end
```

With `presentation2.dir`, the user can navigate through the same content in a very different way. They can select a city and jump right to that screen. Then can then return to the menu and select another city. The next and previous arrow buttons are still there as another option.

UNDERSTANDING MESSAGES AND BEHAVIORS

When you run a Director movie, certain things are put into motion. Sprites are displayed, messages are sent to scripts, and the movie moves forward, frame-by-frame. Or perhaps not, if you have placed Lingo code to stop it.

Understanding what happens when a movie runs is the key to writing Lingo code and controlling the movie.

Movie Event Messages

As the movie runs, events occur. For instance, when a new sprite is encountered for the first time in the Score, the beginSprite event occurs. This triggers an `on beginSprite` message that is sent to the appropriate part of the movie, in this case the sprite's script.

One way to divide these messages is into two groups: messages sent to global movie scripts, and messages sent to frame and sprite scripts. The first group includes prepareMovie and startMovie, which can be used to trigger handlers to perform actions when the movie starts. The stopMovie message, likewise, can be used to trigger commands that happen when a movie is done.

Frame and sprite scripts have another set of messages. The beginSprite message is sent when the frame script or sprite span is first encountered during movie playback. Then the prepareFrame, enterFrame, and exitFrame messages are sent while each frame plays out. Finally, an endSprite message is sent when the sprite span ends.

Table 3.4 shows a run-down, in order, of the messages sent by the movie as it runs.

Table 3.4 Movie Event Messages

Message	Description	Sent To
prepareMovie	Issued before anything else	Global movie scripts
beginSprite (frame)	Initializes the frame script	The frame script
beginSprite (sprite)	Initializes the sprite script	Each sprite script, starting with sprite 1
prepareFrame (sprite)	Sent to each sprite before the sprite is drawn to the Stage	Each sprite script, starting with sprite 1
prepareFrame (frame)	Sent to the frame script before any sprites are drawn	Frame script
startMovie	All sprites in frame 1 are drawn	Global movie script
enterFrame (sprite)	Sent to each sprite just after all sprites have been drawn	Sprite scripts, starting with sprite 1
enterFrame (frame)	Sent to the frame script just after all sprites have been drawn	Frame script
idle	Sent to the frame script at least once every frame. If time allows, this message will be sent repeatedly to the frame script until the frame rate dictates that it is time to move on	Frame script
exitFrame (sprite)	Sent to each sprite when it is time to move to the next frame	Sprite scripts, starting with sprite 1
exitFrame (frame)	Sent to the frame script when it is time to move to the next frame	Frame script
stopMovie	Sent when the movie is halted	Global script
endSprite (frame)	Sent to the frame when the frame script span ends or the movie is halted	Frame script
endSprite (sprite)	Sent to each sprite when the sprite span ends or the movie is halted	Sprite scripts, starting with sprite 1

In a typical sequence, the first few messages are triggered when the movie starts. Then, after the exitFrame messages, the sequence loops back to the prepareFrame messages. The endSprite messages happen whenever a sprite ends, but the stopMovie message only when the movie is done or is stopped.

The exception to this is the idle message. This is repeated several times depending on how much time the movie has between enterFrame and exitFrame messages. If time is tight, then only one idle message will be sent. But if the movie must delay itself between enterFrame and exitFrame so that it can stick to a slower frame rate, then the idle message may happen multiple times.

So now that we know all of the messages sent when a movie plays, the next step is learning how to use them. To do this, you need to write handlers.

An event handler always has the same name as the message it is meant to handle. For instance, if you want to write a movie script that should execute when the movie starts, you would write an on startMovie handler and place it in a movie script. Here is an example:

```
on startMovie
 gScreensVisited = 0
end
```

If you want to write a frame or sprite handler that runs when a sprite span begins, you would write an on beginSprite handler and place it in a script attached to that frame or sprite.

```
on beginSprte
 sound(1).play(member("intro sound"))
end
```

It is important to remember to use handlers in appropriate places. For instance, an on startMovie handler belongs in a movie script and will only work properly there. An on beginSprite handler belongs in a frame or sprite script, and only belongs there.

User Event Messages

There is a whole other set of messages that don't happen automatically. Instead, they happen in reaction to user events.

The most common example is when the user clicks on a sprite. A mouse click can be dissected into two parts: when the user presses down on the mouse button, and when they release it. Both of these events have a corresponding message: mouseDown and mouseUp.

In the case of user event messages, the message is passed from one part of the movie to another until it finds a handler to deal with it. For instance, if the user clicks on a sprite and creates a mouseUp message, the message is sent first to the sprite's script. In there is an on mouseUp handler attached to that sprite, it will trigger that handler. The message does not continue on from that point until special Lingo is used to pass it along to the next level.

However, if the sprite has no behavior with an on mouseUp handler in it, the message continues to look for a receiving handler.

The next place it looks is in the cast member. It checks to see whether an on mouseUp handler has been placed in the cast script. If not, it checks the behavior in the Frame Script channel. Finally, if that fails, it looks for an on mouseUp in a movie script member.

If it still cannot find a handler to receive the message, the message is simply not used.

Messages look for handlers in

- A behavior attached to the sprite acted upon. If there is more than one behavior, it looks at them in the order that they appear in the Behavior Inspector.

- The cast script.

- A behavior in the Frame Script channel.

- Any movie script cast member.

Table 3.5 shows all of the user event messages.

Table 3.5 User Event Messages

Message	User Action
mouseDown	The user presses the mouse button. In Windows, this corresponds to the left mouse button.
mouseUp	The user releases the mouse button after clicking. Every "mouseUp" message is preceded by a "mouseDown" message, although they don't necessarily have to be on the same sprite.
mouseEnter	The cursor enters the area of a sprite.
mouseLeave	The cursor leaves the area of a sprite.
mouseWithin	A message sent continuously, once per frame, as long as the cursor is over a sprite.
mouseUpOutside	A message sent when users click in a sprite, but move the cursor away and then release the mouse button.
keyDown	A message sent when users press a key on the keyboard.
keyUp	A message sent when users release a key on the keyboard.

The keyDown and keyUp messages will only ever happen if the sprite has some sort of link to the keyboard. An example would be a text member set to be editable. The user can click in that text member and type. Each key press generates a keyDown and keyUp message that can be intercepted with an on keyDown or on keyUp handler.

Connecting Messages to Sprites

When a message, such as mouseUp, reaches a sprite's script, it carries with it one piece of information: a reference to the sprite itself. This seems redundant. After all, why does a script need a reference to the very sprite it is attached to? Doesn't it already know which sprite it is attached to?

But this allows us to capture that reference and give it a name. By convention, this name is always me. For instance, look at this script:

```
on mouseUp me
 go to frame 7
end
```

The me is the first parameter of the handler. The event calls the handler and places a reference to the sprite inside of me. We can then use me to get information about the sprite. For instance:

```
on mouseUp me
 put me.spriteNum
end
```

When this button is clicked, the spriteNum property of me is place in the Message panel. This property, which is the one most commonly used for sprites, tells us the sprite number of the sprite that the script is attached to. If the previous script is attached to sprite 3, the result will be a "3" in the

Message panel. Move the same sprite down one channel, and you will get a "4" when the sprite is clicked.

If you are not accessing any properties of the sprite, you don't need to use the me parameter. But since it is so common to need properties such as spriteNum, the me parameter is usually placed after the handler name in every case. This is only true for sprite and frame scripts, as movie script handlers do not get a me parameter passed to them.

Creating Your Own Properties

The spriteNum property is built-in to the script's me object. However, you can also create your own custom properties that will be available to all of the handlers in the script.

Properties are special variables that maintain their values during the life of a sprite. To declare a property, we need to use the property declaration in the script. By convention, it is placed before the first handler.

```
property pJumpFrame
```

Once declared, the variable *pJumpFrame* can be used in any handlers in that script. Any value you set it to will persist for other handlers, or the next time that same handler is called.

For instance, this script will set the property in the on beginSprite handler that runs when the sprite first appears on the Stage. It then uses that property later in the on mouseUp handler.

```
property pJumpFrame

on beginSprite me
 pJumpFrame = 7
end

on mouseUp me
 go to frame pJumpFrame
end
```

While this script doesn't have any advantage over the previous version, it does demonstrate the use of a persistent property. Now, we'll see how properties can be used to make scripts more useful.

Creating Simple Behaviors

In the previous script, when the sprite begins, it sets *pJumpFrame* to 7. It then uses this value in a go command when the user clicks.

What would be great is if you could apply this same script to several buttons, but have each button have a different value for *pJumpFrame*.

So one button would use a *pJumpFrame* of 7, the second would use a value of 9, the third a value of 13. There would only be one script, but it would be used three times, each with a different value for *pJumpFrame*.

The way to do this is with an `on getPropertyDescriptionList` handler. This handler will be used to customize the value of a property on a per-use basis. So each time you apply the script to a sprite, you get to tell the script what value it should use for *pJumpFrame*.

Here is what a script would look like that allows you to customize *pJumpFrame* for each application of the script.

```
property pJumpFrame

on getPropertyDescriptionList me
  return [#pJumpFrame: [#comment: "Jump To:", format: #integer, #default: 1]]
end

on mouseUp me
  go to frame pJumpFrame
end
```

The value returned by the `on getPropertyDescriptionList` function is a property list that contains one or more other property lists. The property name for the first (and only, in this case) item of the list is the name of the property, turned into a symbol by adding a # in front of it.

The list that is its property value contains three items. The first is the `#comment` property. This is the string that the Parameters dialog box will show for this parameter. The second item, `#format`, tells the Parameters dialog box which types of values to accept for this parameter. The last item is a default value for this parameter.

When you drag this script to a sprite, a Parameters dialog box will automatically appear. It will look like Figure 3.9.

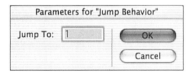

Figure 3.9
The Parameters dialog box appears when you drop a behavior on a sprite and that behavior needs custom parameters set.

This behavior can now be attached to many sprites, but with a different target frame each time. This reusability is one of the powerful features of behaviors. You can have a movie filled with navigation buttons, but you need only this one behavior.

In addition to getting the Parameters dialog when you drag and drop the script on to a sprite, you can also bring it up at any time by selecting the sprite, using the Behaviors tab of the Property Inspector, and clicking the Parameters button at the top of that tab. The Parameters button's icon looks like two gear wheels. This way you can change the value of the parameters at any time.

When a script contains customizable parameters, it is usually referred to as a *behavior*. Some programmers refer to all sprite and frame scripts as behaviors, while others reserve that name only for customizable ones with `on getPropertyDescriptionList` handlers.

For more information about creating behaviors, see "Creating Simple Behaviors," p. 319.

WRITING LINGO CODE

There are many ways to go about creating a Director movie with Lingo. Over time, you will adopt your own method.

For instance, some programmers create one movie script member to hold all their movie handlers. Others break them up into several script members by category. Some people even create one script member per handler.

If you do a lot of programming, you will find that your style adjusts over time. There is no right or wrong way to go about doing it. However, some basic programming guidelines can help you get started.

The Lingo Programmer

Lingo programmers are really of two types. The first type is someone who has a background in computer science or engineering. These programmers probably know languages such as C or Pascal, and took courses such as "Data Structures" and "Linear Algebra" in college.

The second type is far more common. This is the graphic artist or multimedia producer. These programmers may have used presentation tools before, even Director, but have never used a programming language before. They have explored the basic range of Director and want to go beyond the basics. They are now ready to start learning Lingo.

For both types of programmers, starting to learn Lingo can be difficult. For experienced programmers, Lingo takes care of much of the tedious work that they were used to in the past, but gives them control over graphics elements and the user interface. For graphic artists, Lingo can seem like lines and lines of text that stand between them and their end products.

The important point to remember is that programming is an art. Programming languages, such as Lingo, provide a wide canvas for programmers to express themselves. Two programmers given the same task are almost certain to write two different programs. Each one shows the programmer's own style.

For experienced programmers, this means that programming in Lingo provides another type of canvas on which they can create. As an experienced programmer myself, I will even venture to say that Lingo will enable them to be more creative than before.

For graphic artists, this means that Lingo is a new brush with which they can paint. I know many artists who have become Lingo programmers and used it as a way to create the art they envision.

Programming as Problem Solving

Programming is just problem solving. If you want to make a Director movie, think of it as a problem. Your goal is to find a solution.

As with all problems, more than one step is usually needed to solve the problem. You have to examine the problem, take it apart, and find out what you know and what you don't. Then, you need to come up with a plan for solving it.

To solve a programming problem, first define it. What, exactly, do you want to have happen? Saying "I want to animate a sprite" is not a well-defined problem. Saying "I want to move a sprite from the left side of the Stage to the right side" is better. What you really should be going for is something like "I want to move a sprite from position 50,200 to position 550,200 over the period of 5 seconds at the rate of 10fps."

After a problem has been defined, you can start to see how it can be solved. Imagine that your goal is to move a sprite 500 pixels in 5 seconds at 10fps. At 10fps, 5 seconds will be 50 frame loops. So, you want to move the sprite 10 pixels per frame loop.

Only by clearly defining the problem can you start to envision a solution.

Solving Smaller Problems

The key to writing a program in any language is being able to break it down. You start off with a large concept, such as "A quiz that teaches children about geography." That's a fairly tall order. You can bet that Lingo has no `quizKidsOnGeography` command.

So, you break it into smaller parts. Maybe you want to have each question of the quiz show a map of the world with one country lit up. Then, three choices are presented as to what the country might be. So, now forget about the whole program and start to concentrate on just asking one question.

But this part is also too big to tackle all at once. However, it has smaller parts. How does the map display a country? How do the three choices appear? How do you make sure one of the three choices is correct?

A very small part of this might be just having a Lingo program that selects a random country out of a list of 100 names. Now that you have broken the problem down this far, you might begin to program. The result is a handler that selects a random country and outputs it to the Message panel. You build it and test it and you've solved your first small problem.

Then, you continue to identify and solve other small problems in this way. Before you know it, you have a working program.

The concept of breaking big problems into smaller ones is the most important aspect of programming. If you ever get stuck while programming in Lingo, it is likely to be because you have not broken the problem down into small enough pieces. Take a step back from what you are doing and decide how you can break it down before continuing.

Did you read the last paragraph? It just might be the most important one in the book. Check it out again even if you have. Make it your personal mantra while using Lingo.

Many Ways to Do Things

The first thing to realize about programming in just about any language is that there are usually many ways to accomplish the same task. This is particularly true of Lingo.

For instance, suppose you want the movie to loop on the current labeled frame. You could use a `go to the frame` command in an `on exitFrame` handler. Or you could use `go loop`. Or, you could use `go marker(0)`. All of these will work. They have differences when used in other situations, but for a single labeled frame, they will all behave exactly the same way.

So why use one method over the other? You might choose one method because you use it more often, so you want to be consistent. You might choose one because you are using that same method elsewhere, where the slight differences in the commands will bring about different behavior. Or, you might just like how one sounds.

In some cases, one solution is more elegant than another. For instance, there are several ways to change the volume of a sound. One method changes the volume setting for the entire movie, not just that one sound. So you may find that advantageous in some cases and a problem in others. In some cases, that technique is not compatible with certain sound cards. So you fall back on another technique which will work better in your situation.

Calling one of these methods the "right" method is subjective. So don't worry too much if you are doing things the "right" way, as there may be no such thing. Instead, work toward getting your program to correctly solve the problem.

Setting Up Your Script Members

If you are creating a small Shockwave movie or projector, a useful way to organize your scripts is to have one movie script member and several behavior members.

In fact, you might not need to have any movie scripts at all. Well-written behaviors can eliminate the need for movie scripts.

If your movie requires mostly buttons, some behavior scripts can handle it all. Each behavior can be attached to a button and tell the movie what to do when it is clicked.

A larger Lingo project might require a few movie scripts. Movie scripts are needed for items placed in the on startMovie handler, for instance, where commands need to be executed when the movie is initially run.

Movie scripts can also hold handlers that are used by more than one behavior. If you want various behaviors to play a random sound, for instance, you might want them all to call your on playRandomSound handler that is stored in a movie script member. This saves you from having to include a similar handler in many different behavior scripts.

It is always a good idea to keep movie scripts together in the Cast. The same goes for behaviors. There are exceptions, of course. Sometimes, you might want to place behaviors near the bitmap members that they usually control.

Commenting Your Code

Director is equipped with an automatic script color function. This function color-codes different types of words in your scripts. For instance, Lingo keywords are blue and comments are red. The goal is to make it easier for you to read. You can also turn this function off in the Script Preferences dialog box. If you do, you can use the Text Inspector to color and style your code manually.

The most important task to complete when writing code is to remember to add comments. Comments are words, phrases, and even sentences that you can sprinkle throughout your code to help clarify what the code is doing. You can place comments on a new line, or at the end of a line of code. Use a double dash to tell Director that everything after it is a comment and should be ignored when the Lingo runs. Here is an example:

```
-- This handler outputs powers of 2 to the Message panel
on powersOfTwo
 n = 2 -- start with 2
 repeat with i = 1 to 100 -- output 100 numbers
  put n -- send to the Message panel
  n = n*2 -- multiply by 2 to get the next number
 end repeat
end
```

Now compare that with the same exact handler that is not commented:

```
on powersOfTwo
 n = 2
 repeat with i = 1 to 100
  put n
  n = n*2
 end repeat
end
```

The first can be understood immediately. If you wrote the second one, and then saved the file and came back to it a year later, would you be able to remember what it did immediately? Now imagine a 100-line handler that picks random geography quiz questions and modifies a map on the Stage.

⇨ *For more information about commenting your code, see "Writing Good Code," p. 662.*

Use Descriptive Names and Comments

In addition to straightforward commenting, you can also accomplish a lot by using sensible names for handlers and variables. You could name a handler *on convTemp*, for instance, but it would be better if it were named *on convertTemperature*. You could have variables in it called *f* and *c*, but it would be much more readable code if they were named *fahrenheitTemp* and *centigradeTemp*.

Because you can use long variable names in Lingo, take advantage of it to make your code more readable. Because you can copy, cut, and paste in the Script panel, there's really no reason to use short, one-character names.

Using colors, styles, comments, and realistic handler and variable names will save you time and frustration. Get used to using them now, from the beginning, and your work will go much more smoothly.

> A Lingo convention is to use capital letters in the middle of variable names to make them easier to read. For example: "screensVisited" or "dataCalculationList". You'll find most Lingo examples, including the ones in this book, use this convention.

Write Re-usable Code

While writing your code, there will be times when you find yourself solving the same problems again and again. For instance, you may have a game where sprites are always trying to determine how far they are from other sprites.

To solve this problem, you will need to write some code that takes the locations of the two sprites and return the distance between them. If you need to do this in several places in your code, you might be tempted to use copy and paste to duplicate that code everywhere it is needed. Saves typing, right?

But there is a better way. You can instead develop your own custom handler that takes two sprites as input and returns the distance. Then, in every spot where you need to perform this task, just call this function that you created.

You can take this a step further by creating a whole library of functions that you find useful in your current project and grouping them together. You might even find them useful for your next project.

TROUBLESHOOTING

Writing Large Lingo Programs

I've got to write the largest Lingo program that I have tried to date. Where do I start?

Remember that the concept of breaking big problems into smaller ones is the most important aspect of programming. If you get stuck while programming in Lingo, it is likely to be because you have not broken the problem down into small enough pieces. Take a step back and decide how you can break the problem down before continuing.

Changing a Behavior Affects All Instances of the Behavior

I made one change to a frame or button script, and now all of my frames and buttons aren't working right. Why did this happen?

Placing a script in more than one place has advantages. But remember that when you change the code attached to one frame or sprite, the change will also happen for any other frames or sprites where the code is attached.

Old Movies Bring Up Errors

I opened an old Director movie and made some changes to the Lingo code. But now I get errors when I close the Script panel. This code worked fine before. What is wrong?

The backslash (\) continuation character was changed back in Director 8. In earlier versions of Director, the continuation character looks like a lazy L. Older movies that use this character may need to be converted. You may have to manually search through the code and replace the old code continuation character with the new one.

DID YOU KNOW?

- You can change the font in the Message panel by selecting text and using the Text Inspector. This is especially useful when you are teaching Lingo and need to show your students the Message panel on a projection screen.

- Because the Message panel can do math for you using the `put` command, consider using it rather than launching a separate calculator program. I find it useful for computing data, such as the midpoint between two locations on the screen.

- You can use the Script Preferences dialog box to change the default font of the Script panel. You can also turn the auto-coloring function on or off. If you turn the auto-coloring function off, you can color in the text manually with the Text Inspector.

- Handler names can contain some symbols and punctuation marks. You can use a question mark or an exclamation point, for example. You can even have a handler called *on !*. You can also use symbols in handler names or as variable names.

3

BUILDING DIRECTOR MOVIES

IN THIS PART

4

USING SPRITES AND THE SCORE

IN THIS CHAPTER

CREATING ANIMATION

When a Director movie plays, it begins by displaying frame 1 on the Stage. Which members are shown on the Stage is determined by what is in the Score. The positions of the members are determined by how you placed them on the Stage. After frame 1 is displayed, Director waits an appropriate amount of time, usually a fraction of a second, and then displays frame 2.

If frame 1 and frame 2 look the same, you will see no difference. However, if the locations of the sprites differ from frame to frame, they appear to move. As the movie goes from one frame to the next, changes in the locations of sprites create the illusion of movement.

As the movie progresses, each sprite starts and ends. Some sprites exist throughout the entire movie, whereas others begin at a certain frame and end at another. Some sprites may appear in only one frame.

When the last frame is reached, the movie stops. You might want to simply have the movie loop back to the beginning and start again. However, you also can use Lingo to have the movie jump to any other frame.

Placing a Sprite on the Stage

A simple example will help you understand how Director movies are made. It includes three bitmap cast members and 28 frames of animation. Figure 4.1 shows the Cast panel with all three members.

Figure 4.1
The Cast panel with three bitmap members.

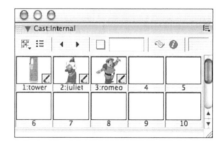

This example can be found in the file `romeo-start.dir`. The finished movie, with the animation we are about to add, can be found as `romeo.dir`.

To continue building the movie, take the first member, the tower, and place it on the Stage by clicking and dragging the member from the Cast panel to the Stage window. Because the image was drawn to be placed on the right side of the Stage, put it there.

Placing the member on the Stage also places it in the Score in the first available channel, which in this case is channel 1. Figure 4.2 shows the Stage with the member placed, as well as the Score panel on top of it. Notice that the sprite appears in channel 1 and stretches from frame 1 to frame 28.

The Stage window contains the bitmap from member 1. The Score shows a sprite that will display member 1 from frames 1 to 28.

If you play the movie now, not much happens. You will see an indicator in the Score panel move from frame 1 to 28. The bitmap stays in the same place on the Stage because you have not told it to do otherwise.

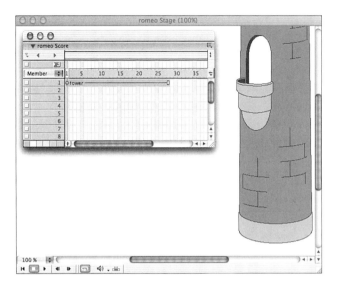

Figure 4.2
The bitmap of the tower corresponds to the sprite shown in
channel 1, from frames 1 to 28.

Working with Multiple Sprites

Now add a second element to the movie. Drag the picture of
the woman onto the Stage. It then appears in channel 2 in the
Score. If you move the woman over to the tower, you see an
interesting result. Figure 4.3 shows the woman and the tower
on the Stage as well as in the Score. The woman appears to
be outside the tower. Her sprite is drawn after the tower's
sprite because it appears in a higher Score channel.

You can fix this problem by swapping the two sprites. If you
move the woman's sprite to channel 1 and the tower's sprite
to channel 2, the tower then covers the woman rather than
the other way around. Swap the sprites by simply dragging
them around the Score panel. Move the tower to channel 3,
the woman to channel 1, and then the tower back to channel 2.

The reason that I show a 28-frame
sprite in the example here is
because Director's default setting
is to make all new sprites 28
frames long. After you get in the
Score, you can adjust the sprite's
length. You can also change the
default sprite span to something
other than 28. Open the Sprite
Preferences dialog to change this
setting.

The desired effect, however, is not to completely cover the woman with the tower, but instead to
have her show through the tower window. You can do this by applying an ink to the sprite.

Sprites are more than just a member, a Stage location, and a frame range. They also have properties,
such as inks. An ink determines how a sprite is drawn on the Stage. The default ink is copy, which
means that a bitmap member blocks out everything under its rectangular boundaries. This is what
you have been using, which is why the woman is completely obscured by the tower.

However, if you set the ink of the tower sprite to Background Transparent, the tower sprite draws
differently. This ink setting causes all pure white pixels in the drawing to appear as transparent, so
the sprites behind them show through. Setting the tower sprite to Background Transparent gives
you the result seen in Figure 4.4.

Figure 4.3
The Stage shows two members: a woman and a tower. The woman is drawn on top of the tower because her sprite is in a higher Score channel.

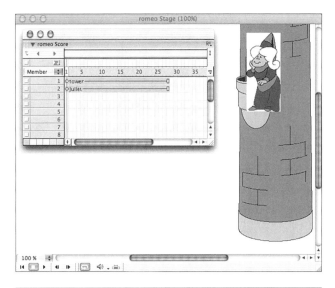

Figure 4.4
Now the woman shows through the window of the tower on the Stage. This effect is achieved by having the tower sprite set to Background Transparent ink.

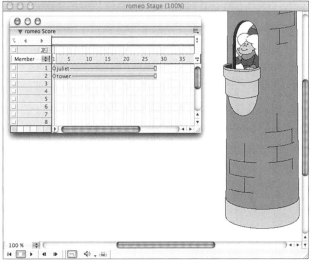

For more information about inks, see "Changing Ink, Color, and Blend," p. 188.

Animating the Sprites

Now you have a movie with two sprites, but it still does not include animation. Drag the bitmap of the man on the Stage and place him somewhere toward the bottom. You want to have him slide in from the left. For now, he appears as sprite 3, which spans the same frames as the other two sprites.

Take a close look at the sprites as represented in the Score. Notice that a small circle appears in the first frame of each sprite and a small rectangle appears in the last frame. The circle signifies a *keyframe*, which describes a frame where the graphic is locked into a position on the Stage. You can see these in Figure 4.4.

In any frame of a sprite that does not include a keyframe, Director positions the sprite on the Stage relative to the last and next keyframe. This process is known as *tweening*. With it, you can create simple animations by just showing Director the starting and ending points of a sprite.

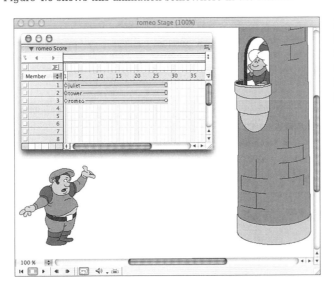 *For more information about tweening, see "Animation Techniques," p. 124.*

The small rectangles at the right side of each sprite span change into a small circle if you grab the sprite on that frame and move it onto the Stage. This turns the last frame into a keyframe. Now, each of the two keyframes of each sprite represent different Stage positions for that sprite. The non-keyframe spaces in between determine how to position the sprite by using a position somewhere between the two keyframes. So, when the frame halfway between the two keyframes is shown, the sprite appears on the Stage halfway between its begin and end positions.

For instance, suppose you have a sprite that is three frames long. The first frame is always a keyframe; otherwise, Director would not know where to start the animation. In most cases, the last frame is also a keyframe, so Director knows where to end the animation. If you position the sprite on the left side of the screen in frame 1, and the right side of the screen in frame 3, you have set the locations of both keyframes.

Director then determines that for frame 2, the sprite needs to be in the middle of the Stage, directly between the first and last locations. You never have to show Director where to place the sprite in frame 2; it just figures it out by looking at the keyframes before and after it.

You can position the man's sprite over to the left of the Stage in frame 1, and then place him closer to the tower in frame 28. Do this by using the Score panel to select which frame to edit. Just click anywhere in that frame's column to move to that frame. Move to frame 1 and position the man at his starting point, and then move to frame 28 and position him at his ending point.

The result is that he will animate from frame 1 to 28, moving across the Stage from left to right. Figure 4.5 shows this animation somewhere in the middle.

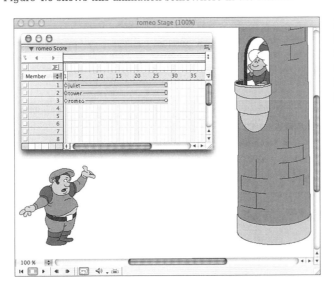

Figure 4.5
Sprite 3 moves from left to right, which results from having different settings for the initial and final keyframes of the sprite in the Score.

SPRITE PLACEMENT TOOLS

On the Stage, sprite positions are measured in pixels. A pixel is equal to exactly one "dot" on the screen; it is the smallest graphic element on computer screens. When one reads that the Stage is 640×480, for example, this means that the Stage is 640 pixels across and 480 pixels down. The pixel at the top-left corner of the Stage is pixel 0,0.

It might help you to know that an inch usually equals 72 pixels. This is an arbitrary standard; the size of a pixel depends on the size of a user's monitor and other settings. To confuse things further, some computer documentation refers to an inch as 96 pixels.

Utilizing the Design Tools

When designing your screens, take advantage of some of the tools that help you position sprites. The following list includes the most useful tools for screen design:

- **Guides and Grid**—Use grids and guides to position your sprites more precisely and quickly. Use them in visible mode to see guidelines on the Stage. Use the Snap To feature to line up items quickly. Choose View, Guides and Grid to access the grids and guides options.

- **Property Inspector**—If you like sprites to be at precise locations, the Property Inspector enables you to manually edit the horizontal and vertical locations, as well as the width, height, rotation, and other properties. Choose Windows, Inspectors, Property to open the Property Inspector.

- **Sprite Overlay**—This tool shows you sprite information and enables you to gain access to the Properties panels without having the Score and Cast panels open. Choose View, Sprite Overlay to access the Sprite Overlay options.

- **Align tool**—You can select groups of sprites and align them horizontally or vertically based on their left, right, top, bottom, center, or registration points. Choose Modify, Align to bring up the Align tool.

- **Tweak tool**—This tool enables you to move a sprite or group of sprites a precise number of pixels in any direction. Choose Modify, Tweak to bring up the Tweak tool.

- **Arrow keys**—You can move any sprite or group of sprites one pixel at a time with the arrow keys. Select a sprite or group of sprites, and then hold the Shift key down to move sprites 10 pixels at a time.

- **The Score panel**—The Score panel combines all the elements of the Sprite Inspector and sprite overlays, plus much more. It's the only tool that enables you to move sprites up and down in the Sprite channels, and thereby over and under other sprites. Choose Window, Score to bring up the Score panel.

➪ For more information about tool panels, see "Working with Tool Panels," p. 22.

Using Menu Commands

To work with sprites effectively, you should become familiar with a few Director commands. The Insert menu, for instance, not only enables you to insert and remove keyframes in a sprite, but it enables you to insert and remove frames for all Sprite channels. Inserting a frame stretches a sprite span that crosses that frame. Any tweening adjusts automatically to reflect this extra frame.

The Modify menu enables you to split and join sprite spans. Splitting a sprite enables you to break free from a previous tweened path and start with a fresh keyframe point. Joining sprite spans automatically tweens their properties provided that those tweening options are turned on for the new sprite.

You can also extend a sprite by selecting the sprite, and then selecting a frame in the Score that is beyond the current sprite span. Choosing Modify, Extend Sprite brings the last frame of the sprite out to the new location.

A variety of other tools exist to help you position sprites on the Stage. The Modify menu contains access to the Align and Tweak tools. The Align tool enables you to line up sprites horizontally or vertically, according to their sides, registration points, or centers. The Tweak tool is a small panel that enables you to specify an exact amount of movement for the sprite. You can set horizontal and vertical numbers, in pixels, and then execute this movement for any sprite or group of sprites.

Tweak Tool

To space out a sprite vertically, access the Tweak tool by choosing Modify, Tweak, while a sprite is selected. Type any number, positive or negative, into the horizontal or vertical change field. Select a sprite in the Score. Click the Tweak button to move the sprite the exact pixel amount. This moves the first sprite that exact amount.

A minor detail is that the sprites are still horizontally aligned to the center of the Stage. You can align the left sides of the sprites with each other, instead, by using the Align tool. Bring it up by selecting Modify, Align, and set the second pop-up menu to Align Lefts. Click the Align button to make the change. You will see some of the sprites shift.

A common shortcut for moving sprites is to use arrow keys along with the Shift key. Doing so moves the sprite 10 pixels at a time. For instance, you could get the same result by selecting a sprite and pressing the up arrow key six times while holding the Shift key as you can get when using the Tweak tool set to -60 vertical change.

WORKING WITH THE SPRITE SPANS

A sprite exists in one sprite channel, but it can stretch between one or many frames. For instance, a sprite can be in sprite channel 7, and stretch from frame 5 to frame 18.

You can adjust this length to a certain number using the Sprite Preferences dialog box, set it to the frame width of the Score panel, or the number of frames from the current frame to the next marker. As a Lingo programmer, I prefer to have the default sprite span set to 1.

Once you have a sprite in the Score, you can adjust the sprite span using a variety of techniques. Table 4.1 shows all of the different ways to adjust a sprite's span.

Table 4.1   Adjusting Sprite Spans

Desired Action	Methods
Select entire sprite span	Click in a non-keyframe frame of the span or click on one keyframe, hold Shift, click on another keyframe
Select a single keyframe	Click on the keyframe
Select a non-keyframe frame of a sprite	(Option-Click) [Alt+Click] on the frame
Insert a keyframe	(Option) [Alt] click on a frame in a span, choose Insert, Keyframe or (Command-Option-K) [Ctrl+Alt+K]
Remove a keyframe	Click on the keyframe, choose Insert, Remove Keyframe or (Delete) [Backspace]
Change last keyframe in span to a null keyframe	Click on the last keyframe so only it is selected, (Delete) [Backspace]
Move a keyframe	Click on the keyframe, drag
Move sprite one channel up	Select sprite span or span segment, (Command-Up) [Ctrl+Up]
Move sprite one channel down	Select sprite span or span segment, (Command-Down) [Ctrl+Down]
Move sprite anywhere in the Score	Click on non-keyframe frame in span and drag
Copy a sprite to another place in the Score	(Option-Click) [Alt+Click] on a non-keyframe frame in the span and drag
Copy a keyframe	(Option-Click) [Alt+Click] on a keyframe and drag left or right
Join two sprites	Select any part of both sprite spans, choose Modify, Join Sprites or (Command-J) [Ctrl+J]
Split a sprite into two pieces	Select the sprite and position the red frame line at the point where you want the second sprite to begin, choose Modify, Split Sprite or (Shift-Command-J) [Shift+Ctrl+J]
Remove a non-keyframe and split a sprite into two pieces	(Option-Click) [Alt+Click] to select a single frame, (Delete) [Backspace]
Extend first/last keyframe in sprite	Select any part of the sprite span, click in the frame number header bar of the Score to reposition the red frame line, choose Modify, Extend Sprite or (Command-B) [Ctrl+B]

Anther way to adjust the sprite span is to use the Sprite tab of the Property Inspector panel. This tab includes a field for the first and last frame of the current span. You can simply type in new numbers here to adjust the span.

> Moving a sprite up one channel will actually move it back visually on the Stage. This is because sprite channel 2 draws in front of sprite channel 1 and so on.

ANIMATION TECHNIQUES

You can use members in the Cast, frames in the Score, and positions on the Stage to animate graphics over time. There are several methods to create these animations.

Step Recording

The easiest type of animation is called *step recording*. It enables you to specify the position of a sprite in every frame.

To perform step recording, you first have to open the correct panels and prepare a sprite to animate. Create or import a bitmap member and place it on the Stage. Be sure that the sprite covers many frames in the Score. If not, stretch it so that it does.

Now close the Cast panel and move the Score panel away from the area on the Stage where the sprite is to animate. Be sure you can see the Control Panel. Although it isn't necessary, turn on the Sprite Overlay, Show Paths function by choosing View, Sprite Overlay, Show Paths. This enables you to see the animation path as you create each step.

To begin animating, select the first frame of the sprite in the Score. Then, choose Control, Step Recording. Now you are ready to begin.

The position of the sprite is probably where you want it to be for frame 1, so proceed to frame 2. Click the Step Forward button in the control panel. The Score should reflect that you are now working in frame 2.

Any tools that enable you to position sprites work while you are using step recording. They can give you more precise control over your animations.

Click and drag the sprite on the Stage. A line should form from the center of the original placement of the sprite to the current placement as you drag. This is the sprite overlay showing you the animation path.

Drop the sprite where you want it to be in frame 2. Click the Step Forward button again to go to frame 3. Set the third position for the sprite. You will see that the sprite overlay feature shows you all the locations of the sprite in each frame. Your screen should look similar to Figure 4.6.

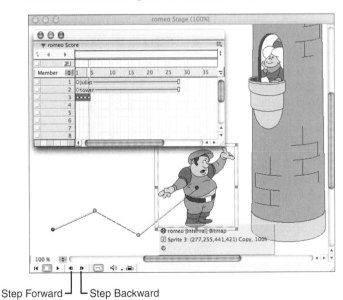

Step Forward ⌐ ⌐ Step Backward

Figure 4.6
The Sprite Overlay feature reflects a step animation in progress.

4

You can continue this way, advancing one frame at a time, until your animation is complete. Then, just deselect the Step Recording menu item to stop recording. You can delete any leftover sprite cells by selecting those frames and deleting them. You can also go back and edit the animation positions on each frame by using the Step Forward and Step Backward buttons or by clicking in the Score. Doing so halts the step recording process, and you will have to reselect the menu item later to continue.

When you are editing an animation path, simply clicking and dragging the sprite results in your dragging the entire animation sequence. Clicking and dragging the sprite overlay circle for each frame enables you to move just that one frame of animation.

After you are finished with step recording, or any animation technique, you can go back and animate other sprites relative to the ones you have completed. As you step through the frames, you will see the sprites you have already worked with move through their paths.

Real-Time Recording

Step recording is good for small animation sequences. However, if you want to animate 200 frames, it can take a long time. For cases such as this, you should use real-time recording.

You set up a real-time recording session in the same way as a step-recording session. After the first frame of the sprite is selected, you can start. Choose Control, Real-Time Recording from the menu. Nothing happens until you click the sprite on the Stage again.

In both step recording and real-time recording, the sprite automatically grows in the Score if you add more frames of animation than the sprite was originally sized to hold.

Click and drag the sprite. The movie starts going and the frame indicator on the Score moves with it. Drag the sprite around the Stage to change its position. This all happens quickly.

When you are finished, the result is similar to step recording. You can go back and edit individual frames of animation. After some practice, you can even combine step and real-time animation techniques to make precisely the animations you want.

Real-time recording happens at the speed of the tempo of the movie. Adjust this in the Control Panel. It is a good idea to lower the tempo for real-time recording, perform your animation in slow motion, and then reset the tempo to play it back. This gives you better control over the placement of each step.

Space to Time Recording

An animation technique that is not used much anymore is called *space to time*. You can place several sprites in the same frame, but in different channels, to represent different steps in the animation. The sprites can use the same cast member, and very often do. You should arrange them so that each step is placed in descending order with the first step in the lowest Sprite channel.

When you have all the sprites in place, select them in the Score. This can be done by clicking the first sprite, holding down the Shift key, and clicking the last sprite. Then choose Modify, Space to

Time. This menu item is active only if you have properly selected consecutive, single-framed sprites in the Score.

You are then prompted by a dialog box asking you how far apart you want the sprites placed. This simply adds extra frames in the Score between each animation keyframe.

The result of a space to time operation is that all the selected sprites are removed from the Score. They are replaced with a horizontal animated sequence consisting of the member and position of each sprite. This sequence exists in one Sprite channel.

Uses for this technique are limited. Because you must place each sprite individually first, it isn't ideal for long animations. However, because you can quickly place sprites that use different members, it's good for multiple-member animation.

For example, you might want to animate a bird flying using three different drawings. You can see each step of the animation on one frame, and easily swap members for some steps before using the space to time command. You can create the same animation using any other animation technique as well, but some people might find it easier to use space to time.

Cast to Time Recording

A similar technique to space to time is *cast to time*. Here, you can use the Cast panel rather than the Score to set up the animation.

To start, place an animated sequence of members in the Cast in consecutive members. For instance, if you have a seven-member sequence that shows a man walking, place each member in member slots 1 through 7. Looking at the Cast panel thumbnails should give you a preview of what the animation will look like, as if it were laid out on individual sheets of paper.

Select all those cast members and then open the Score panel. Select the Sprite channel and frame where you want the animation to start. Choose Control, Cast to Time to place the animation.

This technique is mostly useful for animations where each step uses a different cast member.

Tweening

Each of the preceding techniques relies on each step of the animation being represented by a specific location on the Stage. If you have a 30-frame animation, you will have 30 keyframes, each with a specific location as a property.

However, there is a better way to make animations. With tweening, you set two positions in the animation and have Director automatically fill in the rest. The result is that each frame in between the two positions shows one step in the progression of movement from the first point to the last.

Figure 4.7 shows the Stage and the Score with the simplest of tweening animations. In fact, this is the same example you saw earlier in this chapter. The only difference is that sprite overlay paths have been turned on.

The sprite overlay animation line shows you exactly what is going on here. The two large dots show the two keyframes: the first frame and the last frame. The line between them is the animation path. The small dots on the line show the positions that the sprite will occupy during each frame of the animation. You didn't have to set any of these positions because the tweening function does it for you.

Figure 4.7
A simple animation that uses two keyframes and tweening.

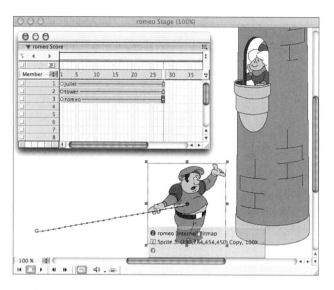

What makes tweening so powerful is that you can reposition any keyframe point and the rest of the animation adjusts automatically. If you move the position of the sprite in the last frame up to the top of the screen, the animation line goes from the initial point up to the top of the screen. All the intermediate points reposition themselves as expected.

You can even lengthen or shorten the sprite span. The example shown previously in Figure 4.7 shows an animation 28 frames long. The first and last frame are keyframes, and there are 26 intermediate frames. If you were to drag the end of the sprite out to frame 40, there would be 38 intermediate frames. The animation would take longer, but it would run smoother because smaller steps would be involved.

But the power of tweening doesn't end there. You can do more than just straight lines. You can actually use tweening to define a curve with three or more points.

Defining a Curve

Figure 4.8 shows an animation with three keyframe points. The first keyframe starts the animation on the left side of the screen and in frame 1. The last keyframe puts the sprite on the right side of the screen and a little lower. A third keyframe is at frame 10. The position of the sprite at this keyframe is higher and to the right of both the start and finish points.

As Figure 4.8 shows, the result is not a straight line between the keyframes. Instead, Director interprets a natural curve for you. But this doesn't mean that you can't make the path a straight line. Nor does it mean that you are stuck with the curve shape shown.

To create a keyframe, click a specific frame in a sprite span in the Score. The red line drawn vertically in the Score shows you precisely which frame of the sprite is selected. To create a keyframe, choose Insert, Keyframe (Command-Option-K) [Ctrl+Alt+K].

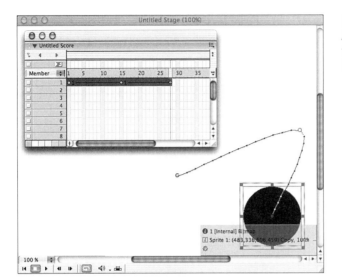

Figure 4.8
A three-keyframe sprite anima-tion. Tweening is used to interpo-late the points in between.

Sprite Tweening Options

Tweened animations have a variety of settings that can be adjusted for each sprite. You can change these settings by choosing Modify, Sprite, Tweening (Command-Shift-B) [Ctrl+Shift+B]. Figure 4.9 shows the dialog box that appears.

At the top of the Sprite Tweening dialog box is a set of check boxes. Use these options to decide which sprite properties are tweened. The examples so far have used only position tweening. However, because you have not changed the size or other properties of the sprite in any keyframe, the other options could be turned on and would have no effect.

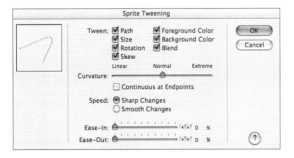

Figure 4.9
The Sprite Tweening dialog box enables you to control which properties of a sprite are tweened and how.

Tweening the other properties has the obvious result. For instance, if you stretch the sprite in the last keyframe, the sprite stretch is applied gradually from the second-to-last keyframe. Rather than becoming a new size suddenly, the sprite changes size over time. You can get the same result by tweening the rotation or skew of a sprite. Changing the foreground color or background color of a sprite affects only sprites in which color changes can change the appearance of the sprite, as in a 1-bit bitmap sprite. Changing the blend gradually alters the blend property of the sprite.

➥ *If you are using skew or rotate in your animations and the movie is now running too slowly, see "Sprite Transformations Slow Animation" in the "Troubleshooting" section at the end of this chapter.*

Below the check boxes is a slider bar that enables you to alter the curvature of the tween. The farther to the left you position the slider, the closer the path comes to being a straight line. Placing the slider on the Normal setting gives you Director's best curved path. If you want a more unusual curve, adjust the slider toward Extreme. The effect varies according to the positions and number of keyframes. In general, you should have at least three keyframes to create curved paths.

> As you adjust the curvature slider, a preview window in the dialog box shows you approximately what the path will look like when you are finished.

The Continuous at Endpoints option is primarily for circular paths. If your animation moves through a circle and ends at the same point where it began (the first and last keyframes have the same position), turn this option on to create a smoother transition between one cycle and the next.

The Ease-In and Ease-Out sliders enable you to alter the apparent speed of the sprite as it moves through the animation. All this really does is space the path points at a slight difference to create the illusion of acceleration or deceleration. The two sliders are related to each other, so they cannot add up to more than 100%. If you try to adjust a slider too far, the other adjusts itself automatically to compensate.

The two options for the speed of the tween affect how abrupt the changes are when the sprite is traveling between keyframes. In most animations, it is hard to tell the difference. The most dramatic effect is when you are using Ease-In or Ease-Out. Try both speed settings to determine which one you like better.

Onion Skinning

When you need to create several bitmap members for an animated sequence, Director's Onion Skinning panel enables you to see two or more members in the same Paint panel. You can draw on only one of those members, but the others remain visible for reference.

To turn on onion skinning, first open the Onion Skin panel by choosing View, Onion Skin. A small tool panel, shown in Figure 4.10, appears. It includes a few buttons and two number settings. You should also have the Paint tab in the Editors panel open, because it's the only panel in which the Onion Skin tool works.

You must have at least two bitmap members for the Onion Skin tool to work. You then need to turn onion skinning on by clicking the leftmost button in the tool (Toggle Onion Skinning).

The default settings for the Onion Skin tool are to show a single preceding bitmap member. You can actually show many more preceding bitmaps and even show many following bitmaps. The two number settings in the tool enable you to set this. Each bitmap shown appears dimmed slightly and always behind the paint image of the bitmap you are editing. If you are showing more than one bitmap in the background, each image is successively dimmed. Figure 4.10 shows two preceding bitmap members.

These images are shown so that you can draw on top of them and create artwork that is relative to another member. You can also adjust the registration point of the current member to match it to the background image.

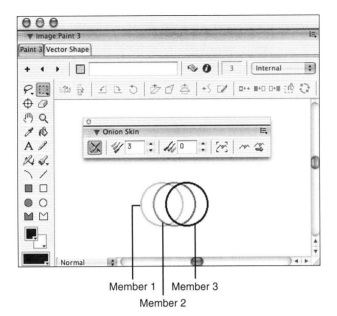

Figure 4.10
The Onion Skin tool enables you to see more than one member in the Paint panel at one time.

Member 1 | Member 3
Member 2

In addition to using the standard method for onion skinning, you can also use the tool to set a fixed background image. This image remains in the background no matter which other member you edit. Use this tool by first selecting the background bitmap. Click the Set Background button in the Onion Skin tool. To use that background image as your background, turn on onion skinning, set both numbers to 0, and then click the Show Background button. You will see that background image used as the background of any bitmap that you edit.

Try using onion skinning while painting with the Reveal ink. It enables you to preview the image that is being revealed before you draw.

You can also combine background onion skinning with regular onion skinning and have several background images. Although normal onion skinning images change as you move from bitmap to bitmap, the background image remains the same.

In addition, you can turn on background tracking and have the background image used by the Paint panel change relative to the bitmap you are editing. For instance, if you choose member 20 as your background, and then edit member 35, you will see member 20 act as the background to member 35, member 21 act as the background to member 36, and so on. Onion skinning is a powerful tool and one you will need to experiment with for a while before you become proficient with it.

USING SCORE EFFECTS CHANNELS

For creating animations, three Score effects channels, the tempo, transition, and sound channels, come in handy.

Tempo Channel

The special Tempo channel, the top channel in the Score, enables you to control the forward flow of the movie. All settings are performed through the Frame Properties: Tempo dialog box shown in Figure 4.11. To access it, just double-click the Tempo channel in the Score.

Figure 4.11
The Frame Properties: Tempo dialog box is the only place to control the Tempo channel in the Score.

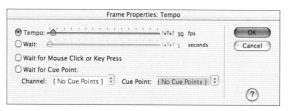

The Tempo button determines how long the movie waits on a frame. You can set this to one of four options. The first is the most common, and causes the movie to wait for a fraction of a second on a frame.

This standard tempo is measured in frames per second (fps). You can set the movie to run from one to 999 frames per second. The movie attempts to run at this speed, but is restricted by the speed of the computer on which it is running. Director displays every single frame, never skipping any. So, if a frame contains a lot of graphic changes, and the computer takes a full half a second to draw it, the relative fps is 2fps, even if you are set to run at 15fps.

If behaviors seem to be reacting slowly in your movie, see "Setting the Tempo to a Low Value" in the "Troubleshooting" section at the end of this chapter.

The Wait button enables you to make the frame wait for between 1 and 60 seconds. This is sort of an extension of the last option. Rates such as these are too slow for real animation. However, for an automatic slideshow that changes images every few seconds, this is perfect. It's also commonly used at the end of an animation to pause the movie on the last frame for a few seconds before continuing to whatever is next.

The Wait for Mouse Click or Key Press option pauses the frame until the mouse is clicked or the keyboard is used. This is a simple non-behavior and non-Lingo way to make presentations.

The Wait for Cue Point setting ties the tempo of the movie to a sound or QuickTime sprite. You can make the movie wait on a frame until a point in the sound is reached. To use it, you need to have one of these two sprites in the Score on that frame. The names of all the channels with cue points appear in the Channel pop-up menu. Select which one you want to use. Then, select the cue point in the next pop-up menu.

In addition to the cue points in sounds and QuickTime sprites, you always have the standard {Next} and {End} choices. They enable you to have the frame end when the next cue point is hit, or when the sound or video is done playing.

Instead of using the Wait tempo or the Wait for Mouse Click or Key Press tempo setting, use the Loop for X Seconds and Wait for Mouse Click or Key Press behaviors that come with Director MX. Both of these behaviors differ from using the Tempo channel in that any frame animation will continue to play. You can find them in the Navigation category of the Library panel.

The {End} choice is very useful, because you can have any frame wait until a sound or video clip is done playing.

➪ *For more information about how to add cue points to sounds, see "Using Cue Points," p. 215.*

Transition Channel

Frame transitions are effects that help usher in a new frame. When placed in the Transitions Frame channel, they control the change from the preceding frame to the current one.

Working with Transitions

When you add a transition to the Score for the first time, it creates a transition cast member automatically. You can then use this cast member again by dragging it from the Cast to a new position in the Transition channel of the Score panel. If you double-click the Transition channel again, it creates another new cast member, even if the transition is exactly the same as the one you previously created. The advantage to having one transition cast member and applying it throughout the Score is that you have to change that one member's settings only once to change all the transitions.

Figure 4.12 shows the Frame Properties: Transition dialog box. Most of the dialog box is used to select the type of transition. You can also control the duration, smoothness, and changing area of a transition.

Figure 4.12
The Frame Properties dialog box for transitions comes up when you double-click the Transitions channel in the Score.

Several transition categories are listed. If you were to add an Xtra that adds some new transitions, those categories would appear as well. Selecting All in the Categories list on the left shows all the available transitions in the Transitions list on the right. Table 4.2 lists all of Director's built-in transitions.

Table 4.2   Score Transitions

Lingo Number	Transition	Lingo Number	Transition
1	Wipe right	27	Random rows
2	Wipe left	28	Random columns
3	Wipe down	29	Cover down

Table 4.2   Continued

Lingo Number	Transition	Lingo Number	Transition
4	Wipe up	30	Cover down, left
5	Center out, horizontal	31	Cover down, right
6	Edges in, horizontal	32	Cover left
7	Center out, vertical	33	Cover right
8	Edges in, vertical	34	Cover up
9	Center out, square	35	Cover up, left
10	Edges in, square	36	Cover up, right
11	Push left	37	Venetian blinds
12	Push right	38	Checkerboard
13	Push down	39	Strips on bottom, build left
14	Push up	40	Strips on bottom, build right
15	Reveal up	41	Strips on left, build down
16	Reveal up, right	42	Strips on left, build up
17	Reveal right	43	Strips on right, build down
18	Reveal down, right	44	Strips on right, build up
19	Reveal down	45	Strips on top, build left
20	Reveal down, left	46	Strips on top, build right
21	Reveal left	47	Zoom open
22	Reveal up, left	48	Zoom close
23	Dissolve, pixels fast*	49	Vertical blinds
24	Dissolve, boxy rectangles	50	Dissolve, bits fast*
25	Dissolve, boxy squares	51	Dissolve, pixels*
26	Dissolve, patterns	52	Dissolve, bits*

*Transitions marked with an asterisk (*) do not work on monitors set to 32 bits.

Not all the transitions enable you to set the duration, smoothness, and changing area. For those that do, the Duration setting is self-explanatory. Note that a transition might actually take longer to complete than the set time if the computer is having trouble making it happen.

The Smoothness setting can be used to help in situations where the transition is taking too long to complete. Moving the smoothness slider to the right makes the steps in the transition more dramatic. Keeping the slider all the way to the left ensures that the transition uses the smallest steps possible. You should move the slider as far left as possible while ensuring that the transition still occurs quickly enough for you.

> **Caution**
>
> Setting a transition on a frame that loops is a bad idea. The transition will occur every time the frame loops, even if this does not make a visible change after the first time. The result will be sluggish performance and maybe a blinking cursor.

The Affects radio buttons at the bottom of the Frame Properties: Transition dialog box enable you to decide whether the transition affects the whole Stage (Entire Stage option) or just the changing area (Changing Area Only option). It makes no difference for dissolve-like transitions. However, for any transition that actually moves images around the Stage, such as the Push category, it matters. If you have changed only one area of the Stage between frames and use a Push transition with Changing Area Only turned on, the push happens only in that rectangle of the Stage that was changed.

⇨ *If transitions seem to be running too slow on some computers, see "Transitions Slowing Playback" in the "Troubleshooting" section at the end of this chapter.*

After you have set a transition in the Score, Director creates a transition cast member in the Cast. You can access the properties of this transition through the Score again, or by double-clicking the cast member. Any changes are applied to the member, which in turn affects how the transition plays in the Score.

You can create a new cast member for every frame transition by double-clicking in empty Transition channel cells in the Score. Or, you can reuse transitions by dragging the member from the Cast onto the Score, or by copying and pasting it around in the Score. If you use a transition member in more than one place in the Score, remember that the transition in each frame is affected by any changes to that one cast member.

This can be a great time-saving technique. If you use a certain transition in several places in the Score, having it as one member enables you to adjust the duration, smoothness, and even the transition type itself in one place and have it affect the whole movie.

4

Sound Channels

You can add sounds to your presentations in a few simple ways. First, you need to import some sounds into the Cast. Choose File, Import to bring in a sound.

⇨ *For more information about the Import dialog, see "Using Bitmaps," p. 34.*

One way to use sounds is to make a sound play when the presentation enters a new frame. All you need to do is place a sound in the Sound channel of any frame. You can double-click the Sound channels and add sounds the same way you add transitions. Or, you can drag a sound from the Cast to the Score. You can even drag and drop a sound member onto the Stage to add it to the Score.

> You can create sounds with Macromedia's SoundEdit 16 or Peak LE on the Mac, SoundForge in Windows, or with many other sound-editing programs. Many are available as shareware on the Internet.

An extension of this is to add a background sound to a frame. Background sounds look the same as any other sound to Director, but they are typically longer pieces with music or some sort of ambient noise, such as wind. Often these background sounds are built so that they loop. When the sound ends, it can start playing again in a manner that makes the loop appear seamless.

When you have a looping sound, you need to tell Director that it is a loop. Do this by editing the properties of a sound cast member. The only available option is to let Director know that it is a looping sound. Director then plays the sound continuously as long as it appears in the Sound channel of the frame currently playing.

Add a background sound to the Score in the same way that you added the previous sound to the Score. Be sure that you are not using this Sound channel for anything else. For instance, if you have a button sound that plays in Sound channel 1, place the background sound in channel 2. Otherwise, the button sound interrupts the background sound.

➪ *For more information about playing sounds, see "Playing Sound Members," p. 208.*

CONTROLLING SPRITE APPEARANCE

When a member is placed on the Stage, its appearance can be altered to make it look different than its member. For instance, the sprite can be stretched, rotated, skewed, or even flipped. In addition, sprite inks, blends, and colors can be used to change how a sprite looks on the Stage.

Sprite Inks

Any sprite is drawn on the Stage according to the rules set by the sprite's ink. The ink takes into account the image itself, often the images and Stage color behind it, and sometimes the sprite's foreground and background colors.

The most common inks are Copy, Matte, and Background Transparent. Anything else can be considered a special effect. However, sometimes a special effect is just what you need to make things work the way you want them to.

You can set the ink of a sprite in many ways. The Score and Property Inspector panel have pop-up menus for setting inks. You can also (Command-click) [Ctrl+click] directly on the Stage to bring up an instant pop-up menu.

To help you understand how inks change the appearance of sprites, Figure 4.13 shows the same pair of sprites 20 times. One sprite is in front of the other. The sprite in front is a black circle that is half filled with a light shade of gray and half filled with white. The second sprite is behind that one and is half dark gray and half light gray. Each of the 20 pairs shows what happens when an ink is applied to the first sprite.

Figure 4.13
Twenty pairs of sprites show how each ink changes the appearance of sprites on the Stage. Note that the Mask ink is shown when no mask bitmap has been provided for Director.

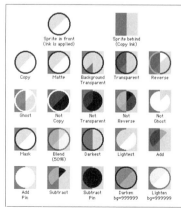

Figure 4.13 does not give the complete picture, however, because it is black and white. Many inks behave differently depending on the color combinations between the sprite and the background image, and the color and background color of the sprite. The figure does give you a basic guide, however.

Table 4.3 includes descriptions of all the inks. The list describes what happens to a single pixel in the image. This description is applied to every pixel in your sprite to create the complete effect. The descriptions also assume that white is being used as the background color of the sprite, which is the default setting for all new sprites.

Table 4.3 Sprite Inks

Ink	Description
Copy	Each pixel, including all white pixels, completely overrides the pixels under the sprite.
Matte	A mask is created for the sprite that makes white pixels on the outside of the image transparent. All other pixels, including white ones completely enclosed in the image, are shown as Copy ink.
Background Transparent	All pixels, except for white pixels, are shown as Copy ink. The rest are transparent.
Transparent	A pixel's red, green, and blue values are compared to the pixel behind it. The darkest value of each color is used. So, a light red on top of a dark red shows up as dark red.
Reverse	Performs a logical "exclusive or" between each red, green, and blue color value of the pixel and the one under it. The resulting value is then reversed. This transforms colors in all sorts of odd ways that are hard to predict.
Ghost	Like Reverse, this performs a complex mathematical transformation of the color values. In this case, a logical "or" is performed between the color under the pixel and the opposite of the pixel's color.
Not Inks	These ink effects are based on the previous four ink effects. First, the color values of the sprite are reversed. Then, the Copy, Transparent, Reverse, or Ghost ink effect is reapplied to the selected sprite.
Mask	Uses the next cast member in the Cast panel to block or unblock background colors. Rules for a Mask are as follows: must be the same size as the masked cast member, must be the next cast member position in the Cast panel, and must be 1-bit. If ther is a black pixel in the mask, the same pixel position of the sprite will be the color of the sprite. Otherwise, it will be completely transparent.
Blend	Applies a blend to the sprite. The amount used in the blend is set in Sprite Properties from the Modify menu or in the Score or Property Inspector. The blend percentage determines the amount of each color used from the sprite and the pixels under it.
Darkest	Takes the darkest color values from the pixel and the pixel behind it.
Lightest	Takes the lightest color values from the pixel and the pixel behind it.
Add	Takes the red, green, and blue color values of the pixel and the pixel under it and adds them. If this is greater than 255, the number wraps back around starting at 0.
Add Pin	The same as Add, with the exception that if the color value exceeds 255, 255 is used.

Table 4.3 Continued

Ink	Description
Subtract	Takes the red, green, and blue color values of the pixel and subtracts them from the pixel under it. If this is less than 0, the number wraps back around from 255.
Lighten	This ink uses the foreground and background colors of the sprite. It does not use color information from the pixels under the sprite. In addition to the color translation, it behaves like the Matte ink by making exterior white pixels transparent. It takes the red, green, and blue values of each pixel and multiplies them by the red, green, and blue values of the sprite's background color. Then it adds the color values from the foreground color.
Darken	The same as Lighten, but in addition, the red, green, and blue values of the background color are reversed and then added to the color for each pixel.

Ink descriptions are quite complex and hard to understand unless you are a mathematician. Almost all Director users stick to the Copy, Matte, and Background Transparent inks.

➪ *If you can't get the Matte or Background Transparent inks to perform like you wish, see "Better Alternative to Matte Ink" in the "Troubleshooting" section at the end of this chapter.*

The real power of the other inks can only be appreciated by experimentation. Figure 4.14, for instance, shows a creative use of the Lightest ink. In this example, a member is placed on the Stage in two places. The sprite on the left uses Copy ink. The sprite on the right uses Lightest ink. Underneath the sprite on the right is a black circle. Because the image is lighter than the black circle, it shows over it. However, the rest of the image is over only the white Stage, which is lighter than the sprite.

Figure 4.14
A member is placed on the Stage in two places. The placement on the right uses the Lightest ink and is positioned over a black circle. The result is that only the pixels over the circle are visible.

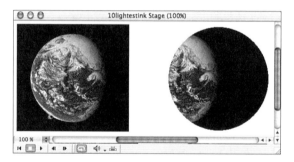

➪ *For more information about sprite inks, see "Changing Ink, Color, and Blend," p. 188.*

Sprite Blend

In addition to inks, you can use blends to modify the appearance of a sprite. Blends enable you to mix the sprite with whatever is behind it. You control the percent of the blend, with 100% being totally opaque.

To use blends, you should set the ink of the sprite to Blend. Director enables you to use other inks, but the use of a Blend overrides them. The Blend ink is similar to Matte in that Director creates a mask to fit the shape of the image. You can also use Copy ink if you want no mask, or use

Background Transparent ink if you want all the white pixels to be transparent. Both these inks work as expected in addition to having the blend.

One effective use of blends is to use images in both the normal way and as background images. You can do this by stretching an image to the size of the Stage, while at the same time reducing its blend to somewhere around 50%. Figure 4.15 shows this type of effect.

Figure 4.15
Two sprites are used to show the same image. One is stretched and faded with a blend.

The Stage in Figure 4.15 shows two sprites. The first one is selected and then stretched on the Stage to cover the whole Stage area. Then its ink is set to Blend. Finally, the blend of that sprite is set to 50%. Both the ink and blend settings can be controlled in the Score or the Sprite Inspector. The second sprite is at normal size with Copy ink.

Sprite Colors

You can also set the foreground and background colors of your sprites. Change these colors by selecting the color chips in the Score panel, Property Inspector, or Tool panel. The defaults are to have the foreground black and the background white.

By changing the colors of sprite, you ask Director to perform a type of tint. Changing the foreground color causes all non-black pixels to be tinted to that color. All black pixels simply become that color. When the background color is changed, all pixels are tinted except for white pixels, which simply become that color.

One way to use this feature is to set 1-bit bitmap colors. Because 1-bit bitmaps contain only black and white pixels, you are essentially changing the two colors from black and white to whatever you want. The display of the sprite also depends on the ink used.

⇨ *If your bitmaps look right on Macs but too dark on PCs, see "Colors Are Darker on PCs Than on Macs" in the "Troubleshooting" section at the end of this chapter.*

Sprite Shape

In addition to changing the appearance and color of pixels in a sprite, you can also distort the sprite in a variety of ways. You can stretch, shrink, rotate, and skew many types of sprites.

Resizing Sprites

To stretch a sprite, select it on the Stage and pull one of the four corners or four sides. You can make the sprite wider or taller, or hold down the Shift key and drag one of the corners to maintain proportions. You can always reset the sprite by choosing Modify, Sprite, Properties, and clicking the Restore button.

You can also set the rectangle of a sprite through the number fields at the top of the Score or in the Sprite Inspector.

Sprites can be resized over time with the same tweening techniques used earlier in this chapter. You can reuse cast members for sprites that need the same image, but at a different size.

Rotating Sprites

Use the Rotate tool rotate bitmap sprites. Choose the Rotate tool in the Tool palette and then click and drag a sprite to pull it around its registration point. Some member types, such as fields and simple shapes, cannot be rotated.

You can also set the rotation of a sprite, a group of sprites, or a single frame in a sprite animation by using the toolbar at the top of the Score or the Sprite Inspector.

You can also rotate with tweening. A sprite can rotate a full 360°. The result is that the sprite spins around its registration point.

You can also use the Rotate tool to grab the sides of sprites to skew them. You can pull one side of the sprite rectangle independent of the other three sides.

Flipping Sprites

While you are using the Rotate tool, you can also pull on the four corners or four sides. Use this method to stretch the sprite just as you can with the Selection tool, but you can go even further. If you pull the left side of the sprite past the right side of the sprite with the Rotate tool, the new image is flipped. The same is true for all four sides, in fact.

Flipping can be accomplished this way, or by simply using the Flip buttons in the toolbar portion of the Score or in the Sprite Inspector. Flipping can cut down the number of images you need. For instance, if you want to have a spaceship in a game fly both left and right, use a "fly right" member for flying right and then flip that member horizontally to show it flying left.

Figure 4.16 brings together the concepts of flipping and rotating to create a whole series of sprites. All these sprites use just one cast member. With earlier versions of Director, you would have had to create a separate cast member of each image.

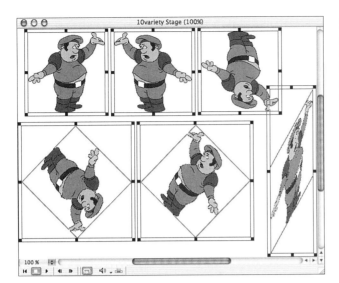

Figure 4.16
A single member is used to create a variety of sprites through sprite flipping, rotation, and skewing. All sprites are selected so you can see the corners and edges.

TROUBLESHOOTING

Setting the Tempo to a Low Value

I've been experimenting with the Tempo channel and I'm running into problems with my movie running too slowly.

Setting the frame tempo below four frames per second is not recommended. Doing so means that some behaviors and other Lingo will react very slowly. Instead, keep the frame rate higher and increase the length of your animation. After all, a 30-second animation can be 30 1 fps frames or 120 4 fps frames.

Transitions Slowing Playback

I have a movie that contains several transitions; it appears to work just fine when I test it, but I'm getting complaints from users that it takes too long to run. What is the problem?

Some transitions, such as dissolves, are processor-intensive. A fast machine, like the one on which you may be developing, might handle it fine, but even a slightly slower computer might take far longer. Decrease the Smoothness property as much as you can to counteract this. Also, transitions lock out animation and user interaction. They actually freeze the whole movie while the transition occurs. Keep this in mind, especially for longer transitions.

Better Alternative to Matte Ink

I want a sprite to be transparent around the edges or in the middle. It seems like background transparent or matte ink is the way to do this. But I can't get the quality of transparency that I need. Is there a better way to do this?

Background Transparent inks and Matte inks look great for some images, and not so great for others. Try using a 32-bit image with an Alpha channel for more control over transparency.

Colors Are Darker on PCs Than on Macs

I'm creating my movie on a Mac and testing my movie on both Mac and Windows to check for consistency. I'm finding that my images look darker on PCs. Is there something I'm doing wrong?

If you are developing for both Mac and Windows, it is important that you check your images to see how they look on both platforms. PC monitors show colors much darker than Mac monitors. Unfortunately, you need to have both types of machines to test on, regardless of which one you use to develop. If PC playback is your primary target, then you may want to make the images brighter than you like on Mac.

Sprite Transformations Slow Animation

I've been using the various tools to skew and resize my sprites, and now the animation takes forever to run. Why?

When you change a bitmap sprite's shape, you make it much harder for Director to draw it. This can slow down animation considerably. If this is happening, you may want to reconsider using these transformations: Use separate bitmaps for each shape instead of transforming one bitmap, or reduce the dimensions of the sprite.

DID YOU KNOW?

- You can use the Darken ink—combined with applying a color other than black or white as the foreground color—to simulate color saturation in an image. Photoshop users can do this with the Hue, Saturation, and Brightness tool. However, in Director you can tween color values to animate the color change!

- While manipulating sprites, keep in mind that Director only has one level of undo. This means you can use (Command-Z) [Ctrl+Z] to undo only the last change you made. Using it a second time in a row will redo the change you undid. So you may want to save your movie often, especially just before trying out a series of steps to change your animation. This way you can revert to the last save if you don't like how the changes turned out.

- If you are working with a movie that has a lot of sound in the sound channels, you can temporarily turn off the sound by selecting the visibility box to the left of the channel in the Score. Hearing your movie's background sound can become annoying to the developer who has to test the movie 1,000 times in a day.

4

5

ADDING USER INTERACTION

IN THIS CHAPTER

TYPES OF USER INTERFACE ELEMENTS

Although animations can go about their merry way without any user input, interaction is needed in most other types of Director movies. There are two main ways to get user input: the mouse and the keyboard. If you are creating interactive movies, you must build interface elements that allow the user to interact with your movie.

Mouse input usually involves buttons. But buttons can perform complex actions. For instance, check boxes and radio buttons don't perform the action immediately, but instead allow the user to select options for a future action.

You can also use mouse clicks to perform special actions such as dragging and dropping elements. This leads to even more complex user interface elements such as sliders and pop-up menus.

In addition to mouse input, the user can use the keyboard to provide input to your movie. Key presses can be used like buttons, mapping an action to a key. They can also be used to enter text information into fields.

MOUSE INPUT

The Director environment keeps constant track of the user's mouse. For instance, try this in the Message panel:

```
put the mouseLoc
```

The result should be the current mouse location as a point. Move the mouse and try it again to see the new value.

Director also knows whether the mouse button is pressed. The properties the mouseUp and the mouseDown return TRUE or FALSE appropriately.

Table 5.1 summarizes some of Director's mouse-related properties.

Table 5.1 General Mouse Properties

Property	Value	Description
the mouseLoc	A point	The current screen location of the mouse.
the mouseH	A number	The current horizontal position of the mouse.
the mouseV	A number	The current vertical position of the mouse.
the mouseDown	TRUE or FALSE	Whether the mouse button is currently pressed down.
the mouseUp	TRUE or FALSE	Whether the mouse button is not currently pressed.
the mouseRightDown	TRUE or FALSE	Whether the right mouse button is currently pressed down.
the mouseRightUp	TRUE or FALSE	Whether the right mouse button is not currently pressed.
the clickLoc	A point	The last spot clicked.

Table 5.1   Continued

Property	Value	Description
the rollover	A sprite number	The topmost sprite under where the user clicked.
rollover(x)	TRUE or FALSE	Whether the cursor is currently over sprite X.
the clickOn	A sprite number	The last sprite clicked. Sprites must have some script attached, or they will not be noticed.

Notice that the three circles in the movie overlap. The property the rollover returns only the top sprite's number if the cursor is at a point where it is actually over two sprites. Also, only sprite 2, the second circle, has a script attached. So only it will set the property the clickOn when it is clicked.

The example movie generalmousedemo.dir on this book's CD-ROM uses all these properties. Check it out if you want to see them in action.

➯ *If* the mouseLoc *and* the clickLoc *look the same to you, see "Differences Between Mouse Location Properties" in the "Troubleshooting" section at the end of this chapter for more information.*

Creating Buttons

The most obvious use for the mouse is to allow the user to click on buttons. To do this, you must use either the on mouseUp or on mouseDown handler in a script attached to that button. For instance:

```
on mouseUp
 go to frame 7
end
```

Buttons can be made out of almost any type of cast member. For instance, you can use a bitmap as a button, a text member as a button, a Flash movie as a button, or even video as a button.

All you need to do to convert most sprites to a button is add a button script like the one just shown. Then, when the sprite receives a mouseUp message, it reacts with whatever code you specify.

More things can happen to a button than just a mouse click. Table 3.5 in Chapter 3, "Writing Lingo Scripts," showed you all the different events that can happen to a button. For instance, you get a mouseEnter message when the cursor rolls over the sprite.

You can use these events to make the button come to life and react as the user moves the cursor over it and away from it. You can also make the button react to the click by changing its appearance.

Button States

A button can be as simple as a single bitmap graphic. But in professional multimedia products, buttons are usually a bit more complex.

5

There are four states to a complex button:

- Normal   The normal state of the button is how the button appears when the cursor is away from it.

- Rollover   The rollover state of the button is how the button appears when the cursor is over it, but the user has not pressed the mouse button.

- Pressed   The pressed state appears when the user has moved the cursor over the button, has clicked down the mouse button, but has not yet released.

- Inactive   This is when a button cannot currently be pressed because of the state of the movie or the user's choices. For instance, a set of video control buttons may have the rewind button inactive if the video is already at the start.

To create an active button, we'll need only the first three states. The fourth state can be placed on the Stage in place of a button in cases where the button doesn't perform any function.

So imagine the normal, rollover, and pressed states of the button as individual cast members. We'll name them Button Normal, Button Rollover, and Button Pressed in the Cast.

If you think it might be a good idea to refer to your cast members by number rather than name, see "Using Member Numbers Could Lead to Trouble" in the "Troubleshooting" section at the end of this chapter.

The Button Normal state gets placed on the Stage and in the Score. We'll attach a script to it that makes it an interactive button.

The first thing this script does is check for the "mouseEnter" event. In that case, it switches the member to the Button Rollover member.

Also, if the `mouseLeave` state occurs, it switches the sprite to the Button Normal state.

Similarly, if the mouseDown message is received, the sprite switches to the Button Pressed state and then back to the Button Rollover state when it is released with a mouseUp. Here is the script so far:

```
on mouseEnter me
  sprite(me.spriteNum).member = member("Button Rollover")
end

on mouseLeave me
  sprite(me.spriteNum).member = member("Button Normal")
end

on mouseDown me
  sprite(me.spriteNum).member = member("Button Pressed")
end

on mouseUp me
  sprite(me.spriteNum).member = member("Button Rollover")
end
```

This works great with one exception. What happens when the user moves over the button, clicks down, holds, moves away from the button while holding down the mouse button, and then moves back over the button? The button will show the rollover state, not the pressed state as it should.

The standards for button behavior were established a long time ago with the early Macintosh and Windows operating systems. When the user clicks on a button, that button is the active button in the interface. The user can either choose to release the button, thus completing the click, or move the mouse away from the button and release it, thus canceling the click.

The user should, in fact, be able to move the mouse away and back over the button as many times as he wants before releasing.

To accomplish this, we'll need to keep track of whether the user has pressed the button and is in the middle of the clicking process: between the mouse down and mouse up.

To keep track, we'll use a variable. But not just any variable—we'll create a property. This way, the value of this variable is maintained from handler to handler as long as the sprite is on the Stage.

```
property pPressed
```

Now we can alter the on mouseDown handler to note that the user has begun the click process.

```
on mouseDown me
  pPressed = TRUE
  sprite(me.spriteNum).member = member("Button Pressed")
end
```

Likewise, you can alter the on mouseUp handler to note that the click process is finished.

```
on mouseUp me
  pPressed = FALSE
  sprite(me.spriteNum).member = member("Button Rollover")
end
```

Now, when the on mouseEnter handler runs, it can make a choice. If the user is in the middle of click process, the button should change to the pressed state. Otherwise, it should just go to the rollover state.

```
on mouseEnter me
  if pPressed then
    sprite(me.spriteNum).member = member("Button Pressed")
  else
    sprite(me.spriteNum).member = member("Button Rollover")
  end if
end
```

One more thing is needed to cover all possibilities. What if the user presses down on the button, moves the mouse, and then lifts up outside the button? In that case, we need to reset the "pPressed" variable. Fortunately, a mouseUpOutside message is built specifically for this case. It will be sent only if the user has clicked the sprite but then releases outside the sprite.

```
on mouseUpOutside me
  pPressed = FALSE
end
```

Now the button handler is complete. You can find it in the file `betterbutton.dir`.

However, the button doesn't do anything. Adding an action to the button is simple: just add it to the end of the `on mouseUp` handler. For instance:

```
on mouseUp me
 pPressed = FALSE
 sprite(me.spriteNum).member = member("Button Rollover")

 go to frame 7
end
```

The problem with this sort of button script is that it is hard-coded for one set of graphics and one action. What if you want a series of buttons that have different labels? What if you want them to perform different actions?

It would be easy at this point to copy-and-paste this code for every button, altering the member names and the `go to` command, but there is a better way. In Chapter 12, "Using Object-Oriented Programming and Behaviors," we'll look at how to create a button behavior that can be used by different buttons.

KEYBOARD INPUT

In addition to the mouse, the keyboard is another way that the user can communicate with your movie. The difference between the mouse and the keyboard is that the keyboard doesn't have a position on the screen, but it does sometimes focus on one sprite.

Detecting Keypresses

There are several ways to determine whether a key is pressed. The simplest is to place a script in the frame to receive keyDown or keyUp messages. Here is a complete frame script that does this, including the loop frame portion that pauses the movie over that one frame:

```
on exitFrame me
 go to the frame
end

on keyUp me
 put "Key pressed!"
end
```

When the movie is resting on that frame and a key is pressed, the message gets sent to the Message panel. You can just as easily tell which key was pressed using the special property `the key`. This property only works within `on keyDown` and `on keyUp` handlers.

```
on keyUp me
 put the key
end
```

If you press the "a" key, you will get an "a" in the Message panel. Most of the keys on the keyboard return exactly what you expect. But what about odd keys such as the arrow keys?

The arrow keys place a value in the key, but it is not a value that can easily be used. Instead, you can get the property the keyCode, which is a sibling property to the key and also is set for every on keyUp and on keyDown.

The arrow keys return the key codes 123, 124, 125, and 126. They correspond to the left, right, down, and up keys, respectively. Here is a variation of the on keyUp handler that deals with arrow keys:

```
on keyUp me
 if the keyCode = 123 then
  put "left arrow"
 else if the keyCode = 124 then
  put "right arrow"
 else if the keyCode = 125 then
  put "down arrow"
 else if the keyCode = 126 then
  put "up arrow"
 end if
end
```

You can also detect other special keys on the keyboard such as the Shift, Command, Option, Ctrl, and Alt keys. These keys do not trigger keyUp or keyDown events. But you can still read their states at any time using a set of properties. Table 5.2 shows a list of these keys and which properties they correspond to.

Table 5.2 Modifier Key Properties

Key	OS	Property
Shift	Mac/Windows	the shiftDown
Command	Mac	the commandDown
Ctrl	Windows	the commandDown and the controlDown
Control	Mac	the controlDown
Option	Mac	the optionDown
Alt	Windows	the optionDown

In addition to waiting for key presses with the on keyUp and on keyDown handlers, you can also check to see whether a key is down by using the keyPressed function. You can ask for any character or key code and test to see whether it has been pressed.

```
on exitFrame me
 if keyPressed("a") then
  put "key a pressed"
 else if keyPressed(123) then
  put "left arrow pressed"
 end if
```

5

```
go to the frame
end
```

Because this is an `on exitFrame` handler, it will run over and over again as the frame loops. So if you hold down the "a" key, you get a stream of "key a pressed" sent to the Message panel, not just one.

You can also ask to find out which key is currently pressed with the property `the keyPressed`. This returns an empty (zero-length) string if no key is pressed. If more than one key is pressed, the most recent key is returned. It only returns characters, not key codes.

Table 5.3 summarizes all keyboard input Lingo.

Table 5.3   Keyboard Lingo

Syntax	Type	Description
`on keyDown`	Handler	Runs when a keyDown message is sent to the sprite. If there is no sprite that handles text, the message is sent to the frame.
`on keyUp`	Handler	Same as `on keyDown`, but runs when the key is released.
`the key`	Property	Present in `on keyDown` and `on keyUp` handlers, this returns a single-character string with the key pressed.
`the keyCode`	Property	Like `the key`, but returns a special cross-platform keyboard code number. Keys 123, 124, 125, and 126 correspond to the left, right, down, and up arrow keys.
`keyPressed("x")`	Function	Whether the key *x* is being held down.
`the keyPressed`	Property	A one-character string with the last key pressed that is still being held down. Returns an empty string if no key is pressed.

Accepting Input

Sometimes you just need to know whether a specific key is pressed and react to that key. But mostly, the keyboard is used to input longer pieces of data. For instance, you may ask the user to type her name into a text member.

To allow this sort of interaction, you don't need Lingo at all. Just create a text member on the Stage and make either the member or the sprite editable. If you also set the tab property of that member, and that is the only editable text member on the Stage, the cursor will automatically appear in that text member and allow the user to type.

Director won't do anything with the text in that member unless you write some Lingo code to read the text and use it. For instance, if you have a text member named "input text" on the Stage and a button next to it, the button script could read what the user typed and send it to the Message panel:

```
on mouseUp me
  userInput = member("input text").text
  put userInput
end
```

The `text` property of a text member is how you take the text and bring it into your Lingo code. You could also set the text in that member using the `text` property.

⇨ *For a closer look at text members,* **see** *"Using Lingo to Alter Text Members,"* **p.357.**

But what if you don't want to have a button next to the text member for the user to push. A more natural thing would be to have the user type something and then press the (Return) [Enter] key when finished. You can write code to a behavior on that text sprite to handle the (Return) [Enter] key.

```
on keyDown me
 if the key = RETURN then
  put sprite(me.spriteNum).member.text
 end if
end
```

This code looks at each key and reacts when the (Return) [Enter] key is pressed. The only problem is that all keys are intercepted by the `on keyDown` handler. When intercepted, those messages will not get passed on to Director and will not be added to the text member.

This is good for the (Return) [Enter] key. It will not be added to the text member to start a second line. Instead, just our code runs. But it is bad for all the other keys because none of them gets returned either. So the user cannot type into the member.

To allow users to enter characters, we'll need to use the `pass` command to release the message from the `on keyDown` handler and allow it to continue:

```
on keyDown me
 if the key = RETURN then
  put sprite(me.spriteNum).member.text
 else
  pass
 end if
end
```

You can find this script in the example movie `waitforreturn.dir`.

The `RETURN` keyword is a constant that represents the (Return) [Enter] key. Whereas you can use "a" to refer to the input from the "a" key, you'll need special keywords such as `RETURN` to refer to some other keys. Table 11.3 in Chapter 11, "Understanding Variables, Operations, and Lists," shows all constants, many of which can be used in situations like this one.

Restricting Input

You can use some of the previous techniques to restrict user input. You might want to do this to make sure that the user enters only characters that you want. For instance, if a field is meant for numerical entry, why would you want to allow the user to enter letters?

Here is a handler that allows only numbers to be entered into the text member:

```
on keyDown me
 if "0123456789" contains the key then
```

```
     pass
   end if
 end
```

The only problem with this script is that there is no way for the user to use the (Delete) [Backspace] key as he would expect when entering data. You can re-enable this key with a slight alteration to the script:

```
on keyDown me
  if "0123456789" contains the key then
    pass
  else if the key = BACKSPACE then
    pass
  end if
end
```

You can find this script in the movie `enteronlynumbers.dir`. You can use this in many situations, such as allowing only standard alphanumeric keys rather than special characters. Or you could allow all characters except for certain ones. This code allows everything but less-than and greater-than signs:

```
on keyDown me
  if "<>" contains the key then
    stopEvent
  else
    pass
  end if
end
```

The `stopEvent` command is the opposite of `pass`. Technically, it is not needed because the message will not pass on by default. But it makes the code easier to read and is obvious in its purpose.

Password Entry

Another common task for text entry is to allow the user to enter a string but not show it on the screen. Instead, each character is replaced by an asterisk or other character.

You can do this with a fairly simple script attached to the sprite. This script keeps track of two strings: one with the characters that the user types and one with just asterisks.

When the user presses a key, the character is added to this first string and an asterisk to the second. The text member never gets the message from the keyDown event, but instead is given the contents of the string of asterisks.

In addition, a special case is made for the (Delete) [Backspace] key. It removes the last character from both strings. The (Return) [Enter] key sends the contents of the real string to the Message panel.

```
property pText, pVisibleText

on beginSprite me
```

```
-- initialize strings
pText = ""
pVisibleText = ""
end

on keyDown me
 if the key = BACKSPACE then
  -- handle backspace
  delete pText.char[pText.length]
  delete pVisibleText.char[pVisibleText.length]

 else if the key = RETURN then
  -- handle Enter/Return key
  put pText

 else
  -- add real key to the end of the string
  put the key after pText
  -- add an asterisk to the end of the visible string
  put "*" after pVisibleText
 end if

 -- put visible string into the text member
 sprite(me.spriteNum).member.text = pVisibleText
end
```

You can find this script in the `passwordentry.dir` movie. Some of this code is new, particularly the `put after` and `delete` commands. But these are pretty self-explanatory. The `char` property allows you to specify a character in a string, and the `length` property gets the number of characters in a string.

➡️ *We'll look at string commands and properties more in-depth; **see** "Understanding Variables, Operations, and Lists," **p.287**.*

Whether you are creating a simple presentation or a complex piece of software, it is primarily through user interface elements that the Director movie and the user interact. These elements can be as plain as pushbuttons, or as complex as slider bars. The rest of this chapter looks at the most common user interface elements and the behaviors that you use to create them.

INTERFACE ELEMENTS

So far, we have seen several simple interface devices, such as buttons and text entry areas. But there are several other, more complex elements that you may need to use in your movies.

Creating Display Rollovers

Earlier in this chapter, you learned how to change the member of a sprite when the cursor moves over it. But what about a situation where the user rolls over one sprite, and another sprite somewhere else on the Stage changes?

A typical use for this interface element is to present a list of items and then show more information about them in another part of the screen when users roll over it. Figure 5.1 shows a screen that does this. Rolling over the three items on the left brings up three different text members in the sprite to the right.

Figure 5.1
The screen shows three sprites on the left and one on the right. The one on the right changes depending on which sprite on the left the cursor is over.

The behavior must know two things to perform its function: the sprite it should affect and the member it should place in that sprite when the rollover occurs. One last parameter should be a default member displayed when the cursor is not over one of the rollover sprites. Here is the start of a behavior:

```
property pRolloverMember, pRolloverSprite, pDefaultMember

on getPropertyDescriptionList me
 list = [:]
 addProp list, #pRolloverMember, [#comment: "Rollover Member",\
  #format: #member, #default: ""]
 addProp list, #pRolloverSprite, [#comment: "Rollover Sprite",\
  #format: #integer, #default: 0]
 addProp list, #pDefaultMember, [#comment: "Default Member",\
  #format: #member, #default: ""]
 return list
end
```

The *pRolloverSprite* parameter defines which sprite is changed. The actual sprite that the users must roll over is the one that the behavior is attached to. The *pRolloverMember* parameter is the member that the *pRolloverSprite* changes to. The *pDefaultMember* is the member that *pRolloverSprite* shows when the cursor is not rolled over the behavior's sprite anymore.

The default member should be the one in the rollover sprite on the Score. You can use on mouseEnter to change this sprite to the desired member. Then, when the cursor leaves the sprite, the on mouseLeave handler can switch it back to the default member.

```
on mouseEnter me
 sprite(pRolloverSprite).member = pRolloverMember
end

on mouseLeave me
 sprite(pRolloverSprite).member = pDefaultMember
end
```

As the cursor moves between the sprites, the mouseEnter and mouseLeave messages control which member the rollover sprite displays. Make sure that the sprites do not overlap; otherwise, the order of the messages can create undesired results. For instance, if sprites 1 and 2 overlap, the cursor can enter sprite 2 before it leaves sprite 1. The result would be that the default member would be displayed rather than the member specified by sprite 2.

To set this up in the Score, you need to attach this behavior to the active sprites and initiate the change in the nonactive sprite. Then, assign the same *pRolloverSprite* and *pDefaultMember* parameters to each, but a different *pRolloverMember* to each. This creates the basic effect discussed in this section. However, you can create more complex interfaces with different values of *pRolloverSprite* and *pDefaultMember* for each rollover.

Because you can attach multiple behaviors to a sprite, you can add a button behavior to these same sprites. That way, the rollovers are handled by the rollover display behavior here, but a click is handled by the button behavior. You can have sprites that display preview information, such as "Click this button to go to the index" in one sprite but also react to the click to go to another frame.

You can see this behavior in action in the `rolloverdisplay.dir` example movie.

Using Check Boxes

A check box is a button that has two states: on and off. Director has a check box member type that is a variant on the button member. You can use this built-in member as a check box, or build your own check boxes with two members per selection.

A behavior for the built-in check box member is almost not needed. The member reacts to a mouse click by itself, placing a mark in the box when clicked and then removing it on a second click. Figure 5.2 shows a small group of check box members.

Figure 5.2
A group of three check box members.

One thing that a behavior can do is to make it easier to determine which check boxes are checked. You can get this as a simple Lingo property of the member. For instance, in this example

```
member("apple check box").hilite
```

the `hilite` property returns TRUE or FALSE.

A behavior can use similar syntax, but because behaviors are assigned to sprites, not members, you can get the state of a check box according to the sprite number. Here is a simple behavior to do this:

```
on isChecked me
 return sprite(me.spriteNum).member.hilite
end
```

You can check the state of any check box by asking `sprite(X).isChecked()`, where *x* is the number of the sprite. Or you can do the same thing with `sendSprite(sprite X, #isChecked)`. A value of TRUE indicates that the check box has a mark in it, and a value of FALSE indicates that the box is empty.

Because the built-in check boxes are rather limited in appearance, it is usually a good idea to create your own multistate buttons with bitmaps. Figure 5.3 shows three such buttons, with the middle one being checked.

Figure 5.3
Three sprites are used to hold bitmap representations of check boxes. Behaviors control these sprites.

Each sprite can contain one of two members: the on state and the off state. So, Figure 5.3 has a total of six members. In this example, the on states look the same as the off states, except for the addition of a check mark next to them.

A behavior to handle these states needs to know what the on and off state members are. It also needs to know whether the sprite should start out in the on or off state. Three properties and parameters take care of this, as follows:

```
property pOnMember, pOffMember, pState

on getPropertyDescriptionList me
 list = [:]
 addProp list, #pOnMember, [#comment: "On Member",\
  #format: #member, #default: ""]
 addProp list, #pOffMember, [#comment: "Off Member",\
  #format: #member, #default: ""]
 addProp list, #pState, [#comment: "Initial State",\
  #format: #boolean, #default: FALSE]
 return list
end
```

When the sprite begins, it should adjust itself to be the proper state, regardless of what is in the Score. This can be done by the `on beginSprite` handler. Because you need to reuse the code that changes the member of the sprite according to the *pState* property, it is a good idea to create a custom handler to do that. The `on beginSprite` handler needs to call that custom handler.

```
on beginSprite me
 setMember(me)
end

on setMember me
 if pState = TRUE then
  sprite(me.spriteNum).member = pOnMember
 else
  sprite(me.spriteNum).member = pOffMember
 end if
end
```

The sprite needs to change its state when users click it. If it's on, it needs to go off, and vice versa. This can be done with one line using the `not` operator:

```
on mouseUp me
 pState = not pState
 setMember(me)
end
```

The `on mouseUp` handler calls the *on setMember* handler to change the member after the state changes.

One final handler can be a function that returns the state of the check box. This can be used by other Lingo handlers in movie scripts or other behaviors.

```
on isChecked me
 return pState
end
```

Note that you can also ask for this property directly in this manner:

```
sprite(X).pState
```

You can see both versions of the check box script in the movie `checkbox.dir`.

Using Radio Buttons

The topic of check boxes naturally leads into the topic of radio buttons. They are similar to each other. Whereas check boxes enable users to select one or more items from a list, radio buttons enable users to select only one item from a list.

Director also has a built-in radio button member in the form of a button member variant. It works the same way as the check box in that it already accepts mouse clicks and turns itself on and off accordingly. Figure 5.4 shows a small group of radio buttons.

Figure 5.4
A group of three radio buttons.

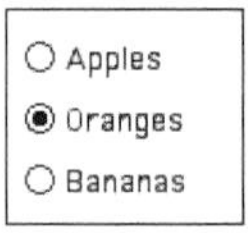

Whereas check boxes don't really need any Lingo to work, radio buttons definitely require some. The reason is that at this point the radio buttons don't know of one another's existence. In the example in Figure 5.4, the Apples button and the Oranges button do not interact in any way. This means that users can select both buttons, which goes against the whole point of radio buttons. Users should be able to select only one of the buttons at a time.

A simple behavior works to restrict the three buttons and get them to work together. To start, the behavior needs to know what other sprites are in its group. It also needs to know whether it begins as selected, which is the equivalent of TRUE.

```
property pState, pGroupList

on getPropertyDescriptionList me
 list = [:]
 addProp list, #pState, [#comment: "Initial State",\
  #format: #boolean, #default: FALSE]
 addProp list, #pGroupList, [#comment: "Group List",\
  #format: #list, #default: []]
 return list
end
```

The property *pGroupList* should contain a linear list of sprites in the group. For instance, if the example's three radio buttons are in sprites 1 to 3, *pGroupList* should be *[1,2,3]*.

The *pState* property should also be set with care. One and only one of the radio buttons in the group should be set to TRUE. Then, in the on beginSprite handler, the sprite needs to be set to the on member if its initial *pState* is set to TRUE.

```
on beginSprite me
 if pState then turnMeOn(me)
end
```

The custom handler *on turnMeOn* is used to set the member of the sprite. Because these are radio buttons, this handler also has to make sure that the other sprites in this group are turned off.

```
on turnMeOn me
 pState = TRUE
 sprite(me.spriteNum).member.hilite = TRUE
 repeat with i in pGroupList
  if i <> me.spriteNum then
   sendSprite(sprite i,#turnMeOff)
  end if
 end repeat
end
```

The `repeat` command in this handler uses the form `repeat with i in`. This special form of the `repeat` command can be used only with lists. Instead of the variable "i" counting from one number to the next, it moves through the values of the list. If the list is *[5,8,14]*, the loop runs three times, and the value of *i* is set to 5, 8, and 14 for those times through the loop.

The `sendSprite` command is used to send the message *#turnMeOff* to each of the sprites in the list. An `if` statement makes sure that this message isn't sent back to the current sprite. The *on turnMeOff* handler is a simple one:

```
on turnMeOff me
 pState = FALSE
 sprite(me.spriteNum).member.hilite = FALSE
end
```

Now that there is a handler to turn on the current radio button, a mouse click is easily handled. It just calls the *on turnMeOn* handler, which turns on the current sprite and turns off all the others.

```
on mouseUp me
 turnMeOn(me)
end
```

One last handler can be used to determine which sprite in the group is currently selected. This handler uses the same repeat loop as the *on turnMeOn* handler, but rather than change the sprite, it just finds one that is on and returns that value.

```
on selected me
 repeat with i in pGroupList
  if sprite(i).pState = TRUE then return i
 end repeat
end
```

This handler relies on the fact that one and only one sprite is turned on. There should never be a time when none, or more than one, are on. The handler also has the unusual capability to return the same answer no matter which sprite in the group is used to call it. If a radio button group is in sprites one to three, a `sendSprite(`*1,#selected*`)` and a `sendSprite(`*2,#selected*`)` should return the same answer because they should have the same *pGroupList* property value.

Although this behavior takes care of the complexity of the radio button group, it does not offer the opportunity to use custom bitmaps as radio buttons rather than the boring built-in radio button member. However, it can be easily modified to do so.

The first step is to add two new properties to represent the on and off state bitmaps. These look the same as they do in the check box behavior:

```
property pOnMember, pOffMember, pState, pGroupList

on getPropertyDescriptionList me
 list = [:]
 addProp list, #pOnMember, [#comment: "On Member",\
  #format: #member, #default: ""]
 addProp list, #pOffMember, [#comment: "Off Member",\
  #format: #member, #default: ""]
```

5

```
addProp list, #pState, [#comment: "Initial State",\
 #format: #boolean, #default: FALSE]
addProp list, #pGroupList, [#comment: "Group List",\
 #format: #list, #default: []]
return list
end
```

Then, the *on turnMeOn* and *on turnMeOff* handlers need to be modified to set the member of the sprite, rather than the `hilite` property of the member:

```
on turnMeOn me
 pState = TRUE
 sprite(me.spriteNum).member = pOnMember
 repeat with i in pGroupList
  if i <> me.spriteNum then
    sendSprite(sprite i,#turnMeOff)
  end if
 end repeat
end

on turnMeOff me
 pState = FALSE
 sprite(me.spriteNum).member = pOffMember
end
```

The rest of the behavior can stay the same. Figure 5.5 shows what this screen might look like. The off members and the on member differ only in that the on member includes an arrow to the right of the picture to signify that it is selected.

Figure 5.5
A set of custom-built radio buttons. A behavior controls which member is used depending on which item is selected.

You can find all the radio button scripts in the movie `radiobuttons.dir`.

Dragging Sprites

Although dragging sprites is possible without Lingo (by setting the `movable` property of a sprite in the Score), Lingo enables you to add all sorts of functionality to dragging. Learning how to drag a sprite with Lingo is the first step, and then you will be ready to try some dragging applications.

Dragging is a useful interface action that all computer users are familiar with. The operating systems on modern computers require you to drag and drop files and folders all the time. Using them in Director movies is a good way to allow the users to manipulate items on the screen.

Simple Drag Script

A drag script can be as simple as setting the sprite to constantly follow the cursor. However, a real drag behavior waits until the user clicks the sprite and then follows the cursor around until the user releases the mouse button.

To do this type of drag, you don't even need any parameters. However, you do need one property to tell the behavior when the dragging is taking place. This should be set to FALSE when the sprite begins.

```
property pPressed

on beginSprite me
  pPressed = FALSE
end
```

When the user clicks the sprite, the behavior needs to change this *pPressed* property to TRUE. When the user lifts up, it needs to be set to FALSE.

```
on mouseDown me
  pPressed = TRUE
end

on mouseUp me
  pPressed = FALSE
end
```

It's possible for the user to lift up the mouse button while the cursor is not over the sprite. The mouse location is updated in real-time, whereas you will be setting the location of the sprite only every frame loop. To make sure that dragging stops whenever the mouse button is lifted, you need to also use the `on mouseUpOutside` handler.

```
on mouseUpOutside me
  pPressed = FALSE
end
```

Finally, the `on exitFrame` handler does all the heavy lifting. It checks to see whether the *pPressed* property is TRUE, and moves the sprite to the mouse location if it is

```
on exitFrame me
  if pPressed then
```

5

```
    sprite(me.spriteNum).loc = the mouseLoc
  end if
end
```

You can find this simple drag behavior attached to the first sprite in the `dragging.dir` movie.

A Better Drag Behavior

The main problem with the simple drag script is a cosmetic one. The sprite appears to snap to center itself on the cursor no matter where users click. So, if you click the upper-right side of the sprite, the sprite immediately shifts so that the center, or actually the registration point, is directly under the cursor.

Fixing this glitch is not a problem. When the initial click is made, the difference in location between the mouse and the center of the sprite can be recorded. This value can then be applied to every change in the sprite's location. The result is that the cursor and the sprite remain synchronized, no matter where the user grabs the sprite. If the user grabs the sprite by the upper-right corner, it then drags by the upper-right corner.

To make this change, first add the property *pClickDiff* to the property declaration. Then, alter the on `mouseDown` handler to record the difference between the click location and the sprite location, as follows:

```
on mouseDown me
 pPressed = TRUE
 pClickDiff = sprite(me.spriteNum).loc - the clickLoc
end
```

Now that the offset is stored in the *pClickDiff*, it can be applied to the position of the sprite in the on `exitFrame` handler.

```
on exitFrame me
 if pPressed then
  sprite(me.spriteNum).loc = the mouseLoc + pClickDiff
 end if
end
```

> The property the clickLoc is similar to the mouseLoc. They both return a point as their value. However, the mouseLoc might change if the mouse moves between the time the click was made and the time the line of Lingo code runs. the clickLoc gives the exact location of the last click in an on mouseDown or similar handler, whereas the mouseLoc is the current mouse position.

If this is still confusing, seeing it in action will help; the second sprite in `dragging.dir` uses this behavior. Compare it to the first sprite to see how the first sprite will lock its center to the cursor, and the second will allow the user to drag the sprite from any point in the sprite.

Click, Drag, and Lock

You can apply what you've learned about dragging by using it to build a matching game or quiz. You have elements of one type on one side of the screen and elements of another type on another side. The game is essentially made up of matching pairs. It's up to the user to drag the sprites on the left over to the sprites on the right. Figure 5.6 shows what this might look like.

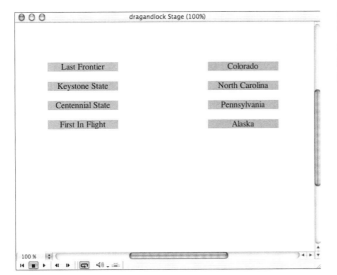

Figure 5.6
The screen shows four pairs of matching items. The user's task is to drag the items on the right onto the correct ones on the left.

Although this can be done with the drag scripts already described, these scripts have no capability to tell the user whether the match is correct. A better way to do it would be to have a script that locks a sprite into position if it is near the place it belongs.

This requires some parameters. The first is the number of the sprite to which that behavior's sprite should lock. The second should be the maximum distance that the dragged sprite can be from the destination sprite before it automatically locks.

Also, an option is needed to tell the behavior what to do in case the sprite is not close enough to its destination to lock. One option is for it to snap back to its original position. The other option is to leave it where it is.

In addition to these new properties, you still need the old properties of *pPressed* and *pClickDiff*. You also need a property to store the original location of the sprite in cases in which it needs to snap back.

```
property pPressed, pClickDiff, pLockToSprite, pOrigLoc, pLockDist, pSnapBack

on getPropertyDescriptionList me
  list = [:]
  addProp list, #pLockToSprite, [#comment: "Lock To Sprite",\
   #format: #integer, #default: 0]
  addProp list, #pLockDist, [#comment: "Maximum Lock Distance",\
   #format: #integer, #default: 25]
  addProp list, #pSnapBack, [#comment: "Snap Back If Not Locked",\
   #format: #boolean, #default: TRUE]
  return list
end
```

The *pLockDist* is a key property for this behavior. Without it, the user would be required to lock the sprite exactly into position over the destination sprite.

The behavior needs to start off by initializing *pPressed* and also setting the *pOrigLoc* property.

```
on beginSprite me
 pPressed = FALSE
 pOrigLoc = sprite(me.spriteNum).loc
end
```

The mouse click handlers are the same as before, except that a custom handler is called from the on mouseUp and on mouseUpOutside handlers. This behavior has more to do than just setting the *pPressed* back to FALSE, so it's best to place it all in a custom handler rather than attempt to duplicate the code between on mouseUp and on mouseUpOutside.

```
on mouseDown me
 pPressed = TRUE
 pClickDiff = sprite(me.spriteNum).loc - the clickLoc
end

on mouseUp me
 release(me)
end

on mouseUpOutside me
 release(me)
end
```

The on exitFrame script is exactly as before.

```
on exitFrame me
 if pPressed then
  sprite(me.spriteNum).loc = the mouseLoc + pClickDiff
 end if
end
```

The custom *on release* handler has to do several things. First, it sets the *pPressed* property to FALSE. Then, it needs to determine whether the sprite is now close enough to its destination to lock into place. It calls yet another custom handler, "on distance," to do this. This function takes two points as parameters and returns the distance between them in pixels.

If the sprite is close enough, the new location of the sprite is set to exactly the location of the destination sprite. Otherwise, if the *pSnapBack* property is TRUE, the location snaps back to the original location. If not, the location remains where the user left it.

```
on release me
 pPressed = FALSE

 if distance(me,sprite(me.spriteNum).loc,sprite(pLockToSprite).loc) \
   < pLockDist then
  sprite(me.spriteNum).loc = sprite(pLockToSprite).loc
 else if pSnapBack then
  sprite(me.spriteNum).loc = pOrigLoc
 end if
end
```

The *on distance* function is a handy tool that is used in a lot of behaviors. It takes two points and uses the square root of the sum of the squares of the differences between horizontal and vertical locations. You might remember this formula from high school trigonometry:

$$\sqrt{(\,(x_2 - x_1)^2 + (y_2 - y_1)^2\,)}$$

```
on distance me, point1, point2
  return sqrt(power(point1.locH-point2.locH,2)+ \
  power(point1.locV-point2.locV,2))
end
```

All that is left to do is apply the behavior to some sprites. In the example shown previously in Figure 5.6, the behavior should be applied to the sprites on the right. They are in higher Sprite channels and appear above the sprites on the left. The *pLockToSprite* of each one of these sprites should be set to the matching item's sprite.

If you were really making a game of this, you could use this movie script to determine whether all the sprites were locked in place.

```
on checkGameDone
  done = TRUE
  repeat with i = 5 to 8
    if (sprite i).loc <> sprite(sprite(i).pLockToSprite).loc then
      done = FALSE
    end if
  end repeat
  if done then beep()
end
```

This movie handler assumes that the game is done by setting the local variable *done* to TRUE. It then looks at sprites 5 through 8, which is where the dragging sprites are located, and compares their locations to the locations of their designated destination sprites. If they all match, "done" is never set to FALSE. In this case, the result is a simple beep. However, you could also make it jump to another frame or play a sound.

The perfect place for a call to this handler is in the *on release* handler of the behavior. The movie needs to check this every time a sprite is locked, so place it after the `sprite(me.spriteNum).loc = sprite(pLockToSprite).loc` line.

Drag and Throw

Another way to apply a drag behavior is to enable users to grab and throw a sprite. They click it and drag it around while the mouse is down, like the other drag behaviors, but then when they release it, the sprite keeps going with some amount of momentum.

This is much more complex than a simple drag behavior. First, you have more than just pressed and nonpressed states. A third state is the state of being thrown. So, the *pPressed* property should be replaced with a *pMode* property that is *#normal*, *#pressed*, or *#throw*.

5

In addition, you need to know how far and in which direction to throw the sprite when it is released. Measuring the distance between the position of the sprite on release and the position of the sprite just before release provides the appropriate information. However, don't take the position of the sprite exactly one frame prior to release, because that can be too short a period of time: It is only one sixtieth of a second if the frame rate is 60fps. Instead, have a parameter that determines how many frames back to look to determine the momentum of the released sprite. A good default for this is five. So, if a sprite is clicked and dragged for 150 frame loops and then released, the position in frame 145 and the position in frame 150 are compared to set the throwing momentum. A list is needed to record the last five positions at any given time. Here is the property list and on getPropertyDescriptionList for this behavior:

```
property pThrowSpan, pMode, pCurrentLoc, pLocList, pMoveAmount

on getPropertyDescriptionList me
 list = [:]
 addProp list, #pThrowSpan, [#comment: "Frame Span of Throw",\
  #format: #integer, #range: [#min: 1, #max: 20], \
  #default: 5]
 return list
end
```

The sprite starts by setting the *pMode* to *#normal*.

```
on beginSprite me
 pMode = #normal
end
```

When the user clicks, the mode must change to *#pressed*, and the list used to store the positions must be initialized:

```
on mouseDown me
 pMode = #pressed
 pLocList = []
end
```

Whenever the mouse button lifts, a custom handler called *on throw* runs. This handler calculates the momentum by taking the current mouse location and the first item in the *pLocList*. It needs to divide that by *pThrowSpan* to get a relative per-frame movement amount. This way, if *pThrowSpan* is set to 5, the *pMoveAmount* is set to the current location of the sprite, minus the location of the sprite 5 frame loops ago, divided by 5:

```
on mouseUp me
 throw(me)
end

on mouseUpOutside me
 throw(me)
end

on throw me
 if pLocList.count > 0 then
```

```
    pMoveAmount = (the mouseLoc - pLocList[1])/pThrowSpan
    pMode = #throw
  end if
end
```

The on exitFrame handler must move the sprite whether it is being dragged or thrown. If being dragged, it needs to set the location of the sprite to the current mouse location. It also needs to record this location in *pLocList*. If *pLocList* has more items than specified by *pThrowSpan*, the oldest item is removed.

If the mode is *#throw*, the *pMoveAmount* is used to move the sprite. In addition, this property is multiplied by .9, thereby decreasing it by approximately 10%. This imitates a sort of friction that one would expect the sprite to exhibit when thrown. If you want, the .9 can be made into a property, say *pFriction*, and altered using the behavior parameter dialog box.

```
on exitFrame me
  if pMode = #pressed then
    pCurrentLoc = the mouseLoc
    sprite(me.spriteNum).loc = pCurrentLoc
    pLocList.add(pCurrentLoc)
    if pLocList.count > pThrowSpan then pLocList.deleteAt(1)

  else if pMode = #throw then
    pCurrentLoc = pCurrentLoc + pMoveAmount
    sprite(me.spriteNum).loc = pCurrentLoc
    pMoveAmount = pMoveAmount * .9
  end if
end
```

Think of the possibilities of a behavior like this. Do you want to add code like that used in the bouncing behavior so that the sprite bounces off the sides of the screen? How about code that adds gravity? How about code that locks the sprite to the position of another if it's close enough? Combine all three and you get something that resembles a basketball free-throw video game.

You can find the drag and throw script attached to the third sprite in the dragging.dir movie.

5

Creating Sliders

A slider is a familiar user interface element used in all major software programs. Sliders offer the best way to enable users to input a number within a small range. They are even used in behavior Parameter dialog boxes for this purpose.

Slider Elements

Creating a slider with several bitmap members and a behavior can be fairly complex. Many actions must be taken into account, and more than one sprite is needed to form the elements of a slider.

Figure 5.7 shows what a slider should look like. This is just a straight imitation of the sliders used in the Director Preferences dialog boxes.

Figure 5.7
A typical slider enables users to
pick a number from a range.

A full slider element contains six parts: a marker, a shadow, a background graphic, two buttons, and a text field. However, you can start by creating the main three parts: the marker, the shadow, and the background graphic. The shadow is the dark coloring to the left side of the marker. It is the only nonbitmap element in this case; it uses a shape sprite instead.

Slider Behavior Properties

You actually need only one behavior script, attached to the marker sprite. Like the button and drag behaviors, this behavior needs a property to tell whether it is in the process of being pressed. It also needs to know how far to the left and right it can move, and what range of values it represents, such as 1 to 3, 0 to 100, or -500 to 500. A relationship with the shadow sprite is needed, so one property should hold that sprite number. Another property needs to record the current value of the slider, as follows:

```
property pPressed -- whether the sprite is being pressed
property pBounds -- the rect of the shadow sprite at start
property pMinimumValue, pMaximumValue -- used by the marker sprite only
property pShadowSprite -- the number of the shadow sprite
property pValue -- actual value of the slider
on getPropertyDescriptionList me
 list = [:]
 addProp list, #pShadowSprite, [#comment: "Shadow Sprite",\
   #format: #integer, #default: 0]
 addProp list, #pMinimumValue, [#comment: "Minimum Value",\
   #format: #integer, #default: 0]
 addProp list, #pMaximumValue, [#comment: "Maximum Value",\
   #format: #integer, #default: 100]
 addProp list, #pValue, [#comment: "Start Value",\
   #format: #integer, #default: 50]
 return list
end
```

The on `getPropertyDescriptionList` needs to use only four of the properties as parameters: the minimum, maximum, and starting value of the slider, as well as the shadow sprite's number.

Setting the Slider's Position

Although the minimum and maximum values are set by the behavior's Parameter dialog box, the behavior also needs to know the physical screen locations of the minimum and maximum values. To determine these locations, a trick is used. The shadow sprite is set to mark the exact bounds of the marker sprite. Because the shadow sprite will be reset by the behavior when it starts anyway, using it to show the boundaries of the slider does not affect its future appearance. In the case of the slider shown previously in Figure 5.7, the shadow sprite is stretched all the way across the inner part of the background graphic. Its `rect` is recorded by the on `beginSprite` handler of the behavior. Then, it is set to display properly, as shown earlier in Figure 5.7:

```
on beginSprite me
 pBounds = sprite(pShadowSprite).rect
 setMarker(me)
 setShadow(me)
end
```

The left and right physical limits of the slider could have been added to the on `getPropertyDescriptionList` handler, but this would mean that you would have had to determine the exact screen locations and type them in. Worse than that, if the slider were moved, even by one pixel, you would have to reenter these numbers. Using the shadow sprite as a "template" of sorts saves you the trouble, and it is easily adjusted on the Stage.

The on `beginSprite` handler includes calls to the custom *on setMarker* and *on setShadow* handlers. These take the current value of the slider and set the position of these two sprites.

The *on setMarker* handler first figures out the value range of the slider. If the slider goes from 0 to 100, the range is 100 (not 101). It computes the value of the slider as a number between 0 and 1, regardless of the real range. It then takes this percentage and applies it to the physical screen range to get the location of the marker:

```
-- this sets the marker sprite
on setMarker me
 -- compute the value as a number between 0 and 1
 valueRange = pMaximumValue - pMinimumValue
 sliderPos = float(pValue)/float(valueRange)

 -- translate to a screen position
 sliderRange = pBounds.right-pBounds.left
 x = sliderPos*sliderRange + pBounds.left

 -- set marker
 sprite(me.spriteNum).locH = x
end
```

The *on setShadow* handler sets the shadow to its original rectangle, but with the right side adjusted to fall under the marker.

```
-- this handler lets the marker sprite set the shadow sprite
on setShadow me
 x = sprite(me.spriteNum).locH
 r = rect(pBounds.left, pBounds.top, x, pBounds.bottom)
 sprite(pShadowSprite).rect = r
end
```

Mouse Input

These handlers accomplish the task of setting the slider to its starting position. Now you need some handlers to enable users to click and drag the marker:

```
on mouseDown me
 pPressed = TRUE
end

on mouseUp me
 pPressed = FALSE
end

on mouseUpOutside me
 pPressed = FALSE
end

on exitFrame me
 if pPressed then
  moveMarker(me)
  setMarker(me)
  setShadow(me)
 end if
end
```

The on *exitFrame* handler checks to make sure that *pPressed* is true and then calls other handlers to handle the work. The *on setMarker* and *on setShadow* handlers are there, but called after an *on moveMarker* handler. The *on moveMarker* handler does the opposite of what the *on setMarker* handler does: It determines the value of the slider based on the mouse location.

Determining the Slider's Value

In addition, the *on moveMarker* handler translates the value to an integer. If you want the slider to show floating point numbers instead, just remove that line:

```
-- this handler takes the mouse position and figures the
-- value of the slider
on moveMarker me
 -- compute the position as a number between 0 and 1
 x = the mouseH - pBounds.left
 sliderRange = pBounds.right-pBounds.left
 pos = float(x)/sliderRange

 -- translate to a value
 valueRange = pMaximumValue - pMinimumValue
 pValue = pos*valueRange + pMinimumValue
 pValue = integer(pValue)
```

```
-- check to make sure it is within bounds
if pValue > pMaximumValue then
 pValue = pMaximumValue
else if pValue < pMinimumValue then
 pValue = pMinimumValue
end if
end
```

The *on moveMarker* also makes sure that the new value of the slider falls within its range. Note that this handler's sole purpose is to set the *pValue* property. After it is called in the *on exitFrame* handler, the *on setMarker* and *on setShadow* handlers update the sprites.

Because the value of the slider is held in the *pValue* property, a handler that returns the value of the slider is quite simple. You can call this handler with sendSprite from other behaviors or movie scripts to get the current value of the slider, even while it is being dragged.

```
-- this handler returns the value of the slider
on getValue me
 return pValue
end
```

If you can't get sliders to show some values, see "Interface Elements Don't Recognize Fractional Values" in the "Troubleshooting" section at the end of this chapter.

Additional Elements

Several elements can be added to a slider to make it as complete as sliders found in other software. For example, a text field can show the current value of the slider, and two buttons can enable users to move the slider one value at a time.

Figure 5.8 shows all these elements. There are a total of eight cast members if you include down states for the buttons.

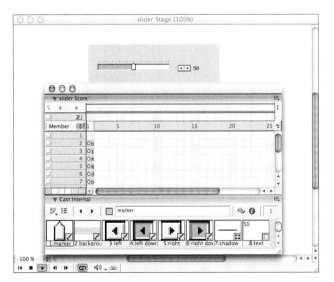

Figure 5.8
The Cast panel shows the eight elements of the slider. The Score shows the sprite placement of each. The Stage shows the assembled slider.

The first bit of extra functionality that you should add to a simple slider, such as this, is a text field that shows the value of the slider. To do this, create a text field and place it on the Stage. You need to tell the marker sprite where this text sprite is located. An extra parameter will do it. Add a *pTextSprite* property to the property declarations at the top of the behavior. Add this to the on getPropertyDescriptionList handler:

```
addProp list, #pTextSprite, [#comment: "Text Sprite",\
  #format: #integer, #default: 0]
```

An *on setText* handler places the current value of the slider in this text field. Just in case no text sprite is used, this handler makes sure that the *pTextSprite* property is not 0. If it is, the *on setText* handler assumes that there is no text sprite and does not place the text:

```
-- this handler sets the text of the text sprite
on setText me
 if pTextSprite <> 0 then -- is there a text sprite?
  sprite(pTextSprite).member.text = string(pValue)
 end if
end
```

Calls to *on setText* need to be added immediately after the calls to *on setShadow* in both the on beginSprite and on exitFrame handlers.

The next elements that the slider needs are the buttons that enable the users to move the slider one value in either direction. You need both normal and down states for these buttons, as shown previously in Figure 5.8.

These buttons need their own behavior, but before you create the behavior, a handler needs to be added to the marker behavior. This handler enables the marker to be moved one value in either direction. It should take one parameter that is either a *#left* or a *#right* depending on which direction the slider should move. It also needs to perform the same boundary check that the *on moveMarker* handler does to make sure that the slider doesn't go past its limits.

```
-- this handler moves the marker one value left or right
on moveMarkerOne me, direction
 if direction = #left then
  pValue = pValue - 1
 else if direction = #right then
  pValue = pValue + 1
 end if

 -- check to make sure it is within bounds
 if pValue > pMaximumValue then
  pValue = pMaximumValue
 else if pValue < pMinimumValue then
  pValue = pMinimumValue
 end if

 setMarker(me)
 setShadow(me)
```

```
 setText(me)
end
```

The *on moveMarkerOne* handler ends by calling the three handlers needed to update the slider. This makes it possible to call this one handler and have the slider changed and updated by the other three automatically.

A handler to take care of the two buttons is similar to any simple button handler. It mostly controls normal and down states for the button sprite. It also has to know where the marker sprite is so that it can send the moveMarkerOne message to it. A key parameter is *pArrowDirection*, which is set to *#left* or *#right* depending on which button is selected:

```
property pDownMember, pOrigMember -- down and normal states
property pPressed -- whether the sprite is being pressed
property pMarkerSprite -- the number of the marker sprite
property pArrowDirection -- 1 or -1 to add to slider

on getPropertyDescriptionList me
 list = [:]
 addProp list, #pMarkerSprite, [#comment: "Marker Sprite",\
  #format: #integer, #default: 0]
 addProp list, #pDownMember, [#comment: "Arrow Button Down Member",\
  #format: #bitmap, #default: ""]
 addProp list, #pArrowDirection, [#comment: "Arrow Direction",\
  #format: #symbol, #range: [#left,#right], #default: #right]
 return list
end
```

The rest of the slider button behavior handles the mouse clicking and calls the *moveMarkerOne* handler in the marker behavior once per frame loop while the button is pressed:

```
on beginSprite me
 pOrigMember = sprite(me.spriteNum).member
end

on mouseDown me
 pPressed = TRUE
 sprite(me.spriteNum).member = member pDownMember
end

on mouseUp me
 liftUp(me)
end

on mouseUpOutside me
 liftUp(me)
end

on liftUp me
 pPressed = FALSE
```

5

```
    sprite(me.spriteNum).member = member pOrigMember
end

on exitFrame me
 if pPressed then
  sendSprite(sprite pMarkerSprite, #moveMarkerOne, \
   pArrowDirection)
 end if
end
```

With eight members and two behaviors, you have all the functionality of the sliders used by other software programs. Even better, you can change the graphics used to anything you want to stylize your sliders to fit your design.

You have a lot of control over how the slider looks and behaves. You can alter your code to place an extra word behind the number in the text field. So, rather than read "50", it can read "50%" or "50 widgets". You can tweak the slider screen boundaries if the shadow sprite isn't working the way you want. You can even remove the shadow sprite.

There is nothing to stop you from taking all the references to horizontal locations and boundaries and converting them to vertical locations and boundaries to make a vertical slider. This is a good example of how much control Lingo behaviors give you as opposed to the drag-and-drop interface elements in other authoring programs.

You can see the slider behavior in the movie `slider.dir`.

Creating Progress Bars

Using some of the same techniques to make the slider bar, you can create a progress bar behavior. A *progress bar* is a rectangle that enlarges to fill a space as a process is completed. An example is the progress bar the Director displays every time you choose File, Save.

If you have a Lingo process that takes more than a fraction of a second to complete, you might want to display a progress bar so that the users know that the computer is not frozen, but simply processing their requests.

Figure 5.9 shows a simple progress bar. It shows two sprites: a hollow rectangle shape and a filled rectangle. To make the progress bar look like others used in various pieces of software, the fill of the rectangle is set to a pattern rather than a solid.

Figure 5.9
A simple progress bar showing a
task about one-half done.

To create a progress bar, you need a process to test it. Here are two movie handlers that work together to compute all the prime numbers between one and 1,000. A prime number is a number divisible only by one and itself.

```
on findPrimeNumbers
 list = []
```

```
  repeat with i = 1 to 1000
   if isPrime(i) then add list, i
  end repeat
  return list
 end

on isPrime n
 repeat with i = 2 to integer(sqrt(n))
  div = float(n)/float(i)
  if div = integer(div) then return FALSE
 end repeat
 return TRUE
end
```

The *on isPrime* function tries every number between two and the square root of the number to see whether it can find a case where there is no fractional remainder to the division. It compares the number to itself converted to an integer to see whether there is a remainder.

This process takes about a second to run on a PowerMac G4 with a 667MHz processor. It also does this calculation in 1,000 steps, so it's a prime candidate for a progress bar.

Of the two sprites involved in the progress bar, only the filled portion needs a behavior. The other sprite is there for merely cosmetic purposes.

Like the slider marker behavior, this sprite needs to know the size of its final, full rectangle. To make that easy to determine, set the sprite up on the Stage to already be its full size. That way, the on beginSprite handler can get the full rectangle size by simply looking at the rect of the sprite when the behavior starts.

```
property pFullRect

on beginSprite me
 pFullRect = sprite(me.spriteNum).rect
end
```

The only other handler needed is the one that sets the progress bar when needed. It will be a custom handler that a process, such as *on findPrimeNumbers*, calls when it can.

```
on setProgress me, currentVal, highestVal
 -- get amount filled as a value between 0 and 1
 percentFilled = float(currentVal)/float(highestVal)

 -- convert to a pixel width
 pixelRange = pFullRect.right-pFullRect.left
 x = percentFilled*pixelRange

 -- set the rect of the sprite
 r = rect(pFullRect.left, pFullRect.top, \
   pFullRect.left + x, pFullRect.bottom)
 sprite(me.spriteNum).rect = r
end
```

The *on setProgress* handler takes two parameters. The first is the current value of the progress bar, and the second is the maximum value of the progress bar. It takes these two values and divides them to get the percentage of fill needed. It then determines the physical width of the progress bar area and determines the point to which the sprite should stretch. Finally, it builds a rectangle from this information and sets the sprite.

To use this behavior, you need to call it from the process taking place. In this case, the *on findPrimeNumbers* handler will use it.

```
on findPrimeNumbers
  list = []
  repeat with i = 1 to 1000
    sendSprite(sprite 2,#setProgress,i,1000)
    updateStage
    if isPrime(i) then add list, i
  end repeat
  return list
end
```

Notice that an `updateStage` is needed because the frame is not looping here. Director is caught inside the `repeat` loop and does not know to update the Stage without you telling it.

Check out the sample movie, `progressbar.dir`, which activates the *on findPrimeNumbers* handler with a button, shows the progress bar as the prime numbers are calculated and then displays the list of prime numbers when it is finished.

You can easily change the color and dimensions of a progress bar such as this. If you prefer a more stylized progress bar, you may want to convert this behavior to use three elements: a left end, a right end, and a stretchable middle piece. Doing so would require the same behavior to control two other sprites, possibly specified as parameters.

You can find this example on the CD-ROM as `progressbar.dir`.

Creating Graphical Pop-Up Menus

Like check boxes, radio buttons, sliders, and progress bars, another item that can be created with bitmaps and a behavior is the pop-up menu.

Pop-up menus are the little menus that appear in windows and dialog boxes, as opposed to the main menu bar that appears at the top of a screen or window. In the Director authoring environment, you can see examples of these in the Score panel and Sprite Inspector. As a matter of fact, just about every window in Director includes some type of pop-up menu.

Pop-up menus are useful when you want the users to choose from a list of items but don't have the space in your interface to show all the choices. The users click to reveal the list of items, select one, and then the list goes away, leaving their choice in that space.

Creating pop-up menus as interface elements in your movies is possible with a behavior. First, create a series of bitmaps in the Cast to be used. Figure 5.10 shows the Cast panel with some example bitmaps. A single bitmap represents the pop-up menu when it is not active, and then five other bitmaps appear under it when it is pressed. All five of these bitmaps have a corresponding `hilite` state.

To create the pop-up on the Stage, place the sprites as you would want to see them when the pop-up is pressed and active. Never mind that the list under the "Choose One" graphic should not be present when the user first comes to the frame; the behavior will handle that.

For the behavior to do that, it needs to know where these sprites are. So, one property of this behavior must be a list of sprites. Another property will be the members initially in these sprites. The behavior itself will be attached to the pop-up menu button, which is the "Choose One" graphic in this case:

```
property pSpriteList, pMemberList, pPressed

on getPropertyDescriptionList me
 list = [:]

 addProp list, #pSpriteList, [#comment: "Sprite List", \
  #format: #list, #default: []]
 return list
end
```

To start, the behavior needs to record the members used by each of the sprites that are part of the pop-up. This example does not include the pop-up button.

```
on beginSprite me
 pMemberList = [:]
 repeat with i in pSpriteList
  addProp pMemberList, i, sprite(i).member.name
 end repeat
 hidePopup(me)
end
```

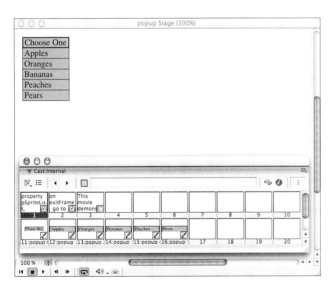

Figure 5.10
The Stage shows a pop-up menu as it appears during creation of the movie. The Cast panel shows these members, as well as the hilite states.

The call to *on hidePopUp* removes the pop-up items before the user sees them. The best way to do this is to set the memberNum property of the sprites to 0:

```
on hidePopup me
 repeat with i = 1 to pSpriteList.count
  sprite(pSpriteList[i]).memberNum = 0
 end repeat
end
```

The mouse click handlers look similar to those used in earlier behaviors. Both on mouseUp and on mouseUpOutside call a custom handler that calls the *on hidePopup* again, as well as an *on select* handler:

```
on mouseDown me
 pPressed = TRUE
end

on mouseUp me
 liftUp(me)
end

on mouseUpOutSide me
 liftUp(me)
end

on liftUp me
 pPressed = FALSE
 hidePopup(me)
 select(me)
end
```

In the on exitFrame handler, a variety of tasks are performed when the pop-up is pressed. First, it calls *on showPopup*, which returns the sprites to the members they used when you set up the movie. Then, it uses the rollover property to determine over which sprite the mouse is currently hovering. It uses getOne on the *pSpriteList* property to determine whether this is one of the pop-up items.

If the mouse is over a sprite in the list, it then changes the member of that sprite to a member of the same name, except with the word "hilite" appended. This is just a convention that this behavior uses to figure out which highlighted members belong to which normal members. You could just as easily have placed all the highlighted members in the next member over from the normal members, and recorded the member numbers of the sprites, using a +1 to find the highlight member, which will be the very next member in the Cast.

The getOne property of a list enables you to find the position of an item in a list. If the item is there, it returns the number of the item, which can also be interpreted as TRUE. If the item is not in the list, a 0 is returned, which is always seen as FALSE.

```
on exitFrame me
 if pPressed then
  showPopup(me)
  s = the rollover
  if (pSpriteList.getOne(s)) then
   sprite(s).member = member (pMemberList.getProp(s)&&"hilite")
  end if
 end if
end
```

The result of this handler is that the pop-up items will be shown if the *pPressed* property is TRUE, and any item that the cursor is currently over will show up as the highlighted member. Figure 5.11 shows this in action.

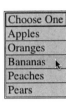

Figure 5.11
The pop-up menu has been selected, and the cursor is over the third item.

The *on showPopup* handler is similar to the *on hidePopup* handler except that the *pMemberList* is used to assign the correct member to each sprite:

```
on showPopup me
 repeat with i in pSpriteList
  sprite(i).member = member pMemberList.getProp(i)
 end repeat
end
```

Finally, the *on select* handler is called when the user releases the mouse button. This handler cannot assume that the cursor is over an item in the pop-up list, so it must check in the same way that the on exitFrame handler checks:

```
on select me
 s = the rollover
 if (pSpriteList.getOne(s)) then
  alert pMemberList.getProp(s)
 end if
end
```

In this case, a simple alert box appears to signify that a choice has been made. However, in your program you will want to set a global, go to a frame, or perform some other action.

This pop-up menu behavior can be customized in many ways. With a little more work, you can even have the selected item appear to replace the "Choose One" graphic, or have sounds play as the pop-up is used.

Notice that nothing in the script specifies that the items must be positioned directly below the original sprite. Why not have them line up to the right of the sprite? Or, have them appear above it? There are many possibilities.

Check the example movie `popup.dir` to see this script in action.

TROUBLESHOOTING

Differences Between Mouse Location Properties

What's the difference between the `clickLoc` *and the* `mouseLoc`? *Aren't they the same thing? Can I use them interchangably?*

Be sure that you understand the difference between the `clickLoc` and the `mouseLoc`. The first is the exact location of the mouse when the user clicked. The second is the current location of the mouse, which might have changed since the user clicked.

Interface Elements Don't Recognize Fractional Values

I'm using a slider or progress bar behavior that I wrote, and I can't get the element to show values between whole numbers. Why won't it do this?

When performing calculations in which the result will be a number between 0 and 1, as in the slider behavior or the progress bar behavior, it is important to convert the numbers to floats before doing division. Otherwise, a calculation such as 3/6 will return a 0, rather than a 0.5.

Using Member Numbers Could Lead to Trouble

Why can't I use member numbers and the sprite's `memberNum` *property to assign members to sprites. That seems like less work than coming up with names for everything.*

The `memberNum` property of a sprite enables you to set the member of a sprite by just referring to it by number. This property is good for setting a sprite to the next member or something similar, but should not be used otherwise. You should use the member property instead and set the sprite to a specific member by name. Otherwise, doing something as simple as reorganizing your Cast could break your scripts.

DID YOU KNOW?

- If you are using floating point numbers in a parameter and assigning a range to that parameter, you can control the number of decimal places used by setting *the floatPrecision* system property. The default is four digits after the decimal point.

- In the `sendSprite` command, the word `sprite` is optional. So, you can write `sendSprite(7,#myHandler)` rather than `sendSprite(sprite 7, #myHandler)`.

- There are two forms of syntax for the keyword `rollover`. The function `rollover(x)` returns a TRUE if the cursor is over sprite *x*. The property `the rollover` returns the number of the sprite directly under the cursor.

- The `memberNum` property does not enable you to set the sprite to a member in another cast library. However, you can change the `castLibNum` to do that.

- The obsolete property `castNum` can still be used. It returns the same value as `memberNum` for members in the first cast library, but returns much higher values for members in other cast libraries. For instance, the first member in cast library 2 would have a `castNum` of 131073.

5

6

CONTROLLING SPRITES

IN THIS CHAPTER

CHANGING THE SPRITE'S MEMBER

Besides navigation, the next most important task that a Lingo command can perform is to change the properties of a sprite. Properties are attributes of sprites that describe anything from their positions on the Stage to their ink types. Changing the sprites' properties is how you use Lingo to animate your sprites.

You will usually set sprite properties in the scripts attached to the sprites, but for now you can examine some sprite properties in the Message panel.

Setting the member of the sprite to something different from the original member is common. This way, rollover and down states for buttons can be different cast members from the normal state of the button, and animations can use different images.

To change the member that a sprite is using, just set the member property of that sprite. You cannot simply set it to the name or number of a member. You have to set it to an actual member object.

Member objects are simply ways of referring to a member that Lingo can understand. If there is a member called "button down state," you need to refer to it as member("button down state"). If that member is member number 7, you could also refer to it as member(7). But you cannot set a sprite to simply "button down state" or 7. You need the member keyword to refer to a member object.

Create a movie with two bitmaps. They can be anything, even just scribbles in the Paint editor. Name them "bitmap1" and "bitmap2". Place the first bitmap on the Stage, as sprite 1. Try this in the Message panel:

```
sprite(1).member = member("bitmap2")
updateStage
sprite(1).member = member("bitmap1")
updateStage
```

You will see the sprite change and then change back with each updateStage. You could have also referred to the members by their numbers.

Here is a script from the example movie memberanimation.dir. This script increases the counter *pAnimationNum* by 1 each frame. When this number gets past 15, the script resets it to 1.

This number is used to determine the member for the sprite. The members should be named *Globe X*, where *X* is a number from 1 to 15.

```
property pAnimationNum

on beginSprite me
  -- start with first member
  pAnimationNum = 1
end

on exitFrame me
  -- display current member
  sprite(me.spriteNum).member = member("Globe"&&pAnimationNum)

  -- move to next member
  pAnimationNum = pAnimationNum + 1
```

```
-- loop back if past last member
if pAnimationNum > 15 then pAnimationNum = 1
end
```

The result is a globe that spins through 15 frames of animation. But the Score isn't doing the animating; it is the script. By swapping out the member each frame, the globe appears to be spinning even while the movie remains on one frame.

CONTROLLING SPRITE LOCATION

For these examples, create a bitmap member and place it on the Stage and in the Score at Sprite channel 1. Then, open the Message panel. Try this:

```
sprite(1).locH = 50
updateStage
```

You should see your sprite jump so that its registration point is 50 pixels from the left side of the Stage. It was the first line of the example that actually did this. It set the property `locH` of sprite 1 to the number 50. The `locH` property is the horizontal location of the sprite.

However, you didn't see any change on the Stage until the second command, `updateStage`. This is a special command that shows changes to sprite properties on the Stage while the movie is not playing. If the movie had been playing, and the change to the property had been inside a behavior script, the Stage would have updated automatically the next time a frame began. But for all the examples here, you need to use `updateStage` to see the sprite properties change because the movie isn't running.

You can also set the vertical location of a sprite. To do this, use the `locV` property:

```
sprite(1).locV = 100
updateStage
```

There is also a way to set both the horizontal and vertical locations of a sprite. This property is just called the `loc` of the sprite. However, it doesn't take a number value, but rather a `point`. A `point` is a special Lingo object that looks like this: `point(x,y)`. The two numbers in the parentheses represent a horizontal and vertical location. Here it is in use:

```
sprite(1).loc = point(200,225)
updateStage
```

6

You can use the location properties of a sprite to give the user control of the sprite's location. In the example found in `location.dir`, the user can use the arrow keys to move the sprite around the Stage. The script that does this is on the sprite itself.

The script uses `keyPressed` to check the arrow keys and move the sprite accordingly. Each `keyPressed` function checks one of the four arrow keys. If it is pressed, the `locH` or `locV` property of the sprite is changed by 1.

> You can use keyPressed of any type of sprite, or in any code that you want. But using the handlers on keyDown and on keyUp only work in frame scripts or field and text member sprites.

```
on exitFrame me

  -- left
  if keyPressed(123) then
    sprite(me.spriteNum).locH = sprite(me.spriteNum).locH - 1
  end if

  -- right
  if keyPressed(124) then
    sprite(me.spriteNum).locH = sprite(me.spriteNum).locH + 1
  end if

  -- down
  if keyPressed(125) then
    sprite(me.spriteNum).locV = sprite(me.spriteNum).locV + 1
  end if

  -- up
  if keyPressed(126) then
    sprite(me.spriteNum).locV = sprite(me.spriteNum).locV - 1
  end if
end
```

You can also compress this script a little by using variables and one-line if then statements. Here is another script that does the same thing:

```
on exitFrame me
  x = sprite(me.spriteNum).locH
  y = sprite(me.spriteNum).locV

  if keyPressed(123) then x = x - 1
  if keyPressed(124) then x = x + 1
  if keyPressed(125) then y = y + 1
  if keyPressed(126) then y = y - 1

  sprite(me.spriteNum).loc = point(x,y)
end
```

CHANGING INK, COLOR, AND BLEND

Three properties, ink, color, and blend all act together to determine the appearance of a sprite on the Stage.

Sprite Inks

Sprite inks were explained in detail in Chapter 4, "Using Sprites and the Score." They determine how the sprite is drawn to the Stage. You can set the sprite ink with the ink property of a sprite.

The ink property takes a number as its value. Unfortunately, you cannot set it to values such as "Background Transparent". So you'll have the refer to a table to match the ink to the number. Refer to Table 6.1 for corresponding ink numbers.

Table 6.1   Lingo Ink Numbers

Number	Corresponding Ink
0	Copy
1	Transparent
2	Reverse
3	Ghost
4	Not Copy
5	Not Transparent
6	Not Reverse
7	Not Ghost
8	Matte
9	Mask
32	Blend
33	Add Pin
34	Add
35	Subtract Pin
36	Background Transparent
37	Lightest
38	Subtract
39	Darkest
40	Lighten
41	Darken

Sprite Colors

Changing the foreground and background colors of a sprite has an effect only some of the time, depending on the ink used. A 1-bit bitmap uses these two colors to set the color of the black-and-white pixels of the bitmap. Color bitmaps that use the Lighten and Darken inks use these colors to alter the shading of the bitmap.

The two color properties of a sprite are color for the foreground color and bgColor for the background color.

You can define colors in several ways. The first is to set them to the red, green, and blue values using a color object. An example of a color object would be rgb(255,128,0). You can also use a string to define a color like you would in HTML: rgb("FFCC33"). You can use a "#" before the color string, but it is optional.

6

For these examples, create a 1-bit bitmap and place it on the Stage. It should be in sprite 1, and it should appear black on the Stage as a default. Try this in the Message panel:

```
sprite(1).color = rgb(0,0,255)
updateStage
```

You can use the rgb object to convert between hexidecimal codes and numbers. For instance, typing put *rgb("FFCC99")* in the Message panel returns *rgb(255,204,153)*.

The color of the black pixels in the bitmap should change to blue. The result of them being set to 0, 0, and 255 is that the color becomes pure blue. When defining rgb like this, keep in mind that the minimum value is 0, and the maximum value is 255.

You also could have accomplished the same thing using a string:

```
sprite(1).color = rgb("0000FF")
updateStage
```

This sets the color to pure blue just as the previous example did. The six digits in the string represent the three colors: a "00" is a 0, and an "FF" is a 255. If you are familiar with hexadecimal values, you can use this system. It also comes in handy if you are used to working with HTML colors. Otherwise, stick to the other version of the rgb structure.

To refer to a color based on the color palette of the movie, use the paletteIndex structure. This enables you to use a palette color number rather than an rgb value:

```
sprite(1).color = paletteIndex(35)
updateStage
```

With both the Mac System palette and the Windows System palette, the color 35 is a red.

The movie coloreffects.dir contains a few sprites with different scripts attached to them. The first has this script, which gradually changes the background color, one component at a time:

```
on exitFrame me
 -- get current color
 currentColor = sprite(me.spriteNum).color

 if currentColor.red < 255 then
  -- increase red until saturated
  currentColor.red = currentColor.red + 1
 else if currentColor.green < 255 then
  -- increase green until saturated
  currentColor.green = currentColor.green + 1
 else if currentColor.blue < 255 then
  -- increase blue until saturated
  currentColor.blue = currentColor.blue + 1
 else
  -- reset to black
  currentColor = rgb(0,0,0)
 end if
```

```
 -- set new color
 sprite(me.spriteNum).color = currentColor
end
```

This sprite starts with a `color` of black, which fades to red, then yellow, and then white. Then it repeats.

The second sprite does something slightly different. It changes all three color registers at the same time. First, it adds five to the `color` each frame, such as taking it from `rgb(15,15,15)` to `rgb(20,20,20)`. Then, when the color reaches its maximum value, it starts to subtract rather than add. The result is a sprite that pulses from black to white and back to black again.

```
property pDirection

on beginSprite me
 -- start by getting lighter
 pDirection = 1
end

on exitFrame me
 -- get current color
 currentColor = sprite(me.spriteNum).color
 currentColor.colorType = #rgb

 if currentColor.red = 255 then
  -- darken
  pDirection = -1
 else if currentColor.red = 0 then
  -- lighten
  pDirection = 1
 end if

 -- change color
 currentColor = currentColor + pDirection*5
 sprite(me.spriteNum).color = currentColor
end
```

In the example movie, a third sprite uses the same color transformation script as the first one. The difference is that this sprite uses a multicolored bitmap. The colors behave differently when the `color` property is changed. To enhance this effect, I set the link to "lighten," so that the foreground color becomes very important in drawing the image seen on the Stage. Give it a look.

Sprite Blend

The `blend` property can be used to make any bitmap, and most other sprite types, semitransparent. For instance, setting the blend to 50 percent, fades the bitmap so that it is only half as bright, while at the same time 50 percent of the background shows through.

You can use `blend` to fade in or out a single sprite. This script does just that. If the sprite member is set to 0 to start, it adds 1 to the `blend` for each frame until the `blend` is 100.

```
on exitFrame me
 if sprite(me.spriteNum).blend < 100 then
  sprite(me.spriteNum).blend = sprite(me.spriteNum).blend + 1
 end if
end
```

The movie `blend.dir` shows this script working on the second of two sprites. The background remains at 100 percent while sprite 2, a bitmap image of a chameleon, fades from 0 to 100 percent. Figure 6.1 shows the movie at the start, middle, and end of the fade.

Figure 6.1
The chameleon sprite is at 0, then 50, and then 100 percent `blend`.

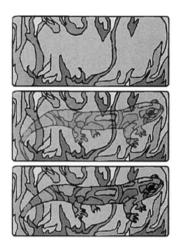

Another example movie, `blendwithdistance.dir`, has five sprites on the screen. Each has the same behavior. This script calculates the distance between the cursor and the sprite and sets the blend between 50 and 100 depending on how far away the cursor is. Here is the script:

```
on exitFrame me
 -- get distance from mouse
 dist = distance(me,sprite(me.spriteNum),the mouseLoc)

 -- invert number for blend
 blend = 100-dist/4

 -- limit blend between 50 and 100
 if blend > 100 then blend = 100
 if blend < 50 then blend = 50

 -- set blend
 sprite(me.spriteNum).blend = blend
end

-- utility function to compute distance
on distance me, p1, p2
 return sqrt(power(p1.locH-p2.locH,2)+power(p1.locV-p2.locV,2))
end
```

You can use this script in conjunction with simple button scripts. As the user gets closer to a button, its blend gets closer to 100. This creates the illusion of the button anticipating the user's click.

DISTORTING A SPRITE'S SHAPE

You can use several properties to distort the shape of a sprite. You can rotate, flip, skew, and stretch a sprite.

> To learn how to distort sprites without using Lingo, see "Controlling Sprite Appearance," p. 136.

The rotation **Property**

The rotation property gives you complete Lingo control over the orientation of the sprite. Bitmaps and text sprites can be rotated, but shapes cannot.

The value of rotation is in degrees. It can range from 0 to 360, but you can use numbers outside that range, and Director can translate them to a number in that range. A new sprite is always set to a rotation value of 0.

```
put (sprite 1).rotation
-- 0.0000
```

You can set the rotation just as easily, as follows:

```
(sprite 1).rotation = 45
updateStage
```

The following shows a one-line behavior that makes a sprite rotate around its center. It rotates one degree every frame:

```
on exitFrame me
  (sprite 1).rotation = (sprite 1).rotation + 1
end
```

A more complex behavior is one that aligns the rotation of the sprite to always point to the cursor. The behavior assumes that the "point" of the bitmap is normally pointing to the right side of the Stage. It reorients it to point toward the cursor, as follows:

```
on exitFrame me
  -- get the mouse location
  p = the mouseLoc
  x1 = p.locH
  y1 = p.locV

  -- get the sprite location
  x2 = (sprite me.spriteNum).locH
  y2 = (sprite me.spriteNum).locV
```

6

```
-- use atan to compute the angle
if x2 = x1 then exit
angle = atan(float(y2-y1)/float(x2-x1))

-- correct the angle
if x1 < x2 then angle = pi()+angle

-- convert the angle to degrees
angle = angle*360.0/(2.0*pi())

-- set the sprite
(sprite me.spriteNum).rotation = angle
end
```

You can use this behavior, found in the movie rotatetomouse.dir, just as easily with other points, as well. For instance, it can align a sprite to the location of another sprite. As that sprite moves, either through user interaction or animation, the controlled sprite follows.

The atan function is at the heart of this behavior. Its purpose is to convert a slope, made by two points, into an angle. The results are limited to only one half of a circle, so an adjustment is made to deal with angles on the left side of the circle. The angle resulting from this is in radians, so there needs to be a conversion into degrees before the angle can be applied to the rotation property.

Radians, if you remember your high school trigonometry, are another way to measure the size of an angle. Whereas there are 360° in a circle, there are 2π, or 6.2832, radians in a circle. In other words, 360° is equal to 2π radians.

⇨ *If you see a performance decrease after rotating some sprites, see "Bogging Down the Animation" in the "Troubleshooting" section at the end of this chapter.*

The flipH and flipV Properties

Bitmap can also be flipped along either the horizontal or vertical axis. Flipping takes place around the registration point of the member. Lingo controls this feature through the flipH and flipV properties. They can be set to either TRUE or FALSE. If the setting is TRUE, the sprite is displayed flipped.

Here is an example. This example flips a sprite horizontally:

```
(sprite 1).flipH = TRUE
updateStage
```

However, if the sprite is already flipped, this last example does nothing. Here is an example that reverses the horizontal flip of a sprite:

```
(sprite 1).flipH = not (sprite 1).flipH
updateStage
```

Here is a behavior that controls a sprite's flip properties according to where the cursor is located relative to the sprite. It flips whenever the cursor crosses one of the sprite's axes:

```
on exitFrame me
 -- get the cursor location
 cLoc = the mouseLoc

 -- get the sprite location
 sLoc = (sprite me.spriteNum).loc

 -- flip horizontally if needed
 if cLoc.locH > sLoc.locH then
  (sprite me.spriteNum).flipH = TRUE
 else
  (sprite me.spriteNum).flipH = FALSE
 end if

 -- flip vertically if needed
 if cLoc.locV > sLoc.locV then
  (sprite me.spriteNum).flipV = TRUE
 else
  (sprite me.spriteNum) .flipV = FALSE
 end if
end
```

You can find this script on the CD-ROM as `flip.dir`.

The `skew` **Property**

The `skew` property can also be set with Lingo. The result is a change in the angle of the vertical sides of the sprite's rectangle. Angles from 0° to 90° tilt the vertical sides to the right, whereas angles from 0° to -90° tilt it to the left. Angles between 90° and 180° and -90° and -180° appear to flip the sprite. Any change of 360° places the `skew` back where it started, which is the same as a skew of 0.

Here is a simple behavior that repeatedly adds 10° to the `skew` of a sprite:

```
on exitFrame me
 (sprite 1).skew = (sprite 1).skew + 10
end
```

The result of the behavior is shown in Figure 6.2.

Figure 6.2
The result of changing the skew of a sprite by 10° several times and having trails turned on to record each step.

You can re-create Figure 6.2 by using the movie `skew.dir` on the CD-ROM.

Setting the Sprite Rectangle

The `rect` property defines the four edges of a sprite. It does this using a special `rect` object. The `rect` object is like the `point` object but includes four numbers: the left, top, right, and bottom of the rectangle.

Another way to think about a `rect` is that the first two numbers indicate the upper-left point, and the last two numbers indicate the lower-right point. Either way, a `rect` defines a rectangular area on the Stage.

You can set the `rect` of a sprite to any size, regardless of how well this corresponds to the dimensions of the actual member. In cases in which the member can be stretched, such as bitmaps, the member is distorted on the Stage to correspond to the sprite's rectangle.

Although Director always thinks of a `rect` as four numbers, you can define a `rect` as two `points`, like this: `rect(point(50,60), point(140,120))`. When you examine a variable set to this value, you will see that it has been converted to `rect(50,60,140,120)`.

With a bitmap member in sprite 1, try this in the Message panel:

```
sprite(1).rect = rect(50,50,175,75)
updateStage
```

In the movie `growrect.dir`, the bitmap in the middle of the Stage has a script on it that enlarges the sprite's rectangle by one point in each direction every frame. This is actually just a one-line script:

```
on exitFrame me
 sprite(me.spriteNum).rect = sprite(me.spriteNum).rect + rect(-1,-1,1,1)
end
```

Although that is a simple script, it takes a little more to make a sprite expand in an unusual way. This next script is found in the same example movie as an alternative to the simple expanding rectangle script. It takes the starting `rect` from the initial dimensions of the sprite and makes that its goal. It then starts as a small `rect` at the upper-left corner of the original area and expands to the right first, and then down.

```
property pFinalRect

on beginSprite me
 -- get final rect from how sprite is in score
 pFinalRect = sprite(me.spriteNum).rect

 -- start rect as only upper left corner
 startRect = duplicate(pFinalRect)
 startRect.right = startRect.left
 startRect.bottom = startRect.top+5 -- add five for some width

 -- reset rect before sprite is drawn
 sprite(me.spriteNum).rect = startRect
end
```

```
on exitFrame me
 -- get current rect
 currentRect = sprite(me.spriteNum).rect

 -- see if it has finished expanding to the right
 if currentRect.right < pFinalRect.right then
  currentRect.right = currentRect.right + 1

  -- see if it has finished expanding down
 else if currentRect.bottom < pFinalRect.bottom then
  currentRect.bottom = currentRect.bottom + 1
 end if

 -- set the new rect
 sprite(me.spriteNum).rect = currentRect
end
```

A bonus behavior in the same movie makes the sprite grow out from the center, first horizontally and then vertically.

The quad **Property**

The last and greatest of the sprite-manipulation properties is the quad property of the sprite. This property contains a list of four items, like rect, but it contains points, not numbers. Each of these points represents one of the corners of a sprite. Here is an example:

```
put (sprite 1).quad
-- [point(184.0000, 126.0000), point(463.0000, 126.0000), point(463.0000, \
302.0000), point(184.0000, 302.0000)]
```

The beauty of the quad property is that you can set the four points to whatever you want. You can essentially "pull" on any of the corners using Lingo.

For instance, if you take a rectangular image, and then push the upper-left corner of the sprite down and to the right, and the upper-right corner of the sprite down and to the left, you can imitate perspective on the Stage and create the illusion of 3D. Figure 6.3 shows this effect.

Figure 6.3
The Stage shows two sprites, both with the same bitmap member. However, one sprite's quad has been changed to imitate 3D perspective.

6

The difference between using quad and skew is that with quad you have total control over the four corners of a sprite. With skew, you control just the angle of the sides of the sprite's rectangle.

You have no way of altering a sprite's quad on the Stage, but this handler enables you to do it while the movie is playing. It enables you to click and grab any corner of the sprite and drag the corner.

```
property pCorner

on beginSprite me
 -- no corner being moved
 pCorner = 0
end

on mouseDown me
 -- see if click was on a corner
 pCorner = 0
 repeat with i = 1 to 4
  if distance(me,the clickLoc,sprite(me.spriteNum).quad[i]) < 10 then
   pCorner = i
   exit repeat
  end if
 end repeat
end

on mouseUp me
 -- corner no longer being moved
 pCorner = 0
end

on mouseUpOutside me
 -- corner no longer being moved
 pCorner = 0
end

on exitFrame me
 if pCorner > 0 then
  -- move this corner to the mouse location
  q = sprite(me.spriteNum).quad
  q[pCorner] = the mouseLoc
  sprite(me.spriteNum).quad = q
 end if
end

-- utility function to find the distance between two points
on distance me, p1, p2
 return sqrt(power(p1.locH-p2.locH,2)+power(p1.locV-p2.locV,2))
end
```

The movie quads.dir on the CD-ROM shows this example in action. Run the movie and click and drag on any of the four corners of the left square.

You can also use quad to form 2D representations of 3D shapes. A cube is a good example. Figure 6.4 shows a cube on the Stage. It is actually drawn with six sprites, one for each side. It uses 3D trigonometry and the quad property to figure out where each side goes.

Figure 6.4
Six sprites are used to draw this 3D cube.

Here is the code that makes this 3D cube. There are actually many different ways to pull this off, but this example uses the following movie script:

This code can be considered complex. If you don't understand exactly what is going on, don't worry. Try the demo file on the CD-ROM called cube.dir to get a better understanding of this example.

```
global gCorners, gCenter, gRectList, gRotate, gPlane

on startMovie
  -- initialize lists for a cube
  initBox
end

on frameScript
  -- add to rotation based on mouse location
  gRotate = gRotate - (float(the mouseH-320)/30)*pi()/100

  -- calc plane tilt based on mouse location
  gPlane = - (float(the mouseV-240)/30)*pi()/20
  drawSides
end

on initBox
  -- list of corners with x, y and z coordinates
  gCorners = [[-60,-60,-60],[60,-60,-60],[60,60,-60],\
       [-60,60,-60],[-60,-60,60],[60,-60,60],\
       [60,60,60],[-60,60,60]]

  -- the screen center
  gCenter = point(320,240)

  -- list of sides
  -- each side has four corners
  gRectList = [[1,2,3,4],[1,2,6,5],[3,4,8,7],\
       [2,3,7,6],[8,5,1,4],[5,6,7,8]]
end

on drawSides
  -- generate a list of screen points and depths based on the
```

6

```
-- gCorners list and the transformation to 2d screen coordinates
list = []
repeat with i = 1 to gCorners.count
 temp = plotPoint(gCorners[i])
 add list,temp
end repeat

-- create a quad list that takes four points to display a side of the cube
repeat with i = 1 to gRectList.count

 -- get the four corners that make this side
 thisRect = gRectList[i]

 -- get the four screen points to draw
 q = [list[thisRect[1]][2],list[thisRect[2]][2],\
    list[thisRect[3]][2],list[thisRect[4]][2]]

 -- get the closest (depth) screen point
 z = min(list[thisRect[1]][1],list[thisRect[2]][1],\
    list[thisRect[3]][1],list[thisRect[4]][1])

 -- draw the side
 sprite(i).quad = q
 sprite(i).locZ = z
 end repeat
end

on plotPoint objectInfo
 -- get x, y, and z from objectInfo list
 x = getAt(objectInfo,1)
 y = getAt(objectInfo,2)
 z = getAt(objectInfo,3)

 -- TRANSFORM BY ROTATION AROUND Z

 -- compute the radius
 radius = sqrt(x*x+y*y)

 -- compute the angle
 if x = 0.0 then angle = atan(the maxInteger)
 else angle = atan(float(y)/x)
 if y < 0 then angle = angle + pi()

 -- rotate
 set angle = angle+gRotate

 -- compute new x, y, and z
 realX = radius*cos(angle)
```

6

```
realZ = radius*sin(angle)
realY = Z

-- TRANSFORM BY ROTATION AROUND X

-- compute the radius
radius = sqrt(realY*realY+realZ*realZ)

-- compute the angle
if realZ = 0 then angle = atan(the maxInteger)
else angle = (atan(realY/realZ))
if realZ < 0 then angle = angle + pi()

-- rotate
angle = angle - gPlane

-- compute the new x, y and z
screenX = realX
screenY = radius*sin(angle)
screenZ = radius*cos(angle)

-- return both z, and the x and y point
return [screenZ,point(screenX,screenY)+gCenter]
end
```

The code uses the mouse position to determine the plane and rotation of the cube. However, you can remove this code and include buttons that enable users to move the cube. You could even have the cube rotate at a constant rate.

⇨ *If you are getting odd results when trying to use the quad property, see "Using Quad Twists the Image" in the "Troubleshooting" section at the end of this chapter.*

OTHER SPRITE PROPERTIES

Many other properties affect bitmap sprites at a less dramatic level than the properties previously discussed. Here is a complete list:

- `useAlpha`—Determines whether Alpha channel information included with 32-bit bitmaps is used in displaying the member. When TRUE, the Alpha channel is used to vary the level of transparency of the bitmap.

- `alphaThreshold`—If an Alpha channel is present, this property can be set to a value between 0 and 255. 0 means that all pixels in the sprite can respond to mouse clicks. Any other setting determines the degree of nontransparency required for a pixel to register a click.

- `locZ`—Sprites normally appear on the Stage with sprites in higher-numbered channels on top of sprites in lower-numbered channels. However, you can change this with the `locZ` property. You can use any integer, even negative numbers, to define in which order the sprites should be drawn. For instance, setting a sprite to have a `locZ` of 500 means that it appears on top of sprites 1 to 499.

➡ *If you are seeing a halo around imported bitmap images, see "Semitransparent Images from Photoshop Have Halos" in the "Troubleshooting" section at the end of this chapter.*

Sprite Property Summary

Table 6.2 shows a list of sprite properties that you can set with Lingo.

Table 6.2   List of Sprite Properties

Property	Description	Example Value
member	The member used by the sprite	member("*myButton*")
locH	The horizontal position of the sprite	50
locV	The vertical position of the sprite	50
loc	The position of the sprite	point(*50,50*)
rect	The rectangle of the sprite, representing the left, top, right, and bottom of the sprite	rect(*25,25,75,75*)
quad	A list of four points that determine where the four corners of a bitmap are drawn on the Stage	[point(*0,0*), point(*100,0*), point(*100,100*), point(*0,100*)]
ink	The sprite's ink, represented by a number	8
blend	The sprite's blend, from 0-100	100
trails	Whether the trails property is on or off	FALSE
color	The foreground color of a sprite	rgb("*#000000*")
bgcolor	The background color of a sprite	rgb("*#FFFFFF*")
useAlpha	Whether the a 32-bit bitmap uses its alpha transparency layer	TRUE
alphaThreshold	With 32-bit bitmaps, how transparent an area needs to be before it cannot be clicked	128
locZ	Overrides sprite channel ordering	1000

MAPPING SPRITES

When you use the quad property to distort a sprite, Director still keeps track of the original member's appearance. In fact, you can use two special functions in Lingo to convert between screen locations and the relative locations of pixels in the original bitmap.

Figure 6.5 shows a good example of why you need to do this conversion. The chessboard has been distorted with *quads* to appear as if it has depth. In reality, the board is a simple 160×160 square with 64 spaces.

Figure 6.5
The chessboard bitmap is actually a straight-down image that has been altered using quads to appear to have depth.

Here is the on beginSprite handler that takes the plain, square board and turns it into the 3D one you see in Figure 6.5. It simply moves the top two quad points. No special math is used—just estimated, hard-coded points for simplicity in this example:

```
on beginSprite me
  q = sprite(me.spriteNum).quad
  q[1] = q[1]+point(-30,100)
  q[2] = q[2]+point(30,100)
  sprite(me.spriteNum).quad = q
end
```

When the movie runs, this sprite appears as it does in Figure 6.5. When it was just a plain rectangle, it would have been easy to get the column and row of a mouse click. Each space on the board is 20×20, so you could just divide the horizontal and vertical location by 20, and add one to get a number between one and eight. However, with the board distorted as shown in Figure 6.5, you need to map the click location with Lingo.

The function needed to map the click location is mapStageToMember. It takes a sprite number and a Stage location and then converts these to a location relative to the bitmap member.

So, if users click the upper-left corner of the distorted sprite, the function returns *point(0,0)*. Here is an on mouseUp handler that uses the mapStageToMember function to calculate where users clicked:

```
on mouseUp me
  p = mapStageToMember(sprite 1, the clickLoc)
  x = 1+p.locH/20
  y = 1+p.locV/20
  put "Row:"&&x&&"Column:"&&y
end
```

The flip side of the mapStageToMember function is the mapMemberToStage function. You can use it to find any Stage location based on a location in the member. Here is a handler that returns the Stage location when given a space on the chessboard:

```
on getPos me, x, y
 p = point(x*20-10,y*20-10)
 return mapMemberToStage(sprite 1, p)
end
```

To position the queen as seen previously in Figure 6.5, you can use this behavior. It assumes that the board is in Sprite channel 1.

```
on beginSprite me
 p = getPos(sprite 1, 4, 5)
 sprite(me.spriteNum).loc = p
end
```

Mapping sprites in this way enables you to distort one sprite and then position other sprites relative to this distortion. It can be used along with the cube example to place an object on the face of a cube. Or, it can be used with the shrinking sprite example to map one sprite onto another, or provide valid clicks on the sprite as it changes size.

TROUBLESHOOTING

Bogging Down the Animation

Why does my animation slow down so much after I've manipulated it by changing the member *properties?*

Nothing is free. When you rotate, skew, or stretch sprites, you take a speed hit. You cannot expect to have dozens of constantly rotating sprites on the Stage and others stretched with quad and still have your animation running as fast as an animation without all that. Keep this in mind when designing.

Using quad **Twists the Image**

When I try to use the quad *property to distort an image, it seems to twist it into a new shape. What am I doing wrong?*

The order of the four points in a quad is important. The first point maps the upper-left corner, the second the upper-right corner, the third the lower-right corner, and the fourth the lower-left corner. A common mistake is to swap the third and fourth points. This would end up twisting the image into a bowtie-like shape.

6

Semitransparent Images from Photoshop Have Halos

I'm importing a nice Photoshop image that uses Alpha channels, and it has this odd halo around it. Can I get rid of the halo?

Using straight Photoshop documents with an Alpha channel produces a "premultiplied" Alpha channel. This just means that a white halo appears around the images. One easy way to correct this is to open the file in Macromedia Fireworks first, save it as a PNG file, and then import that file.

DID YOU KNOW?

- The useFastQuads property, set to TRUE, allows sprites stretched with the quad property to draw more quickly, but they are not stretched in quite the same way. The result is not as good for simulating 3D.

- To convert degrees to radians, divide the number by 360.0 and multiply by 2.0π (or 6.2832). To convert radians to degrees, divide by 2.0π and then multiply by 360.0. Make sure that your original number is a floating point number, not an integer.

- You can make a bitmap semitransparent by using the setAlpha command on its image. If you set it to an integer midway between 0 and 255, you will get an effect to having the blend of the sprite set to 50%.

- Although you can't use quad with non-bitmap members, such as text, you can convert just about any type of member to a bitmap and then perform the distortion. See Chapter 14, "Using Lingo to Create Images," for more information about imaging Lingo.

- You can duplicate the functionality of most of the distortion effects—such as skew, rotate and flip—using quad. However, the math to create the four points can be complex. But if you master the use of quad, you have ultimate control over how the sprite is drawn on the Stage.

6

CONTROLLING SOUND WITH LINGO

PLAYING SOUND MEMBERS

Although the Score can handle background sounds, and behaviors from the library can add sounds to buttons and other simple elements, understanding the Lingo commands that control sound is necessary to use sounds in more advanced Director programs. All three main types of sounds—internal cast members, external files, and compressed Shockwave audio—can be controlled using Lingo. This chapter discusses the ways to control sound using Lingo.

To play sounds using Lingo, you will need to learn about the sound object. A sound object is like a sprite, but it relates to the sound channels in the Score rather than the sprite channels. There are a total of eight sound channels that you can use.

➡ For more information about importing and using sounds, see "Importing and Using Sounds," p. 57.

The play and queue Commands

The most basic sound command is play. You can instantly play a sound in a channel by specifying the channel number and the member. Here is how to play the sound member "mySound" in channel 1:

```
sound(1).play(member("mySound"))
```

The play function takes a sound member as its only parameter. It begins to load the sound and then plays it when it has enough of the sound loaded. You might experience some delay as the sound loads, but not usually.

You can also queue a sound for playing and then trigger it with a play. Here is an example:

> You can use sound channels 1 through 8, even though only the first two are available in the Score.

```
sound(1).queue(member("mySound"))
sound(1).play()
```

You can use multiple queue functions to set up several sounds to play one after the other. When the play command is used, all the sounds play, without any break in between.

> Before Director 8, you played sounds in Lingo with the puppetSound command. Although this method is obsolete, you will still see it in examples and old movies.

```
sound(1).queue(member("ragtime"))
sound(1).queue(member("wacky"))
sound(1).play()
```

After the first sound starts playing, you can force Director to skip to the next sound in the queue using the playNext command:

```
sound(1).playNext()
```

You can get a list of the sounds still in the queue by using getPlayList. Try this in the Message panel:

```
sound(1).queue(member("mysound1"))
sound(1).queue(member("mysound2"))
put sound(1).getPlaylist()
-- [[#member: (member 1 of castLib 1)], [#member: (member 2 of castLib 1)]]
```

This list doesn't just show members. It is actually a list of lists. Each sublist contains the property #member and the member of the sound. You can use this same format to queue or play sounds:

```
sound(1).play([#member: member("mysound1")])
```

You can also manually set the queue using setPlaylist:

```
sound(1).setPlaylist([[#member: member("mysound1")],

[#member: member("mysound2")]])
```

To stop the sound queue from playing, use stop:

```
sound(1).stop()
```

This does not clear the queue but simply stops the current sound, advances to the next in the queue, and awaits another play command.v

⇨ *If you want to use both Score sounds and Lingo sounds, see "Lingo Sounds Cut Off Score Sounds" in the "Troubleshooting" section at the end of this chapter.*

Modifying Sound Playback

Instead of passing a plain member to the queue or play function, you can send it a property list with several other pieces of information. For instance, you could include the #preloadTime property to specify how much of the sound should load before it begins playing. The time is in milliseconds.

```
sound(1).queue([#member: member("mySound"), #preloadTime: 1000])
```

Using the #startTime and #endTime properties, you can play only a segment of a sound. Again, the time is in milliseconds.

```
sound(1).SetPlayList([ \
  [#member: member("ragtime"), \
  #startTime: 7604, \
  #endTime: 10105]])
sound(1).play()
```

You can also make the sound loop for a finite number of times with the #loopCount property.

```
sound(1).queue( \
  [#member: member("ragtime"), \
  #startTime: 10105, \
  #loopCount: 3, \
  #endTime: 15017])
sound(1).play()
```

Does a sound seem to wait a while to start, even when no other sounds are playing? It could simply be that the sound has a second or so of silence at the start. Many sounds that come from CD-ROM sound collections have this. It is recommended that you check all your sounds in a sound-editing program before importing them.

7

The property list used in a `queue` or `play` can get complex. Not only can you specify the start and end times of a sound, but you can also have different start and end times for a loop inside the sound. For instance, suppose that you wanted to have the sound start at the beginning, play until millisecond 10105, loop back to 7604, do that three times, and then continue to the end of the sound. The following code would accomplish this:

```
sound(1).queue( \
  [#member: member("ragtime"), \
  #loopStartTime: 7604, \
  #loopCount: 3, \
  #loopEndTime: 10105])
sound(1).play()
```

Table 7.1 shows a complete list of all these sound object properties.

Table 7.1 Sound Object Properties

Property	Description
#member	The sound member to be played.
#startTime	How much time at the start of the sound to skip, in milliseconds.
#endTime	How much time before the end of the sound to stop, in milliseconds.
#loopStartTime	The starting time for the loop, in milliseconds.
#loopEndTime	The ending time for the loop, in milliseconds.
#loopCount	How many times to loop. A value of 0 makes the sound loop until stopped.
#preloadTime	How many milliseconds of the sound should be loaded into memory before playback starts.
#rateShift	How many tonal half-steps to pitch the sound up or down.

Pitch-Shifting Sounds

By using the `rateShift` property of a sound, you are basically playing back the sound faster or slower than the original. Import a sound into Director and try this in the Message panel:

```
sound(1).play([#member: member(1), #rateShift: 0])
sound(1).play([#member: member(1), #rateShift: 5])
sound(1).play([#member: member(1), #rateShift: -5])
```

The first line plays the sound normally. The second line speeds up the sound, and the third line slows it down. When sounds speed up or slow down, they change pitch.

You can use `rateShift` to make a single sound play back differently in different situations. For instance, in the sample movie `rateshift.dir`, one sound is used in the movie, but each button plays the sound at a different rate. The button scripts look like this:

```
on mouseUp me
  sound(1).play([#member: member("mysound"), #rateshift: 0])
end
```

The only difference between each of the scripts is the #rateShift value. The scripts go from 0 to -4.

If you try out the movie, you can see how easy it would be to make a small music keyboard with just one sound.

Looping Sounds

Looping entire sounds is easy and can even be done without Lingo: Just set the loop property of the sound in the Property Inspector and place the sound in the Score.

But you can do a lot more with looping using Lingo. For instance, you can specify the number of times that a sound will loop. This code plays a sound three times:

```
sound(1).play([#member: member("mysound"), #loopCount: 3])
```

To loop infinitely, you can use a loopCount of 0. Then the sound loops until you do something else with the sound channel, such as issue a stop command.

You can also fine-tune loops by specifying a loopStartTime and loopEndTime. When you do this, you are essentially dividing the sound into three parts: the part before the loop, the looping part, and the part after the loop.

Think of a song that has an introduction, chorus, and finish. You could include all three in a single sound member, use a sound object to play the introduction, loop to play the chorus three times, and then play the finish. Here's how that might look, if each part is 10 seconds long:

```
sound(1).play([#member: member("mysound"), #loopStartTime: 10000,

#loopEndTime: 20000, #loopCount: 3])
```

You can also queue up different parts of the same sound using multiple calls to queue or by using setPlaylist. You can use the same sound member for each part of the queue, but different startTime and endTime properties. Here is an example of how to play the third and fifth seconds of a sound:

```
sound(1).queue([#member: member("mysound"), #startTime: 3000, #endTime: 3999])
sound(1).queue ([#member: member("mysound"), #startTime: 5000, #endTime: 5999])
sound(1).play()
```

The movie playlist.dir shows a few examples of playing and looping sound sections.

Controlling Volume and Balance

A much simpler way to change sounds is by adjusting their volume. You can lower the volume from its default maximum using the volume property of a sound object. This is not a property of the queue item like the loopCount or rateShift, but a normal property of the sound object. For example:

```
sound(1).volume = 128
sound(1).play(member("mysound"))
```

7

Volume values range from 0 to 255. Setting a `volume` to 0 silences the sound channel, but the sound continues playing. You can reset the `volume` at any time while the sound is playing.

This script is from the movie `volumedistance.dir`. It computes the distance from the mouse to the sprite and sets the volume of sound channel 1 accordingly. The sound is set to play and loop in the `on beginSprite` handler.

```
on beginSprite me
 -- play sound, loop
 sound(1).play([#member: member("mysound"), #loopCount: 0])
end


on exitFrame me
 -- get distance from mouse
 dist = distance(me,sprite(me.spriteNum),the mouseLoc)

 -- invert number for volume
 volume = 255-dist

 -- limit volume between 0 and 255
 if volume > 255 then volume = 255
 if volume < 0 then volume = 0

 -- set volume
 sound(1).volume = volume
end


-- utility function to compute distance
on distance me, p1, p2
 return sqrt(power(p1.locH-p2.locH,2)+power(p1.locV-p2.locV,2))
end
```

You can also determine how much sound comes out of each speaker. To do this, set the pan property of a sound object to a value between −100 and 100. A value of 0 balances the sound between both speakers. A volume of −100 shuts off the right speaker completely. This is true only for the sound channel specified. Other sound channels continue to play equally from both speakers unless you also set a pan property for them.

The code in the `pan.dir` sample movie balances the sound in channel 1 based on the mouse location. If you move the mouse to the left, the sound comes out the left speaker. If you move the mouse to the right, it comes out the right speaker. The center region of the screen changes the pan depending on how close the mouse is to the exact center of the screen.

```
on beginSprite me
 --play sound
 sound(1).play([#member: member("mysound"), #loopCount: 0])
end


on exitFrame me
 -- get distance from center
 pan = the mouseH-320
```

```
 -- set pan
 sound(1).pan = pan
end
```

Fading In and Out

You can use the `fadeIn` and `fadeOut` commands to take a playing sound and slowly change its volume. For instance, if a sound is playing in channel 1, you can fade it out like this:

```
sound(1).fadeOut(2000)
```

The 2000 represents the number of milliseconds to fade over. You can fade the sound back in by using the `fadeIn` command in the same way.

Fading does not affect the `volume` of a sound at all. This value will remain the same and be used as the maximum value for both `fadeIn` and `fadeOut`.

When you use the `fadeIn` command, the sound instantly becomes silent and then gradually fades up over the time allotted. The same for `fadeOut`: the sound instantly plays at its `volume` property setting and then fades down to silence. So if you issue a `fadeIn` command while the sound is already fading out, the volume changes abruptly as the `fadeOut` stops and the `fadeIn` takes over.

To fade in a sound when it starts playing, simply issue the `fadeIn` command right after the `play` command. This code, from the movie `fade.dir`, starts the sound with a 2 second fade:

```
on beginSprite me
 sound(1).play([#member: member("mysound"), #loopCount: 0])
 sound(1).volume = 255
 sound(1).pan = 0
 sound(1).fadeIn(2000)
end
```

The buttons in that example movie allow you to fade the sound in and out as you please.

Sound Lingo Summary

Many other sound properties, functions, and commands can alter the way a sound is played. All the commands in Table 7.2 can be used after a `sound` object with dot syntax, in the same way that the `play` and `queue` commands were used. Table 7.2 is a complete list of sound commands.

Table 7.2   Sound Commands

Command	Description
play(*sound*)	Starts the play list. Alternatively, if you include a sound member or a property list describing the sound, you can replace the play list and start playing at the same time.
queue(*sound*)	Adds a sound member or property list describing the sound to the play list.
breakLoop()	When a sound is inside a looping area, this command enables the sound to travel past the end of the loop and continue to play the rest of the sound.

7

Table 7.2 Continued

Command	Description
isBusy()	Returns a TRUE if the sound channel is currently being used to play a sound.
fadeIn(s)	Sets the volume of the sound to 0, and then increases the volume over s milliseconds until the full volume is reached.
fadeOut(s)	Same as fadeIn but in reverse.
fadeTo(v,s)	Moves the volume of the sound to v (a number between 0 and 255) over s milliseconds.
getPlayList()	Returns the play list for the sound channel.
setPlayList(list)	Instead of using multiple queue() commands, you can set the entire play list of a sound channel by sending it a list of sound members or property lists.
pause()	Stops the sound, allowing you to use the play() command to resume it at the same spot.
playNext()	Immediately advances the sound to the next one queued.
rewind()	Brings the current sound back to the beginning.
stop()	Stops the sound. Any sound members still queued in the sound's buffer remain there, ready for the next play() command.
showProps()	Spits out all the sound channel's properties to the Message panel.

In addition to these commands, there are also a number of sound properties. Table 7.3 lists them all. Many of these properties mirror the properties found in Table 7.1. You can grab these properties directly from the sound object, in which case they apply to the currently playing sound. Other properties refer to the sound object in general, or the sound member.

Table 7.3 Sound Properties

Property	Description
channelCount	Returns the number of sound channels in a sound member. For instance, a value of 2 tells you that the sound is in stereo.
currentTime	The current time, in milliseconds, of a sound. This property can be set as well.
elapsedTime	The number of milliseconds that the sound has been playing. This number continues to increase, regardless of looping or changes made to currentTime.
endTime	The ending time, in milliseconds, of the sound currently playing.
loop	A member property. This is the equivalent to the loop property in the Sound Cast Member dialog box. You can change its value with this Lingo property.
loopCount	How many times the current sound is set to loop. A value of 0 means that the sound will loop forever.
loopEndTime	The ending time of the loop in the current sound.
loopStartTime	The starting time of the loop in the current sound.
loopsRemaining	If the sound is currently looping, this property returns the number of loops still to go.
member	The member reference of the currently playing sound.

7

Table 7.3 Continued

Property	Description
pan	Enables you to change the balance of a sound. −100 means that all the sound comes out the left speaker, and 100 means that it all comes out the right speaker.
preloadTime	The number of milliseconds of sound that is loaded before playing begins. The default is 1,500.
sampleCount	The bit rate of the sound, taking into account whether the sound is mono or stereo.
sampleRate	Returns the sample frequency rate of the sound member.
sampleSize	Returns the sample size, in bits, of the sound member. Typical values are 8 or 16.
startTime	The starting time of the currently playing sound in the channel.
status	Returns either 0 for nothing, 1 for loading, 2 for queued, 3 for playing, or 4 for paused.
volume	Enables you to set the volume, from 0 to 255, of a sound channel.

There are also several properties for determining the computer's capability to play sounds. Table 7.4 lists those.

Table 7.4 System Sound Properties

Property	Description
the multiSound	This is TRUE if the computer supports playing more than one sound at a time.
the soundDevice	This property tells you which system device is being used to play sounds. The property can currently have three values: "MacSoundManager," "Macromix," and "QT3Mix." The first is available only on the Mac, and it works quite well. "Macromix" is available only on a Windows machine without QuickTime 3, and it is very slow. If the movie is playing back on Windows and QuickTime 3 is present, you should set this property to "QT3Mix" for best performance.
the soundDeviceList	This property returns a list of the sound devices currently available.
the soundEnabled	This property provides a mute function. If you set it to FALSE, the sound shuts off, but the value of the volume property does not change, so the same volume level is used when the soundEnabled property is reset to TRUE.

USING CUE POINTS

Sounds can include *cue points*, which are little markers in your sound files that specify places in the sound. Sound designers place them there to add comments their sounds. You can also work with a sound designer to place cue points that you can access with Lingo.

7

There are a variety of commands and functions that you can use, as described in Table 7.5.

Table 7.5   Cue Point Lingo

Lingo	Description
cuePointNames	A sound member property that returns a list of cue points in the sound
cuePointTimes	A sound member property that returns a list of times, in milliseconds, when cue points appear
mostRecentCuePoint	Returns the number of the most recently passed cue point from a sound member or a sound channel
isPastCuePoint()	Tells you whether the sound has already passed a cue point number
on cuePassed	A handler that responds to the event of a cue point in a sound being passed

By using cuePointNames and cuePointTimes together, you can have lists of both the names of the cue points and the exact times when they occur. The movie cuepoints.dir contains a sound that has six cue points. You can use the Message panel to get information about them.

> All the cue point syntax can also be used for digital video. Simply specify the sprite channel number that the digital video is in rather than the sound channel number.

```
put member("ragtime").cuePointTimes
-- [0, 2395, 4851, 7603, 10104, 15016]
put member("ragtime").cuePointNames
-- ["Part 1", "Part 2", "Part 3", "Part 4", "Part 5", "Part 6"]
```

Adding cue points to a sound is something that is done in your sound-editing software. The method varies for each piece of software, so consult your documentation to see how to do it. It is usually fairly simple.

To synchronize a presentation or animation to a sound, you can use a basic on cuePassed handler in a frame behavior. Here is an example. The following behavior holds the movie on the current frame while the sound plays. Then, when a cue point arrives, it jumps the movie to a frame labeled exactly the same name as the cue point.

```
on exitFrame me
 go to the frame
end

on cuePassed me, whichChannel, cuePointNumber, cuePointName
 member("cue").text = cuePointName
 go to frame cuePointName
end
```

In addition, this behavior places the name of the cue point into a text member. You can use a technique like this to display song lyrics for a singalong. Just place the lyrics in the sound file as cue points. Then, use the on cuePassed handler to dump the cue points to a text member.

PLAYING EXTERNAL SOUNDS

Playing most external sounds is actually exactly like playing Internet sound members. All you need to do is import them as linked files. The sound member refers to this external file for the sound data, but all the Lingo commands treat it as an internal sound.

However, you can also play a sound file that is not linked as a cast member. Just one two-word command performs this action: `sound playFile`. Here is an example:

```
sound playFile 1, "mySound.aif"
```

This sound plays the file specified in Channel 1. If the file is not in the same folder as the movie, you should specify a full or relative pathname. For instance, "\sound\mysound.aif" would specific the sound down one level in the folder "sound" on a Windows machine.

⇨ *If you are having trouble with sound file pathnames, see "Path Problems" in the "Troubleshooting" section at the end of this chapter.*

The `sound playFile` command can play AIFF or wave sounds, the most common formats for Mac and Windows, respectively. It can also play Shockwave audio files. AU formatted sounds can be played as long as the Sun AU Import Export Xtra is present.

To stop a sound that was started with the `sound playFile` command, you can use the `stop` command, with the sound channel and a 0 for the sound name, such as

> The main advantage to playing external sound files is that Director streams them off the hard drive or CD-ROM. This means that the entire sound does not have to be loaded into memory before being played.

```
sound(1).stop()
```

There is also the obsolete sound `stop` command that does the same thing, but which may not be supported in the future.

USING SHOCKWAVE AUDIO

Playing Shockwave audio is a little different from playing regular sounds. To play Shockwave audio, you need to create a Shockwave audio cast member. You can do this by choosing Insert, Media Element, Shockwave Audio.

The result is a new member that has a Properties dialog box like the one shown in Figure 7.1. The most important part of this dialog box is the Link Address, which specifies the full or relative path of the Shockwave audio file. If the path is relative and the movie is playing in Director or a projector, the path can specify a file on the hard drive or CD-ROM rather than on the Internet.

After a Shockwave audio member has been created, you can also use the `url` property to change the location of the file in Lingo. This means that only one member is needed to play multiple files, as long as the files play at separate times.

7

Figure 7.1
The SWA Cast Member Properties dialog box enables you to set the location of the Shockwave audio file.

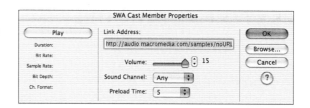

To start a Shockwave audio member playing, just use the play command, as follows:

```
play member "mySound.swa"
```

The stop command halts playback, as follows:

```
stop member "mySound.swa"
```

It is just that simple. The pause command enables you to halt a sound, but then use the play command to resume playing it again at that same point, rather than at the beginning of the sound.

If you want to get more information from a playing Shockwave audio member, you can access many properties. Table 7.6 shows a complete list of member properties.

You can use the Import dialog box to completely import an SWA sound so that it is contained in the internal Cast. However, this defeats the purpose of streaming, which is to play very large sounds without requiring that they be loaded completely into memory first. Internal SWA sounds also do not work in Shockwave.

Table 7.6   Shockwave Audio Properties

Property	Description
bitRate	Returns the bit rate, in Kbps, of the file.
bitsPerSample	Returns the size, in bits, of each sample. Typical values are 8 and 16.
copyrightInfo	Returns the copyright information set when the Shockwave audio file was created.
duration	Returns the length of the sound in ticks (1/60 of a second).
numChannels	Returns the number of channels in the sound. For example, 2 means it is in stereo.
percentStreamed	Returns a value between 0 and 100 that corresponds to how much of the file has been read from the Internet.
percentPlayed	Returns a value between 0 and 100 that corresponds to how much of the file has been played.
preloadTime	The amount of the file that should be loaded into memory before playback begins, displayed in seconds.
sampleRate	The frequency rate of the sound.
soundChannel	The member property that determines which sound channel is used to play back the sound. If the value 0 is given, Director chooses the first available sound channel.
state	Returns a value that tells you what the member is doing at any given time. A list of values is given in Table 7.7.

Table 7.6 Continued

Property	Description
streamName	Same as the `url` property.
url	The location of the Shockwave audio file. You can set and reset this many times to use one member over and over. This way, you can play different audio files but only use one member.
volume	The volume of the sound. A value between 0 and 255.v

The `state` property deserves some more attention. You'll need to use this to track the progress of loading and playing streaming sounds. Table 7.7 shows a complete list of values that `state` can return.

Table 7.7 Values for the State of a Shockwave Audio Member

State	Definition
0	Cast streaming has stopped.
1	The cast member is reloading.
2	Preloading ended successfully.
3	The cast member is playing.
4	The cast member has paused.
5	The cast member has finished streaming.
9	An error occurred.
10	There is insufficient CPU speed.

The `percentStreamed` and `percentPlayed` properties are prime candidates for the progress bar behavior described in "Interface Elements" in Chapter 5 "Adding User Interaction." The `volume` property can be set with the slider behavior discussed in that same chapter.

TROUBLESHOOTING

Lingo Sounds Cut Off Score Sounds

I'm using sounds both in the Score and with Lingo. The Lingo sounds cut off the Score sounds. How can they coexist?

Remember that when you use Lingo to take control of a sound channel, it cuts off any sound being played in the Score using that channel. It is often a good idea to use Channel 3 and above for Lingo commands if you are using Score sounds, also.

Path Problems

I've set up a relative path to a Shockwave audio file, but it's not working when I test the movie. Why?

Using a relative path to a Shockwave audio file can be tricky. It does not work until the movie is located on a server and running from Shockwave. Instead, use the pathname and the relative path to construct a string for the `url` if the `runMode` is "Author". Also, remember that you need to use different pathnames for Mac and Windows, because Mac uses a colon (:) as a path delimiter, and Windows uses a backslash (\).

Mac Sound Doesn't Work in Windows

I've created a sound on my Mac, but it doesn't appear to work when I run the movie in Windows. What could cause this?

If a sound created on the Mac does not work on Windows, make sure that it is in a format that Windows can recognize, such as 16-bit and 22.050KHz. Using an odd setting can result in an unplayable sound in Windows.

Long Sounds Not Working in Projectors

I've got some long sounds that work fine in Director but not in a projector. What is wrong?

If a large internal sound does not work in a projector, it might simply mean that not enough memory is available to play it. Mac users can increase the amount of memory allocated to a Projector by choosing File, Get Info, and then changing the memory allocated to the application. Otherwise, you may want to consider downsampling large sounds to something that will take up less space, or use them as external sounds.

DID YOU KNOW?

- There is no need to create more than one SWA cast member unless you are planning to play more than one sound at a time. Instead, just create one SWA member and use Lingo to set the `url` property to the sound you want to play.

- Shockwave audio file format is similar to the popular MP3 format. In fact, you can link to MP3 files as Shockwave audio, and they will play. MP3 formatted files are usually compressed at too high of a bit rate to be successfully streamed over the Internet, but it is potentially possible.

- Although most PCs are still not capable of mixing more than one sound without a latency effect, Director is capable of mixing sounds almost flawlessly. Director movies can use Microsoft DirectX technology or Apple QuickTime technology to mix sounds. This produces much better results. You need to use one Lingo line: either `the soundDevice = "DirectSound"` or `the soundDevice = "QT3Mix"`. This should be done when the movie starts.

- You can create Shockwave audio compressed files and then import them into Director as internal cast members. You can create sounds that are compressed all the way down to 8Kbps in this way. However, make sure that you don't lose too much quality.

- You can't export sounds from Director normally, but you can copy a sound cast member and then paste it into another sound program. You can also choose an external editor by choosing File, Preferences, Editors, and saving the sound that is referenced when you launch the editor.

- Just because a Shockwave audio file sits on an Internet server doesn't mean that the movie must sit there as well. A Director movie can be run as a Projector, or even in Director, and can still play Shockwave audio over the Internet as long as a connection exists.

7

8

CONTROLLING FLASH MEMBERS

IN THIS CHAPTER

USING FLASH MEMBER LINGO

8

Flash cast members are, no doubt, the most complex type of cast member. After all, they are created in Macromedia Flash, a program all to itself. Flash creates mostly vector-based animations streamlined for the Internet.

Flash members are made up of frames, just like Director movies. Each frame can contain different elements, such as shapes, bitmaps, buttons, and sounds. Rather than being a still media like bitmaps, Flash members are a time-based media like digital video. Most of the Lingo for Flash movies reflects that fact.

Controlling Flash Member Playback

You can use a variety of properties to control the speed at which the Flash movie plays in your Director movie. You can also control playback, stopping and starting the Flash movie as you want. Table 8.1 lists all the Flash properties and commands used to control playback.

Table 8.1 Play Member Playback Lingo

Lingo	Type	Possible Values	Description
findLabel	Sprite command	String	Returns the frame number that corresponds to the frame label.
fixedRate	Member or sprite property	Number	Set this only when you are using the #fixed setting for the playBackMode. It enables you to specify the frame rate for the Flash movie. You can even change it during playback.
frame	Sprite property	Number, read-only	Returns the number of the current frame.
frameCount	Member property	Number, read-only	The number of frames in the Flash movie.
frameRate	Member property	Number, read-only	The Flash movie's original frame rate.
goToFrame	Sprite command	Number or String	Jump to a frame number or label.
hold	Sprite command	None	Stops the Flash movie from animating, but the audio continues.
loop	Member property	TRUE or FALSE	Whether the Flash movie will loop.
pausedAtStart	Member property	TRUE or FALSE	Whether the Flash movie automatically starts playing.
play	Sprite command	None	Enables the Flash movie to continue playing.

Table 8.1 Continued

Lingo	Type	Possible Values	Description
playBackMode	Member or sprite property	#normal, #lockstep, #fixed	The #normal option tells the Flash movie to rely on the settings established when it was created in Flash. The #lockstep setting causes one frame of the Flash movie to play for every one frame of the Director movie. The #fixed setting uses the fixedRate property of the member to determine the Flash movie's frame rate.
playing	Sprite property	TRUE or FALSE, read-only	Whether the Flash movie is currently playing.
rewind	Sprite command	None	Returns the Flash movie to the first frame.
stop	Sprite command	None	Stops the Flash movie.

You can use these properties to build a simple set of playback controls for a Flash movie sprite. The sample movie flashplayback.dir contains such a set. Figure 8.1 shows the controls under a Flash movie sprite.

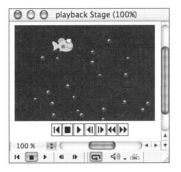

Figure 8.1
This Flash sprite's playback is controlled by the buttons under it.

The Flash sprite, which is in channel 1, has a small script attached to it to make sure that the Flash movie will not start playing automatically, and that it will not loop.

```
on beginSprite me
  sprite(me.spriteNum).member.pausedAtStart = TRUE
  sprite(me.spriteNum).member.loop = FALSE
end
```

You can set both of these properties with the Property Inspector. Doing it in a script, however, ensures that the sprite will behave properly even if you replace the cast member later.

Each of the buttons in the example movie has a small script attached. The Play button simply uses the play command.

```
on mouseUp me
 sprite(1).play()
end
```

Likewise, the Stop button uses the stop command.

```
on mouseUp me
 sprite(1).stop()
end
```

The Rewind button uses the rewind command. In addition it issues a stop command. Otherwise, the Flash movie returns to the first frame and then continues playing if it was playing before.

```
on mouseUp me
 sprite(1).rewind()
 sprite(1).stop()
end
```

For the Step Forward and Step Back buttons, you'll need to stop the movie, get the current frame number, and use goToFrame to move one frame back or one frame forward. Here is one of the scripts:

```
on mouseUp me
 sprite(1).stop()
 currentFrame = sprite(1).frame
 sprite(1).goToFrame(currentFrame+1)
end
```

The example movie includes a Fast Forward button. Unlike digital video, you can't simply set the movieRate to something other than 1 to play the Flash movie at a different speed. But you can use the playbackMode and fixedRate properties to make the movie play back at a faster speed.

```
on mouseUp me
 sprite(1).playbackMode = #fixed
 sprite(1).fixedRate = 30
 sprite(1).play()
end
```

To get a Flash movie to play backward is a tougher assignment. You can't simply give fixedRate a negative number. You would have to build a behavior that uses frame and goToFrame to move backward through the movie frame by frame. The example movie includes such a behavior. Here is the script:

```
property pBackwards

on beginSprite me
 pBackwards = FALSE
end

on mouseUp me
 if pBackwards = FALSE then
  pBackwards = TRUE
  sprite(1).stop()
```

```
  else
   pBackwards = FALSE
  end if
end

on exitFrame me
 if pBackwards then
  currentFrame = sprite(1).frame
  sprite(1).goToFrame(currentFrame-1)
 end if
end

-- if you use this behavior with other controls
-- you must issue a sprite(x).stopBackwards()
-- call on all other controls in order for this
-- behavior to stop rewinding the movie
on stopBackwards me
 pBackwards = FALSE
end
```

Controlling Flash Movie Behavior

You can also control how much like a Flash movie a Flash member should act. Because Flash movies have their own buttons and actions, you will sometimes want to disable those elements in the Flash member when using it in Director.

This could happen in a case where you have a standalone Flash movie that also must exist in a Director movie. The standalone version needs its own scripts to work, but the embedded version will be controlled by Director Lingo.

Table 8.2 lists all the Flash member properties that control its behavior.

Table 8.2   Flash Movie Behavior Properties

Property	Description
actionsEnabled	Determines whether any of the ActionScript scripts in the Flash sprite or member work.
buttonsEnabled	Determines whether buttons in the Flash sprite or member work.
clickMode	This property of a sprite or member can be set to one of three options: #boundingBox, #opaque, or #object. The #boundingBox option enables clicks and other mouse events to be detected over the entire sprite's rectangle. The #opaque option enables clicks to be detected only when the cursor is over an opaque portion of the Flash member. The #object option detects mouse events only when the cursor is over a filled shape in the Flash member. The #opaque option works only when the sprite is set to the Background Transparent ink.
eventPassMode	Determines whether clicks are passed to Lingo behaviors. The four modes are #passAlways, #passButton, #passNotButton, and #passNever. The #passAlways setting is the default.

You can use `clickMode` to use a Flash member as an odd-shaped button. The example movie `oddflashbutton.dir` includes a script that sets the Flash movie in the sprite to use a `clickMode` of `#object`. The Flash movie is an odd-shaped area. The sprite reacts to a click only if the cursor is over the filled area of the sprite.

```
on beginSprite me
 sprite(me.spriteNum).clickMode = #object
end

on mouseUp me
 put "click!"
end
```

Flash Member Interaction

You can detect whether the cursor, or any point, intersects a Flash movie using the `hitTest` function. The function takes one point as its only parameter. It returns `#background`, `#normal`, or `#button`, depending on what the point is over.

The value `#normal` means that the point is over a shape in the Flash movie. The value `#button` means that it is over a button symbol in the movie. The value `#background` means that the point is not over any Flash element. You will get the value `#background` if the point is not over the sprite at all.

The following script, from the movie `hittest.dir`, puts the `hitTest` result into a text member.

```
on exitFrame me
 hitTestResult = sprite(me.spriteNum).hitTest(the mouseLoc)
 member("result").text = string(hitTestResult)
end
```

When you are dealing with Flash movies in Lingo, you may need to translate locations on the Director movie's Stage to locations in the Flash movie. You can use `flashToStage` and `stageToFlash` for this. Each of these sprite functions takes a location point value and returns a location point value. They both take into account the position of the Flash sprite on the Stage and its scaling and rotation.

The mouseOverButton Flash sprite property tells you whether the cursor is over a button in the current sprite. You can determine this with hitTest just as easily.

Controlling Flash Member Appearance

Flash sprites are different from bitmaps in that they are much more malleable. You can stretch and rotate them knowing that the vector graphics that make up most Flash movies will be displayed nicely.

➡ *If you see a performance decrease when using many Flash members, see "Flash Members Slow Down Director Movies" in the "Troubleshooting" section at the end of this chapter.*

You actually have a huge set of Lingo properties that can be used to manipulate the Flash members in various ways. Table 8.3 is a complete list of these properties and commands.

Table 8.3 Flash Member Appearance Lingo

Property/Command	Type	Possible Values	Description
broadcastProps	Member property	TRUE or FALSE	Whether changes to the member properties automatically affect other sprites using the same member.
centerRegPoint	Member property	TRUE or FALSE	Whether the registration point of the Flash sprite is automatically centered if the sprite is scaled.
defaultRect	Member property	rect	The default size of the Flash sprite when placed on the Stage.
defaultRectMode	Member property	#Flash or #fixed	When set to #Flash, the defaultRect will be the original Flash movie rect. When you change defaultRect, this property will automatically change to #fixed.
directToStage	Member property	TRUE or FALSE	Whether the Flash sprite is drawn directly to the screen, appearing on top of all other sprites. This speeds up playback.
flashRect	Member property	rect, read-only	The original rect of the Flash member.
imageEnabled	Sprite and Member property	TRUE or FALSE	Whether the sprite is visible. Audio will play regardless.
obeyScoreRotation	Member property	TRUE or FALSE	Whether sprites using the member will use the Score rotation property or the member rotation property.
originH, originV	Sprite and member property	Floating point number	The location of the origin point used for scaling and rotation. The originMode must be set to #point.
originMode	Sprite and member property	#center, #topleft, #point	Which location to use as the origin point, the point used by rotation and scaling properties.
originPoint	Sprite and member property	point	Same as originH and originV, but points can only use integers.
quality	Sprite and member property	#high, #low, #autoHigh, #autoLow	High quality Flash rendering means antialiased vector lines but slower playback. Low quality uses jagged edges. Using an "auto" setting makes the pla back begin at that quality setting but then adjust depending on whether the frame rate of the movie can keep up.

8

Table 8.3 Continued

Property/Command	Type	Possible Values	Description
rotation	Member property	Floating point number	As long as obeyScoreRotation is set to FALSE, you can rotate the Flash member around its origin point.
scale	Sprite and member property	Floating point number	Scales a Flash sprite centered on its original point.
scaleMode	Sprite and member property	#showAll, #noBorder, #exactFit, #noScale, #autoSize	#showAll fits the Flash movie into the sprite rect and fills empty border spaces on the sides with the movie's background color. #noBorder fits either the vertical or horizontal dimension of the Flash movie into the sprite and crops the rest. #exactFit and #showAll fit the Flash movie to the sprite rectangle, with #showAll even taking into account rotation. #noScale keeps the Flash movie at 100% and crops when necessary.
sound	Member property	TRUE or FALSE	Whether the audio tracks in the Flash movie are heard.
soundMixMedia	Movie property	TRUE or FALSE	Whether the Flash sounds are mixed with the Director movie sounds. If FALSE, Flash movie sounds and Director movie sounds cannot be played at the same time.
static	Sprite and member property	TRUE or FALSE	If you set this to TRUE, the Flash movie image stops updating. This can significantly speed up drawing of Flash sprites that don't need animation.
viewH, viewV	Sprite and member property	Floating point numbers	The center point used by viewScale.
viewpoint	Sprite and member property	point	The center point used by viewScale. Use viewH and viewV to set these to non-integer values.
ViewScale	Sprite and member property	Floating point number	Scaling of the Flash member. The rect of the sprite on the Stage is not changed, so the edges may be cropped.

For many Director applications of Flash movies, you'll want to set the `static` property of any Flash member to TRUE. This includes all Flash members that have just one frame and no animation at all.

⇨ *If you replace current Flash members with new versions and notice that the properties clear, see "Replacing Flash Members Clears Properties" in the "Troubleshooting" section at the end of this chapter.*

In previous versions of Director, you had to set the `static` property using Lingo. With Director MX, you can now set it in the Property Inspector when that sprite is selected.

Using Flash members as static media has become common in Director movies. The vector shape format of Flash means that these members can be rotated and scaled and still look good.

By using the `static` property of the member or sprite, you can spare Director the trouble of redrawing a Flash member that hasn't changed. This translates to a speed increase that is about equivalent to using a bitmap member.

Even if your Flash member has more than one frame, the member can be a good candidate for using the `static` property. For instance, if you have an animated Flash member that is temporarily paused on a frame, you can set the `static` property to TRUE to increase performance. Just remember to set the `static` property to FALSE again before allowing the animation to continue.

Caution

It may seem like a good idea to use Flash for all your sprites. But each Flash sprite uses some overhead that bitmap sprites do not. Using many Flash sprites slows down your movie considerably. Make sure that you use the `static` property set to FALSE whenever you can.

LINGO AND ACTIONSCRIPT INTERACTION

Director MX and Flash MX each have their own scripting language. Lingo can talk to Flash's scripting language, known as *ActionScript*. The simplest examples of this don't involve any Flash member at all, just Lingo calling the Flash Xtra.

Accessing ActionScript Objects

In ActionScript, functions are grouped into categories called *objects*. For instance, all the math functions are grouped together in the Math object. To use a math function, such as the square root function, you would write a line of ActionScript code that looks like this:

```
a = Math.sqrt(4);
```

You can access the Math object in Lingo by using the `newObject` Lingo function. This creates a reference to the Math object and allows you to access functions such as `sqrt`. Here is an example from the Message panel:

```
asMath = newObject("Math")
put asMath.sqrt(4)
-- 2.0000
```

8

➪   *If you are having trouble getting some ActionScript to work in Director, see "Some ActionScript Doesn' t Seem to Work in Director" in the "Troubleshooting" section at the end of this chapter.*

Plenty of other Flash objects can be useful in your Lingo scripts. The next few sections highlight some of these objects.

Arrays

Flash arrays are like Lingo's linear lists. However, you can use `push` and `pop` to add items to the list and remove them. This is similar to JavaScript and some other programming languages. Here's how you would create an array with Lingo, add some items to it, and get the value of one item:

```
asArray = newObject("Array")
asArray.push(5,2,76,2,7,92,34,2)
put asArray[5]
-- 92.0000
```

Note that arrays in ActionScript are zero-based. So the first item in the array is item number 0, the second is item 1, and so on. That is why item number 5 has a value of 92.

See Flash's documentation or a good Flash book for a complete list of Flash array functions. My *Sams Teach Yourself Flash MX ActionScript in 24 Hours* is a good place to start. For a more advanced reference, see *Special Edition Using Flash MX*.

Dates

The ActionScript Date object is a little more complex than the Lingo Date object. It includes functions to retrieve or set all the properties of a moment of time, such as day, month, year, hour, minute, and second. You can also get the time zone. The `toString` function returns a string with almost all this information.

```
asDate = newObject("Date")
put asDate.toString()
-- "Mon Nov 25 07:27:44 GMT-0700 2002"
```

Strings

The String object in Flash handles all string variables. Most of the functions, such as concatenating, can be done in Lingo just as easily. But some utility functions, such as `toLowercase` and `toUppercase`, can be useful.

```
asString = newObject("String","Hello Flash!")
put asString.toString()
-- "Hello Flash!"
put asString.length
-- 12.0000
put asString.toLowercase()
-- "hello flash!"
put asString.toUppercase()
-- "HELLO FLASH!"
```

Notice that to get the initial value of the string back, you need to use the Flash utility function toString. This is because if you simply asked for *asString* you would get an unusable Flash reference to the location of the object in memory.

```
put asString
-- <FlashObject 38F11D4>
put asString.toString()
-- "Hello Flash!"
```

XML

Flash contains a complete XML parser as an object. You can take advantage of this in Lingo by creating an XML object and then using the properties and methods of that object.

```
asXML = newObject("XML")
asXML.parseXML("<TEST>Testing</TEST>")
put asXML.toString()
-- "<TEST>Testing</TEST>"
put asXML.firstChild.nodeName
-- "TEST"
put asXML.firstChild.firstChild.nodeValue
-- "Testing"
```

However, not all the XML object methods and properties seem to work correctly through Lingo. As of this writing, the important childNodes property doesn't seem to be accessible. However, you can always create your own custom ActionScript objects to give you access to anything that doesn't work with this direct method.

Director has its own XML parser that exists as an Xtra. However, it is known as being buggy and difficult to use. Plus, if you are using the Flash Xtra already anyway, using the Flash XML parser will save you from having to include another Xtra.

Custom ActionScript Objects

Flash ActionScript allows the programmer to create his own objects complete with properties and methods. You can then access these custom objects with Lingo.

To do this, you must first start with a Flash MX movie. Here is a script from the Flash MX movie flashfunction.fla. It defines an object called *myFunctions*. The initializing function sets the text in a text field according to the parameter passed in. There are also two other functions: one that sets the text in another text field, and one that duplicates a movie clip that already exists on the Flash Stage.

```
// create asFunctions object type
function asFunctions(initText) {
  showInitText = initText;
```

```
  mcNum = 1;
}

// place Lingo text into field
asFunctions.prototype.showText = function(text) {
  myText = "Text:" + text;
}

// create copy of myMovieClip at x,y
asFunctions.prototype.duplicate = function(x,y) {
  _root.myMovieClip.duplicateMovieClip("mc"+mcNum,mcNum);
  _root["mc"+mcNum]._x = x;
  _root["mc"+mcNum]._y = y;
  mcNum++;
}
```

This movie is then published as a `.swf` file and imported into a Director movie as a cast member. To create a reference to the *myFunctions* object, you'll need to use the `newObject` function as a reference to the sprite that contains the Flash movie. But you can't do that until the sprite is on the Stage. Even when it is on the Stage, the Flash movie needs to start up before the commands that create the custom object run.

So you cannot reference the custom *myFunctions* object in the `on beginSprite` handler. It is too early. The Flash movie has not yet looked at its own ActionScript code to know that the *myFunctions* object exists.

The following behavior sets a property called *pInit* so that the ActionScript object is created the first time `on exitFrame` runs, and only the first time. Then, it continues to call the custom *duplicate* function in each frame.

```
property pInit, pAsFunctions

on beginSprite me
 -- remember to get AS functions
 pInit = FALSE
end

on exitFrame me
 if pInit = FALSE then
  -- get reference to AS functions
  pAsFunctions = sprite(me.spriteNum).newObject("asFunctions","Contact Made!")

  -- try out the 'showText' function
  pAsFunctions.showText("Testing 1, 2, 3")

  -- remember already got AS functions
  pInit = TRUE
 end if
```

```
-- create a copy of the movie clip
pAsFunctions.duplicate(random(550),random(400))

end
```

The example movie `flashfunction.dir` contains this code. When you run it, the Director movie calls the *duplicate* function each frame with random values, thus creating a new red circle each frame.

Flash Variables and Properties

You can also use Lingo to directly access Flash variables stored at the root level of the Flash movie. To do this, use the `setVariable` command. This changes the value of a variable in the Flash movie from Lingo. Here is an example:

```
sprite(1).setVariable("myFlashVariable",7)
```

You can also get a variable value with the `getVariable` function:

```
myLingoVariable = sprite(1).getVariable("myFlashVariable")
```

This returns a string, no matter what type of variable it is in ActionScript. So if you are expecting a number, you may want to use the Lingo `value` function to convert it to a number.

There is also a `getFlashProperty` function that allows you to get the value of a property of a movie clip in Flash. For instance, if you have a movie clip identified as "myClip" and you wanted to find its `_alpha` property, you would use this:

```
a = sprite(1).getFlashProperty("myClip",#alpha)
```

It would be nice if you could use the real names of the Flash properties in your Lingo code. However, for some reason, some of the names are different. For instance, instead of _x and _y, you would need to use #posX and #posY. Most of the other properties are the same, except that you need to remove the underscore character and replace it with a #.

The same is true for the `setFlashProperty` command. So here is how you would move a movie clip to be at horizontal pixel 50:

```
sprite(1).setFlashProperty("myClip",#posX,50)
```

You can also indicate that a set of commands is meant for a specific movie clip. You can do this with the `tellTarget` and `endTellTarget` commands. For instance, you could set a property and then issue a command to the movie clip myClip like this:

```
sprite(1).tellTarget("\myClip")
sprite(1).setFlashProperty(#alpha,50)
sprite(1).goToFrame(7)
sprite(1).endTellTarget()
```

8

Flash Printing

Director can also print Flash graphics. This matches the printing capability of Flash itself, which has actually been around since Flash 4. You can either `print` or `printAsBitmap`. Both commands work the same way, but `printAsBitmap` works in some cases where `print` might not, such as if semi-transparent graphics are present. `printAsBitmap` might not print as nicely, however, depending on the situation.

The `print` command can work with no parameters at all. Frames in the Flash movie must be labeled with a "#p" as the frame label. However, if the "#p" label is not present, every frame is printed. You can also include one argument to specify a movie clip to be printed. A second argument can be `#bframe` or `#bmax`. The first prints each frame as large as it can. The second finds a common size between all the frames and prints each at the same scale.

Here is an example of how the `print` command might be used. Much more detail about Flash printing can be found in the Flash 5 documentation. It pretty much all applies to the Lingo `print` command as well. This will print the Flash sprite in channel 1.

```
sprite(1).print()
```

➡ *For more information about Flash ActionScript objects, see "Using the Flash Communication Server,"*
p. 606.

TROUBLESHOOTING

Flash Members Slow Down Director Movies

I'm using Flash members in my movie, and now it is running slow. What can I do to improve performance?

The most common problem developers have with Flash movies is that they are slow. They are, and there's not much you can do about it except the obvious: Simplify the vector graphics in the movie, reduce the size of the sprite, and set the `static` property to TRUE if the Flash movie isn't animating. Director has a much faster engine than Flash, so you'll want to use Flash members sparingly if speed is important.

Replacing Flash Members Clears Properties

I'm always getting updates of Flash members to replace the old versions in my movies. But when I import the new versions, all the properties are reset. How can I prevent this?

If you using a Flash movie and you want to replace it with an updated version, double-click on the cast member and use the Flash Properties dialog to browse to the new `.swf` to replace it. Doing this preserves all the member's custom properties.

Some ActionScript Doesn't Seem to Work in Director

I'm using a lot of ActionScript in my Flash members, and some of it doesn't work like it does in the Flash player. What am I doing wrong?

Don't be surprised if some Flash functionality doesn't work in Director. To test every Flash function in the Xtra, Macromedia would have had to repeat the entire test process already done when Flash MX was released. In every version of the Flash Xtra so far, there have been a few bugs. But there have also been work-arounds for these bugs.

DID YOU KNOW?

- Flash can be used as an alternative to digital video. Flash MX can import video and export `.swf` files. These files can then be used in your Director movie. These files are ultra-compressed, so in some cases they may be preferable to QuickTime or AVI.

- Flash movies can be edited directly from the Cast with Director MX. Simply select the member, (Control-click) [right-click], and select Edit Cast Member. This will open Flash, allow you to edit the original Flash source file, and then automatically save the compressed Flash movie back into the cast member.

- Flash ActionScript is usually slower than Lingo, but not always. For instance, in a test I conducted, it was faster to call `Math.sqrt` in an ActionScript object than it was to use the Lingo `sqrt` function.

9

CONTROLLING DIGITAL VIDEO
WITH LINGO

IN THIS CHAPTER

USING VIDEO COMMANDS

Whereas most digital video used in Director is simply placed on the Stage with the default control bar, sometimes it's necessary to control video with Lingo. Digital video is not as easy to manipulate as bitmaps are, but a variety of properties can be used to affect how video is displayed. These properties are the subject of this chapter.

There are more member and sprite properties for digital video than for any other media type. Because some of the properties are for the member, and others are for the sprite, it can get confusing. There are even functions involving QuickTime tracks that act like properties. For the sake of clarity, this section separates the properties for the members from the properties for the sprites.

Member Properties

Two groups of member properties are for digital video members: member properties and sprite properties. The first group corresponds exactly to the properties shown in the Property Inspector when you have a video member selected. Table 9.1 is a complete list of digital video member properties.

Table 9.1 Video Member and System Properties

Property	Description
center	A TRUE or FALSE value that determines whether the video is centered in the sprite's rectangle. This works only if the crop property is set to TRUE.
controller	A TRUE or FALSE value that determines whether the default QuickTime or AVI controller is shown.
crop	If this value is set to TRUE, the movie remains the same scale, even if the sprite's rectangle is changed. If it's set to FALSE, the movie adjusts to fit in the sprite's rectangle.
digitalVideoTimeScale	When this system property is set to 0, Director uses the timescale of the movie to play it back. If you have a special need to set the timescale to something else, you can use this property. If you don't know what a timescale is, you will not need to change this value.
digitalVideoType	Returns either #quickTime or #videoForWindows.
duration	Returns the length in ticks (1/60 of a second) of the video.
frameRate	Any value except for -1 or 0 allows you to force the video to play back at a specific frame rate without sound. A value of -2 causes the video to play as fast as possible.
invertMask	This QuickTime member property, when set to TRUE, inverts the 1-bit mask used by the mask property.
loop	This property determines whether the video is to automatically loop back to the beginning when it reaches the end.
mask	This QuickTime property points to a 1-bit bitmap that serves as a mask for the video member. The mask is an overlay where the black pixels determine the shape of the visible area when the video is played back.

Table 9.1 Continued

Property	Description
pausedAtStart	This property determines whether the movie starts playing as soon as it appears on the Stage, or whether it waits for the controller or Lingo to tell it to play.
preLoad	When set to TRUE, this QuickTime property can be preloaded into memory before it plays.
sound	This property determines whether the sound is played.
timeScale	The timescale of the video member. This is a read-only property, but you can use the digitalVideoTimeScale to force the movie to use a different timescale during playback.
translation	If the crop is TRUE, you can use this QuickTime property to offset the video on the Stage. It takes a list of the form *[x,y]*. If center is TRUE, the offset is from the center, otherwise the offset is from the upper left.
video	This property determines whether the video is displayed.

Sprite Properties

Several sprite properties also can be set with Lingo. These properties, listed in Table 9.2, are useful for creating video controls and effects.

To determine whether QuickTime is present, use the quickTimeVersion() function. If QuickTime is not present, it returns a 0.0; otherwise, it returns the version number. The property the videoForWindowsPresent returns TRUE if the computer can play back AVI videos.

Table 9.2 Digital Video Sprite Properties

Property	Description
LoopBounds	This property enables you to set the start and end times of a looping video. Use a short, two-item list, such as [0,240].
MovieRate	This property represents the speed of forward movement of the video. A value of 0 means the video has stopped. A value of 1 means it is playing normally. A value of 2 means it is going at double speed. You can also use negative values to make the video go backward.
MovieTime	This property represents the current time, in ticks, of the video. You can set this to 0 to go to the start, or to the member's duration to go to the end.
rotation	Believe it or not, you can rotate a QuickTime video. Set this property to the angle, in degrees, of rotation. This property works best when the video member is not set to Direct to Stage.
scale	You can also scale the video by setting this property to a small list with the horizontal and vertical scale values, such as [1.5,1.5].
translation	This is the same as the member property translation.
volume	This property works just as it does for sound members, enabling you to change the sound level of the video.

Masks

The mask property of a digital video member allows you to present video in unusual shapes. A *mask* is a 1-bit bitmap that tells Director which pixels of the video to show and which pixels to throw away. Figure 9.1 shows three images: a video (left), a 1-bit bitmap (middle), and the same video with the 1-bit bitmap applied as a mask (right).

Figure 9.1
A 1-bit bitmap can be used as a mask for a digital video member.

To apply a mask, create the 1-bit bitmap and name it. Then use the mask property to apply it to the member. You can even do it in the Message panel to test it. The mask property is a member property, but this command uses the sprite to figure out the member:

```
sprite(1).member.mask = member("myMask")
```

You can also use the invertMask property to have white pixels, rather than black, represent visible pixels in the movie. Keep in mind that the registration point for the mask should be set to the upper-left corner rather than the center.

> The best part about masks is that they can be used when the video is in Direct to Stage mode. This means that the video is not slowed by the mask effect.

> Setting a video mask works best when you do it before the sprite appears on Stage. An on beginSprite handler is a good place for it. To remove a video mask, set the mask property of the member to VOID.

BUILDING VIDEO CONTROLS

Using the video properties explained previously, it's easy to build your own custom controls. As a matter of fact, one behavior can handle 10 types of controls. On the CD-ROM, this next behavior can be found in the movie videocontrols.dir.

The following behavior needs to know which sprite contains the digital video. It also needs to know what type of control is being used.

```
property pControlType, pVideoSprite

on getPropertyDescriptionList me
  list = [:]
  addProp list, #pControlType, [#comment: "Control",\
    #format: #symbol,\
    #range: [#play, #stop, #pause, #stepForward, #stepBackward,\
    #start, #reverse, #fastForward, #fastReverse, #end, #loop],\
    #default: #stop]
  addProp list, #pVideoSprite, [#comment: "Video Sprite",\
    #format: #sprite, #default: 1]
  return list
end
```

Although a more complex behavior might also include button handler–like effects, such as down states and rollovers, this button behavior sticks to doing only what is necessary to control the video sprite.

In the case of a "play" button, all that is needed is for the movieRate to be set to 1:

```
on mouseUp me
 case pControlType of
  #play:
   sprite(pVideoSprite).movieRate = 1
```

A stop button does the opposite, setting the movieRate to 0. The same can be done for the "pause" button. To make the "play" button different, it can also set the movieTime back to 0, which stops and rewinds the video, rather than just stopping it.

```
  #stop:
   sprite(pVideoSprite).movieRate = 0
   sprite(pVideoSprite).movieTime = 0
  #pause:
   sprite(pVideoSprite).movieRate = 0
```

A *#start* or *#end* will take the video to the beginning or end and pause it. Note that this means that the "start" button and "stop" button actually do the same thing!

```
  #start:
   sprite(pVideoSprite).movieRate = 0
   sprite(pVideoSprite).movieTime = 0
  #end:
   sprite(pVideoSprite).movieRate = 0
   sprite(pVideoSprite).movieTime = sprite(pVideoSprite).duration
```

A "reverse" button plays the video at normal speed, but backward.

```
  #reverse:
   sprite(pVideoSprite).movieRate = -1
```

There are two types of "step" buttons: forward and reverse. If the digital video is set to play at a typical 15 frames per second, that means there is one frame every 4/60 of a second, or 4 ticks.

```
  #stepForward:
   sprite(pVideoSprite).movieTime = sprite(pVideoSprite).movieTime + 4
  #stepBackward:
   sprite(pVideoSprite).movieTime = sprite(pVideoSprite).movieTime - 4
```

A "fast forward" or "fast reverse" button can make the video travel at speeds greater than 1 or less than −1. In this case, 3 is used:

```
  #fastForward:
   sprite(pVideoSprite).movieRate = 3
  #fastReverse:
   sprite(pVideoSprite).movieRate = -3
```

One last button type is the loop switch. This determines whether the movie loops at the end. Make this a separate behavior and use some of the same code from the check box behaviors so that the button can change from a looping to nonlooping state. However, to simplify the coding, this button just toggles the `loop` property and does not give any feedback to the users.

```
  #loop:
    sprite(pVideoSprite).member.loop = \
      not sprite(pVideoSprite).member.loop
 end case
end
```

Other video buttons can be made as well. For instance, you can use `loopBounds` to switch between different loops within the same video. A slider can be used as a volume control. Or, you can even use a slider to set the `movieTime` property. Such a slider is just like the one used by QuickTime's default controller, but you can use your own custom graphics.

⇨ *If you notice that your QuickTime controller is a different size when played back on another machine, see "QuickTime Controller Changes Size on Different Platforms" in the "Troubleshooting" section at the end of this chapter.*

USING OTHER VIDEO TECHNIQUES

Another movie on the CD-ROM, `videoeffects.dir`, shows off a set of unusual special effects. These effects are created using various video properties. For instance, the following behavior uses the blend property of the sprite to cause a video sprite to fade in:

```
property pSpeed

on getPropertyDescriptionList me
 list = [:]
 addProp list, #pSpeed, [#comment: "Speed", #format: #integer,\
   #range: [#min: 1, #max: 20], #default: 7]
 return list
end

on beginSprite me
 sprite(me.spriteNum).member.directToStage = FALSE
 sprite(me.spriteNum).member.crop = TRUE

 sprite(me.spriteNum).blend = 0
end

on exitFrame me
 if sprite(me.spriteNum).blend < 100 then
  sprite(me.spriteNum).blend = \
    min(sprite(me.spriteNum).blend+pSpeed,100)
 end if
end
```

Notice that the handler also sets the `directToStage` and `crop` properties of the video sprite. Although this is usually not necessary, it ensures that any changes to these properties from other behaviors are not still in effect.

The same things can be done in reverse. Here is a behavior that fades a video sprite to a blend of 0:

```
property pSpeed

on getPropertyDescriptionList me
 list = [:]
 addProp list, #pSpeed, [#comment: "Speed", #format: #integer,\
   #range: [#min: 1, #max: 20], #default: 7]
 return list
end

on beginSprite me
 sprite(me.spriteNum).member.directToStage = FALSE
 sprite(me.spriteNum).member.crop = TRUE

 sprite(me.spriteNum) .blend = 100
end

on exitFrame me
 if sprite(me.spriteNum).blend > 0 then
  sprite(me.spriteNum).blend = \
    max(sprite(me.spriteNum).blend-pSpeed,0)
 end if
end
```

⇨ *If you are having trouble with these blend behaviors, see "Setting Blend of Video Doesn't Work" in the "Troubleshooting" section at the end of this chapter.*

These behaviors can, of course, be combined into one that provides either function. Note that they can be used for bitmaps and even text members, too.

For a more complex effect, the following behavior causes the video to start off as a small point. It then grows lengthwise until it is a line. Then, it grows up and down until it is the original shape of the video. The result looks something like an old-fashioned television warming up.

```
property pOrigRect, pSpeed

on getPropertyDescriptionList me
 list = [:]
 addProp list, #pSpeed, [#comment: "Speed", #format: #integer,\
   #range: [#min: 1, #max: 20], #default: 7]
 return list
end

on beginSprite me
 sprite(me.spriteNum).member.directToStage = TRUE
 sprite(me.spriteNum).member.crop = FALSE
```

```
  pOrigRect = sprite(me.spriteNum).rect

  -- set rect to center point
  x = pOrigRect.left+(pOrigRect.width/2)
  y = pOrigRect.top+(pOrigRect.height/2)
  r = rect(x,y,x,y+1)
  sprite(me.spriteNum).rect = r
end

on exitFrame me
 if sprite(me.spriteNum).rect.width < pOrigRect.width then
  r = sprite(me.spriteNum).rect
  r.left = max(r.left-pSpeed, pOrigRect.left)
  r.right = min(r.right+pSpeed, pOrigRect.right)
  sprite(me.spriteNum).rect = r

 else if sprite(me.spriteNum).rect.height < pOrigRect.height then
  r = sprite(me.spriteNum).rect
  r.top = max(r.top-pSpeed, pOrigRect.top)
  r.bottom = min(r.bottom+pSpeed, pOrigRect.bottom)
  sprite(me.spriteNum).rect = r

 end if
end
```

Digital video can also be rotated. This next behavior probably has no real use but is a good demonstration. It takes a digital video sprite and rotates it continuously:

```
property pSpeed

on getPropertyDescriptionList me
 list = [:]
 addProp list, #pSpeed, [#comment: "Speed", #format: #integer,\
   #range: [#min: 1, #max: 20], #default: 7]
 return list
end

on beginSprite me
 sprite(me.spriteNum).member.directToStage = TRUE
 sprite(me.spriteNum).member.crop = TRUE
end

on endSprite me
 sprite(me.spriteNum).rotation = 0
end

on exitFrame me
 sprite(me.spriteNum).rotation = \
    sprite(me.spriteNum).rotation + pSpeed
end
```

Here is a very different effect. The following behavior takes the video, shrinks it, and then places it on the left side of the screen. It turns on the `trails` property of the sprite so that the image is left behind. It then moves over to the right and leaves another image. It continues to do this, leaving behind what looks like a filmstrip. When it gets to the right side of the screen, it starts replacing the images to the left.

```
property pOrigRect, pSize, pSpacing, pStart, pDirect

on getPropertyDescriptionList me
 list = [:]
 addProp list, #pSize, [#comment: "Size (%)", #format: #integer,\
   #range: [#min: 5, #max: 100], #default: 25]
 addProp list, #pSpacing, [#comment: "Spacing", #format: #integer,\
   #range: [#min: 0, #max: 25], #default: 5]
 addProp list, #pStart, [#comment: "Start X", #format: #integer,\
   #default: 0]
 addProp list, #pDirect, [#comment: "Direct To Stage", #format: #boolean,\
   #default: TRUE]
 return list
end

on beginSprite me
 sprite(me.spriteNum).member.directToStage = pDirect
 sprite(me.spriteNum).member.crop = FALSE
  sprite(me.spriteNum).trails = FALSE

 pOrigRect = sprite(me.spriteNum).rect
 r = sprite(me.spriteNum).rect
 r = (r*pSize)/100.0
 sprite(me.spriteNum).rect = r
 sprite(me.spriteNum).locH = pStart
 sprite(me.spriteNum).trails = TRUE
end

on endSprite me
 sprite(me.spriteNum).trails = FALSE
 sprite(me.spriteNum).rect = pOrigRect
end

on exitFrame me
 x = sprite(me.spriteNum).locH
 x = x + sprite(me.spriteNum).rect.width + pSpacing
 if x > the stageRight then x = pStart

 sprite(me.spriteNum).locH = x
end
```

Figure 9.2 shows the effects of this code in action.

Figure 9.2
The Film Strip behavior places images of the video in different positions on the Stage.

These are only simple examples of what can be accomplished with the digital video member and sprite properties. You can combine and expand on them depending on your needs. Experimentation is the best way to find what works best for you.

TROUBLESHOOTING

Setting Blend of Video Doesn't Work

I'm trying to use the fade-in and fade-out behaviors in this chapter that set the blend of a video sprite, and it is not working. Why?

It appears that Director MX digital video definitely works much better after the most recent version of QuickTime, version 6 as of this writing, is installed. If you are using an older version, or the user has an older version, don't count on some of the more extreme effects. Also, using Windows AVI video rather than QuickTime may limit your special effects choices. The only way to know for sure is to test in many different environments.

QuickTime Controller Changes Size on Different Platforms

I'm using the built-in default Quicktime Controller, but I can't get it to be exactly the same size in both Mac and Windows. Is there any way to control this?

If you are using the built-in QuickTime controller, check the size on both Mac and Windows; they might be slightly different. It depends on the version of QuickTime. The Windows controller is slightly taller than the Mac in various versions of QuickTime.

QuickTime Sound Overrides Director Sound Channels

I've got a QuickTime movie playing with sound, and it kills the sound in my Director sound channels. Is there any way to have both playing?

This is a common problem. Your best bet is to remove all Director sound on frames that have QuickTime video and only use the sound from the video. Alternatively, if it is just background music, make the video silent and only use Director sound.

DID YOU KNOW?

- You can use the video control scripts to control MIDI-only or sound-only QuickTime video. This way, you can build a jukebox that uses MIDI or supercompressed QuickTime audio.

- In QuickTime, When you set the `movieRate` property to a negative number, not only does the movie play backward, but so does the sound!

- A great alternative to QuickTime or AVI video now is Flash. You can convert video to a Flash `.swf` file in Flash MX or with some third-party tools. You can then import it into Director as a Flash member. See Chapter 8, "Controlling Flash Members," for more information on controlling Flash video and animation with Lingo.

- You can use cue points with QuickTime movies with the same Lingo you use for sound channel cue points: `cuePointNames`, `cuePointTimes`, and so on. Creating cue points for your video is another matter and depends on the capability of your QuickTime authoring software for adding text tracks to the movie.

9

10

CREATING MIAWS AND CONTROLLING THE DIRECTOR ENVIRONMENT

IN THIS CHAPTER

USING MIAWS

Movies in a window, usually referred to as MIAWs (often pronounced "meow," as in the sound a cat makes), are an unusual part of Director. They enable you to open other windows, besides the Stage, that contain Director movies.

You can control MIAWs, and the Stage, with various handlers and commands. You can also use some global properties to find out about the computer the movie is running on and change aspects of movie playback.

MIAWs have many uses. Because they play independently of each other and of the Stage, they are useful for functions that don't fit into the Stage's window. You can create your own custom dialog boxes or message windows with MIAWs. You can even create your own application using several different windows, just as Director and almost every other professional computer application does.

MIAW Lingo can be simple or complex. If you just want to open a window to display some information, only a few lines of code are needed. On the other hand, an entire set of commands, functions, properties, and special event handlers exist to support further use of MIAWs. In any case, you first need to create a MIAW, which is covered in the following section.

Creating a MIAW

To use MIAWs, you first need to have another movie file besides your main movie. When you want to create a small window, the Stage size for the MIAW movie should be set accordingly. The default size of the MIAW's window will be the same size as the MIAW's movie Stage size. Save that file as `miaw.dir` and open another new movie. You can actually use the Message panel to show the MIAW.

```
open window("miaw")
```

This opens the movie in a separate window. This window is not another Stage window in Director, but is a movie playback window. You cannot move sprites around in it, view its Score, or do anything with this window except watch it play back.

You can also open a new MIAW with a series of commands. You can assign the MIAW to a variable and use that variable to reference the MIAW in your Lingo code.

```
miaw = window("My MIAW")
miaw.filename = "miaw.dir"
miaw.visible = TRUE
```

The new window is created and assigned to the variable *miaw*. It is then linked to a movie file. Finally, it is shown by setting the `visible` property to TRUE.

This window shows a title of "Test MIAW." The global variable that is created, *miaw*, holds the reference to that window. You can get its value:

```
put miaw
-- (window "My MIAW")
```

You can refer to this MIAW using both the global variable and the structure `window("My MIAW")`. To close and remove that MIAW, you can also use the Message panel:

```
close(miaw)
forget(miaw)
```

A handler that opens a MIAW for you looks similar to the preceding Message panel code. Here is that handler, and one that closes the MIAW:

```
on startMIAW
 global gTestMIAW
 gTestMIAW = window("Test MIAW")
 gTestMIAW.filename = "miaw.dir"
 gTestMIAW.visible = TRUE
end

on endMIAW
 global gTestMIAW
 close(gTestMIAW)
 forget(gTestMIAW)
end
```

Notice that closing a MIAW takes two commands. The first, `close`, actually just makes the window invisible. The second command, `forget`, erases it from memory. If you issue only the first command, the MIAW is still there, taking up memory—it is just invisible. It can cause potential problems if you plan on using more MIAWs later.

➪ *If you are having trouble debugging MIAW movie Lingo, see "Early Testing for MIAW Code" in the "Troubleshooting" section at the end of this chapter.*

➪ *For more information about MIAWs, see "Creating MIAW Xtras," p. 615.*

MIAW Properties

The simple example described in the preceding section shows some of the basic properties of a MIAW. It has the `filename` and the `visible` property. Table 10.1 is a complete list of the MIAW properties.

Table 10.1   MIAW Properties

Property	Description
drawRect	This powerful property can be used to scale the MIAW, including bitmaps in it.
filename	The filename that corresponds to the Director movie used for the MIAW. If the computer is connected to the Internet, a URL can be used.
modal	When this property of a window is set to TRUE, the window takes over all input and prevents other windows, including the Stage, from receiving clicks or key presses until the MIAW is gone or the modal is set to FALSE.
name	The name of the MIAW. This is used as a default title for the window, and used to refer to the MIAW with the window structure.
rect	This property enables you to crop or expand the MIAW, with no scaling.

10

Table 10.1   Continued

Property	Description
sourceRect	Returns the original coordinates for the MIAW, before changes were made to the drawRect or the rect.
title	Can be used to override the name of the window in the visible title bar.
titleVisible	This determines whether the MIAW shows the title bar.
visible	Determines whether the window is visible or hidden. Even hidden windows can execute Lingo code.
windowType	You can set this to -1, 0, 1, 2, 3, 4, 5, 8, 12, 16, or 49. Tables 10.2 and 10.3 show what is included with each type.

Tables 10.2 and 10.3 show you which elements are visible in which window types. Note the slight differences between windows on Macs and PCs. Windows in Windows have a maximize button. Windows on Macs have a stretch box and a resize box.

MIAWs can position themselves differently for different screen sizes. Be sure to test your MIAWs with different monitor settings and adjust the rect property accordingly.

Table 10.2   MIAW Types for Windows

Type Number	Description	Movable	Close Box	Maximize	Minimize
0	Standard	Yes	Yes	No	No
1	Alert Box	No	No	No	No
2	Rectangle	No	No	No	No
3	Rectangle	No	No	No	No
4	Document	Yes	Yes	No	No
5	Document	Yes	Yes	No	No
8	Document	Yes	Yes	Yes	No
12	Document	Yes	Yes	Yes	No
16	Document	Yes	Yes	No	No
49	Palette (not in projectors)	Yes	Yes	No	No

Table 10.3   MIAW Types for Mac

Type Number	Description	Movable	Close Box	Stretch Box	Resize Box
0	Standard	Yes	Yes	Yes	No
1	Alert Box	No	No	No	No
2	Rectangle	No	No	No	No
3	Rectangle with Drop Shadow	No	No	No	No

Table 10.3   Continued

Type Number	Description	Movable	Close Box	Stretch Box	Resize Box
4	Document	Yes	Yes	No	No
5	Document	Yes	No	No	No
8	Document	Yes	Yes	Yes	Yes
12	Document	Yes	Yes	No	Yes
16	Curved Border Box	Yes	Yes	No	No
49	Palette (not in projectors)	Yes	Yes	No	No

Although Tables 10.2 and 10.3 give you a good idea of what each window type should look like, keep in mind that the look is determined both by your Director version and the version of your operating system. A window type looks different in Mac OS 9 than it does in Mac OS X and different in Windows 98 than it does in Windows XP.

Test your MIAWs on both platforms, and in various versions of operating systems (Windows 95 and 98, for instance), to make sure that they look okay.

Window Commands

open, close, and forget are the primary commands used with MIAWs. Two others, moveToFront and moveToBack, however, are designed to work when more than one MIAW is open at once. Some additional commands enable MIAWs to talk to the Stage and to each other. The important window commands are described in Table 10.4.

Table 10.4   MIAW Commands

Command	Description
open	Creates a new MIAW and returns a reference to it.
close	Makes a MIAW invisible, although the MIAW is actually still present.
forget	Unloads the MIAW from memory.
moveToFront	Takes the MIAW and makes it the frontmost window.
moveToBack	Takes the MIAW and places it behind all others.
tell	Sends a Lingo command or handler call to a MIAW. It can also be used to direct a set of Lingo commands to a MIAW.

MIAWs and the Stage use the tell command to communicate. You can use it to send a single command like this:

```
tell window("Test MIAW") to myHandler
```

You can also send a whole set of lines to the MIAW:

```
tell window("Test MIAW")
  myHandler
  myOtherHandler
  go to frame "x"
end tell
```

MIAW System Properties

In addition to the individual window properties available in Lingo, some system properties relate to windows. Table 10.5 is a complete list of properties that tell you which windows are present, which window is active, and which window is at the front.

Table 10.5 MIAW System Properties

Property	Description
the windowList	Returns a list of all the current MIAWs, including ones that are invisible. If no windows are present, it returns an empty list.
the activeWindow	Returns a reference to the currently active window. If the Stage is the active window, "(the stage)" is returned.
the frontWindow	Returns a reference to the frontmost window. If this is the Stage, "(the stage)" is returned.
windowPresent( )	This function, when given a string with a window name, tells you whether a window with that name is present. It works only with window names, not window references in variables.

You can get good use out of the windowList property by creating a script that closes any and all MIAWs. It determines the number of windows from the windowList and then closes and forgets all the windows, as follows:

```
on closeAllMIAWs
 n = count(the windowList)
 repeat with i = 1 to n
  close window(1)
  forget window(1)
 end repeat
end
```

MIAW Event Handlers

MIAWs can also use many special event handlers. They involve typical window events, such as opening, closing, and moving the window.

Each of these handlers can be used in movie scripts in the MIAW's Director movie. Table 10.6 is a complete list.

Table 10.6 MIAW Handlers

Handler	Description
on activateWindow	This handler is called when the window is not currently the active one and users click it to make it active.
on activateApplication	If the projector is sent to the background or minimized, and then activated again, this handler is called in the main movie and in all the MIAWs.

Table 10.6   Continued

Handler	Description
on closeWindow	This handler is called when users use the close box to close the window, or when the window is closed with the close command.
on deactivateWindow	This handler is called when the window is the active one, and users click another window, thus making this one inactive.
on deactivateApplication	If the projector is sent to the background or minimized, this handler is called in the main movie and all MIAWs.
on moveWindow	This handler is called every time the MIAW is dragged around the screen by users. The call comes when users release the mouse button.
on openWindow	This handler is called immediately after the MIAW opens for the first time.
on resizeWindow	This handler is called whenever users use the corner or sides of the window to resize it.
on zoomWindow	This handler is called whenever users click a zoom, maximize, or minimize box.

CREATING CUSTOM DIALOG BOXES

With MIAWs, you don't have to be stuck with plain, ordinary alert boxes and dialog boxes. After all, if the artwork on your Stage is strange and unusual, why should your dialog boxes look like standard Mac and Windows interfaces? Instead, you can use the window properties and event handlers to construct your own custom dialog boxes and alert boxes. This section shows you how.

Confirmation Dialog Boxes

Confirmation dialog boxes usually ask a yes or no question. In most programs, yes or no is usually expressed as OK and Cancel. However, you can make them anything you want with MIAWs.

Figure 10.1 shows the Stage with a MIAW confirmation dialog box. It is simply a normal MIAW, like the one used in the example earlier in this chapter. The windowType has been set so that the window is a nonmovable rectangle. The modal property has been set to TRUE so that users must interact with it.

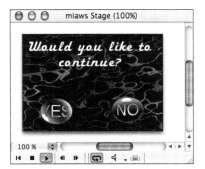

Figure 10.1
Out-of-the-ordinary dialog boxes can be easily created with MIAWs.

The following script opens this MIAW with the correct window type and modal:

```
on mouseUp
  global gFunkyDialog
  gFunkyDialog = window("Funky Dialog")
  gFunkyDialog.filename = "24funkydialog.dir"
  gFunkyDialog.windowType = 1
  gFunkyDialog.modal = TRUE
  gFunkyDialog.visible = TRUE
end
```

Inside the MIAW, the two buttons can be wired up with code that closes the dialog box and also tells the Stage what to do. For instance, here is the code for the Yes button:

```
on mouseUp
  close(the activeWindow)
  forget(the activeWindow)
  tell (the Stage) to continueYes
end
```

The handler *on continueYes* should be in the main movie. You can also have an *on continueNo* that is called by the No button.

In the preceding script, the activeWindow is used as a convenient way to determine which MIAW to close. After all, if the user is clicking it, it should be the active window. Using this function is more convenient than passing a global variable around.

Alert Dialog Boxes

Alert dialog boxes are as simple as MIAWs get. However, you might want to create a MIAW that can handle many types of alerts. To do this, you can use a command to place different pieces of text in a field in the MIAW so that it shows a different message each time. Figure 10.2 shows such a dialog box.

Figure 10.2
MIAWs can be used to create custom alert boxes.

A handler that creates such a MIAW could look like this:

```
on mouseUp
  global gAlertBox
  gAlertBox = window("Alert Box")
  gAlertBox.filename = "24alertbox.dir"
```

```
gAlertBox.windowType = 4
gAlertBox.modal = TRUE

tell gAlertBox
 member("Text").text = "The Jundland wastes are not to be traveled lightly."
end tell

gAlertBox.visible = TRUE
end
```

This code is just like the other handlers that open MIAWs, but the `tell` command is used to change the text in a field in the MIAW. This is done just before the MIAW is made visible so that users don't see the change.

Text Input Dialog Boxes

Another type of MIAW dialog box asks users for more information. You can have radio buttons, check boxes, and even text input fields in these input dialog boxes.

Following is an example of a MIAW that asks users to type their names. Figure 10.3 shows what this dialog box might look like. The field in the middle is a simple editable text field member.

Figure 10.3
MIAWs can gather information through text input and other interface devices.

The MIAW in the main movie is created in the same way as the other MIAWs. However, the code executed when users click the OK button is a little more complex. It takes the text in the field and passes it back to the Stage through a `tell` command:

```
on mouseUp
 text = member("Text Input").text
 close(the activeWindow)
 forget(the activeWindow)
 tell (the Stage) to textInputDone(text)
end
```

The code for the Cancel button is similar, but this button is intended to pass just a VOID constant back rather than text. Then, the main movie handles the input with something like this:

```
on textInputDone text
 if text = VOID then
  put "Cancelled."
 else
  put "Text Entered:"&&text
 end if
end
```

Of course, in real life, *on textInputDone* is likely to store the user's name in a variable or place it in a field. It probably also uses a go command to proceed to the next part of the movie.

CREATING ODDLY SHAPED MIAWS

A hidden feature of Director is its capability to create oddly shaped MIAWs. This was first revealed to developers at the 1999 Macromedia Conference in San Francisco, and then the information spread over the Internet.

Creating oddly shaped windows is an important feature because applications, such as MP3 players and games, use nonrectangular shapes for their windows. Director developers can do this easily.

To create an oddly shaped MIAW, simply set its windowType to a 1-bit bitmap member. This member will then be used as a mask to create the shape of the window.

```
gMyMIAW.windowType = member("MIAW Mask")
```

If you try this in Director, however, it won't work. This function works only in projectors. So, to test your oddly shaped MIAW, you need to build a projector first.

Figure 10.4 shows an oddly shaped MIAW. You can even shape the MIAW to have gaps and holes.

Figure 10.4
An oddly shaped MIAW can be used to create interesting interfaces.

OTHER USES FOR MIAWS

Confirmation dialog boxes, alert boxes, and input dialog boxes are just three of the many possible uses for MIAWs. Just about anything you can do in Director, you can do in MIAWs, so the sky's the limit.

Some developers use MIAWs as the primary screen in projectors. They make the Stage as small as possible, and even stick it out of the monitor's screen area, perhaps at a negative horizontal and vertical location. This way, you can have a movable window as the main screen, even in Mac projectors, which insist on a nonmovable rectangular window for the Stage.

Some other uses for MIAWs include

- A Shockwave player—Because you can use Internet locations as well as filenames for MIAWs, why not open up some Shockwave content in your projectors this way?

- Hyperlinks—In educational programs, MIAWs can be used as glossary windows or windows with additional information. Use hyperlinks in text members to activate them.

- Multiple movies—If you need to have more than one movie playing at a time, you can do so with a single projector that opens two MIAWs.

- Debugging—You can have a MIAW that contains extra information about the main movie that is meant for your eyes only. It can be updated with the `tell` command. When the project is done, just remove the MIAW or make it invisible.

- Stage overlay—If you create a plain rectangle MIAW, it can be placed on top of the Stage, and users won't even know it's a separate window. You can use this to place animation or other external pieces in your movies.

USING LINKED DIRECTOR MOVIES

An alternative to the stage overlay idea is to use linked movies rather than MIAWs. A *linked Director movie* (*LDM*), is simply a cast member that has been imported into the main movie. The linked movie can be placed on the Stage, and users won't know it's a separate movie. The Score and Cast for this linked movie still exist as independent files, but they are represented in your main movie as members.

After you have such a member, you can place it on the Stage and position it. You can even animate its position over a series of frames.

To create an LDM, you need to create an independent movie, just as you would with a MIAW. Then you need to import the movie into your larger movie, but with the Link to External File option selected in the Import dialog box. If you forget to choose this option, the movie will be imported as a film loop rather than an LDM.

> The difference between a linked movie and a film loop is that all the scripts in the linked movie are still active and working. In a film loop, only behaviors and some other scripts work. Film loops are meant more for animation, whereas linked movies are for more complex interactive movies.

The movies `ldm.dir` and `ldmdrag.dir` on this book's CD-ROM are an example of an LDM in action. The `ldm.dir` movie is a small movie that contains a few screen elements and looks like a small dialog box. You can see it in Figure 10.5. It includes a title, a scrolling text member, and a small close button at the upper-right.

Figure 10.5
This linked Director movie can be imported and used inside a larger movie.

The `ldm.dir` movie is then imported into the `ldmdrag.dir` movie as an LDM. This LDM only takes up one cast member in the Cast and only one sprite on the Stage.

The example makes the LDM a draggable element. To do this, a simple drag behavior is attached.

```
property pPressed, pOffset

on beginSprite me
 pPressed = FALSE
end

-- start drag
on mouseDown me
 pPressed = TRUE
 pOffset = sprite(me.spriteNum).loc - the clickLoc
 pass
end

-- end drag
on mouseUp me
 pPressed = FALSE
end
on mouseUpOutside me
 pPressed = FALSE
end

on exitFrame me
 if pPressed then
  -- drag, with offset
  sprite(me.spriteNum).loc = the mouseLoc + pOffset
 end if
end
```

Inside the LDM, we need to create a script for the close button. This presents some challenges, how-ever. Scripting inside LDMs is different than scripting in normal movies because LDMs cannot han-dle mouse messages correctly. For instance, mouseEnter and mouseLeave messages are passed to on mouseEnter and on mouseLeave scripts, but the commands in those scripts cannot reference members inside the LDM. There's no reason for this; it is simply a bug in how LDMs work. Additionally, mouseDown and mouseUp messages are not passed into LDM movies if on mouseDown or on mouseUp handlers are attached to the sprite containing the LDM. There are some other problems with LDM mouse messages as well.

Fortunately, it is possible to write an adequate button behavior without these messages. Here is the close button behavior inside the LDM:

```
property pOver, pPressed

on beginSprite me
 -- start button not over and not pressed
 pOver = TRUE
 pPressed = FALSE
end
```

```
on exitFrame me
 -- if over the button
 if rollover(me.spriteNum) then

  -- not previously over, so change state
  if not pOver then
   pOver = TRUE
   pPressed = FALSE
   sprite(me.spriteNum).member = member("close rollover")
  end if

  if the mouseDown then
   -- remember if mouse is down
   pPressed = TRUE

  else if pPressed = TRUE then
   -- mouse is now up, but was down, so close
   tell the stage
    sendSprite(0,#closeGlossary)
   end tell
  end if

 else if pOver then
  -- mouse was over, but now it is not
  pOver = FALSE
  sprite(me.spriteNum).member = member("close normal")
 end if
end
```

When the user clicks on the close button, the handler on `closeGlossary` in the main movie's frame script is called. LDMs use `tell` commands just like MIAWs. So you can call movie handlers or use `sendSprite` commands inside `tell` statements. In this example, we could have used `sendSprite` to send a command directly to the LDM sprite, but there's no good way of knowing which sprite number to use. So instead the command is sent to the frame behavior, which handles the command.

Back in the main movie, `ldmdrag.dir`, the frame script has a on `closeGlossary` handler. It also has a `showGlossary` handler, which can be used to display the LDM along with new text. Notice that in this case the `tell` command is used with a sprite. This is a special case for the `tell` command, which is usually used to address other MIAWs.

> LDMs and the main movie share the same global variable space. So a global set in the main movie will be accessible by scripts in the LDM as well.

```
on exitFrame me
 go to the frame
end

on closeGlossary me
 -- hide the LDM
 sprite(5).visible = FALSE
end
```

```
on showGlossary me, def
  -- show the LDM
  sprite(5).visible = TRUE

  -- put new text into member
  tell sprite(5)
    member("term").text = def
  end tell
end
```

One last thing you need to know about LDMs is that they have their own tab in the Property Inspector. Figure 10.6 shows this tab. Make sure that Loop and Enable Scripts are both checked for scripts to work properly.

Figure 10.6
The Property Inspector with the Linked Movie (LDM) properties tab shown.

10

Try the movie `ldmdrag.dir`. LDM sprites are not opaque rectangles, even when they are set to Copy ink. So transparent areas in the LDM will be transparent when it is on the Stage. The example movie takes advantage of this by using a background sprite set to 80% blend. So when you drag the LDM over a colored area, you can see a little bit of the main movie's background show through.

USING MUI XTRA DIALOG BOXES

The MUI (pronounced "moo-ee") Xtra that comes with Director is used by various parts of the authoring environment to create dialog boxes similar to the ones that behaviors bring up when dropped onto a sprite. MUI stands for Macromedia User Interface, which is a set of guidelines that Macromedia follows for all its software products.

Macromedia also provides a straight Lingo interface for this Xtra, which enables you to create some standard and custom dialog boxes. All the elements in the dialog boxes look like Macromedia standard interface elements, but that is not necessarily a bad thing. Macromedia has created a good set of cross-platform elements that look like standard dialog boxes.

There are actually five ways to call the MUI Xtra. The first four represent some standard dialog box types: file open, file save, get URL, and an alert. The alert box is customizable. The fifth way to call the MUI Xtra is to create a custom dialog box from scratch.

Creating a File Open Dialog Box

Creating a file open dialog box is simple. All you need to do is create an instance of the Xtra, use its `FileOpen` method to generate the dialog box, and then retrieve its results. The following handler does just that:

```
on muiFileOpen
 gMUI = new(xtra "mui")
 filename = FileOpen(gMUI,the pathname)
 gMUI = 0
 return filename
end
```

> *If Director is crashing often when using MUI dialogs, see "Errors in MUI Xtra Code Can Cause Crashes"*
> *in the "Troubleshooting" section at the end of this chapter.*

The only other parameter for `FileOpen` is the default pathname of the file. The function returns the resulting filename. After that, you should dispose of the Xtra instance by setting it to VOID or 0. Figure 10.7 shows an example of a file open dialog box created on the Mac.

Figure 10.7
The file open dialog box created with the MUI Xtra.

Creating a File Save Dialog Box

The `FileSave` method for the MUI Xtra works similarly. You need to give it two parameters: the default name for the file and a piece of text to be displayed in the dialog box.

```
on muiFileSave
 gMUI = new(xtra "mui")
 filename = FileSave(gMUI,"myfile", "Save Game")
 gMUI = 0
 return filename
end
```

The `FileSave` command returns the pathname to the location of the file to be created. Figure 10.8 shows an example.

Figure 10.8
The file save dialog box created with the MUI Xtra.

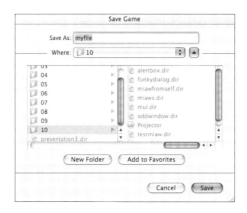

Creating a Get URL Dialog Box

The GetURL method displays a dialog box with the name Open URL. You can specify a default location, and whether the dialog box is movable, as shown in the following code. Figure 10.9 shows an example.

```
on muiGetURL
  gMUI = new(xtra "mui")
  default = "http://clevermedia.com"
  moveable = TRUE
  filename = GetURL(gMUI, default, moveable)
  gMUI = 0
  return filename
end
```

Figure 10.9
The Open URL dialog box created with the MUI Xtra.

Creating Alert Boxes

Creating alert boxes is much more complex because so many more options are available. This handler creates the alert box shown in Figure 10.10. It is a simple alert with a caution icon and an OK button.

```
on muiAlert
  gMUI = new(xtra "mui")
  list = [:]
  addProp list, #buttons, #Ok
  addProp list, #default, 1
  addProp list, #title, "Alert!"
  addProp list, #message, "The Jundland wastes are not to be traveled lightly."
  addProp list, #icon, #caution
  addProp list, #moveable, FALSE
  res = Alert(gMUI,list)
```

```
gMUI = 0
return res
end
```

Figure 10.10
A simple alert dialog box created with the MUI Xtra.

As you can see in the handler, a list is passed into the `Alert` function. This list contains various options that describe how the alert box is to look.

The first property, `#buttons`, can be set to `#OK`, `#OKCancel`, `#AbortRetryIgnore`, `#YesNoCancel`, `#YesNo`, or `#RetryCancel`. Each of these options determines how many buttons the alert box has, and what they are named.

The `#default` property determines which of the buttons is the default one. This button looks different from the others and also reacts to a (Return) [Enter] key press.

The `#title` property enables you to customize the label in the title bar of the alert dialog box. The `#message` and `#icon` properties enable you to determine the contents of the box. Additional options for `#icon` are `#stop`, `#note`, `#caution`, `#question`, or `#error`.

The `#moveable` property enables you to determine whether the alert dialog box is movable.

This type of dialog box returns the number of the button pressed. So, if the buttons are `#OKCancel`, it can return a 1 or a 2.

Creating Custom MUI Dialog Boxes

Custom MUI dialog boxes are even more complex than alert boxes because you can specify every aspect of the window as well as the interface elements inside it.

The best way to learn how to use the custom dialog boxes is to take a look at an example. But even a short example has a lot of Lingo lines associated with it. Figure 10.11 shows a simple custom dialog box that the following handler creates.

Figure 10.11
A custom handler dialog box created with the MUI Xtra.

```
on muiCustom
  global gMUI
  gMUI = new(xtra "mui")
```

Next, the properties for the window must be defined. Instead of requiring you to build the lengthy window properties list from scratch, the MUI Xtra enables you to get a copy of a default property list with the `getWindowPropList` function. This default list contains all the properties needed to define a window, plus their default settings. So, all you have to do is change the settings for the properties you want to alter:

```
windowProps = getWindowPropList(gMUI)
windowProps.type = #normal
windowProps.name = "Custom MUI Dialog"
windowProps.callback = "myCallbackHandler"
windowProps.width = 160
windowProps.height = 230
windowProps.mode = #pixel
```

In this case, the name, callback handler, width, height, and mode of the window were changed. The callback handler is the name of the movie handler called each time the dialog box is touched by users. The mode can be set to `#data`, `#dialogUnit`, or `#pixel`. The `#data` option attempts to do the layout of the dialog box for you, whereas `#dialogUnit` and `#pixel` enable you to specify locations for items.

After the window properties are set, you need to start creating interface elements to be added to the dialog box. Create a list to which these items should be added:

```
list = []
```

Now you can create your first element. Like the window properties, the element properties are so complex that the MUI Xtra includes a special function, `getItemPropList`, which returns a default item property list. Customize this list to become a specific interface element. The following is a label element:

```
element = getItemPropList(gMui)
element.type = #label
element.value = "What size burger do you want?"
element.locH = 10
element.locV = 10
element.width = 140
element.height = 40
add list, element
```

Next, you can add a pop-up menu. This element needs a special `#attributes` property that includes some information specific to that interface element type:

```
element = getItemPropList(gMui)
element.type = #popupList
element.locH = 10
element.locV = 45
element.width = 140
element.height = 20
element.attributes = \
 [#popupStyle: #tiny, #valueList: ["Small", "Medium", "Large"]]
add list, element
```

After another label, the three check boxes can be added:

```
element = getItemPropList(gMui)
element.type = #label
element.value = "What do you want with your burger?"
element.locH = 10
element.locV = 70
element.width = 140
element.height = 40
add list, element

element = getItemPropList(gMui)
element.type = #checkBox
element.title = "Fries"
element.locH = 10
element.locV = 110
element.width = 140
element.height = 20
add list, element

element = getItemPropList(gMui)
element.type = #checkBox
element.title = "Chips"
element.locH = 10
element.locV = 140
element.width = 140
element.height = 20
add list, element

element = getItemPropList(gMui)
element.type = #checkBox
element.title = "Onion Rings"
element.locH = 10
element.locV = 170
element.width = 140
element.height = 20
add list, element
```

The last element needed is the OK button:

```
element = getItemPropList(gMui)
element.type = #defaultPushButton
element.title = "OK"
element.locH = 40
element.locV = 200
element.width = 80
element.height = 20
add list, element
```

After all the elements are ready, a call to `Initialize` creates the dialog box. You need to pass it the window properties and the element properties. Then, use `Run` to create the dialog box.

```
Initialize(gMUI, [#windowPropList: windowProps, #windowItemList: list])
Run(gMUI)
end
```

Unlike the other MUI dialog boxes, a custom dialog box does not return a simple value. Instead, it uses the callback handler defined to send any activity information. It sends every click or item change. It passes this information back as three parameters: what happened, which item it affected, and the property list for that item.

The following handler receives these messages. It is a simple handler that just sends messages to the Message panel:

```
on myCallbackHandler action, elementNumber, elementList
 global gMUI
 put "Action Reported:"&&action
 if action = #itemClicked and elementList.title = "OK" then
  put action, elementList.title
  put gMUI
  Stop(gMUI,0)
  gMUI = VOID

 else if action = #itemChanged then
  newval = elementList.value
  itemName = elementList.title
  put itemName&&"changed to"&&newval
 end if
end
```

In real life, you should record the information provided to this handler in global variables or fields. Each time an item is changed, you can record the change. Or, you can reference the values of all the interface elements through the gMUI global.

The scope of custom MUI dialog boxes does not end with pop-ups, labels, and check boxes. You can have radio buttons, sliders, bitmaps, editable text fields, dividers, and other types of buttons as well.

To see all the possibilities, try this in the Message panel:

```
put interface(xtra "Mui")
```

You will see a huge listing of all the possibilities in the MUI dialog box. This listing is also the most up-to-date one. The MUI Xtra is constantly being updated by Macromedia to accommodate new needs in the software. Just about every update of Director has a slightly different MUI Xtra.

> The MUI Dialog Xtra was not designed for developers to use. Instead, it was made for Macromedia to use for future Director and Xtra development. It's an advanced technique and should not be attempted by beginners. This Xtra is also not fully supported by Macromedia.

USING MENUS

When you create a projector, it runs inside a plain window. On the Mac, it's a simple rectangle. In Windows, it looks like a typical window, but without a menu bar. To make your projector look and act more like a normal program, you have to add a menu bar.

Creating Menus

You can add a menu bar to any projector with the `installMenu` command. This command places the standard Mac menu bar at the top of the screen on Macs, but only with the items you specify. In Windows, it places a standard menu bar at the top of the projector's window.

While you are authoring, the `installMenu` command replaces Director's menu bar from the time the command is issued until the movie stops. This makes it easy to test. In Shockwave, `installMenu` has no effect.

To use `installMenu`, you first need to create a field cast member that contains the menu description. Here are the typical contents of such a field:

```
menu: @
menu: File
Open/O|myOpenHandler
(-
Quit/Q|halt
menu: Edit
Cut(
Copy(
Paste(
Clear(
menu: Navigation
Main Menu/M|go to frame "main"
Chapter 1/1|go to frame "one"
Chapter 2/2|go to frame "two"
Chapter 3/3|go to frame "three"
```

The first line of this text, `menu: @`, tells Director to place the Apple menu, with all its contents, in the menu bar. This is for Macs only. In Windows, this command results in a small menu labeled with a block character.

The second line creates a menu labeled File. The next three lines place three items in this menu. The first is the Open item. The character after the forward slash is the command key shortcut. So, [cmd]+O on the Mac or Ctrl+O in Windows acts as a shortcut for selecting this menu item. After the vertical bar, created while holding down the Shift and the backslash (\) key, is the Lingo command that will execute. In this case, it's a custom movie handler called on `myOpenHandler`.

Don't forget that adding an Apple menu on the Mac means that a Windows projector will have a strange menu added as well. You might want to keep separate Mac and Windows menu description fields. In Windows, place any About menu item in the traditional Help menu rather than in the Apple menu.

The next line, a simple (-, places a dividing line in the menu. The third item in the menu is Quit, which uses "Q" as a shortcut and executes the Lingo `halt` command.

The next menu is the Edit menu. All the items in this menu are grayed out, or inactive, and made so by the (added to the end of each line.

The last menu is called Navigation and contains four lines that take users to four different frames. The resulting menu looks like the one shown in Figure 10.12.

Figure 10.12
This custom menu was created with a field member and the `installMenu` command.

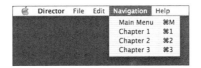

To actually use this menu, you must specify its member in the `installMenu` command. A likely place for this is the on `startMovie` handler:

```
on startMovie
  installMenu member("menu")
end
```

All the special characters in the menu field can be confusing. There are actually a lot more of them. Table 10.7 lists them all and describes what each one does.

You should include File and Edit menus every time you make custom menus. Almost all programs use them, even when the commands in them are grayed out. Having the menus there provides user interface consistency.

Table 10.7　Menu Definition Symbols

Symbol	Example	Description
@	menu: @	Creates the Apple menu on the Mac, complete with the existing Apple menu items.
!v	!vMusic	Places a check mark next to an item
<B	Copy<B	Sets the item to bold
<I	Copy<I	Sets the item to italic
<U	Copy<U	Sets the item to underlined
<O	Copy<O	Sets the item to outlined
<S	Shadow	Sets the item to shadow styled
|	Quit|halt	Associates a Lingo handler or command with the item
/	Quit/Q	Adds a [cmd]/Ctrl key shortcut
(	Copy(	Grays out the item and makes it unselectable
(-	(-	Creates a dividing line in the menu

The styling items listed in Table 10.7 (such as bold, italic, and so on) are available on the Mac only. Windows menus do not accommodate this sort of styling.

Controlling Menus

You can also use Lingo commands to control the custom menu after it has been created by the `installMenu` command. The menu bar itself is treated like an object and is referred to by the keyword menu and the name or number of the menu. For instance, to get the name of the second menu from the left:

> Double-check the text in your menu description fields if you are having trouble. The `installMenu` command is literal and does not forgive many mistakes.

```
put the name of menu 2
-- "File"
```

Note that you must use the old syntax with a `the` rather than dot syntax. The menu functionality in Director was not updated with the new version, so the dot syntax is not recognized.

To get the total number of menus in the menu bar, use `the number of menus`:

```
put the number of menus
-- 4
```

You can also get the name of any menu item in a menu by using the `menuitem` keyword:

```
put the name of menuitem 1 of menu 4
-- "Main Menu"
```

As you might expect, you can use `the number of menuitems` to get the total number of items of any menu. The next example also demonstrates how you can refer to a menu by its name:

```
put the number of menuitems in menu "Navigation"
-- 4
```

You can also set the name of a menu item. However, you cannot set the name of a menu:

```
the name of menuitem 3 of menu 2 = "Exit"
```

Three more properties—the `checkMark`, the `enabled`, and `the script`—enable you to change three other aspects of individual menu items. The the `checkMark` property enables you to place a check mark next to the item. The `the enabled` property enables you to dim an item and make it unusable. The `the script` property enables you to alter the script for an item.

Another method for changing the menu is to update your menu description field by using Lingo string and text member commands and then reapplying `installMenu`.

USING CURSORS

There are three ways to change the cursor in Director. The first is to use the `cursor` command with a built-in cursor. The second way is to use the `cursor` command with one or two bitmaps that represent a black-and-white cursor. The third way is to use the Cursor Xtra to make colored or animated cursors.

Using Built-In Cursors

Using one of the 30 built-in cursors is simple with the `cursor` command. All you need to do is give the `cursor` command one of the cursor numbers to use. For instance, to change the cursor to a watch on the Mac or an hourglass in Windows, use the following:

```
cursor(4)
```

A simple behavior that changes the cursor to a finger when users roll over a sprite looks like this:

```
on mouseEnter me
  cursor(280)
end

on mouseLeave me
  cursor(0)
end
```

Use the cursor number –1 to return control of the cursor to normal. Usually this means that the cursor returns to an arrow.

Table 10.8 shows all the available cursors. Mac and Windows cursors appear slightly different. For instance, the watch cursor appears as an hourglass cursor in Windows. You should test your cursors in a cross-platform environment if consistency is important.

Table 10.8 Cursor Numbers

Cursor Name	Cursor Number
Arrow	–1
I-Beam	1
Crosshair	2
Crossbar	3
Watch/Hourglass	4
Blank	200
Help	254
Finger	280
Hand	260
Closed Hand	290
No Drop Hand	291
Copy Closed Hand	292
Pencil	256
Eraser	257
Select	258
Bucket	259
Lasso	272
Dropper	281

Table 10.8   Continued

Cursor Name	Cursor Number
Air Brush	301
Zoom In	302
Zoom Out	303
Vertical Size	284
Horizontal Size	285
Diagonal Size	286
White Arrow (Mac)	293
Black Arrow with white outline (Windows)	293
Magnify	304
Wait Mouse 1 (Mac)	282
Wait Mouse 2 (Mac)	283

10

Using Custom Bitmap Cursors

The second way to create cursors is to use bitmaps. With bitmaps you can define the cursor any way you want, as long as it is black-and-white and static.

The key to doing this is to create two bitmap members. Each member should be no more than 16×16 pixels in size, and be 1 bit in bit depth. The first member is the actual cursor. The second member is the mask for the cursor. In that second member, the black pixels are the mask for the cursor, whereas the white pixels are transparent.

The two bitmaps should line up with each other according to their registration points. The location of the registration point is the actual hot spot of the cursor, so be careful where you place it. Figure 10.13 shows two Paint windows, one with the cursor and one with the mask.

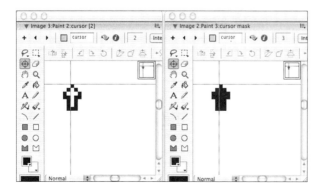

Figure 10.13
Two Paint windows show each of the two parts of a custom cursor. The registration points show the hot spot for the cursor.

After you have these two members, you can use the cursor command, as before, but with a list as the parameter:

```
cursor([member "cursor", member "cursor mask"])
```

If the bitmaps are not 1 bit, or a member name is wrong, the cursor command simply does nothing.

Using the Cursor Xtra

The Cursor Xtra enables you to build custom cursors from one or more 8-bit color bitmaps. The way you create this type of cursor is by using the Cursor Properties Editor, shown in Figure 10.14. You can get this dialog box by double-clicking a cursor member in the Cast.

Figure 10.14
The Cursor Properties Editor enables you to create and modify animated cursors.

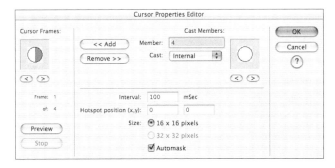

Adding cast members to a cursor is easy. Just use the Cast Members section of the dialog box to find the right member, and then use the Add button to add it. You can also set the speed of the animation and the hot spot location. Check the Automask feature if you do not want the cursor to be transparent.

After you have created the cursor, you can use the `cursor` command, but this time with a single cast member as the parameter:

```
cursor(member("Custom Cursor"))
```

⇨ *If you can't seem to get custom cursors to work, see "Cursor Bitmaps Require Specific Bit Depths" in the "Troubleshooting" section at the end of this chapter.*

LEARNING ABOUT THE COMPUTER

Many movie properties can be accessed to tell you something about the computer on which Director, a projector, or a Shockwave applet is currently running. Table 10.9 lists these properties.

Table 10.9 Computer Properties

Property	Description
the platform	Returns either "Macintosh,PowerPC" or "Windows,32" depending on which platform the movie is running on.
the runMode	Returns either "Author", "Projector", "Plugin", or "Java Applet". The first tells you that the movie is running in Director, the second tells you when it is running as a projector, the third option refers to Shockwave, and the fourth tells you when it is running as a Java applet.
the colorDepth	Returns the bit depth of the current monitor being used by the movie. Examples are 8, 16, 24, or 32.

Table 10.9   Continued

Property	Description
the environment	Returns a list of the values for the three preceding properties and many more.
the desktopRectList	Returns a list of rectangles that correspond to the one or more monitors connected to the computer.
quickTimeVersion()	Not a property, but a function that returns the version of QuickTime on the computer. It returns only "2.1.2" if the version is before version 3.0.
version	Not a property either, but actually a persistent global variable automatically created when Director starts. It contains the version number of the Director engine, whether it is Director, a projector, or Shockwave. An example is "9.0".

You can use these properties to make decisions about what the movie should do if users do not have a computer capable of performing the tasks you want. For instance, to test whether the computer is set to 16-bit color or better, you might do this:

Director MX is actually Director 9. MX is the marketing name for the product, but when using properties such as version, the environment, or Shockwave version numbers in HTML, Director MX is referred to as version 9.

```
on startMovie
 if the colorDepth < 16 then
  alert "Please set your monitor to 16-bit."
  halt
 end if
end
```

Or, if you want to make sure that the user's monitor is at least 800 pixels wide, you can test the width of the first item in the desktopRectList. Because most users have only one monitor, and those with two rarely have their primary monitor set smaller than 800 pixels across, this is a good test.

```
on startMovie
 if (the deskTopRectList)[1].width < 800 then
  alert "Please set your monitor to 800 pixels across."
  halt
 end if
end
```

The system property the environment is a list filled with properties that can describe the playback environment (see Table 10.10).

Table 10.10 Properties of the environment

Property	Description
#shockMachine	TRUE if the movie is running in Macromedia's ShockMachine program.
#shockMachineVersion	Contains a string with the version number of ShockMachine. It is an empty string if the movie is not being played in ShockMachine.
#platform	Same as the platform property. Either "Macintosh,PPC" or "Windows,32".
#runMode	Same as the runMode. Either "Author", "Projector", "Plugin", or "Java Applet".
#colorDepth	Same as the colorDepth. Either 1, 2, 4, 8, 16, or 32.
#internetConnected	The value of this is #online if the computer is currently connected to the Internet, and #offline if not.
#uiLanguage	The language being used to display the operating system's user interface.
#osLanguage	The native language of the computer's operating system.
#productBuildVersion	The number of the Director engine build that is being used. This can be used to determine the exact version of Director's engine used in Shockwave or projectors, even if Macromedia releases several versions with the same version number.
#productVersion	This returns a string like "9.0" that lets you know what version of Shockwave the user is running.
#osVersion	This returns a string that corresponds to the official operating system version. For MacOS 9.2, you get "Macintosh OS 9.2.0"; for MacOS 10.2.2, you get "Macintosh OS 10.2.2"; for one version of Windows 98, you get "Windows 98,4,10,148,1, A".

Look for more properties to be added to the environment in updates of Director. For example, several of the previous elements were not present in Director 7.0, but were added in 7.0.2 and Shockwave version 7.0.3.

➪ *For more ways to get information about the user's computer system about, see "Third-Party Xtras,"* *p. 636.*

TELLING TIME

Lingo has several ways to tell the date and time. First is the date property. This system property is a little different, in that you can preface it with the terms short, long, or abbr:

```
put the date
-- "11/20/02"
put the short date
-- "11/20/02"
put the long date
-- "Wednesday, November 20, 2002"
put the abbr date
-- "Wed, Nov 20, 2002"
```

The `abbr` prefix can also be spelled `abbrev` or `abbreviated`. You can use the returned strings as they are, or use chunk expressions to get pieces of them:

```
put (the long date).item[1]
-- "Wednesday"
put (the long date).item[2].word[1]
-- "November"
the itemDelimiter = "/"
put integer((the date).item[2])
-- 20
```

Another property, called `the time`, works similarly. However, only the long prefix makes any difference in the result:

```
put the time
-- "9:18 PM"
put the short time
-- "9:18 PM"
put the long time
-- "9:18:43 PM"
put the abbrev time
-- "9:18 PM"
```

You can also use chunk expressions to get interesting parts of the time:

```
put (the time).word[1]
-- "9:20"
the itemDelimiter = ":"
put integer((the time).word[1].item[2])
-- 20
put integer((the long time).word[1].item[3])
-- 57
```

> The string format of the date depends on your computer's settings. If you check in the control panels in both Macintosh and Windows, you can see that users have many options as to how dates are displayed. Director reflects these preferences in the date.

Although `the time` and `the date` are great for getting ready-to-use strings and occasionally an integer, there is a better way to work with dates. The property `the systemDate` returns a `date` object:

```
put the systemDate
-- date( 2002, 11, 20 )
```

As you might expect, you can extract the year, month, and day properties from this `date` object:

```
d = the systemDate
put d.day
-- 20
put d.year
-- 2002
put d.month
-- 11
```

☞ *If you are using the date and having trouble on some machines, see "Time Formats Vary On Different Machines" in the "Troubleshooting" section at the end of this chapter.*

What is even more impressive about the date object is that you can add integers to it, and it does all the calculations for you. Here are some examples:

```
put the systemDate
-- date( 2002, 11, 20 )
put the systemDate + 1
-- date( 2002, 11, 21 )
d = the systemDate
put d + 10
-- date( 2002, 11, 30 )
put d + 30
-- date( 2002, 12, 20 )
put d + 365*3
-- date( 2005, 11, 19 )
put d - 365
-- date( 2001, 11, 20 )
```

Using the date object, you can perform all sorts of interesting calculations. The following handler computes the number of days since a certain date. Give it your birth date, as a date object, and it computes the number of days you have been alive:

```
on daysAlive birthDate
  t = 0
  repeat while TRUE
    birthDate = birthDate + 1
    t = t + 1
    if birthDate = the systemDate then
      return t
    end if
  end repeat
end
```

In addition to dates and times, the ticks property is very important. This is the amount of time, in 1/60s of a second, since Director, the projector, or the Shockwave applet started.

Although it isn't useful information to display to users, it's useful for timing animation. This short handler creates a pause for two seconds:

> The property the systemDate also includes a hidden property, seconds. You can get (the systemDate).seconds to determine the number of seconds since midnight.

```
on pauseForTwo
  t = the ticks + 120
  repeat while (the ticks < t)
  end repeat
end
```

The property the milliseconds is a more accurate companion of the ticks. This measures the same amount of time, but with thousandths of a second instead.

The newer timed features added from Director 8 and on, such as sound queuing and timeout objects, use milliseconds to measure time rather than ticks. Many digital video properties use milliseconds as well. Because there is no advantage to using the ticks over the milliseconds, it's better to start using the milliseconds even if you have used the ticks in the past.

Another property, called the timer, also uses ticks. The difference between this property and the ticks is that you can use startTimer at any time to reset the timer. This is more of a convenience, rather than an added feature. There's nothing you can do with the timer that you can't do with a variable, some math, and the ticks. The following handler pauses for two seconds, but uses the timer:

```
on pauseForTwo
  startTimer
  repeat while (the timer < 120)
  end repeat
end
```

QUITTING AND SHUTTING DOWN

Director also has the capability to turn itself off. As a matter of fact, on a Mac, it can even turn the computer off. The quit command does just what you would expect: It acts just like choosing File, Quit or Exit from a typical application. The projector instantly quits. In Shockwave, the movie stops.

The quit command works very well; in fact, it works too well. If you issue a quit command while in Director, the command tries to quit Director. This can be annoying while you are authoring.

Instead, use the halt command in place of quit. In Director, the halt command stops the movie. In projectors, the halt command acts just like the quit command and quits the projector.

If you are building a kiosk on a Mac, you might also want to use the restart or shutDown commands. They perform the same actions as the menu items in the Mac Finder's Special menu. You can use these commands to enable a store owner or museum curator to shut down the computer at night, or restart it. This way, users don't have to exit the projector and then use the Finder.

You can also use these commands in association with code that reads the time. This way, you can automatically shut down or restart the computer at a certain time, or after a period of inaction. For example, the following handler shuts down the computer at 9:00 p.m. It can be called periodically from an on exitFrame handler:

```
on checkTimeShutDown
  if the time = "9:00 PM" then
    shutDown
  end if
end
```

TROUBLESHOOTING

Early Testing for MIAW Code

I'm using MIAWs with a lot of code. There seem to be errors in the MIAW's code, and I'm having trouble tracking them down.

Be sure to test all your code in a MIAW while editing that MIAW by itself in Director. If a Lingo error occurs in the code in a MIAW while it is running as a MIAW, Director might return bad information about what is wrong and where the problem is.

Errors in MUI Xtra Code Can Cause Crashes

Director is crashing a lot since I added MUI dialog boxes. Could my MUI dialog box code be causing it?

Errors in MUI Xtra property lists can cause Director to crash. The Xtra was not created with abuse in mind. Save your movies often when you are working with the MUI Xtra. Check your code carefully before running it.

Time Formats Vary On Different Machines

I'm using the date to determine the local time, and some users outside the U.S. are reporting incorrect values. Why doesn't it work for them?

Don't rely on the playback computer using the same time settings as your computer does. Months and days can easily be reversed in the date, and different item delimiters can easily be set by users. Even if the target machines are in the same country, users sometimes play with the settings. Use the systemDate property when you can.

Cursor Bitmaps Require Specific Bit Depths

I'm trying to use custom cursors, but they refuse to work. What could I be doing wrong?

Make sure that any custom cursor cast members conform to the required bit depths. Plain custom cursors need to be 1 bit, and animated cursor members need to be 8 bits. They won't work otherwise.

DID YOU KNOW?

- You can use one MIAW file to create many MIAWs. Just use the `tell` command to make the MIAW go to another frame in the MIAW movie file before making it visible.

- You can use the `drawRect` property to scale the MIAW, including all bitmaps and other scalable sprites. You can use this to display a MIAW as double-pixel size, for instance.

- You can change items in a custom MUI dialog box while the dialog box is on the screen so that you can have a bitmap in the MUI dialog box that changes in reaction to another interface element.

- You can build the menu description field with Lingo. Just use string commands and other string Lingo to create or alter the field, and then use `installMenu` to make the changes take effect. This way, you can have a dynamically changing menu bar.

- If you want a cursor of unusual size, you can simply use cursor number 200 to turn off the cursor, and then a sprite in the highest channel can be set to follow the mouse around. Users won't be able to tell that the sprite is not a cursor; it will behave just like one.

10

ADVANCED PROGRAMMING CONCEPTS

IN THIS PART

11

UNDERSTANDING VARIABLES, OPERATIONS, AND LISTS

IN THIS CHAPTER

USING NUMBER VARIABLES

Data storage in Lingo consists mostly of variables. Variables in Lingo can store any type of value: integers, floating point numbers, strings, or lists. A variable can switch types as easily as it can switch values. So a variable that holds a string one minute can hold a number the next. Let's look at each value type and what Lingo can do with those types.

You learned how Lingo performs simple math functions in Chapter 3, "Writing Lingo Scripts." However, there are many more ways to work with number variables. Lingo has a full set of commands and functions that work with numbers just as any other programming language does.

Performing Operations

You can add, subtract, multiply, and divide numbers and variables. The symbols you use to do this are the +, -, *, and /. The first symbol, the plus sign, is the only one that makes complete sense, because a plus sign is standard notation used for addition.

The dash is used as a substitute for the minus symbol. An asterisk is used as a multiplication symbol. It is used in just about every programming language for this purpose. The forward slash is used in place of the division symbol because a standard keyboard does not include a division character.

To use these operators, apply them to numbers as you would write them on paper. Here are some examples in the Message panel:

```
put 4+5
-- 9
put 7-3
-- 4
put 6*9
-- 54
put 8/2
-- 4
put 9/2
-- 4
```

➡ *If you are getting unexpected results while dividing numbers, see "Numbers Always Seem to Round Down" in the "Troubleshooting" section at the end of this chapter.*

Integers and Floats

Notice that in one of the previous examples, 9 divided by 2 returned a 4. This is because Director here is dealing in integers only. An integer is a number, positive or negative, with no fractional value. Four is an integer. However, 4 1/2, or 4.5, is not.

Numbers that have fractional parts are called *floating point* numbers. This name refers to the way in which the computer stores these values, using a more complex method than how it stores integers. The number 4.5 is a floating point number, or a *float*.

Be aware that floating point numbers include integers. A 4 is an integer and a floating point number. As a floating point number, it is usually written as 4.0. However, 4.5 is a floating point number but not an integer because it has a fractional component.

In Lingo, floating point numbers are always shown with a decimal point. This way, Director can tell the difference between the two types of numbers.

If Director is asked to interpret an operation such as 9/2, it looks at all the numbers involved and determines whether the result should be an integer or a float. In this case, because you are asking it to perform an operation on two integers, it returns an integer. To do this, it drops the fractional component of the number and returns only the integer component. So, 9/2 returns a 4, not a 4.5.

Director does not round when dividing two integers such as these. Instead, the decimal portion is dropped. So, 7/4 returns a 1, not a 2.

You can force Director to return a floating point value by making one of the numbers in the calculation a floating point number. Try this in the Message panel:

```
put 7/4
-- 1
put 7.0/4
-- 1.7500
put 7/4.0
-- 1.7500
put 7.0/4.0
-- 1.7500
```

You can also use two functions to convert back and forth between integers and floats. A function is a piece of Lingo syntax that usually takes one or more values and returns a value. Try this in the Message panel:

```
put 7
-- 7
put float(7)
-- 7.0000
put 7.75
-- 7.7500
put integer(7.25)
-- 7
put integer(7)
-- 7
put integer(7.75)
-- 8
```

These two functions, `integer` and `float`, convert any number value, either integer or floating point, to the type you want. Notice in the example that applying the `integer` function to an integer value does not change it. Also, notice that the integer function rounds numbers. So, a value of 7.75 produces an integer of 8.

You can use these commands on functions inside operations. Try this in the Message panel:

```
put 8/5
-- 1
put float(8)/5
-- 1.6000
put float(8/5)
-- 1.0000
put integer(float(8)/5)
-- 2
```

Notice that the line put float(8)/5 behaves in the same way as put 8.0/5 would. Also notice that the third example returns what appears to be a wrong answer. It says that the floating point result of 8/5 is 1.000. This is because you are asking it to evaluate 8/5 first, before converting it to a floating point number. As the first example shows, the value of 8/5 is 1. So, the line is simply converting a 1 to a 1.000.

The last example shows how you can use the two functions together to perform an operation and get a rounded result. The division returns a floating point number, which is then rounded to an integer with the integer function.

Precedence

These last two examples bring up an interesting topic: order of operations, also called *precedence*. When more than one operation is performed, or a combination of operations and functions, which operation is performed first? Try this in the Message panel:

```
put 5+3
-- 8
put 8*6
-- 48
put 5+3*6
-- 23
```

Add 5 plus 3, and you get 8. Multiply 8 times 6, and you get 48. However, if you try to do that all at once on the same line, you get 23. Why? Well, some multiplication and division operators take precedence over addition and subtraction. So, in the statement 5+3*6, multiplication is evaluated first, and then the addition. Most programming languages work this way.

However, you can override precedence by specifying which operations you want to perform first. To do this, use parentheses to group together operations. Try this in the Message panel:

```
put 5+3*6
-- 23
put (5+3)*6
-- 48
```

The use of parentheses ensures that the addition is performed first, and then the sum is multiplied by 6. You can use multiple layers of parentheses if you need to:

```
put ((5+3)*6+(7-3)*4)*8
-- 512
```

Operations and Variables

Now that you have all the basic functions for math, the next step is to combine this knowledge with the use of variables. Variables used in mathematical operations are interpreted just as numbers were in the preceding examples.

```
myNumber = 5
put myNumber
-- 5
put myNumber+1
-- 6
put myNumber*7
-- 35
put (myNumber+2)*3
-- 21
```

You can also set a variable to be equal to the result of an operation.

```
myNumber = 7+4
put myNumber
-- 11
myNumber = (7+4)*2
put myNumber
-- 22
myNumber = 5
myOtherNumber = 6
mySum = myNumber + myOtherNumber
put mySum
-- 11
```

The last example shows you how one variable can be set to the result of an operation that involves two other variables. Performing operations on variables and storing the results in other variables is common in Lingo and other programming languages. In this case, it's so obvious what the variable contains, that it almost makes more sense to just use the numbers instead. However, in a real program, the variable holds values that change, such as the score of a game or the age of the user.

Functions

In addition to the integer and float functions, many other functions manipulate numbers. Table 11.1 lists these functions and what they do.

Table 11.1   Lingo Math Functions

Function	Description	Example
abs	Returns the absolute value of the number. It basically strips off the negative sign from numbers less than 0.	put abs(-7) -- 7
atan	Returns the arctangent of the number. It uses radians.	put atan(1.0)4 -- 0.785

11

Table 11.1 Continued

Function	Description	Example
cos	Returns the cosine of the number, using radians.	put cos(3.1416) -- -1.0000
exp	Returns the natural logarithm base (2.7183) to the power provided.	put exp(3) put power(2.7183,3) -- 20.0855 -- 20.0859
float	Converts the number of a floating point number.	put float(1) -- 1.0000
integer	Converts the number to an integer with rounding.	put integer(1.2) -- 1.0000
log	Returns the natural log of the number.	put log(10.0) -- 2.3026
mod	Used to perform modulus arithmetic. It limits a number of a range. The limit always starts with 0, and goes up to the specified number.	put 4 mod 3 -- 1
pi	Returns pi. Works as both a constant and a function	put pi() put pi -- 3.1416 -- 3.1416
power	Returns the first number to the power of the second.	put power(5,3) -- 125.0000
sqrt	Returns the square root of the number. If given an integer, it rounds to the nearest integer. If given a float, it returns a float.	put sqrt(9) put sqrt(10.0) -- 3 -- 3.1623
sin	Returns the sine of the number, using radians.	put sin(3.1416) -- 0.0000
tan	Returns the tangent of the number, using radians.	put tan(1.0) -- 1.5574

Trigonometry Functions

Many of these functions are based on trigonometry. Trig functions are useful for defining curved and circular animation paths with Lingo, but are rarely used by anyone but advanced Lingo programmers. Don't worry if you can't remember your high school math class; you probably won't need it for most things.

The sin and cos functions are the most commonly used trig functions. They define the circumference of a circle. Here's how you can understand what they do:

Imagine drawing a circle with a pencil. Start with the rightmost point and draw down and to the left. Eventually, you will reach the bottom of the circle and be going up and to the left. When you reach the leftmost point, you will start moving your pencil up and to the right. Then, when you reach the topmost point, you will start moving down and to the right. When you reach the rightmost point, you will be back where you started and have a perfect circle.

Now imagine placing markers along the circle as you go, just like the mile markers on highways. You start with 0, go to 1, 2, and so on. Imagine that a circle takes just over 6 mile markers to complete. This would be measuring the circumference in radians. If you were to measure it in degrees, it would take exactly 360 degrees to get around the circumference of a circle. But because trig functions in Lingo use radians, we'll stick with them. Figure 11.1 shows these mile markers.

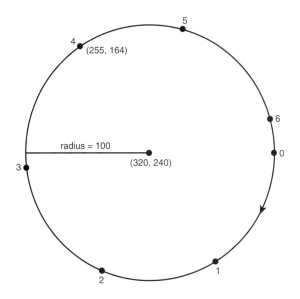

Figure 11.1
A circle marked in radians.

A circle is defined by two facts: the position of the center of a circle and the radius of the circle. The circle in Figure 11.1 is centered at point(320,240) and has a radius of 100.

Now you can locate a point on the edge of the circle by using your mile markers. For instance, one point would be at mile marker 4. However, Director doesn't know where mile marker 4 is; it only knows points: horizontal and vertical locations. So you need to convert mile marker 4 to a point.

This is where sin and cos come in. They take a position along the circumference of a circle and convert it to a screen location. To get the horizontal screen location, you would use cos. The horizontal position of mile marker 4 would be the radius of the circle, times the cos of 4, plus the horizontal center of the circle:

```
x = 100.0 * cos(4.0) + 320
```

Likewise, you can use sin to get the vertical position of the point on the circumference:

```
y = 100.0 * sin(4.0) + 240
```

The result is the point 255,164.

The usefulness of plotting points along a circle is that you can animate sprites along circles with Lingo. All you need to do is to calculate the x and y coordinates as you move along the circumference. So you start at mile marker 0 and move along the edge.

The following behavior does just that. The variable *circPos* starts at 0.0 and moves higher. The cos and sin functions convert *circPos* to a point and then sets the sprite to that location.

```
property circRadius, circCenterX, circCenterY, circPos

on beginSprite me
 circRadius = 100.0
 circCenterX = 320.0
 circCenterY = 240.0
 circPos = 0.0
end

on exitFrame me
 x = circRadius * cos(circPos) + circCenterX
 y = circRadius * sin(circPos) + circCenterY
 sprite(me.spriteNum).loc = point(x,y)
 circPos = circPos + .1
end
```

The `atan` function serves the opposite purpose from `sin` and `cos`. Given a point on the screen, you can find out the angle at which the point is located relative to another point on the Stage.

Figure 11.2 shows a point and its angle and horizontal and vertical distance from the center of a circle.

Figure 11.2
The point can be found on the circumference of a circle using the `atan` function.

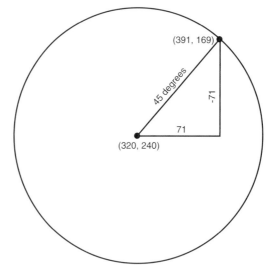

To compute the angle from one point to another, you first need to calculate the horizontal and vertical distance between the points. In Figure 11.2, the difference is 71 pixels horizontally and –71 pixels vertically. You can use these differences to compute the angle.

```
put atan(-71/71)
-- -0.7854
```

One example of what you can use this for would be to point a sprite at a location on the screen no matter where the sprite is located. So the user can move the sprite with the mouse, but it always orients itself toward the center. Check out `pointtocenter.dir` on the CD-ROM to see it in action.

```
on exitFrame me
 sprite(me.spriteNum).loc = the mouseLoc

 -- get distance from center
 dx = sprite(me.spriteNum).locH - 320
 dy = sprite(me.spriteNum).locV - 240

 if dx = 0 and dy >= 0 then
  -- point straight up
  angleRadians = pi/2

 else if dx = 0 and dy < 0 then
  -- point straight down
  angleRadians = -pi/2

 else if dx >= 0 then
  -- point using atan
  angleRadians = atan(float(dy)/float(dx))

 else if dx < 0 then
  -- point using atan + half circle
  angleRadians = pi+atan(float(dy)/float(dx))
 end if

 -- convert to degrees
 angleDegrees = 360.0*angleRadians/(2.0*pi)

 -- set rotation
 sprite(me.spriteNum).rotation = angleDegrees
end
```

Notice that in determining the angle, we actually need to break the possibilities into four cases. The first two cases deal with angles that point straight up and straight down. We can't use atan to calculate these because *dx* would be 0, and you can't divide by 0. So we just hard-code these two cases as pi/2 and -pi/2, which are 90 and –90 degrees.

The third case, in which the sprite points from the right to the left, just needs to use the raw value of atan. But the opposite side, where the arrow points from the left to the right, needs to use atan plus pi, or 180 degrees. By using these four cases, you can compute the angle from any location accurately.

USING STRING VARIABLES

The other basic type of variable is the string, which stores a series of characters. Strings can be as simple as a single character; can be as complex as words, lines, or pages of text; or can even contain no characters at all. The following examples demonstrate different types of strings in the Message panel:

```
myString = "A"
put myString
-- "A"
myString = "Hello"
put myString
-- "Hello"
myString = "Hello World."
put myString
-- "Hello World."
myString = ""
put myString
-- ""
```

Chunk Expressions

You can use Lingo to take strings apart and get single characters or groups of characters from them. A subset of a string is called a *chunk*. To define chunks, use keywords such as char and word. Try this in the Message panel:

```
myString = "Hello World."
put myString.char[1]
-- "H"
put myString.word[1]
-- "Hello"
put myString.char[2..4]
-- "ell"
```

There are more chunk expressions than just char and word. There are also line and paragraph. Paragraph means the same thing as line. Although word returns items based on where spaces are in the string, a line or paragraph returns whole lines, based on return characters in the string.

⇨ *For information about using strings in text and field members, see "Field Properties and Functions," p. 358.*

In addition, there is the item chunk expression. This returns segments of a string based on the location of commas in a string. Try this in the Message panel:

```
myString = "apples,oranges,pears,peaches,bananas"
put myString.item[3]
-- "pears"
```

You can change the character that the item expression uses as its delimiter. To do this, you need to set a value for a special variable called the itemDelimiter. Try this in the Message panel:

```
myString = "walnuts;peanuts;sunflower seeds"
the itemDelimiter = ";"
put myString.item[2]
-- "peanuts"
put myString.item[3]
-- "sunflower seeds"
```

The best thing about chunk expressions is that they can all be used together. You can get a character of a word of a line, for instance. Try this in the Message panel:

```
the itemDelimiter = ","
myString = "red,yellow,blue,green,light brown"
put myString.item[5]
-- "light brown"
put myString.item[5].word[2]
-- "brown"
put myString.item[5].word[2].char[4]
-- "w"
put char 4 of word 2 of item 5 of myString
-- "w"
```

Table 11.2 shows a summary of all the chunk expressions in Lingo.

Table 11.2   Lingo Chunk Expressions

Function	Description	Example
char	A single character or range of characters	myString.char[1] myString.char[2..4]
word	A single group of characters broken up by whitespace	myString.word[1] myString.word[2..4]
item	A single group of characters broken up by the itemDelimiter	myString.item[2..4]
line	A single group of characters broken up by a return	myString.line[1] myString.line[2..4]
paragraph	A single group of line characters broken up by a return	myString.paragraph[1] myString.paragraph[2..4]

Manipulating Strings

In addition to getting pieces of strings, you can also add to or delete pieces of strings. To concatenate, or join together, strings, use the & (ampersand) character. Try this in the Message panel:

```
myString = "Hello"
put myString&"World."
-- "HelloWorld."
myOtherString = "World."
put myString&myOtherString
-- "HelloWorld."
put myString&&myOtherString
-- "Hello World."
```

The first example used a string variable and a string literal, which describes values such as numbers and strings. When you use the & to concatenate the string variable with the word "Hello" and the literal string "World.", you get a result of "HelloWorld." When you use two variables instead, it returns the same thing. Finally, when you use &&, it inserts an extra space in the new string. The double ampersand is used for exactly that purpose: to concatenate two strings with an extra space. You can see how it comes in handy in the final line.

You can also use concatenation to create a new string and store it in a variable. Try this in the Message panel:

```
myString = "Hello"
myOtherString = "World."
myNewString = myString&&myOtherString
put myNewString
-- "Hello World."
```

You can alter the contents of a string in still another way, which involves using the put command. When you use the put command by itself, it places something in the Message panel. However, if you use the put command along with the keywords after, before, or into, it becomes something very different. It actually assigns a new value to a variable. Try this in the Message panel:

```
myString = "Hello"
put "World." after myString
put myString
-- "HelloWorld."
put "I said " before myString
put myString
-- "I said HelloWorld."
```

You see that you can use the put command to add text to strings. You could have done the same thing by concatenating strings together and assigning them to a new (or the same) variable. However, the put command technique is something you should know about.

One special way to use this is to combine the put command with chunk expressions. You can actually insert text into a string.

```
myString = "HelloWorld."
put " " after myString.char[5]
put myString
-- "Hello World."
```

The into keyword can also be used with the put command. It would replace the string. However, that would be the same as just stating the variable name followed by an = and the new value. But you can use put and into to surgically replace characters in the middle of a string.

```
myString = "Hello World."
put "Earth" into myString.char[7..11]
put myString
-- "Hello Earth."
```

In addition to the put command, there is also a delete command. This command removes a chunk from a string variable. Try this in the Message panel:

```
myString = "Hello World."
delete myString.char[2]
put myString
-- "Hllo World."
```

The `delete` command works with character spans, words, lines, and items as well.

String Information

You can find out more about your strings using a series of Lingo functions. For instance, to determine whether a string contains a series of characters, you can use the `contains` function:

```
myString = "Hello World."
put myString contains "world"
-- 1
put myString contains "earth"
-- 0
```

Because the string contains the characters "world", it returns a 1 (TRUE). Notice that `contains` does not care about case.

Similar to `contains` is the `starts` function. As you might guess, `starts` determines whether a string begins with another string:

```
myString = "Hello World."
put myString starts "hello"
-- 1
put myString starts "world"
-- 0
```

You can find the location of one string in another with the `offset` function:

```
myString = "Hello World."
put offset("world",myString)
-- 7
put offset("earth",myString)
-- 0
```

Notice that `offset` doesn't care about case either. It returns the number of the first character in the string that matches the other string. If the string is not present, it returns a 0.

You can get the length of a string with the `length` function or `length` property:

```
myString = "Hello World."
put length(myString)
-- 12
put myString.length
-- 12
```

The property is the more modern Lingo syntax and should be preferred over the older function.

11

ASCII Codes

Strings are nothing more than groups of characters. A character is a single letter, digit, or symbol, such as "A", "z", "8", or "@". Each character is single byte in memory and can be represented by its visible symbol or a corresponding code.

Codes take the form of a number from 0 to 255. For instance, the code 65 represents a capital "A". These codes are well-organized, so code 66 is the next logical character, a capital "B".

These codes are called ASCII codes after the committee that created them decades ago. Table 11.3 shows all these ASCII codes.

Table 11.3 ASCII Character Chart

These are the numbers used by *charToNum* and *numToChar* functions. Some characters, especially those above **127**, vary from font to font and platform to platform.

3	Enter	49	1	76	L	103	g	130	,
8	Delete	50	2	77	M	104	h	131	ƒ
9	Tab	51	3	78	N	105	i	132	„
10	Line Feed	52	4	79	O	106	j	133	…
13	Return	53	5	80	P	107	k	134	†
27	Clear	54	6	81	Q	108	l	135	‡
28	Left Arrow	55	7	82	R	109	m	136	ˆ
29	Right Arrow	56	8	83	S	110	n	137	‰
30	Up Arrow	57	9	84	T	111	o	138	ˇ
31	Down Arrow	58	:	85	U	112	p	139	‹
32	[space]	59	;	86	V	113	q	140	Œ
33	!	60	<	87	W	114	r	141	≤
34	"	61	=	88	X	115	s	142	≥
35	#	62	>	89	Y	116	t	143	Σ
36	$	63	?	90	Z	117	u	144	Π
37	%	64	@	91	[	118	v	145	`
38	&	65	A	92	\	119	w	146	'
39	'	66	B	93	]	120	x	147	"
40	(	67	C	94	^	121	y	148	"
41	)	68	D	95	_	122	z	149	▪
42	*	69	E	96	`	123	{	150	–
43	+	70	F	97	a	124	|	151	—
44	,	71	G	98	b	125	}	152	˜
45	-	72	H	99	c	126	~	153	™
46	.	73	I	100	d	127	DEL	154	π
47	/	74	J	101	e	128	≠	155	›
48	0	75	K	102	f	129	∞	156	œ

Table 11.3 Continued

These are the numbers used by *charToNum* and *numToChar* functions. Some characters, especially those above **127**, vary from font to font and platform to platform.

157	∫	177	±	197	Á	217	Ù	237	í
158	Ω	178	²	198	Æ	218	Ú	238	î
159	Ÿ	179	³	199	Ç	219	Û	239	ï
160	á	180	´	200	È	220	Ü	240	ð
161	¡	181	µ	201	É	221	Ý	241	ñ
162	¢	182	¶	202	Ê	222	Þ	242	ò
163	£	183	·	203	Ë	223	ß	243	ó
164	¤	184	¸	204	Ì	224	à	244	ô
165	¥	185	¹	205	Í	225	á	245	õ
166	¦	186	º	206	Î	226	â	246	ö
167	§	187	»	207	Ï	227	ã	247	÷
168	¨	188	¼	208	Ð	228	ä	248	ø
169	©	189	½	209	Ñ	229	å	249	ù
170	ª	190	¾	210	Ò	230	æ	250	ú
171	«	191	¿	211	Ó	231	ç	251	û
172	¬	192	À	212	Ô	232	è	252	ü
173	–	193	Á	213	Õ	233	é	253	ý
174	®	194	Â	214	Ö	234	ê	254	þ
175	¯	195	Ã	215	×	235	ë	255	ÿ
176	°	196	Ä	216	Ø	236	ì		

Director provides two functions to convert back and forth from single-character strings to ASCII codes. The function `charToNum` converts a single-character string to its number:

```
put charToNum("A")
-- 65
```

The function `numToChar` does the opposite, converting a number to a single-character string:

```
put numToChar(65)
-- "A"
```

You can use these two functions to perform some useful tasks. For instance, if you want to convert a string of letters from uppercase to lowercase, you can do it, keeping in mind that the codes 65 to 90 represent the uppercase characters, and 97 to 122 represent the lowercase characters.

```
on convertToLower myString
  -- loop through characters
  repeat with i = 1 to myString.length

    -- get the character code
    n = charToNum(myString.char[i])
```

```
   -- see if it is a capital letter
   if n >= 65 and n <= 90 then

     -- add 32 to convert the letter
     n = n + 32

     -- replace the character
     put numtoChar(n) into myString.char[i]
   end if
 end repeat

 -- return the new string
 return myString
end
```

You can use the function like this:

```
put convertToLower("Hello World")
-- "hello world"
```

⇨ *If you are having trouble getting special characters to behave cross-platfom, see "Special Characters Are Wrong on Different Platforms" in the "Troubleshooting" section at the end of this chapter.*

CONSTANTS

Constants are special values that are hard-coded into Lingo. Most programming languages have a similar set of constants. In most cases, constants take the place of hard-to-define values, such as the Backspace key or the value for pi.

Table 11.4 runs down all Lingo constants and their uses.

Table 11.4 Lingo Constants

Constant	Type	Description
BACKSPACE	String	The equivalent to the Backspace/Delete key, ASCII 8.
COMMA	String	The comma character (,).
EMPTY	String	A string with the length 0.
ENTER	String	The character created by the Enter key on the numeric keypad, ASCII 3.
FALSE	Boolean	Equivalent to the integer 0, used in logical expressions.
PI	Number	The ratio between a circle's circumference and its diameter, 3.1415926.
QUOTE	String	Straight double quotes (").
RETURN	String	The return character at the end of a line, generated by the Return key on Mac and Enter key in Windows, ASCII 13.
SPACE	String	The space character, ASCII 32.

Table 11.4   Continued

Constant	Type	Description
TAB	String	The Tab character, ASCII 9.
TRUE	Boolean	Equivalent to the integer 1, used in logical expressions.
VOID	Special	The value of a variable that has not yet been set. Also the value returned by many functions when there is an error.

COMPARING VARIABLES

One task that you will want Lingo to do for you is make decisions. For the computer to make decisions, it needs to have information. Information, to a computer, is binary: 1 or 0, on or off, TRUE or FALSE.

Lingo uses the idea of true or false in cases where it needs to make decisions. When you compare variables, for instance, you are asking, "Are they equal?" The answer can either be yes or no, which the computer shows as TRUE or FALSE.

Use the Message panel to try an example. The operator = is the most common comparison operator. Try it out:

```
put 1 = 1
-- 1
put 1 = 2
-- 0
put "abc" = "def"
-- 0
put "abc" = "abc"
-- 1
```

You can see that when a comparison is true, Director returns a value of 1. When it is false, it returns a value of 0. The use of 1 and 0 as true and false is so common that Director even recognizes the words TRUE and FALSE as those numbers.

```
put TRUE
-- 1
put FALSE
-- 0
```

Variables and literals can be compared in a lot of ways besides using the = operator. Table 11.5 shows all of Lingo's comparison operators.

The words TRUE and FALSE are capitalized in the preceding example because they are constants. Constants are Lingo terms that always define the same thing, such as TRUE being 1. Because Lingo is not case sensitive, you don't have to capitalize these terms, but it is a common convention that this book follows.

Table 11.5 Lingo Comparison Operators

Operator	Comparing Numbers	Comparing Strings
=	Are the two numbers equal?	Are the two strings the same?
<	Is the first number less than the second?	Does the first string come before the second alphabetically?
>	Is the first number greater than the second?	Does the first string come after the second alphabetically?
<=	Is the first number less than or equal to the second?	Does the first string come before the second alphabetically or match up exactly?
>=	Is the first number greater than or equal to the second?	Does the first string come after the second alphabetically or match up exactly?
<>	Is the first number different from the second?	Are the two strings different?
contains		Is the second string contained in the first?
starts		Does the first string start with the second?

Here are some examples from the Message panel:

```
put 1 < 2
-- 1
put 2 < 1
-- 0
put 2 <= 1
-- 0
put 2 <= 2
-- 1
put 2 <=3
-- 1
put 2 >= 2
-- 1
put 2 >= 1
-- 1
put 2 <> 1
-- 1
put "this" > "that"
-- 1
```

One important point to note is that when strings are compared with the equals operator, Director rules out capitalization. So, "abc" and "Abc" are seen as equal. However, when using other comparison operators, case is used to break ties. Uppercase letters are seen as coming before lowercase ones. So "Abc" and "abc" are equal when using =, but "Abc" is less than "abc" when using < or >.

USING LIST VARIABLES

In Chapter 3, you learned about lists. There are two types of lists: linear lists and property lists. Many list functions and commands can be used to create and maintain lists.

List Functions

Table 11.6 shows all these commands. Most work with both property and linear lists, but some are specific to one type.

Table 11.6   Lingo List Properties and Functions

Property/Function	Linear or Property Lists	Description
add	Linear	Adds an item to the end of an unsorted list or inserts it into a sorted list.
addAt	Linear	Adds an item at a specific position in a list.
addProp	Property	Adds a property and its value to the end of an unsorted list or inserts it into a sorted list.
append	Linear	Puts a new value at the end of a list.
count	Both	Returns the number of items in a list.
deleteAll	Both	Removes all items from a list.
deleteAt	Both	Removes an item or property and value from a specific location in a list.
deleteOne	Both	Looks for a value in a list and removes the first occurrence, if any.
deleteProp	Property	Looks for a property in a list and removes the first occurrence of the property and its value.
duplicate	Both	Creates a copy of the list with no references back to the original list. This copy can be changed without changing the original.
findPos	Property	Looks for the property in the list and returns the position of the first occurrence of the property in the list.
findPosNear	Property	Looks for the property in the list and returns the position of the first occurrence of the property in the list. If the property is not found, it returns the position where the property would have been found, so long as the list is a sorted one.
getaProp	Property	Returns the value corresponding to the property in the list. If the property is not there, returns a VOID.
getAt	Both	Returns the value at that position in the list.
getLast	Both	Returns the value at the last position in the list.
getOne	Both	Returns the position that corresponds to the first time a value appears in a list. Returns 0 if the item is not in the list.

11

Table 11.6   Continued

Tool	Use	
getPos	Both	Returns the position of a value in a list.
getProp	Property	Returns the value corresponding to the property in the list. If the property is not there, you will get an error message.
getPropAt	Property	Returns the property at a specific position.
ilk	Both	Returns #list or #propList. Can also be used on any other type of variable.
list	Linear	An outdated way to define a list: list(1,2,3).
listP	Both	Returns TRUE for a list and FALSE for any other type of variable.
max	Both	Returns the greatest value in the list.
min	Both	Returns the lowest value in the list.
setaProp	Property	Assigns a new value to a property. If the property doesn't exist, it will be created.
setAt	Both	Sets the value at a specific position.
setProp	Property	Assigns a new value to a property. If the property doesn't exist, you will get an error message.
sort	Both	Sorts a list by values for linear lists or properties for property lists.

Many commands work differently depending on whether a list has been sorted. You sort a list with the sort command. A list of numbers will be sorted numerically, a list of strings will be sorted alphabetically, and a property list will be sorted numerically or alphabetically according to its properties.

Once sorted, a list attempts to remain sorted. For instance, using the add command on a sorted list inserts the new value in its proper place in the list. Using add on a list that is not sorted simply places the new value at the end of the list.

⇨ *If you are using getProp and want to avoid generating error messages, see "getProp Error Messages" in the "Troubleshooting" section at the end of this chapter.*

Creating Lists

Adding to or deleting a list is done with one of the many functions from Table 11.6. But creating one from scratch can be done with bracket notation. For instance, to create a simple linear list of numbers, you can do this:

```
myList = [273,2346,123,2521]
```

You can get or set the value at any position in the list with brackets as well. The number represents the position in the list.

```
put myList[2]
-- 2346
```

If you want to create an empty linear list, just use brackets with nothing in them:

```
myList = []
```

You can create property lists in a similar way, but you must supply both the property and value, separated by a colon:

```
myList = [#prop1: 423, #prop2: 389, #prop3: 242]
```

You can then use brackets to retrieve values by their property:

```
put myList[#prop2]
-- 389
```

To create an empty property list, you can use this:

```
myList = [:]
```

Addressing Items in Lists

As you have already seen, you can use brackets to address a position in a list. For instance to get or set the third item in a linear list, you can use *myList[3]*.

You can also use brackets to address a property in a list. For instance, to get or set the value of the property *#myProp*, you can use *myList[#myProp]*.

Another way to address a property in a list is to use dot syntax. For instance, you can use *myList.myProp*. This is convenient and leads to using lists as multipart variables. You can create a global called *gUserPrefs* and store properties such as *#volume*, *#numVisits*, and *#startingFrame* in it as a list.

```
gUserPrefs = [#volume: 128, #numVisits: 0, #startingFrame: "menu"]
```

You can then set one of the preferences like this:

```
gUserPrefs.numVisits = 1
```

However, you cannot use dot syntax to create a new property in a list. This will return an error. But you can use brackets to do this:

```
gUserPrefs[#name] = "Gary"
```

Duplicating Lists

When you create a list, the variable is actually a pointer to the location in memory where the list is located. This is typical of programming languages.

Usually, this presents no problems because you can treat the variable just as if it *were* the data, rather than a pointer to the data.

But suppose that you create a list in a variable called *myList*. Then you put a list of numbers in it. Then you set another variable to be equal to this list. The two variables now point to the same data. So changing one variable changes both. Here is an example:

```
myList = [242, 46124, 2311, 55]
myOtherList = myList
myOtherList[2] = 7
put myOtherList
-- [242, 7, 2311, 55]
put myList
-- [242, 7, 2311, 55]
```

You can see that changing *myOtherList* also changes *myList* because the data is shared between them. In most cases, you would not want this to happen. Instead, you want the second variable to be a copy of the first, not a second pointer to the same thing.

This is where the duplicate function comes in handy. It creates a new copy of the same list and the two variables will be independent.

```
myList = [242, 46124, 2311, 55]
myOtherList = duplicate(myList)
myOtherList[2] = 7
put myOtherList
-- [242, 7, 2311, 55]
put myList
-- [242, 46124, 2311, 55]
```

11 Nested Lists

Remember that you can also nest lists. For instance, if you want to create a grid of values, 3×3, you can use three lists of three items each. You can then refer to a specific value by using a second set of brackets:

```
myMatrix = [[43,72,38],[32,56,92],[18,63,91]]
put myMatrix[1][3]
-- 38
```

Nested lists can be used to create grids of data. They can also be used to create small databases. A database typically consists of a number of records. Each record contains individual pieces of data in fields. You can do the same thing with a linear list containing property lists.

```
database = []
add database, [#name: "apples", #inventory: 5]
add database, [#name: "pears", #inventory: 12]
add database, [#name: "oranges", #inventory: 3]
put database[2]
-- [#name: "pears", #inventory: 12]
put database[2].name
-- "pears"
```

This preceding example points out how you can combine brackets with dot syntax. We were able to use *database[2].name* to get the #name property of the second list.

List Math

A curious thing about lists is that you can perform math on them. For instance, adding one to a list adds one to each of the values in the list:

```
myList = [345,234,295]
put myList+1
-- [346, 235, 296]
```

Instead of using a single number in the addition, you can also pass a list of the same length, and each value will be added to the corresponding value in the other list.

```
myList = [345,234,295]
put myList+[10,100,1000]
-- [355, 334, 1295]
```

You can also use subtraction, multiplication, and division on lists.

Objects That Act Like Lists

Some objects, such as points and rects, are also treated like lists when it comes to addition. So, for instance, you can expand a rect by 1 in all directions like this:

```
myRect = rect(100,100,200,200)
put myRect+rect(-1,-1,1,1)
-- rect(99, 99, 201, 201)
```

You can add two points together:

```
position = point(100,100)
velocity = point(5,2)
newPosition = position + velocity
put newPosition
-- point(105,102)
```

SYMBOLS

In addition to numbers and strings, Lingo has a third data type called *symbols*. These are unique identifiers that can be used in property lists or to refer to handler or variable names.

Uses for Symbols

Symbols start with a # character, and their names contain no spaces.

Symbols are commonly used in property lists as properties:

```
myList = [#prop1: 423, #prop2: 389, #prop3: 242]
```

When you sort a property list that uses symbols as properties, the list will be sorted according to the alphabetical order of the symbol names.

11

You can also use strings or numbers as property names. Strings have the advantage that they can use spaces or even return characters:

```
myList = ["prop1": 324, "prop two": 389, "Property Three": 242]
```

You also see symbols in some Lingo functions. For instance, to play a sound that loops, you would use this:

```
sound(1).play([#member: member("mySound"), #loopCount: 3])
```

Sometimes symbols take the place of handler names. For instance, in the `sendSprite` command, you would translate the handler name into a symbol:

```
sendSprite(1,#myHandler)
```

You can use symbols in your own code to define variables that have several possible values but never need to be represented as strings or numbers.

For instance, you might have a *pMode* property in a script that defines what an animated sprite is doing at the moment. Possible values could be `#standing`, `#sitting`, `#walking`, and `#running`. This would be much better than using the numbers 1 through 4 and having to remember which number corresponds to which mode.

> **Caution**
>
> Be careful when using strings as property names. They are case-sensitive. So "Prop Two" and "prop two" are different property names and will be treated as such in property list Lingo functions.

Symbols in Lingo

Although symbols might seem like a small feature in Lingo, they are in fact at its very heart. Director keeps a *symbol table* in memory at all times. This symbol table contains every keyword in Lingo, all your handler names, and all your variable names. If you create a new symbol to use in your code, Director adds it to the symbol table.

You can trick Director into revealing its symbol table by using math on a symbol. Try this in the Message panel:

```
put #mouseUp + 1
-- 58
```

This tells us that the symbol `#mouseUp` is number 57 in the table. You can expect the first thousand or so symbols to be Lingo terms. When you add a symbol to the table, Director adds the symbol to the end. This way, we can determine how many symbols are in the table. For instance, if we ask for the symbol `#aaa`, plus one, Lingo adds `#aaa` to the table and returns its value plus one:

```
put #aaa + 1
-- 2193
```

So there must have been 2191 symbols in the table before we added our own.

The curious thing about the symbol table is that you can reuse symbols. For instance, you would expect the symbol `#text` to have already been taken by Lingo because it is a member property. But you can use *text* as a variable name anyway. This means that a variable can be created without adding a new symbol to the table.

Understanding the symbol table is strictly academic. You don't ever need to know that it is there to use Lingo. But knowing that it is there can explain some things. For instance, if you try to use a symbol named #mouseup, you will find that it changes to a capital "U". This is because Director reuses the symbol from the table instead of creating a new one. But the original has a capital "U", so it appears that way from now on.

```
mySymbol = #mouseup
put mySymbol
-- #mouseUp
```

Converting Symbols

You can convert a symbol to a string with the `string` function. This is useful if you ever want to place a symbol value in a text member.

```
put string(#test)
-- "test"
```

You can convert a string to a symbol just as easily with the `symbol` function:

```
put symbol("test")
-- #test
```

Because symbols cannot have spaces in them, only the first word of a longer string will be used:

```
put symbol("this is a test")
-- #this
```

IDENTIFYING VARIABLES

From time to time an expert Lingo programmer will come across variables that can have an indeterminate type. You can test to see whether a variable is the type that you expect it to be by using a variety of functions.

Predicate Functions

Table 11.7 runs down all these functions. They all end with a "P," which stands for the verb form of predicate, meaning "to confirm."

Table 11.7   Predicate Functions

Function	TRUE As Long As the Value Is
floatP	A floating point number
integerP	An integer
listP	A list
objectP	An object, such as a script object, a member, or a behavior reference

Table 11.7   Continued

Function	TRUE As Long As the Value Is
stringP	A string
symbolP	A symbol
voidP	A VOID value, or undeclared variable

The most common predicate function is the voidP function. This is regularly used to determine whether a variable has been used before. If not, it's value is always equivalent to VOID.

The ilk function

The ilk function can be used in place of the predicate functions. It is actually much more specific, returning exactly what type of variable it is examining.

For instance, if ilk is given a property list, the function returns #proplist, whereas a linear list returns #list. The ilk function returns one of the following values:

#castlib	#color
#date	#float
#image	#instance
#list	#media
#member	#picture
#point	#proplist
#rect	#script
#sound	#sprite
#string	#symbol
#transform	#vector
#void	#window

Most of these are self-explanatory. However, #instance will be the result of either a script instance or an Xtra instance. The #media and #picture results are from the media and picture properties of some members. These properties have largely been replaced by the image property.

The ilk function will also return other values at times, such as symbols to represent 3D objects when you pass it models and model resources.

There is a second way to use the ilk function. You can call it with two parameters. The first parameter is the variable you want examined. The second parameter is the type you want to compare it to. So, for instance, you can determine whether *myList* is a list by using ilk(*myList*,#list).

TROUBLESHOOTING

Numbers Always Seem to Round Down

Why am I getting a result of 0 when I perform the operation of 3/4?

Remember that rounding works two different ways in Lingo. If you perform an operation on integers, such as 3/4, the fractional remainder is dropped, giving you a 3/4 = 0. However, if you use the integer function, the result is rounded. So, `integer(.75) = 1`.

getProp **Error Messages**

I'm using `getProp` to get items from a property list, but if the item is not there, I get an error message. Is there a more graceful way to do it?

If you use `getProp` to get the property value in a property list, and for some reason the property does not exist, you get an error message. This halts the program for users. However, if you use `getAProp` instead of `getProp`, you will get a VOID value rather than an error message. You can test for this and handle it in your code.

Special Characters Are Wrong on Different Platforms

I'm using some special characters with accent marks and so on. When I try to view my movie on another platform, these characters show up incorrectly. Why?

ASCII codes for normal letters and numbers are exactly the same for all nonsymbol fonts on both Mac and Windows. As a matter of fact, almost all ASCII characters between 32 and 127 are the same for all fonts. However, characters above 127 can be very different in different fonts and be different even on the same fonts from different platforms. These are special symbols, such as currency symbols and accent marks.

DID YOU KNOW?

- You can set the default number of decimal places that Lingo is to use in floating point values with `the floatPrecision` system property. The default is 4.

- Using a function called `chars` is another way to extract a piece of a string. If you try `chars("abcdefdgh",3,5)`, you get the value "cde".

- You can also use the function `list` to create a list. So, list (4, 7, 8) is the same as [4, 7. 8].

- A function that does not use a `return` command at the end, or instead uses an `exit` command to leave the handler, returns a value of VOID, which is interpreted by Lingo to be equal to FALSE. You can test for VOID with the `voidP()` function.

12

USING OBJECT-ORIENTED PROGRAMMING AND BEHAVIORS

IN THIS CHAPTER

UNDERSTANDING BEHAVIORS

Behaviors have become the standard way of getting things done with Lingo. Understanding behaviors—how to write them, how they work, and how to use them—is the key to powerful Lingo scripting.

Behaviors are reusable pieces of Lingo code stored in a cast member. They are attached either to a sprite span in the Score or a frame or span of frames in the Score. They are used to control the sprite or frame to which they are attached.

Behaviors are single-member complete Lingo programs. They contain properties, which are variables global to that script. If you attach the same behavior to more than one sprite, each sprite uses the same code but can have different values for those properties.

Behaviors are just one type of script object. You can also create script instances that are not attached to sprites using parent scripts.

CONTROLLING A SINGLE SPRITE

All that most behaviors essentially do is control a single sprite. You write them and then attach them to one or more sprites in the Score to have them take control of that sprite.

As the name suggests, a behavior tells a sprite how to behave. For instance, an `on mouseUp` handler in a behavior tells the sprite how to behave when users click the sprite.

Sprite Messages

Many messages are sent to behaviors from different Macromedia Director events. A mouseUp message is a common example. A behavior script is the first script to get such messages, and so it has the capability to use them before frame or movie scripts do.

Here is a complete list of messages that can be sent to behaviors. It is similar to the list in Chapter 3, "Writing Lingo Scripts," but only messages that behaviors can receive are included here:

- mouseDown—The user has pressed down the mouse button while the cursor is over the sprite.

- mouseUp—The user pressed down the mouse button while the cursor was over the sprite and has now lifted the mouse button up while still over the sprite.

- mouseUpOutside—The user pressed down the mouse button while the cursor was over the sprite and has now lifted the mouse button up while no longer over the sprite.

- mouseEnter—The cursor enters the sprite's area. In the case of an ink, such as Copy, the sprite area is the rectangle that bounds it. In the case of an ink, such as Matte, the sprite is the masked area of the sprite.

- mouseLeave—The mouse leaves the sprite's area.

- mouseWithin—This message is sent with every frame loop if the cursor is within the sprite's area.

- prepareFrame—This message is sent with every frame loop just before the frame is drawn on the Stage.

- enterFrame—This message is sent with every frame loop just after the frame is drawn on the Stage.

- exitFrame—This message is sent with every frame loop just before the next frame begins.

- beginSprite—This message is sent when the sprite first appears or reappears on the Stage.

- endSprite—This message is sent just before the sprite leaves the Stage.

- keyDown—This message is sent when the user first presses a key on the keyboard. It is sent for editable text members or fields only.

- keyUp—The user pressed down on a keyboard key and has now lifted it up. It is sent for editable text members or fields only.

Each one of these messages can be handled in a behavior with a handler of the same name. In addition to these event handlers, several special functions, listed next, can be added to behaviors. Each enables you to customize the behavior further.

- getBehaviorDescription—This gives you a chance to define a text description of a behavior. This is the text that appears in the bottom area of the Behavior Inspector panel. It's a simple function; you are expected to create a string and use `return` to send it along.

- getPropertyDescriptionList—This function enables you to create a property list that contains the parameters for the behavior. This function enables the library behaviors to show a dialog box containing parameter settings when the behavior is dragged to a sprite.

- runPropertyDialog—With this function, you can use Lingo to automatically set the parameters of a behavior when it is dragged to a sprite.

- getBehaviorToolTip—ToolTips are those little yellow boxes of help text that appear when you roll over some screen elements. You can add this text to a behavior so that, if it is added to your Library palette, it displays that text as the ToolTip.

12

Properties

A behavior is an object-oriented programming method. *Object-oriented* in this context means that both the program and its data are stored in the same place. In the case of behaviors, the program is composed of the handlers of the behavior. The data is composed of the variables used by the behavior. These variables are called *properties*.

A property is something in between a local and a global variable. A *local variable* exists only inside a single handler, whereas a *global variable* exists throughout the entire movie. A property, however, exists throughout the entire behavior script, accessible to all the handlers in the behavior, but not normally accessible outside it.

You create properties the way you create global variables. Rather than use a `global` command, you use a `property` command. The best place for this is in the first lines at the top of a behavior script.

Properties hold the data that is important to the behavior. For instance, if a behavior needs to move a sprite horizontally across the Stage, two properties might be *horizLoc* and *horizSpeed*. They would correspond to the current horizontal location of the sprite and the number of pixels that the sprite moves each frame, respectively.

Although the first property, *horizLoc*, might just start off from wherever the sprite begins, the second property, *horizSpeed*, might be something that can be set when you drag the behavior to a sprite. In that case, *horizSpeed* might be referred to as a parameter as well as a property.

Using me

Because behaviors are object-oriented, each handler in a behavior must have a reference to the object it is a part of as its first parameter. Sound confusing? It can be.

A behavior script by itself is just a bunch of text in a cast member. When you attach it to a sprite, it's still just a bunch of text with which the sprite knows it has a relationship. However, when you run the movie and the sprite appears on the Stage, an object is created.

The object, called an *instance of the behavior*, is sort of a copy of the behavior. The Lingo code is loaded into a new location of memory, and the property variables are created. This instance is now attached to and controlling the sprite.

If the same behavior is attached to two different sprites, and they both appear on the Stage at the same time, they actually have two different instances of the behavior. Both instances have copies of the same handlers, and both have properties of the same names, but the values of these properties are stored in different locations and can have different values.

The idea of an instance needs to be present in your behavior code. Each handler needs to know that it is part of a behavior. To signify this in your code, you should place the me parameter as the first parameter of all handlers in the behavior.

Create a new script member and set its type to be "Behavior." Now, add this simple script to it:

```
on mouseUp me
 put me
end
```

Name this behavior "Test Behavior" and attach it to any sprite on the Stage. A simple shape will do. Run the movie and click the sprite. You should see something like this appear in the Message panel:

```
-- <offspring "Test Behavior" 4 33b1e64>
```

The actual numbers at the end of this line will vary. They are the memory locations of the instance of the behavior and are not important to your programming. However, the special variable me is important. Because it points to the actual instance of the object, having it as the first parameter of all the handlers in a behavior indicates that the handlers are all meant to be a part of the behavior.

Make sure that if you are creating a behavior, the script type is set to "Behavior." Otherwise, you won't even be able to attach the member to a sprite.

If you are still confused, think of it this way: The common first parameter me of the handlers in a behavior ties all those handlers together. me is a reference to the instance of the behavior where all the handlers and properties exist.

me itself has some properties, the most useful of which is `spriteNum`. You can use `spriteNum` to get the Sprite channel number of the sprite to which the behavior is currently attached:

```
on mouseUp me
 put me.spriteNum
end
```

If you don't place me after the handler name, the script doesn't work. As a matter of fact, it gives you an error message when you try to close the Script panel because Director doesn't even know what me is supposed to refer to if it isn't included after the handler name.

CREATING SIMPLE BEHAVIORS

Simple behaviors can consist of no more than one handler with one Lingo command. Complex behaviors, on the other hand, can be hundreds of lines long with just about every known event handler and many custom handlers.

Navigation Behaviors

A simple navigation handler is usually applied to a button or bitmap sprite. It uses the `on mouseUp` event to trigger a navigation command. Here is an example:

```
on mouseUp me
 go to frame 7
end
```

This handler is no more useful than one created with the Behavior Inspector. However, using a single property, you can create a behavior that can be used on many different buttons.

```
property pTargetFrame

on getPropertyDescriptionList me
 return [#pTargetFrame: [#comment: "Target Frame:",\
    #format: #integer, #default: 1]]
end

on mouseUp me
 go to frame pTargetFrame
end
```

This behavior uses a property *pTargetFrame* to determine to which frame the button will cause the movie to jump. This property is used in the `on getPropertyDescriptionList` function to set things up so that the Parameters dialog box for this behavior enables you to select the frame number.

The list in the `on getPropertyDescriptionList` function is a property list that contains one or more other property

The property *pTargetFrame* can also easily be named just *targetFrame*. However, sometimes it is useful to have your variable names provide a hint as to which type they are. Some programmers like to place a "p" as the first letter of property variables. A common prefix for global variables is "g." Some developers prefer to place an "i" in front of property variables, to stand for instance. These are not really part of Lingo but just convenient conventions.

12

lists. The property name for the first (and only, in this case) item of the list is the name of the property, turned into a symbol by adding a # in front of it.

The list that is its property value contains three items. The first is the #comment property. This is the string that the Parameters dialog box will show for this parameter. The second item, the #format, tells the Parameters dialog box which types of values to accept for this parameter. The last item is a default value for this parameter.

Remember to use return at the end of the on getPropertDescriptionList handler. Without returning the property list defined within, Director cannot make the Parameters dialog box.

When you drag and drop this behavior onto the Stage or Score, the Parameters dialog box appears with a field labeled Target Frame. You can see this dialog box in Figure 12.1. This field takes any number as a value. At first, it shows the default value of 1.

Figure 12.1
The Parameters dialog box appears when you drop a behavior on a sprite and that behavior needs custom parameters set.

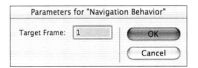

This behavior can now be attached to many sprites, but with a different target frame each time. This reusability is one of the powerful features of behaviors. You can have a movie filled with navigation buttons, but you need only this one behavior.

To complete this behavior, you should add an on getBehaviorDescription function to it. This function displays some informative text in the Behavior Inspector when the script is added to a sprite:

```
on getBehaviorDescription me
  return "Jumps to a frame number on mouseUp."
end
```

Figure 12.2 shows the Behavior Inspector when a sprite with this behavior is attached. Notice the description in the bottom area. You can find this behavior in navigation.dir on the CD-ROM.

Figure 12.2
The Behavior Inspector shows a custom behavior with a description.

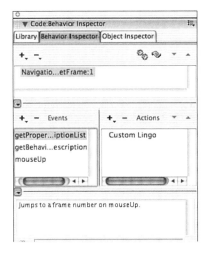

⮕ *If you can't get your parameters to work correctly, see "Completing Parameter Descriptions" in the "Troubleshooting" section at the end of this chapter.*

Rollover Behaviors

A common behavior in Director is one that has a button or other graphic that changes appearance when the cursor is over it. This is commonly referred to as a `rollover`.

Rollover behaviors are easy to do with the `on mouseEnter` and `on mouseLeave` events. The bitmap should change when the cursor enters the sprite's area and then change back when it leaves it. The behavior can be as simple as this:

```
on mouseEnter me
 sprite(1).member = member("button rollover")
end

on mouseLeave me
 sprite(1).member = member("button normal")
end
```

This behavior works fine as long as you use it only on a sprite in Channel 1, and you use only the two members "button rollover" and "button normal" as the bitmaps. So, it is not much of a behavior because it can be used only in one specific instance.

Determining the Sprite Number

The first thing that you can do to improve this behavior is to have it automatically figure out in which sprite it is used. The sprite number is a property of the behavior instance, which you know better as me. Rather than hard-coding the number 1 as the sprite, you can use the syntax *me.spriteNum*. This works as a variable that contains the number of the Sprite channel that this sprite is using. If it happens to be in sprite 1, it will contain a 1; otherwise, it will contain whatever Sprite channel number it is in.

```
on mouseEnter me
 sprite(me.spriteNum).member = member("button rollover")
end

on mouseLeave me
 sprite(me.spriteNum).member = member("button normal")
end
```

Now you have a behavior that can be attached to any sprite in any channel. However, it still uses two hard-coded members as the normal and rollover states. You can easily figure out the normal state of a button because it is probably the member with which that button is initially set. You can get that member and store it in a property in the `on beginSprite` handler.

12

```
property pMemberNormal

on beginSprite me
  pMemberNormal = sprite(me.spriteNum).member
end

on mouseEnter me
  sprite(me.spriteNum).member = member("button rollover")
end

on mouseLeave me
  sprite(me.spriteNum).member = pMemberNormal
end
```

The on beginSprite handler uses the sprite number, through me.spriteNum, to get the member that is assigned to the sprite in the Score. It stores this member in the property variable *pMemberNormal* and then uses it in the on mouseLeave handler as the member of the normal state.

Now you have only one hard-coded element left: the member of the rollover state. It is set to always be the member named "button rollover" no matter which sprite and which normal state member are used.

Using Consecutive Members

Three techniques for completing this behavior are most commonly used. The first is to assume that the rollover member for the button is always in the next cast slot over from the normal member. So, if the normal member is number 67, the rollover member is 68.

```
property pMemberNormal, pMemberRollover

on beginSprite me
  pMemberNormal = sprite(me.spriteNum).member
  pMemberRollover = member(pMemberNormal.number + 1)
end

on mouseEnter me
  sprite(me.spriteNum).member = pMemberRollover
end

on mouseLeave me
  sprite(me.spriteNum).member = pMemberNormal
end
```

The on beginSprite handler gets the current member and places it in *pMemberNormal* as before. It also gets the number of that member and adds one to it to create a new member object. This member would always be the next member in the Cast. It stores that in *pMemberRollover*.

This behavior works only when the normal and rollover states of the sprite are placed in consecutive member slots. It's far more flexible than the previous script. However, you can use the member names to make it even more flexible. You can get the name of the normal member and append something to it, such as "rollover", for instance.

```
property pMemberNormal, pMemberRollover

on beginSprite me
  pMemberNormal = sprite(me.spriteNum).member
  pMemberRollover = member(pMemberNormal.name&&"rollover")
end

on mouseEnter me
  sprite(me.spriteNum).member = pMemberRollover
end

on mouseLeave me
  sprite(me.spriteNum).member = pMemberNormal
end
```

The only difference between the last two behaviors is how they set the *pMemberRollover* property. In the last example, the name of the normal state is taken, and the word "rollover" is appended to it. The double ampersand is used to insert a space between the two. So, if the normal member is named "button1", the rollover member must be named "button1 rollover". It doesn't need to be placed anywhere in particular in the Score as long as it is named appropriately.

Using Parameters

Another way to determine which member is used in the rollover state is to set the property in the Parameters dialog box each time the behavior is applied. Use the on getPropertyDescriptionList handler to do this.

```
property pMemberNormal, pMemberRollover

on getPropertyDescriptionList me
return [#pMemberRollover: [#comment: "Rollover Member:", \
    #format: #member, #default: VOID]]
end

on beginSprite me
  pMemberNormal = sprite(me.spriteNum).member
end

on mouseEnter me
  sprite(me.spriteNum).member = pMemberRollover
end

on mouseLeave me
  sprite(me.spriteNum).member = pMemberNormal
end
```

12

In the `on getPropertyDescriptionList` function, the format `#member` is used. This presents a pop-up menu list of all the current members in the Parameters dialog box for the behavior. You could have also used `#string` to enable yourself to enter a member name manually. Or, the value of `#bitmap` could have been used to restrict the pop-up to bitmap members only. Because no default makes sense here, a value of VOID is used.

You can find this behavior in `rollover.dir` on the CD-ROM.

Animation Behaviors

Now that you know how to change the location of a sprite on the Stage, you can apply that technique to a behavior and have it animate a sprite without tweening it in the Score.

Three events occur regularly and send messages to sprite behaviors: prepareFrame, enterFrame, and exitFrame. The `on exitFrame` handler is the best general-purpose animation handler, because it enables you to show the sprite untouched at first and then altered by the commands in the `on exitFrame` handler the second time the frame loops. Here is a simple example:

```
on exitFrame me
  sprite(me.spriteNum).locH = sprite(me.spriteNum).locH + 1
end
```

This behavior simply takes the horizontal position of the sprite and adds one to it each time the frame loops. If you have a `go to the frame` command in the `on exitFrame` handler of the frame script, the playback head holds on the current frame, and this behavior makes the sprite move one pixel every frame loop.

Instead of hard-coding a 1 as the number of pixels that the sprite moves every frame, you can create a property. You can use the `on getPropertyDescriptionList` function to have this property set when you drag the behavior to the sprite.

```
property pSpeed

on getPropertyDescriptionList me
  return [#pSpeed: [#comment: "Speed:", \
      #format: #integer, #default: 1]]
end

on exitFrame me
  sprite(me.spriteNum).locH = sprite(me.spriteNum).locH + pSpeed
end
```

This behavior now prompts you to enter a number for the speed of movement when you drop it on a sprite. The default is set to 1.

You can use another technique in the `on getPropertyDescriptionList` function that enables you to place a sliding bar in the Parameters dialog box rather than a plain typing field. All you need to do is add the property

> You can use this same behavior to make a sprite move from right to left rather than left to right. All you need to do is use a negative number rather than a positive number for *pSpeed*.

#range to #pSpeed's property list and add a small list with #min and #max properties in it. These properties determine the bounds of the sliding bar.

```
property pSpeed

on getPropertyDescriptionList me
 return [#pSpeed: [#comment: "Speed:", #format: #integer, \
    #default: 1, #range: [#min:-50, #max:50]]]
end

on exitFrame me
 sprite(me.spriteNum).locH = sprite(me.spriteNum).locH + pSpeed
end
```

Figure 12.3 shows the Parameters dialog box with this slider in it. Sliders such as this are great tools for controlling the range of values that a parameter can contain. You can also make it a pop-up menu rather than a slider by placing a linear list, such as [1,5,10,15,–5,–10] as the #range property. Those values would then be the ones available in the pop-up menu for the *pSpeed* property.

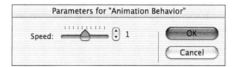

Figure 12.3
The Parameters dialog box can contain interface elements, such as sliders, rather than plain text boxes.

CREATING A SIMPLE BUTTON BEHAVIOR

A simple button behavior should do several things. First, it should make the sprite switch members when users press it. This "pressed" version of the sprite is called the *down state*. Second, it should recognize the difference between the mouse being released above the sprite and it being released outside the sprite. This enables the users to click down, but then move the mouse so that it doesn't activate the button when it's released. Third, the button should perform a task, such as simple navigation, when there is a successful button press.

A behavior such as this should have two parameters. The first is a property that determines the down state of the button. The second defines what the navigation function of the behavior should be. Here is the on `getPropertyDescriptionList` handler for this behavior:

```
property pMemberNormal, pMemberDown, pTargetFrame

on getPropertyDescriptionList me
 list = [:]
 addProp list, #pMemberDown, [#comment: "Down State Member:", \
   #format: #member, #default: VOID]
 addProp list, #pTargetFrame, [#comment: "Target Frame Label:", \
   #format: #marker, #default: VOID]
 return list
end
```

12

First, notice that the variable "list" is built, property by property, and then returned. This makes the code easier to read than a one-line `return` command does.

Two special formats are used for the properties in the list. The first is `#member`, which presents a pop-up menu of all the available members. The second is `#format`, which presents a pop-up menu of available Score markers. It also adds the markers `#next`, `#previous`, and `#loop`, which can be used along with the `go to frame` command to go to the next, preceding, or current marker.

The `on beginSprite` handler gets just the starting member of the sprite, which is used for the normal button state member.

```
on beginSprite me
 pMemberNormal = sprite(me.spriteNum).member
end
```

The next three handlers refer to the three mouse button actions that are possible: mouseDown, mouseUp, and mouseUpOutside. The difference between the `on mouseUp` and `on mouseUpOutside` handlers is that the first also performs the action that the button is meant to do. The second just sets the member of the sprite back to the normal state.

```
on mouseDown me
 sprite(me.spriteNum).member = pMemberDown
end

on mouseUp me
 sprite(me.spriteNum).member = pMemberNormal
 action(me)
end

on mouseUpOutside me
 sprite(me.spriteNum).member = pMemberNormal
end
```

Rather than just perform the action in the `on mouseUp` handler, the handler calls another handler called *on action*. This is a custom handler that you create specifically for this behavior. It does not need to be called *on action*, but it seems like a sensible choice.

```
on action me
 go to frame pTargetFrame
end
```

This custom handler simply needs to execute the command `go to frame` *pTargetFrame*. The property must contain either the name of a frame marker, or one of the special symbols that can be used by `go to frame`: `#next`, `#previous`, or `#loop`.

This completes the simple button behavior. You can find it in the movie `simplebutton.dir` on the CD-ROM. Later in this chapter, you will see how to add a lot more functionality to it, including rollover states, actions other than navigation, sounds, and even different ways of deciding among the members for the down and rollover states.

USING COMPLETE BEHAVIORS

A behavior script has many parts. However, they are all optional. When you are writing quick behaviors to take care of a single action for a single sprite, you might use only one handler with one command. However, for complete behaviors, you will want to include all the optional functions.

Behavior Descriptions

The only use for a behavior description is to have something to appear in the bottom area of the Behavior Inspector. However, because it is in your script as the on getBehaviorDescription function, it can also act as commentary in your script.

All that the on getBehaviorDescription does to accomplish this task is return a string. You can do this with one line:

```
on getBehaviorDescription me
 return "This behavior plays a sound when clicked."
end
```

Chances are, however, that you want to present more information than just seven words. You could expand that line to include as much information as you want, but a better way might be to construct the string in a variable first and then return its value.

```
on getBehaviorDescription me
 desc = ""
 put "This behavior plays a sound when clicked."&RETURN after desc
 put "Choose a sound to play as the Sound parameter."&RETURN after desc
 put "Choose an action as the Action parameter." after desc
 return desc
end
```

This example is easier to write and edit, and will also be easier to read for someone editing the script.

The behavior description is also a good place to include your name or your company's name if the behavior is to be distributed in any way.

Behavior Property Description List

Although the behavior description is cosmetic, the behavior property description list is an essential element for behaviors that require customization. You can use the on getPropertyDescriptionList function to create a Parameters dialog box for any behavior. The Parameters dialog box can contain a wide array of interface elements.

The property list that the on getPropertyDescriptionList returns contains a series of smaller lists. Each smaller list defines a single parameter. It does this through the use of four properties: #comment, #format, #default, and #range. Here is an example from earlier in the chapter:

```
on getPropertyDescriptionList me
 return [#pSpeed: [#comment: "Speed:", #format: #integer, \
    #default: 1, #range: [#min:-50, #max:50]]]
end
```

12

The main list contains the definition of one property: *pSpeed*. In this list, you can see each of the four properties needed to define the way the parameter should appear in the Parameters dialog box.

The `#comment` property is a short string used to label the parameter in the Behavior Parameters dialog box. It's nice to place a colon as the last character if you like that style.

The `#format` property can be set to one of many things. Many settings place a specific type of pop-up menu in the Parameters dialog box. The `#member` setting, for instance, places a pop-up menu that enables you to select any member used by the movie. Table 12.1 shows the different `#format` property settings.

Table 12.1   Settings Used by the `#format` Property

Setting	Parameter Dialog Result	Possible Values
`#integer`	A text entry area	The value is converted to an integer.
`#float`	A text entry area	The value is converted to a floating point number.
`#string`	A text entry area	A string.
`#boolean`	A check box	TRUE or FALSE (1 or 0).
`#symbol`	A text entry area	A symbol.
`#member`	A pop-up menu with a list of all members	A member name.
`#bitmap`	A pop-up menu with a list of bitmap members	A member name.
`#filmloop`	A pop-up menu with a list of film loop members.	A member name.
`#field`	A pop-up menu with a list of field members	A member name.
`#palette`	A pop-up menu with a list of palette members and built-in Director palettes	A string with the name of the palette.
`#sound`	A pop-up menu with a list of sound members	A member name.
`#button`	A pop-up menu with a list of pushbutton, radio button, and check box members	A member name.
`#shape`	A pop-up menu with a list of shape members	A member name.
`#vectorShape`	A pop-up menu with a list of vector graphic members	A member name.
`#font`	A pop-up menu with a list of font members	A member name.
`#digitalVideo`	A pop-up menu with a list of digital video members	A member name.
`#script`	A pop-up menu with a list of script members	A member name.
`#text`	A pop-up menu with a list of text members	A member name.
`#transition`	A pop-up menu with a list of built-in transitions	A transition member name.
`#frame`	A text field	A frame number.

Table 2.1   Continued

Setting	Parameter Dialog Result	Possible Values
#marker	A list of markers in the Score, plus #next, #previous, and #loop	A string or the symbol #next, #previous, or #loop.
#ink	A list of inks An ink number.	

Most of the #format types result in a pop-up menu being placed in the Parameters dialog box. When there are absolutely no values that can be used there, a text field appears instead. For instance, if one parameter is set to #sound and there are no sound members in the movie yet, a text field replaces the pop-up menu.

The #range property is optional at all times but can be useful for narrowing choices. There are two ways to use it: as a pop-up menu list of items or as a slider with minimum and maximum values.

A slider is created in the Parameters dialog box with the format [#min: *a*, #max: *b*]. The values of the slider go from a to b. When used with a linear list, such as *["a", "b", "c"]*, the values of that list are used as choices in the pop-up.

The #default property is required for any parameter. However, you can use values such as VOID, "", and 0 in cases where you really don't plan on using a default.

Automatic Property Setting

In rare cases, you will want to create a behavior that sets its parameters semi-automatically instead of requiring you to set them each time you apply the behavior. The on runPropertyDialog handler enables you to intercept the message that triggers the Parameters dialog box when you apply a behavior. You can use it to examine the properties and even change them. You can also decide whether the Parameters dialog box ever appears.

Here is an example behavior. It has both on getPropertyDescriptionList and on runPropertyDialog handlers. When the behavior is applied to a sprite, the on runPropertyDialog runs and sends a message using the alert command. It takes the property list for the behavior, which is passed in as a second parameter to the handler, and resets one of the properties. It then uses the pass command to signify that the runPropertyDialog message should pass on to open the Parameters dialog box as usual.

```
property pFrame, pBoolean

on getPropertyDescriptionList me
  list = [:]
  addProp list, #pFrame, [#comment: "Frame:", \
    #format: #integer, #default: 0]
  addProp list, #pBoolean, [#comment: "Boolean:", \
    #format: #boolean, #default: TRUE]
  return list
end

on runPropertyDialog me, list
  setProp list, #pFrame, the frame + 1
```

```
alert "I will now set the pFrame property to the next frame."
pass
return list
end
```

The properties in the behavior are passed to the on runPropertyDialog handler through the second parameter, which is the variable *list*. The variable should contain something like this: *[#pFrame: 0, #pBoolean: 1]*.

Because this is just a plain property list, the setProp command can be used to change the value of one of the properties in it. The *pBoolean* property is used only to color up the example a bit. The only property affected by the setProp command is *pFrame*.

> The alert command generates a plain dialog box with a string message and an OK button. It is a quick and easy way to show some information.

After the variable *list* holds a new value, you need to remember to return this value with the return command so that the changes can be applied to the behavior. The pass command can be placed anywhere in the handler, because it just tells Director that when the handler is done, the message that called it (in this case, a runPropertyDialog message) should continue to be used. The result is that the message triggers the normal Parameters dialog box.

Without pass, the Parameters dialog box never appears. This is sometimes desired when the on runPropertyDialog handler is meant to set all the parameters and override any use of the Parameters dialog box.

Controlling Where Behaviors Are Used

Behaviors have the capability to allow themselves to be used only on sprites that are appropriate. The handler on isOKToAttach enables you to execute some Lingo when the Director author first adds a behavior to a sprite. You can then determine whether the behavior really belongs with that sprite. If it does, the handler returns a TRUE. If a FALSE is returned instead, the behavior will not attach itself to the sprite.

The reason you would want to do this is to prevent a behavior from being attached where it doesn't make sense. For instance, if a behavior controls the text in a text member, it would make no sense to attach it to a bitmap sprite.

Two parameters in addition to the me are passed into the handler. The first is the sprite's type: either #script for the Script channel, or #graphic for a normal Sprite channel. The second parameter is the sprite number. You can then use the sprite number to determine whether the sprite is appropriate for the behavior.

Here is a handler that restricts the use of a behavior to only the Script channel:

```
on isOKToAttach me, spriteType
  if spriteType = #script then return TRUE
  else return FALSE
end
```

Here is a handler that restricts the use of a behavior to only a text member:

```
on isOKToAttach me, spriteType, spriteNum
  if spriteType = #script then return FALSE
  else if sprite(spriteNum).member.type= #text then return TRUE
  else return FALSE
end
```

If you do not use the on isOKToAttach handler at all, the behavior can attach to any sprite or the Script channel.

ToolTips

The only use for the on getBehaviorTooltip function is if you plan to use the behavior in the Library palette. If so, placing this function there enables you to define what text appears in that little yellow box called a *ToolTip*.

Here is an example. It basically works the same way as the on getBehaviorDescription handler. You need to simply return a string. In the case of ToolTips, these should be as short as possible so that they fit on the screen nicely and don't cover up too much when they appear.

```
on getBehaviorTooltip me
  return "Button Behavior"
end
```

BUILDING A COMPLETE BUTTON BEHAVIOR

Now you know enough to build a complex button behavior. This behavior needs to perform many tasks, such as the following:

- Changing state when users press down on the button. There should be a choice of how the down state member is chosen: as the next member in the Cast, as a member with the same name as the original member but with the word "down" appended, or as a specific member name.

- Changing state when users roll over the button. There should be a choice of how the rollover state member is chosen: as two members from the original in the Cast, as a member with the same name as the original member but with the word "rollover" appended, or as a specific member name.

- Playing a sound when users press down on the button. The sound name is chosen from the current sound members in the Cast.

- Playing a sound when users roll over the button. The sound name is chosen from the current sound members in the Cast.

- Changing the cursor when users roll over the button. The cursor is chosen from the built-in cursors.

- Playing a sound when the button is successfully clicked.

12

- Taking the movie to another frame with a go or play command when the button is successfully clicked. Also, a play done command can be executed.

- Calling a specific Lingo command or handler when the button is successfully clicked.

A behavior such as this is typical of what you need in a large movie. It takes care of all the different buttons that you may use. It even enables you to create non-button rollover sprites. You can find the result in complexbutton.dir on the CD-ROM.

Creating the Parameters

To begin, create the on getPropertyDescriptionList handler. By making this handler, property by property, you can see how many properties are used and name them appropriately. You can then return to the beginning of the script and add the property declarations.

Start by creating the property list:

```
on getPropertyDescriptionList me
  list = [:]
```

Now, take care of the first course of action: creating a down state for the sprite.

In addition to the three choices previously listed in the bullet item, you should have a fourth choice: no down state. Here is the line of code that adds this property. The name of the property will be *pDownState*, and a pop-up list will be used to let you choose the type of down state. You need to list these choices with the #range property.

```
addProp list, #pDownState, \
  [#comment: "Down State", #format: #string, \
    #range: ["No Down State", "Member + 1",\
        "Append 'down'", "Name Down State"],\
    #default: "No Down State"]
```

Notice that the default state is set to "No Down State". You need to set default states for all the properties.

One of the down state options is to name a down state member. You then need a pop-up menu for the name of this member as a parameter.

```
addProp list, #pDownMemberName, \
  [#comment: "Down Member", #format: #bitmap, #default: ""]
```

You need to provide similar functionality for a rollover state as you did for the down state. However, because you already have a way for the down state to be the next member in the Cast, it makes sense that the rollover state should be the second member after the current one. This way, you can line up normal, down, and rollover bitmaps in the Cast if you want.

```
addProp list, #pRolloverState, \
  [#comment: "Rollover State", #format: #string, \
    #range: ["No Rollover", "Member + 2", "Append 'rollover'",\
        "Name Rollover", "Cursor Change"],\
    #default: "No Rollover"]
```

12

As with the down state, you need to provide a pop-up menu of bitmaps for use in case the "Name Rollover" choice is selected.

```
addProp list, #pRolloverMemberName, \
  [#comment: "Rollover Member", #format: #bitmap, #default: ""]
```

There is an extra option for rollovers: the cursor change. If that option is selected, you want to know which cursor has been chosen as the rollover cursor.

```
addProp list, #pRolloverCursor, \
  [#comment: "Rollover Cursor", #format: #cursor, #default: ""]
```

You also need to provide a way for sounds to play when the button is clicked down and when the button is rolled over. You need to provide a check box for whether the sound is played and then a pop-up menu with a list of sounds.

```
addProp list, #pPlayDownSound, \
  [#comment: "Play Down Sound", #format: #boolean, #default: FALSE]

 addProp list, #pDownSound, \
  [#comment: "Down Sound", #format: #sound, #default: ""]
```

The same properties need to be present for the rollover action:

```
addProp list, #pPlayRolloverSound, \
  [#comment: "Play Rollover Sound", #format: #boolean, #default: FALSE]

 addProp list, #pRolloverSound, \
  [#comment: "Rollover Sound", #format: #sound, #default: ""]
```

All that is left now is to define what happens when the button is successfully clicked. The first option is to have some navigation. This could be either a go to frame, a play frame, or a play done. There should also be an option for no navigation, and that should be the default.

```
addProp list, #pActionNavigation, \
  [#comment: "Action Navigation", #format: #string, \
  #range: ["None", "go to frame", "play frame", "play done"],\
  #default: "None"]
```

If either a go frame or play frame is selected, there needs to be a property that holds the name of that frame. A play done does not need a frame name.

```
addProp list, #pActionFrame,\
  [#comment: "Action Frame", #format: #frame, #default: ""]
```

There should also be an option for a sound to be played when the button is successfully clicked. This requires two more properties, similar to the sound properties for down states and rollovers.

```
addProp list, #pPlayActionSound, \
  [#comment: "Play Action Sound", #format: #boolean, #default: FALSE]

 addProp list, #pActionSound, \
  [#comment: "Action Sound", #format: #sound, #default: ""]
```

12

The last property is another action that takes place when there is a successful click. It is the name of a Lingo command or a custom handler. Using a special command named do, you can execute this command when users press the button. It can be something as simple as a beep or as complex as the name of a custom movie handler that does a variety of things. For the on getPropertyDescriptionList purposes, it just needs to be a string.

```
addProp list, #pActionLingo, \
  [#comment: "Action Lingo", #format: #string, #default: ""]
```

The on getPropertyDescriptionList is now complete. Just top it off with a return list. You should now go back and figure out what the property declarations for the behavior should be. Figure 12.4 shows the Parameters dialog box that results from all this code. You can see each property listed in the on getPropertyDescriptionList.

Figure 12.4
The Parameters dialog box for the complex button behavior shows the properties grouped together by function rather than in the order discussed in the text.

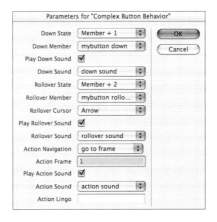

All the properties used in the on getPropertyDescriptionList handler should be present, as well as other properties that you can predict you will need. You should have properties to hold the normal, down, and rollover state member references. You will also need a property called *pPressed* that is TRUE when a button press is in progress and FALSE at all other times.

You can use the property declaration on several different lines (as shown in the preceding example) or one long line. The same is true of the global declaration.

```
property pNormalMember, pDownMember, pRolloverMember, pPressed
property pDownState, pDownMemberName
property pPlayDownSound, pDownSound
property pRolloverState, pRolloverMemberName, pRolloverCursor
property pPlayRolloverSound, pRolloverSound
property pActionNavigation, pActionFrame
property pPlayActionSound, pActionSound, pActionLingo
```

Writing the Event Handlers

Now that all the preliminary steps have been taken to create the behavior, you can actually start writing the event handlers. A logical place to start is with the on beginSprite handler.

The on beginSprite Handler

This handler should be used to set the properties that contain references to the three members used: *pNormalMember*, *pDownMember*, and *pRolloverMember*. Their settings depend on the parameter properties. For instance, if the *pDownState* is set to *member + 1*, you need to get the member number of the original member, add one to it, and get that member.

Here is the on beginSprite handler. It first gets the member currently used by the sprite and stores it as the *pNormalMember*. Then, it looks at the *pDownState* property to determine what to place in the *pDownMember* property. The same thing is done for the *pRolloverState* and *pRolloverMember* properties.

```
on beginSprite me
 pNormalMember = sprite(me.spriteNum).member

 case pDownState of
   "No Down State":
   pDownMember = member pNormalMember
   "Append 'Down'":
   pDownMember = member(pNormalMember.name&&"Down")
   "Member + 1":
   pDownMember = member(pNormalMember.number + 1)
   "Name Down State":
   pDownMember = member pDownMemberName
 end case

 case pRolloverState of
   "No Rollover":
   pRolloverMember = pNormalMember
   "Cursor Change":
   pRolloverMember = pNormalMember
   "Append 'Rollover'":
   pRolloverMember = member (pNormalMember.name&&"Rollover")
   "Member + 2":
   pRolloverMember = member (pNormalMember.number + 2)
   "Name Rollover":
   pRolloverMember = member pRolloverMemberName
 end case

 pPressed = FALSE
end
```

The last thing that the on beginSprite handler does is set the *pPressed* property to FALSE. Note that properties such as *pDownState*, *pDownMemberName*, and *pRolloverMemberName* are no longer needed in the behavior. Their purpose was to determine what *pDownMember* and *pRolloverMember* are supposed to be.

A comprehensive behavior such as this one requires you to use most of the basic event handlers: on mouseDown, on mouseUp, on mouseUpOutside, on mouseEnter, and on mouseLeave. The last two are used to determine when the sprite is being rolled over.

Mouse Event Handlers

In the on mouseDown handler, you need to place the commands that get executed when the sprite is first clicked. Specifically, you need to set the member to the down state, play a sound if needed, and set the *pPressed* property.

```
on mouseDown me
 pPressed = TRUE
 sprite(me.spriteNum).member = pDownMember

 if pPlayDownSound then
  puppetSound pDownSound
 end if
end
```

The on mouseUp handler is the other end of the click. Here you need to call a custom handler that performs the button's actions. You also need to set the *pPressed* property to FALSE. Because you can't assume that the action of the button will be to leave the current frame entirely, it's a good idea to set the member of the sprite back to a nonpressed state. Because the cursor must still be over the sprite when the button is released to get an on mouseUp message, you should set the sprite not to the normal state but to the rollover state.

```
on mouseUp me
 pPressed = FALSE
 sprite(me.spriteNum).member = pRolloverMember
 doAction(me)
end
```

The companion to on mouseUp is on mouseUpOutside. If this handler is executed, it means that the user clicked the button when the cursor was over the sprite at first, but then moved off it before lifting up. This is a standard user interface way of backing out of an action. The user clearly does not want the action to take place, so you should not call the on doAction handler as in the on mouseUp handler. In addition, you know that the cursor is not over the sprite, so you can set the member back to the normal state.

```
on mouseUpOutside me
 pPressed = FALSE
 sprite(me.spriteNum).member = pNormalMember
end
```

The two rollover handlers, on mouseEnter and on mouseLeave, actually have a lot more to do. The first handler needs to set the member to the rollover member. However, if the user has already clicked and is holding down the mouse button, the down state member should be used instead.

In addition, the on mouseEnter handler needs to play a sound if required. If the *pRolloverState* property is set to "Cursor Change", the cursor command should be used to change the cursor.

```
on mouseEnter me
 if pPressed then
  sprite(me.spriteNum).member = pDownMember
 else
  sprite(me.spriteNum).member = pRolloverMember
 end if

 if pPlayRolloverSound then
  puppetSound pRolloverSound
 end if

 if pRolloverState = "Cursor Change" then
  cursor(pRolloverCursor)
 end if
end
```

The companion on mouseLeave handler has to undo what the on mouseEnter handler does. This is fairly simple. It needs to set the member back to the normal state and change the cursor back if needed.

```
on mouseLeave me
 sprite(me.spriteNum).member = pNormalMember

 if pRolloverState = "Cursor Change" then
  cursor(0)
 end if
end
```

> The cursor command changes the cursor to one of many special built-in cursors. In this case, it gets the setting from the Parameters pop-up. You can also use numbers, such as 280 for a hand or 4 for a clock/watch. The number -1 resets the cursor.

Action Handler

That takes care of all the event handlers needed. Only the custom on doAction handler is left. This handler needs to look at three possible values for *pActionNavigation* that need processing. In each case, it performs the necessary commands. Because a navigation command takes the movie immediately away from the current frame where the sprite is, you should use cursor(0) to reset the cursor before that happens.

In addition to navigation, the on doAction handler figures out when a sound is needed. It also determines whether any Lingo command was entered as the *pActionLingo* property. It uses the do command to run that command or handler.

Also notice that instead of just using the *pActionFrame* as a marker name, the code checks to see whether it can be considered a number. It uses the integer function to do this. This function tries to convert the string to a number. If it is successful, it uses the number as a frame to jump to rather than as a marker label string. The same can be done for the "play frame" option if you want.

```
on doAction me
 if pActionNavigation = "go to frame" then
  cursor(0)
  if integer(pActionFrame) > 0 then
   go to frame integer(pActionFrame)
  else
   go to frame pActionFrame
  end if
 else if pActionNavigation = "play frame" then
  cursor(0)
  play frame pActionFrame
 else if pActionNavigation = "play done" then
  cursor(0)
  play done
 end if

 if pPlayActionSound then
  puppetSound pActionSound
 end if

 if pActionLingo <> "" then
  do pActionLingo
 end if
end
```

This behavior is now a powerful multipurpose script that can be used over and over in your current movie and others. Gather any general-purpose behaviors such as this and store them in your own behavior library for future use.

12 CREATING ANIMATION BEHAVIORS

With Lingo, animation does not have to take place over several frames anymore. Instead, it can exist on a single frame as the movie loops on that frame. The possibilities are limitless, but the following two examples show some of them.

Bouncing off Walls

Changing the position of a sprite is easy enough to do. Moving one in a straight line is no great feat, because the Score and tweening already enable you to do this easily. With Lingo, however, you can create a behavior that makes a sprite react to its environment. For example, it can bounce off walls.

A behavior to do this is relatively simple and can be found in bouncing.dir on the CD-ROM. As usual, first create the on getPropertyDescriptionList handler. Three properties should be sufficient: the speed of movement in horizontal and vertical directions, plus a rectangle to bound the object.

```
property pMoveX, pMoveY, pLimit

on getPropertyDescriptionList me
 list = [:]
 addProp list, #pMoveX, [#Comment: "Horizontal Movement",\
  #format: #integer, #range: [#min:-10,#max:10], #default: 0]
 addProp list, #pMoveY, [#Comment: "Vertical Movement",\
  #format: #integer, #range: [#min:-10,#max:10], #default: 0]
 addProp list, #pLimit, [#Comment: "Limit Rectangle",\
  #format: #rect, #default: rect(0,0,640,480)]
 return list
end
```

Using sliders for the horizontal and vertical movement is a good idea, because you probably don't want to be using far-out values anyway. In this case, the properties are limited to plus or minus 10 pixels at a time.

The *pLimit* property is supposed to be a rect structure. Using the format type #rect forces the value of the text entered for this property into a rect.

Figure 12.5 shows the Parameters dialog box that results when this behavior is dropped onto a sprite.

The use of X and Y in variable names is common in Lingo and other languages. The X value is commonly used to denote horizontal positions and movement, whereas Y is commonly used to denote vertical positions and movement.

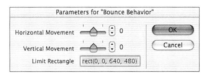

Figure 12.5
The Parameters dialog box for the bouncing behavior.

To make this behavior work, you need only one event handler. The on exitFrame handler is commonly used for animation such as this. You can take the current location of a sprite and add a point to it. Points and rects can be added and subtracted like other variables. Try this in the Message panel:

```
p = point(100,150)
p = p + point(40,20)
put p
-- point(140, 170)
```

This technique makes the coding easy. You don't have to break the location of the sprite into horizontal and vertical components. Here is the handler:

```
on exitFrame me
 -- get the old location
 currentLoc = sprite(me.spriteNum).loc

 -- set the new location
 newLoc = currentLoc + point(pMoveX, pMoveY)
```

```
  -- set the sprite location
 sprite(me.spriteNum).loc = sprite(me.spriteNum).loc + \
    point(pMoveX, pMoveY)
end
```

You will also need to check the *pLimit* property to figure out whether the sprite has hit a side and should turn around. A rect structure, like the *pLimit* property, can be broken into four properties: left, right, top, and bottom. You must check the left and right to see whether a side was hit, and the top and bottom to see whether they were hit.

After a hit is determined, the movement in that direction, represented by either the *pMoveX* or *pMoveY* property, should be reversed. That is, a positive value becomes negative and vice versa.

To make sure that the handler works correctly when the limiting rectangle is tight or the sprite starts outside the limit, each case is handled individually. When the sprite hits the right wall, the *pMoveX* property is taken as an absolute value and made a negative. When it hits the left wall, the absolute value is taken and kept positive. The result in most cases is that the sign of the property changes when a wall is hit.

```
on exitFrame me
 -- get the old location
 currentLoc = sprite(me.spriteNum).loc

 -- set the new location
 newLoc = currentLoc + point(pMoveX, pMoveY)

 -- check to see if it has hit a side of the limit
 if newLoc.locH > pLimit.right then
  pMoveX = -abs(pMoveX)
 else if newLoc.locH < pLimit.left then
  pMoveX = abs(pMoveX)
 end if

 -- check to see if it has hit top or bottom of the limit
 if newLoc.locV > pLimit.bottom then
  pMoveY = -abs(pMoveY)
 else if newLoc.locV < pLimit.top then
  pMoveY = abs(pMoveY)
 end if

 -- set the sprite location
 sprite(me.spriteNum).loc = sprite(me.spriteNum).loc + \
    point(pMoveX, pMoveY)
end
```

You now have a behavior that causes a sprite to move at a constant rate and bounce off walls when necessary. The animation does not stop as long as the sprite is present on the Stage.

Adding Gravity

The bounce behavior seems to act on a sprite as if it were in outer space in a perfect universe. When the sprite hits the side of the screen, it bounces back without losing any speed or being pulled down by gravity.

To create convincing animation, you sometimes need to include elements such as energy loss and gravity. After all, in real life a ball thrown against a wall will hit the wall, fall down to the ground, and bounce back with less energy.

Adding gravity is easy, but it always takes two properties. The first is the amount of force that you want gravity to exert on the sprite. The second is the speed at which the sprite is traveling downward.

When you release an object in real life, it begins falling down slowly at first and then picks up speed as it continues because gravity accelerates the object's speed toward the ground. Acceleration is a change in speed rather than the speed itself.

This acceleration is your first property: *pGravity*. In addition, there needs to be a *pSpeedDown* property that keeps track of how fast the sprite travels downward. For the energy-loss feature of the behavior, all that is needed is a *pLoseEnergy* property that can be either TRUE or FALSE.

To create this behavior, you can start with the "bounce" behavior just described. You need to add a few properties to the property declaration:

```
property pGravity, pSpeedDown, pMoveX, pMoveY, pLimit, pLoseEnergy
```

Now, you need to add two new parameters in the on `getPropertyDescriptionList` handler:

```
addProp list, #pGravity, [#Comment: "Gravity",\
  #format: #integer, #range: [#min:0,#max:3], #default: 0]
 addProp list, #pLoseEnergy, [#Comment: "Lose Energy",\
  #format: #boolean, #default: FALSE]
```

The *pGravity* property works best when it is set to 1, but the slider accommodates values up to 3. The 0 is used as the default, which results in no gravity effect. You can see the resulting parameters dialog box in Figure 12.6.

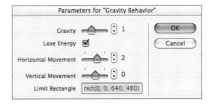

Figure 12.6
The Parameters dialog box for the gravity behavior.

The pSpeedDown property needs to be set when the sprite starts, so you need to create an on beginSprite handler.

```
on beginSprite me
 pSpeedDown = 0
end
```

Then, each time the on exitFrame handler runs, you increase the downward speed by the force of gravity:

```
pSpeedDown = pSpeedDown + pGravity
```

Also, this property must be reversed when the sprite hits the ground, according to Isaac Newton. You can add one line after the line in the on exitFrame handler that reverses the pMoveY property:

```
pSpeedDown = -abs(pSpeedDown)-1
```

The −1 is added to the resulting speed to fix an inconsistency. When the sprite hits the ground and the *pSpeedDown* changes to negative, the location of the sprite is not changed again until the next time through the on exitFrame handler. At that point, a 1 is added to it before the location is changed again. So, if the *pSpeedDown* is 22, and it hits bottom, it changes to a −22. Then, it goes through the handler again and gets 1 added, so now it is a −21.

The result is that the sprite moves 22 one time, and then -21 the next. It gains one pixel because of this. But, by adding a −1 to the *pSpeedDown*, it evens out.

To create the energy loss, first check to see whether *pEnergyLoss* is TRUE. Then, you add 1 to the *pSpeedDown* when the sprite hits the ground. However, be careful not to do this when the speed of the sprite is near 0, because it will slowly suck the sprite under the ground.

```
if pSpeedDown < -1 then pSpeedDown = pSpeedDown + 1
```

Here is the final behavior. Notice that the code that handles the ceiling hit has been taken out. This is because a ceiling hit is less likely now that gravity is involved. Plus, it would further complicate the code that handles the gravity. So, this behavior acts as if there were walls on the sides and ground below, but only sky above.

```
property pGravity, pSpeedDown, pMoveX, pMoveY, pLimit, pLoseEnergy

on getPropertyDescriptionList me
 list = [:]
 addProp list, #pGravity, [#Comment: "Gravity",\
  #format: #integer, #range: [#min:0,#max:3], #default: 0]
 addProp list, #pLoseEnergy, [#Comment: "Lose Energy",\
  #format: #boolean, #default: FALSE]
 addProp list, #pMoveX, [#Comment: "Horizontal Movement",\
  #format: #integer, #range: [#min:-10,#max:10], #default: 0]
 addProp list, #pMoveY, [#Comment: "Vertical Movement",\
  #format: #integer, #range: [#min:-10,#max:10], #default: 0]
 addProp list, #pLimit, [#Comment: "Limit Rectangle",\
  #format: #rect, #default: rect(0,0,640,480)]
 return list
end

on beginSprite me
 pSpeedDown = 0
end
```

```
on exitFrame me
  -- Accelerate due to gravity
  pSpeedDown = pSpeedDown + pGravity

  -- get the old location
  currentLoc = sprite(me.spriteNum).loc

  -- set the new location
  newLoc = currentLoc + point(pMoveX, pMoveY+pSpeedDown)

  -- check to see if it has hit a side of the limit
  if newLoc.locH > pLimit.right then
    pMoveX = -abs(pMoveX)
  else if newLoc.locH < pLimit.left then
    pMoveX = abs(pMoveX)
  end if

  -- check to see if it has hit top or bottom of the limit
  if newLoc.locV > pLimit.bottom then
    pMoveY = -abs(pMoveY)
    pSpeedDown = -abs(pSpeedDown)-1
    if pLoseEnergy then
      if pSpeedDown < -1 then pSpeedDown = pSpeedDown + 1
    end if
  end if

  -- set the sprite location
  sprite (me.spriteNum).loc = newLoc
end
```

COMMUNICATING BETWEEN BEHAVIORS

Behaviors do not have to control only their own sprites; they can actually send instructions and information to other sprites and behaviors as well. Three special commands are used for doing this—sendSprite, sendAllSprites, and call.

Sending a Message to a Sprite

The first command in question is sendSprite, which sends a message to a specific sprite, along with additional information. For example:

```
sendSprite(sprite 1, #myHandler, 5)
```

This line sends the message myHandler to sprite 1. If that sprite has an on myHandler handler, it runs. In addition, the number 5 is passed to it as the first parameter after *me*. It might look like this:

```
on myHandler me, num
  put "I got your message:"&&num
end
```

A more useful example might be to tie two sprites together so that when one is dragged by the mouse, the other follows in sync. The first sprite's behavior might look like this:

```
property pPressed

on beginSprite me
 pPressed = FALSE
end

on mouseDown me
 pPressed = TRUE
end

on mouseUp me
 pPressed = FALSE
end

on mouseUpOutside me
 pPressed = FALSE
end

on exitFrame me
 if pPressed then
  -- calculate move amount
  moveAmount = the mouseLoc - sprite(me.spriteNum).loc

  -- move this sprite
  sprite(me.spriteNum).loc = sprite(me.spriteNum).loc + moveAmount

  -- move another sprite
  sendSprite (sprite 2,#move,moveAmount)
 end if
end
```

This is a fairly basic drag behavior. When users click it, the *pPressed* variable is set to TRUE. This enables three lines to run in the on exitFrame handler. Those three lines calculate the difference between the current location of the cursor and the current location of the sprite, move the sprite that amount so that it matches the cursor, and then send that movement amount to sprite number 2.

The second behavior should be attached to sprite 2, and it can simply be

```
-- get message from another sprite to move
on move me, moveAmount
 sprite(me.spriteNum).loc = sprite(me.spriteNum).loc + moveAmount
end
```

This handler receives a message from the first sprite and uses the point included with the message to change its location. The result is that the two sprites move together when the first one is dragged.

Sending a Message to All Sprites

Another way for behaviors to communicate is to use the `sendAllSprites` command. This is essentially the same as `sendSprite`, but it does not require the first parameter:

```
sendAllSprites(#myHandler, 5)
```

As you can probably guess, this command sends the message and information to all the sprites in the current frame. Any of them that have an `on myHandler` handler receive the message and use it. If a behavior does not have this handler, the message is ignored.

Sending a Message to Specific Behaviors

Another way to send messages between behaviors is by using the `call` command. The difference between `sendSprite` and `call` is that `call` sends the message to a specific behavior attached to a sprite. This is handy when more than one behavior is attached to a sprite.

To use `call`, you need to specify both the sprite number and the behavior. You specify the behavior by using a script instance. You get this special value by using the `scriptInstanceList` of a sprite. Here is how you call the second behavior attached to a sprite:

> The `scriptInstanceList` of a sprite does not exist until the movie is running and the sprite appears in the frame. Until then, the sprite and behavior are just Score information waiting for their chance to appear. When they appear, that is when the script instances are actually created.

```
scriptInstance = sprite(7).scriptInstanceList[2]
call(#myHandler,scriptInstance)
```

Instead of using `call` with a single script instance, you can pass a whole list of script instances. You can also include handler parameters after the script instance in the `call` command.

USING PARENT SCRIPTS

Behaviors are object-oriented scripts customized to fit Director's sprite-oriented nature. But you can also write scripts that exist independent of any sprite. Parent scripts are used to create non–sprite-oriented objects, sometimes called *code objects*.

In Lingo, you define an object template by writing a parent script. *Parent scripts* are like templates for code objects. You then create an object from that parent script by sending a "new" message to the parent script. You can create as many objects as you want from the same parent script. The Director manuals call the objects created from a parent object *child objects*.

> A *code object* is a self-contained unit of code in memory that keeps track of its own internal data. Code objects have internal variables called *properties*, and they respond to messages just as behaviors do. But unlike behaviors, you can't just drop them into the Score to use them.

You get a Lingo object to respond by sending it a message. The object's handler determines which messages it responds to. An object can have a handler for just about anything you can program in Lingo. Director objects also have a built-in data management system, similar to structures in more traditional programming languages. Other than the messages sent to and from an object, the objects are completely isolated from each other.

If you are coming to Lingo with experience in an *OOP* (*object-oriented programming*) language, such as C++, it might take you some time to get your bearings. Lingo does not have a ready-made class library, nor does it impose many rules about object structure, but it uses its own unique terminology. Table 12.2 shows the OOP terms and their Lingo equivalents.

Table 12.2   Object-Oriented Programming Versus Lingo Terms

OOP Term	Lingo Equivalent
Base class	Ancestor script
Class	Parent script
Instance variable	Property variable
Class instance/object	Child object
Method/member function	Method

Reasons to Use Objects

Almost everything you can do with objects in Lingo can be done without much difficulty using Director's Score-based environment. So, why use objects? Objects offer advantages of efficiency, flexibility, and optimal use of processing and memory resources. The following sections give five reasons to use objects.

Objects Organize Your Code

Better organization is achieved with objects because the parent contains both the code and the variables on which the code relies. If all your code and variables related to printing a report or playing digital video are in the same place, it's easier to maintain them using objects.

Objects Persist over Time

Like globals, an object's property variables maintain their state over time; unlike globals, the properties are known only to the object maintaining them. This helps you keep the number of globals used in your program down.

Suppose that you wanted to make a program to keep track of employees. Each employee has a name, a home phone number, and other personal information. These are properties that they all have in common. That is, they have the same properties, even though they have different values from employee to employee. All these variables must be globals, or part of a global list, to be capable of maintaining their contents over time. In this case, you would end up with a lot of global variables all named with some variation of a product section name and counter or timer, all available everywhere in the movie. How long before you accidentally use the same global name twice for two different purposes?

Alternatively, you could make an object for each employee from the same parent script template. They would each have the same properties, but with different values.

If you had some salary employees that are paid monthly, and some hourly employees that are paid weekly, you could create a different parent script for each. Both parent scripts would have properties, such as the employee's name and number, but one would have salary information and the other hourly wage information.

None of these variables is part of the global pool because its scope is restricted to the object to which it belongs. This way, you don't have to worry about using a variable name multiple times for different purposes; instead, you can reference the properties of each object.

Objects Are Easy to Test

An object is self-contained. Because it isn't dependent on any code outside itself, an object can be tested before other parts of the project are finished. After an object is coded, you should be able to test it by sending messages to all its handlers. If the handlers set the correct property variables or return the correct values, you know that the object is functioning properly and can be integrated into the larger project. While in Director, you can even send messages to an object after the movie has been stopped, which can come in handy to test variable names and handler functionality.

Objects Make Coding Easier and More Efficient

Using objects makes coding easier and more efficient through the use of inheritance. *Inheritance* is an OOP term that refers to the capability of one script to incorporate the handlers and properties of another script. Inheritance is a way of reusing existing code for similar programming problems rather than writing code completely from scratch every time.

In Lingo, inheritance works in this manner: A parent script defines the handlers and properties that any object created from it will have. The created object inherits the handlers and properties of the parent. Multiple objects can be created from the same parent and, if appropriate, individualized with their own additional properties and handlers.

An *ancestor script* is another level of script in Lingo that uses inheritance. A parent script can link to an ancestor script. In this way, all the ancestor script's handlers and properties become part of the parent script and are, in turn, passed on to the child object. The child object inherits the ancestor's handlers and properties, plus any of the parent's handlers and properties that are also needed. Ancestor scripts are discussed in more detail in the "Using Ancestors" section later in this chapter.

Objects Can Be Reused

If you create objects with reuse in mind, eventually you will have a library of objects that you can put together to handle much of your routine coding. Director has the capability to link a movie to more than one Cast. This capability enables you to maintain a code library containing library objects that you can easily link to any movie. Almost any object you create has the potential to be reused, and if it's an external cast library, reuse is easy. If you create an object to handle grading a quiz, for example, the same object can be used in any quiz by simply changing a few of the properties.

Creating an Object in Lingo

To create an object, you must first create a parent script. As mentioned in the previous section, a parent script defines the methods and properties of objects created from it. The programming problem you are trying to solve determines the handlers and properties that you should include in your parent script. The basic method required by all parent scripts is the on new handler.

The on new handler creates a new object from a parent script. A parent script is like a template document in a word processing program. Just as you can create any number of identical documents from one template, you can create any number of identical objects by calling the new method of a parent script. Each time you send a parent script a new message, it creates a new object from that parent script.

The syntax for the on new method is as follows:

```
on new me
  return me
end
```

It's important to use the word me in the line beginning with on. The word me holds a pointer to the location in memory of the object created from the parent script. It is also important to include the return line inside the on new method. This line returns a pointer to the object. If you don't include this return, you have no way of communicating with the object after you create it.

Director has a parent script type, available through the Script panel, which is the proper place for creating parent scripts. If you accidentally create an object from a movie script and send it a message, Director looks through all the movie scripts for a handler for that message. If you have a movie script handler with the same name as one of your object methods, the movie script handler, rather than your object, gets the message.

> **Caution**
>
> A common error is to forget the return me at the end of the on new handler.

Global objects, like any other global variable, persist across movies. After an object is created from a parent script, it exists independently in memory. The object no longer references the parent script. If you go to another movie that does not contain the object's parent script, the object still works. The object is using its own copy of the code defined in the parent script that it has stored in memory.

> When you create objects from a parent script, it's a good idea to store them in global variables so that the objects are available to code anywhere in the movie that you want to use them.

If you change a parent script's code after you have created an object from it, you do not change the object already in memory. You must create a new object from the edited parent script; if you want to update multiple objects created from the same parent script, you must create new objects to replace each of the older ones.

With these background facts in mind, we can build an object. Create a new, empty parent by first creating a script cast member. Click the Info button in the Script panel and use the Type pull-down menu in the Property Inspector to change the script's type property to Parent. Enter the name "**minimal**" in the script's name field. A name is not optional for a parent script; it is required because you need to refer to it in other Lingo code.

Enter the following code into your minimalist parent script and name the script member minimal:

```
on new me
  return me
end
```

Create a new object by typing the following Lingo into the Message panel:

```
minimalObj = new(script "minimal")
```

The code line you entered creates a new object from the minimal script and puts it in the global *minimalObj*. You should store your objects in globals so that they will be available to code anywhere in your movie that they are needed.

Enter the following in the Message panel and press (Return) [Enter] to see whether you created an object. Director returns the contents of the object variable, which confirms that the object was successfully created:

```
put minimalObj
-- <offspring "minimal" 2 8daa90>
```

The object *minimalObj* was created successfully, but it can't really do anything yet. It cannot receive any messages other than "new", and it has no property variables to store data.

Add a script so that you can create a new object with the click of a button. This way, you don't have to create a new object by typing commands in the Message panel every time you play the movie. Make an on mouseUp handler that handles creating the object, as follows:

```
on mouseUp
 global gObj
 set gObj = new(script "minimal")
end
```

Rewind and play your movie and create a new object by clicking the button on the Stage. Check to see whether the object was properly created by typing ***put gObj*** in the Message panel and pressing (Return) [Enter].

Create an *on hello* method for the object that makes the object beep. Edit the parent script to contain the following code:

```
on new me
  return me
end

on hello me
  beep
end
```

Rewind and play your movie and create a new instance of the object by clicking the button you created on the Stage. You should now be able to type the following code into the Message panel. If everything worked correctly, your computer should beep.

```
hello(gObj)
```

12

Creating Object Properties

So far, you have created a simple object that beeps if you send it the hello message. This object isn't terribly useful, however. To add greater functionality to an object, it needs more than methods. The minimal object is missing the second component of truly functional objects in Director: properties. The *property* variables of an object can be used to hold any type of data and are unique to each instance of the object.

You declare an object's property variables at the top of the parent script in the same manner as you declare globals and properties in behaviors:

```
property pProp1, pProp2, pProp3...
```

You can refer to the property inside the parent script by just its name. Outside the parent script, you can refer to it using the dot syntax. For instance, if an object is referenced by the variable *gObj* and you want to get the value of its property *pProp1*, *gObj.pProp1* gives you that value.

The following is a simple parent script that sets a property during the new handler. Place it in a script member named "Test Object". Make sure that this member is set to be a parent script, not a movie script or a behavior. You can then use the on test handler to see that the property is there.

```
property pTest

on new me
 pTest = "Hello World."
 return me
end


on test me
 put pTest
end
```

You can try it out in the Message panel:

```
gObj = new(script "Test Object")
test(gObj)
-- "Hello World."
```

As noted earlier in this chapter, you can produce multiple identical objects from the same parent script. You can then individualize the objects by giving them different properties. In this way, you can enjoy the efficiency of not rewriting code for methods and properties that are the same from object to object. Yet, you still have the flexibility to create unique objects as your programming problem demands.

The following is a script parent similar to the last one. In this case, however, it sets the property *pTest* in the new handler according to a parameter:

```
property pTest

on new me, val
 pTest = val
 return me
end
```

```
on test me
 put pTest
end
```

Now, try this in the Message panel. It demonstrates the creation of two separate objects from one parent script and how the values of the properties inside each object can be different:

```
gObj1 = new(script "Test Object 2", "Hello World.")
gObj2 = new(script "Test Object 2", "Testing...")
put gObj1
-- <offspring "Test Object 2" 2 4abfdac>
put gObj2
-- <offspring "Test Object 2" 2 4abfe24>
test(gObj1)
-- "Hello World."
test(gObj2)
-- "Testing..."
```

📎 *If you need to update your parent scripts on-the-fly, see "Changing Parent Scripts On-the-Fly" in the "Troubleshooting" section at the end of this chapter.*

Using OOP

In Director, using OOP is so automatic that you can hardly avoid doing it. Every behavior is OOP code that controls a sprite or frame.

In the past, parent scripts were created to take control of sprites and make them behave in certain ways. Behaviors have taken over this responsibility. As a result, the usefulness of parent scripts has decreased.

You can still use parent scripts for nonvisually oriented tasks. For instance, if you want to create a vocabulary program, you can store words as objects. After all, a word can have many properties: spelling, definition, synonyms, and so on. Here is a simple parent script that can be used to create a word object:

```
property pWord
property pDefinition

on new me, theword
 pWord = theword
 return me
end

on setDefinition me, def
 pDefinition = def
end

on define me
 return pDefinition
end
```

Using the Message panel, you can see how this can be applied:

```
gWord = new(script "Word Object", "Clever")
put gWord.pWord
-- "Clever"
setDefinition(gWord, "Skillful in thinking. ")
put define(gWord)
-- "Skillful in thinking. "
```

Now you can add more properties, such as synonyms, antonyms, homonyms, anagrams, common misspellings, and so on. You can add more handlers to accept and process these properties, or create universal ones that accept and return any property.

This same sort of OOP logic can be applied to any type of data. You can have a database of employees, for instance. Each object can have properties such as the employee's name, address, phone number, date of birth, Social Security number, and so on.

In turn, the handlers in the parent script would be custom built to work with this data.

Using Ancestor Scripts with Parent Scripts

Parent scripts can use a special property, called an *ancestor*, which is a reference to another parent script.

When you define and use the `ancestor` property, you give the object access to all the handlers and properties in that ancestor parent script. In this way, you can have objects created with different parent scripts but that use the same ancestor script. In other words, they can share some handlers but not others.

Suppose that you want to use objects to track items in a store. One problem with items in a store is that they have different properties. A piece of fruit, for instance, has an expiration date. A can of food, on the other hand, might not have an expiration date, but does have a size property: It can fit on some shelves but not others. The following is an *ancestor* script that has all the properties shared by both types of items. It should be in a parent script member named "Property Ancestor". It also has a handler that does something with them:

```
property pProductName
property pAisleNumber

on new me
 return me
end

on whereIs me
 return pProductName&&"is in aisle"&&pAisleNumber
end
```

The shared item is the aisle number. This is the way the store keeps track of where things are. In addition, all products have a name. An *on whereIs* handler returns a string that contains both.

The first type of product that the store stocks is fruit. It is a product, so it uses the ancestor script, and from that gets the use of the *pProductName* and *pAisleNumber* properties, as well as the *on whereIs* handler. In addition, it has an expiration date. Here is a parent script for a piece of fruit. It should be in a parent script member named "Fruit Parent".

```
property ancestor
property pExpires

on new me
 ancestor = new(script "Product Ancestor")
 return me
end

on expiration me
 return me.pProductName&&"expires"&&pExpires
end
```

The first property in the fruit parent script is the ancestor. In the on new handler, this is set to be a new instance of the ancestor script. In addition, this parent script has a *pExpires* property and a handler that uses it. This handler also accesses the *pProductName* property from the ancestor script by using the me property and dot syntax.

You can see how all this works in the Message panel. When an object is created from the fruit parent script, the ancestor is attached to it. You can then assign the object with properties from both its own parent script and its ancestor script. Then you can access handlers from both as well.

```
gApple = new(script "Fruit Parent")
gApple.pProductName = "Apple"
gApple.pAisleNumber = 14
gApple.pExpires = "12/31/98"
put expiration(gApple)
-- "Apple expires 12/31/98"
put whereIs(gApple)
-- "Apple is in aisle 14"
```

The power of this technique comes when you need to create another type of product, such as canned food, for instance. The following is a parent script for cans:

```
property ancestor
property pSize

on new me
 ancestor = new(script "Product Ancestor")
 return me
end

on size me
 return me.pProductName&&"is size"&&pSize
end
```

This script looks similar to the fruit parent script but has a different property. Things such as product name and aisle number are already taken care of because you used the same ancestor script.

```
gYams = new(script "Can Parent")
gYams.pProductName = "Canned Yams"
gYams.pAisleNumber = 9
gYams.pSize = "Medium"
put size(gYams)
-- "Canned Yams is size Medium"
put whereIs(gYams)
-- "Canned Yams is in aisle 9"
```

You can now go on to create dozens or hundreds of types of parent scripts that all use the same ancestor script. If you then want to add another shared property, such as an order number, you can add it to the ancestor script. All the objects that use that ancestor script inherit the property when you run the movie again.

TROUBLESHOOTING

Completing Parameter Descriptions

Why can't I get my on `getPropertyDescription` handlers to work correctly?

When you build a list for an on `getPropertyDescription` handler, each item must have a `#comment`, `#format`, and `#default` property. Even in cases where there is no logical `#default`, you need to put something there, such as a 0, VOID, or an empty string.

Changing Parent Scripts On-the-Fly

I'm trying to change my parent scripts while the movie is running, but I can't figure out how to make the changes take effect.

When you use the `new` command to create an object, it takes the code as it currently exists. If you change the script member, you have to re-create the object with the new command before the change takes effect.

Favor Behaviors Over Parent Scripts

I don't know whether I need to use a parent script or a behavior. Which one is better?

Creating parent scripts might seem natural to OOP programmers, but in many cases a behavior is really what is needed. A good rule of thumb is to use parent scripts only when there is no visual component to the object, or possibly when more than one sprite needs to be controlled by an object.

DID YOU KNOW?

- You can set a #min and #max to a range of values in a behavior parameter description, and also can include an #increment property that determines how much one click of the arrow keys next to the slider will change the value.

- The continuation character was more useful in Director 6 and earlier, when lines in script could only be a finite length before a wrap was forced. A line is considered continued when the last character is a backslash (\).

- If you have overlapping sprites and you want to make sure that your rollover behaviors work only when you roll over a visible portion of the sprite, check to make sure that *the rollover* is the same as the behavior's sprite number (me.spriteNum) before you set the member in the on mouseEnter handler.

- When you are determining the wall, floor, and ceiling positions for the bounce behavior, you might want to compute them relative to the Stage size. Use (the stage).sourceRect to get a rectangle with the Stage size. Use (the stage).sourceRect.width and (the stage).sourceRect.height to get the right wall and floor positions.

- When you create an object and then examine it in the Message panel, the strange-looking result is actually the name of the script, the number of references to the script, and the member location of the object. It might look like this: "<offspring "Can Parent" 2 4abfeec>".

- There is a system property called *the actorList*. If you use add to add objects to this list, the objects begin to receive on stepFrame handler calls exactly once per frame.

- You can assign any object, such as a member, or the systemDate to a script object as its ancestor. For instance, if you assign a sprite as the ancestor of a script object, you can treat properties such as locH and ink as properties of that script object.

- If you assign a sprite as the ancestor of a script object, all the behaviors attached to that sprite also become ancestors of the script object. You can access normal properties in the sprite, as well as properties of the behaviors.

- You can use parent scripts to store handlers in memory to be used when the projector or Shockwave changes movies. Because the code resides in a global variable, it persists beyond the movie. You can use that global to call the handlers that existed in the parent script, even though the script is not present in the current movie.

12

13

USING LINGO TO ALTER TEXT MEMBERS

IN THIS CHAPTER

FIELD PROPERTIES AND FUNCTIONS

A field member's primary property is the text it contains. You can get this text in Lingo with the text property of the member. You can also use the Lingo syntax field to refer to any field's text as if it were a string.

Using `field`, you can use the `put` commands and chunk expressions directly on the field contents without having to first store them in a string variable. For instance, if a field holds the text "Hello World," you can perform this command:

```
put "-" into char 6 of field 1
```

Notice that you cannot use dot syntax with this type of functionality. You cannot write `put "-" into field(1).char[6]`, for instance. However, you can write `put "-" into member(1).char[6]`. This is true because `field` is considered antiquated syntax, so the dot syntax was not implemented for it after Director 6.

Some things can still be done to field members only using the old syntax, such as setting the font of characters inside the field. If you want to set the font of the entire member, you can do that with dot syntax:

```
member(1).font = "Times"
```

However, if you want to set the font of just a few characters, words, or lines in the field, you need to use the field syntax:

```
set the font of word 6 to 9 of field 1 = "Geneva"
```

You can set many properties in a field like this one. Table 13.1 examines all the field properties. The Usage column indicates which properties can be applied to a chunk of a field, an entire field, or only scrolling fields.

Table 13.1   Field Properties

Property	Usage	Description
font	Field chunk	The typeface of the characters. You should specify the font as you would a string, as in Times or Arial, for example.
fontSize	Field chunk	The size of the font of the characters. Should be an integer, such as 9, 12, or 72.
fontStyle	Field chunk	The style of the font. Should be a comma-delimited string that contains all the styles requested. For instance, `"bold"`, or `"bold, underline"`. You can use the styles `"plain"`, `"bold"`, `"italic"`, `"underline"`, `"shadow"`, and `"outline"`. The last two are Mac only. To turn off all styles, use `"plain"`.
foreColor	Field chunk	The color of the characters. You can set the color of any chunk in the field to a color in the movie's color palette.
alignment	Field	This can be set to either `"left"`, `"right"`, or `"center"` to change the alignment of the field.

Table 13.1 Continued

Property	Usage	Description
autotab	Field	Use TRUE or FALSE to change the member property of the same name. When TRUE, and the field is editable, the user can use the Tab key to move quickly between fields.
bgColor	Field	Enables you to set the background color of the field member. You can use rgb and paletteIndex structures.
border	Field	Enables you to set or change the border width around the field. A value of 0 removes the border.
boxDropShadow	Field	Enables you to set or change the drop shadow around the box of the field. A value of 0 removes the drop shadow.
boxType	Field	Enables you to change the type of field member. The options are #adjust, #scroll, #fixed, and #limit, just as they are in the field member's Properties dialog box.
color	Field	The same as foreColor, but you can use rgb and paletteIndex structures. The entire field has to be set at once.
dropShadow	Field	Enables you to set or change the drop shadow around the text of the field. A value of 0 removes the drop shadow.
editable	Field	Enables you to change the editable property of the member. Can be either TRUE or FALSE. When TRUE, and the movie is playing, users can click and edit the text in the field.
lineCount	Field	Returns the number of actual lines in the field, taking into account line wraps.
lineHeight	Field	Enables you to set the line height, in pixels, of the entire text field. Typically, line heights are set to be a few points above the font size.
margin	Field	Enables you to change the inside margin property of the text field.
wordWrap	Field	Enables you to turn automatic word wrapping on or off by setting this to TRUE or FALSE.
scrollByLine	Scrolling field	A command that forces the field to scroll up or down a number of lines. For instance, scrollByLine member(1), 2, scrolls down two lines. Use a negative number to scroll up.
scrollByPage	Scrolling field	The same as scrollByLine, except that it scrolls by pages. A page is the number of lines in the field visible on the Stage. Use a negative number to scroll up.
scrollTop	Scrolling field	This property corresponds to the number of pixels that the scrolling field is from the top. If a field uses the line height 12, and it is scrolled one line, the scrollTop is 12.

The powerful thing about the three scrolling field commands is that they also work on fields set to be a "fixed" type. This means that you can use Lingo to scroll a field even if the scrolling bar elements are not on the screen.

Editable text fields have a special quality in that text can be selected inside them by users. Some Lingo code relates to this. You can get the position of the selection, the selection itself, and even set the selection. Table 13.2 runs down all the Lingo having to do with recognizing text selection in fields.

Remember that the `editable` property works for both members and sprites. To make a field or text member non-editable, make sure that both properties are switched off.

Table 13.2   Field Text Selection

Lingo	Description
hilite	This command enables you to set the selection of an editable text field. For instance: `hilite word 2 of member "myField"`.
the selection	This property returns the text selected in the currently active editable text field. Do not place a member reference after this property; it stands on its own.
the selStart	This returns the number of the first character in the current selection. You can use it to set the selection. Do not place a member reference after this property; it stands on its own.
the selEnd	This returns the number of the last character in the current selection. You can use it to set the selection. Do not place a member reference after this property; it stands on its own.

Lastly, for fields, several functions enable you to find the correlation between a location on the screen and the characters in a field. Table 13.3 shows these functions.

Table 13.3   Field Location Functions

Lingo	Description
charPosToLoc	Takes a field member and a number as parameters and returns a point that corresponds to where that character is located in the member. The point is relative to the upper-left corner of the member, regardless of any scrolling that is taking place.
linePosToLocV	Takes a field member and a number as parameters and returns the distance, in pixels, from the top of the member to where the line is located.
locToCharPos	Takes a member and a point as parameters and returns the number of the character located at that point in the field. The point should be relative to the upper-left corner of the member, regardless of any scrolling that is taking place.
locVtoLinePos	Takes a member and a number as parameters and returns the line number indicating the distance from the top of the field.
the mouseChar	Returns the number of the character that is under the cursor, regardless of what field it is.
the mouseWord	Returns the number of the word that is under the cursor, regardless of what field it is.
the mouseLine	Returns the number of the line that is under the cursor, regardless of what field it is.
the mouseItem	Returns the number of the item that is under the cursor, regardless of what field it is.

Although the mouseChar and similar properties tell you what chunk number is under the cursor, they do not tell you to which field that chunk belongs. You can use the other functions to get a more accurate reading. Here is a function that tells you what field and chunk are under the cursor at any time, regardless of scrolling:

```
on underCursor
 s = the rollover
 loc = the mouseLoc

 -- is there a sprite under the cursor?
 if (s > 0) then

  -- is there a field attached to that sprite?
  if sprite(s).member.type = #field then

   -- subtract the loc of the sprite to get relative loc
   loc = loc - sprite(s).loc

   -- add any field scrolling
   loc.locV = loc.locV + sprite(s).member.scrollTop

   -- get the character number
   c = locToCharPos(sprite(s).member,loc)

   -- figure out the character
   ch = (sprite(s).member.text.char[c])
   put "The cursor is over character"&&c&&"("&ch&")"
  end if
 end if
end
```

TEXT MEMBER PROPERTIES AND FUNCTIONS

Text members have a similar set of properties and functions as fields. However, sometimes the syntax varies.

For instance, you can still set the font, size, style, and color of any chunk in a text member, but you must use the new dot syntax. font and fontSize work much as you would expect. For example:

```
member("myText").char[2..5].font = "Times"
member("myText").char[2..5].fontSize = 18
```

However, fontStyle works a little differently. Instead of giving it a string, such as "bold, underline", you need to give it a list, such as [#bold, #underline]. As is the case elsewhere, using [#plain] removes all styles.

Coloring text is also a little different. You can use the color property to set the color of the whole text member or just a chunk inside it. Here are some examples:

13

```
member("myText").color = rgb(40,120,0)
member("myText").char[2..5] = rgb("#6699CC")
member("myText").word[7].color = paletteIndex(35)
```

The text members do not have any border, margin, or drop shadows. However, they do share some of the other properties of fields. Most of these, however, use different values. They also have some new properties, as shown in Table 13.4.

Table 13.4   Properties Unique to Text Members

Property	Description
alignment	This can be set to either #left, #right, or #center to change the alignment of the member. Text members also have a #full setting that justifies text.
antiAlias	Set to TRUE or FALSE, depending on whether you want the text in the member to display with a smooth, anti-aliased effect.
antiAliasThreshold	A point size at which the member should display text as anti-aliased. Any characters under this point size are displayed normally.
autotab	Use TRUE or FALSE to change the member property of the same name. When TRUE, and the member is editable, users can press the Tab key to move quickly between text members.
bottomSpacing	The number of pixels of spacing after each paragraph in the text.
boxType	Enables you to change the type of text member. The options are #adjust, #scroll, and #fixed.
charSpacing	The number of extra pixels to place between characters. The default is 0.
editable	Enables you to change the editable property of the member. Can be TRUE or FALSE. When TRUE, and the movie is playing, users can click and edit the text in the member.
firstIndent	The number of pixels away from the left edge that the first line of text in a paragraph should start.
fixedLineSpace	The same as the lineHeight property of fields, but you can set different lines to different amounts.
html	The raw data from the text member in HTML format.
kerning	Set this to FALSE if you do not want Director to automatically adjust the character spacing in the text member if the text changes.
kerningThreshold	Set this to the minimum font size that you think the kerning property should default to within that cast member.
leftIndent	The number of pixels away from the edge that the text should start at the left side of the member.
rightIndent	The number of pixels away from the edge that the text should start at the right side of the member.
rtf	The raw data from the text member in Rich Text Format.
selectedText	A reference to the selected text that can be used to get font information.

13

Table 13.4   Continued

Property	Description
tabs	A list containing the tab types and pixel positions. For example: *[[#type: #left, #position: 72]]*. You can create your own list of tabs and set the tabs property of a text member.
topSpacing	The number of pixels of spacing before each paragraph in the text.
wordWrap	Being able to turn off word wrapping by setting this to FALSE in text members, as well as fields, is new to Director 8.

Text members, when set to be editable, can also have a selected area. The Lingo functions to deal with this are different from those that deal with fields.

To get the selected text, use the selectedText property. This returns a ref structure. From that, you can get the text string of the selected area and some font information:

```
r = member("myText").selectedText
put r.text
-- "the"
put r.font
-- "Times"
put r.fontSize
-- 12
put r.fontStyle
[#plain]
```

The selection property returns a list with the first and last character number of the selected area. You can also set the selected area of a text member, as long as the member is editable, the movie is playing, and the text member has focus. This means that you cannot use the Message panel to successfully set the selection.

```
on preselectText
 member("myText").selection = [6,9]
end
```

Text members also have the capability to tell you which character is at a certain spot. The functions for this are quite different than with fields. The basic function is pointToChar, and it tells you which character is under a point. It looks like this:

```
pointToChar(sprite 1, point(x,y))
```

This function has several companions: pointToWord, pointToItem, pointToLine, and pointToParagraph. They perform basically the same way, but with different chunk expressions.

Unlike the field functions, these text member functions figure things out according to the actual Stage location, calculating differences caused by the sprite location and scrolling automatically.

Notice that this function uses the sprite reference, rather than the member reference. To determine which character is under the cursor, use the mouseLoc as the point.

13

Text members also differ from fields in how they are represented in memory. Text members can be either rich text or HTML text. Fields have a text property that holds the plain, unformatted text of the member. So do text members. However, they also have rich text and HTML properties named `rtf` and `html`. Here is what happens if you create a simple text member, place the word "Testing" in it, and then try to access these properties in the Message panel:

```
put member(1).text
-- "Testing"

put member(1).rtf
-- "{\rtf1\mac\deff3 {\fonttbl{\f3\fswiss Geneva;}{\f20\froman
Times;}}{\colortbl\red0\green0\blue0;}{\stylesheet{\s0\fs24 Normal Text;}
}\pard \f3\fs24{\plain\f20\fs24 Testing\par}}"

put member(1).html
-- "<html>
<head>
<title>Untitled</title>
</head>
<body bgcolor="#FFFFFF">
<font face="Times, Times New Roman" size=5>Testing</font></body>
</html>
"
```

The `rtf` and `html` properties are constantly updated to reflect changes in the text member. Even better, you can directly set either of these properties, and the text member re-creates itself to match.

CREATING TEXT LISTS

A few interface elements use fields and text members. One of these is sometimes called a *text list*. It is similar to a group of radio buttons, but only one sprite is needed. This sprite contains a text field on which users can click to select a line of text from a list. Figure 13.1 shows an example of such a text list.

Figure 13.1
A small text list that highlights
the text line selected by the user.

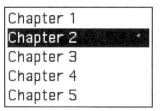

To create one of these text lists, first create the field member. The field in Figure 13.1 has several lines of text and uses a 2-pixel margin and a 1-pixel border. It is not editable, despite the fact that selecting text does highlight it.

The behavior is short and simple. Only one property is needed, and that is one of convenience. You need to reference the member of the sprite several times, so placing it as a property makes it easily available:

```
property pMember

on beginSprite me
 pMember = sprite(me.spriteNum).member
end
```

The selection action can take place on either an on mouseUp or an on mouseDown handler. It calls one custom handler to determine the line clicked and then one to select the line:

```
on mouseDown me
 -- get the number of the line clicked
 clickedLine = computeLine(me,the clickLoc)

 -- select that line
 selectLine(me,clickedLine)
end
```

The next handler calculates the line clicked from the click location, the sprite location, and the scrolling position of the field. The field in this example isn't a scrolling one, but this extra line ensures that the behavior will be ready to go in the future if you want to have a scrolling text list:

```
on computeLine me, loc
 -- get the vertical location minus the top of the sprite
 verticalLoc = loc.locV - sprite(me.spriteNum).locV

 -- add any amount that the field has been scrolled
 verticalLoc = verticalLoc + pMember.scrollTop

 -- return the results of locVtoLinePos
 return locVtoLinePos(pMember,verticalLoc)
end
```

You could replace the entire on computeLine function with the use of the mouseLine, but this can be considered sloppy. If users click one line and then move the mouse quickly away before Director executes the line that includes the mouseLine, the actual line clicked and the line selected differ.

The *on selectLine* handler can be as simple as one line. If you use the command hilite, and refer to the member as a field, nothing more is needed.

```
on selectLine me, clickedLine
 -- use a simple hilite command to highlight the line
 hilite line clickedLine of field pMember
end
```

If you take another look at the image in Figure 13.1, you can see that the highlight goes all the way across the line. This is accomplished by using char references rather than line references with the hilite command. All that is needed is for the invisible Return character at the end of each line to be included in the hilite, as follows:

```
on selectLine me, clickedLine
 --figure out the first and last chars for hilite
```

13

```
if clickedLine = 1 then
 -- first line, start with char 1
 startChar = 1
else
 -- not first line, count chars before line
 -- and add 2 to go past return to the next line
 startChar = (pMember.text.line[1..clickedLine-1]).length + 2
end if

 -- for last char, count chars including line,
 -- and then add 1 for the RETURN character
endChar = (pMember.text.line[1..clickedLine]).length + 1

 hilite char startChar to endChar of field pMember
end
```

The text list can also be accomplished by just using the radio button behaviors and some members that contain one line of text each. Or, you could use text members rather than field members and place a rectangle shape behind the text to act as the highlight. By doing so, you could even add more code and allow for multiple selections in the text list, so the items in the list act like a group of check boxes. You cannot do this using hilite because it allows only for a continuous selection area.

CREATING TEXT POP-UP MENUS

Pop-up menus are a natural extension of text lists. These types of pop-ups are one of those tricks that developers have learned over the years. Because fields can be set to "Adjust to Fit" and can be updated on-the-fly, you can make them imitate pop-ups fairly convincingly.

Figure 13.2 shows a single text field with one line of text. The field has been set to have a 1-pixel border, a 2-pixel margin, and a 2-pixel box shadow to make it look like something that can be clicked.

Figure 13.2
A simple field can be made to look like an inactive pop-up menu.

Choose One

The behavior attached to the field changes its appearance by simply placing more lines of text in it. Because the field is set to "Adjust to Fit," it grows when that happens. Figure 13.3 shows what the field looks like when clicked. Not only is more text added, but a hilite command is used to show which item would be selected if the mouse were released at the moment.

To accomplish this neat trick, the behavior first needs to get the list of items to place in the field when the field is active. This can be done a number of ways. For this sample behavior, the field starts with all the items present. All the lines but the first are hidden from view when the sprite begins. The field should be set to a frame type of "fixed" and contain an extra Return at the end of the last line. Here is the start of the behavior:

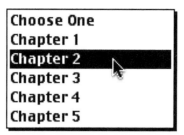

Figure 13.3
The field pop-up expands as more
text is placed in it.

```
property pMember -- the field used in the pop-up
property pText -- the complete text of the pop-up
property pSelection -- the selected text
property pPressed -- whether the user is making a selection
property pLastHilite -- the last line highlighted

on beginSprite me
 -- get some properties
 pMember = sprite(me.spriteNum).member.name
 pText = member(pMember).text
 pSelected = pText.line[1] -- assume first line is default
 pPressed = FALSE

 -- set the field to the selected item
 member(pMember).text = pSelected

 -- set the field rectangle
 setMemberRect(me)

 -- remove any highlight
 hilite member(pMember).char[the maxInteger]
end
```

The action starts when the user clicks the field. Then, the pop-up menu needs to appear. Here are the handlers for that action:

```
on mouseDown me
 pPressed = TRUE
 openPopup(me)
end

on openPopup me
 member(pMember).text = pText
 setMemberRect(me)
 pLastHilite = 0
end

-- This handler will adjust the field to be the size
-- of the text contained in it
on setMemberRect me
```

13

```
 memRect = member(pMember).rect
 numLines = member(pMember).text.lines.count
 if member(pMember).text.line[numLines] = "" then numLines = numLines - 1
 memRect.bottom = memRect.top + (numLines * member(pMember).lineHeight)
 member(pMember).rect = memRect
end
```

The on `exitFrame` handler now needs to keep checking the mouse location to ensure that the correct item is highlighted:

```
on exitFrame me
 if pPressed then
  -- What line is the cursor over?
  thisLine = the mouseLine

  -- is it over a different line than before?
  if (thisLine <> pLastHilite) and (thisLine > 0) then
   selectLine(me,thisLine)
   pLastHilite = thisLine
   pSelection = pText.line[thisline]
  end if
 end if
end
```

When the mouse button is released, the pop-up text needs to go away, and the field should be restored to its former self. In addition, if the mouse is released over the sprite, it probably means that a selection has been made:

```
on mouseUp me
 pPressed = FALSE
 closePopup(me)
 makeSelection(me)
end

on mouseUpOutside me
 mouseUp(me)
end

-- set the pop-up to the current selection
on closePopup me
 member(pMember).text = pSelection
 setMemberRect(me)
end
```

The *on selectLine* handler is the same one used for the text list behavior:

```
on selectLine me, clickedLine
 --figure out the first and last chars for highlight
 if clickedLine = 1 then
  -- first line, start with char 1
  startChar = 1
```

```
else
 -- not first line, count chars before line
 -- and add 2 to go past return to the next line
 startChar = (member(pMember).text.line[1..clickedLine-1]).length + 2
end if

-- for last char, count chars including line,
-- and then add 1 for the RETURN character
endChar = (member(pMember).text.line[1..clickedLine]).length + 1

hilite member(pMember).char[startChar..endChar]
end
```

Finally, the *on makeSelection* handler is the one that actually does something. In this case, just an alert is shown. Note, however, that it must subtract one from the line number to get a corresponding choice number. This subtraction is necessary because the choices start at line two of the field. There is also an `updateStage` just before the `alert` command. If the `updateStage` were not there, the alert dialog box would appear and freeze the Director movie with the pop-up menu still open.

```
on makeSelection me
 if pLastHilite > 0 then
  updateStage -- update stage before alert
  alert "You picked number"&&(pLastHilite-1)
 end if
end
```

One last handler needed is the `on endSprite` handler, which is called when the movie leaves the frame with the sprite. This handler ensures that the original text gets replaced inside the field:

```
on endSprite me
 -- restore the contents of the field
 pMember.text = pText
end
```

Pop-up menus such as this are not as pretty as those created with bitmaps. However, they are easy to create and customize. If you need dozens of different pop-up menus and appearance is not critical, this is the way to go.

USING RICH TEXT FORMAT

By using the `rtf` property of a text member, you have access to its rich text format version. This is an entire language unto itself and is now maintained by Microsoft. Here are the results of creating a text member with the word "Testing" in 18-point Times New Roman font, and using the Message panel to get the `rtf`:

```
put member(1).rtf
-- "{\rtf1\mac\deff3 {\fonttbl{\f3\fswiss Geneva;}{\f20\froman
Times;}}{\colortbl\red0\green0\blue0;}{\stylesheet{\s0\fs24 Normal Text;}}\pard
\f3\fs24{\pard \f20\fs36\sl360 Testing\par}}"
```

13

Rich text format, as you can see, requires many control structures to define styles and colors. Detailing the meaning of each of these structures would take a whole book. Because RTF is so rarely used now and is being replaced by HTML as a text standard, it is hardly worth going into.

However, you should know that you do have the power to create your own rich text formatted code and replace the text in a member by setting the `rtf` property. If you took the messy line shown previously and replaced Times New Roman with Courier, for instance, you could set the text member to look the same, but with Courier font instead.

USING HTML AND TABLES

The `html` property of text members is much easier to use. You can actually create your own HTML code with Lingo and apply it to the member. The following example illustrates how easy this property is to use.

A Simple HTML Application

Here is the same "Testing" member's `html` property:

```
put member(1).html
-- "<html>
<head>
<title>Untitled</title>
</head>
<body bgcolor="#FFFFFF">
<font face="Times, Times New Roman" size=5>Testing<br>
</font></body>
</html>
"
```

You can see that Director likes to make sure that the proper "<html>", "<head>", "<body>", and "<title>" are present. The title is always given as "Untitled," but the "bgcolor" actually reflects the background color of the member.

The `html` property is easy to edit, especially if you already know HTML. You can even ignore some of the tags, and Director fills them in for you. Try this in the Message panel with a text member in cast member position one:

```
member(1).html = "Testing"
put member(1).html
-- "<html>
<head>
<title>Untitled</title>
</head>
<body bgcolor="#FFFFFF">
Testing</body>
</html>
"
```

You can see that most of the proper tags were added by Director. However, these tags are required if you want to use some of your own HTML tags to modify the text. Try this:

```
member(1).html = "<B>Testing</B>"
put member(1).html
-- "<html>
<head>
<title>Untitled</title>
</head>
<body bgcolor="#FFFFFF">
&lt;B&gt;Testing&lt;&#47;B&gt;</body>
</html>
"
```

You can see that Director did not correctly interpret your bold tag to make the text bold. Instead, it took it as a literal. The resulting text on the Stage would look like "<B>Testing</B>". For Director to recognize the bold tag, it needs to see the "<body>" tag.

```
member(1).html = "<HTML><B>Testing</B></HTML>"
put member(1).html
-- "<html>
<head>
<title>Untitled</title>
</head>
<body bgcolor="#CCCCCC">
<b>Testing</body>
</html>
"
```

Now Director correctly identifies the bold tags as tags. However, the background color of the member has been set to gray, which is meant to imitate the default gray background of browsers. To make it something other than gray, you have to set your own body tag as well:

```
member(1).html = "HTML><BODY BGCOLOR=#FFFFFF><B>Testing</B></BODY></HTML>"
put member(1).html
-- "<html>
<head>
<title>Untitled</title>
</head>
<body bgcolor="#FFFFFF">
<b>Testing</body>
</html>
"
```

13

Now the text member appears as you want it to. You can add font tags with sizes and faces to set the font of the text. You can even add table tags to create tables.

➡ *If you need to use HTML text with a background transparent sprite, see "Using HTML and Sprite Inks" in the "Troubleshooting" section at the end of this chapter.*

Creating Tables

Creating tables with HTML is an extremely powerful function of Director. It enables you to create highly formatted text in a way that was nearly impossible before Director 7.

To create a table, all you need to do is construct it in HTML and then apply that to the `html` property of the text member. Here is a simple example. Create a text field, name it "html text," and then place the following text in it:

```
<html>
<body bgcolor="#FFFFFF">
<table border=1>
<TR><TD>
Test1
</TD><TD>
Test2
</TD></TR>
<TR><TD>
Test3
</TD><TD>
Test4
</TD></TR>
</table>
</body>
</html>
```

Now, create an empty text member and place it on the Stage. Name it "html member." Using the Message panel, you can apply the HTML text to the text member:

```
member("html member").html = member("html text").text
```

The text member on the Stage should appear as shown in Figure 13.4.

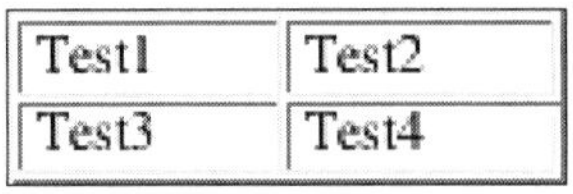

Figure 13.4
A text member that contains some simple HTML has constructed a table with a border.

| Test1 | Test2 |
| Test3 | Test4 |

Just about all the special features of HTML tables are available to the text member. Using a movie handler, you can create tables to suit any need. Here is a handler that takes a few lists and creates a table from them:

```
on makeTable memberName, headings, widths, data
  -- start with <HTML> and <BODY> tags
  htmlText = "<HTML><BODY BGCOLOR=FFFFFF>"

  -- beginning of table
  put "<TABLE BORDER=0><TR>" after htmlText

  -- place headings as TH tags
  repeat with i = 1 to count(headings)
    put "<TH WIDTH="&widths[i]&">" after htmlText
```

```
  put "<B>"&headings[i]&"</B></TD>" after htmlText
 end repeat
 put "</TR>" after htmlText

 -- add each row
 repeat with i = 1 to count(data)
  put "<TR>" after htmlText

  -- add a row
  repeat with j = 1 to count(data[i])
   put "<TD>" after htmlText
   put data[i][j]&"</TD>" after htmlText
  end repeat

  put "</TR>" after htmlText
 end repeat

 -- close table and html
 put "</TABLE></BODY></HTML>" after htmlText

 member(memberName).html = htmlText
end
```

This handler takes a member name and three linear lists as parameters. The first list contains the column heading text. The second list contains the widths of the columns in HTML-based pixels. The third list contains a series of smaller lists, each representing a row in the table. The number of items in these smaller lists should be the same as the number of items in the other two lists. Here is an example handler that uses this on `makeTable` handler:

```
on testTable
 headings = ["Name","Address","Phone","Birthday","City"]
 widths = [100,150,60,60,80]
 data = []
 add data, ["John Doe", "123 Street Road", "555-3456", \
   "7/28/65", "Seattle"]
 add data, ["Betty Deer", "654 Avenue Blvd", "555-1234", \
   "9/11/68", "Los Angeles"]
 add data, ["Robert Roberts", "9346 Dead End Pl.", \
   "555-9999", "1/8/67", "New York"]
 makeTable("html table",headings, widths, data)
end
```

Figure 13.5 shows the result of using these two handlers.

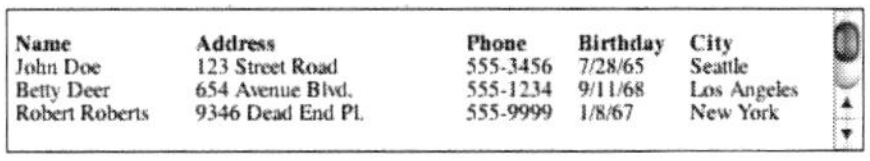

Name	Address	Phone	Birthday	City
John Doe	123 Street Road	555-3456	7/28/65	Seattle
Betty Deer	654 Avenue Blvd.	555-1234	9/11/68	Los Angeles
Robert Roberts	9346 Dead End Pl.	555-9999	1/8/67	New York

Figure 13.5
This table was generated with Lingo and applied to a text member.

One strength of tables such as this is that text can wrap inside a column. This is far superior to using multiple lines with tabs to form a table. You can even place tables such as this into scrolling text members when they are too long to fit on the screen all at once.

USING HTML AND HYPERTEXT

Director also has the capability to easily add hypertext to text members. In fact, it's so simple, you hardly need any Lingo at all.

Setting and Using Hyperlinks

Indicating that some text represents a link only requires the use of the member and the Text Inspector. You can edit the text on the Stage or in the Text Cast Member editing window. Just select some text and then type the hyperlink data in the bottom text field of the Text Inspector.

Figure 13.6 shows this process in action. The Stage contains a text member, with the word "dog" selected. The Text Inspector has been used to place "man's best friend" as the hyperlink data for that text. The result is that the word "dog" in the text member is now underlined and colored blue, as hypertext in Web browsers is typically styled. The word "quick" has already been set as hypertext.

Figure 13.6
The Text Inspector is used to set hypertext in text members.

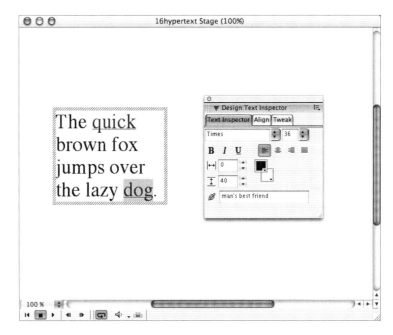

After the hypertext has been set, the hyperlink data is accessible through Lingo whenever the text is clicked. The styling of the text is automatic. Also, the cursor automatically changes into a finger cursor.

You can turn off the automatic styling and cursor change by setting the member property `useHyperlinkStyles`. Then, you can color and style the text independently.

For hypertext to actually do anything, you need to create a simple behavior to capture the messages sent when users click a hyperlink. An `on hyperlinkClicked` handler gets this message as well as the hyperlink data stored for that specific link. Here is an example:

```
on hyperlinkClicked me, data
 put data
end
```

This simple handler places the hyperlink data in the Message panel. That line of code is not very useful by itself but can be used instead to place the data in another field. A handler like this can be used to create a simple glossary function. Users can click a hyperlinked word, and the definition appears at the bottom of the Stage.

```
on hyperlinkClicked me, data
 member("Glossary").text = data
end
```

You can also have this script do something, such as make the movie jump to another frame. The frame name would be the *data* parameter.

```
on hyperlinkClicked me, data
 go to frame data
end
```

If you were creating a Shockwave movie, the hypertext could be used to make the browser go to another location. This would then act just like a normal hyperlink on a Web page. The hyperlink data would have to be a valid location, such as `http://clevermedia.com`.

```
on hyperlinkClicked me, data
 gotoNetPage(data)
end
```

One more parameter can be used with the `on hyperlinkClicked` handler. It returns a small list with the first and last character positions of the hyperlink that was clicked. You can use this to get the actual text of the hyperlink by using a normal chunk expression. Here is a modified version of the hyperlink glossary script:

```
on hyperlinkClicked me, data, pos
 definition = data
 hyperword = sprite(me.spriteNum).member.char[pos[1]..pos[2]]
 member("Glossary").text = hyperword&":"&&definition
end
```

Modifying Hyperlinks with Lingo

In addition to setting hyperlinks with the Text Inspector, you can also set them with Lingo. The `hyperlinks` and `hyperlink` properties of text members enable you to add, modify, and delete hyperlinks and their data.

13

The `hyperlinks` property returns a list of small lists that contain the first and last character positions of each link. For instance, the example in Figure 13.6 shows two hyperlinks. If you use the Message panel to get the hyperlinks, this is the result:

```
put member(1).hyperlinks
-- [[5, 9], [41, 43]]
```

Although this property is useful for determining what hyperlinks are present in the text, you cannot actually set hyperlinks this way. Instead, use the `hyperlink` property. Here is an example:

```
put member(1).char[5..9].hyperlink
-- "fast, speedy"
```

You can set the hyperlink data to something new in a similar manner.

```
member(1).char[5..9].hyperlink = "no definition"
put member(1).char[5..9].hyperlink
-- "no definition"
```

Setting the hyperlinks in this manner without specifying the exact character positions of the hypertext is not a good idea. However, Director does behave in a logical way when this happens. If you try to set a subset of the hyperlink, such as characters 6 to 8 of the previous example, the entire hyperlink is changed.

To remove a hyperlink, set its hyperlink data to "", or the empty string:

```
member(1).char[5..9].hyperlink = EMPTY
```

Setting the hyperlink on a set of characters that does not already have a hyperlink applied to it creates one. Here is a script that searches for a word in a text member and sets all instances of it to act as hyperlinks:

```
on makeHyper memberName, hyperword, hyperdata
 text = member(memberName).text
 repeat with i = 1 to text.word.count
  if text.word[i] = hyperword then
   member(memberName).word[i].hyperlink = hyperdata
  end if
 end repeat
end
```

You can also set hyperlinks simply by setting the entire contents of the text member using the `html` property. You can include <A HREF=""> tags in that HTML code. These tags will be interpreted to add hyperlinks to the text member, just as they add hyperlinks in Web browsers.

13

TROUBLESHOOTING

Using HTML and Sprite Inks

I'm using HTML text in a text member with the sprite set to transparent ink. How can I get it to look good?

Using HTML doesn't work well when the sprite's ink is set to background transparent. To improve its quality, make the background color of the member something similar to the actual background behind the sprite. Then you can use background transparent ink without too many problems. Otherwise, stil to Copy ink whenever possible.

Using Text Styles With Embedded Fonts

Why does text spacing get distorted when I am using an embedded font?

If you are using a text member that uses an embedded font cast member, make sure that you don't change the font style. For instance, making the text bold sometimes screws up the character spacing. This happens often on Windows in Shockwave.

DID YOU KNOW?

- You can force Director to be your own RTF-to-HTML converter by importing RTF files and then getting the `html` property of that member. The same would work in reverse.

- Instead of using `put` to place text before, after, or into a text member, you can use some undocumented Lingo: `setContentsBefore`, `setContentsAfter`, and `setContents`. For instance, you can write

  ```
  member("myText").setContentsBefore("abc")
  ```

  to place "abc" before the text in the member, or

  ```
  member("myText").char[7].setContentsAfter("abc")
  ```

  to place "abc" after character 7 of the member, or just plain
  `member("myText").setContents("abc")` to replace the contents of the member completely.

13

14

USING LINGO TO CREATE IMAGES

THE IMAGE OBJECT

At the heart of imaging Lingo is the *image object*. An image object is a representation of a bitmap in memory. It can be tied to a cast member, exist independently of a member as a variable, or represent the Stage itself.

Accessing Images

To create or modify a bitmap member with imaging Lingo, you first need to reference its image object. This is done with the `image` property of the member. For instance, you can use something like `member("`*`myMember`*`").image` or `sprite(`*`x`*`).member.image`. You can also store a reference to an image in a variable like this:

```
myImage = member("myMember").image
```

In this case, *myImage* is a variable that points to `member("`*`myMember`*`").image`, whereas `member("`*`myMember`*`").image` is the image itself. If you want to replace the image in this member with the image in another member, you can do something like this:

```
member("myMember").image = member("myOtherMember").image
```

The previous line takes the bitmap image in the second member and copies it into the first member. You could have also done this:

```
myImage = member("myOtherMember").image
member("myMember").image = myImage
```

One special type of image that is not from a member is the image of the Stage. You can get this image and modify it just as you can with the image of a member.

```
myStageImage = (the stage).image
```

The great thing about using the image of the Stage is that you can draw right on the Stage without needing to create bitmap members. The problem with this is that when these pixels are disturbed, say by an animated sprite, they will be wiped out. So you can only draw on the Stage temporarily, so long as you don't disturb the area you just drew on with sprites.

> When you set a variable to the image property of a member, you are actually setting that variable to point to that image member, not to receive a copy of it. So any changes to that image affect the original member.

You can also use the image of the Stage to copy portions of the Stage to other images or to examine the color values on pixels.

Creating Images

You can create a new image in a member with the `image` function. This function allocates space in memory for a bitmap image. You can then assign this image to a member, or just manipulate it using the variable that references it.

The `image` function takes three parameters. The first two define the width and height of the image. The last defines the bit depth of the image. This can either be 1, 2, 4, 8, 16, or 32. Typically, you want to use 32, which gives you the full range of colors plus an alpha channel for transparency.

```
myImage = image(240,120,32)
```

The `image` function takes two optional parameters as well. The first is the bit depth of the alpha channel layer. This parameter is used only if the bit depth of the image is 32. You can set the alpha bit depth to either 0 or 8, a 0 indicating that you don't want any alpha channel, and an 8 giving you the full alpha channel.

The fifth parameter is used only if you have a 2, 4, or 8-bit depth image. It specifies which palette the image uses. Acceptable values include symbols such as `#grayscale`, `#web216`, and `#pastels` for one of Director's built-in palettes, or a cast member for a custom palette.

Image Properties

Images have only a few properties. Table 14.1 shows you each of these.

Table 14.1 Image Object Properties

Property	Description
depth	The bit depth of the object. You cannot change this property.
height	The height in pixels of the image.
width	The width in pixels of the image.
rect	The rect of the image.
useAlpha	Whether the image should display using its alpha channel.

None of the image properties can be altered except for the `useAlpha` property. To change the size and depth of an image, you have to copy over the entire image with a new one. You can also use the `crop` command to crop a bitmap to a smaller size.

If you can't get a 32-bit image to display correctly on the Stage, see "Problems with `useAlpha` Property" in the "Troubleshooting" section at the end of this chapter.

> You cannot change the dimensions of an image by simply changing its `rect`, `width`, or `height`. Instead, you need to use director commands, such as `crop`, or create a new image object and copy the old image into it at a new size or location within a larger image.

Image Commands

After you have an image object, you can alter it in many ways. The primary commands for altering images are `copyPixels`, `fill`, `draw`, and `setPixel`. However, there are more than just those four, although some are rarely used. Table 14.2 lists them all.

14

Table 14.2   Image Object Commands

Command	Parameters	Description
copyPixels	sourceImage, destinationRect, sourceRect, modifierList	Copies a rectangle from one image into another. The destinationRect can also be a list of four points to define a quad.
createMask		Creates a special 8-bit mask object to be used by copyPixels to define which parts of the image to copy.
createMatte		Creates a special 1-bit mask object to be used by copyPixels to define which parts of the image to copy.
crop	rect	Cuts the image down to the specified rect.
draw	rect, modifierList	Draws a line, oval, or rectangle in the image.
duplicate		Creates a duplicate of the image that can be changed without affecting the original image.
extractAlpha		Creates an 8-bit grayscale image from the alpha channel of the original image.
fill	rect, modifierList	Draws a filled oval or rectangle in the image.
getPixel	x, y	Returns the color of the pixel at the x and y location in the image.
image	width, height, depth	Returns a new image.
setAlpha	8-bit image object	Sets the alpha channel of the image to the 8-bit image supplied.
setPixel	x, y, color	Sets the color of the pixel at the x and y location in the image.
trimWhiteSpace		Removes any extra whitespace around the image.

The copyPixels, draw, and fill commands allow for a list of modifiers as the last parameter. For instance, you can fill a rectangle in the image *myImage* with a command like this:

```
myImage.fill(rect(10,10,20,20),[#color: rgb("000000"), #shapeType: #rect])
```

The draw and fill commands share three out of four of the same modifiers. Here is a list:

- #color   The fill color for the fill command and the line color for the draw command.

- #bgColor   For the fill command only, this is the color of the line around the edge of the filled area.

- #shapeType   Can either be #oval, #rect, #roundRect, or #line.

- #lineSize   The width of the line used.

Note that the draw command uses #color as the line color, whereas the fill command uses #bgColor as the line color.

Both the fill and draw commands can be used in three different ways. The first is to pass it a rect as the first parameter. Optionally, you can pass four numbers that represent the left, top, right, and bottom of the rect. The third option is to pass it two points. This last option comes in handy when using draw to create lines from one point to another. But all three options are essentially the same.

The copyPixels command also uses a modifier list as the last parameter. However, it has many more possible parameters. Here is a list. Note that all these are optional; in fact, you don't even need to use a modifier list at all.

- #color   A color that provides the same effect as applying a foreground color to a sprite.

- #bgColor   A color that provides the same effect as applying a background color to a sprite.

- #ink   An ink to be used; just a sprite would use it. Can be the ink number or symbol such as #copy or #blend.

- #blendLevel   The blend level, from 0 to 255, to be used.

- #dither   Whether to use a dither when copying pixels into images that are less than 32-bit depth.

- #useFastQuads   Whether to use fast or higher quality calculations when copying pixels with quads.

- #maskImage   The mask or matte image object to be used to copy only a portion of the image.

- #maskOffset   A point offset for the mask that determines where the mask is located relative to the image itself.

We'll be looking at specific examples of using these commands in the next few sections.

▷ *If you have performance issues when using large* copyPixels *commands, see "*copyPixels Requires Power" *in the "Troubleshooting" section at the end of this chapter.*

DRAWING WITH LINGO

There are three commands that you can use to draw pixels onto an image: setPixel, draw, and fill.

Drawing Shapes

The fill and draw commands are nearly identical. The only difference is that the draw command only outlines the area instead of filling it.

Using the fill command is a great way to wipe an image clean and start with a fresh canvas for other Lingo image commands. For instance, if you wanted to blank out a member with white pixels, you could do this:

```
on clearBitmap
 myImg = member("myBitmap").image
 myImg.fill(myImg.rect,rgb("FFFFFF"))
end
```

14

You can draw rectangles, rounded rectangles, and ovals with both the `draw` and `fill` commands. This handler, found in the movie `drawfill.dir`, creates the frame seen in Figure 14.1.

```
on drawFrame
  myImg = image(200,150,32)
  myImg.fill(rect(0,0,200,100),[#shapeType: #rect, #color: rgb("000000")])
  myImg.draw(rect(2,2,198,98),[#shapeType: #rect, #color: rgb("FFFFFF")])
  myImg.fill(rect(5,5,195,95),[#shapeType: #roundRect, #color: rgb("FFFFFF")])

  member("myBitmap").image = myImg
end
```

Figure 14.1
This frame was made with three
`fill`/`draw` commands.

The `fill` and `draw` commands are also good for drawing circles when you use the `#shapeType` of `#circle`. The next example is a behavior that draws circles at the location of the cursor. It keeps track of each circle and continues to redraw and expand each circle. The result is a set of circles that expand out form their original location like ripples on water. Figure 14.2 shows what this looks like when the cursor is moved around the screen. You can see this script in action in `ripples.dir`.

Figure 14.2
These ripples are ovals drawn
with the `draw` command and
maintained by a behavior.

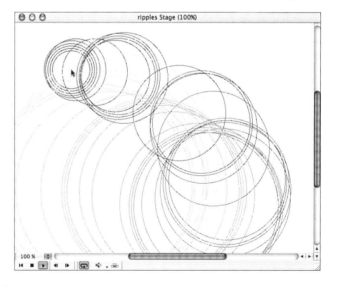

```
property pRipples, pPressed

on beginSprite me
  pRipples = []
end
```

```
-- on click, add a new ripple
on mouseDown me
 addRipple(me)
 pPressed = TRUE
end

-- stop adding ripples
on mouseUp me
 pPressed = FALSE
end

on mouseUpOutside me
 pPressed = FALSE
end

-- add a new ripple to the list
on addRipple me
 add pRipples, [#loc: the mouseLoc, #radius: 0]
end

on prepareFrame me
 -- add a new ripple
 if pPressed then
  addRipple(me)
 end if

 -- draw all ripples and increase their radius
 expandRipples(me)
end

on expandRipples me
 -- remember what the stage looks like
 (the stage).image.fill(0,0,640,480,rgb("FFFFFF"))

 -- loop through all ripples
 repeat with i = pRipples.count down to 1

  -- get the info for this ripple
  loc = pRipples[i].loc
  radius = pRipples[i].radius

  -- determine the rect
  r = rect(loc,loc) + rect(-radius,-radius,radius,radius)

  -- set the color according to the radius
  color = rgb(radius,radius,radius)

  -- draw it
```

```
(the stage).image.draw(r, [#shapeType: #oval, #color: color])

  -- expand the radius
  pRipples[i].radius = pRipples[i].radius + 5

  -- see if the ripple is too big
  if pRipples[i].radius > 255 then
   deleteAt pRipples, i
  end if
 end repeat
end

on exitFrame me
 go to the frame
end
```

The ripples draw directly to the Stage using the Stage image. Each frame, the Stage is cleared with the `fill` command and then all the ripples are drawn onto the Stage, a little larger than the size they were drawn last time. If the mouse is pressed, a new ripple is added.

Drawing Pixels

The `setPixel` command allows you to set the color of a single pixel in an image. This is the most precise command, allowing you to create whatever you want, limited only by the complexity of your code.

For instance, suppose that you wanted to draw dots in 100 random locations in an image. We'll assume that the bitmap is member "myBitmap" and draw 100 black dots in it:

```
myImg = member("myBitmap").image
myImg.fill(myImg.rect,rgb("FFFFFF"))
repeat with i = 1 to 100
 myImg.setPixel(random(myImg.width), random(myImg.height), rgb("000000"))
end repeat
```

Something like this can be used to create a simple star field as a backdrop. Or you can create just plain noise. This code, from `starfieldandnoise.dir`, creates an image of random pixels from three similar colors:

```
on drawNoise
 -- loop through all pixels
 myImg = member("myBitmap").image
 repeat with x = 1 to myImg.width
  repeat with y = 1 to myImg.height

   -- pick random color
   case random(3) of
    1: c = rgb("906000")
    2: c = rgb("966B00")
    3: c = rgb("9B6600")
```

```
    end case

    -- set this pixel
    myImg.setPixel(x,y,c)
   end repeat
  end repeat
 end
```

Filling Odd-Shaped Areas

There is a somewhat undocumented way to use the `fill` command to fill an odd-shaped area. For instance, in the Paint panel or in a program like Photoshop, you might use the Paint Bucket tool to fill an area with a color.

The way to do this with imaging Lingo is to use `fill` with a point object rather than a rect object. The point will be the location of the start of the fill. The command will continue to fill all connected pixels of the same color.

```
member("myBitmap").image.fill(point(100,100),rgb("FF0000"))
```

Figure 14.3 shows an odd-shaped area that has been filled with a command like the preceding one.

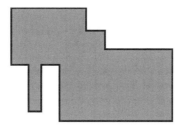

Figure 14.3
The `fill` command can be used to fill odd-shaped areas like this one.

EXAMINING PIXEL COLOR

You can use `getPixel` to get the color value of a picture in an image. This can be any image, including the Stage. In the movie `detectpixel.dir`, the frame script examines the pixel under the cursor and puts the color value into a text member on the Stage.

```
on exitFrame me
 c = (the stage).image.getPixel(the mouseLoc)
 member("loc").text = string(c)
end
```

You can use the `getPixel` command for collision detection. For instance, in the movie `pixelcollide.dir`, the frame behavior draws black pixels on the Stage and moves the pixel according to the *pDirection* property. If the pixel comes near a red pixel on the Stage, the *pDirection* is changed to account for the bounce. Figure 14.4 shows the result.

14

Figure 14.4
The boxes are sprites on the Stage, and the diagonal line is a moving pixel that bounces off them.

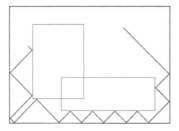

```
property pLoc, pDirection

on beginSprite me
 -- starting point and location
 pLoc = point(100,100)
 pDirection = point(1,1)
end

on exitFrame me
 pLoc = pLoc + pDirection

 -- check each direction for a bounce
 if (the stage).image.getPixel(pLoc+point(1,0)) = rgb("FF0000") then
  pDirection.locH = -1
 end if

 if (the stage).image.getPixel(pLoc+point(-1,0)) = rgb("FF0000") then
  pDirection.locH = 1
 end if

 if (the stage).image.getPixel(pLoc+point(0,1)) = rgb("FF0000") then
  pDirection.locV = -1
 end if

 if (the stage).image.getPixel(pLoc+point(0,-1)) = rgb("FF0000") then
  pDirection.locV = 1
 end if

 -- draw the pixel
 (the stage).image.setPixel(pLoc,rgb("000000"))
end
```

MANIPULATING IMAGES

If you need to use imaging Lingo to alter existing images, your primary tool is the versatile `copyPixels` command. You can use it to copy one image into another, or a portion of one image into a portion of another.

Copying Image Portions

Even without any modifiers in its fourth parameter, `copyPixels` can be very powerful. For instance, if you have a 100×100 image, you can copy a 50×50 image into its upper-left quarter without disturbing the other three-quarters of the image.

```
myImg.copyPixels(myOtherImg,rect(0,0,50,50),myOtherImg.rect)
```

You can also copy only a portion of the second image rather than the whole thing.

```
myImg.copyPixels(myOtherImg,rect(0,0,50,50),rect(25,25,50,50)
```

This second example would automatically scale the portion of the second image to fit into the larger space allocated in the first image. Whenever the destination rect and the source rect are different sizes, the `copyPixels` command automatically shrinks or enlarges the copied portion to fit.

Although the source rect always needs to be a rectangle, you can use a set of four points to represent the destination. These four points, called a *quad*, can represent a four-sided shape of any kind. So you can distort or even rotate your image portion.

This script, from `liftimage.dir`, draws an image with its top two corners down at the bottom of the screen to start, and then brings them up to the corners of the screen. The effect is to make the image appear to "lift up" onto the Stage.

```
property p1, p2, pImg

on beginSprite me
 p1 = point(240,480)
 p2 = point(400,480)
 pImg = member("picture 1").image
end

on exitFrame
 if p1 <> point(0,0) then

  -- move corners up and out
  p1 = p1 + point(-20,-40)
  p2 = p2 + point(20,-40)

  -- draw new image
  (the stage).image.copyPixels(pImg,[p1,p2,point(640,480),point(0,480)],pImg.rect)
 end if
end
```

The four points of a quad list represent the upper-left, upper-right, lower-right, and lower-left corners of the original image. You can rotate and flip the image by manipulating these four points. For instance, swapping the second and third points with the first and fourth points flips the image horizontally.

The movie `distort.dir` contains a script that allows the user to distort the image. The user can click on any point in the image and drag to distort the image starting from that point.

14

The image is divided into four parts, with the click point making the center meeting place of the four parts. Each of the four parts is defined by four points, and they all share that one center point. Then the drag action moves that center point around, thus distorting the image. When the user releases the mouse, the distorted image replaces the original image; this way, the user can implement another distortion on top of the first. Figure 14.5 shows the original image and the image with one distortion applied.

Figure 14.5
The first image is the original, and the second has been distorted by the user.

```
property pSpriteUpperLeft, pFocusPoint, pStartImg, pImg

on beginSprite me
  -- start with original image
  sprite(me.spriteNum).member.image = member("original").image

  -- get reference to image
  pImg = sprite(me.spriteNum).member.image
end

-- start of drag
on mouseDown me
  -- get starting point
  pSpriteUpperLeft = point(sprite(me.spriteNum).rect.left,
➥ sprite(me.spriteNum).rect.top)
  pFocusPoint = the mouseLoc - pSpriteUpperLeft

  -- copy image as it is right now
  pStartImg = duplicate(sprite(me.spriteNum).member.image)
end

-- end of drag
on mouseUp me
  pFocusPoint = VOID
end
on mouseUpOutside me
  pFocusPoint = VOID
end

on exitFrame me
```

```
-- only distort if being dragged
if not voidP(pFocusPoint) then

  -- get relative location of click
  cursorPoint = the mouseLoc - pSpriteUpperLeft

  -- get 8 points along edge of image
  upperLeft = point(0,0)
  upperMiddle = point(pFocusPoint.locH,0)
  upperRight = point(pStartImg.width,0)
  lowerLeft = point(0,pStartImg.height)
  lowerRight = point(pStartImg.width,pStartImg.height)
  lowerMiddle = point(pFocusPoint.locH,pStartImg.height)
  middleLeft = point(0,pFocusPoint.locV)
  middleRight = point(pStartImg.width,pFocusPoint.locV)

  -- drag upper left area
  q = [upperLeft,upperMiddle,cursorPoint,middleLeft]
  r = rect(0,0,pFocusPoint.locH,pFocusPoint.locV)
  pImg.copyPixels(pStartImg,q,r)

  -- draw upper right
  q = [upperMiddle,upperRight,middleRight,cursorPoint]
  r = rect(pFocusPoint.locH,0,pStartImg.width,pFocusPoint.locV)
  pImg.copyPixels(pStartImg,q,r)

  -- draw lower right
  q = [cursorPoint,middleRight,lowerRight,lowerMiddle]
  r = rect(pFocusPoint.locH,pFocusPoint.locV,pStartImg.width,pStartImg.height)
  pImg.copyPixels(pStartImg,q,r)

  -- draw lower left
  q = [middleLeft,cursorPoint,lowerMiddle,lowerLeft]
  r = rect(0,pFocusPoint.locV,pFocusPoint.locH,pStartImg.height)
  pImg.copyPixels(pStartImg,q,r)
 end if
end
```

Rotating an image is more difficult. You need to determine the distance from the center of rotation to each corner. Then you need to determine the original angle from the center of rotation to each corner. Using the distance and angle, you can rotate these four points by increasing the angle uniformly across all four points.

You can find the following behavior `rotateimage.dir`. It makes a list of the four corner points, defining them by their angle and distance from the center. Then, it builds a new set of four points, each frame using this data and `cos` and `sin` functions. The angle changes slightly in each frame, so the four corners rotate around the center. Figure 14.6 shows the result.

14

Figure 14.6
The image has been rotated a little each frame, leaving part of itself behind beyond its edge.

```
property pImg, pCenter, pList, pOriginal

on beginSprite me
  -- make a copy in memory
  pImg = sprite(me.spriteNum).member.image
  pOriginal = duplicate(pImg)

  -- get rotation point
  pCenter = point(pImg.width/2, pImg.height/2)

  -- create list of angles and distances
  pList = []
  repeat with p in [point(0,0), point(pImg.width,0),
➡ point(pImg.width,pImg.height), point(0,pImg.height)]
    d = getDistance(me,pCenter,p)
    a = getAngle(me,pCenter,p)
    add pList, [#angle: a, #radius: d]
  end repeat
end

on endSprite me
  -- when done, replace original image
  pImg.copyPixels(pOriginal,pOriginal.rect,pOriginal.rect)
end

on exitFrame me
  -- create a quad from all corner points
  pQuad = []
  repeat with i = 1 to pList.count
    x = pList[i].radius*cos(pList[i].angle)
    y = pList[i].radius*sin(pList[i].angle)
    add pQuad, point(x,y) + pCenter
    pList[i].angle = pList[i].angle + .1
  end repeat

  -- place new image
  pImg.copyPixels(pOriginal,pQuad,pImg.rect)
```

```
  go to the frame
end


-- convert two points to a distance
on getDistance me, p1, p2
  return sqrt(power(p2.locH-p1.locH,2)+power(p2.locV-p1.locV,2))
end


-- convert two points to an angle
on getAngle me, p1, p2
  dx = p2.locH-p1.locH
  dy = p2.locV-p1.locV

  if dx = 0 and dy >= 0 then
   angleRadians = pi/2
  else if dx = 0 and dy < 0 then
   angleRadians = -pi/2
  else if dx >= 0 then
   angleRadians = atan(float(dy)/float(dx))
  else if dx < 0 then
   angleRadians = pi+atan(float(dy)/float(dx))
  end if

  return angleRadians
end
```

This script makes the image rotate over itself. You could also copy the image to the Stage to avoid writing over the original member. You can use `fill` before each `copyPixels` to erase the previous image and draw a clean one on a solid background.

This code, from `rotatein.dir`, also changes the distance of each point from the center of rotation. The effect is that the image spins in from a distance. It uses *on getDistance* and *on getAngle* from the previous example as well.

```
property pImg, pCenter, pList, pOriginal, pStep


on beginSprite me
  -- make a copy in memory
  pImg = sprite(me.spriteNum).member.image
  pOriginal = duplicate(pImg)

  -- get rotation point
  pCenter = point(pImg.width/2, pImg.height/2)

  -- create list of angles and distances
  pList = []
  repeat with p in [point(0,0), point(pImg.width,0),
➥ point(pImg.width,pImg.height), point(0,pImg.height)]
   d = getDistance(me,pCenter,p)
```

```
   a = getAngle(me,pCenter,p)
   add pList, [#angle: a, #radius: d]
 end repeat

 pStep = 25
end

on exitFrame me
 if pStep >= 0 then
  -- create a quad from all corner points
  pQuad = []
  repeat with i = 1 to pList.count

   -- modify both distance and angle with pStep
   x = (pList[i].radius-pStep*8)*cos(pList[i].angle-pStep*.2)
   y = (pList[i].radius-pStep*8)*sin(pList[i].angle-pStep*.2)
   add pQuad, point(x,y) + pCenter
  end repeat

  -- place new image
  pImg.fill(pOriginal.rect,rgb("FFFFFF"))
  pImg.copyPixels(pOriginal,pQuad,pImg.rect)

  -- next step
  pStep = pStep - 1
 end if

 go to the frame
end
```

The preceding code uses pStep to keep track of the animation. It starts with pStep equal to 25. It counts down to 0. At 25, the distance from the center for each corner is reduced by 25×8, or 200. The angle is spun backwards by 5.0, a bit less than a full circle.

As the animation continues, the image is drawn with its corner distances and angles approaching their original values.

Understanding the Alpha Channel

A 32-bit image has four channels. The first three are the red, green, and blue channels that determine the color of the pixel. The fourth channel, the alpha channel, determines how transparent the pixel is.

By using setPixel, fill, draw, and copyPixels, you can change the first three channels of the pixels in the image. To change the alpha channel, you need to use setAlpha. This command replaces the entire alpha channel at once.

You can pass either a number or an image object to `setAlpha`. Using a number sets all the pixels to use an alpha channel of that value. The values range from 0 to 255, with 0 being completely opaque, and 255 being completely transparent. So, to set an entire image to 50% transparent, you can do this:

```
myImage.setAlpha(128)
```

Using `setAlpha` only works if the image is a 32-bit image and if the `useAlpha` property is set to TRUE.

If you want to replace the alpha channel with an image, you should use a grayscale image. A grayscale image is an 8-bit image with a grayscale palette.

So if you have a 100×100 32-bit image, you can create an 8-bit 100×100 grayscale image, alter it, and then apply it to the 32-bit image as its alpha channel using `setAlpha`.

This code, taken from `alphademo.dir`, creates a grayscale image and applies it to the sprite's image. The grayscale image starts as a completely white image the same size as the sprite's image. Then, another grayscale image, that of a fuzzy circle, is copied into it at the cursor location. Finally, the grayscale image replaces the alpha channel in the sprite's image. The result is that only the area under the cursor is visible, fading out to an invisible area. Try the `alphademo.dir` movie to see it in action.

```
property pImg

on beginSprite me
  -- get image and make it use its alpha channel
  pImg = sprite(me.spriteNum).member.image
  pImg.useAlpha = 1
end

on exitFrame me
  -- make a new alpha image
  alphaImg = image(pImg.width,pImg.height,8,#grayscale)

  -- copy the fuzzy circle at the mouse location
  p = the mouseLoc - point(sprite(me.spriteNum).rect.left,
➥ sprite(me.spriteNum).rect.top)
  r = rect(p-point(49,49), p+point(50,50))
  alphaImg.copyPixels(member("alpha").image,r,member("alpha").image.rect)

  -- set the alpha channel
  pImg.setAlpha(alphaImg)
end
```

You can also get the alpha channel from a 32-bit image with the `extractAlpha` function. This would allow you to make 8-bit images from the alpha channel, or apply the alpha channel from one image to another.

14

Sprite Transitions

A common and simple use for imaging Lingo is to make behaviors that transition a bitmap sprite from one image to another. These sprite transitions are different from Score transitions in that they affect only that one sprite.

This code, taken from `softwipe.dir` uses two images in addition to the image used by the sprite. It copies the first image into the sprite's image and then copies the second image in vertical stripes from left to right. There are actually two vertical stripes, the first at 50% blend and the second at 100%. As the first stripe moves across the screen, it blends in the second image darker and darker. The second stripe makes sure that the image left behind is purely the second image.

```
property pImg, pImg1, pImg2, pPos


on beginSprite me
 -- get images involved
 pImg = sprite(me.spriteNum).member.image
 pImg1 = member("picture 1").image
 pImg2 = member("picture 2").image
 pImg.copyPixels(pImg1,pImg.rect,pImg.rect)
 pPos = 0
end


on exitFrame me
 wipeArea = 50 -- width of fuzzy area
 wipeSpeed = 5 -- amount to move wipe each frame

 if pPos < pImg.width+wipeArea then

  -- blend edge of wipe
  r = rect(pPos-wipeArea,0,pPos,pImg.height)
  pImg.copyPixels(pImg2,r,r,[#blend: 50])

  -- copy beyond edge of wipe
  r = rect(pPos-wipeArea-wipeSpeed,0,pPos-wipeArea-1,pImg.height)
  pImg.copyPixels(pImg2,r,r)

  -- move along
  pPos = pPos + wipeSpeed
 end if
end
```

Another sprite transition example is `digitalfocus.dir`. This loops through a grid of rectangles in the image and copies a single pixel onto a larger square area. Figure 14.7 shows six frames of the transition.

Figure 14.7
This sprite transition brings the image in the sprite into focus a little each frame.

```
property pImg, pOriginal, pArea

on beginSprite me
 -- get images involved
 pImg = sprite(me.spriteNum).member.image
 pOriginal = duplicate(pImg)
 pArea = 20
end

on exitFrame me

 if pArea > 1 then

   -- loop through pixels
   repeat with x = 0 to pImg.width/pArea
    repeat with y = 0 to pImg.height/pArea

      -- copy one pixel into an area
      fromRect = rect(x*pArea,y*pArea,x*pArea+1,y*pArea+1)
      toRect = rect(x*pArea,y*pArea,x*pArea+pArea,y*pArea+pArea)
      pImg.copyPixels(pOriginal,toRect,fromRect)
    end repeat
   end repeat

   -- reduce pixel area
   pArea = pArea - 4

 else if pArea = 1 then
   -- done, so make sure image is complete
   pImg.copyPixels(pOriginal,pOriginal.rect,pOriginal.rect)
   pArea = 0
 end if
end
```

IMAGES OF OTHER MEMBER TYPES

Bitmap members aren't the only members with image objects. Other members have image objects that can be copied, although they can't be altered.

Bringing Text into Images

You can take the image of a text member, including its alpha channel for antialiased text members. This way, you can create images using text. Here's how would you copy the image from a text member to a bitmap member:

```
myText = member("text").image
member("bitmap").image = myText
```

You can also use `copyPixels` to copy the text on top of an existing image. The alpha channel is used to overlay the text smoothly on top of the image. This happens by default, so you don't need to use any modifiers. Here is an example:

```
myText = member("myText").image
myImg = member("picture").image
myImg.copyPixels(myText,myText.rect+rect(0,180,0,180),myText.rect)
```

You can try this code in `textonimage.dir`. Figure 14.8 shows the image with the text copied onto it.

Figure 14.8
The text on this image has been made a permanent part of the image using `copyPixels`.

You could also use a list of four points to rotate or distort the text during the copy. For instance, this code takes an editable text member's image and copies it into a bitmap. But it flips the points in the quad so that the text is copied in reverse, as shown in Figure 14.9.

Figure 14.9
This text is copied using a quad list that flips points 1 and 4 with points 2 and 3.

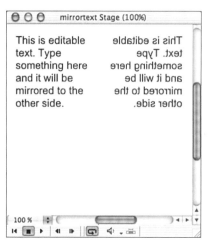

```
on keyUp me
 myBitmap = member("mirror").image
 myText = sprite(me.spriteNum).member.image

 mirrorList = []
 mirrorList[1] = point(myText.rect.right, myText.rect.top)
 mirrorList[2] = point(myText.rect.left, myText.rect.top)
 mirrorList[3] = point(myText.rect.left, myText.rect.bottom)
 mirrorList[4] = point(myText.rect.right, myText.rect.bottom)

 myBitmap.copyPixels(myText, mirrorList, myText.rect)
end
```

Flash Members

You can also grab the image of a Flash member. However, the image property of a Flash member does not get updated while it is running. Instead, it is based on the first frame, called the *poster frame*, of the movie.

To copy the image of the Flash movie into a bitmap member, you can simply do this:

```
member("bitmap").image = member("flashmovie").image
```

If you want to copy any frame besides the first one, you need to set the posterFrame property of the Flash member. Here is a short handler that does this:

```
on getFlashFrameImage frameNum
 member("flashmovie").posterFrame = frameNum
 member("bitmap").image = member("flashmovie").image
end
```

Copying an image of a text member means that Director must render the text just as it does when it is drawing it to the Stage. This can be slow, especially if you are using antialiased smooth text. You'll see a major speed problem is you are copying a lot of text repeatedly. However, you can store commonly used text images in global variables or properties and reuse these images without penalty.

However, this does not take into account any movement or changes performed by ActionScript code in the movie. Those changes are simply not available to the image property of the member.

The only solution for this is to grab the area of the Stage that shows the Flash movie. This handler uses crop to take the full image of the Stage and crop it down to just the Flash movie's area. It grabs anything else in that area too, including sprites that appear on top of the Flash movie sprite.

```
on grabFlashSpriteImage whichSprite
 img = duplicate((the stage).image)
 img.crop(sprite(whichSprite).rect)
 member("bitmap").image = img
end
```

One fundamental difference between grabbing the image of a Flash member and grabbing a copy of that area of the Stage is that you don't end up with a true 32-bit image. The Stage does not have an alpha channel because there is nothing behind it. It is opaque by its nature.

14

This technique of capturing the portion of the Stage where the sprite is located not only works for Flash movies with ActionScript but also any type of visible sprite. So you can use it for digital video, sprites using Xtras, or even combinations of several sprites.

3D Members

Although the `image` property of a Flash member works only for simple Flash movies and not at all for some other member types, 3D members have a robust `image` property. You can capture the image of a 3D sprite at any time, complete with modifications made by Lingo.

```
member("bitmap").image = member("3d").image
```

This can be ideal during production when you are trying to create a movie compatible with computers that don't have any 3D capability. For instance, if you have a spinning product demo, you could take a still image from the `image` property during production and store it as a bitmap for use by non-3D computers.

The example movie `3dmirror.dir` uses imaging Lingo to capture the animated 3D sprite and show it in a flipped bitmap sprite on the other side of the Stage.

One thing to note about the images taken from 3D members is that they are always the size of the member, usually 320×240. So you can scale the sprite, but your `image` property will be the same as the member.

TROUBLESHOOTING

Problems with `useAlpha` Property

I'm using an image with an alpha channel, why doesn't the image doesn't show up right on the Stage?

If you are trying to use alpha channels and they don't seem to work, a common mistake is forgetting to set the `useAlpha` property of the member to TRUE.

`copyPixels` Requires Power

I'm using a lot of copPixels commands, and it is slowing down my movie. Any way to speed it up?

Performing numerous large `copyPixels` commands can slow down your movie. Try using lower bit-depth images where possible to speed up things.

Paint Panel Doesn't Show Some Images Correctly

I've got some 32-bit images that show up as black boxes in the Paint panel.

After you copy the image of a text member into a bitmap, it will appear as a black box in the Paint editor. This is because the Paint editor panel cannot handle images with complex alpha channels.

DID YOU KNOW?

- Copying images to the Stage takes basically the same amount of time as drawing sprites; sometimes it is even faster.

- Some Director developers now use imaging Lingo for everything. They have an empty Score and use `copyPixels` to draw all their content directly to the Stage.

- You can fade an image by simply copying a single color over the entire image using `copyPixels` with a blend less than that of 100%. This keeps a little of the original image. Doing this repeatedly eventually fades the original image completely out.

- The system property `disableImagingTransformation` can be set to FALSE so that Stage images take on the scaling and scrolling positions of the Stage. When set to TRUE, the image of the Stage is always taken at 100%.

14

15

USING LINGO TO DRAW VECTOR SHAPES

IN THIS CHAPTER

VECTOR SHAPE PROPERTIES AND COMMANDS

Vector shape members use the same software engine as Flash members. But they have one major difference from Flash members: They are static images rather than time-based media. However, unlike Flash members, they can be completely controlled with Lingo, right down to the locations of the vector shapes. You can even create a vector shape from scratch in Lingo and design it to look however you want.

The combined vector shape properties enable you to change every aspect of a vector shape. Table 15.1 contains a complete list of these properties.

Table 15.1   Vector Member Properties

Property	Description
antiAlias	Determines whether the member is drawn antialiased. When off, the member may draw a little faster, but the lines do not look as smooth.
backgroundColor	The member's background color.
broadcastProps	Determines whether changes to the member are immediately reflected on the Stage. If not, the sprite shows changes to the member only after it leaves and then reappears on the Stage.
centerRegPoint	If set to TRUE, the registration point of the member changes automatically when the sprite is resized. If you are changing the vector shape with Lingo while the member is visible on the Stage, you should set this property to FALSE to prevent the sprite from jumping around.
closed	Determines whether the first and last point in the vector shape are joined. It must be set to TRUE for the shape to be filled.
curve	Returns a single curve from the vertexList. In the vertexList, curves are separated by [#newcurve] items in the list. To use the curve property, treat it as list a list, using brackets with a number. You can also use count to get the number of curves.
defaultRect	A property that can be used, in conjunction with defaultRectMode, to change the default rectangle for new sprites that use the vector shape member.
defaultRectMode	This property can be set to either #flash or #fixed. The #flash setting sets all new sprites that use the member to the normal rectangle of the member. The #fixed mode instead uses the defaultRect property to set the initial rectangle of the sprite. This setting also affects any existing sprites that have not yet been stretched.
directToStage	Determines whether the member is drawn on top of all other sprites, ignoring the sprite's ink effects. Drawing members in this manner improves performance.
endColor	The destination color of a gradient fill in a vector shape member. Use an rgb or paletteIndex structure to set this. The fillMode must be set to gradient, and the closed property must be TRUE.
fillColor	The color of the interior of a vector shape member if the fillMode is set to #solid, or the starting color if the fillMode is set to #gradient. Use an rgb or paletteIndex structure to set this. The closed property must be TRUE.

Table 15.1   Continued

Property	Description
fillCycles	The number of fill cycles in a vector shape member that have the fillMode set to #gradient. Should be a number from 1 to 7.
fillDirection	The direction of the fill, in degrees. The fillMode must be set to #gradient, and the gradientType should be set to #linear.
fillMode	This can be set to #none, #solid, or #gradient. Only when this is set to #solid will the property fillColor be useful. When it is set to #gradient, other properties, such as fillCycles, fillDirection, fillOffset, fillScale, and endColor, will determine the way the fill is drawn.
fillOffset	This property is a point that corresponds to the horizontal and vertical offsets for the fill. This works only when the fillType is set to #gradient.
fillScale	This corresponds to the "spread" in the vector shape editing window. The fillMode must be set to #gradient for this to work.
flashRect	The original size of the vector member as a member, not as a sprite.
gradientType	Can be set to #linear or #radial. Works only when the fillMode is #gradient.
originMode	This is the relationship between the vertex points and the center of the sprite. It can be set to #center, #topLeft, or #point. The #center option makes the vertex points relative to the center of the member, whereas the #topLeft option makes them relative to the top-left corner. The #point option uses the originPoint property. Set the originMode to #center if you plan to adjust a vertex while the movie is playing.
originPoint	A point indicating the relationship between the vertex points and the member's location. This is used only when originMode is set to #point. You can also use the originH and originV properties.
regPointVertex	If 0, the regPoint and centerRegPoint properties are used to determine the registration point. Otherwise, the regPointVertex specifies the number of the vertex to use as the registration point for the member.
scale	Enables you to scale the member, using a list such as [1.000,1.000], where the first item is the horizontal scale, and the second is the vertical scale. This is an alternative to simply stretching the sprite.
scaleMode	This is the equivalent to the member property in the vector shape's Properties dialog box. It can be set to #showAll, #noBorder, #exactFit, #noScale, and #autoSize. You can also use this as a property of a sprite that contains a vector shape.
strokeColor	The color of the line used by the vector shape. The strokeWidth must be greater than 0 for this to work.
strokeWidth	The width of the line used by the vector member.
vertex	A list of all the vertices in the vertexList. Use this property like a list with brackets and a number, or the count property.
vertexList	The main property of a vector shape. It is a list of all the points that make up the shape.
viewpoint	This point enables you to change the point of the vector shape that appears at the center of the sprite. You can use viewH and viewV as well.
viewScale	Another way to scale the size of the vector shape on the Stage.

15

There are a lot of vector shape properties, as you can see. These don't even include the many sprite properties that also work on vector shapes, such as `rotation`, `flipH`, `flipV`, and `skew`. You can always refer to the list view of the Property Inspector panel to see all the properties of any member.

⇨ *If you can't get the fill property to work as you expect, see "Fills Only Work When the Shape Is Closed" in the "Troubleshooting" section at the end of this chapter.*

VECTOR SHAPE COMMANDS

The key property of any vector shape member is the `vertexList`. Taking a look at one using the Message panel will help you understand how it works. Create a new vector shape and draw a rectangle in it. Then, use the Message panel to view the `vertexList`.

```
put member(1).vertexList
-- [[#vertex: point(-104.0000,-40.0000)], [#vertex: point(104.0000,-40.0000)],\
   [#vertex: point(104.0000,41.0000)], [#vertex: point(-104.0000,41.0000)]]
```

The `vertexList` is a list of lists. Each small list is a property list with one property: `#vertex`. The value of `#vertex` is a point. Each point corresponds to a corner of the vector shape.

You can alter the `vertexList` in a few ways. The `addVertex`, `deleteVertex`, and `moveVertex` commands enable you to do so without dealing with the member's properties directly. For instance, to add a new vertex, just use a command like this:

```
addVertex(member(1),3,point(0,0))
```

This command adds a point at 0,0 after the second vertex point and before the third. You can move an existing vertex by using a relative point and the `moveVertex` command:

```
moveVertex(member(1),3,100,10)
```

This command moves the third vertex point over to the right by 10 pixels. You can also delete a vertex, as follows:

```
deleteVertex(member(1),3)
```

Instead of using these commands, you can replace the entire `vertexList`. This next series of commands moves the third vertex over to the right 10 pixels:

```
vl = member(1).vertexList
v = vl[3].vertex
v = v + point(10,0)
vl[3].vertex = v
member(1).vertexList = vl
```

This is a lot more involved than just using `moveVertex`. However, resetting the entire vertex list actually makes sense in many cases. If you are using Lingo to create a vector shape from scratch, and then you want to replace it with another,

> **Caution**
>
> When setting the `vertexList` with Lingo, make sure that it is a valid vertex list, with all the properties spelled correctly and the values in the proper format.

> The `vertexList` items actually have two elements other than the `#vertex`: `#handle1` and `#handle2`. They are points as well. However, they correspond to the curve handles of the point. These are the same handles that you can see when you edit a point in the vector shape editing window. The values in the `vertexList` are points relative to the actual `#vertex` point.

slightly different, shape, you can use the same handler to create both shapes. This handler uses parameters to make the two shapes different, by simply replacing the entire vertex list each time, instead of trying to figure out which points differ. Tests show that there is no difference in drawing speed either way.

Table 15.2 runs down all vector commands.

Table 15.2   Vector Commands

Command	Description
addVertex	Adds a new vertex to the end of the vector shape. If you include an integer as the first parameter, the new vertex will be inserted at that point in the vertexList.
deleteVertex	Removes a vertex from the vertexList.
moveVertex	Changes the location of a vertex. The first parameter is the position of the vertex in the vertexList. The second parameter is the new location.
moveVertexHandle	Changes the location of the vertex handle. The first parameter is the vertex position in the vertexList. The second parameter is the number of the handle, either 1 or 2. The third parameter is the new handle location.
newCurve	Adds a new curve to the vertexList by adding a [#newcurve] item. The one parameter is the position of the new curve among other curves in the vertexList.

> ⇨ *If you can't seem to change the vertexList without shifting the registration point of the shape, see "Changing Vertex Locations Shifts Registration Point" in the "Troubleshooting" section at the end of this chapter.*

BUILDING VECTORS WITH LINGO

By setting the vertexList property of a vector member, you can create all sorts of interesting things with Lingo. For instance, here is a short behavior that creates a new, simple line and replaces the sprite's vector shape member with this line:

```
on beginSprite me
 sprite(me.spriteNum).member.vertexList = \
  [[#vertex: point(0,0)], [#vertex: point(200,100)]]
end
```

This handler sets the sprite's vertexList to two simple points. You can use strokeWidth and strokeColor to set the line's thickness and color.

You can also have multiple curves. The way to do this is to insert a [#newCurve] element into the vertexList. Here is a behavior that creates a grid using 11 vertical and 11 horizontal lines:

```
on beginSprite me
 mem = sprite(me.spriteNum).member

 vlist = []
```

```
repeat with x = 0 to 10
 add vlist, [#vertex: point(x*10,0)]
 add vlist, [#vertex: point(x*10,100)]
 add vlist, [#newCurve]
end repeat

repeat with y = 0 to 10
 add vlist, [#vertex: point(0,y*10)]
 add vlist, [#vertex: point(100,y*10)]
 add vlist, [#newCurve]
end repeat

mem.vertexList = vlist
end
```

Here is a behavior that creates a curve using the `sin` function. Figure 15.1 shows the results of this handler, placed on the Stage. The member that this sprite is placed on should be a blank vector shape member.

```
on beginSprite me
 mem = sprite(me.spriteNum).member

 list = []
 repeat with x = -100*pi() to 100*pi()
  y = sin(float(x)/100.0)*100
  add list, [#vertex: point(x,y)]
 end repeat
 mem.vertexList = list
end
```

Figure 15.1
This sine curve is a single vector shape member created with Lingo.

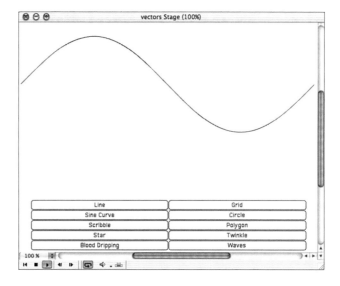

Only a little more work is needed to create a circle. Unlike the circle created with the vector shape editing window, this circle consists of 64 individual points with lines attaching them. The result actually looks round, despite being made up of little lines. Figure 15.2 shows the result.

```
on beginSprite me
 mem = sprite(me.spriteNum).member

 radius = 50

 list = []
 repeat with angle = 0 to 63
  x = cos(float(angle)/10.0)*radius
  y = sin(float(angle)/10.0)*radius
  add list, [#vertex: point(x,y)]
 end repeat
 mem.vertexList = list
end
```

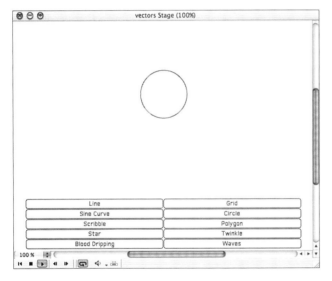

Figure 15.2
This circle is made up of 64 small lines in a single vector shape member created by Lingo.

Simple shapes are not where Lingo vector creation shines. Complex ones, such as polygons, really show off the power of creating vectors with Lingo. Here is a behavior that sets a vector graphic in a sprite to a polygon. You can even choose the number of sides in the polygon.

```
property pNumPoints, pRadius

on getPropertyDescriptionList me
 list = [:]
 addProp list, #pNumPoints, [#comment: "Number of Points",\
   #format: #integer, #default: 5]
 addProp list, #pRadius, [#comment: "Radius",\
   #format: #integer, #default: 100]
 return list
end
```

```
on beginSprite me
  mem = sprite(me.spriteNum).member

  -- how many degrees apart is each point
  angleDiff = 360/pNumPoints

  -- build vertex list
  list = []
  repeat with angle = 0 to pNumPoints
    p = circlePoint(angle*angleDiff,pRadius)
    add list, [#vertex: p]
  end repeat

  -- set the member
  mem.vertexList = list
end

-- the following handler returns the point on any circle
-- given the angle and radius
on circlePoint angle, radius
  a = (float(angle-90)/360.0)*2.0*pi()
  x = cos(a)*radius
  y = sin(a)*radius
  return point(x,y)
end
```

Figure 15.3 shows the use of this behavior. It resets the member used by the sprite as a polygon. If the same member is used in more than one sprite, the behaviors interfere with each other. Instead, create multiple copies of a vector shape and place each one on the Stage only once. The initial vector shapes can be anything, such as small rectangles or circles. The behavior resets the vertexList of the sprite and makes sure that it is closed. However, the fill color and type remain as they were before. A more complex behavior can set these, too.

The more vertex points in a vector shape, the more slowly it draws. Antialiased vector shapes also draw more slowly than non–antialiased shapes.

Figure 15.3
These polygons were created with a polygon behavior that takes any vector shape and molds it into a polygon.

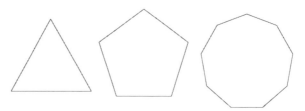

A little modification to this behavior gives you a handler that creates a star rather than a polygon. It just needs to set alternative outer and inner points. Figure 15.4 shows the result of this behavior.

15

```
property pNumPoints, pRadius

on getPropertyDescriptionList me
 list = [:]
 addProp list, #pNumPoints, [#comment: "Number of Points",\
   #format: #integer, #default: 5]
 addProp list, #pRadius, [#comment: "Radius",\
   #format: #integer, #default: 100]
 return list
end

on beginSprite me
 mem = sprite(me.spriteNum).member

 -- how many degrees apart is each point
 angleDiff = 360/pNumPoints

 -- build vertex list
 list = []
 repeat with starPoint = 0 to pNumPoints-1

  -- outer point location
  p = circlePoint (starPoint*angleDiff,pRadius)
  add list, [#vertex: p]

  -- inner point location
  p = circlePoint((starPoint+.5)*angleDiff,pRadius*.5)
  add list, [#vertex: p]
 end repeat

 -- set the member
 mem.vertexList = list
 mem.closed = TRUE
end

-- the following handler returns the point on any circle
-- given the angle and radius
on circlePoint angle, radius
 a = (float(angle-90)/360.0)*2.0*pi()
 x = cos(a)*radius
 y = sin(a)*radius
 return point(x,y)
end
```

15

Figure 15.4
This star was created with a star behavior, which takes any vector shape and molds it into a star.

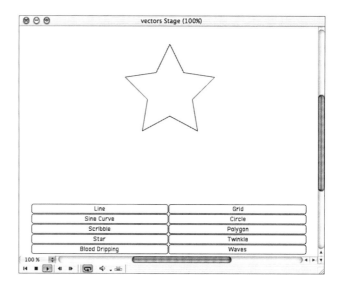

All the previous handlers and behaviors draw a shape once, usually at `on beginSprite`, and leave the vector shape alone. However, Lingo can just as easily redraw the vector shape each and every frame to create animated vector shapes.

A simple example draws a random shape. The following behavior draws a vector between 20 random points. The result is a messy scribble. However, it re-creates itself on each frame to create an unusual animated effect. Check the movie on the CD-ROM (`vectors.dir`) to see it in action.

Notice that the closed property of the vector shape member is set to TRUE. This enables you to also set the `fillMode` property to `#solid` and set the `fillColor` property to the color you want to use. You can also use a gradient by setting the `fillMode` to `#gradient` and then setting the entire collection of fill properties to specify the color, type, direction, scale, and type of gradient fill.

```
on exitFrame me
  mem = sprite(me.spriteNum).member

  list = []
  repeat with i = 1 to 20
    x = random(100)
    y = random(100)
    add list, [#vertex: point(x,y)]
  end repeat
  mem.vertexList = list
end
```

The same idea can be applied to the star shape behavior. Stars are sometimes known to twinkle. The following behavior redraws the star every frame but with a different random point stretched slightly. The result, if done with the right color and size, is an animated twinkling star:

```
property pNumPoints, pRadius, pPointToMove, pPointMoveDiff,\
  pPointMoveAmount, pTwinkleSpeed, pTwinkleAmount
```

```
on getPropertyDescriptionList me
 list = [:]
 addProp list, #pNumPoints, [#comment: "Number of Points",\
   #format: #integer, #default: 5]
 addProp list, #pRadius, [#comment: "Radius",\
   #format: #integer, #default: 25]
 addProp list, #pTwinkleSpeed, [#comment: "Twinkle Speed",\
   #format: #integer, #default: 1]
 addProp list, #pTwinkleAmount, [#comment: "Twinkle Amount",\
   #format: #integer, #default: 3]
 return list
end

on beginSprite me
 moveNewPoint(me)
 mem = sprite(me.spriteNum).member
 mem.centerRegPoint = FALSE
 mem.originMode = #center
end

-- this handler decides which new point of the star
-- to twinkle
on moveNewPoint me
 repeat while TRUE
  r = random(pNumPoints)
  if r <> pPointToMove then exit repeat
 end repeat
 pPointToMove = r
 pPointMoveDiff = 0
 pPointMoveAmount = pTwinkleSpeed
end

on exitFrame me
 mem = sprite(me.spriteNum).member

 -- how many degrees apart is each point
 angleDiff = 360/pNumPoints

 -- build vertex list
 list = []
 repeat with starPoint = 1 to pNumPoints

  -- move twinkling point in or out
  if starPoint = pPointToMove then
   pPointMoveDiff = pPointMoveDiff + pPointMoveAmount
   if pPointMoveDiff > pTwinkleAmount then pPointMoveDiff = -pTwinkleSpeed
   if pPointMoveDiff <= 0 then moveNewPoint
   p = circlePoint(starPoint*angleDiff,pRadius+pPointMoveDiff)
  else
```

```
     -- keep non-twinkling point normal
     p = circlePoint(starPoint*angleDiff,pRadius)
   end if

   add list, [#vertex: p]
   p = circlePoint((starPoint+.5)*angleDiff,pRadius*.5)
   add list, [#vertex: p]
 end repeat

 -- set the member
 mem.vertexList = list
end


-- the following handler returns the point on any circle
-- given the angle and radius
on circlePoint angle, radius
 a = (float(angle-90)/360.0)*2.0*pi()
 x = cos(a)*radius
 y = sin(a)*radius
 return point(x,y)
end
```

The result looks just like the previous star shape behavior, but one point at a time is animating. First it moves a little bit out from the center, and then it moves back into place.

A more dramatic behavior is one that uses the handles of each vertex point. Because these handles measure the curve of the line coming into and going out of the vertex, they are difficult to use. Changing the handles is easy enough, but getting them to do what you want is another matter. Even illustrators who have used vector editing programs for years can sometimes be at a loss to explain exactly how to use handles. They simply use them intuitively. There is mathematics behind these handles, but the complexities are beyond the scope of this book.

The following code shows a behavior that uses #handle1 to create a curved look to many points along the bottom of a vector shape. The behavior then moves the vertex points downward to create a "curtain" or "dripping blood" effect. Figure 15.5 shows the result in mid-animation.

```
property pNumPoints, pRadius, pVlist

on getPropertyDescriptionList me
 list = [:]
 addProp list, #pNumPoints, [#comment: "Number of Points",\
   #format: #integer, #default: 25]
 addProp list, #pRadius, [#comment: "Radius",\
   #format: #integer, #default: 12]
 return list
end

on beginSprite me
 pVlist = []
```

```
-- space between drips
spacing = 640/pNumPoints

-- add top and sides
add pVlist, [#vertex: point(640+spacing,0)]
add pVlist, [#vertex: point(640+spacing,0)]
add pVlist, [#vertex: point(0-spacing,0)]

-- add drip spots along bottom
repeat with i = 0 to pNumPoints
  add pVlist, [#vertex: point(i*spacing,0), \
#handle1: point(spacing/2,spacing)]
end repeat

-- set member
mem = sprite(me.spriteNum).member
mem.vertexList = pVlist
mem.centerRegPoint = FALSE
mem.originMode = #center
mem.closed = TRUE
end

on exitFrame me
  -- change 20 vertex points at a time
  repeat with i = 1 to 20
   r = random(pNumPoints+1)+3
   pVlist[r][#vertex] = pVlist[r][#vertex] + \
    point(0,random(pRadius))
  end repeat
  sprite(me.spriteNum).member.vertexList = pVlist
end
```

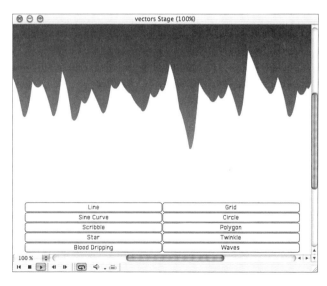

Figure 15.5
The dripping blood effect was created with a vector shape and a Lingo behavior that moves the vertex points down over time.

Another effect uses both the #handle1 and #handle2 properties to direct the curve of many points along a line. With each frame, the angle of the curve changes to make the point appear to roll over, like a wave. The final result, seen in Figure 15.6, is a sea-like graphic.

```
property pNumPoints, pRadius, pList, pOffset, pAngle

on getPropertyDescriptionList me
 list = [:]
 addProp list, #pNumPoints, [#comment: "Number of Points",\
   #format: #integer, #default: 25]
 addProp list, #pRadius, [#comment: "Radius",\
   #format: #integer, #default: 12]
 return list
end

on beginSprite me
 pOffset = 0
 pAngle = 0
end

on exitFrame me
 pList = []
 spacing = 680/pNumPoints
 pOffset = pOffset + 2
 if pOffset > spacing then pOffset = 0

 -- create bottom and sides
 add pList, [#vertex: point(680+spacing,0)]
 add pList, [#vertex: point(680+spacing,100)]
 add pList, [#vertex: point(0-spacing,100)]

 -- add wave points
 repeat with i = 0 to pNumPoints

  -- move the waves
  pAngle = pAngle - 1
  if pAngle < -90 then pAngle = 90

  -- get the handle
  h = circlePoint(pAngle,pRadius)
  h2 = circlePoint(pAngle+180,pRadius)

  add pList, [#vertex: point(i*spacing-pOffset,0), \
#handle1: h, #handle2: h2]
 end repeat

 -- set the member
 mem = sprite(me.spriteNum).member
 mem.vertexList = pList
```

```
  mem.centerRegPoint = FALSE
  mem.originMode = #center
  mem.closed = TRUE
end

-- the following handler returns the point on any circle
-- given the angle and radius
on circlePoint angle, radius
  a = (float(angle-90)/360.0)*2.0*pi()
  x = cos(a)*radius
  y = sin(a)*radius
  return point(x,y)
end
```

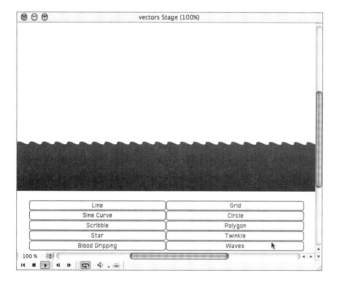

Figure 15.6
The changing locations of the handles for each vertex point create animated waves.

USING VECTORS FOR COLLISION DETECTION

One way in which vector shape members are different from bitmaps is that, with vector shapes, you can actually tell whether a point is inside or outside a vector shape. You can do this with bitmaps and the `rollover` property, but only when the ink is set to matte, and the mouse is at the location you are trying to detect.

The function `hitTest` enables you to specify a sprite and a Stage location. The returned value is either #background, #normal, or #button. The last value can be returned by only a Flash movie, not a vector shape. However, the other two values can be used to determine whether any point is inside or outside a shape, no matter how complex that shape is.

The following code shows a behavior that takes advantage of this feature. It assumes that there is a vector shape in sprite 1 that the behavior cannot move its sprite over. It looks for key presses and then moves its sprite accordingly. If the behavior finds that the new location is inside the vector shape in that sprite, it doesn't allow the move to take place.

```
property px, py

on beginSprite me
 -- get initial location
 px = sprite(me.spriteNum).locH
 py = sprite(me.spriteNum).locV
end

on exitFrame me

 -- assume x doesn't change
 newx = px

 -- see if it does
 if keyPressed(123) then newx = px - 1
 if keyPressed(124) then newx = px + 1

 -- see if new x will hit the shape
 if hitTest(sprite(1),point(newx,py)) <> #normal then
  px = newx
 end if

 -- assume y doesn't change
 newy = py

 -- see if it does
 if keyPressed(125) then newy = py + 1
 if keyPressed(126) then newy = py - 1

 -- see if new y will hit the stage
 if hitTest(sprite(1),point(px,newy)) <> #normal then
  py = newy
 end if

 -- new location for the sprite
 sprite(me.spriteNum).loc = point(px,py)
end
```

A more complex behavior might have a parameter that specifies which sprite the behavior should be looking at. Or, perhaps the behavior can specify an entire range of sprites.

TROUBLESHOOTING

Changing Vertex Locations Shifts Registration Point

When I use Lingo to change the `vertexList` of a vector shape, why does the registration point of the vector shape shift?

If you are animating by using Lingo to change the `vertexList` while the movie is playing, the `centerRegPoint` should be set to FALSE, the `originMode` set to "center", and the vector's scale mode set to "auto-size." Otherwise, the sprite appears to move around the Stage as the shape changes.

Fills Only Work When the Shape Is Closed

Why do some shapes not appear to be filled when I set the `fill` property to TRUE?

If you are trying to apply a fill color to a vector shape, make sure that the `closed` property is set to TRUE. Otherwise, there is no area to fill.

Using the Right Ink for Vector Shapes

Why do all my vector shapes appear on the Stage in a rectangle with the background color of the member?

You usually want to set a vector shape's sprite `ink` to Background Transparent. Leaving it as Copy applies the background color of the member to the whole rectangle on the Stage. Using Matte ink doesn't work.

DID YOU KNOW?

- Although vector shape members have only one fill type, color, stroke width, and other properties, you can create more complex Freehand or Illustrator–like images by using several vector shapes on top of each other.

- EPS files are actually lists of vertex points and handles. If you get to know the EPS file format well enough, you can write a Lingo script that reads these files and creates vector shape members based on the data.

- Vector shapes and Flash members, when placed in a sprite, can be rotated, skewed, and scaled like bitmaps. However, because they are made of curved lines, enlarging them does not degrade the image resolution.

- You can use the Lingo command to put `member(x).showProps()` in the Message panel, where x is a vector shape member, to get a complete list of all its properties. The same is true for Flash members.

IV

CREATING AND CONTROLLING 3D

IN THIS PART

16

CREATING 3D MODELS

IN THIS CHAPTER

3D BASICS

Using 3D worlds and models is almost completely different from the 2D graphics space that Macromedia Director developers are used to. To really be able to use Director's 3D capabilities, you need to understand the basics of 3D computer graphics.

16

The Third Dimension

The three dimensions of 3D are horizontal distance, vertical distance, and depth. These are also referred to with the letters x, y, and z. Locations of objects in a 3D world can be specified by x, y, and z coordinates just as locations in a 2D space can be defined by horizontal and vertical, or x and y, coordinates. Figure 16.1 shows you how to think of this three-coordinate system.

Figure 16.1
The z coordinate usually represents depth.

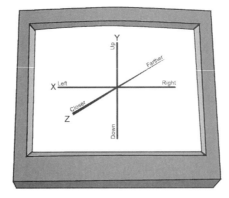

The world we live in is 3D, so you would think that it would be easy to build and manipulate 3D computer models. But it isn't easy because computers really don't display anything in 3D. The computer monitor is hopelessly a flat 2D surface. 3D computer graphics are not really about 3D spaces, but about representing 3D spaces on a 2D screen. This complicates things quite a bit. You can't reach your hand into a computer monitor and move something around in three dimensions. Instead, you have all sorts of expensive complex tools to help you create 3D illusions on a 2D screen.

Two of the three dimensions, x and y, are easy to talk about. They correspond to the horizontal and vertical position on a computer screen. The z dimension, depth, is supposed to represent locations *into* the computer screen. But there is really no such thing. It is all an optical illusion.

So when you are dealing with 3D graphics, you are always dealing with five numbers: the x, y, and z coordinates of the 3D object in 3D space and the x and y coordinates that indicate where the 3D object appears on the 2D computer screen. Fortunately, the 3D engine built in to Director takes care of determining where things appear on the screen. All you need to worry about is where objects are in the x, y, and z coordinate system of the imaginary 3D world.

> **Caution**
>
> The z coordinate usually represents depth, but some 3D graphics programs use z as the vertical coordinate and y as depth. You must remain open to such variations if you want to understand and use 3D graphics.

The Imaginary 3D World

With 2D graphics, usually what you see is what you get. As you create a 2D picture, you know exactly what it will look like on the screen in the final product. You may stretch or shrink the image, but the basic image will look exactly as you created it.

3D graphics are totally different. Instead of a flat painting, 3D graphics are made of models. A *model* is a mathematical representation of a 3D object. For instance, you may have a model of a tea cup or an airplane.

So what does this model look like? Well, it doesn't look like anything. To get a visual representation of the model, you have to create a rendering of it. A *rendering* is a snapshot of the model taken from a particular angle and distance. Other factors are involved in determining what the rendering looks like. For instance, you could use different lighting, a different type of camera lens, or even a different mathematical method of creating the rendering. Figure 16.2 shows several renderings of the same 3D model.

Figure 16.2
All these images use the same model, only the viewpoint has changed.

When you create a 3D graphic in a 3D modeling program, you usually see the model as you create it. This is a preview rendering of the model that is created on-the-fly as the model is being built. This is usually a low-quality rendering because the image needs to be updated constantly as the artist changes the 3D model. If you are a 3D artist, you may request from the 3D program a high-quality rendering of the model. This would usually take a few seconds or minutes to create.

When a 3D engine like the one in Director is used, the purpose is usually to have a live rendering that is updated as the model changes position, or the viewpoint changes. So instead of creating a model and making a single 2D rendering of it, we will be creating a model to place in a live environment.

Shockwave 3D Terminology

You should master certain terms before beginning to work with 3D graphics. Note that we'll be talking about what these terms mean for Shockwave 3D. This may differ slightly from what you may have learned when using other 3D tools. Unfortunately, terms can sometimes mean slightly different things as you use tools created by different companies.

Models

We have already talked about models. A model is a mathematical representation of an object, such as a goldfish or an automobile. A model can also define a smaller sub-object, such as the goldfish's

16

eye or the automobile's front left tire. Or, you can go the other way and have a model that contains many other models, such as the model of a goldfish bowl or a city street.

Cameras

Next to models, the most important thing in a 3D environment is the *camera*. A camera is a viewpoint through which the world is seen. You can have one or more cameras in a 3D world and switch between them. A camera, like a model, can be positioned and rotated in the world. The result would be that the view of the world through that camera changes to reflect the position and rotation of the camera. In addition, cameras have some other minor properties, such as the field of view of the lens.

➯ *For more information about cameras, see "Camera Effects," p. 547.*

Lights

Another important part of 3D worlds is light. In the real world, we can see things because light comes from a source, such as the sun or a light bulb, reflects off a surface, and bounces into our eyes. The same is true for 3D worlds. There needs to be one or more light sources or the world is just completely dark.

A *light source* can be a point of light that radiates in all directions, or a spotlight that shines in a particular direction. A light has a color and intensity.

A light that shines universally throughout a 3D world is called an *ambient* light. The location of such a light doesn't matter because the light is treated like it is coming from all directions and hitting everything evenly.

One model, one light, and one camera make up the bare minimum you need to have a 3D world. Most 3D creation programs start with a default camera and light, so all you need to do is add a model.

Parts of a Model

Models are made up of *faces*, sometimes called *surfaces*. For instance, a cube would have six faces. Each face is made up of *polygons*. These are three-sided planes that fit together to make up a face and thus make up the whole model. Each polygon is defined by its three corner points. These points are called *vertices*. Figure 16.3 shows all these elements as they relate to a cube.

Figure 16.3
A cube model can be broken into faces, then polygons, and then vertices.

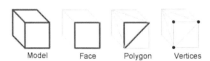

Model   Face   Polygon   Vertices

Shaders and Textures

What the surface of a model looks like is determined by a *shader*. A shader can be defined as a color and how the surface reflects light. Or, a shader can use a texture for a more complex surface. A *texture* is usually a 2D bitmap graphic that represents what the surface looks like if viewed under simple straight-on conditions.

Shaders are one of the most complex aspects of 3D worlds. Shaders also give the world character. Without shaders, the world would be made up of flat-colored polygons.

For instance, if you have a model of a brick, you will probably want to apply a shader to the brick to make it red. Or, you could have a shader that uses a texture to make the surface of the brick look red and resemble rough stone. A brick wall model might be a simple wide and tall box that uses a bitmap texture to represent a whole wall of bricks.

In some 3D graphics programs, shaders and textures are combined and are simply called "textures." In other programs, shaders are called "materials."

Some models use one shader to color in the entire model. More complex models use several shaders to represent different parts of the model.

Now that you know some 3D terminology, let's import a model into Director and work with it a bit.

IMPORTING MODELS

Although Director can manipulate 3D models, no tool in Director can be used to create them. Instead, you would normally use a 3D graphics tool to create the models and then a special exporter to create a Shockwave 3D file that can be imported into Director.

Where to Get 3D Models

Although having a 3D engine in Director is great, it is useless unless you have some 3D media to display. There are three ways to make or obtain models to be used in Director.

Make Them Yourself

If you want to make your own 3D models, you are going to need a 3D graphics program. Dozens of such programs are available, and they range in price from a few hundred dollars to several thousand dollars. Whichever one you choose, make sure that it has a Shockwave 3D export function. Here is a list of 3D graphics programs that have, or are planning to have, Shockwave 3D exporters at the time of this writing:

- Alias | Wavefront: Maya
- Caligari: TrueSpace
- Curious Labs: Poser
- Discreet: 3ds max
- Maxon Computer: Cinema 4D
- NewTek: Lightwave
- RealViz: ImageModeller
- SoftImage: XIS

16

- Tabuleiro: ShapeShifter 3D

- TGS: AMAPI 3D

ShapeShifter 3D stands out as the only tool created specifically for Shockwave 3D model creation. It also is different in that it works as a window inside Director. It is a simple tool, however, whereas tools such as Maya, 3ds max, and Lightwave are used to create high-end 3D graphics you might see on television or in the movies. We'll look more closely at ShapeShifter 3D later in this chapter.

Making 3D models is a skill all to itself. Do not expect to be able to buy one of these tools and instantly create jet fighters and jellyfish. 3D modeling is a skill usually developed over years of work or education.

Because the explanation of how to use a 3D program is a topic for a book all by itself, we won't spend any more time with it here. If you want to make your own models, pick your 3D program of choice and then look for a way to learn it: for instance a good book or a training course. Otherwise, you may want to consider other ways of getting 3D models.

When you create a model in a 3D graphics program, you may be creating it from several different shapes. You must tell the 3D program that you want these shapes grouped together into a single model, or they will all appear as separate models when you get the file into Director.

⇨ *If you are importing models and they come up with odd camera angles, see "Choose the Correct View Before Exporting" in the "Troubleshooting" section at the end of this chapter.*

Shockwave 3D Model Libraries

Just like there are 2D image clip art collections, there are also 3D model collections. You can purchase them on a CD-ROM or subscribe to a Web site that allows you to purchase models a la carte.

The Director MX CD-ROM comes with a folder full of example Shockwave 3D files. These files are examples from 3D model collections that can be purchased. Even though Shockwave 3D is relatively new, several 3D model companies are already offering models in ready-to-use Shockwave 3D format. By the time you read this, many more collections may also be available.

Convert Other 3D Models

A third way to get 3D models is to obtain models in universal 3D formats. Then, import these models into a 3D program that has a Shockwave 3D exporter and export them as Shockwave 3D.

Although this method seems simple, there are some complications. Often, the 3D models you get in collections will be too simple or too complex for what you need. For instance, a detailed model of an airplane may contain tens of thousands of polygons. Although this is required for a film or television rendering of the airplane, it will be too complex for the fast on-the-fly rendering of a Shockwave 3D application. Plus, it may be so huge that the download time for a movie with this model in it may be too long.

Textures are often a problem as well. Often textures from standard 3D formats do not import correctly into a 3D program. Even if they do, these textures may not export correctly to Shockwave 3D.

Converting non-Shockwave 3D models into Shockwave 3D models will sometimes work and sometimes not. It all depends on what you start with and what your expectations are.

Importing into Director

No matter how you create your Shockwave 3D model, you should end up with a Shockwave 3D file, also called a ".w3d" file after its dot-three filename extension. To bring this .w3d file into Director is simple. It is the same process that you use to bring in any other piece of media, such as a picture or a sound.

> If you are using models imported for a 3D program, note that the models inherit all the aspects they obtained while in that external program, so they might be positioned and oriented strangely when you first start.

By choosing File, Import, you can find and select one or more .w3d files. The only options you have at this point are whether to import the 3D models completely into Director or create a cast member that links to an external file. You can do this by using the pop-up menu at the bottom of the Import dialog box.

Now the 3D model is a Shockwave 3D cast member. The fun is just beginning. Next, we'll use Director's 3D member window to inspect the model.

⇨ *If you are having trouble importing .w4d files created by third-party programs, see "Importing Models Doesn' t Work" in the "Troubleshooting" section at the end of this chapter.*

THE SHOCKWAVE 3D PANEL

To open the Shockwave 3D panel, just double-click on the 3D member in the Cast panel. You'll get a window like the one shown in Figure 16.4, except that your model will be shown in the middle area. This middle area is the 3D preview area.

The Shockwave 3D panel is not like Director's Paint editor. You can't actually create or modify models. You can preview your 3D member and make changes to the initial camera position.

All the buttons on the left side of the window control the camera. The first three buttons are Dolly Camera, Pan Camera, and Rotate Camera. Click the button of the function you want to use, and then click and drag in the preview area to move the camera. A dolly move zooms the camera in and out. A pan moves the camera horizontally and vertically.

A rotation movement depends on which of the two buttons on the left is pressed, the Camera Y Up button or the Camera Z Up button. If you rotate using the z-axis, the camera can move above and below the model, and the camera can lean left and right. If you use the y-axis, the camera can move to the left and right around the model as well as above and below it. Give these tools a try. It takes a while to get used to them if you have never used a 3D tool before.

The Reset Camera Transform button, with a picture of a house on it, resets the camera to its default position. The Set Camera Transform button sets the default to match the view you have at the moment. Any changes you make to the camera view will disappear the moment you close the Shockwave 3D panel if you do not use this Set Camera Transform button.

Figure 16.4
The Shockwave 3D panel allows you to view your 3D member and make some changes to the position of the camera.

Reset Camera Transform
Set Camera Transform
Reset world

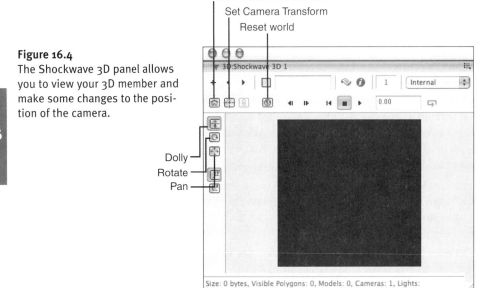

Dolly
Rotate
Pan

The Reset World button, with the little picture of the Earth on it, resets the camera and everything else in the 3D member. This is handy if you have been using Lingo to manipulate models in the 3D member.

The rest of the controls have to do with 3D members that have been created with a 3D animation tool. When imported into Director, these 3D animations can be played just like Flash members. You can use these videotape recorderlike buttons to play the animation and view each frame if you want.

At the bottom of the Shockwave 3D panel, you will see some information about the 3D member. The total size, number of polygons, number of cameras, and number of lights are shown. This helps you judge how complex a 3D member is and how much space it will occupy in the final Shockwave movie.

DISPLAYING A 3D MODEL ON THE STAGE

You can place a 3D member on the Stage just like a bitmap or Flash member. Once there, you can use the Property Inspector to make some adjustments to it. You can also select the member in the Cast and use the Property Inspector to make adjustments before you ever place it on the Stage.

Figure 16.5 shows the Property Inspector's 3D Model pane.

The six number fields at the top of the pane allow you to change the camera position and angle. This has the same effect as moving the camera around in the Shockwave 3D panel, but it is more precise.

Probably the most important setting for any 3D member is whether it is Direct to Stage. If it is Direct to Stage, no other sprites can be placed on top of the 3D member. The benefit is speed. A Direct to

Figure 16.5
The 3D Model pane of the Property Inspector allows you to change the camera position and lighting of a 3D member.

16

Stage 3D member displays much faster than one that is not. Unless you know that your users will have very fast 3D computers, it is best to always have 3D members set to Direct to Stage.

The Play Animation and Loop options only apply if the 3D member contains a 3D animation. The Preload option makes sure that the entire member has been loaded into memory before it is displayed on the screen.

The Revert to World Defaults button comes in handy when you begin to use behaviors or Lingo to change a 3D member on-the-fly. The 3D member always starts with models in their default position when you first run a movie. However, when you are working in Director, changes to a 3D member may persist as you build the movie. It is often useful to press this "Revert to World Defaults" button to manually reset the member so that it looks like it will when a user first runs the final movie.

The next part of the Shockwave 3D panel deals with the default directional light present in the 3D member. The little pop-up menu reads Top Center in Figure 16.5, but you can change it to one of nine positions. You can also select None to have no default directional light at all. After you have selected the position of the directional light, you can set its color. The color also determines the intensity. For instance, to

After a Shockwave 3D member is on the Stage, you can stretch it or shrink it like a bitmap member. However, whereas bitmaps do not look very nice when stretched, Shockwave 3D was built so that it can be stretched without losing any quality. In fact, you should feel free to stretch the sprite to fit any size you want. This should not affect quality or performance.

You can change the 3D software drivers that Director uses by choosing Modify, Movie, Properties. Test your movies with each available driver to make sure that it looks good and is fast enough. You never know what the end-user will have.

have a weak white light, choose a gray color rather than white. A directional light appears to originate from a point in the 3D world. That's why changing its position affects how much light is on certain parts of your model.

An ambient light also is present in every 3D member. You can select its color here as well. If you don't want any ambient light, just set it to black. The ambient light doesn't have a location; it just comes from everywhere and reflects off all surfaces equally.

The Background color chip determines what color is seen in the background of the 3D member. Black is the default and creates the illusion of empty space around the model. However, white can work just as well in many cases.

The final set of controls in the Shockwave 3D panel are the default shader controls. These come into play if a model is imported that has no shader applied to its surface, or if Lingo is used to create new objects in the 3D member.

You can pick a bitmap cast member as the default texture, or use the red and white checkerboard default bitmap. You can also adjust how diffuse light and specular light are reflected on the shader surface. These basically tint the shader to a certain color. The specular color defines what color is used to show highlights, whereas the diffuse color is used to tint the rest of the surface. The reflectivity setting determines how shiny the surface is.

> When I import a 3D file that was made in an external graphics program, the first thing I do is check the directional and ambient lights. Sometimes these are black or turned off, and I need to turn them on to brighten the scene.

The controls in the Shockwave 3D panel and the Shockwave 3D Property Inspector panel are the sum total of what you can do to change the appearance of a 3D member without using behaviors or Lingo. The only benefit of Shockwave 3D so far is the capability to display 3D media on the Stage. Next, we'll look at how to use behaviors to manipulate 3D models.

USING SHAPESHIFTER 3D

Director's 3D functionality displays 3D models and allows you to build them with Lingo. But there is no real 3D model creation tool in Director. This omission is easily corrected, however, thanks to Tabuleiro's ShapeShifter 3D Xtra.

ShapeShifter 3D differs from other 3D modeling solutions in that it is built specifically for Director. Other, much more expensive, modeling programs have all sorts of features that cannot be used with Shockwave 3D. These features not only drive up the cost of these tools but also make them much more confusing to learn. They also tend to generate models that have way to many polygons, thus slowing down your Director movies. ShapeShifter 3D is the perfect fit for Shockwave 3D modeling.

> You can download the Xtra from http://www.shapeshifter3d.com/. The evaluation version is free, and the full version is only $79 at the time of this writing. It is well worth the price if you are going to do any 3D work in Director.

Creating a Simple Model

After you have installed ShapeShifter 3D in your copy of Director MX, you can access it by choosing Xtras, ShapeShifter3D. The ShapeShifter 3D panel then appears. It looks like Figure 16.6 regardless of whether you are on Mac or Windows.

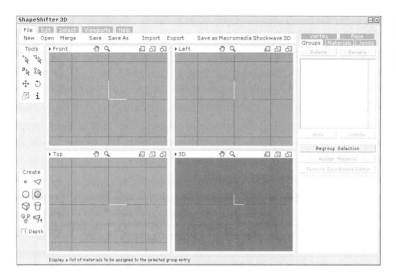

Figure 16.6
The ShapeShifter 3D panel allows you to create models specifically designed for use in Director.

The panel is broken into four panes. Each pane shows a different view of the same space. You can use the pull-down menu at the top of each pane to change its view to one of seven options: top, bottom, left, right, front, back, and 3D. The 3D view allows you to see the space from any angle, whereas the others are locked to being parallel or perpendicular to the x, y, and z axes.

You can click on the magnifying glass and then click and drag in a pane to zoom in or out. You can click on the hand tool and click and drag in the pane to move the view around. Click on these tools again to deactivate them.

You can also change the number of panes by selecting the Viewports tab at the top of the panel. You will then see a list of many pane combinations, including combinations that have 3, 2, or only 1 pane.

To create a model in ShapeShifter 3D, click on one of the shapes, say the box, in the Create toolbar at the bottom left. Then, click in one of the panes, any one but the bottom-right 3D pane, and drag to create a box. The result should look like Figure 16.7.

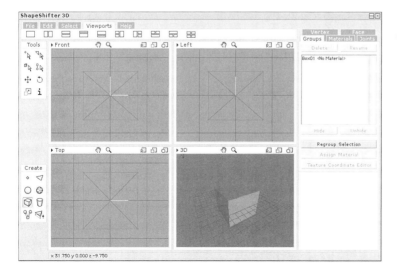

Figure 16.7
A simple box created in ShapeShifter 3D.

To get a better view of the box in 3D, click and drag in the 3D pane to adjust the view to what is shown in Figure 16.7.

You can see in the Groups information area on the right side of the screen that a group has been created, called Box01. You can select this name in the listing and click the Rename button just above it to rename the group. A group becomes a single model after it is imported into Director. So think of groups and models as one and the same thing.

To bring this model into your Cast, first save it. In the ShapeShifter 3D panel, choose File, Save. Name the file `mybox`. The extension `.ss3d` is added to the file automatically.

Now, choose File, Save as Macromedia Shockwave 3D. Don't worry about the Export Macromedia Shockwave 3D Options dialog box for now, just use the default settings. Name this file `mybox` as well. This time it will be saved as a `.w3d` file, the native format of Shockwave 3D. It will also be automatically imported into your Cast.

The reason you need to save the file two different ways is because the `.w3d` format is compressed and does not contain the information that ShapeShifter 3D would need to re-edit the model. So a special ShapeShifter 3D file is saved and then the `.w3d` file is exported for use in Director.

Now close the ShaperShifter 3D panel and look at your model in the Cast. You can double-click on it to view it in Director's 3D viewer. You can drag it to the Stage to see it there.

Creating Complex Models with ShapeShifter 3D

You can create more complex models in ShapeShifter 3D by using multiple shapes, altering them, and then combining them. We'll create a simple rocket ship model.

Open the ShapeShifter 3D panel and select the Sphere creation tool at the bottom left. Drag a sphere in the middle of the space, using the Front, Top, or Left pane. To create a sphere, click where you want the center of the sphere to start and then drag outward to make the sphere larger. The result should look like Figure 16.8.

Figure 16.8
A sphere created in ShapeShifter 3D.

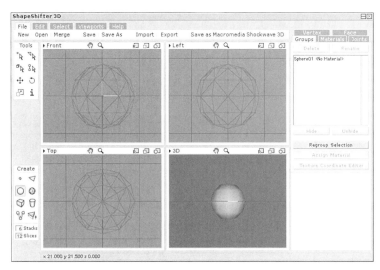

Now choose the Scale tool from the Tools palette. Click and drag in the pane labeled Top to shrink the width and length of the sphere, while keeping the height of the sphere the same. The result should look like Figure 16.9, with the 3D pane adjusted to show an angled view. This will be the rocket ship body.

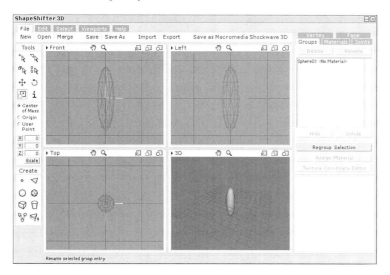

Figure 16.9
The width and the length of the sphere are scaled down to make the sphere oblong.

Now select the Vertex Mode tool, the first in the Tools palette. Using the Left pane, select the vertex point at the bottom of the shape. Then choose Edit, Delete Selected to remove it. The result, shown in Figure 16.10, is that the bottom of the rocket ship body has been truncated.

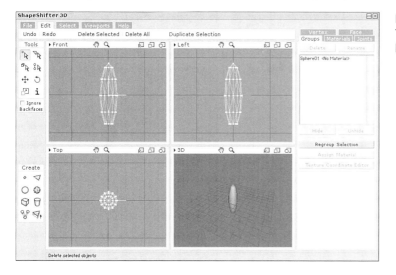

Figure 16.10
The body of the rocket ship now has a flat bottom.

Now choose the Sphere tool again and create another sphere off to the side of the ship. It should be about the size of the sphere in Figure 16.11.

16

Figure 16.11
The second sphere will become the tail fin.

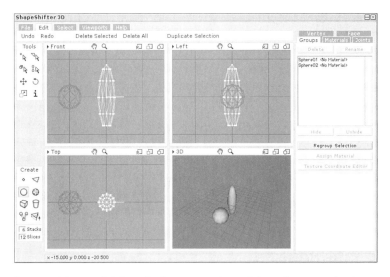

Choose the Vertex Mode tool again. Select and delete the bottom vertices of the sphere, turning it into a half-sphere. Using the Front pane works best for this. Figure 16.12 shows the result.

Figure 16.12
The sphere is cut in half by selecting the bottom vertices and deleting them.

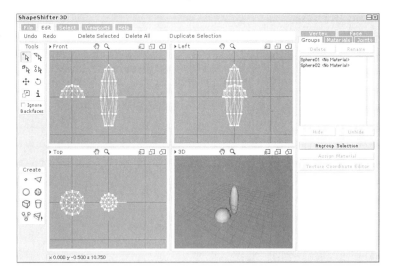

Now choose the Group tool from the Tools palette so that you can reselect the half-sphere. Then choose the Scale tool from the Tools palette and flatten the half-sphere in the Top pane, while making it taller and wider in the Front pane. Figure 16.13 shows the result.

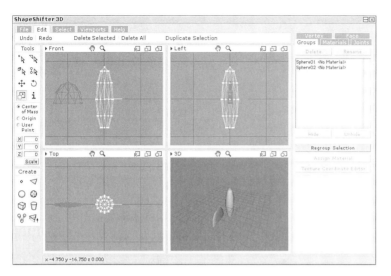

Figure 16.13
The half-sphere is now starting to look like a tail fin.

Now use the Move tool to reposition the tail fin so that it rests at the bottom of the rocket ship. You'll have to move the fin in the Top, Front, and Left panes to make sure that it is centered on the ship. Figure 16.14 shows the result.

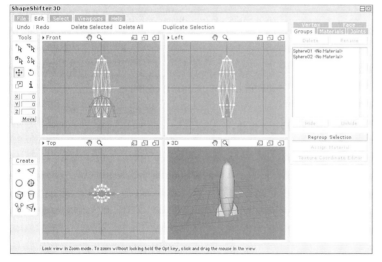

Figure 16.14
The tail fin is now in place at the bottom of the ship.

Now choose Edit, Duplicate Selection with the fin still selected. This creates a duplicate of the fin, sitting in the same place as the original. You can see in the Groups information area to the right that there is a new model named Duplicate01. The selection is now the new model, not the original.

Now choose the Rotate tool. Instead of clicking and dragging in one of the panes to rotate the second fin model, use the number fields at the left to enter a 90° change in the y-axis. Then click the little Rotate button to make the rotation happen. The second tail fin is now at a 90° angle to the first. You can see the rotation fields and the new orientation of the tail fin in Figure 16.15.

Figure 16.15
The second tail fin is perpendicular to the first.

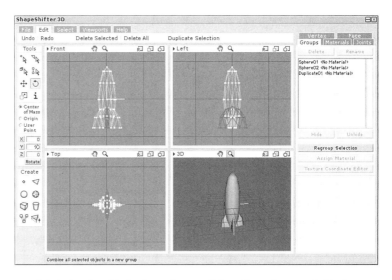

The 3D space now has three models in it: the ship body and two tail fins. If you imported this into Director's Cast, it would look fine at first. But then when you started to move one of the models around, it would not move along with the others. You want to group all three pieces of the ship together so that they act as one model.

To do this, use the Group selection tool again. With the Shift key down, you can select all three shapes. Then in the Groups information area to the right, select Regroup Selection. The three groups listed will change to one group named Regroup01. Select it in the list and change its name to Rocket.

Now, save the model as `rocket.ss3d` and as `rocket.w3d` using the ShapeShifter 3D File menu. Your current movie will now have the rocket model in one of its cast members.

Extruding Models with ShapeShifter 3D

One way to build models is by combining various shapes, as in the previous example. Another way is to take a single shape and mold it into the final object.

We'll make a simple table model. Open the ShapeShifter 3D panel and draw a cube. You should end up with something the size of the cube shown in Figure 16.16.

We want the box to become a relatively flat table surface. We could scale it and reduce its height, but let's demonstrate a different technique. Select the Vertex Mode tool and drag to select the bottom vertices in the Front pane. Then select the Move tool and move those vertices up to make the table top a thin surface. You can see the result get in Figure 16.17.

> Notice that the vertices in Figure 16.16 match the grid perfectly. You can do that by drawing the shape close to the grid lines and then clicking the Snap to Grid button under the Vertex information area to the right.

Now, change the bottom left pane to a Bottom view rather than a Top view. You can do this by using the pull-down menu at the top of the pane. Select the Faces Mode tool. Check the box next to Ignore Backfaces. Then click to select each of the two triangular polygons in the Bottom pane.

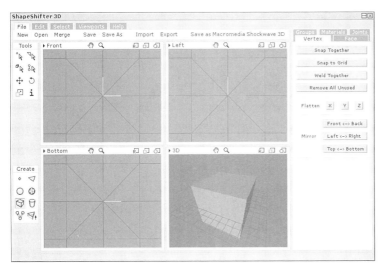

Figure 16.16
This simple cube will be molded into a table.

16

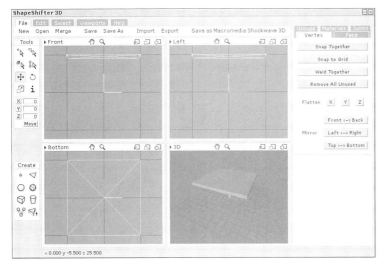

Figure 16.17
The table top was created by taking a cube and bringing its bottom surface up close to its top.

The Ignore Backfaces option is very important. When you use the Faces Mode tool, any click selects any polygon faces under the cursor. This would include both the top and bottom of the cube. But if you select Ignore Backfaces, only the side of the cube facing you in the pane will be selected.

Next, go to the Face tab of the information area to the right of the viewports. Click on the Subdivide 4 button. This takes the square area made up of two polygons and divides it into four squares. Click this button again to get a total of 16 squares.

Figure 16.18 shows what wills look like. The top of the cube is still one square made up of two polygons, but the bottom is now 16 squares and a total of 32 polygons.

Figure 16.18
The bottom of the table top is now 16 squares.

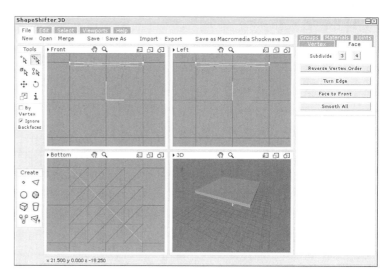

Select the Vertex Mode tool and drag to select the middle 9 vertices of the table's bottom. Make sure that Ignore Backfaces is still selected so that you are only grabbing vertices on the bottom of the table.

Now use the Scale tool on the Bottom pane to shrink the size of this middle portion of the model. The result looks like Figure 16.19.

Figure 16.19
The middle four squares of the table top's bottom have been shrunk to form the beginnings of the table's center column.

.

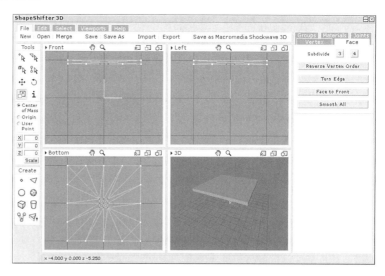

Switch to the Faces Mode tool again. You need to select the eight polygon faces that make up this small center portion of the table top's bottom. Make sure that you are not selecting any faces that are not in this little area.

Then, select the Extrude tool from the Create palette. Click and drag in the Front pane so that you stretch a new set of polygons down from the table to form the table's center column. If you do not get results like in Figure 16.20, you have selected too many or too few polygon faces.

When doing precision editing in ShapeShifter 3D, you may want to use the magnify tools to zoom in on an area. It also helps to use the 3D pane to spin the model around to see exactly what you have selected.

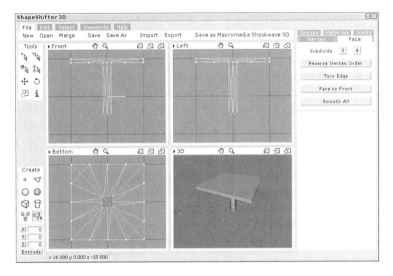

Figure 16.20
The table's center column has been extruded from its top.

Without deselecting the Extrude tool or doing anything else, you can click and drag again to extrude a second section from the first. So you can extend the table column a little farther. Do that so you have something like Figure 16.21.

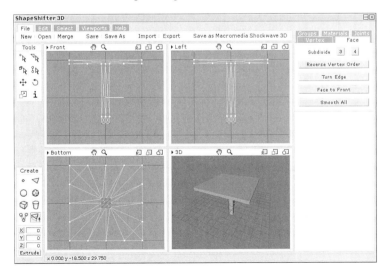

Figure 16.21
This new section of the column will become the table base.

16

Now switch back to the Vertex Mode tool, deselect the Ignore Backfaces option, and select the bottommost set of vertices in the Front pane. Select the Scale tool and use the Bottom pane to stretch these vertices into a larger area. This expands the bottom portion of the column into a table base, as shown in Figure 16.22.

An extrude action pulls away some polygons from the main shape. While doing so, it creates side polygons to connect the original shape to the faces being pulled away.

Figure 16.22
The table now has a base so that it won't fall over.

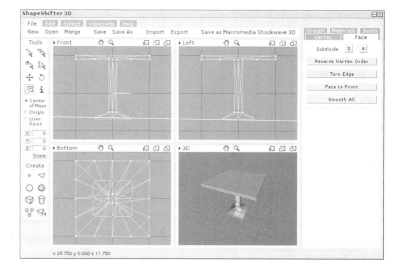

Save this as `table.ss3d` and `table.w3d` so that you can use it in your Director movie.

Applying Textures in ShapeShifter 3D

Applying a texture to your surfaces in ShapeShifter 3D is easy. First, create a simple model, such as a box. You can shrink the depth of the box down to make it look more like a wall.

If you select the Groups tab on the right, you will notice that the words "<no material>" appear next to the group's name. Let's change that.

Select the Materials tab. Click the New button that appears under the tab. Name the new material Brick Wall by using the Rename button. Now click the Choose button in the Texture section at the bottom. Select the `brickwall.jpg` image found on this book's CD-ROM. The whole Materials tab should now look like Figure 16.23.

Now, go to the Groups tab and select the only group there, the one that represents your model. Click Assign Material and select the Brick Wall material.

The wall is now a brick wall. Figure 16.24 shows what you should see.

Figure 16.23
The Materials tab allows you to add textures to your 3D models.

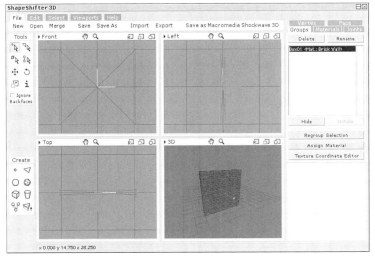

Figure 16.24
The Brick Wall texture has been applied to the model.

In Figure 16.24, you'll notice the Texture Coordinate Editor. This option allows you to map the texture onto your model however you specify. For instance, you could apply the texture only to a portion of the model, or stretch it in one of many ways. Experiment with this feature if you need more control over your textures.

More About ShapeShifter 3D

The preceding sections only touched the surface of what ShapeShifter 3D can do. Its real power lies in the fact that you can edit right down to the vertex and face level. The Create Vertex tool and the Create Faces tool allow you to start by creating your model one vertex at a time. Then you can define each polygon from those vertices.

It takes of lot of patience to create 3D models this way, but you get much more efficient results than you would if you used an expensive 3D modeling program.

The documentation goes into more detail about how to use each tool. There are also tutorials at the http://www.shapeshifter3d.com/ site.

CREATING PRIMITIVES WITH LINGO

So far in this section we have used Lingo to modify models in a 3D world created by an external 3D program. You can also use Lingo to start with a completely blank 3D world and create objects in it.

These simple objects are called primitives. There are four main types of primitives: box, sphere, cylinder, and plane. Figure 16.25 shows them all.

Figure 16.25
These are all four basic primitives.

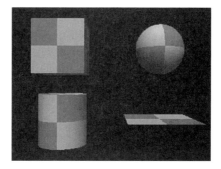

Starting from Scratch

We'll start by creating a completely blank 3D cast member. This is not as easy as it sounds. If you choose Insert, Media Element, Shockwave 3D, a new 3D member is created. However, it disappears as soon as you close the Shockwave 3D panel.

To keep a blank member, you need to name it. Choose Insert, Media Element, Shockwave 3D and then name the member in the Shockwave 3D panel. When you close the panel, the 3D member remains in the Cast.

You could also use Lingo in the Message panel to create a new 3D member. The new command works with the #Shockwave3D symbol to do this. However, you'll have to name the member right away or risk losing it again.

```
my3Dmember = new(#Shockwave3D)
my3Dmember.name = "My 3D Member"
```

Either way you create a 3D member, you'll want to drag it onto the Stage next. If you drag it right into the Score, the member will be centered on the Stage. Or, you could drag it onto the Stage and position it as you want.

Creating a Box

To create a primitive, you need to do two things. First, you need to create a model resource. This is like a template for creating models. Then, you need to use the model resource to create the actual model.

The `newModelResource` command creates one of these templates. You just need to tell it what you want to name the template and what type of primitive it represents. Here is a line of code that creates a box model resource:

```
myModelResource = sprite(1).member.newModelResource("My Box Resource",#box)
```

The model resource can be referred to by its name, or it can be referenced with the variable *myModelResource* that we used in the previous line. Using variable references can greatly reduce the length of your Lingo statements.

To create a model from this resource, use the `newModel` command. The new model will appear in the center of the 3D world.

```
myModel = sprite(1).member.newModel("My Box",myModelResource)
```

Because you are looking straight-on at the box, you can't see any of the sides or the back. Figure 16.26 shows the one face you can see.

Figure 16.26
A single box primitive placed in the middle of the 3D world.

You can now reposition the box and reorient it. For instance, to spin the box around 45 degrees and tilt it 45 degrees, try this in the Message panel:

```
sprite(1).member.model("My Box").rotate(45,45,0)
```

All primitives have unique properties. Boxes, for instance, have the `height`, `length`, and `width` properties. These are not properties of the individual models, but properties of the model resource.

When you create primitives with Lingo, these primitive models only exist until the member is reset. If you quit Director and return to the movie later, they will be gone.

By default, a box is 50 units high by 50 units wide by 50 units long. But you could make a box that has different dimensions. For instance, if you wanted to make a box that is 10 high by 20 wide by 100 long, you could do this:

```
sprite(me.spriteNum).member.resetWorld()

-- create the model resource
myModelResource = sprite(me.spriteNum).member.
➥newModelResource("My Box Resource",#box)
myModelResource.height = 10
myModelResource.width = 20
myModelResource.length = 100

-- create the model
myModel = sprite(me.spriteNum).member.newModel("My Box",myModelResource)

-- rotate to see it better
sprite(me.spriteNum).member.model("My Box").rotate(45,45,0)
```

The example movie `createbox.dir` contains this code if you want to play with the numbers more. Figure 16.27 shows this odd-sized box.

Figure 16.27
This odd-sized box was created by setting the properties of the box resource.

Besides the `height`, `width`, and `length`, there are a few other properties of box resources. Table 16.1 shows a complete list of box resource properties.

Table 16.1 Box Primitive Resource Properties

Property	Default	Description
width	50	X-axis measurement
height	50	Y-axis measurement
length	50	Z-axis measurement
top	TRUE	Whether the box top is present
bottom	TRUE	Whether the box bottom is present
left	TRUE	Whether the box left side is present
right	TRUE	Whether the box right side is present

Table 16.1 Continued

Property	Default	Description
back	TRUE	Whether the box back is present
front	TRUE	Whether the box front is present
widthVertices	2	Number of X-axis vertices
heightVertices	2	Number of Y-axis vertices
lengthVertices	2	Number of Z-axis vertices

The last three properties determine how many vertices will be in the box. More vertices mean more polygons, which means a slower movie. However, it also means that lighting effects will look nicer on the surfaces of the box. In addition, if you wanted to play with the mesh of the box, which we will do later in this chapter, you need to have enough vertices to create the shape you are after.

Note that you can change the properties of a box resource after you have created a model from it. The model will then change to reflect this change. So you could create a model resource, create 100 models from that resource, and then change the model resource. The result would be that all 100 models would change.

Creating a Sphere

Spheres can be created in the same way as boxes. The only difference is that you need to use a #sphere symbol rather than a #box symbol.

```
myModelResource = sprite(1).member.
➡newModelResource("My Sphere Resource",#sphere)
myModel = sprite(1).member.newModel("My Sphere",myModelResource)
```

The default sphere looks like the one in Figure 16.28. Spheres don't use the width, height, and length properties that boxes do. Instead, they use the radius property. The default radius is 25.

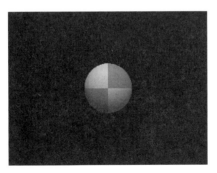

Figure 16.28
The default sphere is 25 units in radius.

In addition to the radius property, there are also startAngle and endAngle properties. Normally, these are set to 0 and 360, respectively. This creates a complete sphere. However, you could set them to other amounts to make an incomplete sphere. Figure 16.29 shows such a sphere.

Figure 16.29
This sphere has a `startAngle` of 0, but an `endAngle` of 330. So 30° have been cut out of this sphere.

You can see the behavior that created this sphere in the example movie `createsphere.dir`. Table 16.2 is a complete list of sphere properties.

Table 16.2 Sphere Primitive Resource Properties

Property	Default	Description
radius	25	The distance from the center of the sphere to the outside
resolution	20	Number of polygons used to create the sphere
startAngle	0	The start of the sweep of the sphere
endAngle	360	The end of the sweep of the sphere

Another thing you can see in Figure 16.29 is that the inside of the sphere is dark. In fact, it is transparent, showing the background color. This is because the surface of the sphere only reflects light on the outside of the sphere. The inner surface is invisible, kind of like a two-way mirror.

You can make both sides of the surface reflect light by altering the `newModelResource` command to include a third parameter. This third parameter tells the 3D engine which side of the surface to make reflective. The default value is `#front`, but you can also use `#back` or `#both`. Using `#both` makes the inside of the sphere reflect light.

Creating a Cylinder

Cylinders are the most complex of the four basic primitives. To create a default cylinder, just use the symbol `#cylinder` in the `newModelResource` command:

```
myModelResource = sprite(me.spriteNum).member.
➥newModelResource("My Cylinder Resource",#cylinder)
myModel = sprite(me.spriteNum).member.newModel("My Cylinder",myModelResource)
```

Figure 16.30 shows the default cylinder created. A cylinder is made up of a circular top, a circular bottom, and a surface wrapped around between the top and the bottom.

You can adjust the cylinder to make it thinner by changing both the `topRadius` and the `bottomRadius` properties of the model resource. You can also make the cylinder shorter by adjusting the `height` of the model resource. Table 16.3 shows all the cylinder properties.

Figure 16.30
A default cylinder is 50 units tall with a uniform radius of 25.

Table 16.3 Cylinder Primitive Resource Properties

Property	Default	Description
topRadius	25	The radius of the top of the cylinder
bottomRadius	25	The radius of the bottom of the cylinder
height	50	The height of the cylinder along the Z-axis
numSegments	2	The number of polygons from top to bottom
resolution	20	The number of polygons around the circumference of the cylinder
topCap	TRUE	Whether the top of the cylinder is present
bottomCap	TRUE	Whether the bottom of the cylinder is present
startAngle	0	The start of the sweep of the cylinder
endAngle	360	The end of the sweep of the cylinder

Because the top and bottom radii of a cylinder are independent properties, it is easy to set them to different values. This would create a cone, or at least a portion of a cone. Here is how it can be done. Figure 16.31 shows the result.

```
myModelResource = sprite(me.spriteNum).member.
➥newModelResource("My Cone Resource",#cylinder)
myModelResource.topRadius = 0
myModelResource.bottomRadius = 40
myModelResource.height = 50
myModel = sprite(me.spriteNum).member.newModel("My Cone",myModelResource)
```

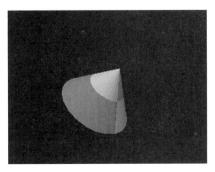

Figure 16.31
A cone was created by using a cylinder with a top radius of 0.

The example movie `createcylinder.dir` has two behaviors. The first creates a default cylinder. The second creates the cone in Figure 16.31. You can play with this behavior to create different cones, even ones that have somewhat flat tops.

Creating a Plane

Planes are the simplest of the primitives. A plane is just a flat surface. A default plane is a 1×1 flat square that is facing the camera. This is too small to be easily seen, so here is the code to create a 10×10 plane.

```
myModelResource = sprite(me.spriteNum).member.
➥newModelResource("My Plane Resource",#plane)
myModelResource.width = 100
myModelResource.length = 100
myModel = sprite(me.spriteNum).member.newModel("My Plane",myModelResource)
```

Because this plane faces you, it just looks like a large square. For all the viewer knows, it may even be hiding a whole cube behind it. To prove that it is just a plane, we can rotate it a bit with this code to produce Figure 16.32.

```
sprite(me.spriteNum).member.model("My Plane").rotate(-60,0,0)
```

Figure 16.32
This 100×100 plane has been rotated from its default position so you can see it better.

The movie `createplane.dir` contains all this code if you want to play with these settings. Table 16.4 lists all the plane properties.

Table 16.4   Plane Primitive Resource Properties

Property	Default	Description
width	50	X-axis measurement
length	50	Z-axis measurement
widthVertices	2	Number of X-axis vertices
lengthVertices	2	Number of Z-axis vertices

Planes, like spheres and all the other primitives, can use a third parameter during the `newModelResource` command. In the case of all the other primitives, the default third parameter is `#front`, which means that only the outside surfaces of the primitives reflect light. However, in the case of the plane, #both is the default property, which means that both the top and bottom of the plane reflect light. You can set it to #front or #back if you don't want to use the default.

Assigning Shaders to Primitives

So far, the primitive shapes we have created have a strange red-and-white checkerboard pattern. This is how it appears by default. A 3D member has a default texture that is used on every new item created. The red-and-white texture is the default texture.

You can change this default texture by bringing up the Property Inspector, looking at the 3D Model tab, selecting the 3D member, and changing the Shader Texture to something else. Then, when you create new primitives, they will use this default texture.

However, it is more likely that you want to create primitives that use varied colors and textures. To do this, you will need to create shaders and textures, and assign them to the faces of the primitives you create.

First, let's create a primitive box:

```
myResource = sprite(1).member.newModelResource("My Box Resource",#box)
sprite(1).member.newModel("My Box",myResource)
```

Now, let's look at the shaderList for this box:

```
put sprite(1).member.model("My Box").shaderList
-- [shader("DefaultShader"), shader("DefaultShader"),
➥shader("DefaultShader"), shader("DefaultShader"), shader("DefaultShader"),
shader("DefaultShader")]
```

You can see that each of the six sides of the box has been assigned the shader "DefaultShader". That's the red-and-white checkerboard.

Now, let's create a new shader and assign that shader to the first side of the box:

```
thisShader = sprite(1).member.newShader("Shader 1",#standard)
thisTexture = sprite(1).member.newTexture("Texture 1",#fromCastMember,
➥member("texture 1"))
thisShader.texture = thisTexture
sprite(me.spriteNum).member.model[1].shaderList[1] = thisShader
```

The example movie primitiveshaders.dir contains a little behavior that creates six shaders with six textures, assigns one shader to each side of the box, and then rotates the box around so that you can see all the sides. Figure 16.33 shows the resulting box.

Figure 16.33
This box was created from a primitive model resource and then new shaders were created for each side.

16

Here is the behavior from that example movie:

```
on beginSprite me
  sprite(me.spriteNum).member.resetWorld()

  -- create a box
  myResource = sprite(me.spriteNum).member.newModelResource
➡("My Box Resource",#box)
  sprite(me.spriteNum).member.newModel("My Box",myResource)

  -- create 6 shaders, each with a texture, and assign
  repeat with i = 1 to 6
    thisShader = sprite(me.spriteNum).member.newShader("Shader"&&i,#standard)
    thisTexture = sprite(me.spriteNum).member.newTexture("Texture"&&i,
➡#fromCastMember,member("texture"&&i))
    thisShader.texture = thisTexture
    sprite(me.spriteNum).member.model[1].shaderList[i] = thisShader
  end repeat
end


on exitFrame me
  -- tumble the box so you can see all sides
  sprite(me.spriteNum).member.model("My Box").rotate(5,5,0)
end
```

If you want to simply color in a side of a box instead of using a bitmap, you can create shaders that don't use any texture at all. Instead, just set the ambient and/or diffuse colors of the shaders.

The example movie primitiveshaders2.dir contains a behavior that assigns a different color to each face of the box. Here is that behavior:

```
on beginSprite me
  sprite(me.spriteNum).member.resetWorld()

  -- create a box
  myResource = sprite(me.spriteNum).member.newModelResource
➡("My Box Resource",#box)
  sprite(me.spriteNum).member.newModel("My Box",myResource)

  -- create shaders for each color
  redShader = sprite(me.spriteNum).member.newShader("Red Shader",#standard)
  redShader.ambient = rgb("FF0000")
  redShader.texture = VOID

  greenShader = sprite(me.spriteNum).member.newShader("Green Shader",#standard)
  greenShader.ambient = rgb("00FF00")
  greenShader.texture = VOID

  blueShader = sprite(me.spriteNum).member.newShader("Blue Shader",#standard)
  blueShader.ambient = rgb("0000FF")
```

```
blueShader.texture = VOID

cyanShader = sprite(me.spriteNum).member.newShader("Cyan Shader",#standard)
cyanShader.ambient = rgb("00FFFF")
cyanShader.texture = VOID

magentaShader = sprite(me.spriteNum).member.newShader
➡("Magenta Shader",#standard)
magentaShader.ambient = rgb("FF00FF")
magentaShader.texture = VOID

yellowShader = sprite(me.spriteNum).member.newShader
➡("Yellow Shader",#standard)
yellowShader.ambient = rgb("FFFF00")
yellowShader.texture = VOID

-- assign shaders to each face
sprite(me.spriteNum).member.model[1].shaderList[1] = redShader
sprite(me.spriteNum).member.model[1].shaderList[2] = greenShader
sprite(me.spriteNum).member.model[1].shaderList[3] = blueShader
sprite(me.spriteNum).member.model[1].shaderList[4] = cyanShader
sprite(me.spriteNum).member.model[1].shaderList[5] = magentaShader
sprite(me.spriteNum).member.model[1].shaderList[6] = yellowShader
end


on exitFrame me
 -- tumble the box so you can see all sides
 sprite(me.spriteNum).member.model("My Box").rotate(5,5,0)
end
```

We'll look at shaders and textures much more closely in Chapter 19, "Modifying Shaders, Textures, and Lights."

PARTICLE SYSTEMS

Particle systems are special 3D elements that are groups of small 2D graphics, usually dots. They emit from a single point or region and usually travel at random speeds. Particles can change color and size while moving, and usually fade and disappear only to be replaced by more particles being emitted. Particles are used to simulate a variety of real-world objects such as running water, smoke, explosions, and visible energy.

Particle System Basics

The default particle system can be created with only two lines of code. The first line creates a new model resource, just like we did with the primitives. The second line adds the particle system to the world.

```
myPartRes = sprite(1).member.newModelResource("My Particle Resource",#particle)
myPartSys = sprite(1).member.newModel("My Particle System",myPartRes)
```

To get this working using the Message panel, you must first place a 3D member in sprite 1 and then set the movie playing.

The default particle system looks like a small blob of particles in the center of the screen. We can make it more interesting by adjusting a few parameters of the particle resource. This next line gets the particles moving faster, and thus gets them to move farther away from the center of the particle system before they dissolve.

```
myPartRes.emitter.minSpeed = 10
```

Now we have a particle system that I can show you an image of. Figure 16.34 shows the default particle system with a `minSpeed` of 10.

Figure 16.34
This particle system uses all the default settings, except for a minimum speed of 10.

For good measure, let's set the maximum speed of the particles to 15. This means that the particles will travel at random speeds between 10 and 15.

```
myPartRes.emitter.maxSpeed = 15
```

Now, let's change the number of particles being generated:

```
myPartRes.emitter.numParticles = 100
```

As soon as you change the number of particles, the particle system resets itself. But pretty soon it is back to full speed. Notice that with 100 particles, there are far fewer particles on the screen at any one time. Try different numbers such as 1,000 or 5,000 to see what you get.

Particle systems are cool, but they are also expensive. If you add a few particle systems to your world, you will find that your movie runs very slowly on slower machines. Try particle systems that have very few particles and a short `lifetime` to speed up things.

You can also play with the color of the particles. Try this:

```
myPartRes.colorRange.start = rgb("FF0000")
```

The particles now start off red, but change to white as they get older. You can adjust the destination color too:

```
myPartRes.colorRange.end = rgb("0000FF")
```

Notice that the `colorRange` properties don't require the `emitter` property to be placed before it. Some particle system properties need the word `emitter` before them, and some don't.

Another fun property to play with is the `lifetime` of the particles. Try changing it to one second:

```
myPartRes.lifetime = 1000
```

So far we have only played with particle systems that emit particles at a constant rate. The particles keep coming. However, you can turn this off by setting the `loop` property to false. So, instead of a constant stream of particles, you get a finite number of particles.

```
myPartRes.emitter.loop = FALSE
```

Particle systems have many properties. Table 16.5 shows them all.

Table 16.5   Particle System Properties

Property	Description
`lifetime`	How long the particles last, in milliseconds.
`colorRange.start, colorRange.end`	A particle starts with one color and changes to the other color over its lifetime.
`tweenMode`	If set to `#velocity`, the color changes according to its speed. Otherwise, the default `#age` setting will have it change over the course of its lifetime.
`sizeRange.start, sizeRange.end`	The particles start at one size and gradually change to the other. The default for both is 1.
`blendRange.start. blendRange.end`	The particles go from one blend setting to the other. For instance, to make the particles fade away, set `blendRange.start` to 100, but `blendRange.end` to 0.
`texture`	This texture will be applied to each particle. The default, VOID, means no texture at all.
`emitter.numParticles`	The number of particles that can exist at one time in a stream, or the number of particles created at once if the system is a burst.
`emitter.minSpeed, emitter.maxSpeed`	The slowest and fastest possible speed for a particle.
`emitter.mode`	If set to `#burst`, all the particles will be emitted immediately. If set to `#stream`, the particles will be emitted gradually.
`emitter.loop`	Whether the particles are recycled or not. If the system is a stream, setting this to TRUE ensures a constant stream of particles. If set to TRUE when the system is a burst, the burst repeats over and over again.
`emitter.angle`	The distribution of directions in which the particles are emitted. A value of 180° means that the particles are emitted from any direction. A value of 90 means that they are distributed from only one hemisphere. A value of 0 means that they all go in exactly the same direction.
`emitter.direction`	The direction of the particles. If the `emitter.angle` is set to 180, this will have no effect.

Table 16.5   Continued

Property	Description
emitter.region	Usually, particles are emitted from a single point. You could set this point using the emitter.region. Instead, if you want the particles to come from a line, give this property a list of two vector points. If you want the particles to come from a larger area, give this property four vector points.
emitter.distribution	Determines the distribution of the particles, either #linear or #gaussian.
emitter.path	A list of vector points that define a path for the particles to follow.
emitter.pathStrength	A value from 0 to 100 of how strictly the particles should follow the path.
gravity	The force and direction of gravity that affects the particles.
wind	The force and direction of wind that affects the particles. This requires that the drag property be set.
drag	How much a particle is affected by wind, from 0 to 100.

Now let's look at how some of these properties can be used to create various interesting effects.

Creating a Simple Fountain

Particle systems can be used to simulate running water. You could use them to show water falling from a faucet or a waterfall. You could also use them to simulate fountains.

Figure 16.35 shows a simple fountain. The particles are streaming out of a point and going straight up.

Figure 16.35
A fountain made with particles.

To achieve this effect, I created a particle system that uses a very narrow angle and direction vector to point the particles up. I also set the gravity so that the particles fall back down. To complete the effect, the blend ranges from 100 to 0, so the particles fade away as they age.

Here is the complete behavior, which can be found in the movie `particlesystems.dir`. The speed and gravity numbers were obtained through trial and error until I had a combination that looked good.

```
on beginSprite me
  sprite(me.spriteNum).member.resetWorld()

  -- create particle system
  myPartRes = sprite(me.spriteNum).member.newModelResource
➥("My Particle Resource",#particle)

  -- range of speeds
  myPartRes.emitter.minSpeed = 20
  myPartRes.emitter.maxSpeed = 30

  -- just enough particles to make it look like water
  myPartRes.emitter.numParticles = 1000

  -- narrow stream, straight up
  myPartRes.emitter.angle = 5
  myPartRes.emitter.direction = vector(0,1,0)

  -- gravity to pull back down
  myPartRes.gravity = vector(0,-0.2,0)

  -- live about long enough to get back down
  myPartRes.lifetime = 7000

  -- start full blend, then fade
  myPartRes.blendRange.start = 100
  myPartRes.blendRange.end = 0

  -- place particle system
  myPartSys = sprite(me.spriteNum).member.newModel
➥ ("My Particle System",myPartRes)
end
```

Smoke

Imagine the smoke coming from a factory smokestack or a locomotive. To create a particle system like this, we can use wind and drag (see Figure 16.36).

Figure 16.36
Smoke created with a particle system.

⇨ *If you can't get wind to work, see "Particle System Wind Needs Drag" in the "Troubleshooting" section at the end of this chapter.*

I've taken a similar approach to making smoke as I did to making the fountain. A narrow stream is pointed up, but gravity is turned off because smoke rises, and wind is turned on. I played with the `drag` property until I found that a value of 5 worked well to make this effect.

```
on beginSprite me
 sprite(me.spriteNum).member.resetWorld()

 -- create particle system
 myPartRes = sprite(me.spriteNum).member.newModelResource
➡ ("My Particle Resource",#particle)

 -- range of speeds
 myPartRes.emitter.minSpeed = 20
 myPartRes.emitter.maxSpeed = 80

 -- just enough particles to make it look like smoke
 myPartRes.emitter.numParticles = 5000

 -- narrow stream, straight up
 myPartRes.emitter.angle = 15
 myPartRes.emitter.direction = vector(0,1,0)

 -- live about long enough to get off the screen
 myPartRes.lifetime = 10000

 -- start full blend, then fade
 myPartRes.blendRange.start = 100
 myPartRes.blendRange.end = 0

 -- wind to blow the smoke away
 myPartRes.wind = vector(15,0,0)
 myPartRes.drag = 5

 -- place particle system
 myPartSys = sprite(me.spriteNum).member.newModel
➡ ("My Particle System",myPartRes)
end
```

To use this behavior, you'll need to remove the current behavior in the `particlesystems.dir` movie and drag and drop the "smoke" behavior onto the 3D sprite.

Creating a Tornado

You can force particles to follow a path. This gives you the artistic license to create all sorts of things. However, finding something that looks good can be tough.

By using just two points in a path, and playing with the number of particles and their speed, I came up with something that looks a little like a tornado. Figure 16.37 is a still image of it, but it looks much better when animating.

Figure 16.37
This tornado effect looks better when animating in Director.

16

Here is the behavior, which can be found in `particlesystems.dir`. Try playing with the number of particles and the speeds to see what else you can make it look like. Also, try inserting other points in the `path`.

```
on beginSprite me
  sprite(me.spriteNum).member.resetWorld()

  -- create particle system
  myPartRes = sprite(me.spriteNum).member.newModelResource
➥ ("My Particle Resource",#particle)

  -- range of speeds
  myPartRes.emitter.minSpeed = 20
  myPartRes.emitter.maxSpeed = 10

  -- just enough particles to make it look like smoke
  myPartRes.emitter.numParticles = 1000

  -- start with narrow stream, straight up
  --myPartRes.emitter.angle = 0
  --myPartRes.emitter.direction = vector(0,1,0)

  -- live about long enough to get off the screen
  myPartRes.lifetime = 5000

  -- define a path to follow
  myPartRes.emitter.path = [vector(0,-30,0),vector(0,30,0)]

  -- place particle system
  myPartSys = sprite(me.spriteNum).member.newModel
➥ ("My Particle System",myPartRes)
end
```

Creating Explosions

One of the main properties of particle systems is the mode, which can be set to #stream or #burst. Changing it to #burst allows you to create quick bursts of particles that look like explosions.

Figure 16.38 shows such an explosion in progress. All the particles are generated at once and expand outward. I also set them to fade away with the blendStart and blendEnd properties.

Figure 16.38
An explosion in progress.

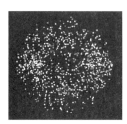

Here is the behavior for this. Note that you can change the loop property to FALSE if you don't want the explosion to repeat again and again.

```
on beginSprite me
 sprite(me.spriteNum).member.resetWorld()

 -- create particle system
 myPartRes = sprite(me.spriteNum).member.newModelResource
➡("My Particle Resource",#particle)

 -- burst, not stream
 myPartRes.emitter.mode = #burst

 -- change loop to FALSE if you don't want it to repeat
 myPartRes.emitter.loop = TRUE

 -- range of speeds
 myPartRes.emitter.minSpeed = 20
 myPartRes.emitter.maxSpeed = 10

 -- just enough particles
 myPartRes.emitter.numParticles = 1000

 -- live about long enough to see real
 myPartRes.lifetime = 5000

 -- start full blend, then fade
 myPartRes.blendRange.start = 100
 myPartRes.blendRange.end = 0

 -- place particle system
 myPartSys = sprite(me.spriteNum).member.newModel
➡ ("My Particle System",myPartRes)
end
```

If you set up an explosion like this, you can always force it to start over again by setting the numParticles again, even if it is to the exact same amount.

Modifying an Explosion to Create Fireworks

Modifying the explosion to make it look like fireworks is simple. All you need to do is add gravity. I've also slowed down the particles quite a bit because fireworks cover a large area and take a long time to expand and fall.

```
on beginSprite me
 sprite(me.spriteNum).member.resetWorld()

 -- create particle system
 myPartRes = sprite(me.spriteNum).member.newModelResource
➡ ("My Particle Resource",#particle)

 -- burst, not stream
 myPartRes.emitter.mode = #burst

 -- change loop to FALSE if you don't want it to repeat
 myPartRes.emitter.loop = TRUE

 -- range of speeds
 myPartRes.emitter.minSpeed = 12
 myPartRes.emitter.maxSpeed = 8

 -- just enough particles
 myPartRes.emitter.numParticles = 500

 -- live about long enough to see real
 myPartRes.lifetime = 10000

 -- start full blend, then fade
 myPartRes.blendRange.start = 100
 myPartRes.blendRange.end = 0


 -- add gravity
 myPartRes.gravity = vector(0,-.2,0)

 -- place particle system
 myPartSys = sprite(me.spriteNum).member.newModel
➡ ("My Particle System",myPartRes)
end
```

These were just a few examples of what you can do with particle effects. I have used them in many different ways. For instance, I have a few particles fly out of a point where two objects collide so that they look like sparks. I have also used them to draw attention to a model, such as a magic item in a game.

If you plan on creating a lot of products with Director's 3D engine, I definitely recommend investing some time playing around with particle systems first. This will give you some good ideas that you can use later.

MODIFYING PRIMITIVE MODELS WITH MESH DEFORM

You have already seen that you can create primitives of various shapes and sizes and even apply your own textures to them. You can also modify the points that make up a primitive model.

To do this, you must attach the mesh deform modifier to the model. After you do that, you can modify every vertex in the model.

For a simple example, let's take a plane. To create a plane, just use a few simple lines in the Message panel. The following code assumes that you have placed a blank 3D member in sprite 1:

```
myModelResource = sprite(1).member.newModelResource("My Plane Resource",#plane)
myModelResource.width = 200
myModelResource.length = 200
myModel = sprite(1).member.newModel("My Plane",myModelResource)
```

This creates a huge plane that just about fills the 3D sprite. Use `updateStage` to update the image on the screen.

To make the plane easier to see, let's rotate it and move it down so that it becomes a ground plane in our 3D world:

```
sprite(1).member.model("My Plane").rotate(90,0,0)
sprite(1).member.model("My Plane").transform.position = vector(0,-50,-50)
```

Figure 16.39 shows this simple plane. Our goal is to alter the plane so that it is not flat, but shows some irregularities.

Figure 16.39
This is a normal flat plane primitive.

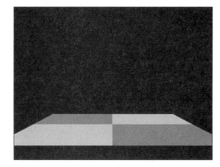

The plane is made up of vertices. In this case, there is one vertex on each corner of the plane. However, we can define the plane to be made up of a whole matrix of vertices instead. To make the plane a grid of 5×5 vertices, just change the `widthVertices` and `lengthVertices` properties of the model resource. But you must do this before you create the model. So it is important to start over again.

```
sprite(1).member.resetWorld()
myModelResource = sprite(1).member.newModelResource("My Plane Resource",#plane)
myModelResource.width = 200
myModelResource.length = 200
myModelResource.widthVertices = 5
myModelResource.lengthVertices = 5
myModel = sprite(1).member.newModel("My Plane",myModelResource)
sprite(1).member.model("My Plane").rotate(90,0,0)
sprite(1).member.model("My Plane").transform.position = vector(0,-50,-50)
```

Now it is time to add the mesh deform modifier. After this is done, the plane becomes a matrix of vertices that you can access and alter.

```
myModel.addModifier(#meshDeform)
```

To see that the model is now made up of a grid of 5 vertices by 5 vertices, look at the count of the vertexList property:

```
put myModel.meshDeform.mesh[1].vertexList.count
-- 25
```

There are 25 vertices in the model. It follows that the thirteenth vertex is the one in the middle of the grid. Let's get the position of that vertex.

```
put myModel.meshDeform.mesh[1].vertexList[13]
-- vector( 0.0000, 0.0000, 0.0000 )
```

That makes sense. The model is at 0,0,0, so the vertex right in the middle of the model should be at 0,0,0. Now, let's try moving that vertex up to create a bump in the plane:

```
myModel.meshDeform.mesh[1].vertexList[13] = vector(0,0,-30)
updateStage
```

You should now see something like Figure 16.40; the middle vertex has been moved up by 30 units. This creates a bump in the middle of the plane.

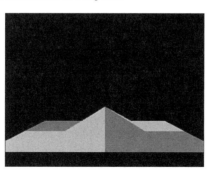

Figure 16.40
The plane has been altered by moving the middle vertex up to create a bump.

Notice that we are altering the first mesh in the meshDeform property. A plane actually has two meshes: the top and the bottom. Other primitives have even more meshes when they are given the mesh deform modifier.

16

The example movie `meshdeform.dir` actually performs a similar set of commands to what you just learned. However, it randomly assigns vertical positions to all the vertices in the mesh, rather than just the middle one. It then assigns a whole new set of vertices in the next frame, and so on. This creates a little earthquake, or water ripple animation.

CREATING COMPLEX SCENES

For the most part, creating complex 3D members in Director relies on a third party 3D program. But the ability to create primitives with Lingo means that you can create complex scenes from scratch as well.

You have already seen how you can create primitives and particle effects with Lingo. Now, let's try to use those commands to create an entire scene from scratch.

With Lingo and a blank 3D member, you can do a lot. Figure 16.41 shows the complete scene that we will create. There is an uneven ground, a volcano complete with spewing ash, a distant planet, and a fireball trailing dust. The fireball is moving, and when it hits the ground, it even causes an explosion.

Figure 16.41
This scene can be created with Lingo.

Each object in this world will be created in its own handler. The `on beginSprite` handler calls each of these custom handlers to create the entire world.

To make the lines of code a bit shorter, I've stored a reference to the sprite in *pSprite* and a reference to the member in *pMember*. I've also create properties to store the references to each object, such as *pFireball*.

```
property pSprite, pMember
property pPlanet, pGround, pVolcano, pFireball
property pViewType

on beginSprite me

  -- choose view type
  pViewType = #normal -- still camera
  --pViewType = #fireball -- follow fireball down
  --pViewType = #orbit -- swing camera around
```

```
-- get easy reference variables
pSprite = sprite(me.spriteNum)
pMember = pSprite.member

-- reset world
pMember.resetWorld()

-- make the elements of the world
makeGround(me)
makeVolcano(me)
makeSmoke(me)
makePlanet(me)
makeFireball(me)
makeBackdrop(me)
makeFireballCamera(me)

-- register for fireball impact
pMember.registerForEvent(#collideAny,#collisionHandler,me)
end
```

The last line of the on beginSprite handler makes sure that collisions get passed to the *on collisionHandler* handler that we'll define later on. We'll be adding the collision modifier to the ground and the fireball so that we know when these two items collide.

The first custom handler makes the ground plane. It starts with a plane resource, but then uses the mesh deform modifier to break it into adjustable polygons. The plane is then rotated to be oriented like a ground plane. The position is set back a bit, and farther down.

To make the ground uneven, all the points in the ground's mesh are given random z values. This makes some ground points higher than others.

Always remember to use a resetWorld command at the start of your movie or behavior. Otherwise, conditions in the world will persist from play to play, and you may end up with different results for that if you started the movie fresh. Also, you will get errors when you try to create models and model resources that are already in place from the previous play.

The handler then creates a texture from the bitmap member "ground". This texture is applied to a new shader, and this shader is then applied to the ground model.

The collision modifier is then added. The mode is set to #mesh to make it the most accurate.

```
on makeGround me
  -- create the model resource
  groundResource = pMember.newModelResource("My Plane Resource",#plane)

  -- make it big enough to be seen
  groundResource.width = 1000
  groundResource.length = 1000
```

```
-- make the mesh out of 10 by 10 vertices
groundResource.widthVertices = 15
groundResource.lengthVertices = 15

-- create the model
pGround = pMember.newModel("My Plane",groundResource)

-- rotate it and reposition it to see it better
pGround.rotate(90,0,0)
pGround.transform.position = vector(0,-50,-250)

-- add the mesh deform modifier
pGround.addModifier(#meshDeform)

-- loop through all of the vertices
repeat with i = 1 to pMember.model("My Plane").
➥meshDeform.mesh[1].vertexList.count
  -- lower vertice by a random amount
  v = pGround.meshDeform.mesh[1].vertexList[i]
  v.z = random(30)
  pGround.meshDeform.mesh[1].vertexList[i] = v
end repeat

-- create ground texture and shader
groundtexture = pMember.newTexture
➥ ("Ground Texture",#fromCastmember,member("Ground"))
groundShader = pMember.newShader("Ground Shader",#standard)
groundShader.texture = groundtexture
pGround.shaderList[1] = groundShader

-- add collision modifier
pGround.addModifier(#collision)
pGround.collision.mode = #mesh
end
```

The volcano is actually a cylinder with a narrower top than bottom. After it is created and placed, the same shader used for the ground is applied to this model as well.

```
on makeVolcano me
 -- create the model resource
volcanoResource = pMember.newModelResource("Volcano Resource",#cylinder)
volcanoResource.topRadius = 5

 -- create the model
pVolcano = pMember.newModel("Volcano",volcanoResource)

 -- place the model
pVolcano.transform.position = vector(-70,-50,0)
```

```
  -- set the ground shader
  pVolcano.shaderList[1] = pMember.shader("Ground Shader")
end
```

The ash coming from the top of the volcano is a particle system. The settings were achieved by trial and error to get the system to look just right. Some wind will blow the particles away. The particle system originates from the inside of the volcano.

```
on makeSmoke me
  -- create the resource
  smokeResource = pMember.newModelResource("Smoke Resource",#particle)
  smokeResource.emitter.angle = 10
  smokeResource.emitter.direction = vector(0,1,0)
  smokeResource.emitter.maxSpeed = 150
  smokeResource.emitter.minSpeed = 75
  smokeResource.drag = 5
  smokeResource.wind = vector(5,0,0)
  smokeResource.lifetime = 10000
  smokeResource.blendRange.start = 100
  smokeResource.blendRange.end = 0

  -- make the model
  pSmoke = pMember.newModel("Smoke",smokeResource)

  -- place the model
  pSmoke.transform.position = vector(-70,-50,0)
end
```

The planet appears to be a small sphere, but it is actually quite huge. It has been placed very far away. This makes the scene more realistic when we move the camera around.

The planet uses a new texture and shader that come from a bitmap that is a flattened picture of Jupiter.

```
on makePlanet me
  -- make the resource
  planetResource = pMember.newModelResource("Planet Resource",#sphere)

  -- a very large sphere
  planetResource.radius = 30000

  -- make the model
  pPlanet = pMember.newModel("Planet",planetResource)

  -- place it a long way away
  pPlanet.transform.position = vector(0,100000,-500000)

  -- create the planet texture and shader
  planetShader = pMember.newShader("Planet Shader",#standard)
  planetTexture = pMember.newTexture
➥ ("Planet Texture",#fromCastmember,member("Jupiter"))
```

```
planetShader.texture = planetTexture
pPlanet.shaderList[1] = planetShader
end
```

The fireball is actually two models. The first is a small sphere. This sphere is oriented so that moving it forward along its z axis moves the sphere diagonally down toward the ground. It is positioned off the screen so that it comes into the scene later.

The other part of the fireball is a particle system that is oriented so that the particles shoot out away from the fireball as it descends. The particle system model is made a child of the sphere so that it moves with the sphere.

The fireball model gets a collision modifier too. Because the tail is a part of the fireball, we want to use the #mesh mode for accuracy because the default #sphere mode will mean too big of a collision area when the particles are included.

```
on makeFireball me
 -- create a small sphere
 fireballResource = pMember.newModelResource("Fireball Resource",#sphere)
 fireballResource.radius = 3
 pFireball = pMember.newModel("Fireball",fireballResource)

 -- place it and rotate it pointed to where it is going
 pFireball.transform.position = vector(150,150,0)
 pFireball.transform.rotation = vector(0,90,45)

 -- use the ground shader
 pFireball.shaderList[1] = pMember.shader("Ground Shader")


 -- create a particle system for the tail
 fireballParticleResource = pMember.newModelResource
➥ ("Fireball Particle Resource",#particle)
 fireballParticleResource.emitter.angle = 20
 fireballParticleResource.emitter.direction = vector(1,0,0)
 fireballParticleResource.emitter.maxSpeed = 150
 fireballParticleResource.emitter.minSpeed = 75
 fireballParticleResource.lifetime = 1000
 fireballParticleResource.blendRange.start = 100
 fireballParticleResource.blendRange.end = 0
 fireballParticles = pMember.newModel
➥ ("Fireball Particles",fireballParticleResource)

 -- place the particle system with the fireball
 --and aim it pointing out the back
 fireballParticles.transform.position = pFireball.transform.position
 fireballParticles.transform.rotation = vector(0,0,45)

 -- add collision modifier
 pFireball.addModifier(#collision)
 pFireball.collision.mode = #mesh
```

```
 -- group the tail with the fireball
 pFireball.addChild(fireballParticles)
end
```

The backdrop is simply a bitmap of stars that adds some realism to the scene. It is added to the main camera for the scene.

```
on makeBackdrop me
 -- create the backdrop texture
 backdroptexture = pMember.newTexture
➡ ("Backdrop",#fromCastmember,member("Backdrop"))

 -- add the backdrop
 pSprite.camera.addBackdrop(backdropTexture,point(0,0),0)
end
```

When the fireball collides with the ground, we'll want to have an explosion. This next handler creates a particle system with a type #burst and places it at the location passed into the handler.

```
on makeExplosion me, loc
 -- create a burst particle resource
 explosionResource = pMember.newModelResource
➡ ("Explosion Particle Resource",#particle)
 explosionResource.emitter.maxSpeed = 150
 explosionResource.emitter.minSpeed = 75
 explosionResource.emitter.mode = #burst
 explosionResource.emitter.loop = FALSE
 explosionResource.emitter.numParticles = 5000
 explosionResource.lifetime = 1000
 explosionResource.blendRange.start = 100
 explosionResource.blendRange.end = 0

 -- make the model and place it
 explosion = pMember.newModel("Explosion Particles",explosionResource)
 explosion.transform.position = loc
end
```

If you change the *pViewType* to *#fireball*, a new camera is created. This camera is set to a point just above and behind the fireball. It is also grouped with the fireball. Then, the sprite's main camera is changed to this new camera. This way, the view will be from this "fireball cam" as the fireball descends.

```
on makeFireballCamera me
 if pViewType = #fireball then
  -- create a new camera
  pMember.newCamera("Fireball Cam")

  -- place the new camera on top of the fireball
  pMember.camera("Fireball Cam").transform.position =
➡pFireball.transform.position + vector(20,30,0)
  pMember.camera("Fireball Cam").transform.rotation =
➡pFireball.transform.rotation
```

```
-- group the camera with the fireball
pMember.model("FireBall").addChild(pMember.camera("Fireball Cam"))

-- change the sprite's camera to this one
sprite(me.spriteNum).camera = sprite(me.spriteNum).
➥member.camera("Fireball Cam")
end if
end
```

As the movie plays, the fireball needs to descend a little bit every frame.

```
on moveFireball me
-- move the fireball one step
if not voidP(pFireball) then
 pFireball.translate(0,0,-1)
end if
end
```

If the *pViewType* is set to *#orbit*, the camera orbits around the center of the scene. To do this, use the `transform.rotate` function. If you were to simply use the `rotate` function, the camera would spin around its own axis. However, by using `transform.rotate`, the camera spins around the center of the world, always pointing at the same location. This creates a nice visual fly-around effect as the scene unfolds. It also brings out the fact that this is a 3D scene, not a 2D scene that is just faking it.

```
on orbitCamera me
-- move the camera one degree
if pViewType = #orbit then
 sprite(1).camera.transform.rotate(0,1,0)
end if
end
```

The `on exitFrame` handler calls *on moveFireball* and *on orbitCamera* every frame:

```
on exitFrame me
-- move fireball
moveFireball(me)

-- move camera
orbitCamera(me)
end
```

When the fireball hits the ground, the *on collisionHandler* is called. Because this is the only collision that will take place in this scene, we don't need to examine modelA and modelB of the "data" parameter to find out which two objects collided. Instead, we can just handle the collision.

The first thing that happens is the camera is restored to the default view if *pViewType* is set to *#fireball*. This is needed because if the camera is riding the fireball down, the camera will cease to exist when we get rid of the fireball. Also, the viewpoint just above the fireball is a lousy place to witness the collision.

The fireball is then removed from the world. This also gets rid of its children, in this case the fireball's particle system tail. The *pFireball* property is set to VOID so that the *on moveFireball* handler ceases to worry about the fireball.

Then, the *on makeExplosion* handler is called to display the explosion particle system.

```
on collisionHandler me, data

  if pViewType = #fireball then
    -- return to default camera view
    sprite(me.spriteNum).camera = sprite(1).member.camera("DefaultView")
  end if

  -- remove fireball
  pFireball.removeFromWorld()

  -- don't need fireball again
  pFireball = VOID

  -- particle system explosion
  makeExplosion(me,data.pointOfContact)
end
```

Try the example movie `complexscene.dir` to see this behavior in action. Try changing the beginning of the behavior to use one of the different *pViewType* values.

I strongly encourage you to tinker with this scene even further. Try different textures. Try having ground that is more or less uneven. Try a volcano that spews more or less, or maybe several volcanoes that spew different colors. Perhaps the collision of the fireball should form a new volcano. The best way to get good at creating 3D scenes with Lingo is to practice.

TROUBLESHOOTING

Importing Models Doesn't Work

I'm creating models in a third-party graphics program, exporting them to .w3d format, but I can't import them into Director. Why?

Almost every 3D graphics program will export Shockwave 3D files in a slightly different way. Be prepared to spend some time getting used to how your 3D program does it. If you are not creating usable .w3d files, try removing advanced features from the models and sticking to simple polygons and textures. Use as few polygons as possible. Check the Web site of your 3D graphics program to see whether there is an update for the .w3d exporter.

16

Choose the Correct View Before Exporting

I'm exporting from 3ds max, but the scene always comes up with a view different from that of what I expect. How can I get the correct view?

When exporting from 3ds max, the camera view is completely dependent on which window is selected when you choose to export. Usually, you want the perspective view window, not the front, back, or side windows.

Particle System Wind Needs Drag

I'm trying to use the wind feature of particle systems, but I can't get it to have any effect. Why?

Either the Director documentation is wrong, or there is a bug: You must use the drag property of a particle system to make wind have any effect at all.

DID YOU KNOW?

- You can stretch the 3D sprite to any size you want without hurting performance. You don't need to stick to 320×240.

- The extrude3d function can be used to take a font member and some text and convert it to a model resource of that text. This is the basic function used by 3D text members. However, by using extrude3D, you can also insert 3D text into your 3D world.

- You can also use extrude3D to convert a vector shape into a 3D model resource. Just replace the vertexList of the model resource created by extrude3D with the vertexList of your vector shape member. This is an undocumented feature, but you can get it to work with some experimentation.

- If you are making a Shockwave movie that will stretch with the size of the browser window, the 3D sprites in your movie will stretch very nicely with the Stage size.

17

CONTROLLING 3D MODELS

IN THIS CHAPTER

SETTING A MODEL'S POSITION

The first aspect of 3D Lingo that we will examine is simply to move 3D models around in the 3D world. This will give you a basic understanding of how to manipulate 3D members.

Referring to Models

Let's start off simple by using the Message panel to examine and then alter a 3D member. Load up the file `movemodels.dir` from this book's CD-ROM. You can see this movie in Figure 17.1.

Figure 17.1
We will be playing with the properties of this simple example movie.

Leaving the Stage visible, open and position the Message panel. Now try this:

```
put sprite(1).member.model.count
-- 3
```

Sprite 1 contains the member "goldfishpair," which is a 3D member. We could refer to this member by name, but instead, I referred to it as the member of sprite 1. The `put` statement gives us the `count` of the member property `model`. This `model` property gives us access to all the models in the member. The output from this `put` statement shows us that there are three models in the member.

Next, let's get the names of these models. We can do this by treating the `model` property like a list. We can then get the `name` of each item in this list.

```
put sprite(1).member.model[1].name
-- "right goldfish"
put sprite(1).member.model[2].name
-- "left goldfish"
put sprite(1).member.model[3].name
-- "plane"
```

Where did these names come from? They were assigned when the 3D world was created. In this case, I used 3ds max to create the world. While building the world, I took the time to name the three objects "right goldfish," "left goldfish," and "plane."

Getting the Model Position

Next, let's find out something about one of these models. We can get the location of a model by looking at the `position` property of the `transform` property:

```
put sprite(1).member.model[1].transform.position
-- vector( 70.8987, 118.1114, 30.6382 )
```

The transform of a model is a long, complex list of numbers that contain information about a model's location, scaling, and orientation. To access just the location information, the position property is used.

The result of transform.position is a *vector*. A vector is a three-part list of numbers that give the location of an object in 3D space. The numbers represent the horizontal position, vertical position, and depth. You can get the components of a vector by using the x, y, and z properties.

```
myModelPos = sprite(1).member.model[1].transform.position
put myModelPos.x
-- 70.8987
put myModelPos.y
-- 118.1114
put myModelPos.z
-- 30.6382
```

If you look at the transform property of a model or other object, you will get a list of 16 numbers. This corresponds to a 4×4 matrix that describes the location, orientation, and scale of the object. However, you will need to use subproperties such as position to effectively alter the transform of an object.

Changing Model Position

To change the position of a model, you can use the same properties. For instance, to move the right fish slightly to the right, try this:

```
sprite(1).member.model[1].transform.position.x = 100
updateStage
```

The updateStage is necessary only because the movie is not running. It forces an update of the Stage, as well as any 3D sprites on it.

You can also refer to the model by name. Use parentheses instead of brackets, and then the model name.

```
sprite(1).member.model("right goldfish").transform.
position.x = 100
updateStage
```

Table 17.1 shows all the properties of the transform of a model.

Caution

Remember that positions in a 3D member depend completely on the orientation of the camera. If you try these commands with a different 3D world, you might get different specific results if the camera is not the same as in the example. However, the basic principles of position and orientation are the same.

Instead of using updateStage, I find that I can update the screen by simply clicking on the 3D sprite on the Stage. However, I'm not positive that this will work with all computer hardware and software configurations. Give it a try.

Table 17.1 Model Transform Properties and Commands

Property/Command	Description
position	Vector describing the position of the model
rotation	Vector describing the rotation of the model around each axis
scale	Vector describing the scale of the model
translate	Command that moves the model according to its current orientation and the vector passed into the command
rotate	Command that rotates the model around each axis according to the vector passed into the command
scale	Command that scales the model according to the vector passed into the command
preTranslate	Command that moves the model relative to the world
preRotate	Command that rotates the model relative to the world
preScale	Command that scales the model relative to the world

Resetting Model Position

To get the fish back to its original location, you can use the resetWorld command. For some reason, this does not need an updateStage to be called after it.

```
sprite(1).member.resetWorld()
```

The resetWorld command comes in handy because a 3D member will remember any changes that you force upon it until you quit Director or reload the movie. If it is important to start off fresh each time your play the movie, you will want to use the resetWorld command at the start of your movie.

World Position

Another way to get the position of a model is to use the worldPosition property. In our example so far, this returns the same value as transform.position:

```
put sprite(1).member.model[1].worldPosition
-- vector( 70.8987, 118.1114, 30.6382 )
```

The worldPosition property has the same three properties as transform.position: x, y, and z. You can set worldPosition or any of these three subproperties just like you can set transform.position.

So what is the difference between transform.position and worldPosition? Right now, they appear to do the same thing. The difference is when models are grouped. Usually when models are grouped, one model or another object is the parent, and the other models in the group are its children. Moving the parent also moves the children.

A model's transform is always relative to its parent. In this case, the transform.position tells you the location of the model relative to the location of its parent. But the worldPosition is always relative to the center of the 3D world, location 0,0,0.

SETTING A MODEL'S ORIENTATION

In addition to moving a model, you can also turn and tilt it any which way you want. A model's orientation is represented by how many degrees it is rotated around each of the three axes.

Getting the Model Orientation

Let's use the Message panel to examine the orientation of a model in the `movemodels.dir` example movie. The `transform` property is used again, but this time the `rotation` subproperty is what we want:

```
put sprite(1).member.model("right goldfish").transform.rotation
-- vector( 0.0000, 0.0000, 0.0000 )
```

As you can see, a vector is returned. Each of the three parts of the vector represents an angle, in degrees.

⇨ *If you are having trouble deciding which axis to rotate a model on to get the right result, see "Transformation By Trial and Error" in the "Troubleshooting" section at the end of this chapter.*

That's right, a vector can sometimes contain positional units, and sometimes contain angular units. So if you are used to the physics definition of a vector as speed and direction, remember that sometimes it is used by Director as just a collection of three numbers.

17

Changing the Model Orientation

To change the orientation of a model, you can set the entire vector. For instance, to turn the fish completely on its side, try this:

```
sprite(1).member.model("right goldfish").transform.rotation = vector(0,0,-90)
updateStage
```

You can also use the x, y and z subproperties of the `transform.rotation` property to affect only one of the three axes.

```
sprite(1).member.model("right goldfish").transform.rotation.z = -90
updateStage
```

The `transform.rotation` property is relative to the model's parent, just as the `transform.position` property is. However, there is no `worldRotation` property. Instead you can use the `getWorldTransform()` function to get the transform of the model relative to the 3D world. From there, you can get the `rotation` relative to the world.

```
worldTrans = sprite(1).member.model("right goldfish").getWorldTransform()
worldRot = worldTrans.rotation
updateStage
```

Unfortunately, this is a one-way operation. There is no way to set the orientation of a model relative to the world except through complex vector math. But setting the rotation of a child or a group of models is not usually needed.

MOVING AND ROTATING MODELS

So far we have seen how we can set the position and orientation of a model, but how about movement?

What's the difference between setting the position of a model and moving it? Moving a model means that you are taking the current position and orientation of a model and moving it from that spot by a certain distance. The starting point is important and so is its orientation.

Using the `translate` Command

To move a model, we use the `translate` command. This takes a vector and moves the model from its current spot by the distance of the vector. The following lines move one of the fish closer by 10 units. Remember to use `resetWorld` first if you have just completed the code in the previous section.

```
sprite(1).member.model("right goldfish").translate(0,-10,0)
updateStage
```

Now, try the same two lines of code again. The model moves closer by another 10 units. You can keep issuing these same commands, and the model will continue to move closer.

The `translate` command is not just using the current location of the model, but it is also using the orientation of the model. Try rotating the model and then moving it.

```
sprite(1).member.model("right goldfish").transform.rotation = vector(0,0,-90)
updateStage
sprite(1).member.model("right goldfish").translate(0,-10,0)
updateStage
```

The model is first rotated to the left and then moved. The result is that the model moves to the left. This is the same `translate` command that moved the model toward you before. So the `translate` command does not just move the model relative to the rest of the world, it moves the model relative to the orientation of the model.

This is the way to get models to move at a constant rate and a consistent direction. First, you orient the model in the direction you want it to go; then you use `translate` to move the model in that direction.

Using the `rotate` Command

Whereas the `translate` command moves a model relative to its current location, the `rotate` command rotates it relative to its orientation.

To rotate one of the models in the example movie, try these lines in the Message panel. They rotate one of the fish by 5 degrees.

```
sprite(1).member.model("right goldfish").rotate(0,0,-5)
updateStage
```

You can keep issuing these lines to make the fish rotate even more. Here is a simple behavior that rotates the model at a constant rate:

```
on beginSprite me
  sprite(me.spriteNum).member.resetWorld()
end

on exitFrame me
  sprite(me.spriteNum).member.model("right goldfish").rotate(0,0,-5)
end
```

You can find this simple behavior in the movie `constantrotate.dir`. You can make the fish rotate in the other direction by changing the –5 to 5.

Making the Fish Swim

To make the fish swim, all you would need to do is write a behavior that moves the fish a little bit every frame. This would be just like the previous rotation behavior, except using the `translate` command rather than the `rotate` command.

However, this would create a problem. The fish would swim right off the screen! That's not much fun. Fish usually swim around in circles, so let's try to make our fish behave that way.

To make a fish swim in a circle, we need to both rotate the fish and move the fish a little each frame. Here is a script that does just that:

```
on beginSprite me
  sprite(me.spriteNum).member.resetWorld()
end

on exitFrame me
  sprite(me.spriteNum).member.model("right goldfish").rotate(0,0,-5)
  sprite(me.spriteNum).member.model("right goldfish").translate(0,-10,0)
end
```

Now the goldfish on the right swims in circles around the goldfish on the left. Changing the numbers in this script makes the goldfish swim in a wider or smaller circle. Check the movie `fishorbit.dir` to see it in action.

User-Controlled Movement

Giving the user control of a 3D model is easy using the `rotate` and `translate` commands. In the example movie `moveteapot.dir`, the user can use the left and right arrow keys to rotate the teapot and the up and down arrow keys to move it.

Because the teapot has been modeled with the spout facing forward, the forward movement of the model always goes in that direction. So the `translate` command doesn't have to worry about which direction the teapot is facing; it always moves forward.

17

Here is the script that allows the user to drive the teapot:

```
property pTeapot

on beginSprite me
  sprite(1).member.resetWorld()
  pTeapot = sprite(me.spriteNum).member.model("teapot")
end

on exitFrame me
  -- rotate
  if keyPressed(123) then
    pTeapot.rotate(0,0,5)
  else if keyPressed(124) then
    pTeapot.rotate(0,0,-5)
  end if

  -- move
  if keyPressed(125) then
    pTeapot.translate(-2,0,0)
  else if keyPressed(126) then
    pTeapot.translate(2,0,0)
  end if
end
```

When you run this movie, use the arrow keys to drive the teapot around the 3D scene.

Pretranslation and Prerotation

Going back to the `constantrotate.dir` movie, go into the code and change the `rotate` command to `rotate` the `transform` of the model rather than the model itself.

```
on exitFrame me
  sprite(me.spriteNum).member.model("right goldfish").transform.rotate(0,0,-5)
end
```

The difference is that the fish now rotates around the center of the world rather than its own center. The result is much like the `fishorbit.dir` movie, but it is achieved with different commands.

Because the `transform` of a model contains all the positional, rotational, and scaling information to determine where the model is relative to its parent, in this case the world, then rotating it rotates it around the center of the world.

We can, however, specify that we want the transform's rotation to occur relative to itself, rather than the world, by using the `prerotate` command. So the following two lines of code produce identical results:

```
sprite(me.spriteNum).member.model("right goldfish").transform.prerotate(0,0,-5)
sprite(me.spriteNum).member.model("right goldfish"). rotate(0,0,-5)
```

The `preTranslate` command also does the same thing to the model's transform as `translate` would do to the model itself. Using `transform.translate`, on the other hand, would move the model forward relative to the model's orientation in the world.

PreRotation and preTranslation are typically used in complex 3D movements. For the most part, you only need to use `rotate` and `transform`.

SCALING MODELS

Besides changing the model's position and rotation, you can also shrink or stretch it using its transform. The `scale` property is all you need to do this. In the case of `position` and `translation`, the vector represents a position in space. In the case of `rotation` and `rotate`, the vector represents the angle around all three axes. But in the case of `scale`, the vector represents the scale amount for all three directions, with 1.0 being 100%.

So a vector of 1.0,1.0,1.0 represents a model at its original size. To scale it up to double its size, you would need to set the scale like this:

```
sprite(me.spriteNum).member.model("right goldfish").transform.scale =
➥vector(2.0, 2.0, 2.0)
```

In the movie scaleteapot.`dir`, you can use the four arrow keys and the A and Z keys to scale the model in all six directions. Here is the code that does this easy task:

```
property pTeapot

on beginSprite me
  sprite(1).member.resetWorld()

  -- get model references
  pTeapot = sprite(me.spriteNum).member.model("teapot")
end

on exitFrame me
  if keyPressed(123) then
    pTeapot.transform.scale.x = pTeapot.transform.scale.x - .1
  else if keyPressed(124) then
    pTeapot.transform.scale.x = pTeapot.transform.scale.x + .1
  else if keyPressed(125) then
    pTeapot.transform.scale.y = pTeapot.transform.scale.y - .1
  else if keyPressed(126) then
    pTeapot.transform.scale.y = pTeapot.transform.scale.y + .1
  else if keyPressed("Z") then
    pTeapot.transform.scale.z = pTeapot.transform.scale.z - .1
  else if keyPressed("A") then
    pTeapot.transform.scale.z = pTeapot.transform.scale.z + .1
  end if
end
```

17

Figure 17.2 shows the teapot scaled to be tall and skinny. The `scale.x` was set lower, whereas the `scale.z` was set higher.

Figure 17.2
This model has been scaled by changing its `transform.scale` property.

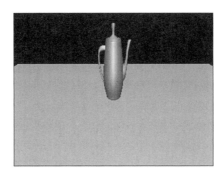

Notice that if you adjust the scale of the model so that either the x, y, or z property is 0, you get an error message. So although this movie is a good demonstration of the `scale` property, it needs to be a little more robust if a real user is to have control of the scale. The values can be negative; they just can't be 0.

DUPLICATING MODELS

After a model is part of a 3D member, you can make a copy of it in that same member. This copy, or clone, has all the same properties as the original. Here is how you would make a copy of a model in the Message panel. This code assumes that you have the movie `scaleteapot.dir` open.

```
m = member(1).model("teapot").clone("teapot2")
member(1).model("teapot2").transform.position.x = 50
updateStage
```

The `clone` command is a method of a model that already exists in the world. The only parameter is the name of the new model, in this case "teapot2".

You need the second line, the one that moves the second teapot over to the right, because the second teapot is created in exactly the same position as the first. So you can't see two different teapots until you move one.

Cloning a model that is already in the world has limited use. But cloning a model from one member to another can be useful. You can have a series of 3D members that contain various objects and clone them into the visible 3D member as you need them.

To clone a model from one member to another, you need to use the `cloneModelFromCastMember` command. This command takes three parameters: the name of the new model, the name of the original model, and the member from which the model is to be cloned.

The following code is from `cloneteapot.dir`. This movie shows a blank 3D member with no models. Then, for each frame that passes, the model "teapot" from the member "teapot" is cloned into the world. The position, rotation, and scale of the new copy are set to random values.

```
property pNum

on beginSprite me
  sprite(me.spriteNum).member.resetWorld()
  pNum = 0
end

on exitFrame me
  -- clone new model
  m = sprite(me.spriteNum).member.\
      cloneModelFromCastmember("teapot"&pNum, "teapot", member("teapot"))

  -- random location ,rotation and scale
  m.transform.position = vector(random(200)-100,random(200)-100,random(200)-100)
  m.transform.rotation = vector(random(360),random(360),random(360))
  scaleAmt = .01*random(50)+.5
  m.transform.scale = vector(scaleAmt,scaleAmt,scaleAmt)

  pNum = pNum + 1
end
```

17

Figure 17.3 shows one random result of this script after it has been running for a while.

Figure 17.3
These teapots are all clones of a
model from another cast member.

When you use `clone` to copy a 3D model in the same 3D member, you are making a copy of the model only. The shaders and model resources of both the original and the clone are one and the same. If you change the model resource of the clone or the original, you change both.

However, you can also use the `cloneDeep` command to make a clone of every part of a model. Any shaders or model resources referenced by the model will be copied into new shaders and model resources. This is similar to using `cloneModelFromCastMember`, where all the shaders and model resources need to be copied along with the model for the model to work in its new member.

A faster but more complex way to do the previous example if you have a lot of identical models to clone would be to use `cloneModelFromCastMember` the first time, which would have copied the model resource and shader for the teapot. Then use `clone` the second and subsequent times to clone only the model itself.

⤵ *If you are having trouble cloning models, see "Unable to Clone Models from Another Member" in the "Troubleshooting" section at the end of this chapter.*

ORIENTING OBJECTS USING POINTAT

Although the transform object of a model allows you to play with the specific numbers behind the position and orientation of a model, there are other ways to reposition models. One way is to use the pointAt function to orient an object so that it is pointed directly at another object.

The first step in using pointAt is to use pointAtOrientation to tell Director what the "up" direction is, according to the object, and what the forward direction is. If you are into 3D math, you can easily calculate these vectors. If you are not into 3D math, you can use trial and error to get these vectors soon enough.

After you set the pointAtOrientation, you can use pointAt to spin the object around to point at a vector location, such as the location of another object.

The movie pointteapot.dir does just this. If you run the movie and click on the sprite, the teapot reorients itself to point at the next object. Here is the behavior from that movie:

```
property pWorld, pNum

on beginSprite me
  sprite(1).member.resetWorld()
  pWorld = sprite(me.spriteNum).member
  pNum = 0

  -- set orientation
  pWorld.model("teapot").pointAtOrientation = [vector(1,0,0),vector(0,0,-1)]
end

on mouseUp me
  -- next model to point at
  pNum = pNum + 1
  if pNum > 4 then pNum = 1

  -- point at model
  pWorld.model("teapot").pointAt(pWorld.model("ball"&pNum),  vector(0,0,-1))
end
```

Figure 17.4 shows this movie in action. The first three models are on the same plane as the teapot, so it just rotates around the vertical axis. However, the last model is above and behind it, so the orientation has to change on more than one axis for it to point at it.

The pointAtOrientation is set so that the forward vector is directly along the x-axis, and the up vector is back along the z-axis. This will be different depending on how you created your world. In this example, 3ds max likes to use the z-axis for up and down, and the teapot happened to have a spout pointed along the x-axis.

Figure 17.4
The teapot is pointing at the frontmost model with the help of the pointAt command.

We needed to restate the up vector as the second parameter to the pointAt command. If the teapot was not oriented so that its "up" was the same as the world's "up," then we might have had to use different up vectors for the pointAtOrientation property and the pointAt command.

You can also use the pointAt command and pointAtOrientation for lights and cameras. Using them with cameras is particularly useful because you can have a camera point directly at an object of interest.

GROUPING MODELS

When you have a 3D world that has more than one model, it is sometimes useful to group them. A group of models has a parent and children. When the parent model is moved, rotated, or scaled, all the children undergo the same transformation.

In addition, when a child model is rotated or repositioned, the operation is performed relative to the parent, not the whole 3D world.

To make one model a parent and the other a child of it, you need to use the addChild command. For instance, to make the model "sphere" a child of "block", you would do this:

```
sprite(me.spriteNum).member.model("block").addChild("sphere")
```

After that command, you would be able to move or rotate both models by just moving the "block" model.

You also could have done the same thing by assigning the "block" model as the parent of the "sphere" model:

```
sprite(me.spriteNum).member.model("sphere").parent =
sprite(me.spriteNum).member.model("block")
```

You can use the parent property to tell which model is the parent of any model. You can also use the child list to tell which models are the children of any model. For instance, sprite(me.spriteNum).member.model("*block*").child[*1*] returns a reference to the "sphere" model.

A parent can have more than one child, but a child can have only one parent. In addition, you can create a dummy model to be used as a parent for a group of models that has no obvious central model. To create a dummy object, use newGroup:

```
myGroup = sprite(me.spriteNum).member.newGroup("myGroup")
```

A group is like a model in that it has a `transform` property with `position`, `rotation`, and `scale` subproperties. However, it has no visible portion like a model. After you create a group, however, you can use `addChild` to assign child models to it.

To refer to a group, use `group` rather than `model`. For instance, to move a group, you would do this:

```
sprite(me.spriteNum).member.group("myGroup").transform.position
= vector(100,0,0)
```

The example movie `planets.dir` uses Lingo to create several spheres. Each sphere is assigned to either a central sphere (the sun) or another sphere (moons assigned to planets) as its parent using `addChild`. Then, when the `transform.rotate` command is issued, the sphere rotates around its parent. Here is the code:

The term *group* can be confusing because some 3D programs use the term to refer to what Shockwave 3D refers to as a model. So in your 3D program, you might create shapes and then group them together. This imports into Shockwave 3D as a model, not a group.

```
property pWorld, pModels, pCount

on beginSprite me
  pWorld = sprite(me.spriteNum).member
  pWorld.resetWorld()
  pCount = 1
  pModels = []

  -- make solar system
  sun = makeSphere(me,0,10)
  mercury = makeOrbit(me,20,3,sun)
  venus = makeOrbit(me,30,5,sun)
  earth = makeOrbit(me,40,5,sun)
  moon = makeOrbit(me,10,2,earth)
  mars = makeOrbit(me,50,4,sun)
  jupiter = makeOrbit(me,70,8,sun)
  io = makeOrbit(me,10,1,jupiter)
  ganymede = makeOrbit(me,12,1,jupiter)
  europa = makeOrbit(me,14,1,jupiter)
  calisto = makeOrbit(me,16,1,jupiter)
end

-- create a sphere model and place it
on makeSphere me, x, r
  -- create resource
  res = pWorld.newModelResource("sphere"&pCount,#sphere)
  res.radius = r

  -- create model and position it
  m = pWorld.newModel("sphere"&pCount,res)
  m.transform.position = vector(x,0,0)
  pCount = pCount + 1
  return m
end
```

```
-- create a sphere that is a child of another sphere
on makeOrbit me, dist, size, orbitPlanet

  -- make a new sphere a distance away from another sphere
  x = orbitPlanet.transform.position.x + dist
  m = makeSphere(me,x,size)

  -- make this a child of another sphere
  orbitPlanet.addChild(m)
  add pModels, m
  return m
end

-- move all models around their parents
on exitFrame me
  repeat with m in pModels

    -- speed determined by distance from parent
    speed = 50/m.transform.position.distanceTo(vector(0,0,0))

    -- move around parent
    m.transform.rotate(vector(0,-speed,0))
  end repeat
end
```

Every model in a 3D member has a parent. If you have not assigned it a parent, it has the world as a parent. If you put the parent of such a model to the Message panel, here's what you get:

```
put sprite(1).member.model(1).parent
-- group("World")
```

> The Director MX printed documentation seems to be lacking when it comes to commands such as addChild. In fact, not only is this command missing from the official *Lingo Dictionary*, but all 3D commands starting with the word add are missing. They are also missing from the index of the official user guide. But these are not undocumented features—they are fully supported and appear in the online help.

CONTROLLING ANIMATION

Director 3D members can contain animated sequences. There are actually two types of animation in 3D members: keyframe player animations and bones player animations.

The bones player animations involve skeletons that map out how the pieces of a model are connected. For instance, if you have a model of a person, the arms, legs, and joints may all form a skeleton map inside the model. The bones player animations can be things such as walking, picking something up, looking around, and so on.

The other type of animation is more what you would be used to with Flash or digital video. Keyframe player animation can be created with a variety of 3D graphics tools. Only a few support exporting to Shockwave 3D, but more will probably do so by the time this book is published.

After an animation has been included in the Shockwave 3D file, you can control it with Lingo. Open the file `animation.dir` to see a simple animated scene. Figure 17.5 shows this scene.

> **Caution**
>
> Creating bones player animations requires a 3D program that supports the exporting of bones and bones player animations to Shockwave 3D. This is not supported by most exporters. Check your exporter documentation.

Figure 17.5
In this animated scene, the ball will bounce through the boxes.

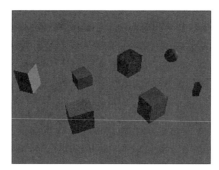

To access the properties of such an animation, you must use the `keyframePlayer` modifier. However, you don't have to add the modifier with the `addModifier` command. Because the member includes an animation, the modifier is automatically attached.

You can use the Message panel to find out about this animation. The model has a `playList` that lists the different animations queued up and ready to play. If you have used Director sound Lingo, you will recognize this sort of list.

```
put sprite(1).member.model("ball group").keyframePlayer.playlist.count
-- 1
put sprite(1).member.model("ball group").keyframePlayer.playlist[1]
-- [#name: "ball group-Key", #loop: 0, #startTime: 0, #endTime: 5000,
➥#scale: 1.0000]
```

The name of the animation is "ball group-Key". This name was assigned when the animation was created in the 3D program. You can see all the animations by using the `motion` property of the member. In this case, there is a blank "DefaultMotion" and the motion above. You can also get the `duration` of a motion.

```
put sprite(1).member.motion.count
-- 2
put sprite(1).member.motion[1]
-- motion("DefaultMotion")
put sprite(1).member.motion[2]
-- motion("ball group-Key")
put sprite(1).member.motion[2].duration
-- 5000
```

When you start playing the movie, the animation begins automatically. To stop that, we'll place a behavior on the sprite that issues a `pause` command to the model's keyframe player modifier:

```
property myModel

on beginSprite me
  -- reset the model
  sprite(me.spriteNum).member.resetWorld()

  -- get easy reference to the ball
  myModel = sprite(me.spriteNum).member.model("ball group")

  -- don't let it play the first time
  myModel.keyframePlayer.pause()
end
```

Now that we have stopped the animation, we can play the movie, and the ball will not bounce. To start the ball bouncing, we can just issue the `play` command. Here is a behavior that will do this when the user clicks on the sprite:

```
on mouseUp me
  myModel.keyframePlayer.play()
end
```

When the user clicks, the animation plays out. If you check the `playList` when it is finished, you will find it empty. This is because the motion has been used and is now over.

The `playList` can contain a whole series of motions. Each will be performed one after the other. You can also add motions with the `queue` command that will be added to the `playList` while the current animation is playing.

The following `on mouseUp` handler checks the `playing` state of the animation. It also checks to see whether an animation is currently in the `queue`. If an animation is there, it uses `playNext` to skip the rest of that animation just after it adds one to the end of the `queue`. This causes the animation to play again when the user clicks the sprite. If no animation was playing, it simply starts a new one. If the animation has never started playing, the `play` command is used to start it.

```
on mouseUp me

  if myModel.keyframePlayer.playing and
➥myModel.keyframePlayer.playList.count > 0 then
    -- if one already playing, then que another and skip to it
    myModel.keyframePlayer.queue("ball group-Key")
    myModel.keyframePlayer.playNext()

  else if myModel.keyframePlayer.playList.count = 0 then
    -- if none queued or playing, start a new one
    myModel.keyframePlayer.queue("ball group-Key")
    myModel.keyframePlayer.play()

  else
```

17

```
      -- not playing yet, so start it
      myModel.keyframePlayer.play()
   end if
end
```

If you run the movie `animation.dir` and click on the sprite several times, you will notice something interesting. The ball will not just pop back into its original position and start again; it actually flies back to its original position.

This is because animation in 3D members uses tweening to make smooth transitions between motions. So the ball will actually travel back to its starting position rather than just teleport there.

You can change this tweening behavior by using the `autoBlend`, `blendFactor`, and `blendTime` properties of the keyframe player modifier. If the `autoBlend` property is set to TRUE, blending between animations is automatic. Otherwise, you can control the amount of blending with the `blendFactor` setting of 0 to 100. The `blendTime` is the time it will take to transition.

17 BONES AND JOINTS

So far we have seen how you can move a model around the 3D world, rotate it, scale it, group it, and even duplicate it. But can you *bend* models?

Adding Joints to Models

Yes, but not just any model. To be able to bend models, you first need a model that has a *skeleton*. A skeleton is a series of joints and bones associated with the vertices of a model. You cannot add a skeleton in Lingo. Instead, you must create the skeleton, along with the model that uses it, in an external 3D program.

ShapeShifter 3D allows you to create bones and export them into Shockwave 3D, and it will even pass the names of the joints in the bones to Director, which is not typically supported by other exporters.

> Most 3D modeling programs allow you to create a skeleton along with your model. However, few of these programs will export the skeleton to Shockwave 3D. Check with your 3D program and read the documentation for its Shockwave exporter.

To create bones in ShapeShifter 3D, first create the model. I've extruded a simple body model, with arms and legs, and placed it in the `robotstart.ss3d file`. You can open this file in ShapeShifter 3D. The result should look like Figure 17.6.

To create the skeleton, first choose the Create Joints tool, which is the bottom left button in the Create palette. Then create the primary joint by clicking right between the shoulders of the model. Use the Front pane for this. This first joint will be the center of the model.

Immediately create the second joint by clicking on the right shoulder. This will create another joint and link it back to the first. Do this again for the right elbow. You should now have three joints like in Figure 17.7.

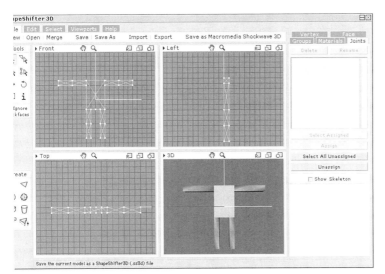

Figure 17.6
This simple body was created from a cube using the extrude techniques in Chapter 16.

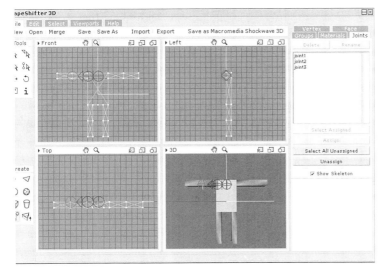

Figure 17.7
The three joints created so far.

Next, click on the Select Joints tool in the Tools palette. Select the first joint. Now click on the Create Joints tool again. Because the first joint is selected, the next joint created connects directly to that one. Create the left shoulder and elbow joints.

Repeat this process to create a joint between the hips. Then create two branches off that joint to create the hips and knees. The final set of joints should look like Figure 17.8.

Notice that in Figure 17.8, I've named all the joints. You can do this by simply selecting the joint name under the Joints tab in the information area to the right. Then click the Rename button.

After all the joints are there, you are still not finished. The model needs to know which vertices are associated with which joints. So you have to sew the skin onto the bones, so to speak.

Figure 17.8
A total of 10 joints create the skeleton.

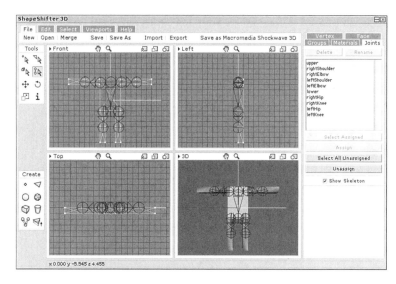

To do this, select the vertices to associate with a joint using the Select Vertex tool. Then, select the joint name in the list to the right and click the Assign button under the list.

To properly assign the vertices to each joint, only think of the vertices that should move when each joint moves. For instance, the elbow vertices do not move when the elbow moves. The elbow stays in place. Instead, the vertices at the end of the arm move.

Open the file `robot.ss3d` in ShapeShifter 3D. By selecting each joint's name, you can see which vertices have been assigned to which joint. The vertices are highlighted in color, so showing them in a figure here will not help. You'll have to look at it in ShapeShifter 3D to get the full effect.

⇨ *If you are getting twisted-looking limbs when using joints, see "Joints Can Easily Be Twisted" in the "Troubleshooting" section at the end of this chapter.*

Using Joints in Lingo

Start a new movie in Director and import the `robot.w3d` model into it. The bones should be a part of this model, but accessing them takes a few steps.

First, you need to tell the model that it should be using its bones. You do this with the `addModifier` command to add the `#bonesPlayer` modifier to it. Then, you need to initialize the bones player by using the `play` command. This would normally start a prebuilt bones-driven animation. However, we have not made a prebuilt animation to go with the bones, so this just initializes the bones player so that we can access the bones afterward.

You cannot create a bones animation in ShapeShifter 3D. In fact, I'm not aware of any 3D program that will export a bones animation to Shockwave 3D. Check your 3D exporter documentation to see whether this has changed.

```
member(1).model(1).addModifier(#bonesPlayer)
member(1).model(1).bonesPlayer.play("defaultMotion",1)
put member(1).model(1).resource.bone.count
-- 11
```

So now we see that Director has recognized the bones in the model. But why are there 11, not 10? There is a default bone for every model. We won't be using that default bone, but it is important to remember it is there so that we know our first bone is bone number 2, not bone number 1.

Also try typing put member(1).model(1).userData into the Message panel. The result is a list of bone names and numbers. This list has been attached to the model by ShapeShifter 3D for your use. Typically, the userData property of a model is nothing more than miscellaneous information passed from the external 3D program to Director. Because bones in Lingo have no names, just numbers, this piece of information can come in handy.

To rotate a joint, thus bending part of your model, all you need to do is change the rotation of the transform of one of the joints. Unfortunately, you can't do this directly. Instead, you need to copy the transform of one of the joints to a variable, change its rotation, and then apply the new transform back to the joint. Here is an example in the Message panel:

```
member(1).model(1).addModifier(#bonesPlayer)
member(1).model(1).bonesPlayer.play("defaultMotion",1)
t = member(1).model(1).bonesPlayer.bone[4].transform
t.rotation.z = 45
member(1).model(1).bonesPlayer.bone[4].transform = t
updateStage
```

Because bone number 4 is the right elbow, this should bend the elbow up 45 degrees. Figure 17.9 shows the result.

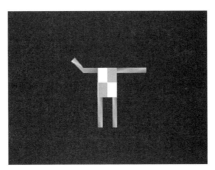

Figure 17.9
The right elbow has been bent 45 degrees by rotating the joint.

Joint Demonstration Movie

The movie robot.dir allows you to use the spacebar to choose between the 10 joints and the left and right arrow keys to rotate each joint around the z-axis. Figure 17.10 shows the movie in action.

Figure 17.10
The robot's joints can be moved with the arrow keys.

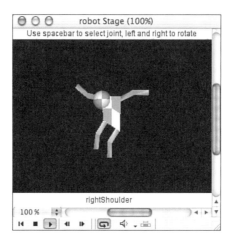

The behavior to do this is surprisingly simple. The selected joint is indicated by moving a sphere model to the location of that joint. The name of the joint is taken from the userData property.

```
property pWorld, pModel, pJoint, pIndicator

on beginSprite me
  -- reset world
  pWorld = sprite(me.spriteNum).member
  pWorld.resetWorld()
  pModel = sprite(me.spriteNum).member.model(1)

  -- acivate bones
  pModel.addModifier(#bonesPlayer)
  pModel.bonesPlayer.play("defaultMotion",1)

  totalBones = pModel.resource.bone.count
  put "Total Number of Bones:"&&pModel

  -- create sphere to indicate selected joint
  r = pWorld.newModelResource("indicator",#sphere)
  r.radius = 2
  pIndicator = pWorld.newModel("indicator",r)

  -- show first joint
  pJoint = 2
  showJoint(me)
end

on keyUp me
  if the key = SPACE then -- next joint
    pJoint = pJoint + 1
    if pJoint > pModel.resource.bone.count then pJoint = 2
    showJoint(me)
```

```
  else if the keyCode = 123 then -- rotate
    t = pModel.bonesPlayer.bone[pJoint].transform
    t.rotation.z = t.rotation.z - 3
    pModel.bonesPlayer.bone[pJoint].transform = t

  else if the keyCode = 124 then -- rotate
    t = pModel.bonesPlayer.bone[pJoint].transform
    t.rotation.z = t.rotation.z + 3
    pModel.bonesPlayer.bone[pJoint].transform = t
  end if
end

on showJoint me
  -- put indicator at joint location
  t = pModel.bonesPlayer.bone[pJoint].worldTransform
  pIndicator.transform.position = t.position

  -- get joint name from user data
  member("joint").text = (pModel.userData)[pJoint+1]
end
```

The most common use for joints is to animate actions that a model might perform. A simple example would be a door model that can swing open and shut. A more complex example would be a human model walking, running, jumping, and dancing.

Creating complex examples requires many steps. Typically, a whole independent system is developed to mark every step of every joint animation. You can work on this yourself, or use a third-party tool such as ReAnimator 3D (http://www.toxi.co.uk/reanimator3d/).

TROUBLESHOOTING

Unable to Clone Models from Another Member

I am trying to clone a model from another 3D member, but the process just isn't working. What could I be doing wrong?

If you find you can't clone models from other cast members, it may be because that member hasn't been loaded into memory yet. To prevent this, you may want to place the member on the Stage, even if it is off to the side and not visible, on some frame before the one where the clone is needed.

Transformation By Trial and Error

I need to transform a model, but I'm not sure which axis to rotate it or which direction to translate it. Is there an easy way to figure this out?

You can rotate and translate a model in many different directions and it is sometimes difficult to tell which direction is the right one. Part of the problem is that the camera can be pointing in any direction as well. But you don't have to know exactly what you are doing. I use trial and error often to figure out the right direction to rotate or translate a model. Just try different vector amounts in your code, and you will hit the right combination pretty quickly. It is usually faster to do this than to contemplate all the factors in your head.

Joints Can Easily Be Twisted

I'm trying to use joints, but when I use Lingo to move the limbs of my model, they seem to twist as well as bend. How can I prevent this?

This usually happens when a joint is rotated in a different direction from the parent joint. You can try to use Lingo to rotate the joint and undo the twist. Or, you can delete and re-create the joint in ShapeShifter 3D and avoid the problem.

DID YOU KNOW?

- If you are experimenting with your 3D world and mess up, you can just use the `resetWorld` command to start over. In fact, make sure that this is the first command your movie executes for each world so that it starts off fresh. You can also use the Reset World button in the Shockwave 3D window to do this manually while you are developing your scripts.

- You can still assign normal behaviors to a 3D sprite. For instance, if you have a small 3D sprite that shows a logo, you can assign an `on mouseUp` behavior to it so that it acts like a button.

- You can permanently save the changes you make to your 3D member by setting the member's `fileSaveMode` property to `#saveAll` and then saving the movie immediately. This is an unsupported and undocumented feature and doesn't always work.

- Try setting the `debug` property of a model to TRUE. This surrounds the model with a spherical mesh and three lines. The three lines show the axes of the model, and the mesh shows its bounds. This can be a useful way to troubleshoot odd rotation and translation movements.

18

IMPLEMENTING 3D USER INTERACTION

CLICK TRACKING

After a 3D scene is on the screen, you may want to have it react to user clicks. But the cursor exists in the 2D space of the screen and the Stage. The models exist in a virtual 3D space inside the 3D member. So how can you tell what model appears at what screen location?

There are several ways to determine which 3D object the user clicked on. The simplest is to use `modelUnderLoc`. This function lets you determine which model is at a specific screen location.

Here is a behavior that uses `modelUnderLoc` to determine which model has been clicked on. First, you need to calculate the upper-left corner of the sprite. Then, you need to subtract that from the screen click location. This gets you the location of the click relative to the upper-left corner of the sprite.

```
on mouseUp me
 -- get upper left corner
 upperLeft = point(sprite(me.spriteNum).left, sprite(me.spriteNum).top)

 -- calculate the click location
 clickLocation = the mouseLoc - upperLeft

 -- get the model there
 model = sprite(me.spriteNum).camera.modelUnderLoc(clickLocation)

 -- send to message window
 alert model.name
end
```

The example movie `modelsunderloc.dir` contains this simple behavior. The movie shows a 3D world with several objects. If you click on the television, chair, table, or remote control, you get an alert box with the name of the model. However, if you click anywhere else, you see a reference to "Room" instead. This is the model that represents the walls, floor, and ceiling. If you click on the window, you also get a reference to "Room," because the window is just part of the "Room" model and not its own model.

The `modelUnderLoc` function only returns a reference to the closest model that is in the click location. You can use `modelsUnderLoc` to get a complete list of models under the click location, ordered by distance from the camera.

Two other commands—`spriteSpaceToWorldSpace` and `worldSpaceToSpriteSpace`—also can be used to convert 2D screen coordinates to or from 3D world coordinates.

COLLISION DETECTION

Objects in 3D worlds tend to be like ghosts: they can move through other objects and even exist inside other objects. This is not typically how things work in the real world. In most cases, you will want to limit the movement of 3D objects so that they do not pass through other objects.

To do this, you need collision detection. There are four ways to do collision detection in 3D Macromedia Director members. The first way is to use the collision modifier, and the second way is to use `modelsUnderRay`. We'll examine both of these next. You could also use pure math to determine when two objects are too close to each other. A fourth way is to use the Havok physics engine, which we'll get to later in this chapter.

The Collision Modifier

You can apply the collision modifier to enable collision detection. After the collision modifier is there, you can get and set properties of the model related to collisions.

Let's start by creating a playground of 3D objects. Figure 18.1 shows a 3D world created in a 3D graphics program. There are four models and a ground plane.

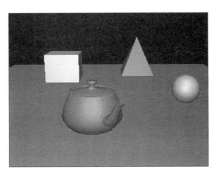

Figure 18.1
This 3D playground is a good place to experiment with collision detection.

To test collisions, you need to be able to move around one of the objects in the world. Here's a behavior that allows us to move the teapot around. You can find this behavior and the other versions of it to come in the file `collision.dir`.

```
property myModel

on beginSprite me
  sprite(me.spriteNum).member.resetWorld()

  -- store reference to the teapot
  myModel = sprite(me.spriteNum).member.model("teapot")
end

on exitFrame me
  -- rotate with left and right arrows
  if keyPressed(123) then myModel.rotate(0,0,5)
  if keyPressed(124) then myModel.rotate(0,0,-5)

  -- move with up and down arrows
  if keyPressed(126) then myModel.translate(5,0,0)
  if keyPressed(125) then myModel.translate(-5,0,0)
end
```

Open the example movie and make sure that only the Quick Movement Behavior is attached to the sprite. If you run the movie, you will be able to use the arrow keys to move the teapot around. You can easily drive the teapot through other objects.

To add collision detection, first add the collision modifier to the teapot. The behavior has stored a reference to the model in *myModel*. Add this code to the on beginSprite handler:

```
myModel.addModifier(#collision)
```

Just adding the modifier to the teapot is not enough. Models with the collision modifier attached can detect collisions only with other models that also have the collision modifier attached. So, here is the code to attach the collision modifier to all the other models:

```
sprite(me.spriteNum).member.model("sphere").addModifier(#collision)
sprite(me.spriteNum).member.model("box").addModifier(#collision)
sprite(me.spriteNum).member.model("pyramid").addModifier(#collision)
```

If you run the movie now, you can still move the teapot around, but it will not be able to pass through the other three objects.

This isn't really collision detection so much as collision prevention. However, you can add another line to have the collision event reported back to your Lingo code. The following line uses the registerForEvent command to tell Director that any collisions should be reported to a handler named *on handleCollision* in the current script object.

```
sprite(me.spriteNum).member.registerForEvent(#collideAny,#handleCollision,me)
```

Now all we need is an *on handlerCollision* handler. Here is a simple one:

```
on handleCollision me, collisionData
 put collisionData.modelA.name&&"collided with"&&collisionData.modelB.name
end
```

The handler you define as the collision handler will get back a parameter, called *collisionData* in the preceding example. The Director documentation refers to this parameter as *collisionData* as well, although you could name it whatever you want.

The *collisionData* parameter is actually an object that has a few properties. The modelA and modelB properties tell you which models were involved in the collision. The previous handler simply displays the model names in the Message panel.

Right now, the code looks just like the behavior Basic Collision Detection in the collision.dir movie. Swap out the previous behavior for this one to see it in action.

One of the things you will notice about the collisions is that they seem to happen when the teapot is still quite a distance from the objects. For instance, Figure 18.2 shows the teapot and the box at the point of collision, but they are not very near each other. In addition, the debug property of both models has been turned on so that you can see the bounding spheres of these models. It is easy to see, then, that the spheres around these models have collided, not the models themselves.

There are actually three different modes for collision detection. The first, #sphere, uses the bounding spheres of the objects. This is the default. It is the quickest method, because the only calculation that needs to be done is to determine how far the center of one object is from the other.

Another fast method is the #box mode. This uses the bounding box of the models rather than the sphere. This comes in handy when you have walls or roads that may be very long or tall, thus making their bounding spheres huge.

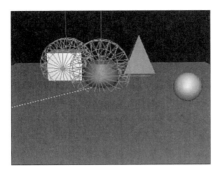

Figure 18.2
The teapot and box collide when their bounding spheres touch.

The ultimate mode for collision detection is #mesh. This gives accurate collision detection right down to the polygon. It is also very slow. Here's how to modify the current behavior to use #mesh mode collision detection. You can find a new behavior in the file as Mesh Collision Detection.

```
myModel.collision.mode = #mesh
sprite(me.spriteNum).member.model("sphere").collision.mode = #mesh
sprite(me.spriteNum).member.model("box").collision.mode = #mesh
sprite(me.spriteNum).member.model("pyramid").collision.mode = #mesh
```

It is important to set all the objects to #mesh as if you set only one object to #mesh and leave the others at #sphere mode. Then #sphere mode will be used to determine any collisions.

When you run the movie with this new behavior applied, you can see that the teapot can get right up to the other objects. As a matter of fact, you can see that collision detection works when you rotate objects as well. Just bring the teapot up alongside another object and try rotating it so that the spout or handle hits the other object. The collision detection works in this case too.

The collisionData object you get back when a collision occurs contains more than just the two models that collided. A pointOfContact property tells you exactly where the collision occurred, and a collisionNormal property tells you the direction of the collision.

Casting Rays

The collision modifier is a great function that is easy to use and has a lot of versatility. However, this versatility comes with a price: It is slow.

The example with the teapot and other shapes is a pretty simple 3D world. If you make a game that has hundreds of models, some that are quite large, the collision modifier is just not fast enough.

One way that I have found to detect and avoid collisions is to use the modelsUnderRay function. This casts a ray from one point in the 3D world in a certain direction. In other words, it draws an invisible line. It then reports back what models this line came in contact with.

Because this is a simpler calculation for the 3D engine to perform, it is much faster than using the collision modifier.

So, if you start at the location of the moving object and then cast a ray in the direction that the object is supposed to move, you can get a list of what objects are in the way. Better yet, you also find out how far away these objects are.

18

For instance, if the teapot is supposed to move 5 units in a certain direction, we can cast a ray before the teapot moves, find out whether anything is in front of the teapot, and then find out how far it is in front of the teapot. If the object in the way is too close, we can simply not allow the teapot to move in that direction.

Defining the Collision Distance

The first step in setting up something like this is to determine how close the moving model can get to something else. If the object is roughly circular, like the teapot, you can get the radius of the object and use that as the minimum distance that the teapot can get to another object. Any closer and the other object and the teapot will overlap, because the distance is measured from the middle of the teapot.

To get the radius of a model, you can use the boundingSphere function. This returns a list where the first item is the center of the object, and the second item is the radius of the object.

```
modelRadius = myModel.boundingSphere[2]
```

Monitoring the Direction of Movement

The next step is to monitor the keyboard for up and down arrow keys so that the requested movement is recorded in a variable. This is different than in the previous example where we just tried the movement immediately. This time, we will record the requested movement and perform calculations on it before doing the movement.

```
if keyPressed(126) then move = vector(5,0,0)
else if keyPressed(125) then move = vector(-5,0,0)
else move = vector(0,0,0)
```

If there is a movement, you can use modelsUnderRay to determine whether an object is in the way. This function requires two parameters. The first is the location of the starting point of the ray. The second is a vector that represents the direction of the ray.

To get the direction, you would think that we could just use the transform.rotation of the model. Not so. This returns a vector with angles, like vector(0,90,0) for a 90° angle. What we need is a real vector, like vector(0,0,1), that shows the movement, sort of like a short arrow pointing in the right direction.

Getting this vector becomes a little complex. First, we create a blank transform variable. Everything is set to 0 in this variable. Then we rotate this transform by the same amount that the model is rotated. Next we move the transform by the amount that the model is to be moved. We can't use translate for this, however, because that will not take into account the rotation of the transform. However, preTranslate rotates the transform first and then moves it.

The result is that the position of the transform is now a certain distance from the origin. This makes a little arrow for us to use, drawn from the center of the world to the position of the "t" transform. Here is the code:

```
t = transform()
t.rotate(myModel.transform.rotation)
t.preTranslate(move)
rayMove = t.position
```

I realize that the concepts here are getting a little deep into 3D mathematics. Unfortunately, this is necessary to use this technique.

Determining the Starting Point

The first parameter of the `modelsUnderRay` function is the location of the starting point of the ray. However, we cannot just use the location of the teapot for this. Why? Well, the teapot rests on the ground plane, at y location 0. If we cast a ray from here, the ray is drawn along the ground. This will miss an object like the sphere, because the sphere barely touches the ground at its bottom point. However, if we simply raise the location of the ray's starting point a little off the ground, it will find the sphere and any other objects that are off the ground.

```
rayLoc = myModel.transform.position
rayLoc.z = 5
```

Detailed Results

The `modelsUnderRay` function returns a list of models. You can set a third parameter to the number of models to return. We'll use 1 so that it returns the closest model. If we used, say, 4, the closest four models would be returned. We'll also use the optional `#detailed` parameter so that we get a list back that includes the distance to the closest model rather than just a reference to the model.

```
list = sprite(me.spriteNum).member.modelsUnderRay(rayLoc, rayMove,1,#detailed)
```

If the *list* contains any items, it means that there is an object in the way. If this object is closer than our *modelRadius*, we will not allow the user to move in that direction.

```
if list.count > 0 then
  d = list[1].distance
  if d < modelRadius then move = vector(0,0,0)
end if
```

You can see this code in action in the movie `raycast.dir`. Play with moving the teapot around to see how it collides with other objects. This method uses fewer resources than the collision modifier method. These simple examples will run at about the same speed on a fast machine. But when you try to create more complex movies, you'll see a huge difference.

Advanced Techniques

There are many flaws in this method of collision detection. For one thing, the moving object can easily sideswipe another object, and the two objects will overlap. This is because only one ray is being cast from the middle of the moving object. If this ray comes from the center of the object and misses an object that is off to one side, no collision occur.

I get around this by using two rays, one from each side of the object. For instance, if the object were an airplane, I would cast a ray from the tip of each wing.

You could also use the `modelsUnderRay` function to determine how far an object is from the ground, or the altitude of the ground at a certain point. Just cast a ray down from above and measure the distance to the "ground" model. This is great for making hover cars that try to maintain a constant distance from the ground, or for having normal cars or characters follow the contours of the ground as they move.

HAVOK PHYSICS ENGINE

In addition to the 3D engine that comes with Director, there is an additional physics engine provided by Havok. Havok makes 3D physics engines for many popular computer games, so having part of this engine included in Director 8.5 is quite a treat.

The Havok physics engine makes it easy to have 3D objects that behave like normal real-world objects. You can assign a mass to a model and apply forces to it. Using Havok is relatively simple.

The Director MX CD-ROM comes with a folder of Havok behaviors. You can use these to quickly create worlds with accurate physics. If you want to write your own Lingo scripts, here is a simple introduction to Havok physics Lingo.

⇨ *If you can't get Havok Lingo to work in Shockwave, see "Havok Not Working in Shockwave" in the "Troubleshooting" section at the end of this chapter.*

The Havok physics engine is really an Xtra. It comes with Director and can easily be added to your projectors. The default download for Shockwave 8.5 and 9 does not include Havok, but it is automatically added when the user runs into the first movie that needs it. Because this is a Macromedia "blessed" Xtra, the user doesn't even see a confirmation dialog box as Havok is installed. It just happens automatically.

Check out the Havok Xtra site at http://www.havok.com/xtra/. It has many open source examples. This is one of the best sites for Director developers.

Turning Models into Rigid Bodies

After you have models in your 3D world, you need to turn them into Havok *rigid bodies* to get them to have physical properties. There are two types of rigid bodies: fixed and movable.

A fixed rigid body is one that never moves. No matter what forces act on it, its location and orientation remain fixed.

Although the real world doesn't have any real fixed bodies, local simulations of small areas do: brick walls, the ground, buildings, and so on. Anything that should be too heavy or is attached to the ground should be considered a fixed rigid body.

The other type of rigid body is a movable one. These are normal objects like balls, blocks, cars, people, and so on.

Whereas fixed rigid bodies don't need a weight, because they never move, movable rigid bodies need a weight value. These weights should be relative to other movable rigid bodies in your world. For instance, a ball should weigh considerably less than a car. If a ball and a car hit each other, the ball should react violently to the impact while the car barely reacts at all.

Before you can create rigid bodies, you need to initialize the Havok physics simulation. The first thing you need to do is add a Havok Physics Scene to the movie. Choose Insert, Media Element, Havok Physics Scene to do this.

This Havok member is referenced by Lingo. You don't have to do anything else with it, such as place it in the score or set its properties. This is just a placeholder for Havok to be able to store information about the physics going on in your 3D world.

The first command you need to issue is the `initialize` command, which starts the physics simulation:

```
pHavok = member("havok")
pHavok.initialize(pWorld,.5,1)
```

The `pWorld` variable references the 3D member that the Havok member will be connected to. You'll see a complete example in a bit.

The two parameters of the `initialize` command are the collision tolerance and world scale of the simulation. The collision tolerance default is .1, but I find that .5 works better. This determines how close objects can be before they are considered touching. The world scale can be used to adjust all units in your simulation. Just leave it at 1 for normal use.

You can actually change several general properties of a Havok physics simulation. They are all listed in Table 18.1.

Table 18.1 Havok Member Properties

Property	Description
initialized	Whether the simulation has been initialized.
tolerance	Current collision tolerance.
scale	Overall scaling factor.
timeStep	Default time step to use if no parameter passed to the `step` command.
subSteps	Default number of substeps to use if no parameter passed to the `step` command.
simTime	The total amount of time that has passed since the simulation started.
gravity	A vector representing the gravitational force acting on all movable rigid bodies at all times. The default is vector(0,0,-9.81).

To create a fixed rigid body, you first need to create the model. In the example movie `rigidbodies.dir`, a small plane is created to be the ground. This plane is moved a little lower than the middle of the world.

```
r = pWorld.newModelResource("ground",#plane)
r.width = 200
r.length = 200
m = pWorld.newModel("ground",r)
m.shaderList = pShader
m.transform.position.z = -50
```

To make this a rigid body, you first have to apply the `#meshDeform` modifier to the model. This reveals all the vertices and polygon faces to Havok. Then use the `makeFixedRigidBody` to add the model to the simulation.

```
m.addModifier(#meshdeform)
pHavok.makeFixedRigidBody("ground",FALSE)
```

The first parameter of the makeFixedRigidBody command is the name of the rigid body. This name is for the Havok object, not the 3D world. The second parameter is whether the object is convex, which means that it has simple geometry where there are no holes or inward dents. A plane, however, cannot be a convex object, so we use FALSE here. If you were using a box, you could specific TRUE, and then optionally use #box or #sphere as a third parameter to provide a simpler geometry instead of the actual model's mesh.

Creating a movable rigid body is almost the same process, but you need to also tell Havok the weight of the object. This example creates a box resource, then a model from that resource, and then a rigid body from that model with a weight of 10.

```
r = pWorld.newModelResource("box",#box)
m = pWorld.newModel("box",r)
m.shaderList = pShader
m.addModifier(#meshdeform)
h = pHavok.makeMovableRigidBody("box",10,TRUE,#box)
```

Because a box can be a convex object, we'll use TRUE as the third parameter and then tell Havok to forget about the actual mesh of the model and use a simple box instead.

The example movie actually uses a repeat loop to create three boxes, one on top of the other. Figure 18.3 shows the three boxes stacked slightly disorderly, on the ground plane.

Figure 18.3
These three boxes fell a short distance to become stacked on each other.

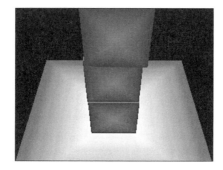

Now that there is a fixed rigid body acting as the ground and a box hovering above it, running the movie should result in the box falling to the ground. However, one more piece of code needs to be added. For each frame that passes, you need to give the Havok engine time to process the simulation. To do that, use the step command along with the amount of time in the simulation that should pass and the number of substeps that should take place.

```
on exitFrame me
  pHavok.step(.5,10)
end
```

A *substep* is a step of the simulation that occurs without the screen being updated. So a value of 10 means that the simulation moves forward 10 small steps before showing the result. The more substeps you have, the more accurate the physics will be in the simulation.

Play with the rigidbodies.dir example movie now. Try changing the parameters of the step command to see how it affects the result.

> If you are trying to use Havok with a Lingo-created mesh, see "Havok Doesn't Work Well with Lingo Mesh Objects" in the "Troubleshooting" section at the end of this chapter.

Havok Rigid Body Lingo

To create a rigid body, you need to use either the `makeFixedRigidBody` command or the `makeMovableRigidBody` command. After you have a rigid body, a number of properties can affect how it behaves in the simulation. Table 18.2 shows all the rigid body properties.

Table 18.2   Rigid Body Properties

Property	Description
active	Whether the object is moving or has momentum. You can set this property to FALSE to stop an object temporarily.
angularMomentum	A combination of the angular velocity and the mass of an object.
angularVelocity	A vector representing the speed and angle, which the rigid body is spinning.
centerOfMass	A vector representing the center of mass for an object.
force	This read-only property tells you the total force being applied to the body at the moment.
friction	How much surface friction the body has. Values range from 0 for slippery to 1.0 for sticky.
linearMomentum	A combination of the linear velocity and the mass of an object.
linearVelocity	A vector representing the speed and direction, which the rigid body is moving.
mass	The mass of a movable rigid body.
pinned	If set to TRUE, the movable rigid body will lock in place until `pinned` is set to FALSE again.
position	The vector position of the body. Use this property rather than the model's transform to move the model or Havok will lose track of it.
restitution	A value representing how much the body bounces. Values range from 0 to 1.
rotation	The vector rotation of the body. Use this property rather than the model's transform to rotate the model or Havok will lose track of it.
torque	This read-only property tells you the total angular force being applied to the body at the moment.

To make a rigid body move, you can do several things. In the previous example, you actually didn't do anything to the models except let them fall. In that case, the constant force of gravity did the action.

But you can apply forces to rigid bodies as well. There are a variety of ways to do this. Table 18.3 shows all the standard ways to apply force to rigid bodies.

18

Table 18.3 Rigid Body Commands

Command	Description
applyForce	Applies a vector force at the center of mass. The force is constant until removed.
applyForceAtPoint	Applies a vector force at a certain point. This causes torque (spin) as well as movement.
applyImpulse	Applies a single hit of force at the center of gravity.
applyImpulseAtPoint	Applies a single hit of force at a specific point.
applyTorque	Applies a constant angular force to the body at the center of mass.
applyAngularImpulse	Applies a single hit of angular force to the body at the center of mass.
attemptMoveTo	Attempts to move the body to a new location and orientation. If other objects are in that location, it does not move the body but returns FALSE. Otherwise, it moves the body and returns TRUE.
interpolatingMoveTo	Like attemptMoveTo, except that if an object is in the destination, it attempts to move the body to a nearby location.
correctorMoveTo	Havok uses impulses to try to bring a body to a desired location, orientation, linear velocity, and angular velocity.

If you are getting unusual results with your rigid body collisions, see "Use Realistic Physics Values" in the "Troubleshooting" section at the end of this chapter.

18

Using Havok to Simulate Ballistics

A simple example of applying an impulse to a body would be to fire a cannonball at a wall of bricks. The example movie cannonball.dir shows this.

The behavior that controls the sprite starts off by creating the ground and making it a fixed rigid body.

```
property pHavok, pWorld, pBullet

on beginSprite me
  -- reset world and camera
  pWorld = sprite(me.spriteNum).member
  pWorld.resetWorld()
  pWorld.camera[1].transform.rotate(90,0,0)

  -- get reference to havok member
  pHavok = member("havok")
  pHavok.initialize(pWorld,.5,1)

  -- make shader
  pShader = pWorld.newShader("shader",#standard)
  pShader.texture =
⮕pWorld.newTexture("texture",#fromCastMember,member("texture"))
```

```
-- create the ground
r = pWorld.newModelResource("ground",#plane)
r.width = 1000
r.length = 1000
m = pWorld.newModel("ground",r)
m.shaderList = pShader
m.transform.position.z = -50
m.addModifier(#meshdeform)
pHavok.makeFixedRigidBody("ground",FALSE)
```

It then creates a set of bricks, all stacked on top of each other. Each row of bricks is staggered so that the bricks interlace. You can see the result in Figure 18.4.

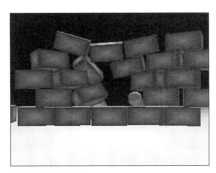

Figure 18.4
The cannonball has just hit the wall of bricks for the second time.

```
-- create bricks
r = pWorld.newModelResource("box",#box)
r.width = 50
r.height = 25
r.length = 25
levelOffset = 1
repeat with y = 0 to 4
 levelOffset = not levelOffset
 repeat with x = -2 to 2
  m = pWorld.newModel("box"&&x&&y,r)
  m.transform.position = vector(x*50.5+levelOffset*25,100,y*25.5-37)
  m.addModifier(#meshdeform)
  m.shaderList = pShader
  h = pHavok.makeMovableRigidBody("box"&&x&&y,10,TRUE,#box)
  h.restitution = 0.0
 end repeat
end repeat
```

The cannonball will be a sphere that has much less mass than the bricks.

```
-- create bullet
r = pWorld.newModelResource("bullet",#sphere)
r.radius = 10
m = pWorld.newModel("bullet",r)
m.addModifier(#meshdeform)
```

```
pBullet = pHavok.makeMovableRigidBody("bullet",2,TRUE,#sphere)
pBullet.pinned = TRUE
end
```

If you run the movie, the cannonball, referred to in the code as a bullet, starts off pinned in place. But pressing down on the sprite results in the bullet being unpinned and then fired with a great impulse at the wall.

```
on mouseUp me
 pBullet.pinned = FALSE
 pBullet.position = vector(0,-150,0)
 pBullet.applyImpulse(vector(0,800,0))
end
```

One hit is not be enough to knock over the bricks. It takes about four. Just click on the sprite again after each impact to reposition and shoot the bullet.

Of course this movie needs an `on exitFrame` handler to give Havok control over the simulation.

```
on exitFrame me
 pHavok.step(.5,10)
end
```

Using Havok to Simulate a Vehicle

The example movie `movingcar.dir` contains a simple scene with a car and some boxes. You can see it in Figure 18.5. If you run the movie, you'll find that you can drive the car around with the arrow keys. You can also smash into the boxes and push them around. This was all done with Havok.

Figure 18.5
This scene includes a car that you can drive and boxes that can be pushed around.

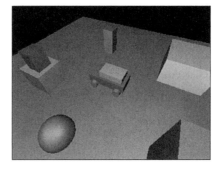

The behavior that controls the car starts off by defining the entire world. It gets a reference to the Havok cast member and then uses `initialize` to start the physics simulation. Next, all the objects in the world are assigned masses. Some objects are fixed in place, whereas others are free to move. Before this is done, the mesh deform modifier needs to be added to all these models.

```
property pHavok, pMember, pCar

on beginSprite me
 -- get the member for easy reference
 pMember = sprite(me.spriteNum).member
```

```
  -- reset the world
  pMember.resetWorld()

  -- get reference to havok member
  pHavok = member("carscene physics")

  -- start havok at scale of 1
  pHavok.initialize(pMember,.5,1)

  -- add mesh deform to all models
  pMember.model("Ground").addModifier(#meshdeform)
  pMember.model("Car").addModifier(#meshdeform)
  pMember.model("Green Box").addModifier(#meshdeform)
  pMember.model("Blue Box").addModifier(#meshdeform)
  pMember.model("Pink Box").addModifier(#meshdeform)
  pMember.model("Top Box").addModifier(#meshdeform)
  pMember.model("Purple Box").addModifier(#meshdeform)
  pMember.model("Sphere").addModifier(#meshdeform)

  -- fix ground, one box and the sphere
  pHavok.makeFixedRigidBody("Ground",TRUE,#box)
  pHavok.makeFixedRigidBody("Blue Box",TRUE,#box)
  pHavok.makeFixedRigidBody("Sphere",TRUE,#sphere)

  -- assign mass to other boxes
  pHavok.makeMovableRigidBody("Green Box",20,TRUE,#box)
  pHavok.makeMovableRigidBody("Pink Box",20,TRUE,#box)
  pHavok.makeMovableRigidBody("Top Box",20,TRUE,#box)
  pHavok.makeMovableRigidBody("Purple Box",40,TRUE,#box)

  -- assign mass to car
  pCar = pHavok.makeMovableRigidBody("Car",1000,TRUE,#box)
end
```

The models in this example were actually created in an external 3D program, so we don't need to worry about making primitives. We just need to know the names of the models to apply the rigid body specifications.

Now that the world is set, we need to look for key presses and move the car when needed. We'll use the `applyImpulse` command to move the car and the `applyAngularImpulse` command to turn the car.

```
on exitFrame me
  -- if up arrow pressed, move forward
  if keyPressed(126) then
    -- calculate forward vector
    t = pMember.model("Car").transform.duplicate()
    t.position = vector(0,0,0)
    v = t*vector(0,1,0)
```

```
 -- move forward
 pCar.applyImpulse(v*2000)
end if

-- if down arrow pressed, move backward
if keyPressed(125) then
 -- calculate forward vector
 t = pMember.model("Car").transform.duplicate()
 t.position = vector(0,0,0)
 v = t*vector(0,1,0)

 -- move backward
 pCar.applyImpulse(v*-1000)
end if

-- if arrows pressed, apply angular impulse to turn
if keyPressed(123) then
 pCar.applyAngularImpulse(vector(0,0,5000))
end if
if keyPressed(124) then
 pCar.applyAngularImpulse(vector(0,0,-5000))
end if

-- set the physics simulation
pHavok.step()
end
```

The last line of the behavior issues the `step` command. In the physics simulation, time does not move forward until you tell it. The `step` command pushes time forward and moves all the objects according to the forces applied to them.

If you play with the movie, you'll see that the car can bump into the boxes and push them away. There is even a box stacked on top of another box that you can knock off.

The sphere embedded in the ground acts as an immovable obstacle for the car. If you hit it hard enough, you can get the car to flip over.

Because the ground plane, really a box in this case, is finite, you can easily run the car off it. In that case, the car falls into the void.

If you want to have the camera follow around behind the car, just add the following code to the end of the `on beginSprite` handler. I've left it in the example movie too, but commented out.

```
-- camera follows the car
pMember.camera[1].transform.position = pMember.model("Car").transform.position
➥+ vector(0,-80,30)
pMember.camera[1].transform.rotation = pMember.model("Car").transform.rotation
➥+ vector(90,0,0)
pMember.model("Car").addChild(pMember.camera[1])
```

Using Havok to Simulate a Rope

Another thing that Havok can do well is tie objects together. For instance, if you want to swing a ball from a wire, you can attach one end of a wire to a fixed body, and the other end of the wire to a heavy ball. Then you can apply an impulse to swing the ball, or just let gravity do the work.

To do this, you need to use *dashpots*, which are links between rigid bodies. A linear dashpot tries to keep two bodies the same distance from each other no matter what other forces are acting on each. This is similar to a string, chain, or wire connecting to objects.

In the example movie wreckingball.dir, the same wall is used from the cannonball.dir example. But instead of shooting a small bullet, we'll let a large wrecking ball do the job of knocking the wall down.

First, let's create the ball. This will be a standard movable rigid body:

```
-- create ball
r = pWorld.newModelResource("ball",#sphere)
r.radius = 20
m = pWorld.newModel("ball",r)
m.addModifier(#meshdeform)
m.transform.position = vector(0,-140,120)
pHavok.makeMovableRigidBody("ball",2)
```

Next, we'll create a fixed body that the ball swings from:

```
-- create hook
r = pWorld.newModelResource("hook",#sphere)
r.radius = 10
m = pWorld.newModel("hook",r)
m.addModifier(#meshdeform)
m.transform.position = vector(0,0,120)
pHavok.makeFixedRigidBody("hook",FALSE)
```

We could connect the hook and ball to each other and tell them to remain a certain distance apart. This causes the ball to swing around the hook by that distance. But in reality, that doesn't happen. So instead we'll create a line, a thin box, that connects the two.

```
-- create line
r = pWorld.newModelResource("line",#box)
r.width = 3
r.height = 140
r.length = 3
m = pWorld.newModel("line",r)
m.addModifier(#meshdeform)
m.transform.position = vector(0,-70,120)
pHavok.makeMovableRigidBody("line",1)
```

Notice that we've positioned the hook, ball, and line so that the hook is exactly at one end of the line, and the ball is at the other. This will be important because Havok will be told that these relationships exist, and if the locations of the models don't match what we tell Havok, then Havok will react violently to try to get the objects in their proper place.

18

First, we establish the relationship between the stable hook and the line:

```
-- set dashpot for top and bottom of line
pHavok.makeLinearDashpot("dash1","line","hook")
pHavok.linearDashpot("dash1").strength = 1
pHavok.linearDashpot("dash1").damping = .05
pHavok.linearDashpot("dash1").pointA = vector(0,70,0)
```

The properties `strength` and `damping` control how strong the dashpot is. Be careful with these settings; too much or too little results in chaotic behavior.

Here is the code that establishes the connection between the other end of the line and the ball:

```
pHavok.makeLinearDashpot("dash2","line","ball")
pHavok.linearDashpot("dash2").strength = 1
pHavok.linearDashpot("dash2").damping = .05
pHavok.linearDashpot("dash2").pointA = vector(0,-70,0)
```

Figure 18.6 shows the wrecking ball in action.

Figure 18.6
The wrecking ball has swung down to gain momentum and then over to smash the wall of bricks.

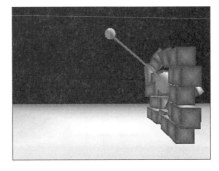

You can also create angular dashpots. These make a body tend toward a specific orientation. They are useful for keeping characters upright. A similar function in Havok is springs, which allow objects to move away or toward other objects but eventually end up at the original distance.

These Havok examples only scratch the surface of what can be done. Check the Web and the Havok site for many more examples. The Havok site, `http://www.havok.com/xtra/`, should be your first stop.

TROUBLESHOOTING

Havok Not Working in Shockwave

I'm using Havok in my movie, but it doesn't work for some users in their Web browsers. How can I make sure that they have the Xtra?

Remember to include the Havok Xtra with your projectors if you need it. Also make sure that it is set to Download If Needed in the Movie Xtras properties.

Havok Doesn't Work Well with Lingo Mesh Objects

I'm can use Havok with many of my models but not with uneven meshes created using only Lingo. What am I doing wrong?

Havok works well with simple objects, such as boxes and spheres. However, if you create your own mesh with Lingo, Havok doesn't seem to be able to correctly represent its shape. It works fine for odd-shaped objects created outside Director, though, like those created with ShapeShifter 3D. If you are an expert at creating your own meshes with Lingo, you can improve Havok's use of those meshes by making sure that the normals for all the polygons are pointed in the correct direction.

Use Realistic Physics Values

How do I know what values to give as the masses for my rigid bodies? Does it really matter?

When using the Havok physics engine, always remember to use realistic values. If you have a huge object that has a mass of 1 and a small object that has a mass of 1,000, you can only expect unusual results.

DID YOU KNOW?

18

- The Havok physics engine included with Director is a subset of the full Havok physics engine used in many A-title games.

- You can get the `boundingSphere` property of a model or a group. This returns a list with the location of the center of the model or group and the radius of the sphere. You can roll your own collision detection this way, or use this information for other purposes.

19

MODIFYING SHADERS, TEXTURES, AND LIGHTS

IN THIS CHAPTER

COLORING MODELS

Shaders are used to color or texture the surface of a 3D model. A shader can be a definition of how the surface reacts to light, such as by reflecting a certain color. Or, a shader can use a bitmap texture to place an image on the surface of the model.

The simplest type of shader is one that simply colors in a model. The color of a surface is determined by both the shader assigned to it and the light being shone on it. We'll focus on lights later in this chapter. For now, we'll consider coloring surfaces using default white ambient and directional lights that can be set with the Property Inspector.

Assigning a Color to a Model's Surface

Let's look at an example of a primitive created with Lingo. The following code creates a plane:

```
on beginSprite me
  pWorld = sprite(me.spriteNum).member
  pWorld.resetWorld()

  r = pWorld.newModelResource("plane",#plane)
  r.width = 100
  r.length = 100
  myPlane = pWorld.newModel("plane",r)
  myPlane.transform.rotation.x = 135
end
```

Figure 19.1 shows this plane with the typical checkerboard pattern you see when you create a new primitive. This pattern is actually the default shader automatically included with every 3D member. When a new primitive is created, each surface of that primitive is given the default shader until you specifically assign it your own shader.

Figure 19.1
The default shader is automatically assigned to surfaces of a new Lingo-created primitive.

To assign your own color to this model, the first thing you need to do is to create a shader. A shader is created with the `newShader` command. You need to give the shader a name and a type. For now, we'll only deal with `#standard` shaders.

```
myShader = pWorld.newShader("myShader",#standard)
```

After you have created a shader, you must assign it to the model. Each surface of the model can take a shader. In the case of a plane, there are two surfaces—the top and bottom.

To see the shaders applied to a surface, get the shaderList of the model. Here is how to do it in the Message panel:

```
put member(1).model(1).shaderList
-- [shader("DefaultShader"), shader("DefaultShader")]
```

Now let's change the shader for one of the surfaces. First, let's modify the new shader we have created so that it is different from the default shader.

When you create a new shader, it is identical to the default shader. We want to change this shader so that it is just a solid color. To do that, we first need to set its texture property to VOID to get rid of the checkerboard texture:

```
myShader.texture = VOID
```

Then, we want to assign a color to the shader. Colors are assigned based on the type of light reflected off the surface. There are two primary types of light: diffuse and ambient. Diffuse light comes from a single light source in the world. Ambient light comes from everywhere in the world. We'll find out more about lights later in this chapter. We want the surface to react to both types of lights by reflecting blue.

```
myShader.diffuse = rgb("0000FF")
myShader.ambient = rgb("0000FF")
```

Now we need to assign the new shader to the surface. To do that, just set the item in the shaderList to the new shader:

```
myPlane.shaderList[1] = myShader
```

You can see the result in the movie colorplane.dir. The plane is blue rather than the red and white of the default shader.

If you want to change both the first and the second shaders of the model at the same time, just assign the shader to the shaderList as a property:

```
myPlane.shaderList = myShader
```

This changes all the shaders used by the model to *myShader*. So if you are working with a box that has six sides and thus six shaders, all of them will use *myShader*.

Simple Shader Effects

If we move away from the simple plane model and use a sphere, we can see that even simple shaders can create complex effects on the surface of a model.

Here is some simple code that creates a sphere and assigns the same plain blue shader to the model:

```
on beginSprite me
  pWorld = sprite(me.spriteNum).member
  pWorld.resetWorld()
```

```
-- create a sphere
r = pWorld.newModelResource("sphere",#sphere)
r.radius = 50
mySphere = pWorld.newModel("sphere",r)

-- create a new shader that reflects blue
myShader = pWorld.newShader("myShader",#standard)
myShader.texture = VOID
myShader.diffuse = rgb("0000FF")
myShader.ambient = rgb("0000FF")

-- assign this shader to the sphere
mySphere.shaderList = myShader
end
```

The result of this simple shader is different on the surface of the sphere than it is on the simple plane. Figure 19.2 shows what it looks like.

Figure 19.2
The surface shows a highlight where the default directional light hits the surface more directly.

As you can see, there is a highlight on the sphere caused by the default directional light above the model. This really helps to bring out the 3D look of the object.

You can change this effect by adjusting the shininess of the shader. A value of 0 turns off the high-light, whereas a value from 1 to 100 changes the level at which the light affects the surface. A value of 1 actually gives the light the greatest effect, making the entire surface reflect the light; a value of 100 minimizes the effect. The movie colorsphere.dir on this book's CD-ROM uses a value of 50. The default, if you do not reset the shininess of a new shader at all, is 30.

You can adjust the way the shine is rendered on the polygons by setting the flat property of the shader to TRUE. Then each polygon of the surface will have a single uniform color. When it is set to the default of FALSE, each polygon uses a gradient like the one seen in Figure 19.2.

Another way you can change the shader is to use the blend property of the shader. This makes the surface semitransparent so that you can see models behind it.

The movi blendshader.dir created both a plane and a sphere. The plane is not given a new shader, but the sphere is. In addition, the blend of the new shader is set to 50.

As you can see in Figure 19.3, the plane cuts the sphere in half. The sphere itself is semitransparent, and you can see the default texture of the plane through the sphere.

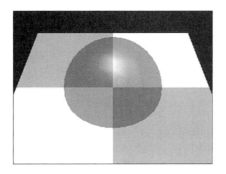

Figure 19.3
You can see the plane through the sphere with a shader that has a 50% blend.

Table 19.1 shows all the shader properties related to special effects like these.

Table 19.1   Shader Special Effects Properties

Property	Possible Values	Description
ambient	color	Reaction to the ambient light.
diffuse	color	Reaction to diffuse lights.
specular	color	Highlight from directional lights with a specular component.
shininess	0, or 1 to 100	How shiny the surface is.
flat	TRUE or FALSE	Whether each polygon should use a single color or a gradient.
emissive	color	Light given off by the surface regardless of other light in the scene.
blend	0 to 100	Amount of transparency.
transparent	TRUE or FARE	Needs to be TRUE to use blend.
renderStyle	#fill, #wire, or #point	If #wire or #point is used, the surface is rendered with a wireframe or set of points rather than the shader.

19

The emissive property is an interesting one if you want to create the illusion that the object is glowing. It seems to generate light and can even be seen in scenes where all lights are black or have been removed. When an emissive light is applied to a shader, it can sometimes appear much brighter than other objects in the 3D world.

⇨ *If you notice that wireframe mode does not work on some machines, see "Wireframe in Software Mode" in the "Troubleshooting" section at the end of this chapter.*

Caution

The renderStyle of the shader can be used to make the model look like a high-tech 3D wireframe. However, this effect doesn't work on all 3D hardware and might not work at all when no 3D hardware is installed. So test this carefully.

APPLYING TEXTURES TO MODELS

Although coloring the surfaces of a model can create better-looking 3D scenes than the default shader can, the best look comes from applying bitmap textures to a model.

Using Bitmap Members at Textures

To do this, you need to use a shader with a `texture` property set to a texture object. So first you need to create the texture object with `newTexture`. This code creates the texture object, applies it to the shader, and then applies it to the model.

```
on beginSprite me
  pWorld = sprite(me.spriteNum).member
  pWorld.resetWorld()

  -- create a plane and tilt it away from the camera
  r = pWorld.newModelResource("plane",#plane)
  r.width = 100
  r.length = 100
  myPlane = pWorld.newModel("plane",r)
  myPlane.transform.rotation.x = 135

  -- create a texture from a bitmap member
  myTexture = pWorld.newTexture("myTexture",#fromCastMember,member("plaster"))

  -- create a new shader
  myShader = pWorld.newShader("myShader",#standard)
  myShader.texture = myTexture

  -- assign this shader to the plane
  myPlane.shaderList = myShader
end
```

The texture, in this case, comes from the bitmap member "plaster". You can see this in the movie `textureplane.dir`. Figure 19.4 shows the textured plane.

Figure 19.4
A plaster texture has been applied to the plane.

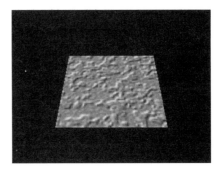

To apply a bitmap member to the model, you first need to create the texture. Next, you need to create the shader, and then you need to set the `texture` property of the shader.

Table 19.2 shows all the shader properties that pertain to applying simple textures.

Table 19.2   Texture-Related Shader Properties

Property	Possible Values	Description
texture	VOID or a texture	This applies the texture to the shader.
transparent	TRUE or FALSE	If TRUE, you can use a blend or the texture's alpha channel.
blend	0 to 100	The amount of uniform transparency.
textureRepeat	TRUE or FALSE	Whether the texture is tiled over the surface.
textureTransform	Transform	A transform, with position, rotation, and scale, that can alter how a texture is mapped onto the surface.
textureMode	#none, #wrapPlanar, #wrapCylindrical, #wrapSpherical, #reflection, #diffuseList, #specularLight	How the texture is mapped onto the surface.

⇨ *If you can't get some textures to work on some machines, see "Odd-Sized Textures" in the "Troubleshooting" section at the end of this chapter.*

Tiling Textures

In many cases, you will want to tile a texture many times across the surface of a model. For instance, if you have a brick wall, you might want to use a texture that shows a small section of bricks, and then apply the texture to a large wall.

There are not many properties of a texture. However, one that is useful is the `quality` property. This can be set to `#low`, `#medium`, or `#high`. Don't assume that `#high` is better than `#low`. In some cases, much more interpolation happens at the higher level, making it look worse. It all depends on the look of your bitmap and what you expect the result to be.

19

Using the basic technique in the previous example, you will end up with a small section of bricks stretched to fit the entire wall. The problem with this method is that each brick will be huge.

Instead, you can scale the texture down and have it repeat over the surface. To do this, you first need to set the `textureRepeat` to TRUE and then set the `textureTransform.scale` to resize the texture. Here is an example:

```
myShader.textureRepeat = TRUE
myShader.textureTransform.scale = vector(0.5,0.5,1.0)
```

Figure 19.5 shows the difference that these two lines of code can make. If you compare it to Figure 19.4, you can see that the texture is tiled four times over the surface.

Figure 19.5
The texture has been scaled down to half its size and then allowed to tile across the surface.

You can scale the texture in only one direction by changing the x or y component of the vector assigned to the `textureTransform.scale` property. The third component, z, should just be a 1.0, because it does not apply to this 2D surface.

Semitransparent Textures

You can also use textures that are semitransparent, meaning that some of the texture is opaque, and other parts of the texture have varying levels of transparency.

You do this by starting off with a 32-bit texture that has an alpha channel layer. You can create these in Fireworks or Photoshop. An example is the Fireworks graphic `semitranstexture.png`. It is a square texture with a transparent hole in the middle.

If you import this into Director, keeping the image's alpha channel intact, you can apply this to a shader, and it will use its alpha channel just as if it were a normal bitmap on the Stage.

The example movie `semitranstexture.dir` is similar to the previous examples. However, the `transparent` property of the shader has been set to TRUE to make sure that the shader uses the alpha channel of the texture. Also, the box model was created with the third parameter of `#both`, meaning that both the front and back faces of each side of the model must be visible. This creates a total of 12 surfaces that need to be shaded.

Finally, the script has a small `on exitFrame` handler that rotates the box around all three axes so that you can clearly see the transparent holes. Here is the complete script:

```
property pWorld

on beginSprite me
 pWorld = sprite(me.spriteNum).member
 pWorld.resetWorld()

 -- create a box
 r = pWorld.newModelResource("box",#box,#both)
 myBox = pWorld.newModel("box",r)

 -- create a texture from a bitmap member
```

```
myTexture = pWorld.newTexture("myTexture",#fromCastMember,
➥member("semitranstexture"))

-- create a new shader
myShader = pWorld.newShader("myShader",#standard)
myShader.texture = myTexture
myShader.transparent = TRUE


-- assign this shader to the plane
myBox.shaderList = myShader
end

on exitFrame me
-- spin the box
pWorld.model("box").rotate(1,1,1)
end
```

Figure 19.6 shows this movie in action. As the box spins, you can see right through the holes in the sides. I've made the background color of the 3D member lighter so that you can see the box more clearly.

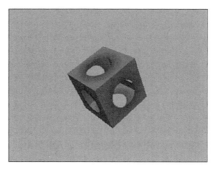

Figure 19.6
The sides of the box use a texture that has an alpha channel hole in the middle.

Layering Textures

So far we have applied shaders to either a single surface on a model or to all the surfaces of a model. You can actually apply up to eight shaders onto the surface of a model.

A shader has a `textureList` property as well as a `texture` property. The `texture` property is the equivalent to the `textureList[1]`, although you can also use items 2 through 8.

The only advantage to using more than one texture comes when you have some textures that are semitransparent or blended.

For instance, you may set the `textureList[1]` texture to one texture and the `textureList[2]` texture to another texture. Then, you can set the `blendConstant[2]` to 50 so that the two texture layers blend together. This would be the equivalent of placing one sprite on top of another and setting the top sprite to a 50% blend so that you can see partially through it to the bottom sprite.

You actually have four properties that affect each texture layer. Table 19.3 shows the `textureList` property, the three blend-related properties, and several others.

Table 19.3 Shader Texture Layer Properties

Property	Single-Layer Equivalent	Description
textureList	texture	Which texture is applied to which layer.
blendFunctionList	blendFunction	Either #multiply, #replace, #blend, or #add. The #blend option uses the blendConstantList to determine the amount of transparency.
blendSourceList	blendSource	Either #constant to use the blendConstantList or #alpha to use the texture's alpha channel.
blendConstantList	blendConstant	A number from 0 to 100 to represent the blend amount.
textureTransformList	textureTransform	Transforms with scale, position, and rotation for orienting a texture on its layer.
textureRepeatList	textureRepeat	Set to TRUE if you want to tile the texture. You'll also need to set the textureTransform.scale to something less than vector(1,1,1).
textureModeList	textureMode	Set to #none, #wrapPlanar, #wrapCylindrical, #wrapSpherical, #reflection, #diffuseList, #specularLight. See the descriptions in the following section.

The single-layer equivalents for each property affect the first layer only. They are useful for when you don't need to mess with more than one layer.

The movie `texturelayers.dir` shows a cube that has two textures applied to the shader. Each texture is set to blend 50%, so you end up with a mixture of the two.

Special Texture Modes

So far, the textures we have applied have been placed on the surfaces as you would expect. However, there are six more ways to map a texture onto a surface. You can control this with the `textureMode` property of the shader, or the `textureModeList` property if you are using more than one texture layer. Here are all the `textureMode` options:

- #none—Normal.

- #wrapPlanar—Texture projected from above.

- #wrapCylindrical—Texture rolled onto the surface.

- #wrapSpherical—Texture wrapped around the surface.

- #reflection—Texture reflected onto the surface, and the texture will not move along with the model.

- #diffuseLight, #specularLight   Map the texture vertex by vertex.

Although most of these texture modes are complex and have limited use for simple 3D models, the #reflection mode can create the interesting effect of seeming to reflect things like the sky.

Try the movie reflectsky.dir. It uses a second layer just like the previous example, except that the textureModeList[2] has been set to #reflection. In addition, the sky texture has been placed in the background using the addBackdrop command.

⇨ *For more information on backdrops, see "Camera Effects" p. 547.*

⇨ *If you need to use a lot of textures but can get your movie to work only in software rendering mode, see "Large Textures Cause Problems" in the "Troubleshooting" section at the end of this chapter.*

Engraver and Newsprint Shaders

So far, we have only used the standard shaders. There are actually a few specialty shaders that you can use as well.

The engraver and newsprint shaders render the model so that they appear as if they have been either carved or printed in a black-and-white newspaper. To me, they appear to be using a printing style called *halftoning*, which is used in newspaper printing.

Figure 19.7 shows the teapot with these effects applied.

Figure 19.7
The left teapot uses the engraver shader, and the right teapot uses the newsprint shader.

19

Because these are the default shaders, I haven't done anything except create new shaders and apply them to the models.

```
on beginSprite me
 -- reset the member
 sprite(me.spriteNum).member.resetWorld()

 -- Create an engraver shader and apply it
 engraverShader = sprite(me.spriteNum).member.newShader("Engraver Shader",
➥#engraver)
 sprite(me.spriteNum).member.model[1].shaderList[1] = engraverShader
```

```
-- Create a newsprint shader and apply it
newsprintShader = sprite(me.spriteNum).member.newShader("Newsprint Shader",
➥#newsprint)
sprite(me.spriteNum).member.model[2].shaderList[1] = newsprintShader
end
```

In addition to all the normal shader properties, these shaders also have other properties. Engraver shaders have brightness, density, and rotation properties. Newsprint shaders have brightness and density.

The movie engraver.dir demonstrates both the engraver and newsprint shaders.

> There is also one other type of shader: the painter shader. This is much like the toon modifier. In fact, the toon modifier is really just a combination of the inker modifier and the painter shader. If you want the surface to have flat colors, use the painter shader.

Dynamic Textures

After you apply a texture to a shader and then to a model's surface, the texture is not permanent. You can change it by simply changing the texture object.

This means that you can have textures that change while the models are visible. So, for instance, if you want to have a clock on the wall, you can change the texture applied to the face of the clock every second to show the clock moving.

The movie rotatingclock.dir goes even further. In it, one side of the clock uses old-fashioned hour, minute, and second hands, and the other side uses numbers. The clock rotates to show both sides.

The hands are generated with imaging Lingo. A small image is created, and the hands are painted on it with lines.

The numbers are generated by using a text member and grabbing the image of that member with imaging Lingo. Those types of images are 32-bit alpha channel images, which would make the clock semitransparent. So instead of using the raw image, the text member image is copied onto a prebuilt opaque image.

⇨ *For more information about imaging Lingo, see "Drawing With Lingo," p. 383.*

Figure 19.8 shows both sides of the clock.

Figure 19.8
Both sides of this clock are dynamically generated and change even while the 3D model rotates.

Here is the code that does this:

```
property pWorld, pClock

on beginSprite me
 pWorld = sprite(me.spriteNum).member
 pWorld.resetWorld()

 -- create plane for clock
 r = pWorld.newModelResource("clock",#plane)
 r.width = 80
 r.length = 80
 pClock = pWorld.newModel("clock",r)

 -- create shader for face clock
 t = pWorld.newTexture("clockface",#fromImageObject,drawClock(me))
 s = pWorld.newShader("clockface",#standard)
 s.shininess = 0
 s.texture = t
 pClock.shaderList[1] = s

 -- create shader for digital clock
 t = pWorld.newTexture("digitalclock",#fromImageObject,drawDigital(me))
 s = pWorld.newShader("digitalclock",#standard)
 s.shininess = 0
 s.texture = t
 pClock.shaderList[2] = s

end


on exitFrame me
 -- update clock textures
 pWorld.texture("clockface").image = drawClock(me)
 pWorld.texture("digitalclock").image = drawDigital(me)

 -- spin clock
 pClock.rotate(0,3,0)
end

on drawClock me
 -- get the time
 the itemDelimiter = ":"
 hour = value((the long time).item[1])
 min = value((the long time).item[2])
 sec = value((the long time).item[3])

 -- create the new image
 img = image(128,128,32)
```

```
-- hour hand
a = 2.0*pi*hour/12-pi/2
img.draw(point(64,64), point(64+30*cos(a),64+30*sin(a)), rgb("000000"),
➥[#lineSize: 3])

-- minute hand
a = 2.0*pi*min/60-pi/2
img.draw(point(64,64), point(64+50*cos(a),64+50*sin(a)), rgb("000000"),
➥[#lineSize: 3])

-- second hand
a = 2.0*pi*sec/60-pi/2
img.draw(point(64,64), point(64+60*cos(a),64+60*sin(a)), rgb("000000"),
➥[#lineSize: 1])

return img
end

on drawDigital me
-- set the text member and get the new image
member("digital clock").text = (the long time).word[1]
textimg = member("digital clock").image

-- make a new opaque image
img = image(128,128,32)
img.copyPixels(textimg,img.rect,textimg.rect)

return img
end
```

The main piece of Lingo to learn here is that the textures are created with the #fromImageObject property rather than the #fromCastMember property. This allows you create images in Lingo and apply them to the texture. It also allows you to grab the image from a text or Flash member to use as a texture.

This example is kept simple to demonstrate dynamic textures clearly. However, it would improve performance if the textures were not reapplied each and every frame. Instead the time could be kept in a persistent property, like *pOldTime*, and then compared to the new time. Only if the time has changed (a second has passed) would the textures be reapplied. This way, the textures update every second, not every frame.

Dynamic textures have all sorts of uses. A 3D character could have moving lips or a whole moving face as it talks. A window could show different views during the day and night. A door lock could change from showing a red light to a green light when the player unlocks it.

UNDERSTANDING AND USING LIGHTS

Lights are a critical part of a 3D world. Without any lights, there would be nothing to see. The brightness and color of surfaces depend on having lights in the 3D world to reflect off the surfaces.

We can deal with lights in Lingo in the same way that we deal with models. They have a position and orientation. They also have a few properties unique to lights.

Examining Lights

First, let's look at the default lights that come with every Shockwave 3D member. Start a new movie in Director and create a 3D member called "world." Take a look at the Property Inspector, shown in Figure 19.9.

Figure 19.9
The Property Inspector shows the two default lights for a 3D member: The Directional and Ambient lights.

19

Each new 3D member comes with two lights. You can see them in the Message panel as well as by accessing the `light` property of the member.

```
put member("world").light.count
-- 2
put member("world").light[1]
-- light("UIAmbient")
put member("world").light[2]
-- light("UIDirectional")
```

There is more information about each light. They have transform properties and type properties and well as their primary property, `color`.

```
put member("world").light[1].type
-- #ambient
put member("world").light[2].type
-- #directional
put member("world").light[1].color
-- rgb( 0, 0, 0 )
put member("world").light[2].color
-- rgb( 255, 255, 255 )
```

Lights can be one of four types, shown in Table 19.4.

Table 19.4   Light Types

Type	Comes From	Direction
#ambient	Everywhere	Every direction
#directional	Everywhere	One direction
#point	Specific point	Away from source
#spot	Specific point	Specific direction

In addition, lights have several other properties, the most important of which is `color`, which represents both color and intensity. For instance, the *color FFFFFF* would be a pure white, whereas *999999* would be a medium gray. *000000* would be black, or the complete absence of any intensity. If you wanted a bright red light, you could use *FF0000*, whereas *990000* would be a darker red light.

Table 19.5 shows all the other light properties.

Table 19.5   Light Properties

Property	Description
type	Either #ambient, #directional, #point, or #spot.
color	In one rgb value, this represents the color and intensity of the light.
transform	The position and orientation of the light.
spotAngle	For #spot lights, the angle of the projected cone of light.
spotDecay	If TRUE, the power of a #spot light becomes less the farther away the camera is.
attenuation	For #spot lights, a vector representing the attenuation factors involved.
specular	If TRUE, the light produces specular effects on some surfaces.

Creating New Lights

To add a new light to a scene, use the `newLight` command. The first parameter is the name of the light, and the second is the type of light. Here is an example:

```
member(1).newLight("myLight",#point)
```

You should then set the `color` and `transform.position` of the light. If it is a `#directional` light, you should set the `transform.rotation` instead.

In the following example, two lights are created in a 3D member that has no directional light and black as its ambient light color. So the only light comes from these two new `#point` lights. Figure 19.10 shows the result.

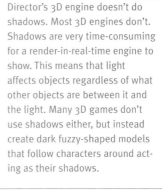

Director's 3D engine doesn't do shadows. Most 3D engines don't. Shadows are very time-consuming for a render-in-real-time engine to show. This means that light affects objects regardless of what other objects are between it and the light. Many 3D games don't use shadows either, but instead create dark fuzzy-shaped models that follow characters around acting as their shadows.

Figure 19.10
The two lights illuminate the top of the painting.

Two spheres also are visible in Figure 19.10. The spheres are optional, but are used here so that you know where the lights are located. Here is the code, taken from `picturelight2.dir`.

```
on beginSprite me
  pWorld = sprite(me.spriteNum).member
  pWorld.resetWorld()

  -- create plane
  r = pWorld.newModelResource("picture",#plane)
  r.width = 80
  r.length = 120
  m = pWorld.newModel("picture",r)
  m.transform.rotation.y = -135

  -- apply painting to plane
  t = pWorld.newTexture("painting",#fromCastMember,member("painting"))
  s = pWorld.newShader("painting",#standard)
  s.texture = t
  m.shaderList[1] = s
```

19

```
-- increase number of polygons
r.widthVertices = 20
r.lengthVertices = 20

-- spheres for lights
r = pWorld.newModelResource("sphere",#sphere)
r.radius = 5
m1 = pWorld.newModel("sphere1",r)
m2 = pWorld.newModel("sphere2",r)
m1.transform.position = vector(20,55,-14)
m2.transform.position = vector(-14,55,20)

-- make lights
l1 = pWorld.newLight("bulb1",#point)
l2 = pWorld.newLight("bulb2",#point)
l1.transform.position = m1.transform.position
l2.transform.position = m2.transform.position
l1.color = rgb("FF6666")
l2.color = rgb("6666FF")
end
```

Notice that one light is red, and the other is blue. You can see the color effect when you look at the example movie. Also notice that lengthVertices and widthVertices are used to give the plane more than the standard two polygons. Because light differences are only shown over the distance covered by one polygon, the more polygons you have, the better a light effect like this will work. Unfortunately, it also slows down the movie.

You might think that #spot lights would work even better for this sort of thing. But #spot lights are actually next to useless. The light only changes from polygon to polygon, so you don't get a good spotlight effect unless you have many polygons. Plus, the #spot light doesn't seem to work on many machines, including Macs with OpenGL.

TROUBLESHOOTING

Wireframe in Software Mode

Why does wireframe camera mode only work on some computers?

In my tests, the wireframe and point shaders do not work in software mode. If a user does not have DirectX or OpenGL, she will not be able to see wireframes but will see normal shaders instead.

Odd-Sized Textures

Why do some of my textures not appear on some machines?

Try to use bitmap textures that have widths and heights that are powers of 2: 8, 16, 32, 64, 128, and 256. Some video cards will not work with textures that are odd sizes.

Large Textures Cause Problems

When I use a lot of textures, why can I no longer run Director with DirectX or OpenGL?

Keep track of your bitmap textures and their sizes. Every bitmap texture you use takes up memory on the video card. If the card runs out of memory, Shockwave 3D switches to software rendering, which is much slower.

DID YOU KNOW?

- There are several shader properties that will automatically set items in the `textureList`, `textureModeList`, `blendFunctionList`, `blendConstantList`, and other shader properties: `refectionMap`, `diffuseLightMap`, `specularLightMap`, and `glossMap`. These are common types of texture layers used in 3D worlds, so these shortcut properties let you add them easily.

- Although textures are compressed with jpeg compression, they can still take up the lion's share of your file. For instance, the difference between a 32×32 texture and a 64×64 is four times the size. So try to use as small a texture as you can.

- You can have a 3D world completely without lights, as long as you use emissive shaders. This will make the models glow by themselves. This technique can create an arcade video game appearance.

19

20

CONTROLLING CAMERA AND RENDERING EFFECTS

IN THIS CHAPTER

MOVING THE CAMERA

Most of the time that a 3D world is used, the camera represents the viewpoint of the user. It is the user's eye into the world.

Moving the camera, then, is like moving the user. Most objects in 3D worlds are stationary; the user's' perspective changes as he walks or flies through the world.

Camera Position

To get the position and orientation of the camera, use the `position` and `rotation` properties just like you would if the camera was a model.

```
put sprite(1).member.camera[1].transform.position
-- vector( 0.0000, 0.0000, 250.0000 )
put sprite(1).member.camera[1].transform.rotation
-- vector( 0.0000, 0.0000, 0.0000 )
```

The default camera is positioned 250 units back from the center of the 3D member's world. It is oriented at 0 degrees around all axes.

You can also address the camera by its name. In this case, the name of the camera was assigned when it was created in the 3D modeling program.

```
put sprite(1).member.camera[1].name
-- "DefaultView"
put sprite(1).member.camera("DefaultView").transform.position
-- vector( 0.0000, 0.0000, 250.0000 )
```

Another way to refer to a camera is directly through the sprite reference. A 3D member can have one or many cameras. The camera currently being used to view the 3D world can be accessed with the `camera` property of the sprite:

```
put sprite(1).camera.transform.position
-- vector( 0.0000, 0.0000, 250.0000 )
```

To move the camera, we could assign a new `position` or `rotation` to it. Another way is to use the `translate` command to move the camera a certain distance from its current location. This is the same process that we used to move models. These commands will move the default camera closer to the center of the world by one unit.

```
sprite(1).camera.translate(0,0,-1)
updateStage
```

Using different `translate` commands, we can assign a direction to each of the four arrow keys. Here is a simple behavior that allows the user to move the camera in four directions. In addition, the A and Z keys move the camera forward and back. You can test it yourself in the example movie `repositioncamera.dir` on this book's CDROM.

```
on beginSprite me
 sprite(me.spriteNum).member.resetWorld()
end
```

```
on exitFrame me
 if keyPressed(123) then -- left arrow
  sprite(me.spriteNum).camera.translate(-1,0,0)
 else if keyPressed(124) then -- right arrow
  sprite(me.spriteNum).camera.translate(1,0,0)
 else if keyPressed(125) then -- down arrow
  sprite(me.spriteNum).camera.translate(0,-1,0)
 else if keyPressed(126) then -- up arrow
  sprite(me.spriteNum).camera.translate(0,1,0)
 else if keyPressed("A") then -- down arrow
  sprite(me.spriteNum).camera.translate(0,0,-1)
 else if keyPressed("Z") then -- up arrow
  sprite(me.spriteNum).camera.translate(0,0,1)
 end if
end
```

If you try this example movie, you see that it works to reposition the camera just fine, but the movement is not natural. That is because the camera is always oriented in the same direction. A better way to move the camera would be to allow the user to spin the camera around left and right, and move forward and backward. This better simulates how we walk.

Natural Camera Movement

To get the camera to change orientation, you can use the `rotation` property. In the previous example, the camera starts off at 0,0,0. This was set when the models were made in a 3D modeling program. We can change the `rotation` of the camera to point in another direction.

```
put sprite(1).member.camera[1].transform.rotation
-- vector( 0.0000, 0.0000, 0.0000 )
sprite(1).camera.transform.rotation = vector(0,5,0)
updateStage
```

The result is that the camera turns slightly to the left. You could use a –5 to turn the camera slightly to the right.

Instead of setting the `rotation` of the camera, we can use the `rotate` command to turn the camera relative to the current orientation.

```
sprite(1).camera.rotate(0,5,0)
updateStage
```

This behavior allows the user to rotate the camera with the left and right arrow keys, and move the camera forward and back with the up and down arrow keys. See the example movie `movecamera.dir` to see it in action.

```
on beginSprite me
 sprite(me.spriteNum).member.resetWorld()
end
```

It is always good to experiment with the `rotate` command in the Message panel because its effect depends on how your 3D world was originally built. The camera in an imported 3D scene may not start at 0,0,0.

20

```
on exitFrame me
 if keyPressed(123) then -- left arrow
  sprite(me.spriteNum).camera.rotate(0,1,0)
 else if keyPressed(124) then -- right arrow
  sprite(me.spriteNum).camera.rotate(0,-1,0)
 else if keyPressed(125) then -- down arrow
  sprite(me.spriteNum).camera.translate(0,0,5)
 else if keyPressed(126) then -- up arrow
  sprite(me.spriteNum).camera.translate(0,0,-5)
 end if
end
```

Complete Camera Movement

A camera actually can be moved in 12 different ways. It can be moved up, down, left, right, forward, and backward. It can also be rotated in any one of these directions.

Most 3D applications restrict the camera movement. For instance, if the user is supposed to be walking through a 3D world, the movement is restricted so that the user can't fly up off the ground or go down into the ground.

However, it is useful to have a behavior that allows all 12 movements. Here is such a behavior. It uses the arrow keys and the A and Z keys to get movement in all directions. Then, if the Shift key is held, you get rotation in all directions with the same keys. The movement and rotation are around the axis that makes the most sense with each set of keys.

```
on beginSprite me
 sprite(me.spriteNum).member.resetWorld()
end

on exitFrame me
 if the shiftDown then
  -- rotation
  if keyPressed(123) then -- left arrow
   sprite(me.spriteNum).camera.rotate(1,0,0)
  else if keyPressed(124) then -- right arrow
   sprite(me.spriteNum).camera.rotate(-1,0,0)
  else if keyPressed(125) then -- down arrow
   sprite(me.spriteNum).camera.rotate(0,-1,0)
  else if keyPressed(126) then -- up arrow
   sprite(me.spriteNum).camera.rotate(0,1,0)
  else if keyPressed("A") then -- A
   sprite(me.spriteNum).camera.rotate(0,0,-1)
  else if keyPressed("Z") then -- Z
   sprite(me.spriteNum).camera.rotate(0,0,1)
  end if

 else
  -- movement
```

20

```
  if keyPressed(123) then -- left arrow
   sprite(me.spriteNum).camera.translate(-5,0,0)
  else if keyPressed(124) then -- right arrow
   sprite(me.spriteNum).camera.translate(5,0,0)
  else if keyPressed(125) then -- down arrow
   sprite(me.spriteNum).camera.translate(0,-5,0)
  else if keyPressed(126) then -- up arrow
   sprite(me.spriteNum).camera.translate(0,5,0)
  else if keyPressed("A") then -- A
   sprite(me.spriteNum).camera.translate(0,0,-5)
  else if keyPressed("Z") then -- Z
   sprite(me.spriteNum).camera.translate(0,0,5)
  end if
 end if
end
```

Take a look at the example movie `movecameraall.dir` to see this behavior in action.

Constant Camera Movement

Moving the camera around as a reaction to a key press makes sense if the user is supposed to be standing or walking. But what if the user is driving a car or flying a plane? In that case, the forward movement doesn't stop immediately when the user lifts up the key on the keyboard.

To get this type of movement, we need to remember the speed and direction in which that camera is moving, and then allow the user to accelerate or decelerate (brake) to change that speed. The movement continues each frame even if the user is not issuing a new command.

The example movie `smoothmove.dir` contains a behavior that does just this. It stores the current speed of the camera movement in the property *pSpeed*. If the user presses the left or right arrow keys, the orientation of the camera turns just like in the last few examples. However, pressing the up or down arrow keys simply changes *pSpeed*. Then, as each frame passes, the camera is moved by *pSpeed*.

```
property pSpeed

on beginSprite me
 sprite(me.spriteNum).member.resetWorld()

 -- user starts standing still
 pSpeed = 0.0
end

on exitFrame me
 if keyPressed(123) then -- left arrow
  sprite(me.spriteNum).camera.rotate(0,1,0)
 else if keyPressed(124) then -- right arrow
  sprite(me.spriteNum).camera.rotate(0,-1,0)
 end if
```

20

```
if keyPressed(125) then -- down arrow
  pSpeed = pSpeed + .1 -- speed up
else if keyPressed(126) then -- up arrow
  pSpeed = pSpeed - .1 -- slow down
end if

-- move every frame according to speed
sprite(me.spriteNum).camera.translate(0,0,pSpeed)
end
```

One simple improvement to this behavior is to add the following lines to the middle of the on exitFrame handler. They check to see whether the speed is positive or negative and decrease or increase the speed slightly so that it tends toward being 0. This acts like friction to slow down the camera when the user is not pressing the up or down arrow key.

```
-- move the speed closer to 0 to simulate friction
if pSpeed >= 0.1 then
  pSpeed = pSpeed - .01
else if pSpeed <= -0.1 then
  pSpeed = pSpeed + .01
else
  pSpeed = 0 -- close to 0, so stop completely
end if
```

In the example movie, smoothmove.dir, if you press the up arrow for a few seconds, the speed increases. When you release, the speed slowly decreases until you stop.

Following an Object

So far we have treated the camera like the eye of the user. It is the portal through which the user sees the 3D world. However, in many 3D applications, the user sees the world from just behind the object that represents the user. For instance, in a racing game, the camera might be just behind and above the player's car. In a first-person shooter, the player's character might be right in front of the camera, so that the player sees the back of his or her head.

To get this type of view, you must lock the camera to the player's character. This means that as the character moves, so does the camera. It stays right in sync with the character, always the same distance from it and always the same viewpoint relative to the character.

The example movie followobject.dir contains three fish. The left and right fish are still there, but there is also a fish in front of the camera, facing the same direction as the camera. The camera is right on top of this fish so that you are looking over it. Figure 20.1 shows this view.

Locking the camera so that it stays in the same position relative to the new fish is easy. The addChild command makes the camera a child of the fish.

Parent and *child* are terms used to describe grouping in 3D members. When we say that a model is a child of another model, we mean that the models are locked to each other. Any change in the parent, such as movement or rotation, also happens for the child. The two models are locked together as if they were one larger model. Note that any movement of the child does not affect the parent.

Figure 20.1
The camera is poised behind a fish that is facing two other fish.

Suppose that model B is a child of parent A. When model A moves, model B moves with it. When model B moves, model A is not affected.

The new fish model is called "character goldfish" because it is the representation of the player's character in the environment. The behavior starts just like the previous example, except for the addChild command:

```
property pSpeed

on beginSprite me
 sprite(me.spriteNum).member.resetWorld()

 -- lock camera to fish
 sprite(1).member.model("character goldfish").
➥addChild(sprite(1).member.camera[1])

 -- user starts standing still
 pSpeed = 0.0
end
```

The rest of the behavior also looks like the previous example. However, instead of the camera moving, the fish is moved. The camera is never even referred to. It doesn't have to be. It is locked to the fish, so as the fish moves, so does the camera.

```
on exitFrame me
 if keyPressed(123) then -- left arrow
  sprite(me.spriteNum).member.model("character goldfish").rotate(0,0,1)
 else if keyPressed(124) then -- right arrow
  sprite(me.spriteNum).member.model("character goldfish").rotate(0,0,-1)
 end if

 if keyPressed(125) then -- down arrow
  pSpeed = pSpeed + .1 -- speed up
 else if keyPressed(126) then -- up arrow
  pSpeed = pSpeed - .1 -- slow down
 end if

 -- move the speed closer to 0 to simulate friction
 if pSpeed >= 0.1 then
```

20

```
  pSpeed = pSpeed - .02
else if pSpeed <= -0.1 then
  pSpeed = pSpeed + .02
else
  pSpeed = 0 -- close to 0, so stop completely
end if

-- move every frame according to speed
sprite(me.spriteNum).member.model("character goldfish").translate(0,pSpeed,0)
end
```

Camera Properties

A camera has a whole set of properties that control how the user sees the world through that camera. We'll be using many of these in upcoming sections about multiple cameras and camera effects. Table 20.1 summarizes the basic ones. We'll be looking at more camera properties later in this chapter.

Table 20.1 Basic Camera Properties

Property	Description
colorBuffer.clearAtRender	Whether the 3D scene is completely redrawn every frame, or whether movements leave trails of color behind them.
colorBuffer.clearValue	The color to use to clear the scene each frame before drawing the models.
fieldOfView	The vertical projection angle of a #perspective view. The default is 30. The same property as projectionAngle.
hither	Models closer than this distance are not drawn.
name	The camera's unique name.
orthoHeight	The size of the view area for #orthographic view. The default is 200 units.
projection	Whether the scene is rendered in #perspective or #orthographic view.
rect	The area of the member that the camera is shown in. Usually this is rect(0,0,320,240), but you can use this to position multiple cameras around and over each other.
rootNode	The parent node for all models shown, usually the whole world. But if you set it to a model or group, only the objects in that group will be shown by the camera.
yon	Models farther than this distance are not drawn.

The fieldOfView and orthoHeight properties determine how much of the scene is seen through the camera. The fieldOfView is used when the projection is set to #perspective, which is the normal camera mode and the one that most closely approximates how we really see the world.

The #orthographic projection, on the other hand, discounts perspective altogether and presents the world as if distance and angle don't affect the size of objects through the camera view. This is similar to how many strategy games show large areas of terrain.

The demo movie cameraroom.dir allows you to view a small room switching between projection types by clicking on the sprite. You can use the left and right arrow keys to adjust the fieldOfView and orthoHeight of the camera as well.

Figure 20.2 shows two views that demonstrate the difference between the two projection angles.

Perspective: 30.0000   Orthographic: 200.0000

Figure 20.2
The same scene with different camera projection types.

MULTIPLE CAMERAS

You are not restricted to one camera. Your 3D world can have has many cameras as you want. You can switch between them to determine which camera the user is actually looking through at any one time. You can even show the user more than one camera angle at a time.

Creating New Cameras

You can add a new camera to the 3D member with newCamera. All you need to do is supply a name.

```
sprite(1).member.newCamera("myCamera")
```

After you have a new camera, you can position it using its transform. For instance, you can reposition the second camera to look straight down at a scene.

When you have more than one camera, you can switch cameras by setting the camera property of the sprite. This is a special sprite property that denotes the one and only camera being used to view the world. It is unusual in that it is a property of the 3D sprite, not the 3D member.

Here's how you would create an overhead camera. Basically, you create the camera, move it directly over the center of the world, and point it down.

```
pCamera2 = pWorld.newCamera("overhead")
pCamera2.transform.position = vector(0,500,0)
pCamera2.transform.rotation = vector(-90,0,0)
```

Assuming that *pCamera2* is a persistent property of the sprite's script, you can switch to this camera like this:

```
sprite(me.spriteNum).camera = pCamera2
```

20

You can also switch to any camera if you know its number. Because the default camera is 1, the new camera should be 2:

```
sprite(me.spriteNum).camera = sprite(me.spriteNum).member.camera[2]
```

To switch back to camera 1, the default camera, you can use the same line, but with *camera[1]* instead.

Showing More Than One Camera

Another way to use more than one camera is to show multiple cameras at the same time. Use the addCamera command to add a second camera view to the sprite.

First, you would want to create your second camera. Then, you would want to set its rect property. This property determines the area of the member that the camera's view occupies. Usually this is rect(0,0,320,240), which is the entire member. But if you set it to rect(220,0,320,100), the view will be positioned in the upper-right corner.

By setting the rect property of different cameras, you can arrange different views around the 3D member. You can also overlap views. The first view can occupy rect(0,0,320,240) and then the second view can be placed over the first in rect(220,0,320,240).

If you ever need to place a view under another view, you can use the addCamera command with an optional second parameter to specify what level the camera should be at. So you can use addCamera(*myCamera*,1) to place the camera under the default camera. This would make sense only if the default camera, now camera number 2, had a rect that did not fill the member.

Here is the code from multiplecameras.dir. The rest of the sprite's behavior deals with moving a ball around the world. But this piece creates a second camera and shows it in the upper-right corner:

```
-- create second camera, color background
camera2 = pWorld.newCamera("overhead")
camera2.colorBuffer.clearValue = rgb("999999")

-- position second camera overhead, pointing down
camera2.transform.position = vector(0,500,0)
camera2.transform.rotation = vector(-90,0,0)

-- show second camera in upper right corner
camera2.rect = rect(220,0,320,100)
sprite(me.spriteNum).addCamera(camera2)
```

Figure 20.3 shows this example movie in action. You can see the second camera in the upper-right corner. The colorBuffer.clearValue property is set to a medium gray so that you can clearly see where the second view overlaps the first.

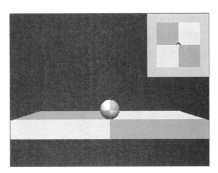

Figure 20.3
This 3D member shows two camera views at the same time.

CAMERA EFFECTS

In addition to the camera basics such as the projection type and the camera's transform, some special properties allow you to change the way the user sees your 3D world.

Fog

Fog is a camera effect that obscures models the farther they are from the camera. You can set up fog with a variety of properties.

Figure 20.4 shows two members, but the fog in the second member is obscuring the pyramid in the distance. The other models are faded from the fog as well.

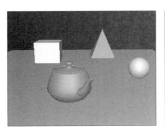

Figure 20.4
This member is the same as Figure 20.3, but fog obscures some of the models.

To turn on fog, you must first set the fog.enabled property of the camera to TRUE. There are also a variety of other settings. Table 20.2 shows all the fog properties.

Table 20.2 Camera Fog Properties

Property	Description
enabled	This turns fog on and off.
decayMode	The decayMode can either be #linear, #exponential, or #exponential2.
color	The color of the fog.
far	The distance where the fog reaches its maximum.
near	The distance where the fog begins.

20

The default value for decayMode is #exponential, which means that the fog starts immediately and grows exponentially until the far distance. #exponential2 is the same, but the fog grows until the near distance. The #linear setting means that the fog grows steadily between the near and far distances.

The code to get the fog to look like Figure 20.4 is in the example file fog.dir. I had to set the near and far properties very carefully to get the pyramid to be almost, but not quite, totally hidden while the teapot was still pretty bright.

```
on beginSprite me
 -- reset the member
 sprite(me.spriteNum).member.resetWorld()

 -- get a reference to the camera
 pCamera = sprite(me.spriteNum).camera

 -- turn fog on
 pCamera.fog.enabled = TRUE

 -- recognize but near and far
 pCamera.fog.decayMode = #linear

 -- set near and far just right
 pCamera.fog.near = 200
 pCamera.fog.far = 320
end
```

A common technique when using fog is to also set the yon property of the camera to just past the far property of the camera's fog. This makes sure that no objects past the limit of the fog are rendered and may speed up things.

Another common technique is to set the bgColor of the sprite to the same value as the fog.color of the camera. Or, alternatively, have the backdrop texture use a similar color. This way, the fog blends naturally with the background.

Backdrops and Overlays

Until now, all our 3D worlds have had solid-colored backgrounds. You can change this by making a bitmap graphic the background for the world. This is called a *backdrop*.

A backdrop is not really a part of the 3D world. It does not rotate around as the camera moves, for instance. It remains a steady image behind the 3D models.

To add a backdrop, just use the addBackdrop command on the current camera. You must first create a texture object, however. You do this in the same way that you would create a texture object to use in a shader. Here are two lines that will add a backdrop:

```
backdropTexture = sprite(me.spriteNum).member.
➡newTexture("my backdrop", #fromCastMember, member("backdrop"))
sprite(1).camera.addBackdrop(backdropTexture,point(0,0),0)
```

The addBackdrop command also wants to have a position and a rotation value. The position is measured from the upper-left corner.

An overlay is just like a backdrop, except that it appears in front of the 3D models in the member. You can have an overlay that is a small graphic floating in front of the 3D world. Or, you can have an overlay that covers the entire member but uses alpha-channels to reveal a part of the world.

In Figure 20.5, I used an overlay bitmap that I made in Fireworks. Only the border is opaque; I simply left the middle part transparent. You can do the same thing in Photoshop, but not in the Director Paint window.

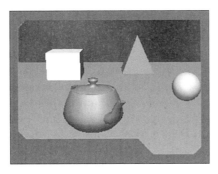

Figure 20.5
This world has been given one backdrop and one overlay.

Here is the behavior used to apply the backdrop and the overlay in Figure 20.5. You can see the movie backdrop.dir as an example.

```
on beginSprite me
  sprite(me.spriteNum).member.resetWorld()

  -- create backdrop texture from bitmap
  backdropTexture = sprite(me.spriteNum).member.
➥newTexture("my backdrop", #fromCastMember, member("backdrop"))

  -- add backdrop to world
  sprite(1).camera.addBackdrop(backdropTexture,point(0,0),0)

  -- create overlay texture from bitmap
  overlayTexture = sprite(me.spriteNum).member.
➥newTexture("my overlay", #fromCastMember, member("overlay"))

  -- add overlay to world
  sprite(1).camera.addOverlay(overlayTexture,point(0,0),0)
end
```

Note that commands are prefixed with the word "add." This is because you are not setting the backdrop and overlay but adding one. You can add more than one backdrop or overlay. For instance, you may want to use the starfield bitmap as the first backdrop and then have a smaller graphic of a planet as a second backdrop. You may want to add a title graphic as a second overlay to appear in the enlarged area of the border to the lower left.

20

Dynamic Overlays

A common problem you may run into when creating 3D worlds is that you need some dynamic information to be displayed over the 3D models. For instance, in a racing game, you may want the user's speed displayed.

You can do this in a text member just outside the 3D sprite, but sometimes you want the 3D member to fill the screen and not have a 2D area at all.

You can apply a dynamically changing texture to an overlay just like we did with the dynamic texture in Chapter 19, "Modifying Shaders, Textures, and Lights."

The movie dynamicoverlay.dir contains a simple 3D scene where you can move a ball around over a plane. In the on beginSprite handler, two overlays are created and positioned at the bottom left and bottom right.

```
-- create time overlay
t = pWorld.newTexture("time",#fromImageObject,member("textrender").image)
sprite(me.spriteNum).camera.addOverlay(t,point(0,210),0)

-- create position overlay
t = pWorld.newTexture("position",#fromImageObject,member("textrender").image)
sprite(me.spriteNum).camera.addOverlay(t,point(160,210),0)
```

The text member "textrender" is used for the image to be displayed by both overlays. Whatever text is in that member will be displayed in both places.

Then, in the on exitFrame handler, the text is replaced in that member, and the new image is taken and applied to the first texture, used by the first overlay. After that, the text is changed again, and the new image is used by the second texture for the second overlay.

```
-- render new time to overlay
member("textrender").text = (the long time).word[1]
pWorld.texture("time").image = member("textrender").image

-- render new position to overlay
member("textrender").text = "X:"&&integer(pModel.worldPosition.x)&&\
            "Y:"&&integer(pModel.worldPosition.z)
pWorld.texture("position").image = member("textrender").image
```

Figure 20.6 shows the result. The left overlay displays the time, whereas the right overlay displays the position of the ball.

As with the dynamic textures in Chapter 19, you probably shouldn't change the textures in each and every frame, but only when needed. So you'll want to store the time and position in a persistent property, compare new values to the old ones, and change the texture only if the values don't match. This will help performance considerably.

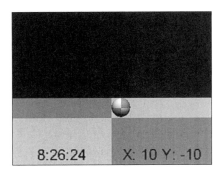

Figure 20.6
Two overlays are dynamically changed with each frame.

USING SPECIAL MODEL MODIFIERS

You can perform many procedures and special effects on models after they are a part of a 3D member. Some of these affect the appearance of models, whereas others have to do with the balance of quality versus performance.

Level of Detail

Level of detail, or lod, is a way to get Director's 3D engine to remove polygons from a model so that it renders faster. It works only on models imported from a 3D graphics program, not primitives.

Normally, the level of detail is handled automatically. Director will remove polygons from a model when the model is far away from the camera and such extra polygons make little difference. When the object is close to the camera, all the polygons will be used.

To take control over the level of detail in a model, you must first add the #lod modifier to the model. Adding a modifier is just a matter of using the addModifier command. Open up lod.dir and try this:

```
sprite(1).member.model("left teapot").addModifier(#lod)
```

Now that the model has an lod modifier, you can access several new properties of the model. The first is the lod.auto property. When set to TRUE, Director handles changes in the level of detail. Set this to FALSE to take control of the level of detail yourself.

```
sprite(1).member.model("left teapot").lod.auto = FALSE
```

Now that you have control, you can use the lod.level property to set the level of detail. A value of 100 means that all the polygons should be used to render the model. Let's set this to 20, so that only 20 percent of the polygons will be used.

```
sprite(1).member.model("left teapot").lod.level = 20
```

The result can be seen in Figure 20.7. The two teapots are identical, but the one on the left has been given an lod modifier, and the lod.level has been set to 20.

20

Figure 20.7
The teapot on the left has a lower level of detail setting.

Another way to use the `lod` modifier is to keep the `lod.auto` setting at TRUE, but set the `lod.bias` setting to something between 0 and 100. This changes how aggressive Director is in adding or removing polygons as the model gets closer or farther from the camera.

The movie `lod.dir` also enables the user to change the `lod` on-the-fly with the left and right arrow keys. By using these, you can see how the `lod` changes the appearance of the model.

Subdivision Surfaces

The subdivision surfaces, or `sds`, modifier is sort of the opposite of level of detail. sds adds geometry to a model rather than takes it away. This added detail comes from information provided by the 3D graphics program.

After adding the `#sds` modifier to a model, set the `sds.depth` property to a value from 1 to 5. A value of 0 is the same as not using `sds` at all. Use the example movie `sds.dir` to test these changes:

```
sprite(1).member.model("left box").addModifier(#sds)
sprite(1).member.model("left box").sds.depth = 3
```

Figure 20.8 shows the result. The box on the left has been given very smooth, rounded corners rather than the sharp ones of the original box.

Figure 20.8
The box on the left has been altered using the subdivision osurfaces modifier.

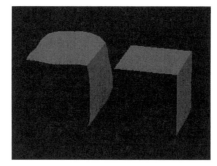

In addition to the `sds.depth` property, you can also set the `sds.tension` to a percentage that indicates how much the new surfaces match the old ones. The `sds.subdivision` property can be set to either `#uniform` or `#adaptive`. Using `#adaptive` means that the changes take place only when there is a major vertex and when that vertex is visible. If you use #adaptive, you can use the sds.error to set the tolerance level for these changes.

The movie sds.dir allows you to play with the sds depth by holding down the left and right arrow keys.

Inker

The inker modifier allows you to accentuate the lines between faces in a model. The effect looks like someone traced the wireframe of a model to make it stand out.

Figure 20.9 shows a simple box model that has been given the inker modifier.

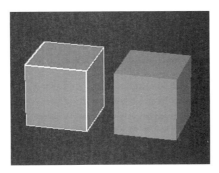

Figure 20.9
The box on the left has been given the inker modifer, and the lineColor has been set to white to make the lines more visible.

To turn on the inker modifier, use the addModifier command. The effect will be rather pronounced right away, but you can alter it in a few different ways.

The lineColor property allows you to set the color of the lines drawn. To create Figure 20.9, I set the line color to white because the default black lines were a little difficult to see in the figure. You can see this code in movie inker.dir.

```
sprite(1).member.model("left box").addModifier(#inker)
sprite(1).member.model("left box").inker.lineColor = rgb("FFFFFF")
```

The lines are drawn along creases in the model. This is typically where one face begins and another ends. However, if the angle between these two faces is shallow, no line will be drawn. Only sharp angles, like the ones at the edges of the box in Figure 20.9, are used for lines.

You can adjust the sensitivity for which creases get lines and which don't using the inker.creaseAngle property. If you set this all the way up to 1.0, lines are drawn at every crease. The default value is .01.

Three different types of lines are drawn: creases, boundary lines, and silhouette lines. You can turn these lines on and off with the inker.creases, inker.boundary, and inker.silhouettes properties. By default they are all on.

Toon

The toon modifier takes a 3D model and flattens it so that it looks similar to a 2D cartoon. Figure 20.10 shows a teapot that has been given the default toon modifier.

Figure 20.10
The teapot on the left has been flattened with the toon modifier.

To get this effect, all you need to do is apply the toon modifier like this:

```
sprite(1).member.model("left teapot").addModifier(#toon)
```

You can customize the toon modifier in many ways. Table 20.3 shows a complete list.

Table 20.3 Toon Modifier Properties

Property	Possible Values	Description
colorSteps	2, 4, 8, 16	This is the number of colors that can be used. Figure 20.10 shows the default two2 colors.
highlightPercentage	0 to 100	This is the percentage of colorSteps to be used for highlights. This number is linked to the shadowPercentage, so changing one will changes the other.
highlightStrength	0.0 to 1.0 and up	The brightness of the highlight colors.
shadowPercentage	0 to 100	This is the percentage of the colorSteps to be used for shadows. A default value of 50 means that half the colors will be used for shadows.
shadowStrength,	0.0 to 1.0 and up	The darkness of the shadow colors.
style	#toon, #gradient, #blackandwhite	The difference between #toon and #gradient is that #gradient provides smoother transitions between colors.

In addition to the properties listed in the table, the toon modifier can also use all the properties of the inker modifier. So you can set lineColor, creases, silhouettes, boundary, and creaseAngle.

OPTIMIZING SHOCKWAVE 3D

After you begin to work with Shockwave 3D, you'll quickly find that you can't get far without worrying about optimizing your 3D member and code.

If you just try to place hundreds of models and dozens of shaders into a 3D member and expect to be able to move objects and the camera around quickly, you're in for a surprise. This is not a limitation of Shockwave 3D so much as a limitation of 3D graphics in general.

Low-Poly Models

When you see 3D computer graphics in movies, those models have thousands and sometimes millions of polygons. There are countless high-resolution textures as well.

In 3D games and simulations, however, models have only hundreds of polygons, and every texture is applied with care.

The difference is that 3D models used in movies are rendered in advance. Sometimes it takes hours to render a few seconds of film, even on expensive computers built specifically for the task. But 3D models in games have to render in real-time to react to the user's interactions. They have to do this on standard computers that most people have at home.

So it is often the mistake of Director developers to expect huge models to be used in Shockwave 3D in real-time. You have to budget your model sizes and textures.

In general, a model used in your 3D world should have only hundreds of polygons. Other models, ones used in the background or on the sidelines, should have even fewer. In addition, textures should be small and used sparingly.

This not only speeds up the 3D member but also reduces the file size of the movie.

At the bottom of the 3D Member viewer panel in Director, you can see the number of polygons in the member, as well as the number of models, lights, and cameras.

Direct-To-Stage

Your 3D world exists inside a sprite that is inside a member. This sprite can either be displayed as a normal sprite or drawn directly to the screen. The latter option, which is the default, is much faster. You can change this setting using the `directToStage` property of the member.

If you decide to turn off `directToStage`, you gain only one advantage: Other sprites can appear on top of the 3D sprite. However, the speed decrease is so profound that the 3D world needs to be pretty simple to get any performance at all.

More Polys Versus More Models

Two main factors determine the speed of your 3D members: the number of models and the number of polygons. Each means a lot, but you would think that the number of polygons would be the overriding factor.

The number of models has a profound effect on the performance of the member. In the movie `optimize.dir`, the behavior can generate two different sets of primitives. The first set would be a grid of 441 models, each with two polygons. They form a solid surface and total 882 polygons. The behavior moves the camera forward one unit every frame, forcing all the polygons to be redrawn.

However, if you switch the behavior to the second mode, it creates one model that is a large plane broken into 882 polygons. So this second model has the same number of polygons but only one model.

The difference is incredible. I get 80-100 fps on the same machine under the same conditions. The results of these

The frame rate is about 13 fps on my computer, a little too low for any serious game or simulation.

20

tests are completely dependent on the speed of your machine and your 3D card. But the relation between the first and second modes will be the same: The second mode will be faster.

This undoubtedly has to do with the different calculations applied on a model-to-model basis. So it is better to combine objects into single models rather than many smaller ones. Examples might be segments of pavement on a sidewalk or small items on a table. You could speed up performance by combining these into one larger model rather than several smaller ones.

You can also improve performance in some situations by grouping models with the addChild command. For instance, if you are moving or rotating several models in unison, it will be better to group them together and move the group rather than each model individually.

Removing Unused Models

Although the preceding four chapters and this one have shown you how to create and add models to your 3D world, you can also delete or remove models. This can help you to improve performance because you can remove models when they are no longer needed.

The difference between deleting models and removing them is that deleting models is permanent, whereas removing models leaves the model in place but stops rendering it to the scene for the time being.

You can use the deleteModel, deleteLight, deleteCamera, and deleteGroup commands to permanently remove items from the 3D member. You can also use deleteShader, deleteTexture, and deleteModelResource to free up memory in your 3D simulation.

The removeFromWorld command takes a model, light, camera, or group and makes it invisible. If you use this command with a group or a model that has children, all the children will also be temporarily removed.

To add the model, light, camera, or group back to the world, use the addToWorld command.

The great thing about removeFromWorld is that after an object has been removed it has absolutely no impact on the performance of the 3D world. So you can have many hidden models waiting to be used later. Using the removeFromWorld and addToWorld commands doesn't hurt performance either, so there is no reason not to use them when possible.

An example of when to use removeFromWorld might be when an object is hidden behind a wall or will not be revealed to the user until she does something else in the simulation. An "enemy" character in the world might disappear temporarily according to the player's actions but reappear later, so you do not want to use deleteModel.

Tweaking Settings

Several small settings affect the way models and textures are shown in 3D members. These quality settings usually only have a slight effect on the performance of a member and a larger effect on how the models look. But you may want to try tweaking them at some point to optimize performance.

Table 20.4 shows a list of these properties and their possible values.

Table 20.4 Quality and Performance Properties

Property	Property Of	Possible Values	Notes
renderer	getRendererServices()	#openGL, #directX5_2, #directX7_0, #software	#software is always available but the slowest. DirectX 7 or better is available on most Windows machines. OpenGL is present on some Windows machine and most Macs.
textureRenderFormat	getRendererServices()	#rgba8888, #rgba8880, #rgba5650, #rgba5550, #rgba5551, #rgba4444	The number of bits used to draw textures in the red, green, blue, and alpha channels.
textureRenderFormat	texture	#rgba8888, #rgba8880, #rgba5650, #rgba5550, #rgba5551, #rgba4444	
quality	texture	#low, #medium, #high	Level of mipmapping for textures. Sometimes #low can produce the best effect.
nearFiltering	texture	TRUE or FALSE	Whether bilinear filtering is used to render the texture.
yon	camera	Distance from camera	The distance from the camera where objects stop being drawn. Not drawing distance objects can speed up frame rates considerably.
bias	model.lod	0 to 100	Decreasing this number makes distant models render with fewer polygons.

20

⇨ *If you want to make sure that your movies play back at a decent speed on different machines, see "The Need for Speed" in the "Troubleshooting" section at the end of this chapter.*

Changing 3D Drivers

In the previous section, you got a peek at the global `getRendererServices()` function. This function can be used to access a few pieces of information about the user's computer. Table 20.5 provides a complete list, plus a few other global 3D properties.

Table 20.5 Global 3D Properties

Property	Possible Values	Get or Set
`getRendererServices().renderer`	`#openGL`, `#directX5_2`, `#directX7_0`, or `#software`	Get
`getRendererServices().rendererDeviceList`	A list containing one or more: `#openGL`, `#directX5_2`, `#directX7_0`, or `#software`	Get
`getRendererServices().textureRenderFormat`	`#rgba8888`, `#rgba8880`, `#rgba5650`, `#rgba5550`, `#rgba5551`, `#rgba4444`	Get
`getRendererServices().depthBufferDepth`	24	Get
`getRendererServices().colorBufferDepth`	32	Get
`getRendererServices().modifiers`	A list containing one or more: `#collision`, `#bonesPlayer`, `#keyFramePlacer`, `#toon`, `#lod`, `#sds`, `#meshDeform`, `#inker`	Get
`getRendererServices().primitives`	A list containing one or more: `#sphere`, `#box`, `#cylinder`, `#plane`, `#particle`	
`the preferred3DRenderer`	`#auto`, `#openGL`, `#directX5_2`, `#directX7_0`, or `#software`	Get and Set
`the active3DRenderer`	`#openGL`, `#directX5_2`, `#directX7_0`, or `#software`	Get and Set

The lists returned by `getRendererServices()` can sometimes change. For instance, if in the future a company comes out with a third party Xtra that adds more modifiers or primitives to Director, and you are using that Xtra, you may get more items in those lists.

The only control you have is which 3D renderer the user is using. For instance, some users on Windows machines may have the ability to use all four rendering engines. In that case, you may want to set their `the active3DRenderer` to `#openGL` if your movie requires a special feature of that renderer. Use `getRendererServices().renderDeviceList` first to make sure that it is available. A more common use might be to force the user into `#software` render mode if he is having trouble with one of the other modes. This slows down performance, but it may increase the graphic quality.

⇨ *If you want to make sure that your 3D models look the same on users' machines, see "Remember to Test with Different Modes" in the "Troubleshooting" section at the end of this chapter.*

Antialiasing

Optimization is not all about speed. Sometimes the quality of the 3D image is more important. In that case, you may want to consider setting the sprite property antiAliasingEnabled to TRUE.

This will smooth the visible edges of the models slightly so that they don't have a jagged appearance. It does this by rendering the 3D member at twice its normal size and then shrinking it down 50%. So four times as many pixels are rendered and then used to create a smoother normal-sized image.

The slow-down in performance is dramatic, but the increase in quality is only slight. Use this property only when needed.

One way to use it is to set antiAliasingEnabled to TRUE when a 3D simulation stops. Then, set it to FALSE when movement begins. Usually, if the models are moving, the user doesn't notice the jagged edges anyway.

> **Caution**
>
> The antiAliasingEnabled property doesn't always work with every 3D rendering engine. It doesn't work with OpenGL on the Mac, for instance. However, it should always work for Software rendering mode.

TROUBLESHOOTING

Remember to Test with Different Modes

How can I best make sure that users will see good quality 3D rendering on their machines?

Sometimes rendering with software mode can produce significantly different results when using DirectX or OpenGL. If you are forced to author in software mode, make sure that you test often on a machine with DirectX or OpenGL. Alternatively, if you are using a machine with DirectX or OpenGL, switch to software mode every once and a while to test.

The Need for Speed

How can I make sure that performance is OK on different machines?

Remember that speed is always an issue. When you use 3D Lingo, be sure to test often on a basic computer that has your minimum requirements for playing the finished product.

20

DID YOU KNOW?

- You can get the image property of a 3D member at any time to take a quick snapshot of the 3D member. You can use this image as a bitmap member. This could allow you to freeze the 3D world and replace it with a bitmap sprite that renders to the screen much faster while other sprites on the Stage are active.

- Instead of having distance objects such as a mountain range or a cityscape exist as models in your 3D member, you can paint them in as backdrops just like in the movies. When the user rotates the camera, you can move the backdrop left or right by adjusting its loc property.

V

EXTENDING DIRECTOR

IN THIS PART

21

READING AND WRITING DATA FILES

IN THIS CHAPTER

FILEIO XTRA BASICS

Using text files has always been more difficult in Director than it should be. Director MX is no different. It requires you to use the FileIO Xtra. This Xtra adds Lingo commands to handle reading and writing files.

Using an Xtra such as this is like using a behavior, except that the Xtra is referenced through a variable, not a sprite. Here is an example. To read a text file, use the following series of commands:

```
fileObj = new(xtra "FileIO")
fileObj .openFile("myfile.txt", 1)
text = fileObj.readfile()
fileObj.closeFile()
```

The variable *fileObj* is used to store an instance of the Xtra. The new command in the first line creates this instance, and a pointer to it is placed in the variable *fileObj*. You can think of *fileObj* as the me in a behavior. It is now needed to refer to this instance of FileIO.

An instance of FileIO is capable of opening, creating, writing, reading, and deleting files. In the preceding example, the object is used to open a file with the openFile command, read the contents of the file with the readFile command, and then close the file with the closeFile command. The 1 at the end of the openFile command signifies that the file is being opened for reading. A 2 would mean that it is opened for writing.

READING FILES

To read text files with the FileIO Xtra, you can use several different commands. The most basic is to use the readFile command to read the entire contents of a text file into a variable. The previous example did just that. You can see all the commands later in this chapter.

You can also read the file a portion at a time with the readChar, readWord, and readLine functions. When you use these, the file object keeps track of the current position in the file. For instance, if you use readLine to get the first line of a file, the current position will be the first character of line 2. You can then use readLine to get line 2, or readChar or readWord to get a smaller portion.

At any time, you can use readFile to get the rest of the current file.

Here is a piece of code that reads a file, one line at a time, until it finds a line with the text "record213" in it:

```
fileObj = new(xtra "FileIO")
fileObj.openFile("myfile.txt", 1)
repeat while TRUE
 text = fileObj.readLine()
 if text contains "record213" then
  put "Record Found:"&&text
  exit repeat
 end if
end repeat
fileObj.closeFile()
```

Notice that the `openFile` command used 1 to signify that the file will be open only for reading. The file needs to be in the same folder as the executable because we have not specified a path, just the name of the file.

To find the current position at any time, you can use the `getPosition` function. You can also set the position with the `setPosition` function.

The previous example will repeat endlessly until it finds that line. However, if the line isn't there, we have trouble. You can avoid this by using `getPosition` and comparing it with the `getLength` value. This tells you the total length of the file.

```
if fileObj.getPosition() >= fileObj.getLength() then
 put "Not found!"
 exit repeat
end if
```

➡ *If you need to read non-text files, see "Reading and Writing Binary Files" in the "Troubleshooting" section at the end of this chapter.*

WRITING FILES

Writing files works similarly to reading files. You can write a whole string out to the currently opened file with `writeString`. You can also write a single character with `writeChar`.

You can continue to write strings and characters out to a file until you are done. However, there are a few common problems with writing out files.

First, there is no direct way to append to a file. You just have to open it for writing, use `getLength` and `setPosition` to jump to the end of the file, and then start writing there.

If you don't want to append to an existing file, but instead replace that file, you will need to delete it first. If you create a file, open it, and write to it, any existing file by that name will remain in place and simply be written over. This could be a problem if the old file was longer than the new one. You'll end up with the last part of the old file stuck to the end of the new one.

So the proper way to create a new file is to first use `openFile` to open the old file, if any. Then use `delete` to delete the file. Then you can use `createFile` to make the new file and `openFile` again to open it. This example makes sure that a new file is written, without any leftovers from an old file.

```
fileObj = new(xtra "FileIO")fileObj.openFile("myfile.txt",2)
fileObj.delete()
fileObj.createFile("myfile.txt")
fileObj.openFile("myfile.txt",2)
fileObj.writeString(mytext)
fileObj.closeFile()
```

CHOOSING FILES

So far, the examples in this chapter have only used hard-coded filenames. But typically, you'll want to prompt the user for a filename both for reading and writing files.

21

The FileIO Xtra has several commands to help handle this. To select a file for reading, you can use the `displayOpen` command. This returns the name of the file. Here is a typical set of commands that allow the user to select a file and then the contents are read into a variable:

```
fileObj = new("FileIO Xtra")
filename = fileObj.displayOpen()
fileObj.openFile(filename,1)
mytext = fileObj.readFile()
fileObj.close()
```

The file open dialog that is displayed is a standard system dialog for both Mac and Windows platforms. You can force this dialog to allow only certain types of files to be opened by using the `setFilterMask` command. This works differently for Mac and Windows. For Mac, you would enter a string of four-letter file types. This example only allows text and jpeg files to be selected.

```
fileObj.setFilterMask("TEXTJPEG")
```

For Windows, you need to pass this function a list of file types. They need to be in pairs, with the first item being a description and the second item being the wildcard file designator. It makes sense when you look at this example that allows `.txt` and `.csv` files to be selected:

```
fileObj.setFilterMask("Text Files,*.txt,Database Files,*.csv")
```

If you want to prompt the user for a filename to save some data, you will need to use the `displaySave` function. This takes two parameters: a text message to put into the dialog box and a default filename.

```
filename = fileObj.displaySave("Save Database To","mydata.txt")
```

The next section takes a look at a complete file read and write solution.

FILEIO UTILITY HANDLERS

Reading and writing files take many lines of code. However, a handler that does this can be reused many times. Here is a handler that prompts users for a text file to read and then returns that text file's contents:

```
on openAndReadText
 -- create the FileIO instance
 fileObj = new(xtra "FileIO")

 -- set the filter mask to text files
 if the platform contains "mac" then
  fileObj.setFilterMask("TEXT")
 else
  fileObj.setFilterMask("Text Files,*.txt,All Files,*.*")
 end if

 -- open dialog box
 filename = fileObj.displayOpen()
```

```
-- check to see if cancel was hit
if filename = "" then return ""

-- open the file
fileObj.openFile(filename,1)

-- check to see if file opened ok
if fileObj.status() <> 0 then
 err = fileObj.error(fileObj.status())
 alert "Error:"&&err
 return ""
end if

-- read the file
text = fileObj.readFile()

-- close the file
fileObj.closeFile()

--return the text
 return text
end
```

If you want to use this handler to read a file that you already know the name of, just pass in the "filename" variable as a new parameter to the handler, and remove the references to the setFilterMask and displayOpen commands. Then take the new parameter and use that as the filename instead.

The opposite of this handler is one that saves any text to a file. This handler takes care of it all, down to setting the file type of the new file to a SimpleText file for the Mac. The text placed in the file is passed in as a parameter.

Oddly, when writing out a new file, you must first open the file and then use the delete command to delete it. Then, you can use createFile and openFile to create and write a new file. If you do not do this, the new file overwrites any file of the same name that already exists, and there might be some parts of the old file left in the new one.

```
on saveText text
 -- create the FileIO instance
 fileObj = new(xtra "FileIO")

 -- set the filter mask to text files
 if the platform contains "mac" then
  fileObj.setFilterMask("TEXT")
 else
  fileObj.setFilterMask("Text Files,*.txt,All Files,*.*")
 end if

 -- save dialog box
 filename = fileObj.displaySave("","")

 -- check to see if cancel was hit
 if filename = "" then return FALSE
```

```
-- delete existing file, if any
fileObj.openFile(filename,2)
fileObj.delete()

-- create and open the file
fileObj.createFile(filename)
fileObj.openFile(filename,2)

-- check to see if file opened ok
if fileObj.status() <> 0 then
 err = fileObj.error(fileObj.status())
 alert "Error:"&&err
 return FALSE
end if

-- write the file
fileObj.writeString(text)

-- set the file type
if the platform contains "Mac" then
 fileObj.setFinderInfo("TEXT ttxt")
end if

-- close the file
fileObj.closeFile()
 return TRUE
end
```

These functions can be found in the sample movie `fileio.dir` on the CD-ROM.

FILEIO COMMANDS

Table 21.1 is a complete list of commands used with the FileIO Xtra.

Table 21.1   FileIo Command List

Command	Description
new	Creates a new instance of the Xtra.
filename	Returns the name of the file currently being controlled by this instance of the Xtra.
status	Returns the error code of the last command used on the Xtra. A 0 means that there was no error.
error	Takes the object and an integer as parameters. It returns a string with the description of the error number passed in as the integer.

Table 21.1   Continued

Command	Description
setFilterMask	Takes the object and a string as parameters. The string defines the type of files to be shown in the Open and Save dialog boxes. On the Mac, pass a string that contains one or more four-letter file types, such as "TEXT" or "JPEGGIFF". In Windows, the string should be a comma-delimited list alternating file descriptions and types, such as "Text Files,*.txt,GIF Files,#.gif".
openFile	Opens the file for reading, writing, or both. You need to call this function before performing most other file functions. It takes an additional parameter, which should be a 1 to read, a 2 to write, or a 0 for both.
closeFile	Closes the file associated with the file object. You must call this when you are finished with the file.
displayOpen	Displays a Mac or Windows Open dialog box and enables users to browse and select a file. It returns that file path.
displaySave	Displays a Mac or Windows Save dialog box and enables users to browse and select the destination of that file. It returns that file path.
createFile	Give this command the object and a string that represents the filename or full path of the file. You must call this before openFile in cases where the file does not yet exist.
setPosition	Takes an integer as an extra parameter. It sets the position in the file where the next read will take place.
getPosition	Returns the current reading position in the file.
getLength	Returns the length of the currently opened file.
writeChar	Writes a single character to the file.
writeString	Writes a complete string into the file.
readChar	Reads a single character from the file.
readLine	Reads from the current position in the file to the next return character. It includes the return character in the returned value.
readFile	Reads from the current position in the file until the end.
readWord	Reads from the current position in the file until the next space or nonvisible character.
readToken	Takes three parameters: the object, a skip character, and a break character. It reads from the current position in the file until the break character, and it skips the skip characters whenever it encounters them.
getFinderInfo	Gets the file type and creator of the currently opened file. It returns it as a nine-character string with a space between the file type and creator. For example: "TEXT ttxt". Mac-only function.
setFinderInfo	Enables you to set the file type and creator of the currently open file. You must use a nine-character string, such as "TEXT ttxt". Mac-only command.
delete	Removes the currently opened file.
version	Returns the version of the Xtra. Use it in this manner: *put version(xtra "FileIO")*.

21

Table 21.1   Continued

Command	Description
getOSDirectory	Part of the Xtra, but does not require a reference to it. Use it in this manner: `put getOSDirectory()`. It returns the path to the Mac system folder or the Windows directory.
setNewlineConversion	This Mac-only function, when passed a TRUE, will set the FileIO instance so that Windows newline/return characters will be converted automatically to normal returns.

FILE-RELATED LINGO PROPERTIES

Several other Lingo commands can help you build handlers that deal with files. These commands don't require the FileIO Xtra, with the exception of the first one: `getOSDirectory()`.

getOSDirectory()

The `getOSDirectory()` command returns the path to the operating system folder. Typically on Windows it will be `C:\windows\`, but it doesn't necessarily need to be that. Using `getOSDirectory()` will make sure that you get the right place.

For Mac systems, it is even more useful. Most Mac computers have a user-specified name for the hard drisk drive. So one user may have a `My Computer:System:` folder, and another might be `TiBook:System:`. So `getOSDirectory()` would be a great way to figure out the drive name for a Mac.

Movie and Application Paths

You can also determine the path to the current movie with `the moviePath`. Similarly, you can determine just the name of the movie with `the movieName`.

In many cases, the movie will be running in a different directory from the application. In the case of a movie, the application can either be Director itself, or the projector. To determine this path, use `the applicationPath`. To get just the name, use `the applicationName`.

Table 21.2 is a summary of all the file-related Lingo.

Table 21.2   File-Related Lingo

Property	Description
the movieName	The filename for the current movie
the moviePath	The full path of the current movie
the movie	Obsolete syntax for `the movieName`
the pathname	Obsolete syntax for `the moviePath`
the applicationName	The filename for the projector
the applicationPath	The full path of the projector
the filename	Returns the full path of a linked member, castLib or MIAW.
the searchPaths	This is a list of paths used by Director to search for linked media.

21

Files in Folder

An interesting function in your Lingo arsenal is `getNthFileNameinFolder`. This function dates back to the early days of Lingo and stands out as a useful function that exists outside the FileIO Xtra.

`getNthFileNameinFolder` returns the name of any file or folder in a directory. For instance, to find the name of the first file in a movie's current path, you can do this:

```
filename = getNthFileNameinFolder(the moviePath, 1)
```

To get a list of all the files in the folder, you can create a loop that starts with file 1 and continues until no file name is returned.

```
fileList = []
fileNum = 1
repeat while TRUE
  fileName = getNthFileNameinFolder(the moviePath, fileNum)
  if fileName = "" then exit repeat
  add fileList, fileName
  fileNum = fileNum + 1
end repeat
```

The list returned includes files that may normally be invisible to the user, as well as folder names.

> **Caution**
>
> The `getNthFileNameinFolder` function usually ceases to work after the 255th file. You may want to test your handler thoroughly for this case if you expect there to be a lot of files in the folder you are searching.

Determining the Path Delimiter

A common problem for CD-ROM developers is the difference between the path delimiter on Macs and Windows machines. On the Mac, the delimiter is a colon (":"), whereas on Windows, it is a backslash ("\").

If you need to determine the path to an external file, or prompt the user to open or save a file with the FileIO Xtra, you might need to construct a path based on the path delimiter.

For instance, you might want to link to a file named `myimage.png` in the subdirectory `media` under the current folder. The property `the moviePath` gets you to the current directory, and you can append `media` to that to get to the `media` directory, but then you'll need a path delimiter after that to get to the file.

One way to get the path delimiter is to simply look at the last character of `the moviePath`:

```
pathDel = (the moviePath).char[(the moviePath).length]
```

After you have that, you can construct a path to the file that will work on both platforms:

```
filePath = (the moviePath)&"media"&pathDel&"myimage.png"
```

Using Network Preference Files as an Alternative

Two file-oriented functions can be used to read and write files that are not part of the FileIO Xtra. These functions, `getPref` and `setPref`, are meant to be used with Shockwave movies, but also work with projectors.

➡️ *If you need to write files from Shockwave, see "Writing Files from Shockwave" in the "Troubleshooting" section at the end of this chapter.*

The `setPref` command writes out a little text file to a `Prefs` directory. You can specify only the filename and the text to be written.

```
setPref("myfile.txt", mytext)
```

The file will be written to a `Prefs` folder in the same folder as the projector. If you are running the movie in Director, the file will be created in a `Prefs` folder in the Director application folder. If the movie is running as Shockwave, the file is created in the `Prefs` folder in the Shockwave plug-in folder, usually in the System folder somewhere. In any of those cases, the `Prefs` folder is automatically created if it does not exist.

➡️ *If you can't get setPref to work, see "Using setPref to Write Files" in the "Troubleshooting" section at the end of this chapter.*

You can read the text back from the file with the `getPref` function.

```
mytext = getPref("myfile.txt")
```

Because neither you nor the user can specify the location of the file, these functions are not good ones to use for saving files that the user will want to access outside your movie. But they are excellent for saving data to be reused by the same movie.

For instance, if you are making educational software, you can ask the child's name when she firsts start. You can then use `setPref` to store this name and `getPref` to get it each time the program is run. This way, the software seems to remember the child.

You can also use `getPref` to quickly access external text information. Just place small text files, such as instructions to a game or licensing information for software, into the `Prefs` folder in the projector's folder. Then use `getPref` to get the text so that it can be displayed in the movie. This way, the data can be edited directly in the text file instead of using Director to edit the movie.

TROUBLESHOOTING

Writing Files from Shockwave

Is there any way for me to use FileIO in Shockwave? If not, what other options are there?

Remember that the FileIO Xtra does not work with Shockwave. This would present a security risk. For small temporary files, you can use `getPref` and `setPref`. However, the correct way to save data from Shockwave is to call the server with `postNetText` and use a server-side database. This is much more difficult, but necessary for Shockwave to be safe.

Reading and Writing Binary Files

Can I use the FileIO Xtra to read other types of files besides text files?

The FileIO Xtra is only meant to be used for text files. Binary files, which are used to store images and other complex data, can't be read or written with the FileIO Xtra. However, third party Xtras can do this.

Using `setPref` to Write Files

I'm trying to use `setPref` to write simple files, but it is not working. Is there something I am missing?

Check the filename you are using. The `setPref` command can only write files that end with a `.txt` extension. Also, if you are using `setPref` from Director, note that the file will appear in a `Prefs` folder in the Director application folder, not in the folder that contains the movie.

DID YOU KNOW?

- Use `put interface(xtra "FileIO")` in the Message panel to get a list of all the FileIO commands and functions. The same function works with most Xtras.

- If you import a text file created in Windows, you might see extra block characters at the start of each line. These are newline characters. Director and most modern word processors do not use them. To get rid of them, write a repeat look that checks each character against `numToChar(10)` and deletes it if it matches. Or, you can use the `offset` function in a repeat look to quickly hunt down and remove them. You can also try to use `setNewlineConversion`.

- Using `getPref` and `setPref` is a great way to pass data between movies in Shockwave. For instance, one movie can ask the user for her name and then store it with `setPref`. Then another movie on your site can access this data with `getPref`.

- If you have XML files, you can read them with the FileIO Xtra and then parse them with the XML Parser Xtra or the Flash Xtra.

22

PROGRAMMING NETWORK
COMMUNICATION

IN THIS CHAPTER

22

CONTROLLING THE WEB BROWSER WITH LINGO

Macromedia Director movies can communicate with files on Internet servers in a similar way that Web browsers do. You can request text documents, send small or large pieces of information, or even command the user's default browser to go to Web pages.

The primary command for forcing the Web browser to go to another Web page is `gotoNetPage`:

```
gotoNetPage("http://garyrosenzweig.com/books/")
```

If the movie is being run in Shockwave, you can use a relative location instead of one starting with `http://`. For instance, if the movie is at `http://clevermedia.com`, these two commands are identical:

```
gotoNetPage("http://clevermedia.com/resources/")
gotoNetPage("resources/")
```

You can also use relative targeting in a projector to get the browser to open an HTML page in the projector's folder or a subfolder.

If you are running the movie as Shockwave in a browser, you can also use a target frame or window with `gotoNetPage`. Web developers are familiar with how to use targets. Basically, every browser window, and every frame inside a window, has a name. A target tag modifier can specify which of these targets should receive the `gotoNetPage` signal.

If you have developed your own set of windows or frames with HTML, you already know the names of these targets. However, a few target names, such as `_blank` and `_top`, are reserved for special purposes. Table 22.1 shows their usage.

Table 22.1   Reserved HTTP Target Names

Name	Action
`_blank`	Creates a new, blank window without a name.
`_self`	The new page loads in the current frame. This works even if the HTML pages use the BASE structure.
`_parent`	Loads the new page one level up in the frame set, replacing the current frame and all its siblings.
`_top`	Loads in the current window, replacing all frames there.

The following are examples of `gotoNetPage` commands that use a target:

```
gotoNetPage("mypage.html","_blank")
gotoNetPage("http://clevermedia.com","_top")
gotoNetPage("http://clevermedia.com","mainframe")
```

If you are planning to use the `gotoNetPage` command in a projector, you might want to have more control over which browser is launched. Director uses the browser specified in

As with any HTML, you should test targets in all browsers that you plan to support. Many browsers, especially the Mac version of Internet Explorer, will behave differently, even for simple HTML-like commands such as `gotoNetPage` with a target specified.

the network preferences, or the system's default browser if none is specified. You can check the path of the browser with the `browserName()` function:

```
put browserName()
-- "Macintosh HD:Netscape Communicator Folder:Netscape Communicator"
```

You can also set this path with the `browserName` command:

```
browserName "Macintosh HD:Other Browser"
```

If, for some reason, you want to disable the projector's capability to launch a browser, use the `browserName` command with this odd syntax:

```
browserName(#enabled, FALSE)
```

Use a TRUE in place of the FALSE to enable browser launching.

> You can let users select the browser application if you use the `displayOpen` function of the FileIO Xtra and then use the `browserName` command with the results.

In addition to telling the browser which page to display, you can replace the current Shockwave movie with a new one. The `gotoNetMovie` command is the network equivalent to `go to movie`. It loads a new movie from the network and replaces the current one directly in the page:

```
gotoNetMovie("newmovie.dcr")
gotoNetMovie("http://clevermedia.com/newmovie.dcr")
```

You can use both relative and absolute pathnames, as you can see. You can even specify a frame in the new movie to jump to. Just place a "#" after the filename and then the name of the frame label:

> If you want to determine whether the user has a connection to the Internet before using a `gotoNetPage` in a projector, you can access the `#internetConnected` property of the environment. If the user is connected, its value is `#online`. Otherwise, you may want to pop an alert box to tell them to log on before continuing.

```
gotoNetMovie("newmovie.dcr#intro")
```

When the `gotoNetMovie` command is used, the current movie continues to play until the new movie has been loaded. If you issue another `gotoNetMovie` command, it cancels the first command and replaces the current movie.

GETTING TEXT OVER THE INTERNET

Network Lingo enables you to get many forms of media over the Internet or an intranet. For bitmaps, getting an external image is as easy as specifying its location. Getting text, however, is a little more complex.

You might get text from another file on the Internet to store textual data in an external file so that non-Director users in your company can update this data. This technique would work with the numbers that make up a chart, for example. You might also import text data from another source, such as a weather report or a small text database.

The primary command for getting text over the Internet is `getNetText`. But this command cannot stand alone. It simply initiates the call to the network. You have to use a series of commands and functions to perform the whole operation.

After `getNetText` is issued, a `netDone` function tells you when the text has been received. Then, you use `netTextResult` to get the text and store it in a variable or member.

However, you can't use `getNetText` and then simply lock the movie in a repeat loop until `netDone` returns TRUE. A repeat loop monopolizes the computer and limits its capability to actually get the text. The computer will be so busy running the repeat loop that it will never have the time to do the network functions.

The proper way to get text is to issue the `getNetText` call and then let the movie run. The movie can even loop on a frame to appear paused. Remember, looping on a frame is completely different from using a repeat loop inside a handler. While looping, the movie enables the network functions to complete and the text to be received.

The following example is in two frames. Each frame has an `on exitFrame` script placed in the Frame Script channel. The first frame initiates the network call:

```
on exitFrame
 global gNetID
 gNetID = getNetText("http://clevermedia.com")
end
```

As you can see, `getNetText` is actually a function. It returns a number that corresponds to the network identification number for this network function. Because Director can perform more than one network function—such as `getNetText`—at a time, these ID numbers are needed to refer to them in the future. This number is likely to be 1 in this case, unless you have already performed a network function.

The next frame contains code that checks to see whether the network function corresponding to the variable *gNetID* is complete. If so, it gets the text and then moves on. If not, it keeps looping on the frame:

```
on exitFrame
 global gNetID

 -- check to see if text has arrived
 if netDone(gNetID) then

  -- it has, so get it
  text = netTextResult(gNetID)
  put text

  -- move the movie forward
  go to the frame + 1
 else

  -- text is not here yet, keep looping
  go to the frame
 end if
end
```

It might also be a good idea to make sure that the system did not experience any problems in getting the text. You can use the `netError` function immediately after confirming that the operation has been completed with `netDone`. For instance, you can add this code:

```
if netError(gNetID) <> 0 then
  alert "An error occurred trying to get the text."
  halt
end if
```

A 0, obviously, means there is no error. However, any other number means there is a problem. Table 22.2 shows all the possible errors.

Table 22.2 The `netError` Codes

Code	Meaning
0	Operation completed successfully.
4	The required network Xtras are not installed.
5	Bad MOA Interface. Probably same as 4.
6	Bad location. Or, could be same as 4.
20	Browser detected an error.
4146	Connection could not be established with the remote host.
4149	Data supplied by the server was in an unexpected format.
4150	Unexpected early closing of connection.
4154	Operation could not be completed due to timeout.
4155	Not enough memory available to complete the transaction.
4156	Protocol reply to request indicates an error in the reply.
4157	Transaction failed to be authenticated.
4159	Invalid URL.
4164	Could not create a socket.
4165	Requested object could not be found.
4166	Generic proxy failure.
4167	Transfer was intentionally interrupted by client.
4242	Download stopped by a `netAbort` command.
4836	Download stopped for an unknown reason, possibly a network error, or the download was abandoned.

➡ *If you get a security alert when using getNetText, see "Security Alert Appears When Using getNetText" in the "Troubleshooting" section at the end of this chapter.*

SENDING TEXT

Since the introduction of Shockwave in 1995, movies have been able to send text over the Internet. However, until Director 7, there were no commands to do this in Director. Instead, a trick was used to send information to server CGI scripts using `getNetText`. This trick is still a great way to communicate with the server. Director MX also includes the `postNetText` command, which enables the movie to post information to a server in the same manner as an HTML page form.

Using `getNetText` to Send Text

It seems confusing, but you can send text by getting text. The `getNetText` command is used to get text information from a server. However, in doing so, you can give information to the server. It is similar to the way that Lingo functions work. A function returns information, but it can also accept information as a parameter.

The following is a typical `getNetText` call asking for an HTML page on a Web server:

```
getNetText("http://clevermedia.com/test.txt")
```

You can also use `getNetText` to call a CGI program. A CGI program is a small computer program, usually written in a language called Perl, which resides on the server. The output of a Perl program is usually text, such as an HTML page:

```
getNetText("http://clevermedia.com/cgibin/echo.cgi")
```

In this case, the CGI program returns text, just as the call to "test.txt" did previously. Neither the browser nor Director cares that the server had to run a program rather than just serve up a text file.

CGI programs can do much more than just serve up static text. They can actually take some data and then use it. For instance, they can store data in a file on the server. Information can be given to a CGI program by simply placing a "?" after the Web location, followed by text:

```
getNetText("http://clevermedia.com/cgibin/echo.cgi?gary")
```

In this case, the information "gary" was sent to the server. The Perl program on the other end just needs to look for it, get it, and then do something with it. The following Perl program sits on the server:

```perl
#!/usr/bin/perl
$invar = $ENV{'QUERY_STRING'};
print "Content-type: text/html\n\n";
print "Input: $invar <BR>\n";
```

Although it is beyond the scope of this book to go into Perl, which has many books of its own, this script works like this:

1. The first line tells the server that this is a Perl program, so when it is called, the server knows to run Perl and use this file as the source code.

2. The second line gets the data from after the question mark in the server call. In this case, that information is "gary".

3. The third line starts the output. It places the line "Content-type: text/html" plus two newline characters into the output stream. This is needed to tell the server and the Web browser what type of output is coming. This line and the extra newline character never appear in the text you get back. However, everything after the newline character does.

4. The last line outputs the word "Input:" followed by the text. So, the result is an echo of what was sent. It is a good test and shows that the server can get information as well as send it. In this case, the server got "gary," processed it, and sent it back. It could also have opened a file and stored the information. It could have even opened another file, such as a database, and used this information to look up other information.

Usually, when you call a CGI program on a server, you want to send a specific piece of information to the server. You can easily construct a URL that reflects this piece of information. For instance, if your CGI script is at `http://clevermedia.com/cgibin/submit.cgi` and you want to send the contents of variable *myVariable* to the script, you do something like this:

```
submitText = "http://clevermedia.com/cgibin/submit.cgi?"&myVariable
getNetText(submitText)
```

As explained earlier in the chapter, after the call to `getNetText`, you need to make periodic checks to `netDone` to see whether the operation was successful. Note that the GET method of sending information has a length limit. It should be roughly 4,000 characters, but this limit is imposed by the browser when the movie is running in Shockwave. So, if the browser has a limit of 250 characters, Shockwave cannot send a longer string. In addition, a 250-character limit on `getNetText` string lengths was a bug that plagued earlier versions of Shockwave and could easily be a problem again in the future.

⇨ *If you can't get Perl scripts to work, see "Getting CGI Scripts to Work" in the "Troubleshooting" section at the end of this chapter.*

Using `postNetText` to Send Text

The `postNetText` command enables you to perform the same function as an HTML form with METHOD=POST. The main advantage of using this command is that it can send much more information than the `getNetText` method, which is limited to about 4,000 characters in most situations. The information also arrives in a different format than the `getNetText` method, which many CGI programmers prefer.

The two required arguments of a `postNetText` command are the location of the CGI script and the data. The data, in this case, is a list. Here is an example:

```
postNetText("http://clevermedia.com/echopost.cgi", ["name": "Gary", "ID": 1])
```

The list should be a property list. Each property corresponds to the name of an item, whereas each value is the value of the item. All properties should be strings, but Director translates them to strings if they are not.

After a `postNetText` call, the same process as used for the `getNetText` function has to be followed. You must use the function's return value as an ID number, check `netDone`, and then use `netTextResult` to get the returned text.

Getting `postNetText` to work in Lingo is the easy part. Getting a CGI program that receives and deals with the data is a little more difficult. Hopefully, if you do not know about server programming, you will have the opportunity to work with someone who does. Otherwise, a good book on Perl or maybe some Web research into the subject will help.

Even if no text is meant to be returned, or you don't need the text, you should go through the steps of using `netDone` and `netTextResult`. Otherwise, the call to the server is never ended, and you can have only so many open-ended calls before network calls stop working.

DOWNLOADING FILES

Two network Lingo commands allow you to download files. The first is `preloadNetThing`. This doesn't allow you to download a file to just anywhere. It takes the file and requests it through the browser. The result is that it is placed in the user's browser cache.

The reason you would want to do this would be to speed up the transition from one Director movie to another. For instance, you can `preloadNetThing` the next Director movie, wait until `netDone`, and then use `gotoNetMovie` to jump to the movie.

Had you not used `preloadNetThing` first, the `gotoNetMovie` command would have not had an immediate effect. Instead, it would have started the download of the new movie but not actually gone to that movie until the download was complete.

The same technique can also be used for external cast libraries and other external media. As a matter of fact, you must use `preloadNetThing` for external image and sound files before assigning them to cast members by changing their `filename` property.

So if you wanted to replace an externally linked image member with a new one, the procedure would be to first use `preloadNetThing`, wait for `netDone` on that operation, and then assign the `filename` property of the image member to the new image.

The `downloadNetThing` command is more powerful. It allows you to download any object from the Internet into a specific location of the user's hard drive. Because this is a security risk at many levels, it is not available in Shockwave. It is, however, available to projectors.

For instance, if you want to give the user the opportunity to download a PDF file to her drive, you could write a button script to do this:

```
on mouseUp
 downloadNetThing("http://www.mysite.com/mydoc.pdf","c:\mydoc.pdf")
end
```

A more versatile script would use FileIO to prompt the user for a location first.

22

TROUBLESHOOTING

Security Alert Appears When Using `getNetText`

What causes the security alert that I get when I use the `getNetText` command?

When a movie attempts to get text from a different server with `getNetText`, a security alert appears. To avoid this alert, place both text and the movie on the same server and use a relative pathname. It is considered a security violation to have a movie on one site pass information to a location on another site.

Getting CGI Scripts to Work

I'm not a Perl programmer, but I thought I could use some simple Perl scripts in my movie. No matter what, I can't get them to work. How can I be sure they work before I upload my movie to my Web site?

Using Perl scripts can be frustrating if you have never used them before. You can test your Perl scripts by typing the CGI calls in your browser. Do this to confirm that they work before trying to use Shockwave movies to call them. Confirm with your Internet service provider that you can use Perl scripts and what you need to do to get them to work with your site. Another option would be to enlist the help of a friend who knows how to write server-side scripts.

DID YOU KNOW?

- You can use a second parameter with `getNetText` to specify a different server character set: "JIS" or "EUC." The default for this parameter is "ASCII," and the setting "AUTO" attempts to automatically determine the server character set.

- The `netMIME` function can be used to determine the file's MIME type after the `netDone` command returns TRUE.

- The function `netLastModDate` can be used to determine the server's time stamp for the file after the `netDone` returns TRUE.

- You can use network Lingo over HTTPS (secure servers).

23

ADDING MULTIUSER COMMUNICATION

IN THIS CHAPTER

SHOCKWAVE MULTIUSER SERVER

The Shockwave Multiuser Server version 3.0 is a program that enables you to connect your users to one another over the Internet. For Macromedia Director, Shockwave, and projectors, a Multiuser Xtra provides this connectivity. The server itself is a compact program that runs on a Mac or Windows machine with a dedicated Internet connection.

To get the Shockwave Multiuser Server, look in the Goodies folder of the Director MX CD-ROM. There is no Mac OS X version, but there is a Mac OS 9 version.

The Multiuser Server can be used to send information to and from users, connect users with chat-room and whiteboard applications, and even make multiplayer games.

This chapter serves as an introduction to and an overview of the capabilities of the Multiuser Server and Xtra. There are also some examples of the server and Xtra at work. To write a complete reference would almost require another book. Macromedia's own documentation takes up quite a bit of space. With this chapter as a starting point and the official documentation as a reference guide, you should be able to use the Multiuser Server and Xtra to create a variety of applications.

SETTING UP THE MULTIUSER SERVER

The Multiuser Server is a program, just like Macromedia Director. When you install the Multiuser Server, it is installed in a folder called Shockwave Multiuser Server 3.0. That folder contains a lot of files that support the server, as well as the application itself.

Running the Multiuser Server

To set up the server, all you need to do is run the program. First, make sure that the computer you are running it on is connected to the Internet. For a deployed product, that computer should have a permanent static IP address, but a temporary IP address is fine for testing.

Figure 23.1 shows what the server program window looks like after you launch it. In addition, the figure includes the output obtained by choosing Status, Server from the menu.

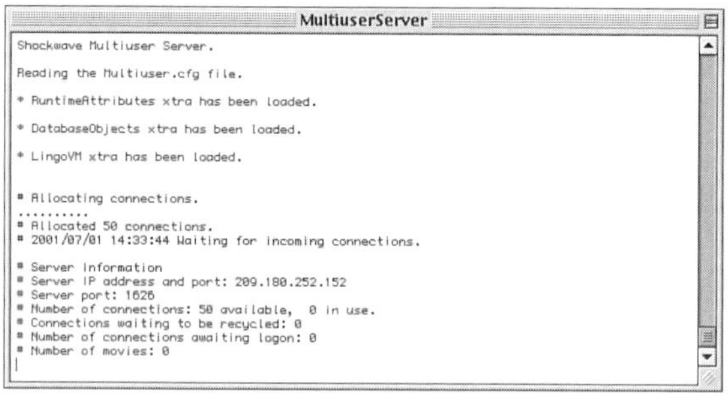

Figure 23.1
The Multiuser Server window after it has been launched and server information has been requested.

The Multiuser Server application is simply a window that displays messages concerning the server. By choosing Status, Server, you can see the computer's IP address and the port that the server is using. You need this information to build multiuser movies.

Configuring the Server

There are many options that you can set to change the way your server works. These can all be found in the `Multiuser.cfg` file in the same folder as the application.

The `Multiuser.cfg` file is well commented, and most settings are described in detail, along with how to change them. One of the first changes you can make in the file concerns `ServerOwnerName` and `ServerSerialNumber`. If you enter your Director serial number, you can go beyond the 50-connection limit of the server, all the way up to 2,000 connections. The actual number of connections can be set using the `ConnectionLimit` parameter, found further down in the file.

The next setting is the port number. A *port* is an addressing technique used by your computer to determine which incoming data goes where. The default port is 1626, which means that any information coming into your computer on port 1626 is routed to the Multiuser Server.

Another useful setting is `IdleTimeOut`. This is set to the default of 600, which is 10 minutes. This means that if a Shockwave movie has not tried to contact the server in 10 minutes, the connection is dropped. This can be a problem if you plan on having long delays between communications, such as you might have in a chess game.

Most of the other settings pertain to user levels. These settings specify which commands a movie can or cannot use on the server. For instance, if a user has a level of 20, but a level of 40 is required to create a record in the database, messages sent to the server that ask it to create a new record are refused.

User levels are a great security feature, but they complicate things for developers who just want to build basic multiuser applications. I don't deal with user levels much in this chapter, but the server documentation contains all the details needed by advanced developers.

If your computer is properly configured, you can set up the server to run on multiple ports. This is called *multihoming*. See your computer's documentation for how to set it up.

You can also set many properties of the server on a movie level, rather than on the server level. This means that as different movies use the same server, they can have different settings. Check the `Movie.cfg` file for an example. You can duplicate this file and rename it to create unique settings for different movies.

It is a good idea to do only the bare minimum changes to the `Multiuser.cfg` file and use multiple `movie.cfg` files to customize the settings for each different movie that connects to the server. To do this, name each customized `movie.cfg` file the same as the movie that will be connecting to the server. Then, the correct `.cfg` file will be read, and, in effect, a custom server will be set up for the movie.

USING THE MULTIUSER BEHAVIORS

After your server is up and running, creating a basic multiuser application takes very little effort. This is because Macromedia has included a set of multiuser behaviors in the behaviors library.

Taking these behaviors and building a simple chat room is easy. It took me less than 10 minutes, and I didn't have to use any Lingo at all.

The first screen simply needs a button and a text member. The text member should be editable and indicate to users that this is where they should enter the name they want to use in the chat room. Figure 23.2 shows what this screen might look like.

Figure 23.2
The sign-in screen for a simple chat room.

After the text member and the button are ready, choose Window, Library Palette, and select the Multiuser subcategory of the Internet category. Drag and drop the Connect to Server behavior onto the button. I used a simple Director pushbutton for the sample movie on the CD-ROM (see librarychat.dir), but you can use a nice bitmap instead.

After you drop the behavior onto the button, a Parameters dialog box appears (see Figure 23.3). It contains most of the information that your server needs to create and maintain the chat room.

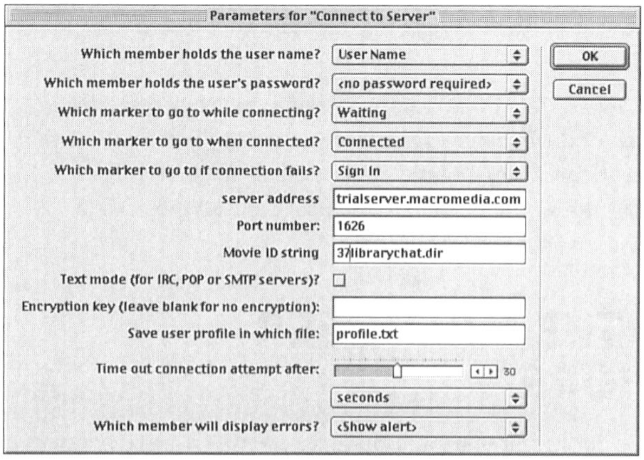

Figure 23.3
The Connect to Server behavior offers many customizable features in its Parameters dialog box.

First, you must specify the name of the text member that is on the Stage. This is where the server gets the user's name. You can also create another text member and have the user type in a password.

Next, you should specify three frames: a wait frame, a frame that the movie goes to when the connection is in place, and a frame to go to if the connection fails. To keep this simple, I have the movie return to the sign-in frame when the connection fails.

To set these three frames, you might want to cancel the behavior Parameters dialog box and place "Sign In," "Connected," and "Waiting" frame labels in the Score. Then, drag and drop the Connect to Server behavior onto the button again to set these parameters more easily.

The Server Address and Port Number parameters should reflect the numbers that you see when you set up the server. Refer to Figure 23.1 to see where these are.

The Movie ID String is simply an identifier for the server. You can use a Multiuser Server to service more than one application. The server uses the movie ID to tell the applications apart. All the people using this chat movie will be connecting to the server with the same movie ID. If something else, such as a game, is using the same server, it should have a different movie ID.

The rest of the parameters can be left as defaults.

The next step in creating the chat room is to place a "please wait" message on the Waiting frame. You need simple `go to the frame` handlers in each frame script for the Sign In, Waiting, and Connected frames. You can use the Go Loop standard behavior if you want to avoid Lingo entirely.

The main frame for the chat room is the chat frame. You can see this frame in Figure 23.4. It contains a title, a chat output text member, a chat input text member, a text member that displays the members in the chat room, a Disconnect button, and a small whiteboard bitmap.

Figure 23.4
The Connected frame is where all the action takes place in the chat room movie.

Most of the elements in the chat room have an associated behavior that makes each element work. For instance, the chat input text member, at the bottom left, needs to have the Chat Input behavior dropped on it. There is also a Chat Output behavior, a Display Group Members behavior, and a Disconnect from Server behavior. To make the whiteboard work, you need to first drop the Canvas behavior, found in the Paintbox behaviors category onto a bitmap sprite. Then, you can drop the Whiteboard (Shared Canvas) behavior on it.

Many of these behaviors have short Parameter dialog boxes that appear when you drop them on the sprites. In all cases, the default settings in those dialog boxes will work just fine to get your chat room up and running.

Caution

This is a bug in the Chat Input behavior that comes with Director that you must fix to get this to work. In the handler on `init`, the following two lines must be switched so that they are in this order:

```
pCurrentGroupID = groupID
me.setMessageSubjects(groupID)
```

After the movie is complete, you can simply rewind and run your movie to see it in action. You need the server to be running on another computer for it to work, of course.

The chat area functions as you might expect. You just type in the input area and press (Return) [Enter]. The text appears in the output area.

For the whiteboard, just click and draw. If you want to create a more complex whiteboard, check out the other behaviors in the Paintbox category. These behaviors enable you to set brushes and colors as well as erase the canvas.

The only loose end is the Disconnect button. It successfully disconnects users from the server, but it does not jump to another frame. The users are left staring at a dead chat-room screen. You have to attach another button behavior to the button to make it go to another frame.

☞ *If you can't get the CD-ROM movies to work, see "Demo Movies Won't Work" in the "Troubleshooting" section at the end of this chapter.*

LEARNING BASIC MULTIUSER LINGO

Although the standard multiuser behaviors enable you to customize your chat room quite a bit, you have to use Lingo to build other types of multiuser applications.

You need to know about several main Lingo commands. They enable you to connect to the server, get messages, and send messages.

Creating an Instance of the Xtra

First, you need to create an instance of the Multiuser Xtra. All the commands you need are part of the Xtra. You can create an instance with the new command like this:

```
gMultiuser = new(xtra "Multiuser")
```

The variable *gMultiuser* should be global so that other handlers in other scripts can access it.

Connecting

After you have an instance of the Xtra, you can establish the connection to the server. You need the connectToNetServer command to do this. It requires the IP address and port number for your server, as well as a movie ID. A common call looks like this:

```
err = gMultiuser.connectToNetServer(userName,"password", \
IPaddress,portNumber,"myMovie")
```

In this case, I use the password "password" to make it simple. You can provide a real password if you want. I use the name "myMovie" for the movie ID, but you can use something more relevant for yours.

You can check the error code that's returned by connectToNetServer to make sure that the connection was successful. If the error code is 0, it was successful. If it is some other number, you can feed that number to the getNetErrorString function to see a description of the problem.

Setting the Callback

After the connection has been established, call `setNetMessageHandler`. This call tells the Xtra which handler should be called every time a communication arrives from the server.

```
gMultiuser.setNetMessageHandler("myMessageHandler")
```

Sending a Message

Now you are ready to send and receive messages from the server. To send a message, use the `sendNetMessage` command. This command takes three parameters. The first parameter is the name of the recipient, the second is the subject, and the third is the message content. Here is an example:

```
gMultiuser.sendNetMessage("@AllUsers","chat","Hello!")
```

Instead of specifying the name of a single user, I use the value "@AllUsers" for the recipient. This means that the message is broadcast to all the users on the server who are using the same movie ID.

The subject and content in this example are simple. In most cases, the subject is used to identify the type of message being sent, and the content is the message itself. The server doesn't really care. Your Lingo code interprets the subject and content.

"@AllUsers" defines a group on the server, as does any recipient that uses an @ before it. "@AllUsers" is set up automatically for you, but you can also define your own groups by using sendNetMessage with "system.group.join", "system.group.leave", and similar commands. See the user documentation for details.

Receiving Messages

When a message is sent with `sendNetMessage`, you need to have a handler in the movies of all the connected users that retrieves this information. This is where the handler defined in `setNetMessageHandler` comes in. It is called whenever a message is sent to the user, whether it is sent specifically to a single user, or to "@AllUsers" as the `sendNetMessage` example does. Here is a simple handler:

```
on myMessageHandler
 message = gMultiuser.getNetMessage()
 subject = message.subject
 content = message.content
 senderID = message.senderID
end
```

The message handler uses the `getNetMessage` function to retrieve a property list that defines the message. This property list includes the properties #subject, #content, and #senderID. In addition, the properties #errorCode, #recipients, and #timestamp are returned should you want to use them.

To disconnect from the server, all you need to do is throw away the Xtra instance. You can do it as simply as this:

```
gMultiuser = VOID
```

Command Summary

That's all the commands that you need to create many multiuser applications. Check the server documentation for more details and for other minor commands and updates. Here is a list of some of the other commands and functions you might use:

- checkNetMessages—Forces the Xtra to check for incoming messages.

- getNetAddressCookie—Returns the IP address of the computer. In Shockwave, this is encrypted as a weird string for security reasons. However, the encrypted string works like a regular IP address for all multiuser commands.

- getNetOutgoingBytes—Returns how many bytes are waiting to be sent.

- getNumberWaitingMessages—Returns how many messages have arrived that have not yet been processed.

- setNetBufferLimits—Sets the limit on how much information can be queued in memory.

Next, let's look at how you might use these commands to create a simple application.

CREATING YOUR OWN MULTIUSER APPLICATION

Using these Lingo commands, you can create a simple multiuser application. This simple example enables users to control a little smiley face in a shared space. It is simple so that the important Lingo syntax is the main feature.

You can do this all in one behavior. This behavior attaches to the frame script. In addition, sprites 1 through 8 hold duplicates of little smiling face graphics.

The behavior starts off with property declarations. You can store the Xtra instance in a property, as well as the user ID. In this case, I use getNetAddressCookie to get a unique username for each person. The first word of every value returned by getNetAddressCookie is "MacromediaSecretIPAddressCookie:". You can discard that and use the second word, which is the encoded address. It is usually something like "be8759e422678e76c855f6fe521ff8".

This unique name guarantees that every user will have a unique ID, and there will be no confusion about where messages are coming from.

You will also have a property that stores the list of user IDs and face locations on the screen. The pLoc property holds the location of the person using the movie.

```
property pMultiuser -- Xtra instance
property pUserID -- unique name
property pPeople -- list of people and positions
property pLoc -- your loc
```

The on beginSprite handler creates the Xtra instance, connects to the server, and places the user at a random location on the screen. It then broadcasts this location to the users already on the server.

```
on beginSprite me
 -- start Xtra
 pMultiuser = new(xtra "Multiuser")

 -- get a unique name
 pUserID = pMultiuser.getNetAddressCookie().word[2]

 -- connect and set up
 pMultiuser.connectToNetServer(pUserID,"",\
   "X.X.X.X",1626,"example")
 pMultiuser.setNetMessageHandler(#messageHandler,me)

 -- init people list and location
 pPeople = [:]
 pLoc = point(random(47)*10,random(31)*10)
 addProp pPeople, pUserID, pLoc

 -- send first message to all present
 pMultiuser.sendNetMessage("@AllUsers","move",pLoc)

 -- draw screen
 drawPeople(me)
end
```

The setNetMessageHandler specifies that the *on messageHandler* will take care of incoming messages. The second parameter in setNetMessageHandler tells the message to look for this handler in this behavior, not in a movie script.

When a message comes in, it is first broken into parts. Then, the subject is checked, and different subjects trigger different events. In the following example, I handle the "move" event by setting a location in *pPeople* and updating the screen.

```
-- handle all incoming messages
on messageHandler me
 -- get message and break into parts
 message = pMultiuser.getNetMessage()
 subject = message.subject
 content = message.content
 sender = message.senderID

 -- handle move messages
 if subject = "move" then
  -- set or add person's location to list
  pPeople.setAProp(sender,content)
  -- update screen
  drawPeople(me)
 end if
end
```

The *on drawPeople* handler takes care of positioning the faces on the screen. The handler is careful to position unused sprites off the screen so that when someone leaves the room, the extra sprite doesn't hang around.

```
-- draw up to eight faces on the screen
on drawPeople me
 repeat with s = 1 to 8
  if s <= pPeople.count then
   -- person exists, place them
   sprite(s).loc = pPeople[s]
  else
   -- no one for this sprite, remove it
   sprite(s).loc = point(-1000,-1000)
  end if
 end repeat
end
```

When the sprite ends, either from the movie stopping or from a navigation button taking the movie off the frame, the Xtra instance is killed. This disconnects the user from the server.

```
-- kill Xtra instance
on endSprite me
 pMultiuser = VOID
end
```

The on keyDown handler accepts arrow keys, moves the person's face, and then broadcasts this move to the other users.

```
-- allow people to move
on keyDown me
 -- arrow keys
 case the keyCode of
  123: dx = -10
  124: dx = 10
  125: dy = 10
  126: dy = -10
 end case

 -- change location
 pLoc = pLoc + point(dx,dy)

 -- broadcast location
 pMultiuser.sendNetMessage("@AllUsers","move",pLoc)
end
```

Finally, as in so many other behaviors, you need a handler that holds the movie on the current frame.

```
-- loop on the frame
on exitFrame me
 go to the frame
end
```

The previous behavior is crude, in a way. All it does is allow nameless faces to float around in an empty space. However, it's important because these faces are controlled by different people, on different computers, possibly from entirely different places in the world.

The basic framework is here to turn this into something much bigger. The on *messageHandler* handler can easily handle more messages, such as "chat" to receive a chat message and append it to a text member. It can get "frown" messages to have faces frown. With a little more Lingo code, there is no reason why you can't have the faces interact: bumping into each other or shooting things at each other, for example.

USING PEER-TO-PEER CONNECTIONS

Not all multiuser programs need to use a server. You can also use the Multiuser Xtra to connect directly with another computer on the Internet. Even though this is a peer-to-peer connection without using an actual server, one computer is considered the "server" and the other the "client." The main difference is that the "server" starts up and waits for connections. The "client" then tries to contact the "server."

This has limited use because the client user must somehow know the IP address of the server user. If they are both Shockwave movies or projectors running on someone's random computer on the Internet, how is one to know the other exists?

There are two ways to use peer-to-peer connections. The first is to use the Multiuser Server to allow two users to meet and decide that they want to connect directly, such as to play a game of chess. Then, the two players can exchange IP addresses and go off to play each other peer-to-peer. With a lot of complex programming, you can achieve this, and the players will not even know the difference.

The other way to use peer-to-peer connections is to have two users who already know that they want to connect. This could work in a business setting. The users might decide in a meeting or via email who will be the server and where that server is located.

> **Caution**
>
> In my experience, setting up a game site using peer-to-peer connections does not work very well. This is because many business firewalls and some ISPs prevent the type of connection needed. Using a central Shockwave Multiuser Server works much better if you plan on allowing the general public to use your application.

Creating the Peer-to-Peer Connection for Users

To create a peer-to-peer connection, you start off by issuing the waitForNetConnection command in the movie that is to be the server. This effectively turns the Shockwave movie or projector into a mini Shockwave Multiuser Server.

```
gMultiuser = new(xtra "Multiuser")
gMultiuser.setNetMessageHandler(#messageHandler,script "MUS Scripts")
myUserID = "server movie"
gMultiuser.waitForNetConnection(myUserID,1627)
```

The client users can connect to the server user in the same way that they connect to a Shockwave Multiuser Server, using connectToNetServer. The trick is, of course, knowing the IP address of the server computer. The user running the server can get this by looking at the appropriate control panel for his operating system. You can also tell this user what his IP address is by using the `getNetAddressCookie()` function. Although this function returns a real IP address if used in a projector, it returns an encoded string of numbers and letters if used in Shockwave. Lingo can interpret either the real IP address or the encoded one, but the encoded one is much harder for client users to type.

When a client movie tries to connect to a server movie, the server movie gets a waitForNetConnection message. It is important that the message handler returns a TRUE with the `return` command. This signals an acceptance of the connection. Otherwise, the connection will be refused by the Xtra.

One other specialized peer-to-peer function is the `getPeerConnectionList()` function. This works for the server movie only. It returns a list of all the users connected to the movie.

Using Peer-to-Peer to Connect Two Movies

One use for peer-to-peer connections has nothing to do with multiuser applications. You can actually establish a multiuser connection between two movies running on the same computer. In fact, you can do it with two movies running in the same Web page.

The way this works is that the movie loaded first uses `waitForNetConnection` to become a server, and the second movie uses `connectToNetServer` to connect to it. They can then send messages back and forth.

Here is a single behavior that demonstrates this. It is on the CD-ROM as `moviecom.dir`. The behavior starts by creating the Xtra. It then checks the "sw1" parameter on the Web page. There are two of these movies in one page. The first instance has an "sw1" tag that states "server". The second instance does not even have an "sw1" tag. Thus, the first movie uses `waitForNetConnection`, and the second uses `connectToNetServer`.

The second movie uses the IP address from `getNetAddressCookie()` to call the server. This returns its own IP address, which is the same as the server's because they are both on the same machine. Although the server started as user "server user", the client starts as "client user".

To complete the connection, the server must return a TRUE when it gets the initial message from the client user. Now that the connection is set, the two movies can communicate between each other with `sendNetMessage`. This simple example sends random numbers back and forth. The numbers are put into text members as proof that the communication is taking place.

```
property pMultiuser

on beginSprite me
 -- create server and get IP address
 pMultiuser = new(xtra "Multiuser")
 pMultiuser.setNetMessageHandler(#messageHandler,me)

 -- the server user waits for a connection while the client user connects
 if externalParamValue("sw1") = "server" then
  pMultiuser.waitForNetConnection("server user",1627)
 else
```

```
    pMultiuser.connectToNetServer("client user","",
➥pMultiuser.getNetAddressCookie(),1627,"37moviecom")
 end if
end


on messageHandler me
 message = pMultiuser.getNetMessage()

 if message.subject = "waitForNetConnection" then
  -- return TRUE to allow client to connect
  return TRUE
 else if message.subject = "number" then
  -- got a new number from other movie
  member("output").text = string(message.content)
 end if
end

on sendNumber me
 -- send random number to other movie
 if externalParamValue("sw1") = "server" then
  pMultiuser.sendNetMessage("client user","number",random(99))
 else
  pMultiuser.sendNetMessage("server user","number",random(99))
 end if
end

on exitFrame me
 go to the frame
end
```

The CD-ROM contains a sample HTML page called `moviecom.html`. You will find two OBJECT/EMBED tags in the file, one with an "sw1" specifying "server" and the other without it. If you open this page with a browser, you'll see the cross-communication in action.

▷ *If you just can't get the Multiuser Server to run, see "Firewall Issues" in the "Troubleshooting" section at the end of this chapter.*

USING THE MULTIUSER DATABASE

A useful feature of the Multiuser Server is its capability to store data. This can be used to store information about the users who connect to the server, or it can contain premade information about a multiuser environment, such as an adventure game.

The Multiuser Server has four types of databases: User data, player data, application data, and read-only application data. The first two can be used to store information about users, the second two about environments.

User data, referred to as "DBUser" in commands, is a good place to store universal information that might cross over to multiple multiuser applications. These could be things such as the user's name and preferences. Player data, "DBPlayer", is similar but is used to store information about a user only as it pertains to the current movie.

The first of the two types of application data, "DBApplication", can be used to store game states and environmental variables about your server that change. The second type, "DBApplicationData", is meant to be read-only by the users, but you can still set it with a movie that has high-level access.

Creating a Database Entry

To create a database entry, use the `sendNetMessage` command with a special recipient. For example, to create a user entry, use `"system.DBAdmin.createUser"`. Here is an example:

```
gMultiuser.sendNetMessage("system.DBAdmin.createUser","",\
  [#userID: userID, #password: password, #userLevel: 20])
```

After there is a record of a user, you can store information about the user in that record. The first step toward doing this is to create the attribute. Then, you can store information with that attribute. Notice in the following example that the first line refers to "DBAdmin" to declare an attribute, but refers to "DBUser" to get the information:

```
gMultiuser.sendNetMessage("system.DBAdmin.declareAttribute","",\
  [#attribute: #userEmail])
gMultiuser.sendNetMessage("system.DBUser.setAttribute","",\
  [#userID: userID, [#userEmail: userEmail]])
```

Retrieving the Data

After the user has a database entry and attributes, you can retrieve data with `"system.DBUser.getAttribute"`. You can also send messages such as `"system.DBUser.getAttributeName"` to get a list of available attributes.

There are dozens of database commands to set and retrieve data from the four types of databases. To see the complete list, check the documentation, which is constantly updated on Macromedia's site to correspond to the latest version of the server.

The biggest problem I have had when creating database entries was that the userlevel of the user was not high enough to allow the creation of users and attributes. If you run into this problem, you can modify the Multiuser.cfg file to give new users a higher userlevel, or lower the userlevel required to perform database modifications.

USING USER DATA PROTOCOL (UDP)

The Multiuser Server and Xtra generally use TCP/IP connections, like most of the rest of the Internet. A connection like this consists of two steps. First, the message is sent to the destination. Then, the destination sends a message back confirming that the message arrived intact.

In fact, each message sent becomes two messages, one there and one back. This can create a long "lag" when sending messages. This lag can be a fraction of a second up to several seconds.

However, there is a way to send a message without this second confirmation step. The Multiuser Server 3.0 supports *User Data Protocol* (*UDP*). With UDP, the message is sent one way, and no checking is done to make sure that it has arrived.

UDP is commonly used for games where many messages will be sent, and mistakes will not matter so much. For instance, if UDP messages are sent every time a player moves a character in a game, then if one never arrives, it is no big deal. In fact, that character position will likely become obsolete in another second when another move is made.

On the other hand, using UDP for a chess game is not a good idea. If a move is missed, the game is ruined. Plus, speed is not that important for chess because it is a turn-based game.

Using UDP messages is not that different from using regular TCP/IP messages. First, you'll need to modify the `Multiuser.cfg` file to allow the server to use UDP. This is done by uncommenting the line that sets the `EnableUDP` property to 1:

```
EnableUDP = 1
```

Right above that line is another that specifies the IP address and port of the server. Uncomment it and set with your own server IP address and a port number other than the one you are using for TCP/IP messages:

```
UDPServerAddress = X.X.X.X:1627
```

When you want to use UDP, you need to connect to the server in a slightly different way. You need to add a `#localUDPPort` property when using `connectToNetServer`.

The following `connectToNetServer` command looks a lot different from `connectToNetServer` commands used previously in this chapter. The `connectToNetServer` command has changed a lot since the first version of the Xtra. However, it maintains backward compatibility with earlier versions of the command. With version 3.0, you can use a single parameter to define all the properties of the connection. This format makes it easy to figure out what is going on. For new functions, like UDP, you'll need to use this format:

> Note that you are specifying a different port on your server for UDP addresses. This means that the server will be using two ports. This also means that every time someone connects to your server, she will be using two connections: one for TCP/IP and one for UDP. A server that is set to allow 50 connections will then only be able to handle 25 users.

```
gMultiuser.connectToNetServer([#remoteAddress:"X.X.X.X",
➡ #logonInfo: [#userID: myUserID, #password: "",
➡ #movieID: "myMovie"], #localUDPPort: 1627])
```

The `#localUDPPort` setting needs to match the setting on the server. Just by using this property, you have set up the movie to allow UDP messages. The next step is figuring out how to send a UDP message. It turns out that this is the same `sendNetMessage` command, but with one more parameter, `#udp`. Set this parameter to TRUE, and the message will be sent via UDP rather than TCP/IP.

```
gMultiuser.sendNetMessage([#recipients: "@AllUsers",
➡#subject: "mySubject", #content: "myMessage", #udp: TRUE])
```

If you set the `#udp` parameter to FALSE, or just leave it out, the message will be sent via TCP/IP.

Note that the speed improvement that UDP messages give you is difficult to demonstrate. If you are connected over a local network, the difference will be almost undetectable. It is over a long distance, such as halfway around the world, where UDP speed is more apparent.

USING SERVER-SIDE LINGO

Another powerful part of the Multiuser Server is server-side scripting. Creating scripts for the server can range in difficulty from relatively easy to very difficult. It all depends on how deep you want to go. For instance, the server can be programmed to use threads. *Threads* are like parent scripts or behaviors, except that they are running virtually at the same time as other scripts. Plus, threads are not, in themselves, scripts. They are created and then told what handlers to run. The handlers themselves come from outside the threads.

Although threads are an advanced topic for anyone who is not an expert programmer, you can also create a server-side script that uses the same basic Lingo that you would use to control a sprite. Before we look at an example, let's examine what server-side scripting can and cannot do.

Lingo Outside Director

So where do these Lingo scripts go? The Multiuser Server does not have a Script panel. Instead, scripts are contained in ordinary text files. One of the server's subfolders is named `Scripts`, and several scripts are already present.

If you open up the `dispatcher.ls` script or the `scriptmap.ls` files, you will see a lot of complex Lingo code. In fact, these two files are well-commented, but the code is expert-level stuff. You'll be relieved to learn that you don't have to know much about these two scripts.

The `dispatcher.ls` and `scriptmap.ls` files are always present with the Multiuser Server. The dispatcher actually handles most server-side scripting. When you create new scripts, it is in charge of passing control of incoming messages onto these scripts. The `scriptmap.ls` tells the dispatcher which movies send messages to which scripts.

To create your own server-side script, start a new text file. Name it with the `.ls` extension and place it in the `Scripts` folder.

You might have trouble editing these files at first. For instance, on the Mac, these `.ls` files are recognized as Director files, and so Director is used to open them if you double-click them. However, Director won't do anything with the files. You can also open them from a text editor such as SimpleText, BBEdit, or WordPad. If you know how to modify your operating system so that it handles `.ls` files by opening them with a text editor, I recommend doing that.

For the server to recognize the new script, the scriptmap needs to be changed. Open the scriptmap with a text editor and take a look. You will see two commented-out examples of scripts being mapped to movies. You can modify one of these or create your own line. Here is a line that maps all messages from the movie "serverside" to the script `serverside.ls`:

```
theMap.append([#movieID: "serverside", #scriptFileName: "serverside.ls"])
```

Now all that is left is to populate `serverside.ls` with a script. You'll need to know more about what events the server responds to first.

New Lingo Syntax

When you are creating a sprite behavior, you know that there are certain messages that the behavior will respond to, such as mouseUp or exitFrame. You would write handlers to handle these messages.

Server-side scripts are the same. They also have a set of possible messages that need handlers if you choose to handle them. Here is a complete list of these handlers:

- on `groupCreate`   This handler gets called when the first user joins a new group.

- on `groupDelete`   This handler gets called when the last user leaves group.

- on `groupJoin`   This handler gets called when a new user joins a group.

- on `groupLeave`   This handler gets called when a user leaves a group.

- on `incomingMessage`   This handler gets called every time a user sends a message to "system.script".

- on `movieCreate`   This handler gets called when the first user logs on to the server.

- on `movieDelete`   This handler gets called when the last user leaves the server.

- on `new`   This handler gets called when the first user logs on to the movie. Use `return(me)` to complete the creation on the script object.

- on `serverShutDown`   This handler gets called just before the server is shut down.

- on `userLogOff`   This handler gets called whenever a user leaves.

- on `userLogOn`   This handler gets called when a new user arrives.

The three most useful of these handlers are the on `incomingMessage` handler, the on `userLogOn`, and on `userLogOff` handlers. With them, most simple tasks can be accomplished.

Server-side scripts look a lot like behaviors. Instead of on `beginSprite`, use on `new` to start it off. You can define properties with the `property` statement that will persist between handlers.

The on `incomingMessage` is the main way to get messages to the script. The Director movie would send a message to "system.script" for the message to reach the on `incomingMessage` handler.

The on `incomingMessage` handler takes four parameters after the me. They are: movie, group, user, and message. The movie, group, and user are three objects that can be used as references to send messages to. The message is a property list of items from the original message sent by the Director movie.

To send a message back to the user, the server-side script would use the `sendMessage` command. This is called using the object that defines where the message should be sent. You can use the movie, group, or user as the object for the `sendMessage` command. Here is an example:

```
on incomingMessage me, movie, group, user, message
  if message.subject = "test" then
    user.sendMessage("system.script.subject","content")
  end if
end
```

When you are using the user as the object, you can just pass two parameters into `sendMessage`: the subject and the content. However, if you use the group or movie object, your first parameter should be the recipients, such as the user id, a list of ids, the group name, and so on.

The subject of any message that comes from the server should start with "system.script" and then a short subject name. The content can be anything you want.

Server-Side Script Limits

Remember that the server is not Director. Things such as sprites, members, and the Stage do not exist. All Lingo that pertains to them doesn't exist either.

You can use standard programming syntax, such as `if`, `repeat`, variables and lists, strings, math functions, and custom handlers. If you like parent/child scripts, there is even a way to do that.

Server-side scripting also has a whole set of new commands that deal with threads and file management. The `exists`, `read`, and `write` commands do what you would expect. For instance, to read a text file into a variable, you can do this:

```
myText = file("myFile").read()
```

You can also use `readValue` and `writeValue` to read and write binary data such as lists. The file functions are powerful and will let your server-side script access or create small databaselike files that can contain valuable data pertaining to your multiuser application.

A Server-Side Script Example

Earlier in this chapter, we looked at a multiuser application where people could log in to the server and move little faces around on the screen. Without server-side scripting, the faces just appeared at random on the screen and could move on top of and underneath each other. With central server control, we can have the server be in charge of making sure that the faces never overlap.

We'll start with a script that looks a lot like the one earlier in the chapter. However, it will be a little simpler. It will not keep track of its own location, so no *pLoc* property is needed. In fact, it will connect to the server and not even establish its location or add itself to the *pPeople* list.

```
property pMultiuser -- Xtra instance
property pUserID -- unique name
property pPeople -- list of people and positions

on beginSprite me
  -- start xtra
  pMultiuser = new(xtra "Multiuser")

  -- get a unique name
  pUserID = pMultiuser.getNetAddressCookie().word[2]

  -- connect and setup
  pMultiuser.connectToNetServer(pUserID,"","X.X.X.X",1626,"serverside")
  pMultiuser.setNetMessageHandler(#messageHandler,me)
```

```
  -- init people list
 pPeople = [:]
end
```

The *on messageHandler* looks different too. It accepts only two messages: "system.script.move" and "system.script.remove". The first adds or replaces the location of a user in the *pPeople* list, and the second removes a user from that list. In both cases, the *on drawPeople* handler is called.

Notice that there is a complete absence of any mention of the real location of the faces. The server will be handling that, not the individual movies.

```
-- handle all incoming messages
on messageHandler me
 -- get message and break into parts
 message = pMultiuser.getNetMessage()
 subject = message.subject
 content = message.content
 sender = message.senderID

 -- handle messages
 if subject = "system.script.move" then
  -- set or add person's location to list
  pPeople.setAProp(content.id,content.loc)
  -- update screen
  drawPeople(me)

 else if subject = "system.script.remove" then
  -- delete user from list
  pPeople.deleteProp(content.id)
  -- update screen
  drawPeople(me)
 end if
end
```

The *on drawPeople* handler is exactly the same as the previous script version. So is the on endSprite.

```
-- draw up to 8 faces on the screen
on drawPeople me
 repeat with s = 1 to 8
  if s <= pPeople.count then
   -- person exists, place them
   sprite(s).loc = pPeople[s]
  else
   -- no one for this sprite, remove it
   sprite(s).loc = point(-1000,-1000)
  end if
 end repeat
end
```

```
-- kill xtra instance
on endSprite me
 pMultiuser = VOID
end
```

The on keyDown handler defines a variable *d* according to how much the face should move. It is not actually changing the location of anything. It simply gets the amount that the face should move and sends that amount on to the server-side script.

```
-- allow people to move
on keyDown me
 -- arrow keys
 case the keyCode of
  123: d = point(-10,0)
  124: d = point(10,0)
  125: d = point(0,10)
  126: d = point(0,-10)
 end case

 -- send new potential location to server-side script
 pMultiuser.sendNetMessage("system.script","move",d)
end
```

```
-- loop on the frame
on exitFrame me
 go to the frame
end
```

A lot seems to be missing from this script. For instance, how is the starting location of the face determined? How is the location of the face changed each time an arrow key is pressed? And how are the faces prevented from colliding? This will all be handled by the server-side script "serverside.ls".

This script starts off by creating an empty property list *pPeople* just like the Director movie. It also puts a nice message to the server text window when the script starts:

```
property pPeople

on new me
  put "Server-side example program loaded and ready!"
  pPeople = [:]
  return(me)
end
```

When a new user logs on, a message is put out to the server window. Then an entry is added to the *pPeople* list. The property name is the user's ID, taken from the "user" object as the *user.name*. The value added to the list contains both the id and the location of the user. This makes it easy to send along in a message.

The *on userLogOn* handler finishes by sending a message to all the users in the movie. This message contains the location of the new face. This location comes from *on getOpenLocation* which we will look at later.

```
on userLogOn me, movie, group, user
  put "User"&&user.name&&"has entered."

  -- put new person into list and give them a unique location .
  pPeople.addProp(user.name, [#id: user.name, #loc: getOpenLocation(me)])
  movie.sendMessage("@AllUsers","system.script.move",pPeople[user.name])
end
```

When a user leaves the server, the "system.script.remove" message is sent to everyone. Also, the user is removed from the *pPeople* list.

```
on userLogOff me, movie, group, user
  put "User"&&user.name&&"has left the arena."
  movie.sendMessage("@AllUsers","system.script.remove",pPeople[user.name])
  pPeople.deleteProp(user.name)
end
```

The only custom message that is sent to the server script is the "move" message. The content of this message is a point representing the direction of movement. This is used to calculate the *newloc* variable. Then the handler *tooClose* is used to determine whether this new location is too close to another face. Only if it is not is the new location placed into *pPeople* and a "system.script.move" message sent to all the users.

```
on incomingMessage me, movie, group, user, message
 if message.subject = "move" then
  newloc = pPeople[user.name].loc + message.content
  if not tooClose(me,user.name,newloc) then
   pPeople[user.name].loc = newloc
   movie.sendMessage("@AllUsers","system.script.move",pPeople[user.name])
  end if
 end if
end
```

The handler *on getOpenLocation* creates a random point and then calls *tooClose* to see whether that overlaps with another face.

```
on getOpenLocation me
  repeat while TRUE
    loc = point(random(350)+25,random(250+25))
    if not tooClose(me,VOID,loc) then return(loc)
  end repeat
end
```

The *on tooClose* handler loops through the existing faces to see whether any is closer than 25 pixels from a point. The *username* variable is passed in so that the handler can avoid comparing a new location to the present location of the same face:

```
on tooClose me, username, loc
  repeat with i = 1 to pPeople.count
    if username = getPropAt(pPeople,i) then next repeat
    if distance(me,pPeople[i].loc,loc) < 25 then return(TRUE)
  end repeat
  return(FALSE)
end
```

The *on distance* handler is a utility function that returns the distance between two points:

```
on distance me, loc1, loc2
  return sqrt(power(loc1.locH-loc2.locH,2)+power(loc1.locV-loc2.locV,2))
end
```

The outcome of the `serverside.ls` script is that it handles the initial placement and all forthcoming movements of the users. The user simply requests a movement, and the server determines whether it is valid. The server keeps the master list of user and locations, and passes that information on to the clients when a change is made.

This is just a simple example of a server-side script. Developers have only begun to tap the power of master control scripts such as this. They allow Director developers to basically create a custom server to do specifically what an application requires.

USING THE FLASH COMMUNICATION SERVER

The alternative to the Shockwave Multiuser Server is the Flash Communication Server. A "Personal Edition" of the server comes on the Director CD-ROM.

The Differences Between the Servers

Whereas the Shockwave Multiuser Server was built specifically for use by Director movies, and it has gone through three versions, the Flash Communication Server is brand new and was built for Flash movies, not Director.

Using the Flash Communication Server with Director and Lingo is no less than an expert-level task. An easier solution might be to use Flash to create your multiuser application and embed that Flash movie into Director. While existing as a Flash member, the Flash movie will be able to communicate with the server just as if it were playing standalone.

The Flash Communication Server runs only on Windows NT or Windows 2000. It can also work on Windows XP, but the documentation states that this is only for development purposes. In addition, the server runs as a background process on these machines. To see what the server is up to, you need to use the supplied administrative tools and log in to the server.

Another difference is the price. To set up a Flash Communication Server for hundreds of people, you need to pay a large licensing fee to Macromedia. The Shockwave Multiuser Server can be used at no additional charge.

One way in which the Flash Communication Server surpasses the Director server is that it can stream video and audio, and even use live video and audio. So you can do videoconferencing.

The video and audio portions of the server functionality are best left to the insides of Flash movies. So if you want to use the Flash Communication Server that way, you should program that part of your application in Flash and then import the Flash movie into your Director movie.

You can even use some of the Flash Communication Server example movies this way. Just import them and use them. Example chat rooms, videoconferencing, and broadcast presentation movies come with the install.

Using the Flash Communication Server with Lingo

It's beyond the scope of this book to go too deeply into using the Flash Communication Server. Programming for this server is a subject that could fill a whole book by itself. Plus, it mostly involves Flash MX ActionScript expertise, not Director or Lingo expertise.

However, it is possible to do simple multiuser applications without using any Flash member at all.

The example movie `flashcommchat.dir` is such an example. To use it, you first need to get the Flash Communication Server running on a Windows 2000/NT/XP machine with a static IP address. That could be a monumental task all by itself. But if you follow the installation procedure carefully, you can get it running. Confirm that it is working by using the administration movie that comes with the server. Refer to the server's documentation as needed.

> **Caution**
>
> You might need some patience to get the Flash Communication Server up and running if you are not familiar with servers and Windows NT-like processes.

After the server is running, you'll need two more machines to test the chat movie. They both need to run `flashcommchat.dir`, which can be seen in Figure 23.5.

Figure 23.5
This simple chat application is powered by the Flash Communication Server.

Before you run the movie, you need to go in and insert the IP address of the server where I have left the *XXX.XXX.XXX.XXX*.

To establish a connection with the server, you first need to use `newObject` to create a Flash object from the Flash Xtra. This will be a `NetConnection` object. You can use this object to connect to the server with the `connect` command.

```
global commServer, sharedObject
```

```
on startMovie
 -- connect to the server
 commServer = newObject("NetConnection")
 commServer.connect("rtmp://XXX.XXX.XXX.XXX/dmxtest", "username")
```

The name "dmxtest" is the name of the application we are creating. This is like the movie name for the Shockwave Multiuser Server. However, you need to create a folder in the Flash Communication Server's machine called "dmxtest" for the server to accept connections using this name. Create it in the `flashcom/applications` folder.

Next, you need to create a *shared object*. This is where the Flash Communication Server becomes much different from the Shockwave Multiuser Server. A shared object is a variable object, much like a Lingo property list. However, this object exists on the server and is shared by all logged-in users. So when one user sets a property in the shared object, the rest also get that property set.

```
 -- create a shared object
 so = newObject("SharedObject")
 sharedObject = so.getRemote("mySharedObject",commServer.uri,false)
 sharedObject.connect(commServer)
```

When the shared object changes, each user is notified with a special onSync message. But for that message to go anywhere, you need to use the setCallBack command to assign it to a handler name, in this case *on getChat*:

```
 -- set callback for when shared object changes
 setCallBack(sharedObject,"onSync",#getChat)
end
```

When the movie starts up, the on startMovie handler logs the user in to the Flash Communication Server. Any changes to the *sharedObject* global will be indicated by a call to *on getChat*. This handler copies the *chat* property of the shared object and uses it as the incoming chat text.

```
on getChat
 -- send chat to text member
 newChatLine = sharedObject.data.chat
 member("chatout").text = member("chatout").text&RETURN&newChatLine
 member("chatout").scrollTop = the maxInteger
end
```

The property scrollTop is set to a large number so that the text scrolling area will show the last line.

To send text, all that is needed is to change the shared object:

```
on sendChat text
 sharedObject.data.chat = text
end
```

The example movie calls *on sendChat* from the editable text member. The script attached to this member will intercept all RETURN characters, send the text, and clear the member:

```
on keyDown me
 if the key = RETURN then
  sendChat(member("chatin").text)
  member("chatin").text = ""
 else
  pass
 end if
end
```

This movie is a good example of how to use Lingo, without any Flash member at all, to communicate. But it is only one way of doing it. Using the `NetStream` object is probably a better way to send text messages than by changing the value of one shared object.

However, a shared object is an excellent way of dealing with player piece positions in games or graphical chat areas.

Be warned, however, that the Flash Communication Server is still new, and the Flash MX Xtra is even newer. You may encounter plenty of bugs and oddities. Just testing this simple movie, I ran into many problems that were simply cleared up when I restarted Director. I noticed that even using `clearGlobals` did not get rid of shared object data at times.

The key to using the Flash Communication Server is to learn how to program it on the server. This uses a Java-like programming language that is closer to ActionScript than to Lingo.

To learn more about the Flash Communication Server, I recommend working with it in Flash for a while before trying to incorporate communication into your Director movies.

TROUBLESHOOTING

Demo Movies Won't Work

I think I set up my server correctly; why won't the movies from the CD run?

The IP address of the server in many cases is set to "X.X.X.X". You need to run your own server and set this IP address to match that server for any these movies to work.

Firewall Issues

Why can't I run the Multiuser Server?

If you are behind a firewall, you might not be able to connect to a Multiuser Server, or run one. Talk to the administrator of that firewall and let him know the port number of your server. He might be able to allow access to it.

DID YOU KNOW?

- You can also use the Multiuser Xtra to communicate with text-based servers. For example, you can communicate with a text-based mail server to send email. Search the technotes on Macromedia's site for examples of this.

- You can run the Multiuser Server on the same computer that you are using to run Director, a projector, or a Shockwave movie that accesses the server. That way, with two computers, you can run the server and one movie on one computer, and the other movie on the other computer and check out how your application works with two users connected to the server.

- Many ISPs are now offering Flash Communication Server access through their systems, so you may not need to set up your own server. Check the Macromedia site for links to ISPs that offer this service.

24

BUILDING AUTHORING TOOLS

IN THIS CHAPTER

TYPE OF AUTHORING TOOLS

Many times, the Lingo programmer's job in a company is not to develop content directly, but to build templates and tools for others, usually referred to as *multimedia authors*. These tools can take the form of Lingo-based Xtras, a behavior library, or even a set of Macromedia Director movie templates.

One type of authoring tool helps animators create complex or repetitive Score sequences. These use Lingo's Score recording commands to alter the sprites in the Score.

Another type of tool uses small Director movies as movies in a window (MIAWs). Although MIAWs are used in completed projects as dialog boxes or such, they can also be used in the Director environment to perform a variety of tasks to help in movie creation.

A third way to build elements to help multimedia authors would simply be to add elements to the Director library. These would include reusable Lingo behaviors and other media elements.

We'll take a look at each of these types of tools.

SCORE RECORDING

Although behaviors can change the properties of a sprite while the movie is running, these properties all return to their default Score settings when the movie is finished. Lingo does have the capability, however, to effect real changes in the Score.

To make changes in the Score, you need to use Score recording commands. You can define the beginning of a Score recording session and then make changes to sprites. These changes then become "real," because the Score is permanently changed. You can even insert and delete frames.

Animators can use this technique to build Score-based animations instead of just having Lingo control the animation during playback. This enables Lingo developers to make tools for animators that result in visible Score changes.

Writing to the Score

Creating or modifying sprites in the Score is fairly simple. First, you must use the `beginRecording` command. Every change to a sprite between the `beginRecording` and the `endRecording` command effects a change in the Score.

After a Score recording session begins, you can use regular Lingo commands, such as `go`, to jump around in the Score. When you start using sprite properties, you begin to make real changes.

The following is a handler that adds the member number 1 to the Score in sprite 7. It uses `go` to make sure that it is placing it in frame 1:

```
on simpleChange
 beginRecording
  go to frame 1
  sprite(7).member = member(1)
  sprite(7).loc = point(100,100)
  updateFrame
 endRecording
end
```

The command `updateFrame` is actually where the change is made. You need to issue either an `updateFrame` or an `insertFrame` command. The first command places all your changes in the current frame and advances the movie to the next frame. The `insertFrame` command places the movie in the current frame, makes a copy of that frame, changes and all, and then inserts it after the current frame. The playback head is now in the inserted frame.

The following handler performs a more complex task. It inserts frames, beginning with the current one, and moves sprite 1 over to the right 10 pixels each time. It does this until the sprite reaches the horizontal location of 600:

> Because Score recording can change many things in the Score and is not undoable by the normal undo command, you might want to warn multimedia authors about saving their movie before using a score recording handler. You can also make your own undo function by setting a variable to the `score`, which makes a copy of the score as it currently exists. You can then undo a Score change by setting the `score` back to that variable value.

```
on recordMove
  sNum = 1
  minX = 0
  maxX = 600
  stepSize = 10

  beginRecording
    x = minX
    repeat while TRUE
      sprite(sNum).locH = x
      insertFrame
      x = x + stepSize
      if x > maxX then exit repeat
    end repeat
  endRecording
end
```

Although this handler doesn't really do anything that a behavior can't do while the movie is running, it demonstrates creating animation in the Score with Score recording. A tool such as this can enable animators to easily add common animations to the Score, while also using traditional Score animation techniques in other sprites.

⇨ *If you can't get Score recording to change the Score, see "Score Recording Won't Stick" in the "Troubleshooting" section at the end of this chapter.*

Score Recording Tools

A more useful Score recording handler takes existing sprites and manipulates them in a way that no other tool can. Director includes the Align tool, which enables you to lock horizontal and vertical positions of sprites to each other. However, what is missing is a tool that evenly spaces sprites.

The next handler does just that. It takes three or more sprites in the same frame, finds the minimum and maximum horizontal and vertical positions, and then uses that information to evenly space them. For simplicity, the handler assumes that the first sprite should be positioned first, the second should be positioned second, and so on. Therefore, it does not work in cases where you have the sprites out of order.

The first thing that this handler does is get the `scoreSelection`. This is a list of lists that tells you what the author has selected in the Score. For instance, if sprite 7 of frame 5 is selected, you get [[7,7,5,5]]. The first two numbers of each item are the sprite, and the third and fourth numbers represent the frame range. To get this handler to work, three sprites in the score need to be selected.

```
on evenlySpace
  set ss = the scoreSelection

  if ss.count < 3 then
    alert "You must select at least 3 items"
    exit
  end if

  -- find max and min locations
  minX = sprite(ss[1][1]).locH
  maxX = minX
  minY = sprite(ss[1][1]).locV
  maxY = minY
  repeat with i = 2 to ss.count
    x = sprite(ss[i][1]).locH
    y = sprite(ss[i][1]).locV

    if x < minX then minX = x
    if x > maxX then maxX = x
    if y < minY then minY = y
    if y > maxY then maxY = y
  end repeat

  -- figure out spacing
  spaceX = (maxX - minX)/(ss.count-1)
  spaceY = (maxY - minY)/(ss.count-1)

  -- record all changes
  beginRecording

    -- space in order of sprite number
    x = minX
    y = minY
    repeat with i = 1 to ss.count
      sprite(ss[i][1]).loc = point(x,y)
      x = x + spaceX
      y = y + spaceY
    end repeat

    -- set changes and end recording
    updateFrame
  endRecording
end
```

This handler is meant for three or more sprites all in the same frame. It is not meant for sprites that span more than one frame.

You can also use `the selection of castLib` to determine which members are selected in the Cast. If the author has selected members 2 through 5 and member 8, for instance, you get this result:

```
put the selection of castLib 1
-- [[2, 5], [8, 8]]
```

Using `the selection of castLib` and `the scoreSelection`, you can determine which members and sprites the author is pointing to at any time. This property can be used to build tools that react to different author selections.

➡️ *If you don't see the Score updating immediately, see "Score Recording Doesn't Appear in Score" in the "Troubleshooting" section at the end of this chapter.*

Setting Behaviors and Parameters Through Lingo

You can also set the behaviors attached to a sprite and the values of the parameters in them. This is represented as a list, which can be read with `the scriptList` property of a sprite:

```
put sprite(2).scriptList
-- [[(member 2 of castLib 1), "[#jumpframe: 7]"], [(member 3 of castLib 1), 0]]
```

You can set this entire list with the new `setScriptList` command. You can use the format returned with `the scriptList` property. Each behavior is a sublist of two elements: the behavior member and a property list of parameters and values. The parameters list has quotation marks around it for some strange reason.

```
sprite(2).setScriptList([[member("My Behavior"), "[#jumpframe: 12]",
➥[member("My Other Behavior"),0]]
```

Another strange fact about this command is that you cannot use it inside a score recording session. So, to truly create sprites in the Score with behaviors attached, you need to do some work within Score recording, such as adding the sprites, and some after it, such as setting the script list.

CREATING MIAW XTRAS

After you have built a handy routine like the *on evenlySpace* handler described previously, it can be used to create an Xtra. These are not the sort of Xtras discussed in Chapter 26, "Using Xtras." Instead of creating an Xtra using C or some other programming language, you are simply creating a Director movie and then placing it in the Xtras folder.

After a Director movie is in the Xtras folder, it appears in the Xtras menu. When selected, it appears in a Movie in a Window (MIAW). It can then tell the Stage to do things, such as initiate Score recording.

The *on evenlySpace* handler can be turned into a simple Xtra by placing it in its own movie. Make the Stage size of that movie very small, maybe 240×160. Then, add a button that calls the *on evenlySpace* handler. This handler needs one change: The `tell the stage` command must be added before the first line, and an `end tell` must be added at the end. With this change, this handler directs all the commands at the Stage, not the MIAW Xtra itself.

All that is left is to place the Director movie in the `Xtras` folder. You can even compress it into a `.dcr` file before doing this. Doing so makes the Xtra available to be used, but makes the scripts unavailable to other developers. Therefore, you can produce Lingo-based Xtras for distribution without worrying about someone stealing your code.

If you need to refer to the MIAW itself, you can't use `the stage`, but should instead use `the activeWindow`. This returns a reference to the MIAW as long as it is the frontmost window. It will almost certainly have to be the frontmost window if the user is performing an action in it, such as typing or clicking.

⇨ *If you want to make sure that you close your MIAW tool properly, see "Leftover MIAW Xtras" in the "Troubleshooting" section at the end of this chapter.*

⇨ *For more information about making MIAWs, see "Using MIAWs" p. 252.*

USING BEHAVIOR LIBRARIES

Just as a Director movie can be placed in the `Xtras` folder, a Director cast library file can be placed in the `Libs` folder. This makes it available in the Library palette.

Director MX already comes complete with a large set of behavior libraries that appear in this palette. Take a look at the `Libs` folder in the Director folder to see how these are arranged. Some cast libraries are just sitting in the folder, whereas others are in subfolders. This structure determines how the libraries appear in the Library palette pop-up menu.

You can use this structure by creating a new folder in the `Libs` folder for your own custom behaviors. The same structure relates the `Xtras` folder to the Xtras menu.

You are not restricted to just behaviors. You can also place any other type of cast member in a library Cast. You can store clip art, common sounds, and even movie scripts. Depending on the type of member, you can drag these members from the Library palette onto the Stage, Score, Cast, or all three.

You can even provide custom icons for cast members in a library. When you are building the members of the cast library to be used as a library, select the member in the Cast, open the Property Inspector, and (Control-click) [right-click] on the icon at the top of the Property Inspector to bring up a pop-up menu, which enables you to copy, cut, and paste

Many developers have a behavior library that they constantly update as needed. The `Libs` folder is the perfect place to keep this cast library so that the behaviors are always accessible. But don't compress your cast library into a `.cct` file because this removes the raw Lingo code. Just use a plain `.cst` file.

If you want to prevent multimedia authors from using behaviors in places where they are not wanted, use the `on isOkToAttach` handler. It can analyze the sprite that the behavior is being dropped onto and prevent it from going onto one that it was not made for. See Chapter 12, "Using Object-Oriented Programming and Behaviors," for more details.

icons. The special icons with the behaviors in Director's built-in libraries were given their special icons in this way.

TROUBLESHOOTING

Score Recording Won't Stick

I'm using Score recording and it seems to be doing something, but when my handler is done, the Score remains unchanged. What am I doing wrong?

Score recording always requires an `insertFrame` or `updateFrame` command to make the changes stick. Forgetting this is a common mistake.

Score Recording Doesn't Appear in Score

I'm using Score recording, but I notice that the Score does not update immediately. The Stage shows the new sprite positions, but the Score doesn't. Why?

Score recording has been known to correctly update the Score but not show the changes in the Score panel until the movie has been rewound and played again. Keep this in mind if it doesn't seem to work at first.

Leftover MIAW Xtras

I suspect that when I close my MIAW tools they are really still there, just invisible. Is there any way to make sure that they are really gone?

MIAW Xtras are easy to create and open, but not so easy to eliminate. If you permit users to click the close box in the window to make the Xtra go away, the window is actually still there. You can even see it in `the windowList`. A good idea is to place a `forget(the activeWindow)` in the `on closeWindow` handler. This forces the window to be discarded when users click the close button.

DID YOU KNOW?

- If you don't want users to see each change in a Score recording session as it occurs, you can set `the updateLock` to TRUE at the beginning of the session. This causes the Stage to freeze while changes are made.

- You can set `the windowType` of a MIAW Xtra after it has been opened. The programmer will see this change occur, however.

- You can also set the MIAW Xtra's screen position after it has been opened.

25

ADDRESSING ACCESSIBILITY
ISSUES

IN THIS CHAPTER

UNDERSTANDING ACCESSIBILITY

Almost since the beginning of computer multimedia, presentations and applications have been created with disabled users in mind. More recently, this has become even more important as U.S. government regulations have mandated that government projects adhere to special standards of accessibility.

The term *accessibility* describes features of computer applications that allow users with disabilities to have as much access as all users of the software.

For instance, spoken audio portions of a presentation might also be presented as captions for users who have trouble hearing. Conversely, text portions of the presentation might be spoken by text-to-speech software for users who have trouble seeing the screen. Users who have trouble using a mouse might be able to use one key on the keyboard to move between buttons and other selectable items, and another key to select the item.

For many developers, adding accessibility features to their movies is not an option. For instance, many government contracts require that you follow a specific set of guidelines. You can find these guidelines at http://www.section508.gov/.

Macromedia Director MX adds some new behaviors and an Xtra that will help you make your movies accessible. First we'll look at an example of building an accessible movie and then take a closer look at the new Speech Xtra, which can be used for many things besides accessibility features.

⮕ *If you need to make sure that your movie follows accessibility guidelines, see "Making Sure Accessiblity Is Done Right" in the "Troubleshooting" section at the end of this chapter.*

BUILDING ACCESSIBLE MOVIES

The Director engineers have provided a set of behaviors and a new Xtra to help make your movies accessible. You can make a simple accessible presentation with these behaviors by using only a little bit of Lingo and a few cast members.

Building a Simple Accessible Presentation

The movie accessible.dir found on this book's CD-ROM is a simple example of an accessible presentation movie. It contains five frames, a collection of buttons, and a few text members. Figure 25.1 shows the first frame, a simple menu.

The movie is an example of a simple presentation that has several accessibility features. The buttons can be selected by using the Tab key to select the button and then using the (Return) [Enter] key to press the button. Text-to-speech functionality will speak information about each button as well as read some text elements aloud.

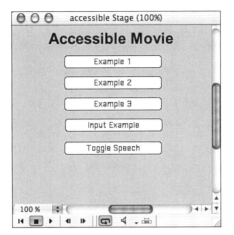

Figure 25.1
This menu can be completely controlled with only the Tab and (Return) [Enter] keys.

Accessibility Behaviors

To make the buttons in the movie functional and accessible, first open the Library panel by choosing Window, Library Palette. Then use the pop-up menu at the top of that panel to select the Accessibility category. Figure 25.2 shows the Library panel. It contains all the behaviors we'll need. Table 25.1 shows all the behaviors to be used in this movie.

Figure 25.2
The Library panel's accessibility behaviors are all you need to make an accessible movie.

25

Table 25.1   Accessibility Library Behaviors

Behavior	Where It Goes	What It Does
Accessibility Target	Box shape	Moves this box around the currently selected sprite
Accessibility Keyboard Controller	Off-Stage editable text sprite	Accepts keyboard input and passes it on to other behaviors
Accessibility Item	On buttons or other sprites that can be selected	Indicates that a sprite has an accessibility component
Accessibility Group Order	On buttons or other sprites that can be selected	Allows you to specify the order in which sprites can be tabbed through
Accessibility Text Edit Item	One editable text sprite	Speaks the keys as the user types into an editable text sprite
Accessibility Speak	On buttons or other sprites that can be selected	Speaks some text when this item is selected
Accessibility Speak Enable Disable	Button	Allows a button to toggle between speech on and off
Accessibility Speak Member Text	Text sprite	Speaks the text in the member when selected
Accessibility Captioning	Text sprite	Allows spoken text to be passed from the Accessibility Synch Caption behavior and displayed in this sprite
Accessibility Synch Caption	On buttons or other sprites that can be selected	Spoken text is also displayed in a caption text member

Creating the Supporting Sprites

Before adding any behaviors to the movie, you'll need to create two sprites. The first is an editable text member. It doesn't have to be any particular size or use any special font. Just make sure that its editable property is turned on with the Property Inspector. Then, drag it off to the side of the Stage so that it is not visible. In the example movie, you can find this editable text sprite in channel 9.

Next, you need to create a sprite to be used to highlight the active button or other element on the Stage. A simple rectangle is perfect for this. It should also be dragged off to the side of the Stage. In the example movie, it is a single-pixel wide red rectangle in channel 10.

Now apply the behavior Accessibility Keyboard Controller to the editable text sprite. Apply the behavior Accessibility Target to the rectangle. Use the default parameters for each.

An accessible movie always has a target. A *target* is the current active sprite, such as a button or editable text member.

The rectangle sprite is used to outline the current target in the movie. The editable text sprite is used to capture any and all keyboard input. When the user presses the Tab key, the target advances to the next button. When the target is a button, and the user presses (Return) [Enter], this activates the button like a mouse click normally would.

Making Buttons Accessible

Now that we have a keyboard control sprite and a target sprite, we can apply behaviors to the buttons. First, drop the Accessibility Item behavior onto each of the buttons. When asked for parameters, use the default Accessibility Group, but enter a different Command to Execute? parameter for each: `go to frame "1"`, `go to frame "2"`, `go to frame "3"`, `go to frame "input"`, and `nothing` for that last button.

Before these buttons will work, they also need to have the Accessibility Group Order behavior dropped on them. This asks for a Tab Order. Use 1, 2, 3, 4, and 5 for these values.

If you are building this movie step-by-step, you will need to attach a `go to the frame` script onto this first frame. Then try the movie. The red rectangle appears around the first button. You can Tab from button to button.

Adding Speech

Next, we'll add speech to the movie. Drag and drop the Accessibility Speak behavior onto each button. Enter the text you want to be spoken when the button is selected. For instance, the first button could say `Select this to go to example one`.

Now when you run the movie, Tabbing between the buttons will activate the Speech Xtra, and the descriptions of each button will be spoken by the computer.

The Toggle Speech button should have an additional behavior: Accessibility Speak Enable Disable. Use the default options.

Now when you run the movie, the last button will toggle speech on and off and speak "Speech On" and "Speech Off" while doing so.

Completing the Movie

To complete this movie, create four more frames: "1," "2," "3," and "Input." Stretch the Toggle Speech button across all frames. Add a Return button to these new frames but not the first one. Add the same behaviors to this button as are applied to the menu buttons on the first frame. Use `go to frame "main"` for its Command to Execute? and 6 as its group order number. Remember to label the first frame of the movie "main". Also, place the `go to the frame` script on each of these frames.

If you are building this movie step-by-step, the movie's Score should now look a lot like Figure 25.3 except for the "caption" member in the last sprite.

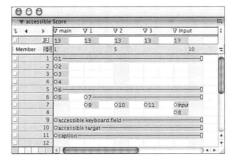

Figure 25.3
This Score shows five frames of a presentation.

25

Each of the first three new frames should include a static text member that contains some text. Attach the Accessibility Item and Accessibility Group Order behaviors to these three text sprites. Leave the Command to Execute? for all these at nothing. Give them all the group order number 1. So on these three frames we'll have the two buttons at the bottom of the screen as numbers 5 and 6, and the text member as number 1. Fortunately, the behaviors will be able to handle this without a problem. Figure 25.4 shows the first of these new frames.

Figure 25.4
This frame contains two accessible buttons and an accessible text member.

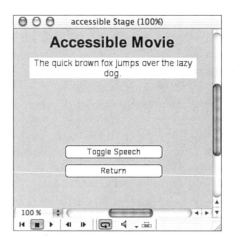

To the text members, attach an Accessibility Speak Member Text behavior. Select the text member from the pop-up list in the Parameters dialog box. Now, when the user tabs to this text member, the contents of the member will be spoken.

The last frame of the movie is named "input." It also has a text member, but this one is editable. The member is named "input" in the Cast. Instead of attaching an Accessibility Item behavior to this one, attach the Accessibility Text Edit Item to it. Then add an Accessibility Group Order behavior and use 1 as the group order number.

An editable text sprite with these behaviors acts like any other accessible sprite, but the user can type text into the member. As each letter is typed, the letter is spoken.

Let's add one more button to the movie. This will appear under the editable text sprite on frame "input." Add Accessibility Item and Accessibility Group Order behaviors, with order number 2. Also add an Accessibility Speak behavior that will speak "Select this to test your text."

Now, return to the Accessibility Item behavior and change the nothing to voiceSpeak(member("input").text). This is the Lingo syntax to send a string to the Speech Xtra. When this button is activated, it simply speaks the text the user has entered.

The last piece needed to complete this movie is to add a text member to the bottom of the movie, across all frames. This is for captioning. Attach an Accessibility Captioning behavior to it.

Now, go back and add an Accessibility Synch Caption behavior to every button in the movie on every frame. This behavior sends the text that would normally be spoken to this caption text member.

Now you have an accessible movie. Each button produces spoken text and a caption explaining its use. Each text member is spoken by the Speech Xtra. The user can navigate through the entire contents of the movie with only the Tab and (Return) [Enter] keys. Text entered into the editable text member is confirmed by having each letter pronounced and has a button that reads back the complete contents.

Play with the example movie for a while to get a feel for all that these behaviors do to make it easier to navigate.

➡️ *If you are worried about accessibility working for all your users, see "Giving the User a Way to Test Accessibility" in the "Troubleshooting" section at the end of this chapter.*

The default settings for Accessibility Synch Caption are to have the first 10 words of the spoken text placed in the caption. You can also adjust this so that it places more or less text in the caption, or advances the caption as the text is spoken. I've had to do this for the Toggle Speech button in the example movie.

USING THE SPEECH XTRA

The Speech Xtra is a simple yet potentially powerful new feature of Director MX. It is incredibly easy to use. For instance, if you want your computer to speak some words, just try this in the Message panel:

```
voiceSpeak("Hello World")
```

That's how easy it is.

The Speech Xtra actually uses the Macintosh system's text-to-speech functionality and Windows' Speech API (version 4 and newer). Windows XP comes with version 5, but owners of older Windows machines can get the Speech API at `http://www.Microsoft.com/speech/`. Anyone with Macintosh system 8.6 and later has the Mac text-to-speech software by default.

Both the Mac and Windows speech functionality can be turned off by the computer's owner, so you might want to check to make sure that speech is available. You can do this with the `voiceInitialize()` command. This returns TRUE only if speech is working on the machine.

Speech Functionality

Here is a simple piece of code that checks for speech functionality. If it doesn't find it, it gives the user more information.

```
if not voiceInitialize() then
 if the platform contains "win" then
  alert "You'll need to have Windows Speech API installed."
  gotoNetPage("http://www.microsoft.com/speech/")
 else
  alert "You'll need to enable text-to-speech on your computer."
 end if
end
```

When you just use `voiceSpeak`, you get the default voice for the user's computer. However, you can control the voice in many ways. Table 25.2 shows all the speech commands.

Table 25.2   Speech Xtra Commands and Functions

Command or Function	Description
voiceSpeak(*text*)	Speaks the text
voiceCount()	Returns the number of voices available on the user's system
voiceGet()	Returns a property list with information about the current voice
voiceSet(*n*)	Allows you to set the voice to voice number *n*
voiceGetAll()	Returns a list of property lists with information about all voices
voiceGetVolume()	Returns a number representing the voice volume
voiceSetVolume(*n*)	Allows you to set the volume of speech
voiceGetPitch()	Returns a positive, negative, or 0 number that determines the pitch of the voice
voiceSetPitch(*n*)	Allows you to set the pitch of the voice to a positive, negative, or 0 value representing the difference from the default
voiceGetRate()	Returns the rate, or speed, of the voice
voiceSetRate(*n*)	Allows you to set the rate of the voice to a negative, positive, or 0 value representing the difference from the default
voicePause	Temporarily pauses the speech
voiceResume	Resumes paused speech
voiceStop	Stops the speech
voiceState()	Returns #playing, #paused, or #stopped
voiceWordPos	Returns the word number that is currently being played

> If you can't get the Speech Xtra to pronounce some words properly, see "Speaking Properly" in the "Troubleshooting" section at the end of this chapter.

One of the problems in working with the Speech Xtra is that you don't really know the range of values for volume, pitch, and rate. These vary depending on the operating system and version of the speech system software.

But you can get a list of the available voices with `voiceGet` and `voiceGetAll` and then choose which voice to use based on the value of the returned list.

When you use `voiceGet`, you get a short list back that describes the voice. Here is an example:

```
put voiceGet()
-- [#name: "Agnes", #age: "35", #gender: "Female", #index: 1]
```

The `#index` property can be used to determine which voice number it is in the total list of voices. You can use `voiceCount` to determine the number of the last voice.

Here is a button script from the example movie `changevoice.dir` that advances to the next voice, displays information about that voice, and speaks a short sentence:

```
on beginSprite me
 -- get current voice and display
 voiceInitialize()
 currVoice = voiceGet()
 showVoice(me,currVoice)
end

on mouseUp me
 -- get voice number and add 1
 currVoiceNum = voiceGet().index
 currVoiceNum = currVoiceNum + 1
 if currVoiceNum > voiceCount() then currVoiceNum = 1

 -- set the voice by number
 voiceSet(currVoiceNum)

 -- get current voice and display
 currVoice = voiceGet()
 showVoice(me,currVoice)
end

on showVoice me, currVoice
 -- put voice info into text member
 info = "Current Voice:"&RETURN
 put "Name:"&&currVoice.name&RETURN after info
 put "Age:"&&currVoice.age&RETURN after info
 put "Gender:"&&currVoice.gender&RETURN after info
 put "Index:"&&currVoice.index after info
 member("display info").text = info

 -- test the new voice
 voiceSpeak("Hello World. I am"&& currVoice.name)
end
```

> Although Mac users typically have about 22 voices installed with their system, Windows users will only have one. You can manually add more voices from Microsoft's site, but you shouldn't count on them having any more than the default voice.

You can use the voiceWordPos function to track the speech as it moves through the text. The obvious use for this is to display the words in a text member as they are spoken.

Here is a simple script that adds a word to a text member when each word is spoken. It can be found in the movie caption.dir.

> **Caution**
>
> In testing the Speech Xtra, I found that if you do not use the voiceInitialize command, you sometimes get a number, rather than a list, returned by voiceGet().

```
property pCurrentWordNum
property pText

on beginSprite me
 -- start speaking
 voiceInitialize()
 pText = "The quick brown fox jumps over the lazy dog."
 voiceSpeak(pText)
```

25

```
  -- currently word 0
 pCurrentWordNum = 0
end

on exitFrame me
 -- get current word according to Xtra
 n = voiceWordPos()

 if (pCurrentWordNum <> n) and (n > 0) then -- new word, add word
  pCurrentWordNum = n
  member("caption").text = pText.word[1..n]

 end if
end
```

This behavior only works with short pieces of text that can fit in a small text member. For longer passages of text, you may want to consider using a longer text member. You can also look for a period in the word being spoken and only display the text one sentence at a time. Here is how this script would work:

```
property pCurrentWordNum
property pStartWord, pText

on beginSprite me
 -- start speaking
 voiceInitialize()
 pText = "Hello World. The quick brown fox jumps over the lazy dog."
 voiceSpeak(pText)

 -- currently word 0
 pCurrentWordNum = 0
 pStartWord = 1
end

on exitFrame me
 -- get current word according to Xtra
 n = voiceWordPos()

 if (pCurrentWordNum <> n) and (n > 0) then -- new word, add word
  pCurrentWordNum = n
  member("caption").text = pText.word[pStartWord..n]

  -- if end of sentence, reset starting word to next word
  if pText.word[n] contains "." then pStartWord = n+1

 end if
end
```

Another use for the `voiceWordPos` would be to animate a mouth on a character. Unfortunately, there is no way to determine whether the voice is speaking or pausing between sentences. But at least you can determine when a new word begins. This behavior, found in `mouth.dir`, uses this information to animate a simple mouth:

```
property pCurrentWordNum
property pTimeDelay

on beginSprite me
 -- start speaking
 voiceInitialize()
 voiceSpeak("The quick brown fox jumps over the lazy dog.")

 -- currently word 0
 pCurrentWordNum = 0
end

on exitFrame me
 -- get current word according to Xtra
 n = voiceWordPos()

 if n = 0 then -- done speaking
  sprite(me.spriteNum).member = member("Mouth Closed")

 else if pCurrentWordNum <> n then -- new word, open mouth
  pCurrentWordNum = n
  pTimeDelay = the milliseconds + 100
  sprite(me.spriteNum).member = member("Mouth Open")

 else if the milliseconds > pTimeDelay then -- close after time has passed
  sprite(me.spriteNum).member = member("Mouth Closed")
 end if
end
```

TROUBLESHOOTING

Making Sure Accessiblity Is Done Right

How can I make sure that I am correctly following government accessibility guidelines?

If accessibility is critical to your project, you may want to bring in an expert to advise you when designing your interface.

Giving the User a Way to Test Accessibility

Some of my users are saying that they don't hear the speech. Is there any way to make sure that it works for everyone?

Even if speech software is correctly installed on the user's machine, speech can be disabled by something as simple as having the volume turned down too low. You probably want to state that your movie uses speech and even provide a test screen for users.

Speaking Properly

The Speech Xtra is neat, but sometimes it pronounces words incorrectly. Is there any way I can teach it proper pronunciation?

Some words just don't sound right when spoken by the computer. Consider using phonetically spelled words rather than their real spelling. For instance, "question" doesn't sound as good as "kwestshon." To get my Mac to pronounce my name correctly, I need to use "Rosensw-eyeg".

DID YOU KNOW?

- Macs come with about 22 different voices, but some are more for novelty purposes than for serious accessibility functionality. Your main factor in selecting a voice for accessibility features should always be clarity.

- After you get to know the accessibility behaviors well, you may want to try writing your own behaviors, custom tailored to your needs. The existing behaviors are by no means the only way to meet accessibility standards. Some developers were writing their own behaviors several versions of Director ago, before these behaviors existed.

- Instead of using alert boxes for small pieces of information, consider using `voiceSpeak` instead. It can even be used as a debugging tool. For instance, you can have your movie speak to your when the code reaches certain conditions. It could even read the values of a variable when you press a button or reach a point in the code.

26

USING XTRAS

WHAT ARE XTRAS?

Xtras serve three purposes. First, they give Macromedia a way to develop pieces of Director independently, without requiring it to make a whole new version of Director. Features such as QuickTime support, Flash support, animated cursors, image filters, and vector graphics are all made possible by Xtras, not anything inside the Director program itself.

Second, Xtras are used by Macromedia to add features that not all developers may need in their finished products. Network Lingo, for instance, is not needed in a projector that does not communicate with the Internet. Because network Lingo is enabled through Xtras, these Xtras can be left out when a projector is created, and the resulting projector is smaller.

Finally, Xtras can be developed by third parties to add functionality to Director that Macromedia has not provided. Many companies produce Xtras commercially, and you can purchase them. At other times, companies develop Xtras for their own use in a single product.

> Even with all the features in Director, most developers, at one time or another, need to use an Xtra. Many standard items in Director, such as vector members, network Lingo, and bitmap importing, are made possible by Xtras already installed in Director.

XTRAS SHIPPED WITH DIRECTOR MX

Macromedia provides many Xtras that come installed with Director. You can find these in the `Xtras` folder inside the `Director` folder. Still more are on the Director MX CD-ROM in the `Xtra Partners` folder. Most are Xtras that add functionality to the authoring environment, but some can be used in projectors as well.

> If you are thinking about making your own Xtra, beware of the trap into which many developers fall: They often assume that a task cannot be done with Lingo alone, when it can. Director Lingo is so powerful that you should always carefully consider the option of using Lingo before commissioning an Xtra.

The following list includes most of the Xtras that come with Director:

- ActiveX—Also known as the Control Xtra, this Windows-only Xtra enables you to access and use ActiveX controls, such as the Internet Explorer browser engine, or custom-built ActiveX programs.

- Cursor Asset Xtra—This Xtra allows you to use animated cursors.

- MacroMix—This Windows-only Xtra enables Director movies to play more than one sound at a time in Windows.

- Photoshop Filters—This Xtra enables you to use Photoshop-compatible filters on bitmap cast members. Many filters will not work in Director, and they must be compatible with Photoshop 3.1.

- Flash Asset—This Xtra enables you to import Flash movies as cast members. It is also used as the engine for vector shape members.

- Intel Effects—This Windows-only Xtra enables you to perform a variety of processor-intensive special effects.

- Animated GIF Asset—This Xtra enables you to import and use animated GIFs.

- FileIO—This Xtra adds Lingo commands to enable you to open, save, and modify text files.

- Font Asset Xtra and Font Xtra—These Xtras enable you to import fonts as cast members and use these fonts in text members.

- Import Xtra for PowerPoint—This Xtra enables you to import Microsoft PowerPoint files. It converts the file to a Score and a Cast, complete with all the items in the original presentation.

- MUI—This Xtra contains code to generate many of the dialog boxes used in Director. You can also use it to create your own dialog boxes.

- SWA Xtras—These Xtras enable you to import and create Shockwave audio files and use them in your movies. They also enable you to compress internal sounds with Shockwave audio compression.

- Text Asset—This Xtra drives the text member, as well as all the text-based authoring windows, such as the Script panel.

- XMLParser—This Xtra contains additional Lingo commands for dealing with XML code, such as HTML.

- Mix Xtras—These Xtras enable you to import all sorts of different file types, including images and sounds.

- Multiuser—This Xtra enables you to communicate with the Director Multiuser Server program. It also communicates with other Director projectors or Shockwave movies as long as they are networked.

- Net Support Xtras—These Xtras add the network Lingo commands and the protocols to support them.

- Sound Control—This Xtra in enables you to use modern sound Lingo, such as `queue` and `play`.

- QuickTime 6—This Xtra enables you to use any QuickTime 4 movie, including QuickTime VR movies, as a cast member.

- Shockwave 3D Asset Xtra—This is the main engine behind Shockwave 3D.

- RealMedia Asset—This allows you to add RealMedia streams on Windows.

- Havok—The Havok physics Xtra works with the Shockwave 3D Xtra to allow you to easily make models in the 3D world. This gives your objects real physical properties such as mass, momentum, and friction.

- Speech Xtra—Enables simple Lingo commands to access speech software on the Windows and Mac operating systems.

- Zip Xtra—Create simple zip-compressed files from files on the hard drive.

26

Many of the Xtras in the Director Xtras folder are not meant to be used in projectors. The Xtras simply extend the authoring environment. The Mix Xtras, for instance, are used only to import images and sounds. However, sometimes this Xtra is required when you are importing new images in your projector while it is running on the user's machine.

Some Xtras cannot be used in projectors at all. The QuickTime Asset Options Xtra, for instance, supplies the Options dialog box that the author uses during authoring. There are also "options" Xtras for the Flash and Animated GIF Xtras. Including these with a projector results in an error message. These three Xtras are all named with the word "options," so you know not to include them.

⇨ *If you are getting an error about a duplicate Xtra when launching Director, see "Duplicate Xtra Error" in the "Troubleshooting" section at the end of this chapter.*

USING XTRA LINGO

A few Lingo properties and functions help you work with Xtras. You can, for instance, determine whether an Xtra is working simply by trying to use it. If the initial new command does not return a valid object, you know there has been an error. Use the objectP function to determine whether you have a valid object:

```
xObj = new(xtra "FileIO")
put objectP(xObj)
-- 1
```

If you want to determine whether an Xtra is present before you try to use it, you can take a look at each Xtra present by using the name property, as well as the number property, of the xtras object. Here is a handler that checks for the existence of an Xtra:

```
on checkForXtra xtraname
 repeat with i = 1 to the number of xtras
  if the name of xtra i = xtraname then
   return TRUE
  end if
 end repeat
 return FALSE
end
```

You can test this handler in the Message panel:

```
put checkForXtra("FileIO")
-- 1
put checkForXtra("xxx")
-- 0
```

Two other properties also tell you what Xtras are available. The the xtraList property returns a long list of available Xtras. Each item in the list contains a #name and #version property.

There is also a the movieXtraList property that corresponds to the dialog box you get when you choose Modify, Movie, Xtras. Each item is a list that contains either a name, a #packageFiles list, or both. The #packageFiles list contains a #name and a #version, which give the movie the information it needs to download the Xtra from the Internet for use in Shockwave.

For most Xtras, you can use the interface function to get a list of all the possible commands, properties, and usage guidelines. The results vary from Xtra to Xtra, depending on what the developer decided this function should return. You can use it in the Message panel by typing something like this:

You can also use the pull-down Scripting Xtras menu on top of the Script panel to find commands and functions used by some Xtras.

```
put interface(xtra "FileIO")
```

USING XTRAS IN SHOCKWAVE

It used to be nearly impossible to use Xtras in Shockwave. Shockwave itself worked fine with them. However, to use them it had to have a copy of the Xtra. This meant that the end users had to download the Xtra and place it in their Shockwave folders.

Easy enough for a developer, but nearly impossible for the general public, who might not know about browser plug-ins and where to find the right folders on their hard drives.

Starting with Director 7, you can use some Xtras through the automatic downloading function in Shockwave. This means that when a movie signals Shockwave that it needs an Xtra, Shockwave downloads it from the Internet and installs it.

For this to happen, the Xtra developer first has to go through the proper channels with Macromedia so that the Xtra is authorized to be downloadable. This is to prevent someone from making a virus-like Xtra that would cause harm. These Xtras are considered "Safe for Shockwave" by Macromedia. But you can skip this process if you just want users to download and install the Xtra manually.

Many of the Xtras mentioned earlier in this chapter are downloadable. Check with the Xtra manufacturer to find out whether the one you need is downloadable. Because this is a desirable feature, most Xtra developers note this on their Web pages and documentation.

To enable your movie to download Xtras, your first stop is choosing Modify, Movie, Xtras. This brings up the dialog box shown in Figure 26.1 with the names of Xtras that your movie needs. If the Xtra you need is not listed, click the Add button to add it.

26

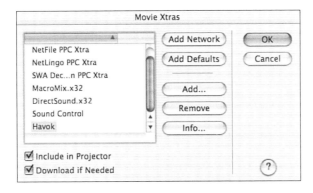

Figure 26.1
The Movie Xtras dialog box allows you to specify that an Xtra should be added to a user's Shockwave folder if needed.

After it's in the list of needed Xtras, select it and click the Download If Needed check box below the list. At this point, Director calls out to the Internet to check the location of the Xtra. You will see a short-lived Downloading progress bar.

Now that your movie is set to download the Xtra if needed, you can check to see exactly what it will do. In the Message panel, use `put the movieXtraList` to display a list of Xtras that the movie thinks it needs. This should be the same as the Modify, Movie, Xtras dialog box list, but with more information.

For instance, the item in the list that represents the QuickTime Xtra looks like this:

```
[#name: "QuickTime Asset", #packageUrl:
"http://download.macromedia.com/pub/shockwave8/xtras/QuickTime3Asset/
➥QuickTime3Asset", #packageFiles:
➥ [[#fileName: "QuickTime Asset", #version: "8.0"]]]
```

You can see that the Director movie knows which file to download and where it is located on the Internet. Other Xtras may include multiple files if they are needed by the Xtra.

When you run the movie for the first time in a browser, you will see a dialog box that asks whether you want the Xtra installed. Clicking OK causes the installation to proceed. Then the movie will run. It is as simple as that.

The Xtra install dialog box is necessary because of Internet security concerns. An Xtra developer can easily make an Xtra that would do harm to a user's machine. This is why Xtras must be certified by Macromedia before they can be made downloadable. The security dialog box is a second form of protection, allowing the user to abort the addition of the Xtra to Shockwave. You should put a warning about this on your Web pages so that users know to expect the Xtra install dialog box and do not feel that it will cause a security problem.

> Although you can package Xtras into a projector, this will slow down the projector at launch and increase the projector size. It is better to make an xtras folder and place the xtra in there instead if you can.

THIRD-PARTY XTRAS

If someone needs something done in Director that isn't built-in to Director, usually an Xtra exists to fill the need. More than a dozen Xtra development companies are out there, and several people have created single Xtras for a single purpose.

Most of these Xtras work on both Mac and Windows platforms. However, different versions of the Xtras will be needed for each platform just as different versions of projectors are needed for each platform.

The rest of this section categorizes and describes most of the Xtras currently available. But there are even more. The three main sources to check for Xtras are Macromedia's site, The UpdateStage.com list of Director-related products, and the Director Web list of Xtras.

- Macromedia—http://macromedia.com/software/xtras/director/

- UpdateStage—http://www.updatestage.com/products_table.html

- Director Web—http://www.mcli.dist.maricopa.edu/director/xobj.html

⇨ *If you can't get Xtras to work cross-platform, see "Remember to Include Cross-Platform Files" in the "Troubleshooting" section at the end of this chapter.*

> **Caution**
>
> The biggest problem at the start of 2003 is that many cross-platform Xtras work with Mac OS 9 projectors but not Mac OS X. However, the Xtra developers are working hard to bring them to the Mac OS X platform. Check the Web site for each Xtra to see whether it is available for OS X.

Multipurpose Utility Xtras

These Xtras perform a wide variety of tasks, usually having to do with communicating with the computer's operating system or files.

Buddy API Xtra

The Buddy API Xtra adds a bunch of Lingo functions that deal with the computer operating system. Because the Mac and Windows operating systems differ so much, many of these functions work on only one platform or the other.

To be available for use, the Buddy API Xtra merely needs to be present in the Xtras folder. You don't have to create an instance of the Xtra or do anything else. Just use the functions as you would any other Lingo syntax.

A basic example uses this Xtra to get the operating system version. For instance, on a Mac, in the Message panel, you can do this:

```
put baVersion("mac")
-- "10.2.3"
```

All functions of the Buddy API Xtra start with "ba" to distinguish them from other Lingo functions. Here are some more useful functions:

```
put baVersion("os")
-- "Mac10"
```

Other possible values for this function would be "Win95", "Win98", "WinNT", "WinXP", and "Mac9". The following function tests to see whether a font is installed:

```
put baFontInstalled("Arial","Plain")
-- 1
```

On Windows, you can even use Buddy API to install a font. You can also get Windows Registry information, INI files, or command-line arguments to Windows projectors, as well as restart Windows, set the default DOS directory, restrict the cursor to an area, and set screensaver information.

Buddy API can also create a folder and copy and rename files—tasks sadly missing from the FileIO Xtra.

Take a look at the Buddy API documentation on the CD-ROM to see a complete list of commands and functions. It is a truly impressive list. Here is a small sampling. Visit the Web site for a complete list.

- SysFolder—Returns the location of system folders
- DiskList—Returns a list of mounted disks

26

- FontList—Returns a list of installed fonts

- CommandArgs—Returns the command-line arguments the application was started with

- DisableSwitching—Disables/enables task switching

- DisableScreenSaver—Disables/enables the screensaver

- SetWallpaper—Sets the desktop wallpaper

- RunProgram—Runs an external program, with command-line arguments

- WinHelp—Shows a Windows help file

- PlaceCursor—Positions the cursor

- PrinterInfo—Returns information about the installed printer

- CreateFolder—Creates a new folder

- CopyFile—Copies a file

- MakeShortcut—Creates a shortcut/alias

- SendKeys—Sends simulated key presses to the active window

Web site: http://www.mods.com.au/budapi/

DirectOS Xtra

This Xtra is similar to the Buddy API Xtra. It enables you to get and set information about the user's operating system and hardware. Here's a small sampling of what you can do according to the documentation:

- Retrieve the operating system type and exact version.

- Create, display, and operate a message box.

- Find an application associated with a specific file type.

- Manipulate the external application's windows.

- Set cursor position or confine it to a rectangular area of the screen.

- Generate a mouse click for any of the three mouse buttons.

- Log off, shut down, or restart the system.

- Launch external applications at a specified state with command-line support.

- Retrieve information about disk drives, such as type, name, size, and free space.

- Retrieve a list of subfolders and files in a folder, with wildcard support.

- Read from, write to, and delete from INI files.

- Easily read, write, and delete strings, integers, and binary data to and from the Windows Registry.

- Install screensavers; get and set their activity and time out.

- Disable/Enable Ctrl+Alt+Del, Alt+Tab, Microsoft key, and other system keys in Windows.

- Encrypt/decrypt text and string variables.

Web site: `http://www.directxtras.com`

Enhancer Xtra

This Xtra combines the Resolution Xtra and the Move Cursor Xtra, and adds several other functions. You can check and use joystick devices and create pop-up menus.

Web site: `http://andradearts.com/`

File Xtra

The File Xtra picks up where the FileIO Xtra leaves off, giving you tons of commands to access all sorts of file functions. As of the time of this writing, no OS X version yet. Here is a list of all the commands in the version that ships on the CD.

- `fx_FileOpenDialog`—Presents an open dialog to the user and returns the file the user selects

- `fx_FileSaveAsDialog`—Presents a save dialog to the user and returns the path and filename the user selects

- `fx_FileExists`—Checks to see whether a file exists

- `fx_FileIsLink`—Checks to see whether a file is a Windows shortcut or a Mac alias.

- `fx_FileRename`—Renames a file

- `fx_FileDelete`—Deletes a file

- `fx_FileRecycle`—Places the file in the recycle bin or trash

- `fx_FileCopy`—Makes a copy of a file to a new location

- `fx_FileMove`—Moves a file to a new location

- `fx_FileGetWriteState`—Checks to see whether the file is read-only

- `fx_FileSetWriteState`—Sets whether the file is read-only

- `fx_FileGetModDate`—Returns the modification date of the file

- `fx_FileGetSize`—Returns the size of a file

- `fx_FileGetType`—Returns the Mac creator and file type or the Windows dot-three extension

26

- `fx_FileSetType`—Allows you to set the Mac creator and file type or the Windows dot-three extension

- `fx_FileCompare`—Tells you whether two files have the same size and modification date

- `fx_FileOpenDocument`—Opens a file with the application associated with it

- `fx_FilePrintDocument`—Prints a file using the application associated with it

- `fx_FileGetAppPath`—Returns the path of the application associated with the document

- `fx_FileRunApp`—Launches the application associated with the document

- `fx_LinkCreate`—Creates a Mac alias or a Windows shortcut

- `fx_LinkResolve`—Returns the actual file that an alias or shortcut links to

- `fx_FolderSelectDialog`—Opens a dialog that lets the user select a folder

- `fx_FolderGetSpecialPath`—Returns the path to special system folders, such as the preferences folder, the favorites folder, the control panels folder, and so on

- `fx_FolderExists`—Checks to see whether a folder exists

- `fx_FolderCreate`—Creates a new folder

- `fx_FolderDelete`—Removes a folder

- `fx_FolderRecycle`—Places a folder in the Windows recycle bin or the Mac trash folder

- `fx_FolderCopy`—Copies a folder to a new path

- `fx_FolderMove`—Moves a folder to a new path

- `fx_FolderSyncOneWay`—Modifies the contents of one folder to match the contents of another

- `fx_FolderSyncBothWays`—Modifies the contents of two folders to make them both match

- `fx_FolderToList`—Creates a list of files and folders at a location

- `fx_VolumeExists`—Checks to see whether a hard drive or other volume exists

- `fx_VolumeGetFreeBytes`—Checks to see how much space is left on a hard drive or other volume

- `fx_VolumeGetTotalBytes`—Returns the size of a hard drive or other volume

- `fx_VolumeIsCDROM`—Checks to see whether a volume is a CD

- `fx_VolumeIsRemovable`—Checks to see whether a volume is removable media, such as a Zip disk

- `fx_VolumeEject`—Ejects a volume, such as a Zip disk or CD

- `fx_VolumesToList`—Returns a list of all volumes

- `fx_ErrorNumber`—Returns an error number for the last File Xtra operation

■ `fx_ErrorString`— Returns an error string for the last File Xtra operation

Web site: `http://www.kblab.net/xtras`

OSUtil

This utility Xtra performs a variety of OS and file functions. You can move, rename, or copy files. You can get just about any property or flag of a file, folder, or volume.

Web site: `http://www.powerup.com.au/~farryp/`

RavKitchenSink Xtra

This new utility Xtra, under development as I write this, can do a variety of things such as create memory files, asynchronous file access, network content streams, a variety of encryption schemes, email support, compression algorithms, com port access, and other goodies.

Web site: RavWare, `http://www.ravware.com/`

System Tools Xtra

This is a scripting Xtra for accessing common Windows API functions for Windows. Here are a few functions that are available.

■ Add and remove fonts

■ Copy files

■ Create directories

■ Determine whether a given drive is a CD-ROM device

■ Get and set environment variables and strings

■ Launch an application or URL

■ Read registry integers and strings

Web site: Media Shoppe, `http://www.mediashoppe.com/xtras/`

26

Application Control Xtras

These Xtras allow you to launch and control other applications. Also check the section "Multipurpose Utility Xtras" earlier in the chapter for Xtras that can do this.

MasterApp Xtra

This Xtra is a more reliable alternative to the `open` command in Director. With MasterApp, you can reliably open documents in applications without knowing the exact path of the application. You can even do things such as open documents in applications that are already running, or open documents in applications that did not create the document.

This Xtra also enables you to get information about running applications and to send messages to some applications.

Web site: `http://www.updatestage.com/xtras/masterapp.html`

Relaunch Utility

You might have run across this situation before: You want Director to run a program, perhaps an installer, and then quit. The user then interacts with the other program for a while, until the user quits or the program ends. Then, it would be great if the Director projector would automatically relaunch.

The Relaunch Utility does just that. It can be particularly useful to get a user to run the QuickTime installer, and then have the user safely return to her projector.

Web site: `http://www.updatestage.com/xtras/`

BrowserController 2

This Xtra provides comprehensive control of Windows browsers from your projector, as well as control of the projector from the browser. For instance, you can have links back from the browser to your movie, and form data can be passed from the browser back to your movie.

Web site: Magister Ludi, `http://www.magisterludi.com/`

RavWare PPViewer Xtra

Description: Allows you to control Microsoft PowerPoint Viewer. You can get information such as the number of sliders and the current slide number. You can also move back and forth between slides.

Web site: RavWare, `http://www.ravware.com/`

zOpen, zPrint, and zLaunch

This Xtra allows you to open and print documents in Windows using external programs. You can use it to open a document with its associated application; print documents with Acrobat, Word, or other applications; pass a document to an open application; or locate an application associated with a file. Also check out zLaunch and zScript for Macs.

Web site: Zeus Productions, `http://www.zeusprod.com/`

zScript

This Xtra allows you to pass instructions to the Mac OS using AppleScript.

Web site: Zeus Productions, `http://www.zeusprod.com/`

User Interface Xtras

These Xtras allow you to add buttons, menus, sliders, and other user interface items to your movies. You can also control the way MIAWs and projectors are displayed and change the resolution of the monitor.

OSControl Xtra

Want to add beveled buttons, progress bars, arrow buttons, sliders, radio buttons, and check boxes to your Director movies? Sure, you can do all of these with complex behaviors and a lot of bitmaps, but the OSControl Xtra allows you to add them much more easily.

You can even add elements such as buttons and have them change to reflect the user's operating system: Mac or Windows. This is the type of functionality that really should be part of Director but isn't. This Xtra fills the gap.

Web site: `http://www.peghole.com/xtras/`

Border Xtra and BorderPatch

This Xtra turns off the borders around the Stage or any MIAW. This helps if you plan to use MIAWs over other MIAWs, if the 1-pixel black border just doesn't fit in with your design.

Web site: Media Connect, `http://www.mcmm.com`

Dialogs Xtra

This Xtra displays Open, Save, and Pick Folder file dialog boxes.

Red Eye Software/UpdateStage

Web site: `http://www.updatestage.com/xtras/xtrahome.html`

Popup Xtra

This Xtra allows you to create custom pop-up menus, including multilevel pop-ups. You can control just about any aspect of the pop-up, including fonts and colors.

Web site: Scott Kildall/UpdateStage, `http://www.updatestage.com/xtras/xtrahome.html`

RavWinShaper Xtra

This Xtra Enables Director developers to change the shape of the display window for a projector into an elliptical, polygonal, textual, or spline-shaped window. You can also use a bitmap cast member as a transparency mask. Stage borders can be completely removed, and the projector window's corners can be rounded. The Xtra allows developers to add a user-defined activation area to act as a handle bar for dragging the projector around the desktop.

Web site: RavWare, `http://www.ravware.com/`

26

Resolution Xtra

This Xtra allows you to change the screen resolution and depth and then change it back without disturbing the position of the desktop icons. You can also turn off application switching.

Web site: Andrade Arts, `http://andradearts.com/`

Database Xtras

These Xtras allow you to use external database files as well as process data inside Director members faster.

V12-Database Engine Xtra

This Xtra is useful if you need to connect your Director movie to a large database. You can maintain and search the database, which can be local or across the Internet.

This Xtra is packed full of database features. There is a full version and a cheaper "light" version available.

Web site: `http://www.integration.qc.ca`

Datagrip

The Datagrip Xtra enables Director to communicate with Microsoft Access databases to read and write data to them. You can use SQL queries and search and sort functions.

Sight and Sound Software, `http://www.datagrip.com/`

Also look into DAOTable Xtra, a complement to the Datagrip Xtra that enables you to see more information about Microsoft Access databases.

Web site: Paul Farry, `http://www.powerup.com.au/~farryp/`

EasyBase

EasyBase enables you to create and use a Tab-separated text file as database. It includes fast full-text searching, multi-expression searching, variable field size up to 16,384 characters, quick sorting formatted lists of records for fast displaying inside one single field, relations to other databases, quick evaluation on selections, and cross-platform data files. The data files can also be encrypted.

Web site: Klaus Kobald Software Design, `http://www.kobald.com/EasyBase/`

FileFlex

FileFlex is a relational database engine for Director projects that is compatible with FoxPro and Access. FileFlex can directly exchange files from these programs, without conversion, and neither database engine is required at runtime. The Xtra also includes dynamic, live encryption and full-text search and retrieval.

Web site: Component Software, `http://www.fileflex.com`

Index Xtra and HTML Xtra

The Index Xtra consists of an indexer, which reads the HTML documents according to several formatting criteria and creates an index file that can then be searched, delivering file number within index, the title tag of the document, filename, and the number of matches to the search string. The complimentary HTML Xtra allows import of the HTML documents as HTML cast members and displays them on the Stage.

Web site: Media Connect, `http://www.mcmm.com`

TextCruncher Xtra

If you have ever had problems processing text with Lingo's string commands because they are too slow, TextCruncher is for you. When you drop it into your `Xtras` folder, it simply adds Lingo commands to your arsenal.

I tried the `FindFirst` command, which is a substitute for the Lingo `offset` command. In my tests, `FindFirst` was five times faster. In addition, TextCruncher also includes a host of other text-processing commands. Here is a partial list:

- `FindFirst`
- `FindNext`
- `FindAll`
- `GetWordOfCharPosition`
- `GetLineOfCharPosition`
- `GetItemOfCharPosition`
- `ReplaceFirst`
- `ReplaceNext`
- `ReplaceAll`
- `GetListOfWords`
- `GetListOfLines`
- `GetListOfItems`
- `ToUpperCase`
- `ToLowerCase`
- `HardWrapText`
- `HardCenterText`
- `HardAlignTextRight`

Web site: UpdateStage, `http://www.updatestage.com/xtras/`

26

Input Device Xtras

These Xtras allow your movies to use different input devices such as joysticks.

Direct Communication Xtra

This Xtra provides direct access to communication resources such as serial ports, parallel ports, fax machines, and modems.

Web site: DirectXtras Llc., `http://www.directxtras.com/`

DirectControl

This Xtra enables Lingo control of analog and digital joysticks.

Web site: DirectXtras Llc., `http://www.directxtras.com/`

Move Cursor Xtra

This Xtra simply allows you to set the position of the user's cursor.

Web site: Andrade Arts, `http://andradearts.com/`

RavJoystick Xtra

This Xtra gives you the ability to use regular and force feedback joysticks, steering wheels, touch screens, and other gaming devices.

Web site: RavWare, `http://www.ravware.com/`

SetMouse Xtra

This Xtra sets the mouse to any location on the screen.

Web site: Scirius Development, `http://www.scirius.com/HNorm/index.html`

Media Xtras

These Xtras allow you to use more media types in your Director movie.

Using Adobe Acrobat PDF Files in Director

Adobe Acrobat files have been around for a while but are still gaining popularity. They present text in a highly formatted way on the screen, so they look more like printed pages than screen text.

Many online versions of documents are given in Acrobat format, also called PDF after the dot-three extension that the files use. Companies use them for reports, and publications use them for articles and books.

With these Xtras, you can embed Acrobat files right into Director. But it doesn't stop there. You can also control the presentation of the files via Lingo. This means that you can build your own page-turning buttons and such.

Here are some Xtras that allow you to use and control PDF files:

- PDF Xtra—Integration New Media, `http://www.integration.qc.ca/`
- AcroViewer Xtra—XtraMedia International, `http://www.xtramedia.com/xtras.shtml`

XtrAgent

This Xtra enables the use of Microsoft's Agent technology in Director movies. It creates a new member type that allows you to use an animated character. It can speak with text-to-speech technology or prerecorded audio and accept voice commands.

Web site: DirectXtras Llc., `http://www.directxtras.com/`

Graphics Xtras

These Xtras allow you to manipulate bitmaps, import graphics in special ways, and display them.

PhotoCaster

For some developers, PhotoCaster from As Is Software has been their best friend since Director 5. This Xtra enables you to import Photoshop files. No big deal, right? After all, you can import Photoshop files normally. However, PhotoCaster enables you to import layers from a Photoshop file. It even preserves the alpha channel.

Using this tool, an artist can create a many-layered document in Photoshop, and a Director developer can import the file as layers. This means that these layers can all be placed on the Stage together. They can be made background transparent so that higher layers show through to lower ones. The result looks just like the original Photoshop document, but each layer is still independent and can be moved or removed as the developer wants.

This technique is often used so that an artist can create an entire array of art—backgrounds, buttons, animated actors, and so on—all in one Photoshop document. This makes the art easy for the artist to maintain and also easy for the Director developer to import.

Web site: `http://www.medialab.com`

PhotoCaster also takes 32-bit images and converts them to 8-bit images. It can actually take a set of images and convert them all to a new 8-bit color palette optimized for use across all the images.

AlphaMania

The AlphaMania Xtra from Media Lab also deals with images. It enables you to import high-quality 32-bit images with alpha channels. Then, you can use effector sets to apply visual effects to the sprites. Such effects include ripple, blur, bevel, and drop shadow.

Web site: `http://www.medialab.com`

PiMz ImageImport Xtra

The ImageImport Xtra enables you to import Photoshop files. You can select from a variety of options.

I particularly like the idea that you can import many images with the registration point somewhere other than the center. For instance, you can set the registration point to the upper left for every image.

Web site: http://www.peghole.com/

AdjustColors

The AdjustColors Xtra performs color adjustments on graphics, including brightness, saturation, and RGB values of cast members. It can do this on-the-fly, allowing you to create and display the altered image to the user.

Web site: Smoothware Design, http://www.smoothware.com

BlurImage

This Xtra enables you to apply filters such as blur, motion-blur, emboss, invert, and find-edges to images in the Cast and display them live to the user.

Web site: Smoothware Design, http://www.smoothware.com

DirectImage Xtra

This Xtra enables you to export bitmap members, image objects, or the Stage into a wide variety of formats. Formats include JPEG, GIF, TIFF, BMP, PICT, PSD, and animated GIF.

The Xtra can also import more than 30 file formats and convert an image from one format to another. You can perform a variety of functions on an image, such as: resize, scale, magnify, minify, flip, flop, roll, chop, crop, rotate, and shear images.

There are also a variety of special image effects: blur, sharpen, oil paint, charcoal paint, implode, explode, motion blur, morph, shade, spread, swirl, wave, raise, edge, emboss, solarize, contrast, modulate, reduce noise, normalize, and more. With some image types, you can even access and manipulate image frames or layers.

Web site: DirectXtras Llc., http://www.directxtras.com/

DirectXport Xtra

This Xtra allows you to export a bitmap member as a file. With Director's image Lingo enhancements, this Xtra is more valuable than ever. You can save a member as a BMP, DIB, EPS, GIF, JPEG, PICT, PSD, TIFF, or one of many other formats.

You can also use image effects such as Blur, OilPaint, AddNoise, Despeckle, Emboss, Sharpen, Flip, Flop, Magnify, Minify, Scale, Sample, Zoom, Roll, Edge, Implode, Solarize, Spread, Swirl, and Transparent.

There are other image export Xtras, but this is the only one I know of that is cross-platform. However, it does suffer from a very large file size, being more than 1 MB.

Web site: DirectXtras, `http://www.directxtras.com`

RavImageExport Xtra

This Xtra allows you to save a bitmap member or the Stage to one of several supported graphic file formats such as JPEG, PNG, TIFF, CUR, ICO, BMP, and others. You can save the whole image or part of it, at any bit depth.

Web site: RavWare, `http://www.ravware.com/`

ShapeShifter 3D

This Xtra adds a complete 3D modeling environment to Director. See Chapter 16, "Creating 3D Elements," for more information.

Web site: Tabuleiro da Baiana, `http://xtras.tabuleiro.com/`

Network Xtras

These Xtras allow you to connect movies over the Internet to sources of data or other types of servers.

CDLink

This Xtra connects to the Internet and synchronizes data between your CD-ROM application and a remote location.

Web site: Ideogram Design, `http://www.cdlink.com/`

DirectConnection Xtra

This Xtra helps you control the process of allowing Mac and Windows users to connect to the Internet. Basically, here's what it can do:

- Tell you whether there is a live dial-up connection to the Internet
- Connect and disconnect the computer to the Internet as-needed, without interaction from the user
- Activate and deactivate dial-up connections
- Create, delete, and modify dial-up connection profiles
- Get and set dial-up connection properties

Web site: DirectXtras Llc., `http://www.directxtras.com/`

DirectEmail Xtra

This Xtra enables you to compose and send email messages with attachments. It doesn't need any other mail application to work. It can send mail through a server, or directly from the client machine. It can also send faxes.

Web site: DirectXtras Llc., `http://www.directxtras.com/`

DirectFTP Xtra

This Xtra allows you to save or retrieve files from FTP servers, get FTP file listings, and more. It even works with Shockwave movies.

Web site: DirectXtras Llc., `http://www.directxtras.com/`

WebXtra

With this Xtra you can create your own Web browser by using the Internet Explorer engine inside Director movies.

Web site: Tabuleiro da Baiana, `http://xtras.tabuleiro.com/`

Development Xtras

These Xtras add functionality to the Director development environment, allowing you to be more productive.

Autocomplete Xtra

This author-time Xtra works with the Script panel. As you type a Lingo keyword, it tries to predict what you are typing and complete it for you. This is similar to how some browsers try to complete the URL you are typing.

For Lingo programmers, this Xtra can save a lot of time and also help avoid typos.

Web site: Peghole, `http://www.peghole.com/xtras/`

Speller, SpellerPro, and SpellerRT2

This Xtra adds a spell checker to Director. You can check the spelling of words in field and text members. The pro version also suggests alternatives. The SpellerRT2 Xtra allows you to add spell checking to your finished projects to help the user.

Web site: Design Lynx, `http://www.designlynx.co.uk/xtras/`

Gamma Xtra

This Xtra solves the problem of images made on the Mac looking too dark when viewed in Windows. It goes through your cast and automatically adjusts all the graphics to make them lighter.

Web site: Magister Ludi, `http://www.magisterludi.com/`

Sound and Music Xtras

These Xtras allow you to import and play different sound and music formats.

Audio Xtra

The Audio Xtra by Red Eye Software enables you to record sounds on a Mac or PC, in Director or projectors. You can save these sounds as AIFF or WAV files. You can even examine the data in the sound.

The Audio Xtra is full of Lingo options, such as setting the bit depth and frequency.

Web site: `http://www.updatestage.com/xtras/`

Beatnik Xtra

The Beatnik Xtra is much more than just a MIDI player. It enables you to control and mix all sorts of music and sounds. Beatnik is also a plug-in for Internet browsers. It includes small files, similar to MIDI, that play music, plus a file that represents a bank of instruments.

You can use Beatnik to play simple MIDI files, if you want. The Lingo code is typical for an Xtra. First, you have to create an instance of the Xtra. Then, you have to give it some initial information. In this case, the Xtra needs to know the location of the instrument bank it is to use. This instrument bank is known as a `.hsb` file. You need to set the Xtra instance to look for a `.hsb` file. There is also a `stub.hsb` file that contains empty instruments. This file can be used if the Beatnik music file, called a `.rmf` file, has been created with its own set of internal instrument sounds.

When the Xtra instance is ready, a simple `play` command kicks off a MIDI file. To stop it, the `stop` command is used, and setting the Xtra instance to 0 clears memory.

Unfortunately, the company that created the Beatnik Xtra has abandoned it. The Windows version still works fine in Director MX, but there is no OS X version of the Xtra. Macromedia may release a new version of the Xtra itself in the future, but for now, this is a Windows and OS 9-only Xtra. In addition, it might be hard to find the Xtra; you'll need to look on a Director 8 CD.

26

CD Pro Xtra

This Xtra from Penworks enables you to play music from the user's CD-ROM drive. You can re-create an entire CD player interface with commands such as Play, Stop, Loop, NumTracks, CurrentTrack, TotalTimeRemaining, and many more.

Web site: Penworks, `http://www.penworks.com`

bkMixer

This Xtra controls CD audio, WAVE, and the system master volume on Windows machines.

Web site: `http://www.updatestage.com/xtras/`

VolumeController Xtra

This Xtra allows you to control the Windows system volume from your movies. You can also control the volume of each channel.

Web site: Magister Ludi, `http://www.magisterludi.com/`

DirectSound Xtra

This Xtra enables the use of Microsoft's DirectSound API. By using it, you can get low-latency mixing, hardware acceleration, and direct access to sound devices. You can also mix as many sounds as you want; get and change the sound's position, volume, panning, and frequency; and also control 3D sounds and retrieve the hardware capabilities of the sound card.

DirectXtras Llc., `http://www.directxtras.com/`

Promix Xtra

This is a comprehensive set of tools dealing with sound cards. Lingo can be used to detect whether a user has a sound card installed, and get and set mute states for any mixer device including master, wave, MIDI, CD, auxiliary, line in, PCS Peaker, DVD, and microphone. You can use it with looping structures to create fades.

Web site: Media Shoppe, `http://www.mediashoppe.com/xtras/`

Printing Xtras

These Xtras allow you to send information to the user's printer.

26

mPrint Designer Xtra

mPrint Designer enables you to generate elaborate reports from Authorware and Director.

The mPrint Xtra can print RTF (Rich Text Format) files with images from Director. You can also print an area of the screen, images, shapes, live data, and cast members. You can prepare your printable content with a visual interface and preview your document.

Web site: Media Shoppe, `http://www.mediashoppe.com/xtras/`

Print-O-Matic

Director's printing functionality is restricted to the `printFrom` command. Although this is a nice feature for animators who want a frame of animation printed to help with development, it has little use in projectors.

All that the `printFrom` command can do is print a screenshot of the Stage. You can set a reduction amount, or choose to print one frame or a series of frames.

The Print-O-Matic Lite Xtra adds the `print` command to Lingo. You can use this command to print any cast member or text string.

Although this is already an improvement over the `printFrom` command, Print-O-Matic does a lot more when you create an instance of the Xtra and use more of its commands. A typical handler looks like this:

```
on printPage
 gPrintDoc = new(xtra "PrintOMatic_Lite")
 if not objectP(gPrintDoc) then
  alert "Unable to use Print-O-Matic"
  exit
 end if
 setDocumentName gPrintDoc, "My Document"
 setMargins gPrintDoc, Rect(36,36,36,36)
 setLandscapeMode gPrintDoc, TRUE
 append gPrintDoc, member "myMember"
 if doJobSetup(gPrintDoc) then print gPrintDoc
 gPrintDoc = 0
end
```

The handler first needs to create the Xtra instance. Then it checks to make sure that it was created. It then uses the `setDocumentName` command to name the print job. It uses the `setMargins` and `setLandscapeMode` commands to set the margins to about a half-inch and to print in landscape mode instead of vertically.

The `append` command is used to add items to the print job. In this case, just one member is added. However, you can add members, sprites, and even plain text.

Finally, the `doJobSetup` command is used to bring up the operating system's Print dialog box. This function returns TRUE if the user clicks the OK button. Then, the `print` command sends the whole thing to the printer.

The full version of Print-O-Matic enables you to perform more functions and even draw lines directly to the print buffer.

Web site: `http://www.printomatic.com`

Transition Xtras

These Xtras add transitions to Director. You can then place these in the transitions channel in the Score.

DirectTransitions/DirectTransitions 3D Xtras

These two sets of Xtras give you several additional types of transitions. The first set, DirectTransitions, is similar to the sprite transitions included with Director's behavior library.

However, the second set, DirectTransitions 3D, has some unique and interesting transitions. Here is a list taken from the README file:

- Bubbles—Simulates the before image bubbling and popping to reveal the after image

- Flipboards—Simulates boards with the before image on the front and the after image on the back flipping

- Fractal Fade—Simulates the before image randomly and unevenly fading into the after image

- Fractal Morph I—Simulates the before image randomly morphing into the after image with an unclearly defined center

- Fractal Morph II—Simulates the before image randomly morphing into the after image with a clearly defined center

- Fracture—Simulates the before image exploding into spinning fractures to reveal the after image

- Peel—Simulates the before image peeling or unpeeling to reveal the after image

Web site: http://www.directxtras.com

DM Tools

DM Tools is another set of transitions that can be easily added to Director. DM Tools is actually three sets of transitions and two Xtras that add effects.

The first transition pack contains a fade, various transitions that fade with coloring, and many variations of wipe. The second pack contains close, cover, page turn, swap, twirl, and zoom in.

None of these transitions is overly spectacular, but the third pack, called DM Xtreme Transitions, contains glass, laser wipe, pixelate, ripple fade, roll, threshold, and wormhole. All these are spectacular and interesting.

DMTools, http://www.dmtools.com

Video Xtras

These Xtras allow you to display different formats of video in your movies, or bring in video from live sources.

MPEG Advance Xtra

This cross-platform Xtra displays high-performance video minimizing configuration and installation issues, and driver incompatibilities. You can create cue points and use imaging Lingo. It uses Microsoft's DirectShow and Apple's QuickTime engines to display MPEG video using only software decompression.

Web site: Tabuleiro da Baiana, http://xtras.tabuleiro.com/

TrackThemColors Xtra

This Xtra takes a live video feed and tracks objects as they move around. The Xtra takes care of displaying the video as well and can return the color of any pixel in the video area.

There is also a TTC-Pro Xtra for Mac that has video filters and other advanced functionality.

Web site: Smoothware Design, http://www.smoothware.com

Video Mask

This Xtra lets you apply video masks to live video. You can use it for effects such as chroma keying, where an object in front of a blue screen can be placed in front of another background.

Web site: Smoothware Design, `http://www.smoothware.com`

OnStage

The OnStage Xtra allows you to play back DVD content in your Director movies. Lingo commands give you access to the standard DVD features. You can even play back DVD content stored on CD-ROM or the hard drive for kiosks. There are standard and professional editions of this Xtra.

Web site: Visible Light, `http://www.visiblelight.com/onstage/products/director/dvd/`

Streaming Media Xtra

This Xtra plays Windows Media files inside Shockwave movies.

Web site: Tabuleiro da Baiana, `http://xtras.tabuleiro.com/`

VCap, VideoSprite, and VSnap Xtras

The VCap, VideoSprite, and VSnap Xtras allow you to capture the content from a video input card. The VCap Xtra provides video capture from a Video for Windows capture card and allows you to save to the formats used by the video card drivers.

The VideoSprite Xtra allows you to display live video in a sprite. You can alpha-mask the video to blend it with the background and apply other effects such as chroma filtering. The video is displayed as a sprite, which makes it possible to place other sprites on top of it and grab single frames.

The VSnap Xtra allows you to take a single snapshot from a video source.

Web site: Penworks Corporation, `http://www.penworks.com`

Other Xtras

Many Xtras don't fit in with any major category. Sometimes an Xtra is so good at what it does that no other Xtra arises to compete with it. The following sections cover Xtras that perform a variety of tasks.

BinaryIO Xtra

This Xtra allows you to read and write binary files. The difference between a binary file and a text file (like the ones that the FileIO Xtra can handle) is that a binary file is not normally readable by word processors or text editors. Binary files can contain values that would normally be used by text files for formatting or an end-of-file indicator.

26

You need the BinaryIO Xtra if you plan on reading or writing complex files that contain more than just text—for instance, if you want to create image files using an image file specification that states exactly what bytes should be present on the file.

Web site: http://www.updatestage.com/xtras/

ChartsInMotion and TableMaker Xtra

These two Xtras enable you to place dynamic charts and tables in your movies. The charts and tables are close in appearance to the ones seen in spreadsheet programs.

Web site: XtraMedia International, http://www.xtramedia.com/xtras.shtml

Installed Fonts Xtra

This Xtra simply returns a list of the user's installed fonts.

Web site: Scott Kildall/UpdateStage, http://www.updatestage.com/xtras/xtrahome.html

Ncrypt Xtra

The Xtra encrypts and decrypts external text files using key-based encryption. This works well for commercial CD-ROMs that unlock files when a user registers or purchases a specific product. You can also encrypt and decrypt Windows registry and INI files.

Web site: Media Shoppe, http://www.mediashoppe.com/xtras/

RavWare GLU32 Xtra

This Xtra allows you to call Windows 32-bit DLLs and Mac shared libraries from Lingo. Provides for direct access to system calls. A developer can use the Xtra to access thousands of functions present in the APIs and thousands more provided by third parties.

Web site: RavWare, http://www.ravware.com/

Propsave

This free little Xtra saves binary Lingo data, such as lists or the media of members, to a file for later use.

Web site: Peghole, http://www.peghole.com/xtras/

TROUBLESHOOTING

Remember to Include Cross-Platform Files

I've built a cross-platform projector but can't get the Xtras to work on both platforms. Why?

Remember that Xtras require different files for different platforms. If you use the Buddy API Xtra, for instance, you have to bundle the Mac version with your Mac projectors and the Windows version with Windows projectors.

Duplicate Xtra Error

Why do I get an error when starting Director that says "A duplicate Xtra has been found"*?*

When you get this message, you have to go to your `Xtras` folder and find the duplicate. Unfortunately, Director does not always point you in any direction. Because the same Xtra can have different filenames, it might be difficult to find the culprit. Many times, you have to remove one Xtra at a time and restart Director until the mystery is solved.

DID YOU KNOW?

- The `xtrainfo.txt` file contains information that determines which Xtras are bundled with projectors by default. You can change this each time you make a projector, or edit this file to change the defaults.

- While authoring, you can use the `showXlib` command in the Message panel to see a simple list of all the Xtras present. It isn't as detailed as `put the xtraList`, but most of the time it is what you need to see which Xtras are there.

- If you want to access an Xtra that is not in the Xtras folder, you can open it with the `openXlib` command, followed by the full or relative pathname. You can also use `closeXlib` to free up memory when you are finished with the Xtra.

26

VI

PRODUCTION PROCESS

IN THIS PART

27

ERROR HANDLING
AND DEBUGGING

WRITING GOOD CODE

If you create a Macromedia Director movie that has more than a few lines of Lingo in it, chances are that you will have to do some debugging. This means, literally, getting rid of bugs. Bugs can be as obvious as error messages generated by a faulty Lingo line, or as vague as "something just not working right."

An ounce of prevention goes a long way when programming. This means commenting your code, using descriptive handler and variable names, and dividing your code into sensible script members.

The reason program errors are called "bugs" is that the first bug was actually, well, a bug. An early computer produced an error when a moth flew in and short-circuited it. The name stuck.

Well-written code has much less chance of containing an error. If it does contain bugs, well-commented code increases the chance that these bugs can be located and fixed.

Commenting Your Code

Knowing when to comment in your code is the trick. You can't add code comments for every line because it clutters up your Script panel and makes it even harder to read. At the same time, no commenting at all makes it difficult to debug or to alter your code in the future.

A comment is anything on a line that follows a double dash: (--). You can place comments in lines by themselves, or follow lines of actual code with a comment.

You can add three types of comments to your code. You can write blocks of comments before a handler or a section of code, write comment lines before a line or group of lines, or write a short comment at the end of a line of code.

You can also use commenting to temporarily deactivate a line of code. This is called *commenting out*.

Block Comments

Writing several lines of commentary before a handler is a common technique in Lingo and other programming languages. As shown in the following commentary, you can state what the handler does, talk about which parameters it needs and which type of value it returns, and specify when and how the handler is used.

Here is an example:

```
-- This handler will add a number to the gScore global
-- and place the global in the text member. It will
-- also check to make sure that the score is not less
-- than 0, and make it 0 if it is. The number passed in
-- should be an integer.
-- INPUT: integer
-- OUTPUT: none
-- EFFECTS: gScore, member "score"
```

```
on changeScore n
 gScore = gScore + n
 if gScore < 0 then gScore = 0
 member("score").text = string(gScore)
end
```

The main advantage of block comments is that they stay out of the way of actual code. Because Lingo code is written in English anyway, individual line comments are not always necessary.

Block comments are also good for situations in which other programmers will take your code and use it in their programs. They can read the block comment rather than the code itself. In these cases, the block comments should include information about the parameters; the return value; and perhaps a list of globals, members, and sprites affected by the handler.

Comment Lines

Placing a single line of commentary before important lines of code is another commonly used technique. The idea is to use the comments to clarify what the following line does and why it does it.

Here is an example:

```
on changeScore n

 -- add n to the score global
 gScore = gScore + n

 -- make sure score isn't less than 0
 if gScore < 0 then gScore = 0

 -- place score in text member on Stage
 member("score").text = string(gScore)
end
```

Although the preceding example uses a comment line before each code line, a more typical example would use a comment line only before some of the lines. This way, the code doesn't get too cluttered with comments.

Comment lines are useful to remind you of what is going on inside the handler. This helps in debugging and in altering the handler in the future.

Short Line Comments

Line comments appear on the same line as the code and explain what is going on in that line. Sometimes the comment points out a specific piece of information about a variable or function in that line.

Here are some examples:

```
on changeScore n
 gScore = gScore + n -- gScore is a global
 if gScore < 0 then gScore = 0 -- make sure it is less than 0
 member("score").text = string(gScore) -- show on screen
end
```

The first line of the handler demonstrates using a short line comment to point out something specific about a part of the line. The other comments serve the same purpose as the full comment lines.

Line comments are useful when you don't feel that full explanations are needed and would rather just use short, helpful "hints" for the person reading the code. Like comment lines, they are useful when you need to go back and alter the code later.

The best strategy for commenting is often to combine all three types of comments. You might place a block comment at the start of a behavior, or before each handler in a movie script, and then use comment lines and line comments in tricky parts of the code.

Using Descriptive Names

Chapter 11, "Understanding Variables, Operations, and Lists," contains some information about using descriptive handler and variable names. I cannot stress the importance of this enough. Several techniques that you can use to make your names more descriptive are described next.

Using Multiple Word Names

A convention among Lingo coders is to use multiple words, all run together, as handler names. Each word, except the first, is capitalized.

Here is an example:

```
on addNumberToScore numberToAdd
 gTotalScore = gTotalScore + numberToAdd
end
```

The handler name and both variable names are descriptive little phrases all run together. You can see that this makes additional commenting almost unnecessary. It is obvious what the handler does and how it does it.

It might seem that using the long word has the disadvantage of taking up more space in your Script panel and taking longer to type. However, if it eliminates the need for a comment on that line or before it, it more than pays for itself in keystrokes.

Using First-Letter Conventions

Throughout this book, you might have noticed the letter "g" at the beginning of all global variables and a "p" in front of all property variables. This convention makes it easier to remember where a variable originated and the range through which it is available.

You can use other conventions for the first letter of a variable. Sometimes the letter "l" is used in front of local variables. Most developers prefer to make local variables the only variable types without a letter prefix, however.

You might also see the letter "i" used in front of property variables in parent scripts. The "i" stands for instance.

You can also use a single-letter prefix in front of handler names. This used to be common in parent scripts, where "m" would be used to mean method, another term for a handler in a parent script. You can use "m" in front of handlers in behavior scripts as well.

If you are the only one to look at your code, or you have a small team that can agree on standards, you might want to implement your own prefixes. A "b" for behavior handlers, an "m" for movie handlers, and a "p" for parent script handlers might be a helpful combination. A custom set of prefixes such as this should be explained in your documentation somewhere, in case other programmers work on the code.

Using Descriptive Member Names

If you are being descriptive when it comes to variable names, you should apply the same techniques to member names. The only difference is that you can actually use separate words, not divided by spaces.

It's tempting to not use any name for a member. After all, a member placed on the Score and referenced by its sprite number doesn't need to be referenced by name in Lingo code. However, you can still benefit from naming that member. Just try cleaning up a Cast panel that has dozens of unnamed members, and you will learn why.

Member names should be descriptive and unique. It's useless to have a bunch of text members named "text." You can mention where and how these members are used in a name. For instance, if one text member shows the score during a game and another shows it in the "game over" frame, name the first "Score Text in Game" and the other "Score Text for Game Over."

Also, it is helpful to arrange your members in the Cast in a useful manner. You can arrange them by member type, or by how or when they are used in the Score.

Using Variable Constants

Another way to make your code more usable and readable is to use variables to represent commonly used numbers and objects. For instance, if the number 2 is used several times in your code for similar reasons, you might want to set a variable to 2, and then use that variable. Look at this example:

```
on moveFromKeyPress charPressed, position
 case charPressed of
  "i": position.locV = position.locV - 2
  "m": position.locV = position.locV + 2
  "j": position.locH = position.locH - 2
  "l": position.locH = position.locH + 2
 end case
 return position
end
```

This handler is used in a program to change the position of a sprite on the Stage when a key is pressed. It makes the position change by 2 in any direction. However, if you want to change this code to make the position differ by three, you need to change it in four places. Instead, the following handler enables you to make the change in only one place:

```
on moveFromKeyPress charPressed, position
 diff = 2
 case charPressed of
  "i": position.locV = position.locV - diff
```

27

```
  "m": position.locV = position.locV + diff
  "j": position.locH = position.locH - diff
  "l": position.locH = position.locH + diff
 end case
 return position
end
```

As another example, consider the need to refer to a sprite several times. You can place a sprite object in a variable and use that instead. For instance, you can code:

```
thisSprite = sprite(34)
```

Then, anywhere in that handler, you can refer to *thisSprite* rather than `sprite(34)`. If you ever need to change the code to refer to sprite 33, for example, you have to change it in just one place.

You can also use this technique with globals. You can set a global to a constant number, string, or object, and then refer to that global throughout your code. If you want to change that constant later, you need to change it in only one place. The disadvantage of using this method with globals, however, is that you must declare the global variable with the `global` command in every script in which it is used.

Member Comments

Another way to comment your movie is to add a comment to each member. You can do this for script members too, adding commentary about what the script does and what it is used for.

> You can even use member comments in Lingo. Just access the `comments` property of the member.

To add a comment, use the Property Inspector. You will also see the created date, modified date, and modified by information. Although you can't change these fields, they do contribute to the information you have about scripts and other types of members.

Writing Error-Proof Code

Impossible, you say? Well, maybe. But you can get awfully close. Many Lingo handlers can be changed in such a way as to catch errors before users are affected by them.

Many times this involves writing code that recognizes something is wrong, tells the users about it if they can do anything, and stops the code before it can do any harm. This sort of error-checking can and should be an integral part of your code.

Bug-Free FileIO Code

If you want to write some code to create a file and place some text in it, all that is required are a few short commands that use the FileIO Xtra. Here is an example:

```
on writeFile name, text
 fileObj = new(Xtra "FileIO")
 fileName = displaySave(fileObj, "Save"&&name, name&".txt")
```

```
 createFile(fileObj,fileName)
 openFile(fileObj,fileName,2)
 writeString(fileObj,text)
 closeFile(fileObj)
 fileObj = 0
end
```

This code works well most of the time. But what if there is a problem? For instance, what if the user clicks the Cancel button when the Save dialog box appears? In the preceding handler, the code marches directly to the `createFile` command with a bad filename. The result is that the file is never created and nothing happens. But the user doesn't know that.

It would be better to check to see whether the Cancel button has been clicked. If it has, the "file-name" variable will contain an empty string. You can test for that and report it to the user. You can then exit the handler before the other commands are used.

But what if the movie cannot create the file for some reason? Imagine that the user chooses a file that has the same name as one already present. You can check for this as well. If you don't check for this sort of thing, your program can be easily crashed by the user.

FileIO has two functions that enable you to test for errors. The first is the `status` function, which returns a number. If that number is 0, everything is fine; otherwise, there has been an error. You can then take the error number and feed it into the second function, the `error` function, to get a string that represents the error in plain English.

Here is the same handler as previously shown, but with comprehensive error checking. Every step of the file-creation process is checked to see whether there is a problem and is handled accordingly.

```
on writeFile name, text
 fileObj = new(Xtra "FileIO")

 -- check to make sure object was created
 if not objectP(fileObj) then
  alert("FileIO failed to initialize")
  return FALSE
 end if

 fileName = displaySave(fileObj, "Save"&&name, name&".txt")

 -- check to see if a filename was returned
 if filename = "" then
  alert "File not created."
  return FALSE
 end if

 createFile(fileObj,fileName)

 -- check to see if file was created ok
 errorNum = status(fileObj)
 if errorNum <> 0 then
  alert "Error:"&&error(fileObj,errorNum)
```

```
  return FALSE
 end if

 openFile(fileObj,fileName,2)

 -- check to see if file was opened ok
 errorNum = status(fileObj)
 if errorNum <> 0 then
  alert "Error:"&&error(fileObj,errorNum)
  return FALSE
 end if

 writeString(fileObj,text)

 -- check to see if file was written to ok
 if errorNum <> 0 then
  alert "Error:"&&error(fileObj,errorNum)
  return FALSE
 end if

 closeFile(fileObj)

 -- check to see if file was closed ok
 if errorNum <> 0 then
  alert "Error:"&&error(fileObj,errorNum)
  return FALSE
 end if

 fileObj = 0
 return TRUE
end
```

Notice that every error found returns a FALSE from the handler. However, if the handler completes its task, it returns a TRUE. This doesn't need to be present, but it is a nice feature. Any handler that calls this `on writeFile` handler can then call it as a function and get an answer back as to whether the file was actually saved.

About 18 different error messages can be returned. Table 27.1 shows a complete list of errors that can be returned by the FileIO Xtra. If the error function is used, and the error number does not correspond to one of the numbers listed here, the text "Unknown Error" is returned.

Table 27.1   Error Codes Used by the FileIO Xtra

Code	Message
124	File is opened write-only
-123	File is opened read-only
-122	File already exists

Table 27.1   Continued

Code	Message
-121	Instance has an open file
-120	Directory not found
-65	No disk in drive
-56	No such drive
-43	File not found
-42	Too many files open
-38	File not open
-37	Bad filename
-36	I/O error
-35	Volume not found
-34	Volume full
-33	File directory full
0	OK
1	Memory allocation failure

Bug-Free Shockwave Code

Although FileIO has the `status` and `error` functions, other categories of Lingo commands also have error-handling functions. Shockwave Lingo commands have the `netError` function. You can use this function to determine what has happened after the `netDone` function returns TRUE.

Here is an `on exitFrame` script that replaces the one from the section "Getting Text over the Internet" in Chapter 22, "Programming Network Communication." It checks the `netDone`, as it did before, but then goes a step further and checks `netError`. This function returns an OK if the operation was successful. If not, it returns a number. That number corresponds to the numbers in Table 22.2 in Chapter 22.

```
on exitFrame
 global gNetID
 if netDone(gNetID) then
  err = netError(gNetID)
  if err = "OK" then
   text = netTextResult(gNetID)
   put text
   go to the frame + 1
   exit
  else
   if err = 4165 then
    alert "Could not find that URL."
   else
   -- handle error somehow
   end if
  end if
```

27

```
  end if
  go to the frame
end
```

This example looks for error code 4165, which usually happens when a file is not found. You might want to replace the comment line with some code that handles other errors too.

Shockwave Audio Error Lingo

Error codes can also be returned by Shockwave Audio members. They return errors through use of the getError function. The parameter that it takes is the name of the SWA member.

Whereas getError produces a number, getErrorString returns a string that you can display to the users. Table 27.2 shows a list of these errors.

Table 27.2   Shockwave Audio Error Codes

GetError	getErrorString	Meaning
0	OK	No error
1	memory	Not enough memory available to load the sound
2	network	A network error occurred
3	playback device	Unable to play the sound
99	other	

Flash Error Lingo

You can also use getError with Shockwave Flash members that stream over the Internet. Rather than return a number, these return symbols. Table 27.3 shows them all.

Table 27.3   Flash Member Errors with getError

Symbol Returned	Meaning
FALSE or 0	No error.
#memory	Not enough memory available to load the member.
#fileNotFound	Could not locate the file.
#network	A network error occurred.
#fileFormat	File is not a Flash movie.
#other	Some other return error occurred.

Error-Handling Lingo

Even after implementing error checking along every step of the way, there is always a chance that a bug will persist and end up in your final product.

There is one way you can minimize the effects of these nasty things, however. Director enables you to intercept errors when they happen.

You can use this power to send your own error message rather than the standard Director message. You can also use this power to display no error message at all. In many cases, the program can continue with little problem after a minor error.

The way it works is a little complicated. First, you set a system property called the alertHook to a parent script. A good place to set it is during the on prepareMovie or on startMovie handlers. In this case, the alertHook is set to a parent script that has the member name "Error Handling":

```
on prepareMovie
  the alertHook = script("Error Handling")
end
```

Then, you need to create the parent script itself. This script needs to contain an on alertHook handler. Here is an example:

```
on alertHook me, error, message
  alert "Error:"&&error&RETURN&message
  return 1
end
```

The on alertHook handler should have a first parameter of *me*, and then it can accept two more: the error and the message. They are actually both messages. They correspond to the two pieces of information displayed with every Director Lingo error. The first message is usually something like "Script runtime error" and is very general. The second message contains specific information about the error, such as "Handler not defined" or "Cannot divide by zero."

You can use these two strings to determine what to do next. For instance, if you want to handle an "Index out of range" error a specific way, you can look for that error and handle it one way, and then handle other errors another way.

The one last thing that the on alertHook handler needs to do is to return a value. If a value of 0 is returned, Director proceeds to display the error message that it wanted to show in the first place. A value of 1 suppresses the error message as long as it is not a fatal error.

If you plan to suppress error messages completely, it might be a good idea to at least check whether the runMode is "author" and handle that by returning 0. Otherwise, you could be getting errors while creating or altering the movie, and not know about it.

If you need to turn off the alertHook error handling, just set the alertHook to 0.

USING LINGO DEBUGGING TOOLS

The best thing to do when you find a bug, of course, is to fix it. Fixing bugs is actually a major part of coding. A Lingo program of any size is certain to need some debugging. It doesn't matter how experienced you are. Expert Lingo programmers tend to write more code, and this code is more complex. Thus, they have just as many bugs as beginning programmers, who are more conservative in their programming.

When a bug appears, it is usually in the form of an error message. Figure 27.1 shows a typical error message dialog box. The important items to notice are the Debug and Script buttons. These buttons take you to the Script panel, which also doubles as a debugger.

Figure 27.1
A typical error message dialog box in Director shows the error type; the error message; and the Cancel, Script, and Debug buttons.

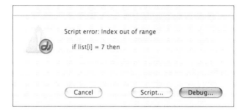

In addition to the Script panel, an Object Inspector displays the values of variables in your movies as they change. The Message panel is also a valuable debugging tool.

Using the Debugger

The debugger can be used on two occasions. The first is when you get an error message and then click the Debug button in that message dialog box to bring up the Script panel in debug mode. The result looks like Figure 27.2.

Figure 27.2
The Script panel in debug mode.

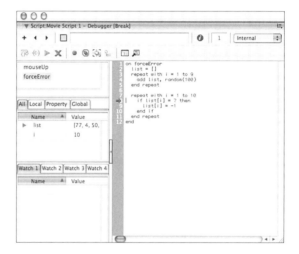

The Script panel in debug mode contains four panes and a set of buttons that enable you to examine the current state of the movie or walk through code step by step. You can see the code of a handler called on forceError in the Debugger window, in Figure 27.2. This is the code executed at the time the error occurred. The error message was the one shown earlier in Figure 27.1.

The upper-left pane in the Script panel (called the History pane) shows a list of handler names. The last one in the list is the handler currently executing—in this case, on forceError. The handlers listed above it are the handlers called that lead to the current situation. In this case, on mouseUp initiated the action, and that called on forceError.

The next pane down (called the Variables pane) contains a list of local and global variables used in the current handler. Next to each is its value. You can not only see these values but change them as well.

The third pane on the left is the Watcher pane. You can type in segments of Lingo code and get the values of those segments. For instance, you can simulate the math or string operations going on in the script.

The largest pane, appearing on the right side of the panel, is the Script pane. This pane displays the script that contains the current handler, along with a green arrow next to the line that was just executed.

In this case, you can see that the Debugger has stopped on the line:

```
if list[i] = 7 then
```

The error was "Index out of range," so the first suspect would be that the *i* used to reference the *list* is a larger number than the number of items in *list*. Sure enough, that is the case because *i* is 10, but *list* has only nine items.

Another way to use the Debugger is to set a breakpoint. You can see the Toggle Breakpoints button in Figure 27.2, it appears as a small red octagon. The same button appears in the Script panel while in normal mode. You can also set breakpoints in the Script panel by clicking in the gray area to the left of any line of Lingo code.

Setting a breakpoint causes a movie to stop and open the Script panel in debugger mode when the line containing the breakpoint is executed. This is different from using the Debugger when an error occurs, because you can start to step through the code line by line.

The three arrow buttons shown in Figure 27.2 are Step, Step Into, and Run Script, which enable you to move the program forward in different ways. Step simply advances you to the next line. The Lingo code executes normally, changing variables and objects on the Stage. You can use this to slowly watch the progress of your code as it runs.

If, as you are stepping through code, you encounter a line that calls another handler, it executes that handler all as one step. However, if you use the Step Into button instead, it enables you to step, line by line, through that handler as well.

The last arrow button, Run Script, enables the program to run again at full speed. The Debugger does not track it anymore. However, if it encounters another breakpoint, it stops again.

This is why there is a Toggle Breakpoint button in the Debugger itself, so you can set a new breakpoint further down in the code and click the Run button to have the program advance to that point.

Using the Object Inspector

Director MX includes a new tool called the Object Inspector, which can be brought up by choosing Window, Object Inspector. It is similar to the Watcher window in previous versions of Director. However, instead of just listing one variable per line, the Object Inspector uses a tabbed list to allow you to drill down into objects and lists to see the complete contents of complex variables.

Figure 27.3 shows the Object Inspector with a simple variable and a list. The list has been expanded to show each of its values. After the list are some system properties. The Object Inspector can look at almost any object, including sprites and instances of parent scripts. It can also dig down many levels to see values that are properties of properties and so on.

Figure 27.3
The Object Inspector can be used during debugging or to tweak values while a movie is running.

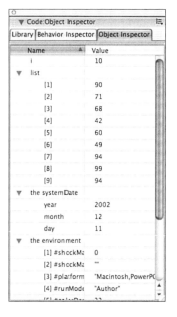

The Object Inspector is particularly useful for 3D members because you can see each model, camera, light, shader, and resource. Not only can you examine the complete 3D member this way, but you can change values while the movie is running.

> You can drag sprites and members to the Object Inspector panel to quickly add them and their properties.

Using the Message Panel for Debugging

The Message panel can serve many purposes when it comes to writing error-free code and debugging code that is not so error-free.

First, you can use the Message panel to test short bits of Lingo code that you are not quite sure about. The Message panel is known as a command-line interpreter in other programming environments. So, for instance, rather than just assume that a text member's type is #text, you can test it:

```
put member("score").type
-- #text
```

Forget what the items in the systemDate are? Just try it out:

```
put the systemDate
-- date( 2000, 1, 5 )
```

Now you can program with confidence.

In addition, you can use the Message panel to test individual movie handlers. Just type their names, add any parameters, and press (Return) [Enter]. If the handler is a function, you can place `put` before it to have the result placed in the next line of the Message panel.

```
put addTwoNumbers(4,5)
-- 9
```

You can also test global variables in the Message panel. So, if you want to see what the global *gScore* is currently set to, just try it:

```
put gScore
-- 405
```

You can even set globals in the Message panel:

```
gScore = 10000000
```

Another way to use the Message panel is to place the `put` command inside scripts. You can send variable contents to the Message panel. This is similar to using the Object Inspector, but you get to keep a record of values.

> Make sure that you comment out or delete debugging `put` statements before finishing your movie. Sending a lot of information to the Message panel slows down your movie considerably.

Using Trace

The Message panel is also the primary tool for using a debugging method known as `tracing`. With tracing, Director sends a message to the Message panel every time a line of Lingo executes, and every time a variable changes. Figure 27.4 shows a sample trace session.

Figure 27.4
Trace information is displayed in the Message panel.

Note that the first line in the Message panel is actually typed. After you press (Return) [Enter], the trace begins. To turn on tracing, simply click the Trace button at the top of the Message panel. It is the middle button of the five shown in Figure 27.4.

In addition, you can set `the trace` to TRUE or FALSE, to turn tracing on or off. You can do this in the Message panel, or you can insert it in your handlers. Doing either one enables you to start the trace before a sensitive piece of code, and stop it afterward.

Using Other Debugging Methods

Debugging works great in Director, but what if the bug only appears when the movie is running as a projector or in Shockwave?

There is no debugger for these situations, but you can still output messages at points in your code to let you know the settings for your variables, or at what point in the code your movie currently is.

In projectors, the `alert` command comes in handy for this. You can use `alert` at a sensitive part of your code to figure out what is going on. For instance, if your program isn't working correctly after a `getNetText` series of commands, you might want to check to see whether the text that your Shockwave movie is getting is actually the text you expect. Instead of just getting the text and moving on, you might want to try this:

```
text = netTextResult(gNetID)
alert text
```

Now, you can see the text and make sure that it is what you expect. Of course, you should remove the `alert` command after the testing is finished.

Shockwave also offers you the chance to use the `netStatus` command. This command places a message in the Netscape Navigator message space at the bottom of the browser window.

You can also use `netStatus` to display useful information to users, such as the potential destination or action of a button over which the user's cursor is hovering. This is similar to how it is used by plain HTML and JavaScript code.

TESTING YOUR CODE

It is a sad fact that most major software is released with bugs in it. Maybe it's not so much sad as unavoidable. After all, how do you thoroughly test software? Thousands of different computer configurations are available that vary by one item or another: processor type, processor speed, operating system type, operating system version, video card manufacturer, video card driver version, video settings, hard drive speed, CD-ROM speed, RAM size, system settings, system extensions, and so on.

It's impossible to test on every machine available. However, you can test on a variety of machines and find a majority of the problems. The key is to test on all target platforms and on as many configurations of hardware and operating systems as possible.

Test Early and Often

Any computer science professor or software project manager will tell you: Test early and test often. Take these words to heart.

Start your testing as soon as you have something that can be tested. If you are writing handlers, test each one individually if you can. For instance, if you write a handler that takes two points and finds the distance between them, why not use the Message panel to try it out? Did you get an error? Did the result come out as expected?

Although this method of testing might seem tedious, consider the alternative. A large Lingo program might have a few dozen movie handlers, many behavior scripts, and a lot of named (or misnamed) members. If you try programming it all at once, never testing any piece individually, chances are slim that it will work when you are initially finished. However, if you perform a minute of testing here and there, the program could work as soon as you write your last line of code.

Testing In-House

In-house testing is sometimes called *alpha testing*. It starts when the program is "done," and you give it a thorough test yourself. Run the program through its paces. Most of your bugs actually show up right away.

The next step is to let others in your company or organization test it. In a classroom situation, lab partners or classmates make good alpha testers. Maybe some of your friends, too.

This level of testing gives you a lot more control than the next stage. You can personally talk to people who use the software, and maybe even have them show you firsthand what went wrong.

You might even want to use the `alertHook` Lingo to give detailed reports when errors occur. This makes it easier for you to track down the problem, but it does not affect the final product because you can remove this code before the product is finished.

Beta Testing

After your program seems to work for you, and everyone in your company has tested it, you can start a *beta test*. This means that you can give out a copy of your program to people outside your company or organization. Many times these are people you don't even know.

Some developers do a private beta test, whereby only a few selected individuals get to test. These individuals can be found among the company's loyal customers, or among applications received from simply advertising.

Some companies do a public beta test, where anyone can download and test the software. This usually results in many people downloading, but few actually reporting errors. It does give you the widest range of testers, however.

Although I recommend that beta tests occur after the product is fully developed and somewhat tested, many companies hold beta tests during development. This enables them to test out new features and get feedback from actual users while they develop.

Beta testing can be overkill if you have a small project, however. Also, if you are developing a Shockwave applet, consider how easy it is to update your movie after you make it live. The applet really exists only in one place: your Web site. If an error, even a big one, is found, you can correct it and upload a new version immediately.

27

DID YOU KNOW?

- Try using the Lingo command `nothing` as a place to put breakpoints. `nothing` does just that. You can place `nothing` inside a conditional statement and set a breakpoint on it to have the Debugger start at only a particular time. For instance:

```
if i = 8 then
  nothing
end if
```

- You can use the Lingo system property `the  traceLogFile` to set a filename that will be used to write the contents of the Message panel to the hard drive. This is useful for viewing Message panel statements while playing back in a projector.

- You can also place `nothing` inside a conditional statement that looks for a keyboard function, such as `the  shiftDown`. This way you can have the Debugger start when the code is at a certain spot, but only when you want it.

```
if the shiftDown then
  nothing
end if
```

- You can click in the handler History pane of the Debugger window to see the previous handlers and the point to which the program will return as soon as the more recent handler is finished. This also changes the variables in the second pane to reflect the state of the handler selected.

28

CREATING APPLICATIONS

IN THIS CHAPTER

CREATING A STANDALONE PROJECTOR

Before the Internet and Shockwave, the primary way to deploy Macromedia Director movies was with projectors. Director is still the main tool used for creating multimedia presentations and CD-ROMs.

A *projector* is a standalone application that other people can play on their computers without having Director. If the movie is authored correctly, it should run fine on all similar computer systems.

To create a projector, you need to choose File, Create Projector. This brings up the Create Projector dialog box shown in Figure 28.1.

Figure 28.1
The Create Projector dialog box is the first step in making standalone applications from Director movies. This is the Macintosh version of the dialog box. The Windows version is slightly different but offers the same settings.

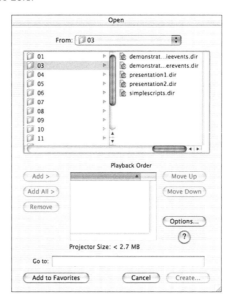

In the Create Projector dialog box, you need to specify which file or files you want to incorporate in the projector. The Create Projector dialog box prompts you to add movie and cast files. Do this by selecting the files and clicking the Add button. In most cases, you will add only one movie file. However, you can have a projector play several movie files sequentially by adding more than one.

Next, you need to decide on the projector options by clicking the Options button to go to the Projector Options dialog box, shown in Figure 28.2.

The Projector Options dialog box has the following options to choose from:

Director cannot create a cross-platform projector. There is no such thing. A Mac version of Director can create a Mac projector, and a Windows version of Director can create a Windows projector. You'll have to buy two copies of Director to create projectors on both platforms.

- Play Every Movie—This option causes the projector to play each movie in the list sequentially. If this option is not selected, only the first movie is played. The other movies included in your list can still be called from Lingo.

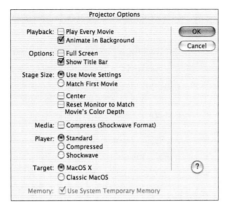

Figure 28.2
This is the Mac version of the Projector Options dialog box. (The Windows version is similar.)

- Animate in Background—This option determines whether the movie continues to play if it is not the frontmost application on the computer. If this option is not turned on and the user clicks another application, or uses the Windows Alt+Tab function, the movie pauses. Unless your movie is a straightforward animation, you should turn on this option.

- Full Screen—You can choose to have your movie take over the full screen when the projector runs. This means that the rest of the screen will be blanked out, using the background color of the Stage. If you are creating a presentation or an animation, this is a desired option. However, if you are creating something that you want to look like a normal Mac or Windows application, don't use this option.

- Show Title Bar—This option puts a standard title bar above the projector's window. The user can see the windows's title and use the bar to move the window.

- Stage Size (Use Movie Settings and Match First Movie options)—The two options for Stage size enable you to decide how the projector handles multiple movies that are different sizes. If you have two movies in your projector, for instance, and the first is 640×480 and the second is 320×240, choosing the Match First Movie option forces the second movie to be contained in a larger, 640×480 Stage. The Use Movie Settings option resizes the Stage when the other movie starts.

- Center—This option should always be selected unless you want the Stage to appear at a specific location on the user's monitor. If Center is not selected, the Stage appears at the same location as it does when you are authoring in Director. This can be dangerous if you are not sure what size monitor the playback machine will have.

- Reset Monitor to Match Movie's Color Depth—This option is available only for Mac projectors. On the Mac, a program such as a projector can automatically adjust the monitor itself. This means that you can switch the monitor to thousands or millions of colors, if that is what your movie requires.

- Media: Compress (Shockwave Format)—You have several options that affect the size of the final projector. You can choose to have Director compress media for you before placing the movie in the projector. This uses the same compression technique that you use when you create a Shockwave movie.

28

- Player: (Standard, Compressed, and Shockwave options)—You can also choose to make a Shockwave projector that relies on the user's computer system having Shockwave installed. Users would get Shockwave from Macromedia's Web site, if they do not already have it from playing Shockwave content off the Web. The Shockwave engine contains most of the code that a projector needs to run. It is a standalone application that does not require a browser to run. A Shockwave projector will be a lot smaller in size because it uses the Shockwave engine. If users do not have Shockwave, the projector prompts them to download it.

- Use System Temporary Memory—This option is available only on the Mac. It enables the projector to steal memory not being used by other programs. It is not used if virtual memory is turned on, so it isn't likely to be a factor in most cases. However, it might give a large presentation a speed boost on some machines.

The Macintosh version of Director MX has an additional option, which you can see in Figure 28.2. You can choose to make either a Mac OS X projector or a Mac OS 9 projector. Although you can't run Director MX in OS 9, you can at least build projectors for that platform.

When you finish with the options, the only thing left to do is choose a filename. The result is an application program on the Mac and an .exe file in Windows.

⇨ *If your projectors are having trouble on some machines, see "Projector Doesn't Work on Client's Computer" in the "Troubleshooting" section at the end of this chapter.*

> **Caution**
>
> Shockwave projectors should only be used for temporary purposes. There's no guarantee that if you make a Director MX Shockwave projector that it will work with future versions of Shockwave. For instance, any Shockwave projectors created with Director 7 don't work with current versions of Shockwave.

STUB PROJECTORS

You also have some alternatives to the simple projector. You can build what is called a *stub projector*, which can run any external Director movie. Director also enables you to build Shockwave projectors, which rely on Shockwave components on the user's system.

The need for a stub projector is obvious after you think about it. Rather than create a new projector each time you make a change to a movie, just create a simple projector that runs your movie as an external file.

The projector can have one movie that contains a `go to movie` command as the sole command of an `on exitFrame` script. This script is placed in the first frame of the movie:

```
on exitFrame
 go to movie "myrealmovie.dir"
end
```

Take this one-frame, one-member movie and create a projector from it. Then, when you run it, it jumps directly to the first frame of the external movie, which is the main (or first) movie of your presentation or program.

If you make a change to your movie later, you don't have to rebuild the projector. Just run it again, and it will use the new, modified version of your movie.

You can even make more complicated stub projectors by having your Lingo code read in the name of the stub projector with the `movieName` property, removing an `.exe` if there is one. This will then be the name of the movie it should run. The projector is smart enough to look for either `.dir` or `.dcr` files, the latter being a compressed movie made with the Publish command.

This way, a projector named `present.exe` looks for and runs `present.dir`. If you then create a movie called `myprogram.dir`, you can copy the `present.exe` projector, change its name to `myprogram.exe`, and it can run the new movie.

Here is a script that does this:

```
on exitFrame
 moviename = findMyMovie()
 go to movie moviename
end

on findMyMovie
 myname = the applicationName
 if myname contains ".exe " then
  myname = myname.char[1..offset(".",myname)-1]
 end if
 moviename = myname
 return moviename
end
```

A more complex projector script can even check to make sure that the file is there before running it. You use the `getNthFileNameInFolder` command to do this. Look for a `.dir` file first, a `.dxr` file next, and then a `.dcr` file if neither of the first two is there. This way, the projector works while you are testing and also works when you decide to create a protected version of your movie.

BUILDING CD-ROMS AND DVDS

Next to the Internet, the most common way to deliver Director content is on CD-ROMs. The steps involved in making a CD-ROM depend on your CD-ROM burner and your CD-ROM burning software. Usually, the software comes with documentation. Because software varies greatly, it is impossible to go into complete detail here.

If you are making a cross-platform CD-ROM, this usually involves building two descriptions of the CD-ROM contents. The popular CD-ROM burning software, Roxio Toast, requires you to make the Mac description first by creating a temporary hard drive partition and copying all the files to it.

Next, you can describe the Windows side of the CD-ROM to it, pointing to files both on the Mac temporary partition and elsewhere. The program is then smart enough to place shared files on the CD-ROM once, in such a way that both platforms can read them.

This way, if you have a 650 MB CD-ROM, you might have just a few megabytes of Mac-only data and a few megabytes of PC-only data. The Mac-only data and PC-only data can be the projector and all the Xtras. The rest can be nearly 650 MB of shared data.

28

Toast and other CD-ROM software can now also make cross-platform CDs This means that you can place one set of files on the CD-ROM and people using either platform can see these files. This makes CD-ROM creation much easier.

Optimization used to be an important topic for CD-ROM creators. Today's software is so advanced that it does a good job of optimizing the positions of the files on the CD-ROM even without more information from you. Check your software's documentation for more information.

Now that DVD burners are more common, you can also make a DVD using your Director files. This is just like making a CD-ROM, except that you have more than 4 GB of space to fill, and the disc will only work in DVD-ROM drives, not CD-ROM drives.

> If you are making a cross-platform CD with one set of files, note that you still need to include both a Mac projector and a Windows projector. These projectors are not cross-platform and will only work on the system they were built for. You'll want to name and arrange the files on the CD so that the user finds the right projector to run. They will be able to see both projectors, but only use the one build for their system.

Note that these DVD discs are not the same as DVDs that you place in your home DVD video player. Those need to be authored using special DVD software, not Director. Home DVD video players cannot play Director projectors.

➩ *If your media can't be read in some machines, see "Some Computers Can't Read CD-ROMs and DVDs" in the "Troubleshooting" section at the end of this chapter.*

MAKING INSTALLERS

If you are building a professional CD-ROM product, you might want to create an installer, instead of just having the projector play from the CD-ROM. Installers are created not with Director, but with third-party programs.

These programs do not care that you used Director to make your product. They will work with just about any type of standalone application, such as projectors.

Each third-party application works differently, so describing the steps needed to use one is beyond the scope of this book. The products all come with instructions and are relatively easy to use. Here is a list of some third-party applications:

- CreateInstall (Windows)—http://createinstall.com/

- InstallerMaker (Mac)—http://www.stuffit.com/installermaker/

- InstallerVise and FileStorm (Mac and Windows)—http://www.mindvision.com

- InstallShield (Windows)—http://www.installshield.com/

- Wise(Windows)—http://www.wise.com/

BUILDING SCREENSAVERS

You can also turn your Director movies into screensavers. These are popular as promotional items.

Projectors, or any other executable, can be used as screensavers if the user knows how to manipulate the Windows screensaver resources. However, because the people in the target audience for screensavers probably don't know how to do that, a little help is needed.

> If you are actually looking for the opposite functionality—disabling the screensaver while your Director movie runs—use the Buddy API Xtra or the Resolution Xtra.

A third-party program can be used to build an installer that creates a screensaver from a Director movie. Other third-party programs can be used to "bridge the gap" between projectors and screensavers. Some of these products are listed here:

- Active Screen Saver Dev Kit—http://www.automatedofficesystems.com/

- AnySaver (Windows)—http://dgolds.com/

- AutoLaunch (Mac)—http://www.stclairsoft.com

- BitBull—http://www.wanpatan.com/bitbull/

- Buddy Saver (Windows)—http://www.mods.com.au/

- DirSaver (Windows)—http://www.goldshell.com/

- Screen Time (Mac and Windows)—http://www.screentime.com/

- ScreenSaver Wizard—http://www.score.de/

- ShowTime (Windows)—http://www.alienzone.com/

TROUBLESHOOTING

Some Computers Can't Read CD-ROMs and DVDs

Why can some computers read my CD-ROM or DVD, and others can't?

Some computers, especially older ones, do not recognize CD-ROMs that have been created in one-off CD-ROM burners, such as the ones that you would typically have attached to your home or office computer. They still work well with CD-ROMs created in factories. The same problem can be found in some DVD-ROM drives. There's not much you can do about it. Often, it helps to use higher quality blank CD and DVD media.

28

Projector Doesn't Work on Client's Computer

How can I make sure that my projector works on all possible playback machines?

It is important to test your projectors on computers that are more basic than your development machine. Chances are you have many fonts, drivers, extensions, and optimizations. However, a cheap test machine with nothing beyond the default install of Windows or OS X is what you need to test on in most cases. You need to decide on what your minimum system requirements are and test on a machine that matches that. Then you want to make sure that potential users know what the system requirements are.

DID YOU KNOW?

- If you include a text file called LINGO.INI in the same folder as your projector, the projector will open this file and read it as Lingo. Any commands inside an on startUp handler will be executed. You can declare and set globals using this file.

- In my tests, OS X projectors will work on Mac OS 9.2.2 as long as the latest system drivers are in place. So making an OS X version of your projector might be all you need if you want to support some machines with 9.2.2 as well. Best to test on a target machine, however.

- You can build CD-ROMs that automatically launch a projector when they are inserted into the CD-ROM drive. This has nothing to do with Director or the way you make your movie. You just need to build the CD-ROM with the proper auto-run files in place. See your CD-ROM burning software documentation.

- For OS X, Apple recommends that you do not use installers at all. Instead, they advocate a drag-and-drop install where the user simply drags your projector or folder onto her hard drive. You can search the developers section of the Apple Web site for more information.

29

PUBLISHING SHOCKWAVE MOVIES

IN THIS CHAPTER

PUBLISH AS SHOCKWAVE

To put your Macromedia Director movies on a Web site, you need to compress them into Shockwave files and then create HTML pages to contain these files. Doing this is easy with the Publish command, but there are many ways to customize your Shockwave movies as well.

A big misconception about Shockwave movies is that you have to "shock" (compress) them. This is not true. You can take a normal Director movie file and play it back in a Web browser with Shockwave.

What is normally referred to as "shocking a movie" is actually just compressing it. The new file is a copy of the movie with images, text, sounds, and Score information compressed. The difference is usually very large; often the file is less than half the size of the original. This makes it much easier for Internet users to download Director movies, especially when they are using modems. The code in a Shockwave file is also protected so that users cannot see the source code.

Using the Publish Command

To make a Shockwave movie, simply choose File, Publish. This outputs the movie as a compressed Shockwave movie, along with a sample HTML page.

Shockwave movies, as these compressed files are called, always have .dcr as a file extension. Web servers use this extension to identify them as Shockwave movies and tell the browser to use the Shockwave plug-in to play them.

> **Caution**
>
> Compressing a Director movie also protects it from being opened by other people who have Director. Otherwise, they could steal your code and media.

You can customize both the .dcr file and the HTML page created by the Publish command. To do this, use the Publish Settings dialog accessed by choosing File, Publish Settings.

This dialog box has several tabs, each dealing with a different aspect of the files.

The Formats Tab

To access the Publish Settings dialog box (see Figure 29.1), choose File, Publish Settings. This multi-tabbed dialog box has many options, starting with the options on the Formats tab.

Figure 29.1
The Publish Settings dialog box starts in the Formats tab. Here, you can set the HTML template that Director uses to create a sample HTML page.

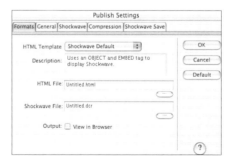

In the Formats tab, you can choose from a number of different HTML templates. Director uses these templates to create a sample HTML page every time you use the Publish command. The following list describes these template options:

- No HTML Template—No HTML sample file is created. Use this when you just want Publish to output a compressed movie, nothing more.

- 3D Content Loader—Displays a loader movie as your movie downloads. This loader movie includes a mention of the Intel 3D Engine.

- Shockwave Default—Makes an HTML page with both an <OBJECT> tag for Internet Explorer and an <EMBED> tag for Netscape Navigator.

- Detect Shockwave—Uses browser scripting to make sure that the users have Shockwave, and tells the users to get it if they don't have it.

- Fill Browser Window—Takes the Shockwave movie and makes it fill the entire browser window, regardless of the size of the window. Use this if you plan to have a scalable Shockwave movie that acts as the entire interface on the page.

- Loader Game—Loads a small Macromedia-created game that the users can play while they wait for your movie to download.

- Progress Bar with Image—With this option, you can specify an image to be shown that appears in place of the Shockwave movie while the movie loads. A progress bar appears with the image. You can specify the image in a new field that appears at the bottom of the Publish Settings dialog box when you select this option.

- Shockwave with Image—If the users don't have Shockwave installed, a JPG image is displayed instead. You can specify the image.

- Simple Progress Bar—Displays a simple progress bar, without any special image, while your movie loads.

- Center Shockwave—Contains HTML code to center your Shockwave movie in the browser window.

After you choose your HTML format, you can specify the name of both the Shockwave movie and the HTML page. If you selected an HTML template that uses an image, you can also specify an image filename.

If you select the No HTML Template option, all the tabs in the Publish Settings dialog box that are not needed disappear. The only tabs that will be left are Formats and Compression.

The General Tab

The General tab in the Publish Settings dialog box enables you to alter the dimensions of the movie according to the HTML that is generated. In other words, the General settings affect only the HTML page, not the movie itself. Figure 29.2 shows the General settings.

Figure 29.2
The General settings portion of the Publish Settings dialog box enables you to alter several parameters in the sample HTML page generated.

You can change the dimensions of the movie to match the movie, to fit into a percentage of the size of the browser window, or to match a specific pixel size. This changes the numbers used in the <EMBED> and <OBJECT> tags; it doesn't change anything about your Shockwave movie. You can also set the background color of the HTML page created in the Page Background text box.

The Shockwave Tab

The Shockwave tab in the Publish Settings dialog box has many options that affect how Shockwave allows users to access your movie. You can see these settings in Figure 29.3.

Figure 29.3
The Shockwave settings portion of the Publish Settings dialog box enables you to set how much access to your movie users have.

The first four options, Volume Control to Save Local, set parameters in the <OBJECT> and <EMBED> tags of the sample HTML. They each restrict what users can do by (Control-clicking) [right-clicking]. With all the options on, users can change the volume of the movie, step through frames of the movie, zoom in and out, and save the movie as a local file to be used in Macromedia's ShockMachine product.

The two loading options allow you to turn off the default logo and progress bar that appear in place of your Shockwave movie as it loads. The options here add "progress" and "logo" parameters to your <OBJECT> and <EMBED> tags.

ShockMachine is a standalone Shockwave player that Macromedia has developed and now offers free on the Web. You can find out more about it at http://www.shockwave.com/sw/help/shockmachine_faq.html assuming they don't change this URL.

The Stretch Style options also result in parameters being added to the <OBJECT> and <EMBED> tags. These options determine exactly how the movie fits into the rectangle created by the use of the <OBJECT> and <EMBED> tags. The four Stretch Style options are as follows:

- No Stretching—Shows the movie at 100%, no matter what

- Default (Preserve Proportions)—Stretches the movie to fit but does not change its dimensions

- Stretch to Fill—Stretches the movie to fit in the rectangle exactly

- Expand Stage Size—Keeps the movie at 100% but allows users to see more of the Stage if the rectangle is larger than the movie

With the Expand Stage Size option selected, the Stretch Position settings come in handy so that you can decide how the movie is positioned within the larger rectangular space.

The Background Color option enables you to set the background color of the Shockwave rectangle before the movie loads. After the movie loads, the background color of the Stage is the color specified by the movie's properties and not the color specified here.

If the last option, JavaScript, is selected, the proper tags are added to the <OBJECT> and <EMBED> tags to ensure the browser knows that the Shockwave movie will attempt to communicate with JavaScript.

The Compression Tab

The Compression tab contains items that actually change properties of your movie, as opposed to just something on the sample HTML page.

Using standard compression means that the image will look exactly the same as your original cast member. However, JPEG compression sacrifices quality for file size.

Figure 29.4 shows this portion of the Publish Settings dialog box. The Image Compression settings enable you to determine the default compression technique used by images in the movie. Each image can be set to use standard or JPEG compression, or it can be set to use the movie's default compression, which is this setting here in the Compression tab. If you choose JPEG, you can set the quality percentage.

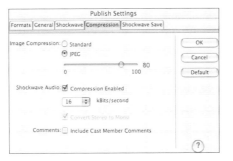

Figure 29.4
The Compression tab of the Publish Settings dialog box enables you to control image and sound compression.

You can also set the compression amount for Shockwave audio. Like JPEG compression, Shockwave audio compression trades quality for file size. You also have the option to not use any sound compression, which guarantees large Shockwave files. Use at least 128 Kbps compression to save some file size. A 32 Kbps setting gives you much smaller Shockwave movies and still sounds pretty good for most purposes.

The last option on the Compression tab falls under the Comments setting. The Include Cast Member Comments option enables you to keep the cast member comment fields that you added to organize your media. Use this option only when you have written some Lingo code to access this information.

The Shockwave Save Tab

The last tab in the Publish Settings dialog box is Shockwave Save. Here, you find places to include information about your Shockwave movie should you be interested in having users download the file for their ShockMachine program. Figure 29.5 shows this tab of the dialog box.

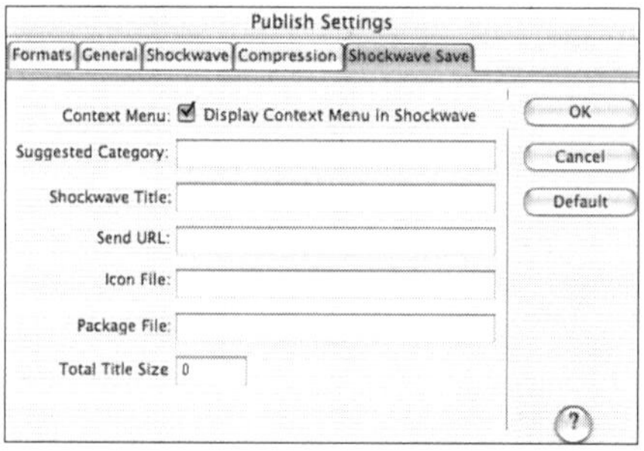

Figure 29.5
The Shockwave Save tab of the Publish Settings dialog box enables you to specify information about your movie for use by ShockMachine.

The Display Context Menu in Shockwave option enables you to control whether users can bring up a pop-up menu by (Control-clicking) [right-clicking]. If users can bring up a pop-up menu, they can choose to save the movie locally, provided that the Save Local setting has been turned on in the Shockwave tab of the Publish Settings dialog box.

If users try to save your movie, Shockwave uses the information in this part of the Publish Settings dialog box to categorize it. You can also specify an icon for the movie, which ShockMachine uses to display the movie. The Package file enables you to create a complex download, such as one that includes external casts and other media. The use of all this information is subject to change as Macromedia continues to develop ShockMachine. Your best bet is to check the Macromedia site to find the latest developer guidelines for creating ShockMachine-compatible movies.

Publishing

After you select all the settings under each tab of the Publish Settings dialog box, you are ready to use the Publish command. Just choose File, Publish, to save your movie as a Shockwave file. The HTML page, if you have selected a template, is saved as well.

The process for placing Shockwave movies on your Web server depends on your file transfer protocol (FTP) software. In most cases, you have the option to upload the file in text or binary format. You must select binary for the file to be properly transferred.

To place the Shockwave movie inside a Web page, you need to use an <OBJECT> tag for Internet Explorer on Windows, an <EMBED> tag for Netscape on Windows and Mac, and Internet Explorer on Mac. However, you can just view the HTML code in the same page that the Publish command outputs.

You can also edit these tags manually using an HTML editor. To do so, you should understand each part of these tags.

WORKING WITH SHOCKWAVE HTML TAGS

Although you can use the Publish HTML output as sample code that can be cut and pasted into your own HTML code, you should also know the basics about how Shockwave is placed into HTML.

There are two main browsers: Netscape Navigator and Microsoft Internet Explorer. Shockwave has versions for both. For Navigator and IE on the Mac, Shockwave is a plug-in that handles Director movies inside a Web page. For Explorer on Windows, Shockwave is an ActiveX control, which is like an extension to the browser.

The result is the same: The Director movie appears in the browser directly on the Web page. However, the information needed to place the movie on the page differs for each browser.

Netscape Navigator <EMBED> Tag

With Navigator, a movie is placed in a page with the <EMBED> HTML tag. Here is an example:

```
<EMBED SRC="mymovie.dcr" WIDTH="400" HEIGHT="200">
```

This tag simply states that the movie file is named `mymovie.dcr` and the size of the movie is 400×200. You can use a more complex path for the file if the movie is not in the same directory as the HTML page.

In addition to the SRC, WIDTH, and HEIGHT parameters shown in the previous piece of code, you can also include several others. Here is a complete list:

- SRC—The relative or absolute location of the movie.

- WIDTH, HEIGHT—The screen size of the movie. The actual movie can be larger or smaller, but this parameter reserves a rectangle exactly this size on the page.

- BGCOLOR—Set to the hexagonal value for the color you want the rectangle to display while the movie downloads.

- NAME—This parameter is more for the HTML page and JavaScript than for use by the movie itself. It is how you refer to the movie object in HTML code.

- SWREMOTE—Contains a string that contains yet more parameters.

- SWSTRETCHSTYLE—Set to either "none" or "fill". The fill option stretches the Shockwave movie to fill the browser window.

- TYPE—Some versions of Netscape enable you to specify the MIME type of the object in the <EMBED> tag. You should set this to "application/x-director". This way, if your server is not set up for Shockwave movies, some users can still see the movie.

- PLUGINSPAGE—You can set the location of the download page for Shockwave here. Newer versions of Netscape use this to direct users to the place where they can get the plug-in. A good URL to use is `http://www.macromedia.com/shockwave/download/`.

If you use the <SWREMOTE> tag, you must include even more parameters inside it. These can be all set to TRUE or FALSE. Here is a list of what you can use:

- swSaveEnabled—Whether the movie can be saved and used in ShockMachine.

- swVolume—Whether the user can change the volume of the movie by right-clicking or using the Shockwave Remote.

- swRestart—Whether the user can restart the movie by right-clicking or using the Shockwave Remote. Set this to TRUE only when the movie is a plain animation.

- swPausePlay—Whether the user can pause the movie by right-clicking or using the Shockwave Remote. Set this to TRUE only when the movie is a plain animation or you are sure that pausing will not hurt your Lingo code.

- swFastForward—Whether the user can fast forward through a movie by right-clicking or using the Shockwave Remote. Set this to TRUE only when the movie is a plain animation.

- swContextMenu—Whether the user gets a context menu when right-clicking on Windows or Control-clicking on the Mac.

The following complex <EMBED> tag contains all the possible standard parameters:

```
<embed src="mymovie.dcr" name="myMovie" bgColor=#FFFFFF width=70 height=50
swRemote="swSaveEnabled='true' swVolume='true' swRestart='true'
swPausePlay='true' swFastForward='true' swContextMenu='true' "
swStretchStyle=none type="application/x-director"
pluginspage="http://www.macromedia.com/shockwave/download/">
</embed>
```

⇨ *If you notice that your movie doesn't appear in Netscape and some other browsers, see "Shockwave Movie Not Appearing in Some Browsers" in the "Troubleshooting" section at the end of this chapter.*

Microsoft Internet Explorer <OBJECT> Tag

To achieve the same result as a Netscape <EMBED> tag, you need to write a different type of tag for Internet Explorer.

The <OBJECT> tag is used to embed an object for which an ActiveX control provides the engine. In this case, the ActiveX control is Shockwave.

The <OBJECT> tag specifies the identification code for the ActiveX control. Microsoft assigned this number to Shockwave. The browser uses the number to determine whether it already has this ActiveX control. If not, the browser uses an Internet address, also specified in the tag, to download and install it.

The following is a sample <OBJECT> tag:

```
<OBJECT classid="clsid:166B1BCA-3F9C-11CF-8075-444553540000"
codebase="http://download.macromedia.com/pub/shockwave/cabs/director/
sw.cab#version=8,0,0,0"
ID=Credits WIDTH=400 HEIGHT=200>
<PARAM NAME=src VALUE="mymovie.dcr">
</OBJECT>
```

The first part of the <OBJECT> tag is the classid, which is the identification code mentioned earlier. The second part is the location on the Internet where the browser can get this ActiveX control if it is not already installed.

Notice that the last part of the location contains version=8,0,0,0, which tells Macromedia's Web site which version of the control is needed.

After those two pieces, the ID parameter is used in the same manner as the NAME parameter in the <EMBED> tag. It identifies the Shockwave movie object to any JavaScript or VBScript that needs to know about it.

The WIDTH and HEIGHT options are next, and they serve the same purpose as the equivalent parameters in the <EMBED> tag. This ends the first part of the <OBJECT> tag.

However, this is not the end of the <OBJECT> tag as a whole. It requires an </OBJECT> tag to end it. In between, there can and should be some <PARAM> tags. You can see one in the preceding example. Each <PARAM> tag specifies a parameter name and a value. In the example, the parameter is src, and the value is mymovie.dcr. This of course, denotes the location of the Shockwave movie itself.

You can also include other <PARAM> tag parameters such as bgColor and swRemote that do the same things as their <EMBED> counterparts. Here is a more complex <OBJECT> tag:

```
<object classid="clsid:166B1BCA-3F9C-11CF-8075-444553540000"
➥codebase="http://download.macromedia.com/pub/shockwave/cabs/
➥director/sw.cab#version=8,0,0,0"
ID=mymovie width=70 height=50>
<param name=src value=" mymovie.dcr">
<param name=swRemote value="swSaveEnabled='true' swVolume='true'
swRestart='true' swPausePlay='true' swFastForward='true' swContextMenu='true' ">
<param name=swStretchStyle value=none>
<param name=bgColor value=#FFFFFF>
</object>
```

➯   *If you can't see the latest version of your movie in your browser, see "Cache Settings and Testing" in the "Troubleshooting" section at the end of this chapter.*

Using Both the <EMBED> and <OBJECT> Tags

Most of the time, you want to build an HTML page for both browsers. This requires you to use both the <EMBED> and <OBJECT> tags.

This works fine for Netscape Navigator, in which the <EMBED> tag is used, and the <OBJECT> tag is ignored.

However, Internet Explorer recognizes both tags. The <OBJECT> tag is used to show the Shockwave movie as you expect. But Internet Explorer can also use the <EMBED> tag to use Netscape Navigator plug-ins. So, it attempts to display the Shockwave movie a second time with the <EMBED> tag. Chances are that the browser does not have the Shockwave plug-in available, but the rectangular area for the Shockwave movie is still reserved for its use, and users might even be prompted for a download.

Fortunately, there is a simple solution for this problem. Just place the <EMBED> tag inside the <OBJECT> tag. Microsoft Internet Explorer is smart enough to ignore <EMBED> tags inside <OBJECT> tags, so the movie will not be displayed twice.

For example:

```
<object classid="clsid:166B1BCA-3F9C-11CF-8075-444553540000"
➥codebase="http://download.macromedia.com/pub/shockwave/cabs/
➥director/sw.cab#version=8,0,0,0"
ID=mymovie width=70 height=50>
<param name=src value=" mymovie.dcr">
<param name=swRemote value="swSaveEnabled='true' swVolume='true'
swRestart='true' swPausePlay='true' swFastForward='true' swContextMenu='true' ">
<param name=swStretchStyle value=none>
<param name=bgColor value=#FFFFFF>
<embed src="mymovie.dcr" name="myMovie" bgColor=#FFFFFF width=70 height=50
swRemote="swSaveEnabled='true' swVolume='true' swRestart='true'
swPausePlay='true' swFastForward='true' swContextMenu='true' "
swStretchStyle=none type="application/x-director"
pluginspage="http://www.macromedia.com/shockwave/download/">
</embed>
</object>
```

☞ *If you see two copies of your movie on the Web page, see "EMBED Tag Needs to Be Inside OBJECT tag" in the "Troubleshooting" section at the end of this chapter.*

TROUBLESHOOTING

Shockwave Movie Not Appearing in Some Browsers

I'm trying to upload my first Shockwave movie to my server, but it does not appear on the page when I try it in my browser. What have I done wrong?

If a Shockwave movie still does not appear on a page after you upload it to a server, it might be because the MIME type for Shockwave is not set on the server. MIME types enable the server to tell the browser what a media element is. Search the Macromedia Web site for MIME to find the latest information about setting MIME types for different servers. This won't happen for Internet Explorer browsers on Windows because the <OBJECT> tage does not need a MIME type, only the EMBED tag.

Cache Settings and Testing

When I upload a new version of my Shockwave movie, I can't see this new version in my browser to test. Why does the old version appear when it is no longer on the server?

Check your browser cache, sometimes called temporary Internet files, settings before testing. Many browsers come with a default setting that has the movie check for new content only once per session. If you are uploading new versions constantly and then testing, you might actually be looking at the cached version of your old movie. Set the cache to check the server every time.

More about caches: Even when you have the browser set to check the server each time for a new version, it still sometimes uses a cached version. Versions of both Internet Explorer and Navigator have exhibited this behavior for developers in the past. To make absolutely sure that you are using a new version of the Shockwave movie on your server, you must go to another page, clear the cache, and then return to the Shockwave page.

EMBED Tag Needs To Be Inside OBJECT Tag

When I test my Shockwave movie, I see two copies of the movie on the page instead of just one. What could be causing this?

Although Netscape and compatible browsers ignore the OBJECT tag, Internet Explorer recognizes both the OBJECT and EMBED tags. This could lead to two copies of your movie on one page. The trick is to make sure that the complete EMBED tag is inside the OBJECT tag, ending before the </OBJECT> tag. Internet Explorer knows to ignore EMBED tags inside OBJECT tags.

DID YOU KNOW?

- You can modify the HTML templates used by the Publish command to suit your own needs. You will find these files in the `Publish Templates` folder in your `Director` folder. You can even find the loader movies there. Be careful when messing with these, however, they contain special tags and code that are required if the templates are to work correctly.

- Keep in mind that if you enable ShockMachine downloading, you are allowing people to remove the content from your site and use it on their own hard drives without returning to your site. If you have an advertising-supported site, this could cut into your revenue. Clients may also have issues with this functionality because it may cut into their site traffic and may go against their site's user agreement.

29

- You can place an <IMG> tag inside an <OBJECT> tag for Internet Explorer users. If the browser is unable to display the Shockwave movie, the image appears instead.

30

ADDRESSING PERFORMANCE
AND CROSS-PLATFORM ISSUES

IN THIS CHAPTER

THE IMPORTANCE OF PERFORMANCE

Performance can be the difference between a good Director movie and a great one. Issues that you may not think about can sometimes spoil a multimedia experience for the users. For instance, issues such as a long download over the Internet, too long of a pause before a digital video starts, poor color quality in a picture, or a sound that isn't synchronized with the animation can spell disaster for your product.

Solving performance issues is usually about fine-tuning. Most of the time it is left for the last stage of development. However, at some point, performance issues must be examined and solved before a project can be considered finished.

DESIGNING FOR A TARGET MACHINE

Every time you create a Director movie, you should think about the type of computer that will run it when it is finished. You not only need to decide what a typical system will be, but what the minimum system requirements are.

Compromise

Kiosk builders have it easy. They know on exactly what computers the movie will run, and usually even get to test it on that machine during development.

Developing a project for yourself or for a co-worker, or even developing a movie that will be seen by only a few co-workers and friends makes the job easier. The best situation is when you are creating a presentation and plan to run the finished product only on your own computer, the same one on which you are developing it.

However, CD-ROM and Shockwave developers are typically not that fortunate. If you are creating a CD-ROM, you will usually have to decide what the minimum specifications are for a computer that can use the CD-ROM. That information goes on the packaging.

The operative word is *minimum*. You can expect most of your users to have fairly fast computers, but you always have to think of that one user who buys the product and has a machine with the bare minimum.

Shockwave developers have it even tougher. People use all sorts of computers to surf the Web. You have to think about your target audience and what they might have. Even if you specify minimum requirements, users with less powerful computers are still going to try to use your movie.

On one hand, you probably want to make the Shockwave experience available to as many people as possible. On the other hand, you don't want to build something that lacks quality, just so that the movie works for a few more people with five-year-old computers. It is definitely a situation for compromise.

Sample Requirements

The computer industry is moving amazingly fast. A system that would have been typical two years ago is almost unacceptable today. Knowing that this book will be on shelves for many years makes it difficult to talk about specifics.

In the beginning of 2003, computers are less expensive than ever. For less than $1,000, you can get a Windows machine running at 2GHz, with a video card and monitor capable of supporting millions of colors and 3D graphics acceleration. Stereo speakers are almost always included.

However, that doesn't mean that everyone who bought a computer in 1999 ran out and upgraded. People hang on to old machines that work just fine for most things.

Worse yet, educational institutions often get hand-me-down computers. So, a 1997 machine will find its way into a school in 2003. A student might sit down and use that computer to try to run a movie made by you. You must decide whether it will work reasonably well on those machines.

Director projectors can be made for only a 32-bit Windows system or a Macintosh PowerPC with OS 9 or OS X. Shockwave runs on only these two platforms as well. 32-bit Windows systems include Windows 95, 98, ME, NT, 2000, and XP. At least this eliminates any worry about having to create movies for Windows 3.1 or Macintosh 68 KB machines.

So, what should the minimum requirements be? If I were to make a mass-market CD-ROM right now, the minimum requirements for Windows would be as follows:

- Pentium 400MHz processor

- CD-ROM drive

- 800×600 monitor with 32-bit color

- 32 MB of RAM

- 2 GB hard drive

- Windows 98

These requirements can be found on just about any new PC purchased during the last three years. On the Mac side, the requirements would be as follows:

- G3 or G4 processor

- CD-ROM drive

- 32 MB RAM

- 800×600 monitor with 32-bit color

- 2 GB hard drive

- System 9.0 or OS X

These requirements are fairly conservative. But the idea is that the CD-ROM is supposed to be mass-market, possibly even educational. If I were creating something that contained a lot of digital video and other high-end effects, such as an adventure game, my Windows requirements would be

- 1 GHz Pentium III processor

- 16x or better CD-ROM drive

- 64 MB of RAM

- 800×600 monitor with 32-bit color

- 2 GB hard drive

- Windows XP

This would be a typical Dell or Gateway computer. On the Macintosh side, my requirements would be

- G4 processor

- 16x or better CD-ROM drive

- 64 MB of RAM

- 800×600 monitor with 32-bit color

- 2 GB hard drive

- OS X

This would be a typical low-end iMac. In early 2003, either a PC or an iMac that meets these requirements costs about $1,000.

Screen Size

One important specification is the monitor screen size. In the CD-ROM multimedia industry, 640×480 was the standard for years. But 800×600 and even 1024×768 has been available on low-end machines for years. Plus, many video cards are no longer supporting 640×480 resolution, especially when running under Windows XP. Therefore, not only do I think 800×600 or 1024×768 should be the standard Stage size for full-screen movies, but you should avoid 640×480.

Another thing to consider is that many people are using flat-screen LCD monitors now. The iMac comes standard with them, and many PC manufacturers are shipping LCD monitors by default. LCD monitors don't change resolutions very easily. A standard small LCD monitor is 1024×768, and a large is 1280×1024. Although they can be reset to 800×600 and other resolutions, the monitor's performance suffers. This is because a pixel on an LCD display is actually a single dot in the matrix of the display. If there are 1024 pixels across the display, resetting the monitor to 800 pixels across will mean that a single pixel in your movie will stretch across more than one pixel, making the image look fuzzy.

If you plan on delivering to machines that use LCD monitors and want your presentation to look good, I suggest not resetting the monitor depth, but instead presenting full-screen at the current depth. So a 800×600 movie would take up the 800×600 rectangle in the middle of the screen and leave a black border around it.

Sometimes, a client or supervisor will specify the system requirements. Usually, they are fairly conservative: 8-bit color, 640×480 screen, and so on. It's important that you tell them about how much those specifications will degrade the movie for a majority of users. Sometimes, when a client or boss finds out that the colors will be poor and the screen will look tiny for most users, they decide to revise their minimum requirements.

3D Requirements

With the 3D capabilities of Director, a separate set of minimum system requirements is needed. Using 3D cast members requires that the computer have both advanced hardware and software.

Hardware

On the hardware side, the computer must have a 3D video graphics card. There are many different manufacturers of these types of cards. Most inexpensive computers come with a video card made by the computer manufacturer. Some even come with a video card as part of the motherboard. Few of these low-power cards will work well with Shockwave 3D or any 3D application.

Most higher-end computers, especially those owned by graphic professionals or game players, will have a third-party video card. Here is a list of third-party cards that Macromedia has tested and found to work well with Shockwave 3D:

> You can find updated 3D driver information at the Macromedia site. Several technotes and other documents cover this subject. You can easily find them by going to http://www.macromedia.com/ and searching for "3D Video Drivers."

- 3Dfx Voodoo 3, 4, 5, and Banshee

- 3D Labs Permedia 2, 3

- ATI Radeon, Rage, All-in-Wonder, XPERT

- Intel i740

- Matrox Millennium G450, G400, G200

- Nvidia GeForce3, GeForce2, GeForce256, TNT2, Riva

- Rendition V2100, V2200

- S3 Virge, Savage

Each one of the cards listed has its own idiosyncrasies when playing back Shockwave 3D. 3D scenes rendered with each card will look slightly different. This is completely different than 3D graphics where you can be assured that things look the same from machine to machine. In the 3D world, the card handles screen display, and each card handles it slightly differently.

One factor you will see when buying a 3D card is a measurement of how much memory the card has. Anything less than 8 MB of video RAM will not work very well. I recommend at least 16 MB.

Even with the previous list, there are no guarantees. Each type of card has many variations. The ATI Rage Mobility card, for example, has different configurations and drivers for each notebook it is on. This means that there are dozens of variations.

To the Director developer used to working in the 2D graphics world, this all must seem incredible. How can you create a product that will look different from machine to machine, and may not even work on some machines that would seem to fit the minimum requirements?

This is reality in the 3D graphics world, and many people with 3D-capable computers already know it. Gamers, for instance, are usually familiar with what the card in their computer can and cannot do.

Mac Video Cards

For the Macintosh world, the hardware issue is much simpler. All modern Macs come with a card from ATI or NVIDIA. Apple has made sure that Mac OpenGL drivers work fine on these cards. This makes it simple to test your Shockwave 3D content on Macs. However, other 3D cards are available for Macs. In fact, almost all cards will work in a Mac, as long as the company has written Mac drivers for the card. So you will run into some people—particularly graphics professionals—who use another type of card. Most older cards will not support 3D at all, whereas many newer ones do.

Testing is an important part of 3D development. However, even a well-funded shop can't afford to get several rooms full of computers and graphics cards to test each possibility. But if you have a small range available, such as one card from each manufacturer, you will get a good idea whether your program will work well on a majority of computers.

Software

The second requirement of a 3D computer is software. You need an extension to your computer's operating system to handle 3D graphics. There are only two choices when it comes to Shockwave 3D: DirectX and OpenGL. The first is made by Microsoft and will run on any modern Windows computer. You can download the latest version from Microsoft's site. At the time of this writing, it is DirectX 9.0.

The other alternative is OpenGL. This is the only choice for Mac users, and Apple goes a long way to support OpenGL on the Mac. In fact, Mac users cab find OpenGL for Mac right on the Apple Web site. OpenGL also works for many Windows cards.

DirectX or OpenGL will be the bridge between Shockwave 3D and the video card. Shockwave 3D knows how to talk to DirectX and OpenGL, and these in turn talk to the video card.

If you are using a Windows machine, I encourage you to download the most recent versions of both DirectX and OpenGL from the Internet. You can easily switch which one Director is using in the Movie Properties dialog box. While playing back content in Shockwave, you can switch by right-clicking on the content.

Macromedia recommends using DirectX 7 or 8 for the best performance. It rates DirectX 5.2 as the second best, and OpenGL as third. In my tests, OpenGL and DirectX 8 were pretty close, whereas DirectX 5.2 performance was poor. However, I was not able to test on a machine that had only DirectX 5.2 on it, and not a later version "dumbed-down" to act like DirectX 5.2. In fact, it will be impossible for users to even get anything earlier than DirectX 8 from normal public channels.

RECOGNIZING ISSUES AFFECTING PERFORMANCE

Many things affect performance on a computer. Think about all these issues when developing your movie, and when writing the system requirements, if any.

To do this, it helps to understand each part of a computer system that could affect performance. You can break these into the categories of hardware, software, and network.

To really get into these issues, you need a knowledge of computer engineering. However, it helps to understand the basics. This way, you can know what to look for when testing and have some idea of what might be happening in situations in which performance varies from machine to machine.

Hardware Considerations

The term *hardware* represents the computer itself. Just about everything except the case can affect performance.

Processor

All computer manufacturers love to talk about the processor speed of the latest machines in their ads. In early 2003, these speeds have topped 2.5 GHz for PCs and dual-processor 1 Ghz for Macs. More importantly, low-priced consumer PCs are usually above 1.5 GHz for PCs and 800 MHz for Macs.

Processor speed, of course, does affect the performance of your movies. Higher processor speeds enable you to attain higher frame rates and smoother transitions. Lingo computes faster.

Also, keep in mind that there are different types of processors. You can find an Intel Pentium III, Pentium IV, and also lower-priced Celeron processors, each one offering slightly different performance. There are also processors made by other companies, such as AMD. On the Mac side, the G3 and G4 series of chips offer increasing speeds as well. The G4 processors can be found in almost all new Macs, except the iBook, and include a wider path for data to enter and leave the processor, giving speed increases over a G3 processor of the same rating.

> Director MX includes many optimizations for G4 processors, particularly when using complex sprite inks.

RAM

Random Access Memory (RAM) is usually just referred to as *memory*. The more a computer has, the more programs it can run at one time. Also, for memory-intensive programs, such as movies with large cast members, RAM is very important.

Director stores all cast members in the file. However, as each one is used, it loads that cast member into memory. The more memory available to Director, the more cast members can be stored in memory. When no more memory is left, a cast member that has not been used recently is erased to make room for others. If the erased member is needed again, it has to be loaded again. This repeated loading slows down things.

Virtual Memory

Virtual memory is used by just about every home computer. The idea is for the computer to pretend that it has more RAM than it really does. It uses hard drive space to pull this off.

The hard drive stores a large file that is actually the total contents of the virtual memory that the computer thinks it has. The real RAM is used as a cache to store the most recently used parts of this virtual memory. Because recently used parts of memory are the most likely parts to be used again soon, a slowdown is caused only when new parts of memory need to be loaded into RAM.

Virtual memory therefore makes a computer slower, but it also increases the amount of memory, at least virtually. For many users, virtual memory is the only option, because their computers came with only 32 MB or 64 MB of RAM.

Disk Speed

All hard drives are not equal. Some hard drives read and write data faster than others. Although this is usually not an issue for consumer-based products, it can be for kiosks. If your kiosk includes media that needs to stream from the hard drive, such as full-screen video, you need to take this under consideration.

CD-ROM Speed

Although CD-ROM speed is not an issue for more recent machines, older ones came with single-speed (1x) or 2x CD-ROM drives. 1x CD-ROMs read data off the CD at the same rate as audio CD players.

At 1x, you can only hope to get to 150 Mbps, which means an average of more like 90 Mbps. This is too slow for decent digital video, and you will definitely see a performance hit in loading large cast members. 2x CD-ROMs double these numbers, but still make it difficult to deliver high-quality video or fast-loading movies. At speeds above that, however, you can expect decent performance. In early 2003, even budget computers come with 32x CD-ROM drives, which perform very nicely for Director movies.

However, CD-ROM drives are still slower than regular hard drives. One way to compensate for this is to require users to install the projector onto their hard drives before running it.

Bus Speed

Although processor speed is the subject most frequently discussed when it comes to buying a new computer, bus speed is another concern. A bus is the vehicle through which the various parts of the computer, such as the processor, cache, keyboard, video, sound cards, and other pieces, communicate. It is usually set to match the speed of the processor.

Video Cards

Video cards also have different capabilities. Director does a lot of drawing to the screen. Drawing occurs as a result of communication between the software and the video card. If the video card is slow, drawing a frame takes longer, and the frame rate suffers.

3D performance relies mostly on the video card. If the video card is not optimized for 3D, you have little hope that 3D cast members will be displayed with any speed at all. The amount of memory on a 3D video card also affects speed. You need at least 16 MB video RAM, but 32 MB or 64 MB is much better.

Sound Cards

Although a slow sound card may not slow down the frame rate, it could mean that sounds are delayed in starting. More commonly, a bad sound card just makes for poor-quality sound. Also, remember that on PCs, MIDI sounds are processed by the sound card. Cheap sound cards can make music sound as if it were being played on a child's toy keyboard. Some high-end sound cards, on the other hand, can make MIDI sound as if the music were being played on professional keyboards.

Speakers

Speakers are easy to overlook. If your movie has CD-quality sound in it, it will still sound only as good as the user's speakers. If the user has the cheap speakers that come with so many bargain computers, you can expect the worst.

Many developers have a great set of speakers, complete with subwoofers and a good range. They design sound for these speakers because that is what they have. Then, the end-user's machine tries to play these sounds, which come out like mere noise. This usually occurs because the sound relies too much on the low- or high-end frequencies.

It is worth the $14.95 to buy a pair of cheap speakers to use for testing if you expect to make movies for users who have them.

Software Considerations

Hardware is only half the picture when it comes to an individual computer. The software is the other half. Your projector, or Shockwave, will be running your movie. It talks to the operating system, which in turn talks to the hardware. Every step of the way there is the potential for a performance problem.

Operating System

PCs will be using Windows 95, 98, Me, NT, 2000, or XP to play back Director movies. There were two major releases of Windows 95, known as A and B. There are also many different versions of Windows NT. As of early 2003, all Macs come with OS 10.2, but some, particularly Macs in education, are still being booted into Mac OS 9.

Windows NT, in particular, seems to be problematic for Director projectors and Shockwave. Sound problems and crashes seem to occur more frequently. Hopefully, users with the latest version of any operating system will not experience any problems, and Macromedia works closely with Apple and Microsoft to minimize problems.

Each upgrade of the operating systems incorporates better performance. Upgraded operating systems handle memory better, handle disk drive access better, and display your graphics better.

Extensions

Beyond the basic operating system, extensions add more functionality to a computer. Typically, the more extensions, the worse performance is. Extensions take up disk space, increase the amount of memory needed by the operating system, and slow down the machine with more information to process on a regular basis.

However, some extensions are designed specifically to increase the performance of the computer. QuickTime, for instance, makes QuickTime media available to the computer and also gives Director movies a better way to mix sound on PCs. An extension such as DirectX enables a Windows machine to process graphics better and faster.

Drivers

Unlike extensions, drivers are a necessary part of the operating system. They tell it how to communicate with various pieces of hardware, such as video cards, sound cards, and printers.

What most users do not know is that drivers have updates. The driver that comes installed on their machines is usually the original driver for the hardware, such as a sound card. A few months later, the hardware company may release a newer version of the driver and make it available for download on the Web. The new version fixes bugs and increases performance.

Sometimes developers are savvy enough to know about driver upgrades and install them on their machines. But you cannot assume that about the end-user. Testing with lowest-common-denominator drivers is a good idea for a mass-market product.

If you are using 3D cast members, the user really should have DirectX or OpenGL drivers on her computer. Without them, Director cannot communicate with the 3D video card.

Display Settings

The two main display settings are screen resolution and color depth. One user may have the display set to 800×600 at 8-bit color, whereas another has the display set to 1024×768 and 32-bit color.

The difference? Well, the first user can see only one palette of 256 colors at a time. Also, that user cannot fit a projector larger than 800×600, or a Shockwave movie larger than 800×600 minus the 200 pixels vertically and the 50 pixels horizontally that the browser uses.

However, the 800×600 8-bit setting is usually faster than the 1024×768 32-bit setting, because there is less display information to process. Multiplying 800 by 600, and then by 8, you get 3.8 million bits of information. On the other hand, 1,024 times 768 times 32 gives you 25 million bits, or 6 times the first number.

On Macs, you can use the `colorDepth` property to change the user's color depth. A few Windows machines enable you to do this, too, but most do not. However, on both Mac and Windows, you can use the Resolution Xtra to change the color depth and screen resolution. You might want to consider that for super-fast, arcade-style movies.

Network Activity

Although this is no longer much of a problem, it used to be that computers hooked up to a network were slowed down by the overhead of staying in touch with the network. Processors are so fast now that this is not a problem. However, if the hard drive on a computer is being accessed by the network, it does slow down a projector or Shockwave movie currently running.

Browsers

Browsers stand between your Shockwave movie and the rest of the computer. Although Shockwave draws most graphics and sounds directly to the portion of the browser window it owns—making it fairly fast—some activity does need to pass through the browser.

Internet text retrieval and media linking, for instance, rely on the browser for the connection. Browsers vary in their performance for this task. In some cases, such as in very old Microsoft Internet Explorer versions on the Mac, they will not even allow you to use network Lingo.

Basically, the newer the browser version, the more compatible it is with the complex features of Shockwave. However, new versions can also introduce new bugs. As of this writing, there are several offshoots of the old Netscape browser to consider, such as Mozilla. In addition, browsers such as iCab and Opera are used by some. Safari is the latest browser for the Mac. At the time of this writing, it is still in beta. Shockwave works for the most part, though some network Lingo seems to be broken.

Network Considerations

Hardware and software describe what is inside a computer, but many factors outside a computer can also affect performance. This is especially true when the movie is a Shockwave movie that needs to be loaded from the Web. Keep in mind that projectors also sometimes call on the Internet for information or media.

Modems

In early 2003, a 56K modem is still the lowest common denominator. There are a lot of them out there. For these users, movies load at the top rate of about 4 Kbps, which means that a 240 KB movie takes a full minute to download.

Even people with digital subscriber line (DSL) modems or cable modems still have limits. They can expect a normal rate of maybe 20 Kbps. This means that a 1 MB file still averages about a minute to download.

The Internet

In a perfect network situation, the user's computer and your server with the Shockwave movie on it would be directly connected. This is not true on the Internet. Chances are the data routes through all sorts of systems, and probably comes in and out of other servers. This is true even when the client and server are in the same town.

Data can even travel in different paths at different times. So, a user might experience a great connection to your server one time, and then a very slow one the next.

You can't do much about this as a Director developer. However, you can plan for it, and make sure that the movie-loading process works well at slow speeds.

Servers

If you or your company own your own servers, you should consider performance on those as well. Can your server handle 20 users? A hundred? A thousand? What happens when it goes down in the middle of the night? Although these are not issues that can be solved with Lingo, they are still important to the end-user looking for your Shockwave game.

IMPROVING PERFORMANCE

30

Plenty of things can degrade the performance of your movie. But how can you improve performance? There are many ways.

Member Loading

When you display a member on the Stage, the member has to first be loaded from the file on the user's hard drive into memory. Because the computer didn't know in advance that you would be using that member, it has to do that loading on the spot. This can slow down your movie. You can use property settings and Lingo to load members into memory before they are needed, thus speeding up performance in critical areas of your presentation.

All cast members are present in either the Director movie's internal Cast, an external Cast, or an external file that is linked in a Cast. Simply put, they are in a file on the hard drive or CD-ROM. For cast members to be displayed on the Stage, they first have to be loaded into the computer's memory.

Director takes care of this automatically. If a sprite needs a cast member, Director checks to see whether it is present in memory, and if not, loads it into memory. As Director uses up more and more memory, it occasionally removes a cast member from memory if it's no longer present on the Stage. This clears room for other members to be loaded.

Although this is automatic, you do have a set of Lingo commands and properties that give you control over this loading and unloading. This control can come in handy when speed is critical. After all, it takes time for Director to load and unload. If you know you will need a cast member soon, and have the time to load it now, a Lingo command forces the load, and the member will be ready to go when needed.

Before looking at the Lingo commands, take a look at a typical Property Inspector display for a member, as shown in Figure 30.1.

There are four Unload options: 3-Normal, 2-Next, 1-Last, or 0-Never. The last option, 0-Never, keeps the member in memory, after it's loaded the first time, and ensures that it's never unloaded. The 1-Last setting keeps the member in memory as long as possible. The 2-Next setting flags the member for removal as soon as it isn't needed. The 3-Normal setting removes the member after all 2-Next members are removed, but before 1-Last members are removed.

It's almost never worthwhile to use any setting other than 3-Normal. However, if you have a member that is constantly being put on and pulled off the Stage, and the speed of the movie seems to be affected by the loading and unloading, setting this member to 1-Last might be a good idea.

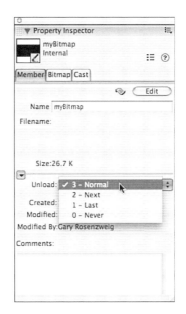

Figure 30.1
The Property Inspector for almost all member types includes an Unload setting as a pop-up menu.

You can set this property with the Lingo `purgePriority` property. Just use the number, such as 0, 1, 2, or 3:

```
member("large image").purgePriority = 2
```

The Lingo commands to control loading and unloading are fairly straightforward. To load a member into memory, issue a `preLoadMember` command:

```
preLoadMember "large image"
```

You can also specify a range of members to preload. This command loads both members specified by the range numbers, plus any members that are in between them in the Cast:

```
preLoadMember "large image 1", "large image 7"
```

You can even use the `preLoadMember` command by itself. In this case, Director attempts to load all members in the Cast until it runs out of memory.

There is also a `preLoad` command. This takes frame numbers rather than member names. By itself, it tries to load all the members used in the current frame of the movie to the last frame of the movie. This includes only members actually in the Score. Any members not in the Score but used by Lingo (such as button state images) are not loaded.

You can also specify two frames in the `preLoad` command, and it loads all the members used in those two frames and any in between. Specifying only one frame loads all the members from the current frame to the one specified.

But what if you are about to jump to another movie with the `go` or `play` command? Because those members are not in the current movie, you cannot use the `preLoadMember` or `preLoad` commands. However, you can use the `preLoadMovie` command. This command loads all the members in the first frame of the new movie.

The commands unLoad, unLoadMember, and unLoadMovie work the opposite of the previous commands by unloading members from memory.

A good rule of thumb with manually loading and unloading members is to experiment. Try running the movie with no special memory management commands, and then try it with your commands. See whether it really makes a difference.

Memory Information

Several functions can tell you how much memory is available. The simple freeBytes() function returns the number of available bytes in Director or the projector's memory space.

A more useful function is freeblock(), which returns the size of the largest contiguous block of memory. Because cast members need to be loaded in a continuous block of memory, you can use this function to make sure that such a block exists.

The size property of a member returns the size, in bytes, of a member. You can combine this with freeblock() to determine whether there is enough room for the member in memory. For instance, if you find that a huge sound member is having trouble playing on a machine with low memory, you can also have a smaller sound ready to play in its place. The following bit of code can decide which sound to use:

```
if freeBytes() > member("large sound").size then
 puppetSound "large sound"
else
 puppetSound "small sound"
end
```

You can also use the ramNeeded function to determine how much memory is needed for a series of frames. This handler measures how much memory is available to determine whether the movie jumps over a set of frames:

```
if ramNeeded(10,14) > the freeBytes then
 go to frame 15
else
 go to frame 10
end
```

A system property, the memorySize, returns the number of total bytes available to Director or the projector. You can use this to test that the program is running with enough memory to perform a memory-intense function.

You can also get the movie's file size using the movieFileSize property. Another property, the movieFileFreeSize, returns the amount of space in the file that is not in use. This extra space is thrown away when you choose File, Save And Compact.

Shockwave File Size and Streaming

If the movie is playing from the Web in Shockwave, you should always take the download time of the movie into account. Does the value of the movie to the end-user make the download time worth it?

Consider a Shockwave movie that introduces a Web site. You want it to look very cool, so it has all sorts of bitmap images and sounds. It is 300 KB. But the movie is really nothing more than an animated introduction. There is very little information for the users; that is all further down in the site.

Well, if 28.8 Kbps-modem users are coming into the site wondering what is there, they are going to be forced to wait for about three minutes to see the Shockwave movie. Then, they are going to be disappointed to learn that the movie does not tell them anything they want to know. The movie is clearly not worth the download time for the users. However, a 30 KB movie might have been just fine.

On the other hand, if the Shockwave movie is a real program, such as a game, a business application, or a presentation of some information, it might be worth a 300 KB download.

The first thing you should do with Shockwave movies that are too large is to use some trimming techniques to get the file size down to something more reasonable. See the "Trimming Media" section later in this chapter. After trimming, you should look at streaming techniques.

Streaming Movies

With the introduction of cable modems, digital subscriber lines, and other modes of fast Internet access, people can download and view larger and larger pieces of media over the Internet. However, even at these high speeds, the loading process is still much slower than from a hard drive or CD-ROM drive. Plus, many people will continue to use 33.6 Kbps or 56 Kbps modems for a long time to come.

For these reasons, you may want to consider streaming your Shockwave movies rather than asking users to download the entire movie before it begins playing. This is especially useful for linear animations, where the first frames of animation need only a few images.

Streaming is the process whereby a movie begins before all the media is loaded through the network. The movie starts with a minimum amount of media and then adds more as it continues. This enables the movie to start sooner instead of requiring users to wait for the entire movie to download.

However, you do not want to use streaming unless you have a good reason. If you expect the whole movie to load quickly, for instance, there is no advantage to streaming, and it may cause an undesirable effect because images appear at random on the first few frames as they are being loaded. In my experience, streaming also increases nonreproducible bug reports from your users, including crashes and such, especially if you are using a lot of Lingo.

Streaming your Director movies is as easy as selecting the streaming option in the Movie Playback Properties dialog box. You can access this dialog box by choosing Modify, Movie, Playback. From there, just choose Play While Downloading Movie.

You can also choose to have the movie wait until a certain number of frames is downloaded before the animation begins by entering the number in the Download Frames Before Playing text box. This helps the movie play more smoothly. If you have a 1-minute movie at 15fps, you might decide that you want 300 frames (one-third of the movie) to download before playing. Shockwave makes sure that all the members it needs for those frames are present before it begins playing.

30

When the movie needs to display a member that has not yet been loaded, it will simply not show that member. However, if you choose Show Placeholders, Director places a rectangle in place of the not-yet-loaded members.

You can also use a number of behaviors to control streaming. Director's built-in library has a whole set of streaming behaviors. Most of them wait on the frame until some other media is ready. You can specify a certain frame or a specific piece of media that you want to make sure has been loaded before continuing.

> You can also place some more members in these first frames but position them off the Stage, which ensures that they download before the movie begins.

A typical way to use these behaviors is to have an opening animation sequence. Set the movie to start playing only when that many frames have been loaded. Then, at the end of this loop, use a behavior to have the movie wait until all the members used by the last frame in the next sequence have been loaded. Because Director loads members in the order in which they are used in the Score, you can be sure that the whole animation sequence is available when the last frame in the sequence has been loaded.

Compensating with Alternatives

Another method of improving performance is to have alternatives to items that might not work well on some systems. A simple example is to create two Shockwave movies, one that uses some very small 1-bit graphics and plain-colored backgrounds, and one that is a much larger movie with sounds and all the images you want.

Then, just ask the users to choose to look at the "slim" movie, which you can recommend for 28.8 modem users, or the "full" version, which is recommended for people with faster connections. This also gives 28.8 users the option to select the full version if they really want. In that case, they will expect the long download time rather than be upset by it.

> There is no way to tell the speed of a user's connection. Some developers have tried a method wherein they have the user load a small movie or external sound first, and the movie times how long it takes to download. The results can easily be misleading, however.

You can also offer alternatives at a smaller level. For instance, you can have a 32-bit image and an 8-bit image in your projector, and use the first if the user's monitor is set to 32-bit color depth, and the second otherwise. This maximizes performance for both users.

The same is true with sound and video. You can have alternative versions of these kinds of media in your movie, and play the appropriate one based on information you have about the user's system. You can check the `freeBlock` for instance, and see whether it is too small to fit a large, stereo sound, and instead play the smaller, mono sound. This way, both types of users can hear the sound at levels their machines support.

Trimming Media

Of course, you always want to trim your media as much as possible in a Shockwave movie to make the file size smaller. Even if you are delivering your product on a CD-ROM, you should pay attention to this. Smaller bitmaps and sounds load and display more quickly.

Bitmaps

With bitmaps, first make sure that you are using every part of every image. For instance, if you have a background image that is 700 pixels wide, but only 640 of those pixels are visible on the Stage, 60 pixels' worth of data in the image will never be seen by users. Cut the excess out.

Next, determine whether the color depth you are using for an image is as low as it can be. If you expect the end-user to be at 32-bit color, you may be using 32-bit color images for your bitmaps. However, in most cases you can use 8-bit color with a custom palette. An image of a forest might have a palette that is mostly greens and browns, whereas an ocean view might use blues and grays. You can display as many graphics as you want on the screen in as many different palettes as you want if the user is in 32-bit color. These 8-bit images with custom palettes are smaller and draw more quickly.

Also, consider 1-bit images when the image contains only one or two colors. Remember that you can set the foreground and background colors of a 1-bit image after it is placed on the Stage. Just select the sprite and use the color chips in the Tool Palette.

Sounds

With sounds, consider whether the sound is too high-quality. Did you try it at a lower quality to see whether it was acceptable? If you are using Shockwave audio compression, which is recommended, try different settings. Try it at 16 Kbps. This is acceptable for many uses.

Make sure that you are using compact, trim sounds. Many developers make the mistake of leaving a second or two of silence at the start or end of a sound. They probably do so because many sound effects collections store their sounds in this manner. Trim away this excess, and your sounds will start when you want them to and use only as much file space as needed.

Video

The same is true for video and any other time-based media. Does a digital video sequence have excess seconds at the beginning or end? Also, is it stored at too high a quality setting for the use that you need? Consider these issues.

Cutting Out Unused Media

One obvious thing to do to reduce the file size of your movie is to look for unused cast members. While developing, you may create or import members that don't end up being used. You should cut away these useless members.

30

One way to make these cuts is to use the Find Cast Member window, shown in Figure 30.2. You can access this window by choosing Edit, Find, Cast Member, or by using (Command-;) [Ctrl+;].

Figure 30.2
The Find Cast Member window enables you to search for members using all sorts of criteria.

If you use the Usage setting in this window, a list of all the members not used in the Score is shown. If you select one or more of these member names, you can use the Select All button to return to the Cast and have all the unused members selected for you automatically.

But don't press Delete right away. The Find Cast Member window does not take into account any members referenced strictly in Lingo scripts. So, down states for buttons, for instance, may not be selected. You will have to look at each member on a case-by-case basis.

OPTIMIZING PROJECTOR PERFORMANCE

One of the biggest complaints that developers have when it comes to projector performance is that it takes a long time for the projector to start. This can be alleviated in a number of ways.

First, don't use embedded Xtras. Embedding Xtras just bundles the Xtras into your projector to make a single file instead of requiring you to have an Xtras folder that comes along with the projector. However, when the projector runs, it extracts the Xtras from itself and places them in an Xtras folder. It removes this folder when the projector quits.

You can eliminate the need for this whole process by choosing Modify, Movie, Xtras and making sure that none of the Xtras are selected to be included in the projector. Then, you must make an Xtras folder that sits next to your projector and contains copies of all the Xtras that you need. You can copy these from the Director Xtras folder.

Of course, it also speeds up things a bit if you don't include Xtras that aren't necessary. You can very often look at projector's Xtras folders and see Xtras such as QuickTime and Flash, even when QuickTime and Flash are not used in the projector.

Projectors also typically run faster from the user's hard drive than from their CD-ROM drive. So, if performance is critical, you may want to make sure that the user has a projector on his hard drive. You can use an installer to do this.

Another great way to speed up projector launching is to limit the size of the movie contained inside the projector. If you have a 40 MB movie inside your projector, then the user is launching a 42 MB projector. Instead, have very little in your projector and have the 40 MB movie as a `.dcr` file outside the projector. Then, your projector is only 2 MB and loads quickly. You can then use Lingo to call the large movie.

OPTIMIZING LINGO PERFORMANCE

If your movie is Lingo-intensive, you might want to consider looking at the performance of your Lingo handlers. There is almost always more than one way to do tasks in Lingo, but that does not mean that different tasks are equal. Some methods take longer, and use more system resources, than others.

For instance, if you have a handler that runs many times in your movie, and refers to all the cast member names in a cast library, you might want to consider placing these names in a list when the movie starts, and referring to the list, rather than to the members themselves.

There are as many ideas for optimizing Lingo as there are tasks that can be accomplished with Lingo. The best way to learn how to optimize is to test.

Benchmark tests compare two methods of accomplishing the same task. Benchmarks are commonly used by expert Lingo programmers to determine the fastest method of doing something.

The idea is that you set up a fake handler that accomplishes a task. Chances are that it takes only a fraction of a tick to accomplish the task, so the task is repeated many times to get a better reading of how long it takes.

The following handler benchmarks a simple `if` statement. It runs the `if` statement 10,000 times, and marks the time before it began and then reports the total time to the Message panel.

```
on testIf
  startTime = the milliseconds
  repeat with i = 1 to 10000
   r = random(3)
   if r = 1 then nothing
   else if r = 2 then nothing
   else if r = 3 then nothing
  end repeat
  totalTime = the milliseconds - startTime
  put totalTime
end
```

Of course, the `random` function takes up a large chunk of the time in this handler. However, the handler that you race this script against should also use the same `random` function, as well as the same `nothing` commands. The only difference between the two handlers is the Lingo syntax used to branch on the value of "r".

This next benchmark handler tests the `case` statement:

```
on testCase
 startTime = the milliseconds
 repeat with i = 1 to 10000
  r = random(3)
  case r of
   1: nothing
   2: nothing
   3: nothing
  end case
 end repeat
 totalTime = the milliseconds - startTime
 put totalTime
end
```

You can see that the two handlers are identical, except that the first uses `if` and the second, `case`. This is important because any other difference, other than the command you are testing, can skew the results.

When the first handler is run on my computer, it takes 64 ticks. I actually ran the handler several times from the Message panel and averaged the results.

The second handler averaged about 68 ticks. This means that it is a little more than 5% slower to use a `case` statement rather than an `if` statement.

However, remember that the handlers were testing the commands 10,000 times apiece. So, don't stop using the `case` statement based on this. However, if a `case` statement is being executed in an `on exitFrame` script in a behavior attached to hundreds of sprites on the Stage, you might want to consider this sort of optimization.

The purpose of this example is not to show the speed difference between `if` and `case`, but to demonstrate how to do your own benchmark tests. If you are trying this on something that will have a larger effect, such as using different inks to draw animating sprites, chances are that you will see a much larger difference.

MAC AND WINDOWS CROSS-PLATFORM ISSUES

If you are developing for just the Mac or just Windows, you might not have to worry about cross-platform compatibility. However, this is usually not the case. Most of the time you need to consider both platforms.

The issues that you need to consider for cross-platform compatibility are the differences in the two operating systems: fonts, system palettes, display brightness, non–cross-platform Lingo commands, and so on. Each of these issues is discussed in more detail in the following sections.

Fonts

Although the issue of Font compatibility across platforms was important in Director 6.5 and before, the capability to have font cast members makes this less of an issue now.

If you import all the fonts that your movie needs, and then use only text members that use these font members as fonts, you won't run into a cross-platform font problem.

However, if you use any fields, you have to worry about fonts. Or, if you use text members that have fonts in them that are not imported fonts, you have to worry, too. After all, the same fonts don't appear across the two operating systems.

For instance, Arial is a popular font in Windows. However, there is no Arial on the Mac by default. The Mac uses a font named Helvetica instead. Many users still have Arial on their Macs, probably because they have installed a Microsoft program such as Word. However, you can't rely on this.

The Font Map

The Font Map is how Director decides which fonts on one operating system map to which fonts on the other. To access the Font Map, choose Modify, Movie, Properties. At the bottom of the Property Inspector are two buttons for saving and loading font maps.

To make a change to the Font Map, you need to use the Save Font Map button to create a text file. Then you can edit it in a program such as SimpleText on the Mac or Notepad in Windows. Then, you must use the Load Font Map button to implement the change.

The Font Map file contains a lot of comment lines, all starting with a semicolon. It basically explains how to use the active part of the file, which consists of lines that map Mac fonts to Windows fonts, and vice versa. Here is the first set:

```
Mac:Chicago      => Win:System
Mac:Courier      => Win:"Courier New"
Mac:Geneva       => Win:"MS Sans Serif"
Mac:Helvetica    => Win:Arial
Mac:Monaco       => Win:Terminal
Mac:"New York"   => Win:"MS Serif"
Mac:Symbol       => Win:Symbol Map None
Mac:Times        => Win:"Times New Roman" 14=>12 18=>14 24=>18 30=>24
Mac:Palatino     => Win:"Times New Roman"
```

Each line consists of a three-letter abbreviation for the name of the system, followed by a colon and the name of the font. The name of the font should be surrounded by quotes if it is more than one word. Then, any number of spaces separates the instructions for the first system from the three-letter abbreviation for the other system, and the name of the font to which it should map.

So, for instance, the font Helvetica on the Mac is mapped to Arial on Windows. If you make a movie on the Mac and you have a text field in your movie that contains text using Helvetica, and you run it on Windows, it is converted to Arial. If you want it, instead, to map to MS Sans Serif, you can just replace the "Helvetica" text with "MS Sans Serif" and then load the Font Map into your movie.

Also note the numbers listed after the Times to Times New Roman mapping. These numbers identify specific font sizes of text that use that font and change them. So not only is text using Times converted to Times New Roman, but any of that text that is 14-point is converted to 12-point at the same time. You just need to specify the two sizes, with the => between them.

In addition to this mapping from Mac to Windows, the file also contains a mapping from Windows to Mac. Here it is:

```
Win:Arial          => Mac:Helvetica
Win:Courier        => Mac:Courier
Win:"Courier New"  => Mac:Courier
Win:"MS Serif"     => Mac:"New York"
Win:"MS Sans Serif"  => Mac:Geneva
Win:Symbol         => Mac:Symbol Map None
Win:System         => Mac:Chicago
Win:Terminal       => Mac:Monaco
Win:"Times New Roman" => Mac:"Times" 12=>14 14=>18 18=>24 24=>30
```

You can see that this is just the opposite of the other mapping. It is important that you coordinate the two mappings. If not, you could end up in an odd situation. Suppose that you map Times on the Mac to Times New Roman on Windows. Then, you move your movie to a Windows machine and open it to test. The conversion takes place. Then, if you take that movie back to the Mac and have the conversion of Times New Roman to New York, you don't end up with the same fonts as before.

The Font Map file also includes character mappings, which are necessary because special characters, such as Yen signs and other symbols, are not in the same locations in Mac and Windows fonts. This mapping converts characters appropriately so that your symbols match up.

Some lines also deal with Japanese fonts. Comments around these lines explain their use if you need to alter them.

One way to make your Shockwave movies a little smaller is to edit the Font Map down to the bare minimum. You can get rid of font mappings that you don't use—such as the Japanese character translations and the other ASCII character translations—as long as you don't need them. You can trim 1 KB or more from your files this way. Doesn't sound like much, but if you are expecting a million people to play your movie, it adds up.

Text Member Bitmaps

Another way to get text members to appear identical across platforms is to use the Save As Bitmap feature. This is an option you can set in the Property Inspector for text members, under the Text tab. First, choose either Copy Ink or Other Ink from the Pre-Render pop-up menu. Then, you can check the Save As Bitmap box.

The Copy Ink option should only be used when the member is displayed on the Stage only using Copy ink. If you are using any other ink at all, choose Other Ink. If you are using the member in multiple frames, sometimes with Copy ink and sometimes with something else, choose Other Ink and then place a white background behind the sprite when you want to simulate Copy ink.

Caution

You would think that if all your text members were set to Save As Bitmap, you wouldn't need the Text Xtra to be included with your projector. Unfortunately, this isn't true. The Xtra still needs to be there. So you won't be able to trim file size off your projector that way. You can, however, use normal bitmaps with text in them, or use fields. Then you can get rid of the Xtra.

Director then saves a copy of the text member as a graphic. When the movie is opened in a projector or in Shockwave, the graphic is used rather than the text. This means that the actual font is not needed.

The disadvantage is that the text cannot be edited and cannot be changed with Lingo. Another disadvantage is that the member increases the file size considerably. But the text member looks identical from platform to platform.

> Another way to do this is to choose Modify, Convert to Bitmap, which permanently converts a text member to a bitmap member. The bitmap member cannot be edited, even in the authoring environment, ever again. This technique also works for fields.

Display Brightness

One common cross-platform mistake is made by Mac developers. The Macintosh display is much brighter than a typical Windows display. Developers working in dark colors are surprised by how much darker they appear in Windows.

You can adjust for this by using your Mac's Monitors and Sound control panel and changing the Gamma setting. Then, compare a dark image on both Mac and Windows platforms before you get too far into your development. Many newer Macs are missing this functionality, however. In OS X, you can adjust your Gamma somewhat by using the Color portion of the Display part of the System Preferences.

Digital Video

Although QuickTime 6 is available on both Mac and Windows platforms, you might want to consider the situation in which Windows users do not have QuickTime. You can certainly ask them to install it, or you can simply have a substitute Video for Windows movie waiting to be played instead.

Use `quickTimeVersion()` to determine whether users have QuickTime installed.

File Pathnames

If you are using FileIO to read any text files, or you are using Lingo to set the `filename` property of a linked member, you need to think about pathnames. On the Mac, the character that goes between folder names in a path is a colon. On Windows, it's a backslash.

If you have an image in a folder that is at the same level as your projector, you might use a command like this one on the Mac:

```
member("linkedimage").filename = "images:newimage.jpg"
```

However, in Windows, you might use this command:

```
member("linkedimage").filename = "images\newimage.jpg"
```

If you try to use the wrong one on the wrong platform, the image cannot be found. Instead, first determine on which platform the movie is running and use the appropriate command, as follows:

```
if the platform contains "mac" then
 member("linkedimage").filename = "images:newimage.jpg"
else
```

```
    member("linkedimage").filename = "images\newimage.jpg"
end if
```

You can also use a variable to store an item delimiter character and then refer to that character later. This works best if you need to set multiple pathnames.

```
if the platform contains "mac" then pathDel = ":"
else pathDel = "\"
member("linkedimage1").filename = "images"&pathDel&"newimage1.jpg"
member("linkedimage2").filename = "images"&pathDel&"newimage2.jpg"
member("linkedimage3").filename = "images"&pathDel&"newimage3.jpg"
```

Non–Cross-Platform Lingo

Many Lingo commands are just not available in both platforms or work differently in different platforms. The following list includes some of the most common ones:

- shutdown—Exits a projector on Windows, but exits the projector and shuts down the computer on Mac.

- restart[md]Exits a projector on Windows, but exits the projector and restarts the computer on Mac.

- cursor—The command and property work the same, but be aware that some cursors look different. For instance, the Watch cursor on the Mac is the equivalent to the Hourglass in Windows.

- optionDown—Examines the state of the Option key on a Mac, but the Alt key on Windows.

- commandDown—Examines the state of the Command (Apple) key on the Mac, but the Ctrl key on Windows.

- controlDown—Examines the state of the Ctrl key on Windows, but only the Control key on Mac, not the Command key.

- on rightMouseDown—You can use the emulateMultiButtonMouse system property to accept Ctrl+click on the Mac as a right-click.

- on rightMouseUp—See previous entry.

- colorDepth—Can be tested in both platforms, but set only on the Mac and some, but not all, Windows machines.

Also, all commands that depend on the operating system for execution behave differently on different platforms. So, the alert command brings up a different-looking alert box for each platform (and does not beep in Windows). The FileIO and MUI Dialog Xtra dialog boxes look slightly different to reflect the different systems.

BROWSER CROSS-PLATFORM ISSUES

Shockwave developers have to deal with a whole other set of issues because of the different browsers being used. The dominant browser is Internet Explorer, but there are different versions of that browser and even customized versions for different Internet services. In addition, you have to worry about people using Netscape, Mozilla, and a variety of other browsers.

The biggest difference between Shockwave in different browsers is the way that the Shockwave plug-in is installed. In Internet Explorer in Windows, Shockwave is wrapped inside an ActiveX control. ActiveX controls are files that extend the functionality of the operating system or of a program. In this case, the ActiveX control adds Shockwave to the browser. Shockwave for Internet Explorer downloads and installs almost automatically.

Users of other browsers, including Internet Explorer for Mac, have to download a Shockwave installer program and run it. This places a plug-in in their browser's plug-in folder that prompts them to download (and automatically install) all of Shockwave's components the next time they browse over to a Shockwave movie.

In addition to installation differences, you need to prepare your HTML pages that contain Shockwave to send the correct signals to both Netscape and Internet Explorer. Netscape needs an <EMBED> tag, whereas Internet Explorer needs an <OBJECT> tag.

If you want to talk to the browser through JavaScript, you also have to do it differently with each browser. In Internet Explorer, JavaScript cannot receive messages from Lingo. Instead, you have to route these messages through VBScript, Internet Explorer's alternative browser language.

One final consideration is screen size. As Netscape and Internet Explorer change, they have different elements at the top, bottom, and sides that take away screen space from the content. If you want your Shockwave movies to fit on the screen, you have to take into account a lot of different potential configurations by users.

Experiment with different Stage sizes and how they look inside both browsers on both platforms. Try the 800×600 monitor setting and any others that you think your users might have. There is no ideal solution, because people with large monitors will think a 600×300 applet is too small, whereas people with small monitors will barely be able to fit it in their browsers.

THE CROSS-PLATFORM CHECKLIST

Developers need to have a checklist of potential problem areas for cross-platform development. Don't use this checklist only when the project is finished. Review it before you begin and occasionally as the development continues.

- Lingo—Are you using any commands that might not work on another platform? Will commands that work differently on another platform still perform adequately?

- Xtras—Are you using Xtras that might not be available on another platform? Do all your Xtras behave the same on each platform?

- Pathnames—Are you using the colon or backslash (: or \) item delimiters to describe pathnames in your code? If so, does the code recognize when it is running on each platform and adjust as needed?

- Color palettes—If you are making an 8-bit color presentation, does it work cross-platform if it's set to 8-bit?

- Fonts—Are you using fields? If so, are the fonts that you are using properly mapped to fonts on the other platform?

- Text—Do you notice any difference between platforms for your text members? Do any extend too far? Do any need to be precisely lined up with other graphics on the Stage?

- Screen size—Does your Stage fit in the screen? How about with the Windows taskbar at the bottom? Do you want it to fit inside both browser windows without requiring the users to scroll? Does it?

- Digital video—Are you using digital video that might work on only one platform? How do you deal with situations in which users do not have the correct extensions, such as QuickTime?

- Transitions—Some transitions are slower on Windows than on the Mac. Be sure to test all your animations for speed.

DID YOU KNOW?

- If you are developing for the Mac, and you have a fast one, you can buy an emulator that runs Windows. Emulators are commonly used by Mac developers to test Windows projectors. The ones that emulate an actual Pentium chip, and then run Microsoft's version of Windows on top of that, are reliable testing devices because they are usually more typical of a Windows configuration than a randomly selected Windows machine.

- When you create a new movie, the `fontmap.txt` file is read in from the `Director` folder and used as the Font Map. You can change that file so that the default font map settings for any new movie you create also change.

- There are companies that specialize in taking your nearly finished product and testing it on different machines in a testing lab. They then report on bugs and performance issues.

- A cheap way to test your projector or Shockwave movie on other machines is to find public computers that you can use. For instance, you can find older machines in libraries. You can also use computers in Internet cafés.

- Use the system property `the traceload` to have member loading and unloading information to the Message panel. Set it to 1 to just see the members, and to 2 to see the members plus all sorts of other information.

- If you are a serious Shockwave developer, you might want to pay for a few $9.95-per-month dial-up Internet connections, even if you have a faster connection available. Then, every once in a while, try the applets on your site using these various services to see what your users are seeing.

VII

APPENDIXES

IN THIS PART

WHAT'S ON THE CD-ROM

The book's CD-ROM contains source files for the movie examples used throughout the book. In addition, there are some bonus chapters, a complete Lingo reference, and some third party Xtras.

BOOK SOURCE FILES

In the folder labeled "Source" you will find the source files from the examples in this book. For every chapter that has examples, there is a folder named after the number of that chapter. Inside that folder you will find .dir source files and any other supporting materials.

BONUS CHAPTERS

The folder labeled "Bonus Chapters" contains seven bonus chapters and a Lingo reference guide. The first six, Chapters 31 through 36, are packed with detailed examples according to category. Chapter 37 covers some miscellaneous topics.

Chapter 31—Educational Applications

- Creating a Matching Game
- Making a Drawing Activity
- Creating Overlays

Appendix A

- Creating a Geography Quiz
- Creating Standardized Tests

Chapter 32 — Business Applications

- Creating a Database Application
- Creating Graphs and Pie Charts
- Creating Questionnaires
- Producing Computer-Based Training Programs

Chapter 33 — Graphics Applications

- Creating Slideshows
- Panning Large Images
- Making Scrollbars for Large Images
- Zooming In on Large Images
- Utilizing Ink and Color Manipulation

Chapter 34 — Sound Applications

- Creating a Piano Keyboard
- Creating a Player Piano
- Simulating 3D Sound
- Creating Volume Controls

Chapter 35 — Shockwave Applets

- Creating Navigation Pages
- Creating Navigation Bars
- Creating Shockwave Ads
- Processing and Displaying Information

Chapter 36—Games

- Creating a Matching Game

- Creating a Sliding Puzzle Game

- Creating a Falling Objects Game

- Emulating a Shooting Gallery Game

- Creating Sprite Invaders

- Creating Trivia Games

- Creating a Blackjack Game

Chapter 37—Miscellaneous Topics

This chapter contains miscellaneous additional topics that were left out of the main book for various reasons. Most of the content here is from earlier revisions of this book. Here, you will find sections on

- Sound quality

- Digital video formats

- Color palette members

- Using 3D text

Chapter 38—Complete Lingo Reference

The last bonus chapter is a complete reference section containing an alphabetized list of all Lingo syntax. In previous editions of this book, this reference section appeared in the appendix section in the back of the book. But the list of commands has grown so much with the addition of 3D that there just isn't room. The advantage of using a PDF file instead is that you can search the file for the specific information you need as well as browse through it page by page.

SOFTWARE APPLICATIONS, XTRAS, AND GOODIES

If you don't have a copy of Director MX, there's a trial edition on the CD for your evaluation. Install the trial edition to start a 30-day evaluation of Director MX. We have also included 30-day trial editions of other Macromedia products: Dreamweaver MX, Fireworks MX, Flash MX, and FreeHand MX.

Also included on the CD is an evaluation copy of ShapeShifter3D, which is a cross-platform modeling tool designed for the Shockwave 3D platform, including full support for the creation of Shockwave 3D bones.

B

GLOSSARY

Accessibility   Features of a multimedia presentation that allows easier access to the content for people with disabilities.

Action   A script in Macromedia Flash.

ActionScript   The programming language of Macromedia Flash.

ActiveX   ActiveX controls are files that extend the operating system or a program, such as Internet Explorer. Shockwave is available as an ActiveX control for Microsoft Internet Explorer for Windows. The ActiveX Xtra enables projectors to use other controls.

AIFF   Audio Interchange File Format. The most common sound format used on Macintosh computers. It is also used in the digital music recording industry. You will see these files on both Mac and Windows machines, usually represented with a .aif extension.

Alpha channel   An extra channel of information in an image file. (The other channels are usually red, green, and blue color amounts.) This channel determines how transparent each pixel is.

Ambient light   A light in a 3D world that doesn't come from a specific spot, but instead illuminates all objects in the world equally from all sides. *See also* Light.

Anchor   A tag in an HTML page that can be used to allow a link to go directly to that line on the HTML page instead of starting at the top and requiring that users search for it.

Animated GIF   A file using Graphic Image Format that contains more than one frame of animation.

Antialiasing   A technique that takes the edges of a text graphic and blends them with the background colors to make a smooth edge.

ASCII   American Standard Code for Information Interchange. The number system that corresponds to the 255 characters. In Director, it is used in the charToNum and numToChar functions.

Author   *See* Multimedia author.

AVI   *See* Video For Windows.

Axis   An imaginary line through the center of a 3D world. You can rotate a model or the world around an axis, or move it along an axis. The X-axis is a line usually going from left to right, representing the horizontal; the Y-axis is a line usually going up and down, representing vertical; and the Z-axis is a line going straight into the screen, representing depth.

Backdrop   A 2D image that appears as a static background in a 3D scene.

BASIC   Beginners All-Purpose Symbolic Instruction Code. A simple programming language popular in the '70s and '80s that was a good first language for new programmers.

Behavior   A script member that controls a sprite or a frame. You can have only one behavior attached to a frame, but multiple behaviors can be attached to a sprite. You can create one with the Behavior Inspector or by writing raw Lingo, or use one from the Library palette.

Bézier   A curved line that is generated with a mathematical formula based on a series of points.

Bevel   When a 3D shape or text is extruded with a round or angled edge.

Bit depth   The number of bits used to represent a single unit in a file. In an 8-bit image, for instance, each pixel is represented by 8 bits of information. In a 16-bit sound, each sound sample is represented by 16 bits of information. Higher bit depth usually means higher quality, but may be slower to view and download because of a larger file size.

Bitmap   An image cast member. You can edit most bitmaps in Director by using the Paint editor.

Blend   A sprite property also used in image Lingo. It determines the amount that each pixel should blend with the pixels behind it. A blend of 100 makes the pixels in a bitmap opaque, whereas a blend of 0 makes it invisible. A blend of 50, for instance, would mean that the screen would show the user 50% of the color in the bitmap and 50% of the color behind the bitmap.

BlendLevel   The same as blend, except that the scale goes from 0 to 255 rather than 0 to 100.

BMP   Windows format for plain bitmap files.

Bones   Lines running throughout a 3D model that define which parts of the model link to which other parts. With bones, parts of a model can be manipulated without it breaking apart. You can use bones to animate movements such as walking.

Boolean   Math involving only two states true and false. Used in programming to determine branching, as in `if` statements.

Braces   The term sometimes used to define {} characters, also called "curly brackets."

Buttons   Can refer to the quick, simple buttons made in Director with the Tool palette. It is also a term used to describe any bitmap or other member assigned a script that reacts to a mouse click.

C/C++   A general programming language used to create operating systems, applications, and even Macromedia Director. C++ is the object-oriented version of the language and is used most often today.

Cache   When a browser loads a document or a media element, it places it in a folder called the cache. When users want that document again sometime very soon, they can get it from the cache rather than load it again from the Internet. This is much faster. The same principle is applied to computer memory contents when you are using virtual memory on your machine.

Callback   When an Xtra or other process is called and left running, it sometimes communicates back with the movie by calling a handler, called a callback handler.

Camera   A point through which a 3D world is viewed. A camera has a location and a direction, as well as some other properties. A 3D world can have one or more cameras, and the view of that 3D world can switch between them.

Cast   The list of cast members used in a movie. All movies have at least one internal Cast, but movies can have many other internal Casts and external Casts. An external Cast is its own file, usually with a `.cst` extension.

cct   The file extension for a Director external cast library that has been compressed for use on the Internet. These cannot be reopened in Director.

Cell   Sometimes used to refer to the intersection of a frame and a sprite channel.

CGI   Common Gateway Interface. Scripts that run on servers to handle communication between the users and the server. CGI scripts are used to receive information in HTML forms, such as requests for more information or online transactions. CGI also stands for Computer Generated Image, as in the special effects used in modern films.

Channel   A numbered position in the Score. The Score has channels 1 through 1,000, as well as a few special channels at the top of the Score. Which channel a sprite is in determines whether it gets drawn on top of or under another sprite.

Check box   A button that has an on or off state. The state of the button is usually reflected by a check mark or X that is visible only when the button state is on.

Child   An instance of a parent script, stored in a variable or list. Created with the `new` command.

Chunk   A piece of a string, such as a character or series of characters, a word or series of words, or a line or series of lines.

Client   In the realm of multiuser communication, a client is a computer that communicates only with the server and not directly with other computers. *See also* Server.

Clip art   A set of graphics, usually created by a third-party company, which are used in print and multimedia.

Codec   A piece of hardware or a software algorithm that converts sound or video to digital code and then back again. You compress audio and video files with codecs.

Collision   Usually used to describe when two graphic objects touch or overlap on the screen. This can refer to 2D or 3D graphics.

Color cycling   This describes when the Stage is using an 8-bit palette to define its colors, and then the palette is shifted to redefine those colors. The color in each pixel then adjusts to fit the new palette, thus shifting all the colors on the screen. The term also describes the simpler process of taking a graphic and shifting its colors through a rainbow.

Color depth   The amount of information stored per pixel in an image or on the screen. With 8-bit color depth, for example, 8 bits (256 possible values) are stored per pixel.

Color palette   A set of 256 colors used to define the colors available to an 8-bit bitmap image.

Compression   When a file is changed in such a way that the information can be stored in less space. Compressed files may have to be decompressed before they can be used. Director compresses bitmaps, text, and sounds when a movie is made into a Shockwave movie.

Constant   A Lingo value such as PI or QUOTE that represents a specific value, usually one that is difficult to represent with normal syntax.

CSS   Cascading Style Sheets. *See also* Style Sheets.

cst   The file extension for a Director external cast library. These external cast libraries can also be used as files in the Lib director to add more elements to your Director Library palette.

Cue point   A marker in a sound or digital video file. These markers can be read and reacted to with Lingo.

cxt   The file extension for a Director external cast library that has not been compressed but has been protected from being reopened in Director.

Dancing Baloney   A slang term used to describe a purely cosmetic element in a multimedia presentation or Web page.

Database   A collection of organized information that can be accessed and altered. Examples are a collection of names and addresses, or a description of levels in a game.

dcr   The file extension for a Director movie that has been compressed for use on the Internet. These files can be used on Web pages, by Ppojectors, or even as Xtras, but cannot be reopened in Director

Debugging   The process of seeking out and fixing problems in a program.

Depth: The third dimension in computer graphics. The horizontal and vertical dimensions correspond to the horizontal and vertical dimensions of your screen, but depth is the illusion of graphics being closer to or farther from the camera.

DHTML   Dynamic Hypertext Markup Language. Using JavaScript and Style Sheets to create complex Web pages, often with interactivity. *See also* Style Sheets.

Diffuse   Light that is spread evenly over an area.

Digital video   An external file that is linked to the Director movie. It can display video or a time-based animation, such as a 3D rendering. Video members can come in a variety of formats but are usually in Apple QuickTime format or Windows AVI format. The definition can be extended to hold a variety of QuickTime formats, such as QuickTime VR and MIDI files. *See also* DV.

dir   The file extension for a Director movie.

Direct To Stage   Refers to sprites drawn directly to the screen, ignoring any sprites in the same location. Director To Stage sprites always appear on top of other sprites regardless of their sprite channel location.

DirectX   A set of extensions to the Microsoft Windows operating system that improves the graphics and sound capabilities of PCs. Parts are called DirectSound, Direct3D, and DirectDraw.

Dithering   The process whereby pixels in an image are colored with available colors to simulate a color that is not available. For instance, two pixels next to each other might be colored two shades of red to produce the visual effect of the shade of red exactly between the two colors.

Dolly   A camera movement that takes the camera closer to or farther from its original position.

DOS   Short for disk operating system. The underlying code that enables PCs to access files.

Dot syntax   Refers to Lingo code that uses dots, or periods, to specify properties or functions performed on an object.

Down state   A graphic used to portray a screen button when it is in the process of being pushed by users.

Dreamweaver   A popular HTML authoring package from Macromedia that specializes in adding interactivity to Web pages.

DV   Digital video. Also used to describe the standard digital video format used by camcorders and FireWire devices.

dxr   The file extension for a protected Director movie. These are not compressed, but are still protected against being reopened in Director.

Easter egg   A hidden function in a piece of software. A common example would be a hidden button that reveals the names of the software engineers who built the product.

Engraver   A 3D shader that gives the model the appearance of an engraved metal surface.

Extrude   To take a 2D shape, such as a circle, square, or even text, and expand it into a 3D model.

Fields   The original text member from before Director 5. It still has a few properties that text members do not, such as borders and drop shadows.

Film loop   A cast member that contains a complete animation. Any Score selection can be copied and pasted into the Cast as a film loop and used as a single cast member.

Filters   Defines plug-ins to imaging programs, such as Photoshop. Some Photoshop-compatible filters can be used as Xtras in Director to extend the functionality of the Paint editor.

FireWire   A high-speed connection method for digital video and high-speed hard drives. Common on newer Macintosh computers. Also available on PCs, but it is called IEEE 1394.

Fireworks   A popular image-editing tool from Macromedia that specializes in creating graphics for the Web. It's also an excellent tool to use to create graphics for Director.

fla   The file extension for a Flash movie file. *See also* swf.

Flash   A program and the files it creates. Flash is another Macromedia tool that enables you to create mostly vector-based animation for the Web. Flash files can be imported and used as Director members.

Float   A floating point number. This is a number that contains a fractional component. For instance, 4 is an integer, but 4.5 is a float. Also, 4.0 is a float because it has a defined fractional component, even though that component is 0.

Fog   A 3D effect that obscures models farther away from the camera just like natural fog would.

Font   The description of how a set of characters appears on the screen. In Director, fonts can be imported so that they can be used in the movie even if the font does not exist on the user's computer.

FPS   Frames Per Second, such as in the tempo of movement through a Director movie.

Frame   An instant of time in Director. Also, a column in the Score. While you are working on a movie, the Stage shows a single frame. While the movie is animating, the Stage moves through frames to create the visual effect of animation.

Frame script   A script that controls a frame. It appears in the script channel. Only one script can be attached to a frame. In the Cast, frame scripts are shown as behaviors.

FTP   File Transfer Protocol. This is the technology used to send raw files over the Internet. It is commonly used by developers to send files back and forth when they are too large to comfortably send via email.

GIF   Graphics Interchange Format. This is an image format that stores 8-bit images with a custom palette.

Global variable   A variable that can be accessed by any script in Director, as long as it is declared in a global command in that script.

GUI   Graphical user interface. Pronounced "Goo-ee."

Handle   One or two points applied to a vertex point used to define the curvature of the lines in a vector shape.

Handler   A Lingo function or procedure. Sometimes incorrectly referred to as a "script," which is actually a collection of handlers.

Home page   The main index page of a Web site. Also used to describe a personal Web site created by an individual.

Hot spot   An active part of a user interface. An area of the screen on which users can click is a hot spot.

HTML   Hypertext Markup Language. The language used to compose Web pages. It consists of plain text with special tags that are interpreted by Web browsers and other programs. The tags style and position the text, and add elements such as links, images, and other media.

HTTP   Hypertext Transport Protocol. This is the technology used to access Web pages over the Internet.

Hyperlink   A piece of text that, when clicked, takes users to another page, frame, or piece of information.

Icon   A small graphical element that helps define a file, action, tool, or other part of a computer's interface.

IDE   Integrated Drive Electronics. A common method for connecting hard disk drives inside computers. Also known as ATA.

IEEE 1394   *See* FireWire.

IMAP   Internet Messaging Access Protocol. An up-and-coming method for receiving email over the Internet. It's a little more sophisticated than POP3. *See also* POP *and* SMTP.

Ink   The rules by which a sprite is drawn on the Stage. Copy ink places the sprite on the Stage as an opaque rectangle.

Background Transparent ink treats white pixels as transparent. You can also choose from dozens of other inks.

Inspectors Small, palette-like Windows in Director that enable you to see and change information about selected items. An example is the Property Inspector. (Others include the Text and Behavior.)

Integer A number that has no fractional component. A 4 is an integer, but a 4.5 or a 4.0 are floats. *See also* Float.

Java applets Small programs created in Java that are usually presented on Web pages.

JavaScript The scripting language built into the Netscape Navigator browser that enables Web authors to create interactive content. *See also* JScript *and* DHTML.

JPEG The Joint Photographic Experts Group format for images. It takes 32-bit images and compresses them a variable amount, depending on the decisions you make concerning file size versus quality.

JScript The version of JavaScript included in the Microsoft Internet Explorer browser. Very similar to JavaScript, but not completely compatible. *See also* JavaScript *and* DHTML.

Kerning Modifications made to the spacing of characters in a text member.

Keyframe A frame in a sprite that denotes a specific position and other properties of the frame that the Stage must show exactly when that frame is reached. Between keyframes, the position and state of a sprite is tweened. *See also* Tweening.

Keyword Any command, function, property, or constant in Lingo.

Kiosk A single computer set up in a public place running a multimedia program.

Label A label is a name given to a frame in the Score. Frames in the Score can be labeled and referred to by that label. Also called *markers*. *See also* Marker.

LAN Local area network. What you would call the network in your office.

Level of detail Refers to the number of polygons used to render a model. The more polygons used, the higher the level of detail.

Light An object in a 3D world that creates light. The light bounces off objects to make them viewable. 3D worlds can have one or many lights. *See also* Ambient light.

Lingo The programming language of Director.

Link *See* Hyperlink.

List A series of values stored in Lingo. In other programming languages, this is called an *array*.

Loading movie The term used to describe a small movie that loads before a Shockwave movie. A loading movie loads quickly and then entertains or distracts users while the larger movie downloads in the background. When the larger movie is finished downloading, it replaces the loading movie.

Local variable A variable available only inside the handler. When the handler is finished, the variable ceases to exist, although variables with exactly the same name can be used in other handlers.

Mac OS The operating system used by Macintosh computers. The most recent version is 9.0, as of this writing, but 10.0, otherwise known as Mac OSX, is due out soon.

Marker A name given to a frame in the Score. Frames in the Score can be labeled and referred to by that marker. Also called *labels*. *See also* Label.

Mask   An image used to define the opaqueness of another image. The black pixels in a mask image would map onto the other image and define which pixels are seen.

Matte   Taking an image and making the white (or background color) pixels transparent, while all other pixels are opaque.

Member   A single element, such as a bitmap, a bit of text, a sound, a shape, a vector drawing, or a piece of digital video, stored in the Cast.

Mesh   An interconnected network of points that creates a 3D model surface.

MIAW   Movie in a Window. A Director movie that exists in a window other than the Stage. Sometimes pronounced "meow."

MIDI   Musical Instrument Digital Interface. The means by which computers communicate with keyboards and other instruments. MIDI files contain musical compositions that can be played back with a MIDI device, such as a Windows sound card or QuickTime.

MIP mapping   The use of both large and small textures that map to a 3D surface, where the smaller texture is used for speed, and the larger is only used when needed.

Model   A 3D object, such as a simple shape or a complex object such as a car, an airplane, or a character. Models are usually created in third-party 3D programs and imported into Director inside a Shockwave 3D member.

Movie   The primary Director file; contains one or more cast libraries and a Score. It is the only Director file you need for most productions.

Movie In A Window   Also known as a MIAW (pronounced meow), this is an independent Director movie that is opened in a new window by the main movie.

Movie script   A script that controls the entire movie. You can have as many movie scripts as you want. They do not appear in the Score.

MP3   A popular audio compression format. Actually means MPEG 1, Level 3. This is similar to Shockwave Audio. MP3 can be used in Director just as Shockwave Audio can.

MPEG   Motion Picture Experts Group. A digital video format that uses a lot of compression, but still retains high quality.

Multimedia author   A term used to describe someone who uses Director, or a similar tool, to create animation and presentations. They may use Lingo scripts created by others, but do not do much programming themselves.

Multithreading   When an application runs several programs at once. Because there is only one processor, the programs are not actually all running at once, but they are taking turns using the processor. Lingo running as server-side scripts on the Shockwave Multiuser Server can use multithreading.

Node   A model, group, light, or camera in a 3D scene.

Normal   A vertex that indicates which direction a vector is facing.

Object movie   A term used to describe a QuickTime VR movie that contains a three-dimensional object. *See also* QuickTime VR.

Onion skinning   The technique used by animators to create animation by seeing a shaded copy of the previous or next step in the animation underneath the image that they are currently working on.

OOP   Object-oriented programming. A method of programming that assigns code to objects, such as sprites or data.

Overlay A 2D graphic that is shown in front of the 3D scene.

Palette A list of colors that can be used by an image or by the whole screen to display graphics using only those colors.

Palette window A small window in a user interface, such as Director, which floats above other windows. Examples are the Property Inspector, the Control Strip, and the Library palette.

Pan To move the camera across a 3D scene, usually horizontally.

Panoramic image An image that shows the scene in a 360-degree view around the camera. Typically, users interact with the image to change the view angle because only a portion of the image can be shown at a time.

Parent script A script member that is not used directly, but is instead used to create a script instance or instances. It is used for object-oriented programming.

Particle system A 3D object that is actually a large number of small moving objects. Particle systems can be used to simulate things such as fireworks, running water, smoke, and dust.

Pascal A basic object-oriented programming language used mostly in colleges.

PDA Personal Digital Assistant. Refers to handheld devices, such as the Palm Pilot.

Peer-to-peer A system where users are connected directly to each other through a network, as opposed to both users connecting through a third-party computer server.

Perl A simple text-handling programming language used on many Web servers to create CGI scripts. *See also* CGI.

PICS A single file that contains multiple images. It can be imported into a variety of programs. It can also be imported into

Director as a film loop and series of members. Available on the Mac only.

PICT The standard image file for Macintosh computers.

Pixel The smallest possible dot on a computer screen. The screen is actually made up of rows and columns of pixels.

Plug-in An extension to Netscape Navigator that is used to add new media types to the browser. Shockwave for Director is a plug-in that adds to browsers the capability to display Director movies.

PNG Portable Network Graphics. This is an up-and-coming format that newer browsers support. It's the native format of Macromedia Fireworks.

POP Post Office Protocol. Also called POP3. The most used way to receive email over the Internet. The messages are stored on the server until users request that they be transferred to their computer. *See also* SMTP and IMAP.

Pop-up menu Describes a button that, when clicked, changes to a list of items that can be selected.

Port Although computers usually have a single IP address to identify them on the Internet, a computer will have many ports used for communication. Port 80, for instance, is used for HTTP (HTML pages). The Shockwave Multiuser Server defaults to using port 1626.

Primitive A simple 3D shape, such as a cube, sphere, cylinder, or plane. Primitives can be created by Lingo and inserted into a 3D member.

Progress bar A graphic element that shows the progress of a download or other long computer action. A rectangular-shaped element grows to fill a space on the screen as the process nears completion.

Projector   A standalone application program created from a Director movie.

Property Inspector   A palette window that contains information about the element currently selected. The Property Inspector, sometimes abbreviated PI, can contain information about sprites, members, the Stage, the movie, and a number of other things.

Pull-down menu   Describes a menu at the top of the screen or window that expands to a list of items that the users can select.

QuickTime   The standard video format for Macintosh computers and also used by about half of all Windows machines. Currently version 4.02.

QuickTime VR (QTVR)   A QuickTime movie that contains a panoramic image or a three-dimensional object. Instead of simply playing the movie, users interact with the image to see a different view of the panoramic image or object.

Radians   A definition of an angle, like degrees. Whereas 360 degrees make a complete circle, 6.28 (two times pi) radians make a complete circle.

Radio button   A button that is part of a set of buttons that display an on or off state. Only one button out of a set can be on at one time. When another is chosen, the previous choice is turned off.

RAM   Random access memory. This is usually just referred to as "memory" in the computer.

Registration point   The location in a bitmap image or other member that is used to position the sprite on the Stage. When the sprite is set to an X,Y location, the registration point of the image appears at that exact location.

Rollover   An element on the screen that performs an action when the cursor is over it. The element itself can change, or another element on the screen can change as a reaction to the rollover.

RTF   Rich Text Format. An old standard format for transferring styled text between word-processing programs. It consists of plain text, with special tags that are interpreted as styles and media elements.

Sample frequency   In a sound file, the measurement describes how often a sound sample was taken of the original file to build the data that exists in the current file. The higher the sample frequency, the better the quality.

Score   A chart showing which members appear on the Stage at what times.

Script   Used to describe a Lingo cast member. Sometimes used to describe a single handler.

SCSI   Small Computer System Interface. Pronounced "scuzzy." A method for hooking up external devices, such as CD-ROM drives and scanners, to your computer. This used to be the main external hookup for Macintosh computers but has now been replaced with FireWire and USB.

Server   In the realm of multiuser communication, a server is a computer that enables many other computers to communicate with one another. Of course, a server is also any computer that answers requests for information, such as a Web server or a file server. *See also* Client.

Shader   Something that describes the surface of a 3D object. A shader can be a bitmap texture or a simple color.

Shapes   Director has a few special cast member types called shapes. You can draw lines, ovals, rectangles, and rounded rectangles. All but lines can appear either filled or as outlines. You can use these shapes to add quick graphic elements to your movies without having to create bitmaps for them.

Shockwave   Technology that enables Director movies to play back inside Web browsers. "Shockwave" usually means "Shockwave for Director," whereas "Flash" usually means "Shockwave Flash."

Shockwave Audio   A sound file format that can be used by Director to stream sound over the Internet. Similar to the MP3 format. Also called SWA.

Slider   A graphical interface element that enables users to slide an element across a line to define a number among a range of numbers. A typical example is a slider that enables users to control volume.

SMTP   Simple Mail Transfer Protocol. This is the technology that enables you to send mail over the Internet. *See also* POP and IMAP.

Sorenson   A video compression algorithm available in QuickTime that compresses digital video to very small files.

Sounds   Director can import many different types of sound formats, but does not really have the capability to create or edit sounds. Sounds can be quick, simple buzzes and beeps, or long music pieces.

Sprite   The description of what member is shown, where it is in the Score, where it appears on the Stage, and many other properties.

Stage   The main Director screen where all the action takes place.

Streaming   The process by which a movie or other media is played for users while the file is gradually loaded in from a network or the Internet.

String   A variable that contains alphanumeric characters.

Style Sheets   Information contained in an HTML document, or linked from the HTML document, that describes how text should be displayed under various circumstances in Web browsers.

swf   The file extension for a Shockwave Flash movie. These can be imported into Director or used on a Web page. However, they cannot be reopened in Flash.

Targa   A bitmap graphics format used by some 3D programs.

TCP/IP: Transmission Control Protocol/Internet Protocol. The technology used to send information over the Internet.

Tempo   The speed at which the movie plays. Usually measured in frames per second.

Text member   A text member contains formatted characters. You can create them in Director with the text-editing window, or you can import files created in word processing programs. Director has the capability to display graphically pleasing antialiased text. In antialiased text, the edges of characters are smooth rather than jagged. Also in Director, you can create text members that use fonts that don't need to be on the user's machine to display properly.

Texture   A bitmap image used as the surface of a 3D object. In Director, a texture is usually the property of a shader, which in turn is applied to a surface. *See also* Shader.

Thread   A single program running in a multithreaded environment. *See also* Multithreading.

Thumbnail   A small image that represents the cast member in the Cast.

TIFF   Tagged Image File Format. An older image file format.

Toolbar   The strip of buttons that appears at the top of the Director screen.

Transform   An object that defines the position, rotation, and scale of a model in a 3D world.

Transition   A method of changing the screen, such as a dissolve or wipe.

Tweening   The process whereby you tell Director to place a sprite in a certain location and with certain properties in one frame, and then in a new location and new properties in another (keyframes). Then, Director animates the sprite between the two positions and the property sets in the frames in between. *See also* Keyframe.

URL   Uniform Resource Locator. This is the address of an item on the Internet.

USB   Universal Serial Bus. The modern method for hooking up low-bandwidth devices to Macintosh computers and PCs. It replaces standard serial connections used for digital cameras, MIDI devices, and small removable drives. On Macintosh computers, it can also be used for keyboards and mice.

Variables   Storage areas for values. *See also* Global variable, Local variable.

Vector shapes   Vector shape members are similar to the media created with programs such as Macromedia Freehand and Adobe Illustrator. A vector member is one long line that can be bent and curved. A closed loop in a vector member can be filled. Vector members can be scaled to any size and still maintain their shape and clarity.

Vertex   A single point in a vector shape.

Video For Windows   The video format built into Windows. Sometimes called AVI files. Available in Windows only.

Watermark   A small mark in photographs and other media that identifies the origin of the content. Used primarily to prevent people from using the content without permission.

WAV   A Windows sound format.

Windows   The name of the operating system used on most PCs. Developed by Microsoft, Windows comes in many flavors the obsolete Windows 3.1, the old Windows 95, the modern Windows 98, the high-tech Windows NT, and the new Windows XP.

Wizard   A feature of a piece of software that enables you to use a function of the software while being walked, step-by-step, through the process.

World   A complete 3D environment. A world can be completely empty, or can contain many models and primitives. Worlds include models, lights, cameras, and other elements. A 3D world corresponds to a Shockwave 3D cast member.

WYSIWYG   What You See Is What You Get. Pronounced "wiz-ee-wig." Used to describe an authoring environment that lets users work with information in the same way the information will later be displayed. For instance, an HTML editor is WYSIWYG if you can edit the HTML and see exactly what the page will look like in the browser while you are editing.

XML   Extensible Markup Language. Similar to HTML, but instead of using predefined tags, such as <P>, it enables you to define your own tags and what they mean. An Xtra that comes with Director enables you to parse such documents.

Xtras   Extensions to Director, developed by Macromedia and by third parties, that add or enhance functionality. Some Xtras enable you to have new types of cast members, such as cursor cast members or 3D graphics.

C

ONLINE RESOURCES

TOP RESOURCES

The Macromedia Director world is constantly changing. New Xtras are released constantly. Developers discover new techniques and share them with the rest of the community. New updates of Director and Shockwave produce new features.

To keep up-to-date, developers should check Internet sources of Director information frequently.

The following lists the best places to find and share information about Director. There are actually more than 100 sites, but because most of these sites have links to others, you are only a few clicks away from all of them.

Director Online Users Group (DOUG)

http://www.director-online.com/

This site has quickly become the leading independent resource site for Director developers. You can find the latest news about Director and Director-related products. There are how-to columns, message boards, and job listings. It also has a lot of interviews and articles written by developers.

Director Web

http://www.mcli.dist.maricopa.edu/director/

This is an intense, yet well-organized and often-updated site put together by Alan Levine at Maricopa Center for Learning and Instruction. It is sometimes referred to as the *Maricopa site*. This resource is completely independent of Macromedia and has different information and technical notes than Macromedia's site. It includes tips and tricks, lists of known bugs, links to other resources on the Web, and a huge list of Shockwave sites.

Macromedia

http://www.macromedia.com/software/director/

This is the official Macromedia site. You'll find technical notes, the latest updates, and an excellent list of Xtras.

The most important part of the site for developers is the TechNotes. They are currently located in the support section of the Director product pages. They include some valuable information on how to perform difficult tasks in Director. Just make sure that the TechNote you read is for Director MX, not an earlier version. This is also where to go to get upgrades, the latest Shockwave plug-ins, and some cool free Xtras.

Developer Dispatch

http://www.developerdispatch.com/

Okay. So, I am a little biased with this one. At least I restrained myself from placing it first. My site includes all sorts of Director, Lingo, and Shockwave information. The main feature is an email newsletter I send out as often as I can. It also includes message boards for both Director and Flash. You can also find a huge collection of Shockwave games at http://clevermedia.com/.

Direct-L

DIRECT-L@UAFSYSB.UARK.EDU

This is a mailing list with more than 2,000 subscribers. To subscribe, send email to the above address with "SUBSCRIBE DIRECT-L *YOUR_NAME*" in the body of the message. Be sure to check out its Web site at http://www.mcli.dist.maricopa.edu/director/direct-l/manners.html first. Mailing lists are a great way to stay in touch with the Director community around the world. However, it can be a bit overwhelming, because 2,000 people can generate a lot of email over the course of a day.

To search the archives of this mail list, go to
http://www.mcli.dist.maricopa.edu/director/digest/. If you are an advanced user, you might want to remember that this list is full of novices, and you might find yourself answering questions, not asking them (which is not all bad—it's a great way to land consulting gigs).

DirectOregon

http://www.moshplant.com/direct-or/

Darrel Plant, author of a few books on Director and Flash, runs this site. He is also the technical editor of the *Macromedia User Journal*. He likes to play around a lot with new features in Director and has posted many features, such as his EPS-to-vector-shape converter tool. You can also search the Direct-OR list, an Oregon-based developer mailing list.

MediaMacros

http://www.mediamacros.com

This site contains a huge list of open source behaviors and a large list of Xtras. It also has frequent news updates.

MultiMedia Help

http://www.multimediahelp.org/

This site offers a lot of demo files to download, a forum, free audio links, and free 3D models.

GENERAL DIRECTOR RESOURCES

Here are some sites that have various bits of information, news, sample movies, tutorials, and Xtras:

Lots of Xtras, other products, and Director quirks: http://www.updatestage.com
Message board and chat: http://clubs.yahoo.com/clubs/macromediadirector
Lingo-based Director tools: http://brennan.young.net/Comp/tools.html
Code examples: http://www.the-castle.com/
Chicago Area Users Group: http://www.mmugchicago.org/
Source code examples: http://perso.planetb.fr/newton/
Changing projector icons: http://etosoftware.hypermart.net/Minirun.htm
Director examples: http://users.aol.com/jrbuell/index.html
A tutorial on how to write Director ActiveX controls: http://www.mods.com.au/ActiveX/
Expert Lingo programming technotes:
http://venuemedia.com/mediaband/collins/technotes.html
Advanced Imaging Lingo examples: http://setpixel.com/
Information and Articles: http://www.zeusprod.com/
Demos, source code, and articles: http://www.lingoworkshop.com/
Tutorials and notes: http://www.fbe.unsw.edu.au/Learning/Director/
Multiuser Server information: http://poppy.macromedia.com/multiuser/
Shockwave 3D examples: http://www.director-3d.com/
Shockwave 3D examples: http://cleoag.shockteam.com/sw3d/
Shockwave 3D examples: http://www.theburrow.co.uk/
Articles and source code:
http://www.tetonmultimedia.com/tetonmultimedia/lessons.cfm

NON-ENGLISH DIRECTOR RESOURCES

There are general sites about Director or local user groups. They are all in non-English languages.

Macromedia User Group Argentina: `http://www.mmug-ar.com.ar/`

A German Director site: `http://www.lingopark.com/`

A German Director site: `http://www.director-workshop.de/`

A German Director site: `http://www.lingo.de/`

A French Director site: `http://www.yazo.net/`

A French Director site: `http://www.director-fr.com/`

A French Director site: `http://perso.wanadoo.fr/g.hocquet/`

DIRECTOR-RELATED MAILING LISTS

Here are some mailing lists you can subscribe to:

Direct-L, the largest list: `http://www.mcli.dist.maricopa.edu/director/`

Dir3D-L, Director 3D Mailing List:
`http://nuttybar.drama.uga.edu/mailman/listinfo/dir3d-l`

Director game development mailing list:
`http://nuttybar.drama.uga.edu/mailman/listinfo/dirgames-l/`

Lingo Programmers mailing list and Xtra developers mailing list:
`http://www.penworks.com/maillist.cgi`

Shockwave-L, Shockwave developers mailing list: `http://www.chinwag.com/shockwave/`

3D-RELATED RESOURCES

Here are some 3D-related information sites:

Lots of information, links, and free textures and models:
`http://www.3dcafe.com/asp/default.asp`

Models, textures, and other things, with some available in Shockwave 3D format:
`http://www.turbosquid.com`

Home of the Maya Shockwave 3D exporter: `http://www.aliaswavefront.com/sw3d`

Home of TrueSpace, another 3D tool with a Shockwave 3D exporter:
`http://www.caligari.com/`

Home of a 3D exporter of Poser: `http://www.daz3d.com/`

3D exporter for SoftImage: `http://www.softimage.com/download/xsi/converters/`

A 3D modeling tool made specifically for Shockwave 3D: `http://www.shapeshifter3D.com/`

Developers page for the Havok Xtra: `http://www.havok.com/xtra/`

MAJOR XTRA DEVELOPERS AND DISTRIBUTORS

Here are some of the major Xtra developers. Most of these sites are the home of more than one Xtra.

```
http://www.updatestage.com/xtras/
http://www.directxtras.com/
http://www.ravware.com/
http://andradearts.com/
http://www.xtramedia.com/
http://www.peghole.com/
http://www.mods.com.au/
http://www.penworks.com
http://cxtra.colsup.net/
http://xtras.tabuleiro.com/
http://www.dmtools.com
http://mediashoppe.com
http://printomatic.com
http://www.integrationnewmedia.com/
```

D

LINGO INDEX

Appendix D

F

G

T

U

Appendix D

INDEX

A

How can we make this index more useful? Email us at indexes@quepublishing.com

gradient settings, 38
Hand tool, 37
ink options, 39-40
Lasso tool, 37
Line tool, 38
line weight settings, 39
Marquee tool, 37
Paint Bucket tool, 37
patterns, 39
Pencil tool, 38
Polygon tool, 38
Registration Point tool,
  37
Text tool, 38
Zoom tool, 37

drawPeople handler, 594

drawRect property, 253

dripping blood effect, 414-415

drivers, 558, 708

dropShadow property, 359

DTS property, 48

duplicate command, 305, 308, 382

duplicate Xtra (error message), 657

duplicating. *See* copying

duration property, 218, 240

DVDs
  creating, 683-684
  troubleshooting, 685

dynamic overlays, 550

dynamic textures, 528-530

E

EasyBase Xtra, 644

Edit menus, 272

editable property, 48, 359, 362

editing
  bitmaps, 36
    Air Brush tool, 38
    Arc tool, 38
    Brush tool, 38
    color chips, 38
    Distort tool, 41

Ellipse tool, 38
Eraser tool, 37
Eyedropper tool, 37
Fill tool, 41
Flip Horizontal tool, 41
Flip Vertical tool, 41
gradient settings, 38
Hand tool, 37
ink options, 39-40
Invert tool, 41
Lasso tool, 37
Lighten and Darken tool,
  41
Line tool, 38
line weight settings, 39
Marquee tool, 37
Paint Bucket tool, 37
Paint panel preferences,
  40-41
patterns, 39
Pencil tool, 38
Polygon tool, 38
Rectangle tool, 38
Registration Point tool,
  37
registration points, 41-42
Rotate tool, 41
ruler, 40
Smooth tool, 41
Switch Colors tool, 41
Text tool, 38
Trace Edges tool, 41
Zoom tool, 37
models
  orientation, 477
  position, 475-476
text members, 45-46

editors
Cursor Properties Editor, 71,
  276
Editors Preferences dialog
  box, 27-28
Field Editor, 53-55
Paint panel, 36
  Air Brush tool, 38
  Arc tool, 38
  Brush tool, 38
  color chips, 38
  Distort tool, 41
  Ellipse tool, 38

Eraser tool, 37
Eyedropper tool, 37
Fill tool, 41
Flip Horizontal tool, 41
Flip Vertical tool, 41
gradient settings, 38
Hand tool, 37
ink options, 39-40
Invert tool, 41
Lasso tool, 37
Lighten and Darken tool,
  41
Line tool, 38
line weight settings, 39
Marquee tool, 37
Paint Bucket tool, 37
patterns, 39
Pencil tool, 38
Polygon tool, 38
preferences, 40-41
Rectangle tool, 38
Registration Point tool,
  37
Rotate tool, 41
ruler, 40
Smooth tool, 41
Switch Colors tool, 41
Text tool, 38
Trace Edges tool, 41
Zoom tool, 37
Text Editor, 45-46

Editors Preferences dialog box, 27-28

Effects toolbar, 41

efficiency of objects, 347

elapsedTime property, 214

Ellipse tool, 38

else keyword, 88-89

email mailing lists, 744-746

<EMBED> tag (HTML), 693-696

embedding Shockwave movies, 693-696

emissive property, 521

emitter.angle property, 455

emitter.direction property, 455

mouseRightDown property, 146

mouseRightUp property, 146

mouseUp handler, 81, 104, 147-150, 180, 319
  alert dialog boxes, 258
  complex button behavior, 336
  confirmation dialog boxes, 258
  pop-up menus, 368
  simple button behavior, 326
  text dialog boxes, 259

mouseUp message, 105, 316

mouseUp property, 146

#mouseUp symbol, 310

mouseUpOutside handler, 180
  pop-up menus, 368
  simple button behavior, 326

mouseUpOutside message, 105, 316

mouseV property, 146

mouseWithin message, 105, 316

mouseWord property, 360

mouth.dir file, 629

movable rigid bodies, 504

Move Cursor Xtra, 646

Move tool (ShapeShifter 3D), 437

movecamera.dir file, 539

movecameraall.dir file, 541

moveMarker handler, 172-173

moveMarkerOne handler, 175

movemodels.dir file, 477

moveteapot.dir file, 479

moveToBack command, 255

moveToFront command, 255

moveVertex command, 406-407

moveVertexHandle command, 407

moveWindow handler, 257

Movie menu commands
  Playback, 30
  Properties, 29

Movie Playback Properties dialog box, 30-31, 713

movie property, 570

movie scripts, 10, 78

movieFileFreeSize property, 712

movieFileSize property, 712

movieName property, 570

moviePath property, 570

movieRate property, 241

movies. *See also* animation; files
  accessibility
    accessible.dir example, 620
    behaviors, 622-625
    buttons, 623
    defined, 620
    Section 508 guidelines, 620
    speech, 623
    Speech Xtra, 625-630
    sprites, 622
    testing, 630
  defined, 9
  Flash members, 14, 64
    ActionScript objects, 231-235
    appearance of, 228-231
    behavior, 227-228
    error checking, 670
    Flash printing, 236
    Flash variables, 235
    images, 399-400
    importing, 64
    interaction, 228
    playing, 224-227
    playing backward, 226-227
    properties, 65-66, 224-230, 399
    replacing, 237
    rewinding, 225-226
    stopping, 225-226
    troubleshooting, 236-237
    variables, 235
  frames, 399
  LDMs (linked Director movies)
    compared to film loops, 261
    creating, 261-264
  messages, 102, 104
  MIAWs (Movies in a Window)
    closing, 253-255
    creating, 252-255
    dialog boxes, 257-260
    event handlers, 256-257
    MIAW Xtras, 615-616
    moving to background, 255
    moving to foreground, 255
    oddly shaped MIAWs, 260
    opening, 252
    properties, 253-256
    testing, 282
    type numbers, 254-255
    unloading from memory, 255
    uses for, 260-261
    window commands, 255
  navigating
    example, 99-100
    go command, 96-98
    menu screens, 101-102
    play command, 98
    play done command, 98
  paths, 570
  peer-to-peer connections, 596-597
  performance optimization
    alternative versions, 714
    available memory, 712
    member loading, 710-712
    reducing file sizes, 715-716
    Shockwave files, 712-713
    streaming movies, 713-714
    trimming media, 715

readLine command, 564, 569

readToken command, 569

readWord command, 564, 569

real-time recording, 126

ReAnimator 3D, 495

recompiling scripts, 26

recording
animation recording techniques
cast-to-time recording, 127
real-time recording, 126
space-to-time recording, 126-127
step recording, 125-126
Score recording
on evenlySpace handler, 614-615
on recordMove handler, 613
on simpleChange handler, 612
sprite behaviors, 615
starting, 612
stopping, 612
troubleshooting, 617
writing to Score, 612-613
sounds, 58

recordMove handler, 613

rect property, 196-197, 202, 253, 381, 544

Rectangle tool, 38

Red Eye Software Audio Xtra, 651

reducing file sizes, 715-716

#reflection texture mode, 527

reflectivity, 53

reflectsky.dir file, 527

registerForEvent command, 500

Registration Point tool, 37

registration points
changing, 42
default registration points, 42

defined, 37, 41
Registration Point tool, 37

regPointVertex property, 405

Relaunch Utility, 642

Remap Palettes If Needed option (movie properties), 30

removeFromWorld command, 556

removing. *See* deleting

renderer property (getRendererServices command), 557

rendering
defined, 425
special effects
2D cartoon effect, 553-554
backdrops, 548-549
fog, 547-548
#inker modifier, 553
level of detail, 551
overlays, 548-552
subdivision surfaces, 552-553

renderStyle property, 521

repeat command, 161

repeat while loops, 91

repeat with loops, 90-91

replacing
characters in strings, 298
Flash members, 237

Reset Camera Transform button (Shockwave), 429

Reset Monitor to Match Movie's Color Depth option (Projector Options dialog box), 681

Reset World button (Shockwave), 430

resetWorld command, 465, 476, 496

resizeWindow handler, 257

resizing
sprites, 140
Stage, 16

resolution property, 448-449

Resolution Xtra, 644

restart command, 281, 722

restitution property, 507

restricting keyboard input, 153-154

RETURN keyword, 153, 302

return values (functions), 87

reusing
code, 111-112
objects, 347
scripts, 81

Reveal ink, 39

revealer (panels), 11

Reverse buttons (digital video), 243

Reverse ink, 39, 137

rewind command, 214, 225

Rewind control, 18

rewinding
Flash members, 225-226
sounds, 214

rgb object, 189

rich text format (RTF), 46-47, 369-370

right property, 446

rightIndent property, 362

rightMouseDown handler, 722

rightMouseDown, 722

rightMouseUp handler, 722

rightMouseUp, 722

rigid bodies (Havok)
commands, 507-508
creating, 504-506
fixed rigid bodies, 504
movable rigid bodies, 504
properties, 507

rigidbodies.dir file, 505

robot example, 493-495

robot.dir file, 493

How can we make this index more useful? Email us at indexes@quepublishing.com